BARRON'S

NEW
GRE®

GRADUATE RECORD
EXAMINATION

19TH EDITION

Sharon Weiner Green, M.A.
Former Instructor of English

Ira K. Wolf, Ph.D.
President, PowerPrep, Inc.
Former Professor of Mathematics
Former Director of University Teacher Preparation Program

BARRON'S

All inquiries should be addressed to:
Barron's Educational Series, Inc.
250 Wireless Boulevard
Hauppauge, New York 11788
www.barronseduc.com

Library of Congress Catalog Card Number: 2011010753

ISBN: 978-0-7641-4616-9 (Book)

ISBN: 978-1-4380-7078-0 (Book/CD-ROM Package)

PRINTED IN THE UNITED STATES OF AMERICA
9 8 7 6 5 4

10%
POST-CONSUMER
WASTE
Paper contains a minimum
of 10% post-consumer
waste (PCW). Paper used
in this book was derived
from certified, sustainable
forestlands.

Contents

Acknowledgments

The authors gratefully acknowledge the following for permission to reprint reading passages in the book or on the CD.

Book Passages

Page 34: From *Classic Authors of the Gilded Age* by Darrel Abel. Copyright © 1963 by Barron's Educational Series.

Page 37: Excerpt from pp. 140–1 from *The Indian in America (New American Nation Series)* by Wilcomb E. Washburn. Copyright © 1975 by Wilcomb E. Washburn. Reprinted with permission of HarperCollins Publishers.

Page 38: From the National Biological Information Infrastructure.

Page 107: From "So Many Female Rivals" by Christine Froula, *The New York Times Book Review*, February 7, 1988.

Page 108: Ladislas Segy, "African Sculpture Speaks," Dover Publications, New York, 1958. By permission of Helena Segy.

Page 450: From *From Slavery to Freedom* by John Hope Franklin and Evelyn Higginbotham. Reprinted with permission of the McGraw-Hill Companies, Inc.

Page 454: Showalter, Elaine; *A Literature of Their Own.* © 1977 Princeton University Press, 2005 renewed PUP, 1999 exp. Paperback edition. Reprinted with permission of Princeton University Press.

Page 462: From *Black Leaders of the Twentieth Century.* Copyright 1982 by the Board of Trustees of the University of Illinois. Used with permission of the University of Illinois Press.

Page 492: From [Van Ghent] *English Novel, Form and Function* 1E. Copyright © 1953. Heinle/Arts & Sciences, a part of Cengage Learning, Inc. Reproduced by permission. *www.cengage.com/permissions*

Page 495: From Vol. 15 of *Americas,* Copyright © 1963 by the Organization of American States.

Page 502: From *Literary Women: The Great Writers* by Ellen Moers. Copyright © 1976, 1977 by Ellen Moers. Used by permission of Doubleday, a division of Bantam Doubleday Dell Publishing Group Inc.

Page 504: From Vol. 15 of *Americas.* Copyright © 1963 by the Organization of American States.

Page 505: From *Eyes on the Prize: Civil Rights Years*, edited by Clayborne Carson et al. Copyright © 1987 by Penguin Books. Blackside, Inc. 1991, with permission.

CD Passages

Preface

As a prospective graduate student concerned with professional advancement, you know the importance of using good tools and drawing on solid research. In this Nineteenth Edition of *Barron's GRE*, we offer you both.

This revision contains the fruits of our close study of the major changes effective August 1, 2011, to the GRE General Test announced by the Educational Testing Service (ETS). We have scrutinized hundreds of actual GRE questions, traced dozens of GRE reading passages to their sources, analyzed subsets of questions by order of difficulty and question type. We have gone through all the topics in the new analytical writing section, categorizing the actual issues you will encounter on your test and analyzing the argument passages, pinpointing their logical flaws. In the process, we have come up with the following features, which should make this Nineteenth Edition particularly helpful to you:

Typical GRE Questions Analyzed

The Nineteenth Edition takes you step by step through more than 1,000 practice verbal and mathematical questions that simulate actual GRE questions, showing you how to solve them and how to avoid going wrong.

Testing Tactics

The Nineteenth Edition provides you with dozens of proven, highlighted testing tactics that will help you attack the different types of questions on the GRE.

Comprehensive Mathematics Review

The Nineteenth Edition presents you with extensive mathematical review of all the topics that you need to know. This is especially valuable for college students and adults who haven't taken math since high school.

GRE-Modeled Tests

The Nineteenth Edition offers you a Diagnostic Test geared to the current GRE, a test that will enable you to pinpoint your areas of weakness right away and concentrate your review on subjects in which you need the most work, plus two Model Tests, all with answers completely explained, that in format, difficulty, and content echo today's GRE. Two additional tests are on the accompanying CD-ROM (optional).

Computer GRE Update

The Nineteenth Edition introduces you to the latest version of the computer-based GRE—and, along with the accompanying CD-ROM (optional), explains everything you need to know about how to take the computerized GRE.

Analytical Writing Update

The Nineteenth Edition also provides you with an introduction to the GRE analytical writing section, familiarizing you with the range of topics covered and giving you helpful hints on how to write clear, cogent essays in no time at all.

This Nineteenth Edition once more upgrades what has long been a standard text. It reflects the contributions of numerous teachers, editors, and coaches, and the dedication of the staff at Barron's. It also reflects the forensic and rhetorical skills of Lexy Green, Director of Debate at the College Preparatory School, to whom we owe special thanks. We, the authors, are indebted to all these individuals for their ongoing efforts to make this book America's outstanding GRE study guide.

Timetable for a Typical Computer-Based Graduate Record Examination

Total Time: 4 hours

Section	Time Allowed	Description
1	60 minutes	*Analytical Writing* Essay 1: Giving one's perspective on an issue Essay 2: Analyzing an argument (30 minutes each)
	1-minute break	
2	30 minutes	*Verbal Ability* 6 text completion questions 5 sentence equivalence questions 9 reading comprehension questions
	1-minute break	
3	35 minutes	*Quantitative Ability* 8 quantitative comparison questions 9 discrete quantitative questions 3 data interpretation questions
	10-minute break	
4	30 minutes	*Verbal Ability* 6 text completion questions 5 sentence equivalence questions 9 reading comprehension questions
	1-minute break	
5	35 minutes	*Quantitative Ability* 7 quantitative comparison questions 10 discrete quantitative questions 3 data interpretation questions
	1-minute break	
6	30 or 35 minutes	*Experimental Section* a third verbal or quantitative section

NOTE: Sections 2 through 6 can come in any order—for example, Section 2 could be a Quantitative Ability section and the Experimental Section could be any section except Section 1. Although the Experimental Section will not count in your score, it will look identical to one of the other sections—you won't know which section it is, so you must do your best on every section of the test.

PART 1

INTRODUCTION/ DIAGNOSTIC TEST

What You Need to Know About the GRE

CHAPTER 1

AN OVERVIEW OF THE COMPUTER-BASED GRE GENERAL TEST

The GRE General Test is an examination designed by the Educational Testing Service (ETS) to measure the verbal, quantitative, and analytical writing skills you have developed in the course of your academic career. High GRE scores strongly correlate with the probability of success in graduate school: the higher you score, the more likely you are to complete your graduate degree. For this reason, many graduate and professional schools require applicants to take the GRE General Test, a test now given only on computer. (They may also require you to take a GRE Subject Test in your particular field. Subject Tests currently are available in 14 fields.)

The computer-based GRE General Test you take will have five or six sections. There will always be

- one Analytical Writing section composed of two 30-minute tasks (60 minutes)
- two 20-question Verbal Ability sections (30 minutes each)
- two 20-question Quantitative Ability sections (35 minutes each)

In addition, there *may* be

- an unidentified Experimental Section, which would be a third verbal or quantitative section

Occasionally, there *may* be

- an identified optional research section (but *not* if there is an Experimental Section)

The verbal section measures your ability to use words as tools in reasoning; you are tested not only on the extent of your vocabulary but on your ability to discern the relationships that exist both within written passages and among individual groups of words. The quantitative section measures your ability to use and reason with numbers and mathematical concepts; you are tested not on advanced mathematical theory but on general concepts expected to be part of everyone's academic background. The mathematics covered should be familiar to most students who took at least two years of math in a high school in the United States. The writing section measures your ability to make rational assessments about unfamiliar, fictitious relationships and to logically present your perspective on an issue.

COMMONLY ASKED QUESTIONS ABOUT THE COMPUTER-BASED GRE

How Does the GRE Differ from Other Tests?

Most tests college students take are straightforward achievement tests. They attempt to find out how much you have learned, usually in a specific subject, and how well you can apply that information. Without emphasizing memorized data, the GRE General Test attempts to measure verbal, quantitative, and analytical writing skills that you have acquired over the years both in and out of school.

Although the ETS claims that the GRE General Test measures skills that you have developed over a long period, even a brief period of intensive study can make a great difference in your eventual GRE scores. By thoroughly familiarizing yourself with the process of computer-based testing, the GRE test format, and the various question types, you can enhance your chances of doing well on the test and of being accepted by the graduate school of your choice.

What Is It Like to Take a Computer-Based GRE?

If you purchased the version of this book that comes with a CD-ROM, then by using that CD, you can familiarize yourself with the icons that appear on the screen, practice navigating around the screen, and take two Model Tests, either in practice mode or test-taking mode. Whether or not your version of the book came with the optional CD-ROM, you can go to the ETS's official GRE website— *www.ets.org/GRE/*—and download their free *POWERPREP® II* software, which includes a test preview tool and a practice test.

When you actually take the GRE, you sit in a carrel in a computer lab or testing center, facing a computer screen. You may be alone in the room, or other test-takers may be taking tests in nearby carrels. With your mouse, you click on an icon to start your test. The first section of the test is the Analytical Writing section, and you will have 60 minutes in which to complete the two writing tasks. When you have finished the writing section, you will have a one-minute break to take a few deep breaths and get ready for the next four or five sections, each of which will consist of 20 multiple-choice verbal or quantitative questions. When the break is over, the first question in Section 2 appears on the screen. You answer it, clicking on the oval next to your answer choice, and then, ready to move on, you click on the box marked Next. A new question appears on screen, and you go through the process again. Be sure to answer every question. Because there is no penalty for an incorrect answer on the GRE General Test, when you don't know an answer, try to make an educated guess by eliminating clearly incorrect choices; if you can't eliminate any choices, make a wild guess, and move on.

At the end of the second section, you are given another one-minute break. After finishing the third section, you have a ten-minute break. There will be two more one-minute breaks—after the fourth and fifth sections.

Why Do Some People Call the Computer-Based General Test a CAT?

CAT stands for Computer-Adaptive Test. What does this mean? It means that the test adapts to your skill level: it is customized.

What happens is that after you complete the first quantitative or verbal section, the computer program assesses your performance and adjusts the difficulty level of the questions you will have to answer in the second quantitative or verbal section. The more questions you answer correctly in the first section, the harder will be the questions that you will be given in the second section. However, the harder the questions are, the more they are worth. So your raw score depends on both the number of questions you answer correctly and the difficulty level of those questions.

Actually, the GRE is much less computer-adaptive than it used to be. It used to adapt the level of questions you received continuously; after every question the program would assess your performance and determine the level of difficulty of the next question. Now, it doesn't make that determination until you have completed an entire section.

Can I Tell How Well I'm Doing on the Test from the Questions the Computer Assigns Me?

Don't even try; it never pays to try to second-guess the computer. There's no point in wasting time and energy wondering whether it's feeding you harder questions or easier ones. Let the computer keep track of how well you're doing — you concentrate on answering correctly as many questions as you can and on pacing yourself.

Should I Guess?

Yes, you must! You are not going to know the correct answer to every question on the GRE. That's a given. But you should *never* skip a question. Remember, there is no penalty for an incorrect answer. So if a question has you stumped, eliminate any obviously incorrect answer choices, and then guess and don't worry whether you've guessed right or wrong. Your job is to get to the next question you *can* answer. Just remember to use the process of elimination to improve your guessing odds.

How Can I Determine the Unidentified Experimental Section?

You can't. Do not waste even one second in the exam room trying to identify the Experimental Section. Simply do your best on every section. Some people claim that most often the last section is the Experimental Section. Others claim that the section with unusual questions is the one that does not count. Ignore the claims: you have no sure way to tell. If you encounter a series of questions that seem strange to you, do your best. Either these are experimental and will not count, in which case you have no reason to worry about them, or they will count, in which case they probably will seem just as strange and troublesome to your fellow examinees.

TIP

After taking one of the Model Tests in the back of this book and/or on the optional CD-ROM, it is impossible to calculate exact scores, because there is no way to factor in the difficulty level of the questions. To give yourself a rough idea of how you did, on both the verbal and quantitative sections, assume that your raw score is equal to the number of correct answers, and that your scaled score is equal to 130 plus your raw score. For example, if you answered correctly 30 of the 40 quantitative questions, assume that your raw score would be 30 and that your scaled score would be 160.

NOTE

For all of the multiple-choice questions in the verbal and quantitative sections of the tests and practice exercises in this book, the answer choices are labeled A, B, C, D, and E, and these letters are used in the Answer Keys and the answer explanations. On an actual GRE exam, these letters never appear on the screen. Rather, each choice is preceded by a blank oval or square, and you will answer a question by clicking with the mouse on the oval or square in front of your choice.

How Are GRE Scores Calculated and When Are They Reported?

On both the verbal and quantitative sections of the GRE, your *raw score* is the number of questions you answered correctly, adjusted for the difficulty level of those questions. Each raw score is then adjusted to a *scaled score*, which lies between 130 and 170. The written score report that you will receive in the mail will include both your scaled scores and your percentile rank indicating the percent of examinees scoring below your scaled scores on the General Test.

Your analytical writing score will be the average of the scores assigned to your essays by two trained readers. These scores are rounded up to the nearest half-point. Your combined analytical writing score can vary from 0 to 6, with 6 the highest score possible.

As soon as you have finished taking the test, the computer will calculate your *unofficial* scaled scores for the verbal and quantitative sections and display them to you on the screen. Because your essays are sent to trained readers for holistic scoring, you will not receive a score for the analytical writing section on the day of the test. You should receive in the mail an *official* report containing all three scores approximately three weeks after the test date.

GRE TEST FORMAT

Verbal Reasoning

The two verbal sections consist of a total of 40 questions. These questions fall into two basic types: sentence completion questions and critical reading questions.

Here is how a 20-question verbal section generally breaks down:

- 10 sentence completion questions
- 10 critical reading questions (including logical reasoning questions)

Although the amount of time spent on each type of question varies from person to person, in general, sentence completion questions take less time to answer than critical reading questions.

SENTENCE COMPLETION QUESTIONS

In sentence completion questions, you are asked to choose the best way to complete a sentence or short passage from which one, two, or three words have been omitted. These questions test a combination of reading comprehension and vocabulary skills. You must be able to recognize the logic, style, and tone of the sentence so that you will be able to choose the answer that makes sense in context. You must also be able to recognize differences in usage. The sentences cover a wide variety of topics from a number of academic fields. They do not, however, test specific academic knowledge. You may feel more comfortable if you are familiar with the topic the sentence is discussing, but you should be able to handle any of the sentences using your knowledge of the English language.

Here is a typical sentence completion question, using one of the new sentence completion formats. In this question, you are asked to find *not one but two* correct answers; both answers must produce completed sentences that are like each other in meaning. This is what the test-makers call a **sentence equivalent** question.

| Quit Test | Exit Section | Review | Mark | Help | Back | Next |

Select the <u>two</u> answer choices that, when used to complete the sentence,
fit the meaning of the sentence as a whole <u>and</u> produce completed sentences that are alike in meaning.

Although the two mismatched roommates are the proverbial odd couple—Felix is pedantic where Oscar is imprecise, _____ where Oscar is slovenly, cultivated where Oscar is uncouth—they nevertheless manage to share a small apartment without driving each other crazy.

☐ taciturn
☐ fastidious
☐ ebullient
☐ nice
☐ stoical
☐ egregious

Click on your choices.

Unlike Oscar, Felix is *not* slovenly (messy and untidy); instead, he is a compulsive neatnik. Felix is *fastidious* or *nice* in his habits, excessively sensitive in matters of taste. (Note the use of *nice* in a secondary sense.)

Look at the same question, restructured into what the test-makers call a **text completion** question. In this type of question, you are asked to find only one correct answer per blank. However, you must have a correct answer for each and every blank.

| Quit Test | Exit Section | Review | Mark | Help | Back | Next |

For each blank select one entry from the corresponding column of choices. Fill all blanks in the way that best completes the text.

Although the two (i)_____ roommates are the proverbial odd couple—Felix is pedantic where Oscar is imprecise, (ii)_____ where Oscar is slovenly, cultivated where Oscar is (iii)_____—they nevertheless manage to share a small apartment without driving each other crazy.

Blank (i)	Blank (ii)	Blank (iii)
compatible	curious	refined
peripheral	unkempt	taciturn
mismatched	fastidious	uncouth

Click on your choices.

See page 56 for sentence completion question tactics and practice exercises that will help you handle both of the new sentence completion question types.

CRITICAL READING QUESTIONS

Critical reading questions test your ability to understand and interpret what you read. This is probably the most important ability that you will need in graduate school and afterward.

Although the passages may encompass any subject matter, you do not need to know anything about the subject discussed in the passage in order to answer the questions on that passage. The purpose of the question is to test your reading ability, not your knowledge of history, science, literature, or art.

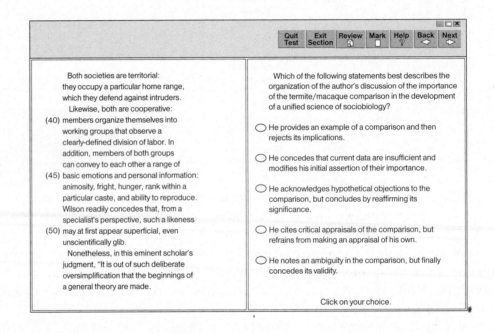

The key lines here are the passage's final sentences. Does the author *acknowledge hypothetical objections* to the comparison? Definitely. Does the author conclude by *reaffirming the significance* of the termite/macaque comparison? Clearly he does: he concludes by quoting Wilson (whom he calls an eminent scholar), in doing so giving implicit support to Wilson's assertion that such oversimplified comparisons can provide the basis for an important general theory. The correct answer is the third choice.

The New GRE contains both familiar and unfamiliar question types. Some of the unfamiliar questions involve logical reasoning and argument analysis. See page 82 for critical reading tactics that will help you handle the new logical reasoning questions. In addition, see Chapter 5 for additional tactics and practice exercises that will prepare you for the remainder of the critical reading portions of the test.

Quantitative Ability

The quantitative part of the GRE consists of two math sections, each with 20 questions. Of the 40 questions, there are

- 15 quantitative comparison questions—7 or 8 per section;
- 19 discrete quantitative questions, consisting of about 11 multiple-choice questions, 4 multiple-answer questions, and 4 numeric entry questions, approximately evenly split between the two sections;
- 6 data interpretation questions—3 per section—all of which are discrete quantitative questions, mostly multiple-choice.

In order to answer these questions, you need to know arithmetic, some very elementary algebra, and a little geometry. Much of this material you learned in elementary and middle school; the rest you learned during the first two years of high school. You do not need to know *any* advanced mathematics. The questions are intended to determine if you have a basic knowledge of elementary mathematics, and if you have the ability to reason clearly.

If you haven't done any mathematics in a while, go through the math review in this book before attempting the Model Tests, and certainly before registering to take the GRE. If you feel that your math skills are still pretty good, you can try the Diagnostic Test first, and then read only those sections of the math review relating to those topics that gave you trouble.

QUANTITATIVE COMPARISON QUESTIONS

Of the 40 mathematics questions on the GRE, 15 are what is known as quantitative comparisons. Unless you prepared for the SAT before 2005, it is very possible that you have never even seen such a question. Even if you have had some contact with this type of question, you need to review the basic idea and learn the essential tactics for answering them. Therefore, read these instructions *very* carefully.

In these questions there are two quantities—Quantity A and Quantity B—and it is your job to compare them. For these problems there are *only four possible answers*:

Quantity A is greater;
Quantity B is greater;
The two quantities are equal; and
It is impossible to determine which quantity is greater.

In this book, these four answer choices will be referred to as A, B, C, and D, respectively. In some of the questions, information about the quantities being compared is centered above them. This information *must* be taken into consideration when comparing the two quantities.

In Chapter 9 you will learn several important strategies for handling quantitative comparisons. For now, let's look at three examples to make sure that you understand the concepts involved.

EXAMPLE

Quantity A	Quantity B
$(3 + 4)^2$	$3^2 + 4^2$

- Evaluate each quantity: $(3 + 4)^2 = 7^2 = \mathbf{49}$, whereas $3^2 + 4^2 = 9 + 16 = \mathbf{25}$.
- Since $49 > 25$, Quantity A is greater. The answer is **A**.

EXAMPLE

$$a + b = 16$$

Quantity A	Quantity B
The average (arithmetic mean) of a and b	8

Quantity A is the average of a and b: $\dfrac{a+b}{2}$. Since we are told that $a + b = 16$,

Quantity A is $\dfrac{a+b}{2} = \dfrac{16}{2} = \mathbf{8}$.

So, Quantity A and Quantity B are equal. The answer is **C**.

NOTE: We cannot determine the value of either a or b; all we know is that their sum is 16. Perhaps $a = 10$ and $b = 6$, or $a = 0$ and $b = 16$, or $a = -4$ and $b = 20$. *It doesn't matter.* The average of 10 and 6 is 8; the average of 0 and 16 is 8; and the average of -4 and 20 is 8. Since $a + b$ is 16, the average of a and b is 8, *all the time, no matter what*. The answer, therefore, is **C**.

EXAMPLE

Quantity A	Quantity B
a^3	a^2

- If $a = 1$, $a^3 = 1$, and $a^2 = 1$. *In this case*, the quantities in the two columns are equal.
- This means that the answer to this problem *cannot* be A or B. Why?
- The answer can be A (or B) only if Quantity A (or B) is greater *all the time*. But it isn't — not when $a = 1$.
- So, is the answer C? *Maybe.* But for the answer to be C, the quantities would have to be equal *all the time*. Are they?

- No. If $a = 2$, $a^3 = 8$, and $a^2 = 4$, and *in this case* the two quantities are *not equal*.
- The answer, therefore, is **D**.

DISCRETE QUANTITATIVE QUESTIONS

Of the 40 mathematics questions on the GRE, 19 are what the ETS calls discrete quantitative questions. More than half of those questions are standard ***multiple-choice questions***, for which there are five answer choices, exactly one of which is correct. The way to answer such a question is to do the necessary work, get the solution, and then look at the five choices to find your answer. In Chapter 8 we will discuss other techniques for answering these questions, but for now let's look at one example.

EXAMPLE

Edison High School has 840 students, and the ratio of the number of students taking Spanish to the number not taking Spanish is 4:3. How many of the students take Spanish?

Ⓐ 280   Ⓑ 360   Ⓒ 480   Ⓓ 560   Ⓔ 630

To solve this problem requires only that you understand what a ratio is. Ignore the fact that this is a multiple-choice question. *Don't even look at the choices.*

- Let $4x$ and $3x$ be the number of students taking and not taking Spanish, respectively.
- Then $4x + 3x = 840 \Rightarrow 7x = 840 \Rightarrow x = 120$.
- The number of students taking Spanish is $4 \times 120 = 480$.
- Having found the answer to be 480, *now look at the five choices*. The answer is C.

A second type of discrete quantitative question that appears on the GRE is what the ETS calls a "multiple-choice question—more than one answer possible," and what for simplicity we call a ***multiple-answer question***. In this type of question there could be as many as 12 choices, although usually there are no more than 7 or 8. Any number of the answer choices, from just one to all of them, could be correct. To get credit for such a question, you must select *all* of the correct answer choices and *none* of the incorrect ones. Here is a typical example.

EXAMPLE

If *x* is negative, which of the following statements *must* be true?
Indicate *all* such statements.

☐ A $x^2 < x^4$

☐ B $x^3 < x^2$

☐ C $x + \dfrac{1}{x} < 0$

☐ D $x = \sqrt{x^2}$

To solve this problem, examine each statement independently, and think of it as a true-false question.

A. For many negative values of x, x^2 is less than x^4, but if $x = -1$, then x^2 and x^4 are each 1, so it is *not* true that x^2 *must* be less than x^4. A is false.

B. If x is negative, x^3 is negative, and so *must* be less than x^2, which is positive. Statement B is true.

C. If x is negative, so is $\dfrac{1}{x}$, and the sum of two negative numbers is negative. Statement C is true.

D. The square root of a number is *never* negative, and so could *not possibly* equal x. Statement D is false.

You must choose B and C and neither A nor D.

The third type of discrete quantitative question is called a ***numeric entry question***. The numeric entry questions are the only questions on the GRE for which no answer choices are given. For these questions, you have to determine the correct numerical answer and then use the number keys on the keyboard to enter the answer. There are two possibilities: if the answer is an integer or a number that contains a decimal point, there will be a single box for your answer; if the answer is to be entered as a fraction, there will be two boxes—one for the numerator and one for the denominator.

Here is a typical numeric entry question.

EXAMPLE

Directions: The answer to the following question is a fraction. Enter the numerator in the upper box and the denominator in the lower box.

On Monday, $\dfrac{1}{5}$ of the students at Central High went on a field trip to a museum. On Tuesday $\dfrac{5}{8}$ of the students who hadn't gone to the museum on Monday had the opportunity to go. What fraction of the students in the school did not go to the museum either day?

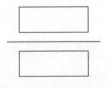

In Section H of Chapter 11, we will discuss the algebraic way to solve a problem such as this one, but on the GRE the best approach is just to assume that the school has 40 students, 40 being the least common multiple of 5 and 8, the two denominators in the problem. Then, 8 students ($\dfrac{1}{5}$ of 40) went to the museum on Monday, and of the remaining 32 students, 20 of them ($\dfrac{5}{8}$ of 32) went on Tuesday. So,

28 students went to the museum and 12 did not. So the fraction of the students in the school who did not go to the museum either day is $\frac{12}{40}$.

Enter 12 in the upper box for the numerator and 40 in the lower box for the denominator. Note that $\frac{12}{40}$ can be reduced to $\frac{6}{20}$ and $\frac{3}{10}$ and you would get full credit for either of those answers, but on the GRE it is *not* necessary to reduce fractions.

DATA INTERPRETATION QUESTIONS

In each of the two quantitative sections there are three consecutive questions that are based on the same set of data. Most data interpretation questions are multiple-choice questions, but you may have a multiple-answer and/or a numeric entry question. No data interpretation questions are quantitative comparisons. As you might guess from their name, all of these questions are based on information provided in graphs, tables, or charts. The questions test your ability to interpret the data that have been provided. You will either have to do a calculation or make an inference from the given data. The various types of questions that could arise will be explored in Chapter 10. Here is a typical data interpretation question.

EXAMPLE

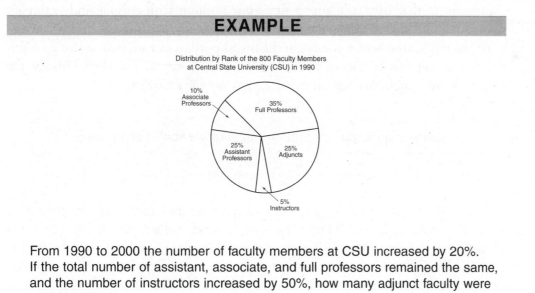

Distribution by Rank of the 800 Faculty Members
at Central State University (CSU) in 1990

From 1990 to 2000 the number of faculty members at CSU increased by 20%. If the total number of assistant, associate, and full professors remained the same, and the number of instructors increased by 50%, how many adjunct faculty were there in 2000?

This question is not difficult, but it requires several calculations.

- Since the number of faculty members increased by 20%, in 2000 there were 960 people on the faculty (20% of 800 = 160, and 800 + 160 = 960).
- In 1990, 70% (35% + 10% + 25%) of the faculty were professors, and 70% of 800 = 560.

So in 1990 and also in 2000, there were 560 professors.

- In 1990, there were 40 instructors (5% of 800 = 40); since that number increased by 50%, and 50% of 40 is 20, there were 60 instructors in 2000.
- Of the 960 faculty members in 2000, 560 were professors and 60 were instructors. The remaining **340** were adjuncts (960 − 560 − 60 = 340).

Enter 340 in the box.

Analytical Writing

The analytical writing portion of the New GRE consists of two tasks:

- Writing an essay presenting your point of view on an issue of general intellectual concern.
- Writing an essay analyzing the line of reasoning in an argument.

You are allotted 30 minutes to complete the issue task, and 30 minutes to complete the argument analysis task. You must finish one task before you begin the other. You will find suggestions for tackling both writing tasks in Chapter 6.

THE ISSUE TASK

In this task, you are asked to respond to a particular issue, clearly presenting your viewpoint on that issue and supporting your position with reasons and examples. This task is intended to test your ability to write logically, persuasively, and effectively.

At the test center, before you begin the timed portion of your issue writing assignment, you will first be shown a set of directions on screen. The directions for the issue task are straightforward. In essence, they say the following:

> **Develop an argument supporting your viewpoint on an issue.**
> **30 Minutes**

Each topic is presented as a one- to two-sentence quotation commenting on an issue of general concern. Your essay may support, refute, or qualify the views expressed in the quotation. Whatever you write, however, must be relevant to the issue under discussion, and you must support your viewpoint with reasons and examples derived from your studies and/or experience. What is more, you must carefully analyze the issue, following the specific instructions given. Your task is not to be creative but to be analytic.

Faculty members from various institutions will evaluate your essay, judging it on the basis of your skill in the following areas:

- Analysis of the question's implications
- Organization and articulation of your ideas
- Use of relevant examples and arguments to support your case
- Handling of the mechanics of standard written English

To begin the timed portion of this task, click on the box labeled Continue. Once you click on Continue, a second screen will appear. This screen contains some general words of advice about how to write an issue essay:

- Think before you write. Plan what you are going to say.
- Work out your ideas in detail.
- Be coherent.
- Leave yourself enough time to revise.

None of this is rocket science. You already know what you are supposed to do. Don't waste your time reading pro forma advice, Just click on the Continue box and get to work.

Here is an issue topic modeled on the sample issue tasks on the Revised GRE's General Test prelaunch update. Please note that this is not an official GRE issue topic, although it does resemble official topics closely in subject matter and form.

SAMPLE ISSUE TASK

Greatness in Art

The great artists in any medium—painters, poets, choreographers, sculptors—are those who create works of art that the majority of people can comprehend.

THE ARGUMENT TASK

In this task, you are asked to critique the line of reasoning of an argument given in a brief passage, clearly pointing out that argument's strengths and weaknesses and supporting your position with reasons and examples. This task is intended to test both your ability to evaluate the soundness of a position and your ability to get your point across to an academic audience.

Again, before you begin the timed portion of your argument analysis task, you will first be shown a set of directions on screen. The directions for the argument task are straightforward. In essence, they say the following:

Evaluate an argument.
30 Minutes

In 30 minutes, prepare a critical analysis of the argument expressed in a short paragraph. You may not offer an analysis of any other argument.

As you critique the argument, think about the author's underlying assumptions. Ask yourself whether any of them are questionable. Also, evaluate any evidence that the author brings up. Ask yourself whether it actually supports the author's conclusions.

In your analysis, you may suggest additional kinds of evidence to reinforce the author's argument. You may also suggest methods to refute the argument or additional data that might be useful to you as you assess the soundness of the argument. You may not, however, present your personal views on the topic. Your job is to analyze the elements of an argument, not to support or contradict that argument.

Faculty members from various institutions will judge your essay, assessing it on the basis of your skills in the following areas:

- Identification and assessment of the argument's main elements
- Organization and articulation of your thoughts
- Use of relevant examples and arguments to support your case
- Handling of the mechanics of standard written English

Here is an argument analysis topic modeled on the sample argument analysis task on the Revised GRE's General Test prelaunch update. Please note that this is not an official GRE argument analysis topic, although it does resemble the official topics closely in subject matter and form.

The following was written as part of an application for a parade permit made by a special event production company in San Francisco.

A televised Christmas parade held in San Francisco would be a sure fire source of profits and publicity for the city. Currently the only nationally televised pre-Christmas parade is the New York Macy's Thanksgiving Day Parade in late November. Our proposed early December Santa Day Parade would both capitalize on the Macy's Parade publicity and attract shoppers to San Francisco: over 10,000 people attended the St. Patrick's Day parade, while last October's Halloween parade through the Haight-Ashbury District drew at least twice that number. Finally, a recent marketing survey shows that people who come to New York to attend the Thanksgiving Day Parade spend over $1,000 that weekend on restaurant meals, hotel rooms, and Christmas shopping.

Test-Taking Tactics for the Computer-Based GRE

> If you purchased the version of this book that comes with a CD-ROM, you can use it *later* to familiarize yourself with the computer-based GRE, but do not use it until you have completed the bulk of your preparation, including going through each chapter in this book and doing the Model Tests in the back of the book. At that point, before taking one of the tests on the CD-ROM, *reread* this chapter.

In this chapter, we will take you step by step through a discussion of all the calculator screens you will see as you take the computer-based GRE. But first let's look at a few sample questions to show you what the screens actually look like, to familiarize you with the various icons, and to demonstrate how to use the mouse to navigate the screen.

Here is a simple ***multiple-choice*** math question as it would appear on a computer screen. Right now the arrow is off to one side.

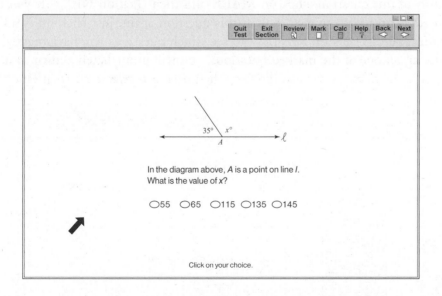

Suppose that in looking at the diagram, you see that the angle is a little greater than 100° and so decide that the answer must be 115. Move the mouse until the arrow is on the circle next to 115 and click. Note that the circle on which you clicked is now black.

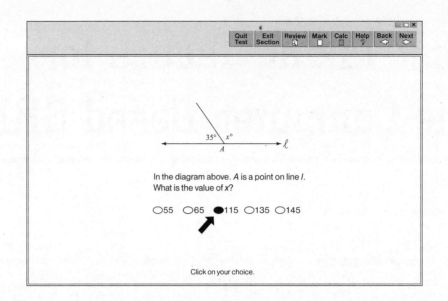

Suppose that just as you are about to click on NEXT to go to the next question, you remember that diagrams on the GRE are not drawn to scale, and so the answer may not be 115. Hopefully, you realize that the sum of the measures of the two angles in the diagram is 180°, and so to get the answer, you have to subtract 35 from 180. You can do the subtraction mentally, you can do it on your scratch paper, or you can click on the CALCULATOR icon and do it on a calculator. As soon as you click on the icon, a four-function calculator will appear on the screen. If the calculator opens up on top of the question or the answer choices, click on the top of it and drag it to wherever is convenient for you. You can either enter the numbers from your keyboard or click the numbers on the calculator. Since $180 - 35 = 145$, you want to change your answer. Simply click on the circle next to 145. That circle is now black, and the one next to 115 is white again. If you think that you might want to return to this question, click on MARK and then click on NEXT. If you know that there is no reason to ever look at this question again, just click on NEXT. At any time, you can click on REVIEW to see which questions you have marked, and by clicking on one of the marked questions, you will immediately return to it.

Suppose the question we just discussed had been a ***numeric entry*** question.

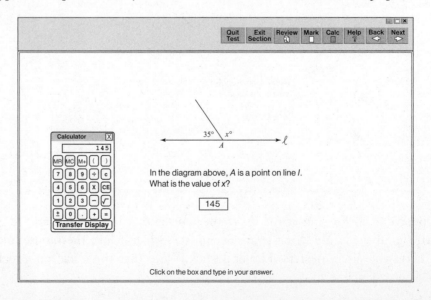

If you subtracted 35 from 180 in your head, and you knew that the answer was 145, you could click in the box and type 145. If you used your calculator to subtract, you could still type 145 in the box, but if you prefer, instead of typing 145, you could click on the bar labeled TRANSFER DISPLAY at the bottom of the calculator, and the 145 that is in the calculator's digital readout will automatically appear in the box. Note that the only time you can click on the TRANSFER DISPLAY bar is when the question on the screen is a numeric entry question; at all other times that bar is greyed out.

Finally, let's look at a ***multiple-answer*** question. Notice that on multiple-answer questions there are squares, instead of circles, in front of each answer choice.

On multiple-answer questions, when you click on a square in front of an answer choice, an X appears in the square. In this question, suppose you clicked on 17, 37, and 57, the screen would then look like this.

TIP

If you use the calculator to answer a question and then click on NEXT to go to the next question, the calculator will remain on the screen (with whatever your previous answer was still in the digital readout). You may leave it there, but it is better to close it, by clicking on the X in the upper-right-hand corner, and then just clicking on the calculator icon the next time you need it.

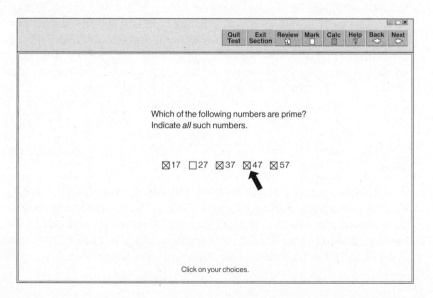

If you then realize that 47 is also a prime, just click on it; an X will appear in its square.

Finally, if you realize that you made another mistake, by including 57 (57 = 3 × 19), just click on the square in front of 57 and the X will go away.

HELPFUL HINTS

1. You should *never* click on the EXIT SECTION icon. This is tantamount to saying, "I give up. I can't deal with this section anymore." At the very least go through each question, taking a wild guess if necessary, get to the end of the section, and click CONTINUE to go to the next section.

2. You should *never* click on the HELP icon. All this will do is bring up a page of directions. Learn the directions for every type of question now, and review them, if necessary, when they appear before each section begins. Once you begin a section, the clock starts and clicking on HELP to reread the directions is just a waste of time.

3. Don't click on REVIEW until you have gotten to the end of the section. When you click on REVIEW, all you will see is a list numbered from 1–20, indicating for each question whether it has been ANSWERED or UNANSWERED and whether or not it has been MARKED. *No question should be unanswered.* If you are completely stumped and have no idea what the right answer is, just guess something before clicking on NEXT. Remember, your raw score is simply the number of correct answers you have. It would be terrible if you skipped a few questions, planning to come back to them, and then ran out of time. Instead of having a few guesses, which might result in a correct answer or two, you would have a few blanks, which earn no points whatsoever.

4. If time hasn't run out after you have answered Question 20, click on REVIEW to see which questions you marked. Click on one of them. That question will immediately appear, and you can give it a little more time. Perhaps you will figure it out; perhaps you will be able to eliminate some choices and make a better guess than you did originally.

A GUIDED TOUR OF THE COMPUTER-BASED GRE

The following outline tells you exactly what you will see, screen by screen, when you take the computerized GRE. To some extent you can alter the flow of screens. For example, after answering the fourteenth math question, we assume that you would click on NEXT to bring up the screen for Question 15. However, at that point, if you chose to, you could click on MARK to put a check mark next to Question 14 in the list of questions you have looked at; you could click on BACK to return to Question 13 or click on BACK repeatedly to return to any previous question in the section; you could click on REVIEW to see exactly which questions you had already answered, which ones you had skipped, and which ones you had marked; or you could click on HELP to reread the directions for the math questions. As you will see shortly, most of those would be poor choices, but you could do any of them.

When you are ready to begin the test, the first screen you will see is a page of TEST CENTER REGULATIONS. You may take as much time as you like to read over this list of rules—no eating, no drinking, no smoking, no creating disturbances, no tampering with the computer—but you shouldn't need to because you should have already read it when you looked at *POWERPREP II* on the GRE website. When you are through looking at this screen, click on CONTINUE.

The second screen is a CONFIDENTIALITY AGREEMENT. This is where you promise not to cheat or to take any test materials or scrap paper out of the room. The way you say "I agree" is to click on CONTINUE.

The third screen contains GENERAL TEST INFORMATION. Much of this information—when you can take breaks; how long the breaks are; when you can leave the room—is included in this book, but feel free to take as much time as you like to read it over. When you are ready to proceed, click on CONTINUE.

This screen gives you the DIRECTIONS FOR THE ANALYTICAL WRITING section of the GRE. Again, once you read this book, you should know all of these directions. When you are ready to move on, click on CONTINUE.

This screen has the DIRECTIONS FOR TASK 1 (ANALYZE AN ISSUE). The most important point to remember is that although you have 60 minutes for Section 1, you have a maximum of 30 minutes for each of the two tasks. If, for example, you finish Task 1 in 23 minutes, you may move on to Task 2, but once you do, you can never return to Task 1 to write for 7 more minutes. Nor can you tack those 7 minutes on to the time you have for Task 2. Once you leave Task 1, you will have exactly 30 minutes for Task 2. Once you are ready to leave this screen, TAKE A DEEP BREATH: as soon as you click on CONTINUE, the test officially begins.

This screen has Task 1. On the left of the screen will be the issue you are to analyze; on the right of the screen will be a blank page on which you are to type your analysis. In the upper-right-hand corner of the screen, below the row of icons, you will see a digital readout of the amount of time remaining. If you find that distracting, you may click on HIDE TIME to make it go away, but it will reappear when there are only five minutes left. During every section, the countdown clock will be visible unless you choose to hide it. Even if you do, in every section, the clock will reappear during the last five minutes. If you finish your essay in less than 30 minutes, read it over and make any changes you like. If you still have time left, and don't want to look at the essay any more, you *can* hit NEXT, but you don't have to. You can relax. When the 30 minutes are up, the computer will automatically close that screen and take you to the next one. If you do click on NEXT, the computer will give you one last chance to change your mind.

If your full 30 minutes for Task 1 has not expired, this screen will remind you that you still have time left and give you the option of returning to Task 1 (RETURN) or moving on (CONTINUE).

Once you have left Task 1, the next screen has the DIRECTIONS FOR TASK 2 (ANALYZE AN ARGUMENT). Note: the clock in *not* running while you read these directions. So if you want an extra minute or so before starting your second essay, wait before clicking on CONTINUE.

This screen has Task 2. The argument you are to analyze will be on the left, and just as in Task 1, on the right there will be a blank page on which you are to type your analysis. And as in Task 1, the moment this screen appears, the clock will start counting down from 30:00. When you have finished your essay, you may look it over, rest a while, or click on NEXT.

If your full 30 minutes for Task 2 has not expired, this screen will remind you that you still have time left and give you the option of returning to Task 2 (RETURN) or moving on (CONTINUE).

Once you have left Task 2, the next screen will tell you that you have finished Section 1 and are about to begin Section 2. When you are ready, click on CONTINUE.

This screen will tell you that the next section will begin in 60 seconds. This is your first official break. You *should* take this short break to relax before beginning Section 2, but you don't have to. At any time before your 60 seconds are up, you can click on CONTINUE to move on.

NOTE

Section 2 will either be a 30-minute verbal section or a 35-minute quantitative section. In the practice tests in this book, Sections 2 and 4 are verbal and Sections 3 and 5 are quantitative. On an actual GRE, however, the sections can come in any order, and it is very likely that there will be an Experimental Section—either a third verbal section or a third quantitative section—which can come at any point in the test. The Experimental Section will not affect your score, but there is no way to know which section it is, so you must do your very best on each section.

This screen gives you the DIRECTIONS FOR THE VERBAL ABILITY sections of the GRE. Reading this screen, slowly, if you like, gives you a little longer break before resuming the test. When you are ready to begin Section 2, click on CONTINUE.

Screens 14–33 will be the 20 verbal questions in Section 2, one question per screen. Go through the section, answering *every* question, guessing whenever necessary. If, when you click on CONTINUE after Question 20, your 30 minutes for Section 2 aren't up, the next screen you see will give you the option of returning to Section 2, by clicking on RETURN, or going on to Section 3, by again clicking on CONTINUE.

This screen will tell you that the next section will begin in 60 seconds. This is your second official break. You *should* take this short break to relax before beginning Section 3, but you don't have to. At any time before your 60 seconds are up, you may click on CONTINUE to move on.

This screen gives you the DIRECTIONS FOR THE QUANTITATIVE ABILITY sections of the GRE. Reading this screen, slowly, if you like, gives you a little longer break before resuming the test. When you are ready to start Section 3, click on CONTINUE.

Screens 36–55 will be the 20 quantitative questions in Section 3, one question per screen. Go through the section, answering *every* question, guessing whenever necessary. If there is a question that has you stumped, you can MARK it, but still answer it (even if your answer is a wild guess) before clicking on NEXT. Just as in Section 2, after answering Question 20, you may click on CONTINUE, but if you still have time left, a screen will appear that will give you the chance to change your mind: you

can click on RETURN to go back to the questions in Section 3 or you can really end the section by once again clicking on CONTINUE.

This screen will tell you that the next section will begin in 10 minutes. This is your third official break, and the only one that lasts more than 60 seconds. TAKE THIS BREAK! Whether you need to or not, go to the restroom now. If you have to go later during the test, the clock will be running. Outside the room, you can have a drink and/or a snack. And, of course, you can use this break to take some deep breaths and to relax before beginning the rest of the test. Having said this, you should know that you don't have to take the full 10-minute break. At any time before the 10 minutes are up, you may click on CONTINUE to move on.

At this point, the screens essentially repeat. There will be at least two more sections (one verbal and one quantitative), and probably three (the third section being yet another verbal or another quantitative one). Remember that if there are six sections, any section other than the writing section can be the experimental one, even Section 2 or 3. Each verbal section will have 20 questions and be 30 minutes long, just like Section 2, and each quantitative section will have 20 questions and be 35 minutes long, just like Section 3.

After you have answered Question 20 in Section 6 and clicked on CONTINUE, the test is over. At this point you will see the following screen.

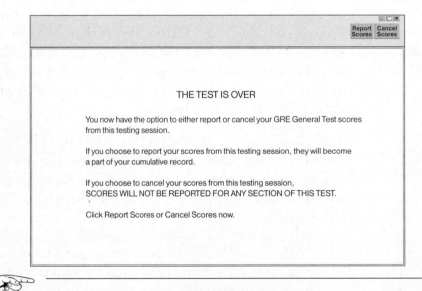

👉 ───────────────────────────────

NOTE

If you click on CANCEL, the next screen will give you a chance to avoid a disaster, in case you clicked CANCEL accidentally. Once again, you will be asked to REPORT or CANCEL, your scores, and this time your decision is irreversible.

If you choose to REPORT your scores, the next screen will give you your unofficial scores for the verbal and quantitative sections. Your official scores will arrive in the mail about three weeks after you take the test and, of course, will include your writing score, as well.

───

A Diagnostic Test

The Diagnostic Test in this chapter consists of three complete sections: one each of analytical writing, verbal ability, and quantitative ability. The format of each section is identical to that of the corresponding section of an actual GRE. The main difference between this Diagnostic Test and the Model Tests at the back of the book, the model tests on the optional CD-ROM, and the real GRE is that it is shorter—one verbal section and one quantitative section instead of two of each. Of course, unlike a real GRE, this Diagnostic Test isn't computerized. If you purchased the version of this book that contains a CD-ROM, then later in your preparation, to get a feel for what it is like to take a computerized GRE, do one or two model tests on the CD-ROM.

After taking the test, score your answers and evaluate your results, using the self-rating guides provided. (Be sure also to read the answer explanations for questions you answered incorrectly and questions you answered correctly but found difficult.)

You should now be in a position to approach your review program realistically and allot your time for study. For example, you should know which topics in mathematics require review and drill. You should also know which of your verbal and analytical skills require concentrated study.

SIMULATE TEST CONDITIONS

To best simulate actual test conditions, find a quiet place to work. Have a stop watch or a clock handy so that you can keep perfect track of the time. Go through each section by answering the questions in the order in which they appear. If you don't know the answer to a question, guess (making an educated guess, if possible) and move on. Knowing how much time you have for each section and how many questions there are, try to pace yourself so that you have time to finish each section in the time allowed. Do not spend too much time on any one question. Again, if you get stuck, just guess and go on to the next question. If any time remains, you may return to a question that you were unsure of or check your work.

Answer Sheet
DIAGNOSTIC TEST

Section 2

1 Ⓐ Ⓑ Ⓒ Ⓓ Ⓔ Ⓕ   6 Ⓐ Ⓑ Ⓒ Ⓓ Ⓔ Ⓕ   11 Ⓐ Ⓑ Ⓒ Ⓓ Ⓔ   16 Ⓐ Ⓑ Ⓒ Ⓓ Ⓔ Ⓕ

2 Ⓐ Ⓑ Ⓒ Ⓓ Ⓔ Ⓕ   7 Ⓐ Ⓑ Ⓒ Ⓓ Ⓔ   12 Ⓐ Ⓑ Ⓒ Ⓓ Ⓔ   17 Ⓐ Ⓑ Ⓒ Ⓓ Ⓔ

3 Ⓐ Ⓑ Ⓒ Ⓓ Ⓔ Ⓕ   8 Ⓐ Ⓑ Ⓒ Ⓓ Ⓔ   13 Ⓐ Ⓑ Ⓒ Ⓓ Ⓔ Ⓕ   18 Ⓐ Ⓑ Ⓒ Ⓓ Ⓔ

4 Ⓐ Ⓑ Ⓒ Ⓓ Ⓔ Ⓕ   9 Ⓐ Ⓑ Ⓒ Ⓓ Ⓔ   14 Ⓐ Ⓑ Ⓒ Ⓓ Ⓔ Ⓕ   19 Ⓐ Ⓑ Ⓒ

5 Ⓐ Ⓑ Ⓒ Ⓓ Ⓔ Ⓕ   10 Ⓐ Ⓑ Ⓒ Ⓓ Ⓔ   15 Ⓐ Ⓑ Ⓒ Ⓓ Ⓔ Ⓕ   20 Ⓐ Ⓑ Ⓒ Ⓓ Ⓔ

Section 3

1 Ⓐ Ⓑ Ⓒ Ⓓ   6 Ⓐ Ⓑ Ⓒ Ⓓ   11 Ⓐ Ⓑ Ⓒ Ⓓ Ⓔ   16 ☐

2 Ⓐ Ⓑ Ⓒ Ⓓ   7 Ⓐ Ⓑ Ⓒ Ⓓ   12 ☐   17 Ⓐ Ⓑ Ⓒ Ⓓ Ⓔ

3 Ⓐ Ⓑ Ⓒ Ⓓ   8 Ⓐ Ⓑ Ⓒ Ⓓ   13 Ⓐ Ⓑ Ⓒ Ⓓ Ⓔ Ⓕ   18 Ⓐ Ⓑ Ⓒ Ⓓ Ⓔ
                                Ⓖ Ⓗ Ⓘ

4 Ⓐ Ⓑ Ⓒ Ⓓ   9 Ⓐ Ⓑ Ⓒ Ⓓ Ⓔ   14 Ⓐ Ⓑ Ⓒ Ⓓ Ⓔ   19 Ⓐ Ⓑ Ⓒ Ⓓ Ⓔ

5 Ⓐ Ⓑ Ⓒ Ⓓ   10 Ⓐ Ⓑ Ⓒ Ⓓ Ⓔ   15 Ⓐ Ⓑ Ⓒ Ⓓ Ⓔ   20 Ⓐ Ⓑ Ⓒ Ⓓ Ⓔ

Section 1 Analytical Writing

TIME: 60 MINUTES—2 WRITING TASKS

Task 1: Issue Exploration
30 MINUTES

Directions: In 30 minutes, compose an essay on the topic below. You may not write on any other topic. Write your essay on the lined page that follows.

The topic is presented in a one- to two-sentence quotation commenting on an issue of general concern. Your essay may support, refute, or qualify the views expressed in the quotation. Whatever you write, however, must be relevant to the issue under discussion, and you must support your viewpoint with reasons and examples derived from your studies and/or experience.

Faculty members from various institutions will evaluate your essay, judging it on the basis of your skill in the following areas.

- Analysis of the quotation's implications
- Organization and articulation of your ideas
- Use of relevant examples and arguments to support your case
- Handling of the mechanics of standard written English

Topic

"We venerate loyalty—to our schools, employers, institutions, friends—as a virtue. Loyalty, however, can be at least as detrimental an influence as it can be a beneficial one."

Task 2: Argument Analysis
30 MINUTES

Directions: In 30 minutes, prepare a critical analysis of an argument expressed in a short paragraph. You may not offer an analysis of any other argument. Write your essay on the lined page that follows.

As you critique the argument, think about the author's underlying assumptions. Ask yourself whether any of them are questionable. Also evaluate any evidence the author brings up. Ask yourself whether it actually supports the author's conclusion.

In your analysis, you may suggest additional kinds of evidence to reinforce the author's argument. You may also suggest methods to refute the argument, or additional data that might be useful to you as you assess the soundness of the argument. *You may **not**, however, present your personal views on the topic.* Your job is to analyze the elements of an argument, not to support or contradict that argument.

Faculty members from various institutions will judge your essay, assessing it on the basis of your skill in the following areas:

- Identification and assessment of the argument's main elements
- Organization and articulation of your thoughts
- Use of relevant examples and arguments to support your case
- Handling of the mechanics of standard written English

Topic
The following appeared in an editorial in the *Bayside Sentinel.*

"Bayside citizens need to consider raising local taxes if they want to see improvements in the Bayside School District. Test scores, graduation and college admission rates, and a number of other indicators have long made it clear that the Bayside School District is doing a poor job educating our youth. Our schools look run down. Windows are broken, bathrooms unusable, and classroom equipment hopelessly out of date. Yet just across the Bay, in New Harbor, school facilities are up-to-date and in good condition. The difference is money; New Harbor spends twenty-seven percent more per student than Bayside does, and test scores and other indicators of student performance are stronger in New Harbor as well."

Section 2 Verbal Reasoning

TIME: 30 MINUTES—20 QUESTIONS

Questions 1–6 (Sentence Equivalent)

Directions: For each of the following sentences, select the **two** answers of the six choices given that, when substituted in the sentence, both logically complete the sentence as a whole **and** create sentences that are equivalent to one another in meaning.

1. Many of us attempt to rewrite our personal stories to present ourselves in the best light; indeed, we are almost universally _____ to do so.

   - [A] reluctant
   - [B] illuminated
   - [C] apt
   - [D] prone
   - [E] intimidated
   - [F] comprehensive

2. Far from condemning Warhol for his apparent superficiality and commercialism, critics today _____ him for these very qualities, contending that in these superficial, commercial artworks he had captured the essence of American culture in the 1970s.

   - [A] belittle
   - [B] chastise
   - [C] tolerate
   - [D] extol
   - [E] flaunt
   - [F] hail

3. A born trickster, he was as inclined to _____ as an embezzler is inclined to fraud.

   - [A] bravado
   - [B] chicanery
   - [C] cowardice
   - [D] candor
   - [E] ingenuousness
   - [F] artifice

4. Paradoxically, the very admonitions intended to reform the prodigal served only to _____ his wicked ways.

   - [A] turn him from
   - [B] confirm him in
   - [C] distress him about
   - [D] absolve him of
   - [E] reinforce
   - [F] transform

5. Although no two siblings could have dis-agreed more in nature—where she was gregarious, he was introverted; where she was outspoken, he was _____—the twins nevertheless got on amazingly well.

- [A] reserved
- [B] discreet
- [C] garrulous
- [D] insensitive
- [E] imprudent
- [F] fluent

6. Amusingly enough, lawyers sometimes drive their sport cars in the same fashion that they construct their cases: a lawyer noted for the _____ of his arguments, for example, may also be known for the circuitousness of his routes.

- [A] brevity
- [B] pertinacity
- [C] judiciousness
- [D] deviousness
- [E] conciseness
- [F] indirectness

Directions: The next questions are based on the content of the following passage. Read the passage and then determine the best answer choice for each question. Base your choice on what this passage *states directly* or *implies*, not on any information you may have gained elsewhere.

For each of Questions 7–11, select *one* answer choice unless otherwise instructed.

Questions 7–9 are based on the following passage.

James's first novels used conventional narrative techniques: explicit characterization, action that related events in distinctly phased
Line sequences, settings firmly outlined and
(5) specifically described. But this method gradually gave way to a subtler, more deliberate, more diffuse style of accumulation of minutely discriminated details whose total significance the reader can grasp only by
(10) constant attention and sensitive inference. His later novels play down scenes of abrupt and prominent action, and do not so much offer a succession of sharp shocks as slow piecemeal additions of perception. The cur-
(15) tain is not suddenly drawn back from shrouded things, but is slowly moved away. Such a technique is suited to James's essential subject, which is not human action itself but the states of mind that produce and are pro-
(20) duced by human actions and interactions. James was less interested in what characters do, than in the moral and psychological antecedents, realizations, and consequences which attend their doings. This is why he
(25) more often speaks of "cases" than of actions. His stories, therefore, grow more and more lengthy while the actions they relate grow simpler and less visible; not because they are crammed with adventitious and secondary
(30) events, digressive relief, or supernumerary characters, as overstuffed novels of action are; but because he presents in such exhaustive detail every nuance of his situation. Commonly the interest of a novel is in the
(35) variety and excitement of visible actions building up to a climactic event which will settle the outward destinies of characters with storybook promise of permanence. A James novel, however, possesses its character-
(40) istic interest in carrying the reader through a rich analysis of the mental adjustments of characters to the realities of their personal situations as they are slowly revealed to them through exploration and chance discovery.

7. The passage supplies information for answering which of the following questions?
   (A) Did James originate the so-called psychological novel?
   (B) Is conventional narrative technique strictly chronological in recounting action?
   (C) Can novels lacking overtly dramatic incident sustain the reader's interest?
   (D) Were James's later novels more acceptable to the general public than his earlier ones?
   (E) Is James unique in his predilection for exploring psychological nuances of character?

8. In which sentence of the passage does the author use figurative language to clarify James's technique in his later novels?

   NOTE: *In the computer-based GRE, the directions would be:* **Click on the sentence in the passage.**

   (A) The first sentence ("James's first novels ... described.")
   (B) The second sentence ("But this method ... inference.")
   (C) The fourth sentence ("The curtain ... moved away.")
   (D) The fifth sentence ("Such a technique ... interactions.")
   (E) The sixth sentence ("James was ... doings.")

9. In the context in which it appears, "attend" (line 24) most nearly means
   (A) take care of
   (B) watch over
   (C) pay attention to
   (D) accompany
   (E) celebrate

Questions 10–11 are based on the following passage.

According to the theory of plate tectonics, the lithosphere (earth's relatively hard and solid outer layer consisting of the crust and
Line part of the underlying mantle) is divided
(5) into a few dozen plates that vary in size and shape; in general, these plates move in relation to one another. They move away from one another at a mid-ocean ridge, a long chain of sub-oceanic mountains that forms a
(10) boundary between plates. At a mid-ocean ridge, new lithospheric material in the form of hot magma pushes up from the earth's interior. The injection of this new lithospheric material from below causes the phe-
(15) nomenon known as sea-floor spreading.

Given that the earth is not expanding in size to any appreciable degree, how can "new" lithosphere be created at a mid-ocean ridge? For new lithosphere to come into
(20) being in one region, an equal amount of lithospheric material must be destroyed somewhere else. This destruction takes place at a boundary between plates called a subduction zone. At a subduction zone, one
(25) plate is pushed down under another into the red-hot mantle, where over a span of millions of years it is absorbed into the mantle.

10. According to the passage, a mid-ocean ridge differs from a subduction zone in that
    (A) it marks the boundary line between neighboring plates
    (B) only the former is located on the ocean floor
    (C) it is a site for the emergence of new lithospheric material
    (D) the former periodically disrupts the earth's geomagnetic field
    (E) it is involved with lithospheric destruction rather than lithospheric creation

11. It can be inferred from the passage that as new lithospheric material is injected from below
    (A) the plates become immobilized in a kind of gridlock
    (B) it is incorporated into an underwater mountain ridge
    (C) the earth's total mass is altered
    (D) it reverses its magnetic polarity
    (E) the immediately adjacent plates sink

Questions 12–16

Directions: Each of the following sentences or groups of sentences contains one, two, or three blanks. These blanks signify that a word or set of words has been left out. Below each sentence are columns of words or sets of words. For each blank, pick the *one* word or set of words from the corresponding column that *best* completes the text.

12. By _____ strict rules of hygiene in maternity wards, Ignaz Semmelweis saved many women from dying of childbed fever, a fate that many expectant mothers feared.

Ⓐ challenging
Ⓑ instituting
Ⓒ intimating
Ⓓ invalidating
Ⓔ sanitizing

13. The earth is a planet bathed in light; it is therefore (i) _____ that many of the living organisms that have evolved on the earth have (ii) _____ the biologically advantageous capacity to trap light energy.

Blank (i)

Ⓐ anomalous
Ⓑ unsurprising
Ⓒ problematic

Blank (ii)

Ⓓ encapsulated
Ⓔ divested
Ⓕ developed

14. To contrast the demeanor of Austen's clergy-man brothers James and Henry with that of Mr. Collins, the much-abused figure of fun in *Pride and Prejudice*, is instructive, for where the Austen brothers were properly (i) _____ to their social superiors and benevolent to their dependents, the odious Mr. Collins was invariably (ii) _____ to his betters, fawning in particular on his patron, Lady Catherine de Burgh.

Blank (i)

Ⓐ deferential
Ⓑ disingenuous
Ⓒ demonstrative

Blank (ii)

Ⓓ responsible
Ⓔ sycophantic
Ⓕ sardonic

15. The reclassification of the solar system that demoted Pluto to a "dwarf planet" did not go (i) _____, for several hundred indignant astronomers petitioned the International Astronomical Union to (ii) _____ its decision.

Blank (i)

Ⓐ astray
Ⓑ uncontested
Ⓒ unrewarded

Blank (ii)

Ⓓ reconsider
Ⓔ initiate
Ⓕ promulgate

16. Relatively few politicians willingly (i) _____ center stage, although a touch of (ii) _____ on their parts now and again might well increase their popularity with the voting public.

Blank (i)

Ⓐ forsake
Ⓑ embrace
Ⓒ endure

Blank (ii)

Ⓓ garrulity
Ⓔ misanthropy
Ⓕ self-effacement

Directions: The passage below is followed by questions based on its content. Once you have read the passage, select the answer choice that *best* answers each question. Answer all questions on the basis of what is *stated* or *implied* in the passage.

For each of Questions 17–20, select *one* answer choice unless otherwise instructed.

Questions 17–18 are based on the following passage.

The stability that had marked the Iroquois Confederacy's generally pro-British position was shattered with the overthrow of James II
Line in 1688, the colonial uprisings that followed
(5) in Massachusetts, New York, and Maryland, and the commencement of King William's War against Louis XIV of France. The increasing French threat to English hegemony in the interior of North America was
(10) signalized by French-led or French-inspired attacks on the Iroquois and on outlying colonial settlements in New York and New England. The high point of the Iroquois response was the spectacular raid of August
(15) 5, 1689, in which the Iroquois virtually wiped out the French village of Lachine, just outside Montreal. A counter-raid by the French on the English village of Schenectady in March 1690 instilled an appropriate
(20) measure of fear among the English and their Iroquois allies.

The Iroquois position at the end of the war, which was formalized by treaties made during the summer of 1701 with the British
(25) and the French, and which was maintained throughout most of the eighteenth century, was one of "aggressive neutrality" between the two competing European powers. Under the new system the Iroquois initiated a peace
(30) policy toward the "far Indians," tightened their control over the nearby tribes, and induced both English and French to support their neutrality toward the European powers by appropriate gifts and concessions.

17. The author's primary purpose in this passage is to
    Ⓐ denounce the imperialistic policies of the French
    Ⓑ disprove the charges of barbarism made against the Indian nations
    Ⓒ expose the French government's exploitation of the Iroquois balance of power
    Ⓓ describe and assess the effect of European military power on the policy of an Indian nation
    Ⓔ show the inability of the Iroquois to engage in European-style diplomacy

18. With which of the following statements would the author be LEAST likely to agree?
    Ⓐ The Iroquois were able to respond effectively to French acts of aggression.
    Ⓑ James II's removal from the throne preceded the outbreak of dissension among the colonies.
    Ⓒ The French sought to undermine the generally positive relations between the Iroquois and the British.
    Ⓓ Iroquois negotiations involved playing one side against the other.
    Ⓔ The Iroquois ceased to receive trade concessions from the European powers early in the eighteenth century.

Questions 19–20 are based on the following passage.

A recent assessment of the status of global amphibian populations identified habitat loss as the single greatest identifiable factor
Line contributing to amphibian declines. Habitat
(5) loss primarily results from the residential, agricultural, arboricultural, or recreational development of an area.
Anthropogenic conversion of land has caused significant reductions in the wetland,
(10) forest, and grassland habitat that amphibians require for their survival. Outright habitat loss probably has the greatest effect on amphibians, but habitat degradation, or the general decline in the health of a habitat,
(15) often results from environmental contamination, the introduction of exotic invasive species, or a reduction in required resources within a habitat, and similarly affects amphibians. Likewise, habitat fragmentation
(20) (the disruption or fragmentation of habitat into discontinuous or isolated remnants of viable habitat) emerges from isolated patches of habitat loss and can often have delayed effects on animal populations.

Directions: For the following question, consider each of the choices separately and select *all* that apply.

19. Which of the following statements about habitat loss is supported by the passage?
    A The role of habitat loss in the decline of global amphibian populations is the subject of current evaluation.
    B Outright habitat loss causes less damage to amphibian populations than either habitat degradation or habitat fragmentation.
    C Introducing non-native species to an area may prove detrimental to the native animal populations.

20. In the course of the passage, the author does all of the following EXCEPT
    Ⓐ define a term
    Ⓑ cite an authority
    Ⓒ state a probability
    Ⓓ qualify a statement
    Ⓔ make an assertion

Section 3 Quantitative Ability

TIME: 35 MINUTES—20 QUESTIONS

Directions: In each of Questions 1–8, there are two quantities—Quantity A and Quantity B. You are to compare those quantities, taking into consideration any additional information given. The correct answer to such a question is

Ⓐ if Quantity A is greater;
Ⓑ if Quantity B is greater;
Ⓒ if the two quantities are equal;
Ⓓ if it is impossible to determine which quantity is greater.

Note: The given information, if any, is always centered above the two quantities. In any question, if a symbol or letter appears more than once, it represents the same thing each time.

$$a > 0$$

Quantity A	Quantity B
1. $a^4 a^5$	$(a^3)^2$

Quantity A	Quantity B
2. $a + b - c$	0

$$0 < a < b < 1$$

Quantity A	Quantity B
3. $\sqrt{a+b}$	$\sqrt{a} + \sqrt{b}$

There are 250 people lined up outside a theater. Jack is the 25th person from the front, and Jill is the 125th person from the front.

Quantity A	Quantity B
4. The number of people between Jack and Jill	100

$$90 < x < 180$$

Quantity A	Quantity B
5. The perimeter of $\triangle AOB$	17

$$\frac{a-b}{c-a} = 1$$

Quantity A	Quantity B
6. The average (arithmetic mean) of b and c	a

Quantity A	Quantity B
7. The average (arithmetic mean) of the measures of the three angles of a triangle whose largest angle measures 75°	The average (arithmetic mean) of the measures of the three angles of a triangle whose largest angle measures 105°

The three circles have the same center. The radii of the circles are 3, 4, and 5.

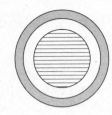

	Quantity A	Quantity B
8.	The area of the shaded region	The area of the striped region

Directions: Questions 9–20 have three different formats. Unless a question has its own directions that specifically state otherwise, each question has five answer choices, exactly one of which is correct.

9. In the figure below, what is the value of $a + b + c$?

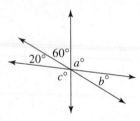

  Ⓐ 210
  Ⓑ 220
  Ⓒ 240
  Ⓓ 270
  Ⓔ 280

10. What is the value of n if $4^{10} \times 64^2 = 16^2 \times 4^n$?
  Ⓐ 6
  Ⓑ 10
  Ⓒ 12
  Ⓓ 15
  Ⓔ 30

11. Twenty children were sharing equally the cost of a present for their teacher. When 4 of the children decided not to contribute, each of the other children had to pay $1.50 more. How much did the present cost, in dollars?
  Ⓐ 50
  Ⓑ 80
  Ⓒ 100
  Ⓓ 120
  Ⓔ 150

Directions: For the following question, enter your answer in the box.

12. Of the 200 seniors at Monroe High School, exactly 40 are in the band, 60 are in the orchestra, and 10 are in both. How many seniors are in neither the band nor the orchestra?

Directions: For the following question, consider each of the choices separately and select *all* that apply.

13. Benjamin's average (arithmetic mean) on the six biology tests he took last semester was 89. On each of his first five tests, his grade was between 90 and 100, inclusive. Which of the following could have been his grade on his sixth test?

   Indicate *all* such grades.

A 15	D 45	G 75
B 25	E 55	H 85
C 35	F 65	I 95

Questions 14–16 refer to the following graphs.

1993
Total Exports to Eastern Europe = $98 Billion

1996
Total Exports to Eastern Europe = $174 Billion

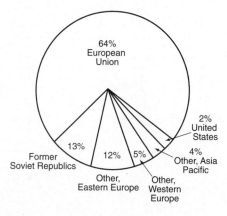

14. Which of the following statements concerning the value of exports to Eastern Europe from other Eastern European countries from 1993 to 1996 is the most accurate?

   Ⓐ They increased by 2%.
   Ⓑ They increased by 12%.
   Ⓒ They increased by 20%.
   Ⓓ They increased by 50%.
   Ⓔ They increased by 100%.

15. France is one of the countries in the European Union. If in 1996 France's exports to Eastern Europe were four times those of the United States, then what percent of the European Union's exports to Eastern Europe came from France that year?

   Ⓐ 5%
   Ⓑ 8%
   Ⓒ 12.5%
   Ⓓ 20%
   Ⓔ 25%

Directions: For the following question, enter your answer in the box.

16. If from 1996 to 2000 the percent increase in total exports to Eastern Europe was the same as the percent increase from 1993 to 1996, and the percent of exports from the European Union remained the same as in 1996, to the nearest billion, what was the value, in dollars, of exports from the European Union to Eastern Europe in 2000?

   ☐ dollars

17. Let the lengths of the sides of a triangle be represented by $x + 3$, $2x - 3$, and $3x - 5$. If the perimeter of the triangle is 25, what is the length of the shortest side?

    Ⓐ 5
    Ⓑ 6
    Ⓒ 7
    Ⓓ 8
    Ⓔ 10

18. In 1990, twice as many boys as girls at Adams High School earned varsity letters. From 1990 to 2000 the number of girls earning varsity letters increased by 25% while the number of boys earning varsity letters decreased by 25%. What was the ratio in 2000 of the number of girls to the number of boys who earned varsity letters?

    Ⓐ $\dfrac{5}{3}$

    Ⓑ $\dfrac{6}{5}$

    Ⓒ $\dfrac{1}{1}$

    Ⓓ $\dfrac{5}{6}$

    Ⓔ $\dfrac{3}{5}$

19. If $x + 2y = a$ and $x - 2y = b$, which of the following expressions is equal to xy?

    Ⓐ ab

    Ⓑ $\dfrac{a+b}{2}$

    Ⓒ $\dfrac{a-b}{2}$

    Ⓓ $\dfrac{a^2 - b^2}{4}$

    Ⓔ $\dfrac{a^2 - b^2}{8}$

20. A square and an equilateral triangle each have sides of length 5. What is the ratio of the area of the square to the area of the triangle?

    Ⓐ $\dfrac{4}{3}$

    Ⓑ $\dfrac{16}{9}$

    Ⓒ $\dfrac{\sqrt{3}}{4}$

    Ⓓ $\dfrac{4\sqrt{3}}{3}$

    Ⓔ $\dfrac{16\sqrt{3}}{9}$

Self-Appraisal

Now that you have completed the Diagnostic Test, evaluate your performance. Identify your strengths and weaknesses, and then plan a practical study program based on what you have discovered.

Use the Answer Key on the next page to check your answers. Your raw score for each section is equal to the number of correct answers you had. Once you have determined your raw score for each ability area, use the conversion chart that follows to get your scaled score. Note that this conversion chart is provided to give you a very rough estimate of the GRE score you would achieve if you took the test now without any further preparation. When you take the computer-based GRE, your scaled score will be determined not only by the number of questions you answer correctly, but also by the difficulty level of those questions. The unofficial conversion chart presented here gives you only an approximate idea of how raw scores convert into scaled scores.

Use this Diagnostic Test to identify areas you may be weak in. You may find that you had trouble with a particular question type (for example, you didn't do well on the reading comprehension questions in the verbal section), or with particular subject matter (for example, you didn't do well on the geometry questions, whether they were quantitative comparisons or discrete quantitative). Determining what you need to concentrate on will help you plan an effective study program.

Remember that, in addition to evaluating your scores and identifying weak areas, you should read all the answer explanations for questions you answered incorrectly, questions you guessed on, and questions you answered correctly but found difficult. Reviewing the answer explanations will help you understand concepts and strategies, and may point out shortcuts.

Score Conversion Chart for the Verbal and Quantitative Sections

Raw Score	Scaled Score	Raw Score	Scaled Score
20	170	9	148
19	168	8	146
18	166	7	144
17	164	6	142
16	162	5	140
15	160	4	138
14	158	3	136
13	156	2	134
12	154	1	132
11	152	0	130
10	150		

Diagnostic Test
ANSWER KEY

Section 1–Analytical Writing

There are no "correct answers" to this section.

Section 2–Verbal Reasoning

1. **C, D**	6. **D, F**	11. **B**	16. **A, F**
2. **D, F**	7. **C**	12. **B**	17. **D**
3. **B, F**	8. **C**	13. **B, F**	18. **E**
4. **B, E**	9. **D**	14. **A, E**	19. **A, C**
5. **A, B**	10. **C**	15. **B, D**	20. **B**

Section 3–Quantitative Ability

Note: The letters in brackets following the Quantitative Ability answers refer to the sections of Chapter 11 in which you can find the information you need to answer the questions. For example, 1. **C** [E] means that the answer to question 1 is C, and that the solution requires information found in Section 11-E: Averages. Also, 14. **E** [10] means that the answer to question 14 is based on information in Chapter 10: Data Interpretation.

1. **D** [A]	6. **C** [E,G]	11. **D** [G]	16. **198** [10]
2. **C** [J]	7. **C** [E,J]	12. **110** [O]	17. **C** [G]
3. **B** [A,B]	8. **C** [L]	13. **C, D, E, F, G** [E]	18. **D** [C,D]
4. **B** [O]	9. **B** [I]	14. **E** [10]	19. **E** [G]
5. **A** [J,L]	10. **C** [A]	15. **C** [10]	20. **D** [J,K]

ANSWER EXPLANATIONS

Section 1—Analytical Writing

There are no "correct answers" to this section.

Section 2—Verbal Reasoning

1. **(C), (D)** Both *apt* and *prone* have several meanings. *Apt*, for example, can mean appropriate, as in an apt remark, or it can mean unusually quick and intelligent, as in an apt pupil. *Prone* can mean prostrate; it can also mean having a downward slope. Here both *apt* and *prone* are used in the sense of inclined or liable.

   Note the use of *indeed* to both confirm and emphasize the preceding statement. Not only do many of us try to rewrite our lives, but we are almost universally inclined to do so.

2. **(D), (F)** *Far from* is a contrast signal. It indicates that you are looking for an antonym for *condemn*. The critics do not condemn Warhol for what seems to be superficiality and commercialism. Instead, they *extol* or *hail* him for having captured the superficial, commercial nature of American culture during the 1970s.

   Note that *hail* in this context is synonymous with acclaim or approve enthusiastically (secondary meaning).

3. **(B), (F)** By definition, embezzlers are inclined to fraud. By definition, tricksters are inclined to trickery, that is, to *chicanery* or *artifice*. Here *artifice* means subtle but base deception, not skill or ingenuity.

4. **(B), (E)** *Paradoxically* inherently signals a contrast. It indicates that something unexpected and unwanted has occurred. An admonition or warning intended to reform a spendthrift failed to have the desired result. Instead, it *reinforced* his profligate behavior, *confirming* or strengthening *him in* his wasteful habits.

5. **(A), (B)** You are looking for an antonym for *outspoken* (frank and unreserved in speech). To be *reserved* is to be restrained or reticent in manner. To be *discreet* is to be judicious in conduct or speech.

6. **(D), (F)** The key word here is *circuitousness*. The writer here is developing an analogy between the way lawyers drive their cars and the way they build or construct their legal arguments. Thus, someone known for choosing circuitous (roundabout; twisty) routes might also be known for coming up with *devious* (tricky; oblique) or *indirect* (roundabout; not direct) arguments.

7. **(C)** The author states that the later novels of James play down prominent action. Thus, they lack *overtly dramatic incident*. However, the author goes on to state that James's novels *do* possess interest; they carry the reader through "a rich analysis of the mental adjustments of the characters to the realities of their personal situations." It is this implicitly dramatic psychological revelation that sustains the reader's interest.

Question A is unanswerable on the basis of the passage. It is evident that James wrote psychological novels; it is nowhere stated that he originated the genre.

Question B is unanswerable on the basis of the passage. Although conventional narrative technique relates "events in distinctly phased sequences," clearly separating them, it does not necessarily recount action in *strictly* chronological order.

Question D is unanswerable on the basis of the passage. The passage does not deal with the general public's reaction to James.

Question E is unanswerable on the basis of the passage. The passage talks of qualities in James as a novelist in terms of their being *characteristic*, not in terms of their making him *unique*.

8. **(C)** In the third sentence the author describes James's later novel as offering "slow piecemeal additions of perception." To clarify the process, he goes on in sentence four to paint a picture in words, using figurative language. No literal curtain is drawn away here; however, the image of a curtain being slowly drawn away helps the reader develop a feeling for James's method of psychological revelation.

9. **(D)** The word "attend" here is used in the sense of "to accompany or go with as a concurrent circumstance or result." People's actions inevitably involve moral and psychological realizations and consequences; they go with the territory, so to speak.

10. **(C)** The subduction zone is the site of the destruction or consumption of existing lithospheric material. In contrast, the mid-ocean ridge is the site of the creation or emergence of new lithospheric material.

    Choice A is incorrect. Both mid-ocean ridges and subduction zones are boundaries between plates.

    Choice B is incorrect. Both are located on the ocean floor.

    Choice D is incorrect. It is unsupported by the passage.

    Choice E is incorrect. The reverse is true.

11. **(B)** Choice B is correct. You are told that the new lithospheric material is injected into a mid-ocean ridge, a suboceanic mountain range. This new material does not disappear; it is added to the material already there. Thus, it is *incorporated into* the existing mid-ocean ridge.

    Choice A is incorrect. "In general the plates are in motion with respect to one another." Nothing suggests that they become immobilized; indeed, they are said to diverge from the ridge, sliding as they diverge.

    Choice C is incorrect. The passage specifically denies it. ("The size of the earth is essentially constant.")

    Choice D is incorrect. It is the earth itself whose magnetic field reverses. Nothing in the passage suggests the new lithospheric material has any such potential.

    Choice E is incorrect. At a mid-ocean ridge, the site at which new lithospheric material is injected from below, the plates diverge; they do not sink. (They sink, one plate diving under another, at a subduction zone.)

12. **(B)** How did Semmelweiss save women from dying of childbed fever? He did so by establishing or *instituting* strict rules of hygiene.

13. **(B), (F)** Given the ubiquity of light, it is *unsurprising* that creatures have *developed* the biologically helpful ability to make use of light energy.

   Note the use of *therefore* indicating that the omitted portion of the sentence supports or continues a thought developed elsewhere in the sentence.

14. **(A), (E)** Here the author is contrasting appropriate clerical behavior with inappropriate clerical behavior. The Austen brothers behave appropriately: they are properly *deferential* to their social superiors, paying them proper respect. The fictional Mr. Collins, however, behaves inappropriately: he is *sycophantic* (obsequious, fawning) to his social superiors.

15. **(B), (D)** To *contest* an action is to dispute it or call it in question. The reclassification of Pluto did not go *uncontested*, for a large number of astronomers asked the International Astronomical Union to *reconsider* or rethink its decision, calling the union's action in question.

   Note the use of *for,* indicating a relationship of cause and effect.

16. **(A), (F)** The politicians are unwilling to *forsake* or abandon center stage. However, if they did leave center stage once in a while, the public might like them better for their *self-effacement* (withdrawal from attention).

17. **(D)** The opening sentence describes the shattering of the Iroquois leadership's pro-British policy. The remainder of the passage describes how Iroquois policy changed to reflect changes in European military goals.

   Choice A is incorrect. The passage is expository, not accusatory.

   Choice B is incorrect. Nothing in the passage suggests that such charges were made against the Iroquois.

   Choice C is incorrect. It is unsupported by the passage.

   Choice E is incorrect. The passage demonstrates the Iroquois were able to play European power politics.

   Remember, when asked to find the main idea, be sure to check the opening and summary sentences of each paragraph.

18. **(E)** Lines 22–34 indicate that in the early 1700s and through most of the eighteenth century the Iroquois *did* receive concessions from the European powers. Therefore, Choice E is the correct answer.

   Choice A is incorrect. The raid on Lachine was an effective response to French aggression, as was the Iroquois-enforced policy of aggressive neutrality.

   Choice B is incorrect. James II's overthrow was followed by colonial uprisings.

   Choice C is incorrect. In response to the Iroquois leaders' supposed favoring of the British, the French initiated attacks on the Iroquois (lines 7–13).

   Choice D is incorrect. This sums up the policy of aggressive neutrality.

19. **(A), (C)** Choice A is supported by the passage: the opening sentence of the passage discusses a "recent assessment" of the status of global amphibian populations. Likewise, Choice C is supported by the passage: habit degradation, which negatively affects amphibians, can be caused by "the introduction of

exotic invasive species," that is, *non-native species.* Note that to receive credit for this question you must have chosen *both* correct answers, not just one.

20. **(B)** The author never *cites* or quotes *an authority.*

    Choice A is incorrect. The author *defines* the term habit fragmentation.

    Choice C is incorrect. The author *states a probability.* He asserts, "Outright habitat loss *probably* has the greatest effect on amphibians."

    Choice D is incorrect. The author *qualifies a statement.* He first states, "Outright habitat loss probably has the greatest effect on amphibians." He then qualifies what he has said by stating that habitat degradation similarly affects amphibians.

    Choice E is incorrect. The author *makes* several *assertions.*

Section 3—Quantitative Ability

1. **(D)** Use the laws of exponents.
   Quantity A is $d^4 d^5 = d^{4+5} = d^9$.
   Quantity B is $(d^3)^2 = d^{3\times2} = d^6$.
   If $a = 1$, the quantities are equal; but if $a = 2$, Quantity A is much greater. Neither quantity is always greater, and the two quantities are not always equal (D).

2. **(C)** Since the measure of an exterior angle of a triangle is equal to the sum of the measures of the two opposite interior angles,
   $$c = a + b \Rightarrow a + b - c = 0.$$

   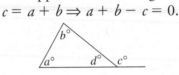

   The quantities are equal (C).

   Alternative Solution. Plug in easy-to-use numbers. If $a = 60$ and $b = 70$, then $d = 50 \Rightarrow c = 130$, and $60 + 70 - 130 = 0$.

3. **(B)**

	Quantity A	Quantity B
	$\sqrt{a+b}$	$\sqrt{a}+\sqrt{b}$
Since both quantities are positive, we can square them.	$a + b$	$a + 2\sqrt{ab} + b$
Subtract $a + b$ from each quantity	0	$2\sqrt{ab}$

Since a and b are positive, $2\sqrt{ab}$ is positive. Quantity B is greater.

4. **(B)** From the 124 people in front of Jill, remove Jack plus the 24 people in front of Jack: $124 - 25 = 99$. Quantity B is greater.

5. **(A)** Since OA and OB are radii, they are each equal to 5. With no restrictions on x, chord AB could be any positive number less than 10 (the length of a diameter). If x were 90, AB would be $\sqrt{50}$; since $x > 90$, $AB > \sqrt{50} > 7$. Therefore, the perimeter of $\triangle AOB$ is greater than $5 + 5 + 7 = 17$. Quantity A is greater.

6. **(C)** $\dfrac{a-b}{c-a} = 1 \Rightarrow a - b = c - a \Rightarrow 2a = b + c \Rightarrow a = \dfrac{b+c}{2}$.

   The quantities are equal (C).

   Alternative Solution. Since you have an equation with three variables, you can choose values for two of them and find the third. Let $a = 2$ and $b = 1$. Then $\dfrac{2-1}{c-2} = 1 \Rightarrow c = 3$. The average of b and c is 2, which equals a.

7. **(C)** The average of the measures of the three angles of *any* triangle is $180° \div 3 = 60°$. The quantities are equal (C).

8. **(C)** The area of the shaded region is the area of the large circle, 25π, minus the area of the middle circle, 16π: $25\pi - 16\pi = 9\pi$. The striped region is just a circle of radius 3. Its area is also 9π. The quantities are equal (C).

9. **(B)** The unmarked angle opposite the 60° angle also measures 60°, and the sum of the measures of all six angles in the diagram is 360°. So,

   $$360 = a + b + c + 20 + 60 + 60$$
   $$= a + b + c + 140.$$

   Subtracting 140 from each side, we get that $a + b + c = 220$.

10. **(C)** $4^{10} \times 64^2 = 4^{10} \times (4^3)^2 = 4^{10} \times 4^6 = 4^{16}$.
    Also, $16^2 \times 4^n = (4^2)^2 \times 4^n = 4^4 \times 4^n = 4^{4+n}$.
    So, $4^{16} = 4^{4+n}$ and $16 = 4 + n$. Then $n = 12$.

11. **(D)** Let x be the amount in dollars that each of the 20 children were going to contribute; then $20x$ represents the cost of the present. When 4 children dropped out, the remaining 16 each had to pay $(x + 1.50)$ dollars. So, $16(x + 1.5) = 20x \Rightarrow 16x + 24 = 20x \Rightarrow 24 = 4x \Rightarrow x = 6$, and so the cost of the present was $20 \times 6 = 120$ dollars.

    Alternative Solution. Since each of the 16 remaining children had to pay an extra $1.50, the extra payments totaled $16 \times \$1.50 = \$24$. This is the amount that would have been paid by the 4 children who dropped out, so each of the 4 would have paid $6. The cost of the gift was $20 \times \$6 = \$120$.

12. **110** Draw a Venn diagram. Since 10 seniors are in *both* band and orchestra, 30 are in band only and 50 are in orchestra only.

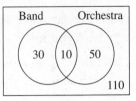

Therefore, 10 + 30 + 50 = 90 seniors are in at least one group, and the remaining 110 are in neither.

13. **(C)(D)(E)(F)(G)** On the six tests, Benjamin earned a total of 6 × 89 = 534 points. On his first five tests, he earned at least 5 × 90 = 450 points, but no more than 5 × 100 = 500 points. So his grade on the sixth test was at least 534 − 500 = 34 and at most 534 − 450 = 84.

Only answer choices C, D, E, F, and G are between 34 and 84.

14. **(E)** Exports to Eastern Europe from other Eastern European countries increased from $9.8 billion (10% of $98 billion) to $20.88 billion (12% of $174 billion)—an increase of slightly more than 100%.

15. **(C)** If France's exports to Eastern Europe were four times those of the United States, then France accounted for 8% of the total exports. Since 8% is $\frac{1}{8}$ of 64%, France accounted for $\frac{1}{8}$ or 12.5% of the exports from the European Union.

16. **198** The percent increase in total exports to Eastern Europe from 1993 to 1996 was

$$\frac{\text{the actual increase}}{\text{original amount}} \times 100\% = \frac{174 - 98}{98} \times 100\% = \frac{76}{98} \times 100\% = 77.55\%$$

So, in billions of dollars, the increase in total exports to Eastern Europe from 1996 to 2000 was 0.7755 × 174 = 134.94, making total exports 174 + 135 = 309 billion dollars. The value of exports from the European Union was 64% of 309 = 197.76 billion dollars. To the nearest billion, the figure was 198.

17. **(C)** Set up the equation:

$$(x + 3) + (2x - 3) + (3x - 5) = 25$$

Collect like terms: $6x - 5 = 25$
Add 5 to each side: $6x = 30$
Divide each side by 6: $x = 5$
Plugging in 5 for *x*, we get that the lengths of the sides are 8, 7, and 10. The length of the shortest side is 7.

18. **(D)** A nice way to answer this question is to pick easy-to-use numbers. Assume that in 1990 there were 200 boys and 100 girls who earned varsity letters. Then in 2000, there were 150 boys and 125 girls. So, the ratio of girls to boys was 125:150 = 5:6 or $\dfrac{5}{6}$.

19. **(E)** The easiest way to solve this is to plug in numbers. Let $x = 2$ and $y = 1$. Then $xy = 2$, $a = 4$, and $b = 0$. Now, plug in 4 for a and 0 for b and see which of the five choices is equal to 2. Only (C) and (E) work:

(C) $\dfrac{a-b}{2} = \dfrac{4-0}{2} = 2$

(E) $\dfrac{a^2-b^2}{8} = \dfrac{4^2-0^2}{8} = \dfrac{16}{8} = 2.$

To determine whether (C) or (E) is the correct answer, plug in different numbers. If $x = 3$ and $y = 1$, then $xy = 3$, $a = 5$, and $b = 1$. Now choice (C) doesn't work: $\dfrac{a-b}{2} = \dfrac{5-1}{2} = \dfrac{4}{2} = 2 \neq 3.$

Choice (E) does work: $\dfrac{a^2-b^2}{8} = \dfrac{25-1}{8} = \dfrac{24}{8} = 3.$

Here is the correct algebraic solution.
Add the two equations:

$$\begin{array}{r} x + 2y = a \\ +\ \ x - 2y = b \\ \hline 2x = a + b \end{array}$$

Divide by 2: $\qquad\qquad x = \dfrac{a+b}{2}$

Multiply the second equation by –1 and add it to the first:

$$\begin{array}{r} x + 2y = a \\ +\ -x + 2y = -b \\ \hline 4y = a - b \end{array}$$

Divide by 4: $\qquad\qquad y = \dfrac{a-b}{4}$

Then $xy = \dfrac{a+b}{2} \cdot \dfrac{a-b}{4} = \dfrac{a^2-b^2}{8}.$

This is the type of algebra you want to avoid.

20. **(D)** Since you need a ratio, the length of the side is irrelevant. The area of a square is s^2 and the area of an equilateral triangle is $\dfrac{s^2\sqrt{3}}{4}$. Then the ratio is

$$s^2 \div \dfrac{s^2\sqrt{3}}{4} = s^2 \times \dfrac{4}{s^2\sqrt{3}} = \dfrac{4}{\sqrt{3}} = \dfrac{4\sqrt{3}}{3}.$$

Of course, you could have used any number instead of s, and if you forgot the formula for the area of an equilateral triangle, you could have used $A = \dfrac{1}{2}bh.$

PART 2

VERBAL ABILITY: TACTICS, REVIEW, AND PRACTICE

Sentence Completion Questions

S entence completion questions are those old favorites, fill-in-the-blank questions. The new GRE presents some variations on this familiar form. The packaging is different, but the task remains the same.

We sometimes refer to the first question type, the **sentence equivalence question**, as the **double or nothing question**. To get credit for answering a sentence equivalence question correctly, you must come up with not one correct answer choice, but *two* correct answer choices that work equally well.

Sentence equivalence questions look like this:

> The medical researchers replied to the charge that their proposed new treatment was _____ by demonstrating that it in fact observed standard medical practices.
>
> A deleterious
>
> B untested
>
> C unorthodox
>
> D expensive
>
> E intricate
>
> F unconventional

Your Clue

The answer choices to sentence equivalence questions are marked with **square boxes**, not with circles or ovals. **Square boxes** are your clue that you must select **two** answer choices to get the question right.

The medical researchers defend their new treatment by saying that it follows accepted, standard practices. What, therefore, must have been the critic's charge or accusation about the treatment? They must have alleged it was nonstandard, violating acceptable medical practices. The two words that best complete this sentence are *unorthodox* and *unconventional.*

We refer to the second question type, the **text completion question,** as the **mix and match question.** In a text completion question, you will be presented with a sentence or group of sentences containing one to three blanks. Instead of seeing a single list of answer choices, you will see one, two, or three independent columns of choices; for each blank in the sentence, you must select one correct answer choice from the appropriate column, mixing and matching your choices until you come up with a combination that makes sense.

Text completion questions look like this:

Her novel published to universal (i)_____, her literary gifts acknowledged by the chief figures of the Harlem Renaissance, her reputation as yet (ii)_____ by envious slights, Hurston clearly was at the (iii)_____ of her career.

Blank (i)	Blank (ii)	Blank (iii)
indifference	belittled	zenith
derision	resented	extremity
acclaim	untarnished	ebb

Think about the structure of the sentence. It begins with three parallel absolute phrases, each telling about some aspect of Hurston's literary position at a particular time in her career. All three phrases are positive in tone. The concluding independent clause ("Hurston clearly was at the _____ of her career") should be positive as well.

Now examine the first blank. What reaction did people have to Hurston's novel? Look at the part of the sentence without any blanks: "her literary gifts (were) acknowledged by the chief figures of the Harlem Renaissance." In acknowledging Hurston's gifts, these literary luminaries were praising her novel. Her novel clearly had been published to great *acclaim* (approval).

Next, study the second blank. You know that, at the time this writer is discussing, Hurston's standing in the literary world was high. Her novel was acclaimed; her gifts were acknowledged (recognized). This third absolute phrase also must state something positive about Hurston. Recast it as a sentence: Her reputation (was) as yet _____ by envious slights. Envious slights (insults or slurs, prompted by jealousy) would have had a negative effect on Hurston's reputation. However, *as yet*, at the time under discussion, no negative comments had besmirched Hurston's reputation, which was *untarnished* (spotless; unblemished).

Finally, consider the third blank. How would you describe Hurston's career at the time under discussion? It was at its highest point: in years to come envious slights would tarnish her reputation and her novels would be forgotten, but for the moment Hurston was riding high: she was at the *zenith* (peak) of her career.

Testing Tactics

The Sentence Equivalence Question

To answer this type of sentence completion question correctly, you must come up with a pair of words, both equally fit to complete the meaning of the sentence as a whole. *If you fail to get both answers correct, you get no credit for the question.*

These are the GRE website's directions for these double or nothing sentence equivalence questions:

*For the following questions, select the **two** answer choices that, when used to complete the sentence, fit the meaning of the sentence as a whole **and** produce completed sentences that are alike in meaning.*

TACTIC

1 Before You Look at the Sentence, Look Over the Answer Choices to Locate Any Obvious Synonyms

Your task is to find two words that can complete the sentence in thought and style, and that can function interchangeably in the context. In other words, you may be looking for synonyms; you definitely are looking for words that complete the sentence in the same fashion.

Before you look at the sentence itself, examine the answer choices. See if you can spot a pair of synonyms. Then substitute these two words in the sentence. If both make logical sense in the context, you may well have found your answer pair. To check yourself, look over the other four choices. Try each of them in the sentence. Satisfy yourself that the synonyms you spotted work better than any of these other words.

Here are six answer choices to a sentence equivalence question.

A	extravagant
B	tawdry
C	parsimonious
D	optimistic
E	profligate
F	pedestrian

Extravagant and *profligate* are synonyms; both mean spendthrift or wasteful.

Now here is the sentence. Do the synonyms that you spotted work in this context?

Although the young duke's trustees had tried to teach him fiscal prudence,
they feared he would never learn to curb his _____ ways.

Clearly, they do. If the young duke has not learned to be careful about his finances, it is understandable that his trustees might worry about his inability to curb or restrain his *profligate* and *extravagant* ways.

NOTE: *Be very careful when you apply this tactic.* The test-makers are very aware that some examinees simply scan the answer choices looking for synonyms. Therefore, often they will deliberately plant obvious synonym pairs among the answer choices. These eye-catchers or distractors are there to trick the unwary. Because you will recognize these words as synonyms, you may want to select them without reading the sentence closely. However, the test-makers are not testing your knowledge of vocabulary *per se.* They are testing your reading comprehension. The words you choose do not have to be synonyms. However, they must both make sense in the sentence in an equivalent way.

TIP

Every sentence equivalence question has *two* correct answer choices. To get credit for the question, *you must get both answers right*.

TACTIC 2   If You Fail to Detect a Pair of Synonyms Right Away, Read the Sentence and Think of a Word That Makes Sense

This tactic is helpful because it enables you to get a sense of the sentence as a whole without being distracted by any misleading answers among the answer choices. You are free to concentrate on spotting key words or phrases in the body of the sentence and to call on your own "writer's intuition" in arriving at a stylistically apt choice of word.

See how the process works in a typical model question.

> Because experience had convinced her that Hector was both self-seeking and avaricious, she rejected the possibility that the motivation behind his donation had been wholly _____.
>
> A redundant
> B frivolous
> C egotistical
> D ephemeral
> E altruistic
> F benevolent

This sentence presents a simple case of cause and effect. The key phrase here is *self-seeking and avaricious.* The woman has found the man to be selfish and greedy. *Therefore,* she refuses to believe his motivation for donating money can be _____. She expects selfishness (*self-seeking*) and greed (*avaricious*), not their opposite.

You are looking for words that are antonyms for *selfish.* What words immediately come to mind? *Selfless, generous, charitable?* The missing words are, of course, *altruistic* and *benevolent.* They are the correct answer pair.

Practice Tactic 2 extensively to develop your intuitive sense of the *mot juste*—the exactly right word.

TACTIC 3   Consider Secondary Meanings of the Answer Choices as well as Their Primary Meanings

Frequently, the test-makers attempt to mislead you by using familiar words in an unfamiliar way. Suppose you have found one answer choice that perfectly fits the meaning of the sentence as a whole but cannot find a second answer choice that seems exactly right.

Reread the sentence, substituting that perfect answer choice for the blank. Then take a fresh look at the other answer choices. Remember that these words or phrases may have multiple meanings. Think of contexts in which you have heard these words or phrases used. That may help you come up with additional meanings for them.

See how this tactic helps you answer the following sentence equivalence question.

Snakes are the most stationary of all vertebrates; as long as a locality _____ . them a sufficiency of food and some shelter to which they can readily retreat, they have no inducement to change it.

- A provides
- B constitutes
- C affords
- D denies
- E disallows
- F withholds

Snakes tend to be stationary creatures. Why? They stay put because a particular locality meets their needs: it *provides* or offers them food and shelter.

Look at the other answer choices. Can you rule out any of them? *Denies, disallows,* and *withholds* are all negative terms; none of them seem appropriate in this context. After all, if a locality *denied* or *disallowed* the snakes food and shelter or *withheld* food and shelter from them, that would not be an inducement or incentive for the snakes to stay put. Likewise, *constitutes* (composes; establishes) does not seem appropriate in the context. It feels awkward, even ungrammatical (the verb does not normally take an indirect object).

Only *affords* is left. Here it clearly is *not* used with its primary meaning, "to be able to meet the expense of," as in affording to buy a new car.

Try to think of other contexts for *afford*. "It affords me great pleasure to be here." "Gustavo's Facebook entries afford us a glimpse into the daily life of a musician on tour." These sentences use *afford* with a secondary meaning: to give, offer, or provide. The correct answers to this sentence equivalence question are *affords* and *provides*.

TACTIC
4 Look at All the Possible Choices Before You Choose an Answer Pair

Never decide on your answer before you have read all the choices. You are looking for *two* words that *both* make sense in the sentence. What is more, not only do both these words have to make sense in the sentence, but they have to make the same kind of sense. You have to be able to substitute one for the other in the sentence without changing the meaning of the sentence as a whole.

In order to be sure you have not been hasty in making your decision, substitute all the answer choices for the missing word. Do not spend a lot of time doing so, but do try them all. Then decide which two of these words function in the same way. That way you can satisfy yourself that you have come up with the *best* possible pair.

See how this tactic helps you deal with another question patterned on examples from the GRE.

The evil of class and race hatred must be eliminated while it is still in _____ state; otherwise, it may grow to dangerous proportions.

A an amorphous

B an overt

C a rudimentary

D a threatening

E an independent

F an embryonic

On the basis of a loose sense of this sentence's meaning, you might be tempted to select the first choice, *amorphous*. After all, this sentence basically tells you that you should wipe out hatred before it gets too dangerous. Clearly, if hatred is vague or *amorphous*, it is less formidable than if it is well-defined. However, this reading of the sentence is inadequate: it fails to take into account the sentence's key phrase.

The key phrase here is "may grow to dangerous proportions." The writer fears that class and race hatred may grow large enough to endanger society. He wants us to wipe out this hatred before it is fully grown. Examine each answer choice, eliminating those answers that carry no suggestion that something lacks its full growth or development. Does *overt* suggest that something isn't fully grown? No, it suggests that something is obvious or evident. Does *rudimentary* suggest that something isn't fully grown? Yes, it suggests that something is unfinished or immature. This may well be one of your two correct answer choices.

Look for a second word that suggests a lack of full growth. Does *independent* suggest that something isn't fully grown? No, it suggests that something is free and unconstrained. Does *threatening* suggest that something isn't fully grown? No, it suggests that something is a source of danger or cause for alarm. Only one word is left: *embryonic* (at an early, incomplete stage of development). If you substitute *embryonic* for *rudimentary* in the sentence, you will not change the sentence's essential meaning. The correct answer choices are *rudimentary* and *embryonic*.

TACTIC
5 Watch for Signal Words That Link One Part of the Sentence to Another

Writers use transitions to link their ideas logically. These transitions or signal words are clues that can help you figure out what the sentence actually means.

GRE sentence equivalence and text completion questions often contain several signal words, combining them in complex ways.

CAUSE AND EFFECT SIGNALS

Look for words or phrases explicitly indicating that one thing **causes** another or **logically determines** another.

Cause and Effect Signal Words

accordingly	in order to
because	so . . . that
consequently	therefore
given	thus
hence	when . . . then
if . . . then	

SUPPORT SIGNALS

Look for words or phrases explicitly indicating that the omitted part of the sentence **supports** or **continues a thought** developed elsewhere in the sentence. In such cases, a synonym or near-synonym for another word in the sentence may provide the correct answer.

Support Signal Words

additionally	furthermore
also	indeed
and	likewise
as well	moreover
besides	too

EXPLICIT CONTRAST SIGNALS

Look for function words or phrases (conjunctions, sentence adverbs, etc.) that explicitly **indicate a contrast** between one idea and another, setting up a reversal of a thought. In such cases, an antonym or near-antonym for another word in the sentence may provide the correct answer.

Explicit Contrast Signal Words

albeit	nevertheless
although	nonetheless
but	notwithstanding
despite	on the contrary
even though	on the other hand
however	rather than
in contrast	still
in spite of	while
instead of	yet

IMPLICIT CONTRAST SIGNALS

Look for content words whose meaning inherently indicates a contrast. These words can turn a situation on its head. They indicate that something unexpected, possibly even unwanted, has occurred.

Implicit Contrast Signal Words

anomaly	anomalous	anomalously
illogic	illogical	illogically
incongruity	incongruous	incongruously
irony	ironic	ironically
paradox	paradoxical	paradoxically
surprise	surprising	surprisingly
	unexpected	unexpectedly

Note the function of such a contrast signal word in the following question.

Paradoxically, the more _____ the details this artist chooses, the better able she is to depict her fantastic, other-worldly landscapes.

- [A] ethereal
- [B] realistic
- [C] fanciful
- [D] mundane
- [E] extravagant
- [F] sublime

The artist creates imaginary landscapes that do not seem to belong to this world. We normally would expect the details comprising these landscapes to be as fantastic and other-worldly as the landscapes themselves. The truth of the matter, however, is *paradoxical*: it contradicts what we expect. The details she chooses may be *realistic* (true to life) or *mundane* (ordinary, everyday), yet the more lifelike and unremarkable they are, the more fantastic the paintings seem. The correct answers are *realistic* and *mundane*.

TACTIC

Use Your Knowledge of Word Parts and Parts of Speech to Get at the Meanings of Unfamiliar Words

If a word used by the author is unfamiliar, or if an answer choice is unknown to you, two approaches are helpful.

1. Break down the word into its component parts—prefixes, suffixes, roots—to see whether they provide any clues to its meaning. For example, in the preceding list of Implicit Contrast Signal Words, the word *incongruous* contains three key word parts. *In-* here means not; *con-* means together; *gru-* means to move or come. *Incongruous* behavior, therefore, is behavior that does not go together or agree with someone's usual behavior; it is unexpected.

2. Change the unfamiliar word from one part of speech to another. If the adjective *embryonic* is unfamiliar to you, cut off its adjective suffix *–nic* and recognize the familiar word *embryo*. If the noun *precocity* is unfamiliar to you, cut off its noun suffix *–ity* and visualize it with different endings. You may come up with the adjective *precocious* (maturing early). If the verb *appropriate* is unfamiliar to you, by adding a word part or two you may come up with the common noun *appropriation* or the still more common noun *misappropriation* (as in the misappropriation of funds).

Note the application of this tactic in the following example.

This island is a colony; however, in most matters it is _____ and receives no orders from the mother country.

   A synoptic
   B independent
   C methodical
   D autonomous
   E heretical
   F disinterested

First, locate any answer choices that are obviously correct. If a colony receives no orders from its mother country, it is *independent* to act according to its own wishes: it is essentially self-governing. It is not necessarily *methodical* (systematic), nor is it by definition *heretical* (unorthodox) or *disinterested* (impartial). Thus, you may rule out Choices C, E, and F.

The two answer choices remaining may be unfamiliar to you. Analyze them, using what you know of related words. *Synoptic* is related to the noun *synopsis*, a summary or abridgement. Does this term have anything to do with how a colony might govern itself? Definitely not. *Autonomous*, however, comes from the prefix *auto-* (self) and the root *nom-* (law). An autonomous nation is independent; it rules itself. Thus, the correct answers are *independent* and *autonomous*.

The Text Completion Question

To answer this type of sentence completion question correctly, you must come up with the right word for each and every blank in the sentence or group of sentences. As in a Cloze procedure, you have to insert words in a text, monitoring for meaning as you read. Your goal is closure: the completion of a partly finished semantic pattern.

These are the GRE website's directions for text completion questions:
For the following questions, select one entry for each blank from the corresponding column of choices. Fill all blanks in the way that best completes the text.

TIP

Remember, if you can eliminate two or more answer choices, it pays to guess.

Strategy for Analyzing Question Types

There is **no** partial credit for text completion questions: to get any credit, you must fill in every blank in the text correctly.

Testing Tactics for Text Completion Questions

TACTIC
7
In Double- and Triple-Blank Texts, Go Through One Column at a Time, Eliminating the Answer Choices That Don't Fit

In a text completion question with two or three blanks, read through the entire text to get a sense of it as a whole. Pay special attention to the parts of the text (subordinate clauses, participial phrases, etc.) *without* any blanks. See whether you can predict what the first missing word may be. Then go through the first column, inserting each word in the sentence's first blank. Ask yourself whether a given word would make sense in this blank. If it makes no sense, eliminate it. If it makes possible sense, keep it in mind as you work on filling in the next blank.

Critics of the movie version of *The Color Purple* (i)_____ its saccharine, overoptimistic tone as out of keeping with the novel's more (ii)_____ quality.

Blank (i)
acclaimed
decried
echoed

Blank (ii)
acerbic
cloying
sanguine

For a quick, general sense of the opening clause, break it down. What does it say? *Critics _____ the movie's sugary sweet tone.*

How would critics react to something sugary sweet and overly hopeful? Most likely they would *not* acclaim (praise) it. You are probably safe to cross out the word *acclaimed.* However, they might well *decry* or disparage it. They might even *echo* or copy it, although that answer choice seems unlikely.

You have two possibilities for the first blank, *decried* and *echoed,* with the former more likely than the latter. Now consider the second blank. The movie's sugary, overly hopeful tone is out of keeping with the novel's quality: the two tones disagree. Therefore, the novel's tone is not *sanguine* (hopeful) or *cloying* (sickly sweet). It is instead on the bitter or sour side; in a word, *acerbic.*

Now that you are sure of your second answer choice, go back to the first blank. Reread the sentence:

Critics of the movie _____ its saccharine, overoptimistic tone as out of keeping with the novel's more acerbic quality. Clearly, the critics would not echo the movie's tone. Instead, they decried or disparaged it. By rereading the text you have confirmed your answer choices.

TIP

Do *not* assume that you have to work your way through the blanks sequentially. It may be easier to fill in the second blank first!

TACTIC
8   Break Down Complex Passages into Simpler Components

In analyzing long, complex text completion items, you may find it useful to simplify the texts by breaking them down. Rephrase dependent clauses and long participial phrases, turning them into simple sentences.

See how this tactic helps you to analyze the following complex sentence.

> Museum director Hoving (i)_____ refers to the smuggled Greek urn as the "hot pot," not because there are doubts about its authenticity or even great reservations as to its price, but because the (ii)_____ of its acquisition is open to question.

Blank (i)	Blank (ii)
characteristically	timeliness
colloquially	manner
repeatedly	expense

What do we know?

1. The urn has been smuggled.
2. Hoving calls it a "hot pot."
3. It is genuine. (There are no doubts about its authenticity.)
4. It did not cost too much. (There are no great reservations as to its price.)

In calling the smuggled urn a "hot pot," Hoving is not necessarily speaking *characteristically:* we have no information about his typical mode of speech. Similarly, we have no evidence that Hoving has *repeatedly* called it a hot pot: we know only that he called it a hot pot at least once. Hoving is speaking *colloquially*, that is, informally. (*Hot* here is a slang term meaning stolen or illegally obtained.) You have your first correct answer choice, *colloquially.*

Now consider the second blank. The urn's *expense* is not being questioned, nor is the *timeliness* (well-timed occurrence) of its acquisition. However, because the urn has been smuggled into the country, there clearly are unresolved questions about how it got here, in other words, about its mode or *manner* of acquisition. The second correct answer choice is *manner.*

TACTIC
9   If a Sentence Contains a Metaphor, Check to See Whether That Metaphor Controls the Writer's Choice of Words (and Your Answer Choice)

Writers sometimes indulge in extended metaphors, complex analogies that imaginatively identify one object with another.

In the following example, the mind of a prejudiced person is compared to the pupil of an eye in its response to light or illumination.

The mind of a bigot is like the pupil of the eye: the more light you pour upon it, the more it will _____.

| blink |
| veer |
| stare |
| reflect |
| contract |

The image of light unifies this sentence. In choosing an answer, you must complete the sentence in such a way as to develop that metaphor fully and accurately. Exactly what takes place when you shine a light into someone's eye? The person may stare back or blink; you may see the light reflected in the person's eye. But what happens to the pupil of the eye? It neither blinks nor reflects. Instead it shrinks in size: it *contracts*. Likewise, exposed to the light of tolerance, the bigot's mind resists illumination, shrinking from light. *Contract* completes the metaphor; it is the correct answer choice.

TACTIC 10

Once You Have Filled In All the Blanks to Your Satisfaction, Reread the Completed Passage to Make Sure It Makes Sense

No matter how confident you are that you have filled in an individual blank correctly, you cannot be sure you have successfully completed the passage until you have confirmed your word choice(s) by rereading the entire text. This is what you did in working out the answers to the sample question in Tactic 4. Remember: you are aiming for closure. Do not omit this stage in the procedure.

Practice Exercises

Sentence Completion Exercise A (Sentence Equivalence)

Directions: For the following questions, select the **two** answer choices that, when used to complete the sentence, fit the meaning of the sentence as a whole **and** produce completed sentences that are alike in meaning.

1. Normally an individual thunderstorm lasts about 45 minutes, but under certain conditions the storm may _____, becoming ever more severe, for as long as four hours.

   A wane
   B moderate
   C persist
   D endure
   E vacillate
   F disperse

2. Perhaps because something in us instinctively distrusts such displays of natural fluency, some readers approach John Updike's fiction with _____.

   A wariness
   B indifference
   C suspicion
   D veneration
   E bewilderment
   F remorse

3. We lost confidence in him because he never _____ the grandiose promises he had made.

   A forgot about
   B reneged on
   C carried out
   D tired of
   E delivered on
   F retreated from

4. We were amazed that a man who had been heretofore the most _____ of public speakers could, in a single speech, electrify an audience and bring them cheering to their feet.

   A prosaic
   B enthralling
   C accomplished
   D pedestrian
   E auspicious
   F iconoclastic

5. Despite the mixture's _____ nature, we found that by lowering the temperature in the laboratory we could dramatically reduce its tendency to vaporize.

   A resilient
   B homogeneous
   C volatile
   D insipid
   E acerbic
   F unstable

6. In a revolutionary development in technology, some manufacturers now make biodegradable forms of plastic; some plastic trash bags, for example, gradually _____ when exposed to sunlight.

   A harden
   B stagnate
   C inflate
   D propagate
   E decompose
   F disintegrate

7. Aimed at curbing European attempts to seize territory in the Americas, the Monroe Doctrine was a warning to _____ foreign powers.

- [A] pertinacious
- [B] cautionary
- [C] credulous
- [D] rapacious
- [E] predatory
- [F] remote

8. Few other plants can grow beneath the canopy of the sycamore tree, whose leaves and pods produce a natural herbicide that leaches into the surrounding soil, _____ other plants that might compete for water and nutrients.

- [A] inhibiting
- [B] distinguishing
- [C] nourishing
- [D] suppressing
- [E] harvesting
- [F] fertilizing

9. The child was so spoiled by her indulgent parents that she pouted and became _____ when she did not receive all of their attention.

- [A] discreet
- [B] suspicious
- [C] elated
- [D] sullen
- [E] tranquil
- [F] grumpy

10. The reasoning in this editorial is so _____ that we cannot see how anyone can be deceived by it.

- [A] unsound
- [B] coherent
- [C] astute
- [D] dispassionate
- [E] scrupulous
- [F] specious

11. Because Inspector Morse could not contain his scorn for the police commissioner, he was imprudent enough to make _____ remarks about his superior officer.

- [A] ambiguous
- [B] impartial
- [C] unfathomable
- [D] contemptuous
- [E] scathing
- [F] pertinent

12. Though he was theoretically a friend of labor, his voting record in Congress _____ that impression.

- [A] implied
- [B] confirmed
- [C] created
- [D] belied
- [E] tallied
- [F] contradicted

13. Modern architecture has discarded _____ trimming on buildings and has concentrated on an almost Greek simplicity of line.

- [A] flamboyant
- [B] ornate
- [C] austere
- [D] inconspicuous
- [E] aesthetic
- [F] derivative

14. The young clerk was quickly promoted when his employers saw how _____ he was.

- [A] indigent
- [B] assiduous
- [C] autocratic
- [D] industrious
- [E] intractable
- [F] self-serving

15. Because it arrives so early in the season, before many other birds, the robin has been called the _____ of spring.

    A prototype

    B hostage

    C harbinger

    D herald

    E progeny

    F newcomer

Sentence Completion Exercise B (Sentence Equivalence)

Directions: For the following questions, select the **two** answer choices that, when used to complete the sentence, fit the meaning of the sentence as a whole **and** produce completed sentences that are alike in meaning.

1. Truculent in defending their individual rights of sovereignty under the Articles of Confederation, the newly formed states _____ constantly.

    A digressed

    B conferred

    C bickered

    D dismembered

    E rebuffed

    F squabbled

2. In Anglo Saxon times, the monastic scribes made _____ distinction between Latin texts and texts in the vernacular by assigning the former an Anglo-Caroline script and reserving the pointed insular script for texts in Old English.

    A a nice

    B a subtle

    C a pointless

    D an obvious

    E an unconventional

    F a judgmental

3. Written in an amiable style, the book provides a comprehensive overview of European wines that should prove _____ to both the virtual novice and the experienced connoisseur.

    A inviting

    B tedious

    C engaging

    D inspirational

    E perplexing

    F opaque

4. Shy and hypochondriacal, Madison was uncomfortable at public gatherings; his character made him a most _____ orator and practicing politician.

    A conscientious

    B unlikely

    C fervent

    D gregarious

    E improbable

    F effective

5. Alec Guinness has few equals among English-speaking actors, and in his autobiography he reveals himself to possess an uncommonly _____ prose style as well.

    A ambivalent

    B infamous

    C felicitous

    D happy

    E redundant

    F ephemeral

6. Because Pauling stubbornly continued to believe in the power of Vitamin C to cure cancer despite much evidence to the contrary, his colleagues felt he had lost his scientific _____.

   A tenacity

   B inventiveness

   C contrariness

   D impartiality

   E hypothesis

   F objectivity

7. The distinctive qualities of African music were not appreciated or even _____ by Westerners until fairly recently.

   A deprecated

   B discerned

   C ignored

   D revered

   E remarked on

   F neglected

8. Bored by the verbose and rambling prose of the typical Victorian novelist, the student welcomed the change to the _____ prose of Ernest Hemingway.

   A consistent

   B terse

   C florid

   D equivocal

   E pithy

   F discursive

9. She is a pragmatist, as _____ to base her future on impractical dreams as she would be to build a castle on shifting sand.

   A determined

   B disinclined

   C loath

   D quick

   E diligent

   F foolhardy

10. Although eighteenth-century English society as a whole did not encourage learning for its own sake in women, it illogically _____ women's sad lack of education.

    A decried

    B postulated

    C criticized

    D tolerated

    E vaunted

    F legitimized

11. Unlike the gregarious Capote, who was never happier than when he was in the center of a crowd of celebrities, Faulkner, in later years, grew somewhat _____ and shunned company.

    A dispassionate

    B infamous

    C reclusive

    D ambivalent

    E withdrawn

    F notorious

12. Studded starfish are well protected from most predators and parasites by _____ surface whose studs are actually modified spines.

    A a vulnerable

    B an armored

    C an obtuse

    D a brittle

    E a concave

    F a rugged

13. Traffic speed limits are set at a level that achieves some balance between the desire of most people to travel as quickly as possible and the danger of _____ speed.

    A inordinate

    B marginal

    C inadvertent

    D inadequate

    E regulated

    F excessive

14. Baldwin's brilliant *The Fire Next Time* is both so eloquent in its passion and so penetrating in its candor that it is bound to _____ any reader.

A embarrass
B disgust
C disquiet
D unsettle
E disappoint
F bore

15. Glendon provides a dark underside to Frederick Jackson Turner's frontier thesis that saw rugged individualism as the essence of American society—an individualism that Glendon sees as _____ atomism.

A antithetical toward
B skeptical of
C degenerating into
D aspiring to
E regressing to
F revitalized by

Sentence Completion Exercise C (Text Completion)

Directions: For the following questions, select one entry for each blank from the corresponding column of choices. Fill all blanks in the way that best completes the text.

1. Unlike other examples of _____ verse, Milton's *Lycidas* does more than merely mourn the death of Edward King; it also denounces corruption in the church in which King was ordained.

Ⓐ satiric
Ⓑ elegiac
Ⓒ free
Ⓓ didactic
Ⓔ pedestrian

2. Just as disloyalty is the mark of the renegade, (i)_____ is the mark of the (ii)_____.

Blank (i)	Blank (ii)
Ⓐ avarice	Ⓓ craven
Ⓑ cowardice	Ⓔ laggard
Ⓒ vanity	Ⓕ misanthrope

3. Because she had a reputation for (i)_____, we were surprised and pleased when she greeted us so (ii)_____.

Blank (i)	Blank (ii)
Ⓐ graciousness	Ⓓ affably
Ⓑ credulity	Ⓔ disdainfully
Ⓒ petulance	Ⓕ irascibly

4. Despite an affected (i)_____ that convinced casual observers that he was (ii)_____ about his painting and cared only for frivolity, Warhol cared deeply about his art and labored at it (iii)_____.

Blank (i)	Blank (ii)	Blank (iii)
Ⓐ fervor	Ⓓ indifferent	Ⓖ ambivalently
Ⓑ gloom	Ⓔ passionate	Ⓗ diligently
Ⓒ nonchalance	Ⓕ systematic	Ⓘ intermittently

5. Although a few years ago the fundamental facts about the Milky Way seemed fairly well (i)_____, now even its mass and its radius have come into (ii)_____.

Blank (i)	Blank (ii)
Ⓐ diminished	Ⓓ disrepute
Ⓑ established	Ⓔ prominence
Ⓒ disparaged	Ⓕ question

6. One of the most (i)_____ educators in New York, Dr. Shalala (ii)_____ a controversy in 1984 by calling the city public schools a "rotten barrel" in need of (iii)_____ reform.

Blank (i)	Blank (ii)	Blank (iii)
Ⓐ indifferent	Ⓓ diverted	Ⓖ partial
Ⓑ outspoken	Ⓔ ignited	Ⓗ superficial
Ⓒ eclectic	Ⓕ defused	Ⓘ systemic

7. The newest fiber-optic cables that carry telephone calls cross-country are made of glass so _____ that a piece 100 miles thick is clearer than a standard windowpane.

Ⓐ	fragile
Ⓑ	immaculate
Ⓒ	iridescent
Ⓓ	tangible
Ⓔ	transparent

8. The texts as we have them were written down and edited carefully by Christians proud of their ancestors but unable to bear the thought of their indulging in heathen practices; thus, all references to the ancient religion of the Celts were (i)_____, if not (ii)_____.

Blank (i)		Blank (ii)	
Ⓐ	aggrieved	Ⓓ	ironic
Ⓑ	detailed	Ⓔ	overawed
Ⓒ	muddied	Ⓕ	suppressed

9. To alleviate the problem of contaminated chicken, the study panel recommends that the federal government shift its inspection emphasis from cursory bird-by-bird check to a more _____ random sampling for bacterial and chemical contamination.

Ⓐ	discreet
Ⓑ	perfunctory
Ⓒ	rigorous
Ⓓ	solicitous
Ⓔ	symbolic

10. The orator was so (i)_____ that the audience soon became (ii)_____.

Blank (i)	Blank (ii)
Ⓐ bombastic	Ⓓ drowsy
Ⓑ inaudible	Ⓔ irresolute
Ⓒ soporific	Ⓕ moribund

11. Her true feelings (i)_____ themselves in her sarcastic asides; only then was her (ii)_____ revealed.

Blank (i)	Blank (ii)
Ⓐ anticipated	Ⓓ anxiety
Ⓑ concealed	Ⓔ bitterness
Ⓒ manifested	Ⓕ charm

12. The sugar dissolved in water (i)_____; finally all that remained was an almost (ii)_____ residue on the bottom of the glass.

Blank (i)	Blank (ii)
Ⓐ gradually	Ⓓ fragrant
Ⓑ quickly	Ⓔ imperceptible
Ⓒ subsequently	Ⓕ problematic

13. After the Japanese attack on Pearl Harbor on December 7, 1941, Japanese-Americans were (i)_____ of being spies for Japan, although there was no evidence to (ii)_____ this accusation.

Blank (i)	Blank (ii)
Ⓐ acquitted	Ⓓ back up
Ⓑ reminded	Ⓔ carry out
Ⓒ suspected	Ⓕ shrug off

14. Mencken's readers enjoyed his (i)_____ wit, but his victims often (ii)_____ at the broad, yet pointed satire.

Blank (i)	Blank (ii)
Ⓐ cutting	Ⓓ connived
Ⓑ kindly	Ⓔ smiled
Ⓒ subtle	Ⓕ winced

15. After having worked in the soup kitchen feeding the homeless, the volunteer began to see her own good fortune as (i)_____ and her difference from the destitute as chance rather than (ii)_____.

Blank (i)	Blank (ii)
Ⓐ a fluke	Ⓓ destiny
Ⓑ an omen	Ⓔ resolution
Ⓒ a reward	Ⓕ tradition

Sentence Completion Exercise D (Text Completion)

Directions: For the following questions, select one entry for each blank from the corresponding column of choices. Fill all blanks in the way that best completes the text.

1. Chaotic in conception but not in _____, Kelly's canvases are as neat as the proverbial pin.

Ⓐ conceit
Ⓑ execution
Ⓒ intent
Ⓓ origin
Ⓔ theory

2. During the middle of the eighteenth century, the (i)_____ style in furniture and architecture, marked by elaborate scrollwork and (ii)_____ decoration, flourished.

Blank (i)	Blank (ii)
Ⓐ abstract	Ⓓ austere
Ⓑ medieval	Ⓔ excessive
Ⓒ rococo	Ⓕ functional

3. Tocqueville decided to swear the oath of loyalty to the new Orleanist king in part (i)_____ (he wanted to keep his position as magistrate), and in part (ii)_____ (he was convinced that the democratization of politics represented by the new regime was inevitable).

Blank (i)	Blank (ii)
Ⓐ opportunistically	Ⓓ altruistically
Ⓑ selflessly	Ⓔ irresolutely
Ⓒ theoretically	Ⓕ pragmatically

4. In seeking to rediscover Zora Neale Hurston, it is intriguing to look at the figure she cut in the minds of her contemporaries, the high regard she (i)_____ before shifting aesthetic values (ii)_____ her to curio status.

Blank (i)	Blank (ii)
Ⓐ deplored	Ⓓ elevated
Ⓑ enjoyed	Ⓔ relegated
Ⓒ offered	Ⓕ suspended

5. The tapeworm is an example of (i)_____ organism, one that lives within or on another creature, (ii)_____ some or all of its nutrients from its host.

Blank (i)	Blank (ii)
Ⓐ an autonomous	Ⓓ converting
Ⓑ a hospitable	Ⓔ deriving
Ⓒ a parasitic	Ⓕ sublimating

6. Ms. Sutcliffe's helpful notes on her latest wine discoveries and her no-nonsense warnings to consumers about (i)_____ wines provide (ii)_____ guide to the numbing array of wines of Burgundy.

Blank (i)	Blank (ii)
Ⓐ overpriced	Ⓓ an inadequate
Ⓑ superior	Ⓔ a spotty
Ⓒ vintage	Ⓕ a trusty

7. Measurement is, like any other human endeavor, a complex activity, subject to (i)_____, not always used properly, and frequently misinterpreted and (ii)_____.

Blank (i)	Blank (ii)
Ⓐ correlation	Ⓓ analyzed
Ⓑ error	Ⓔ incorporated
Ⓒ legislation	Ⓕ misunderstood

8. Just as insincerity is the mark of the (i)_____, boastfulness is the mark of the (ii)_____.

Blank (i)	Blank (ii)
Ⓐ zealot	Ⓓ glutton
Ⓑ skeptic	Ⓔ autocrat
Ⓒ hypocrite	Ⓕ braggart

9. For Miró, art became (i)_____ ritual; paper and pencils were holy objects to him, and he worked as though he were (ii)_____ a religious rite.

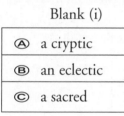

Blank (i)	Blank (ii)
Ⓐ a cryptic	Ⓓ absolving
Ⓑ an eclectic	Ⓔ performing
Ⓒ a sacred	Ⓕ protracting

10. If the *Titanic* had hit the iceberg head on, its watertight compartments might have saved it from (i)_____, but the great liner swerved to (ii)_____ the iceberg, and in the collision so many compartments were opened to the sea that disaster was (iii)_____.

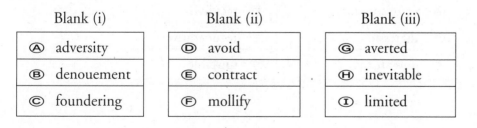

Blank (i)	Blank (ii)	Blank (iii)
Ⓐ adversity	Ⓓ avoid	Ⓖ averted
Ⓑ denouement	Ⓔ contract	Ⓗ inevitable
Ⓒ foundering	Ⓕ mollify	Ⓘ limited

11. We have become so democratic in our habits of thought that we are convinced that truth is (i)_____ through a (ii)_____ of facts.

Blank (i)	Blank (ii)
Ⓐ assimilated	Ⓓ hierarchy
Ⓑ determined	Ⓔ plebiscite
Ⓒ exculpated	Ⓕ transcendence

12. The writer's (i)_____ use of language renders a usually uninspiring topic, economics, known as "the dismal science," uncommonly (ii)_____.

Blank (i)	Blank (ii)
Ⓐ pedestrian	Ⓓ engaging
Ⓑ felicitous	Ⓔ abstruse
Ⓒ grandiloquent	Ⓕ contentious

13. The leader of the group is the passionately committed Crimond, whose (i)_____ politics is (ii)_____ proportional to his disciples' lapsed political faith.

Blank (i)	Blank (ii)
Ⓐ engagement in	Ⓓ critically
Ⓑ indifference to	Ⓔ inversely
Ⓒ retreat from	Ⓕ marginally

14. Although the economy suffers (i)_____, it also has strong (ii)_____ and self-correcting tendencies.

Blank (i)	Blank (ii)
Ⓐ contradictions	Ⓓ recidivist
Ⓑ digressions	Ⓔ recuperative
Ⓒ downturns	Ⓕ unstable

15. Faced with these massive changes, the government keeps its own counsel; although generally benevolent, it has always been _____ regime.

Ⓐ	an altruistic
Ⓑ	an indifferent
Ⓒ	a reticent
Ⓓ	a sanguine
Ⓔ	an unpredictable

ANSWER KEY

Sentence Completion Exercise A

1. C, D
2. A, C
3. C, E
4. A, D
5. C, F
6. E, F
7. D, E
8. A, D
9. D, F
10. A, F
11. D, E
12. D, F
13. A, B
14. B, D
15. C, D

Sentence Completion Exercise B

1. C, F
2. A, B
3. A, C
4. B, E
5. C, D
6. D, F
7. B, E
8. B, E
9. B, C
10. A, C
11. C, E
12. B, F
13. A, F
14. C, D
15. C, E

Sentence Completion Exercise C

1. B
2. (i) B; (ii) D
3. (i) C; (ii) D
4. (i) C; (ii) D; (iii) H
5. (i) B; (ii) F
6. (i) B; (ii) E; (iii) I
7. E
8. (i) C; (ii) F
9. C
10. (i) C; (ii) D
11. (i) C; (ii) E
12. (i) A; (ii) E
13. (i) C; (ii) D
14. (i) A; (ii) F
15. (i) A; (ii) D

Sentence Completion Exercise D

1. B
2. (i) C; (ii) E
3. (i) A; (ii) F
4. (i) B; (ii) E
5. (i) C; (ii) E
6. (i) A; (ii) F
7. (i) B; (ii) F
8. (i) C; (ii) F
9. (i) C; (ii) E
10. (i) C; (ii) D; (iii) H
11. (i) B; (ii) E
12. (i) B; (ii) D
13. (i) A; (ii) E
14. (i) C; (ii) E
15. C

Reading Comprehension Questions

GRE reading comprehension questions test your ability to understand what you read — both content and technique. Each verbal section on the GRE includes two to five relatively short passages, each passage followed by one to four questions. A passage may deal with the **sciences** (including medicine, botany, zoology, chemistry, physics, geology, astronomy); the **humanities** (including art, literature, music, philosophy, folklore); or the **social sciences** (including history, economics, sociology, government). Some passages are strictly objective, explaining or describing a phenomenon or process neutrally. Others reflect a particular bias or point of view: the author is trying to convince the reader to share his or her opinion about the subject being discussed.

The GRE tends to take its reading passages from *The New York Review of Books*, from prestigious university presses (Harvard, Princeton, Oxford), from government publications, and from scholarly journals. Often the test-makers hit academically "hot" topics — biodiesel fuels, plate tectonics, damage to the ozone layer, Arthurian romance, the status of women's literature — that have aroused controversy over the past several decades. Frequently they edit these passages to make them more demanding both in vocabulary level and in grammatical complexity.

Some of the reading comprehension questions on the GRE are factual, asking you about specific details in the passages. Others ask you to interpret the passages, to make judgments about them. Still others ask you to recognize various techniques used by the authors or possible applications of their ideas to other circumstances. Some questions include lengthy and complex statements, as lengthy and complex as any sentences in the passage. Read the questions closely, as closely as you read the text. Be sure, in answering reading comprehension questions, that you read *all* the answer choices before deciding which is correct.

The reading comprehension portions of the new GRE contain some surprises for test-takers. A few reading comprehension questions have brand new formats—some require you to click on a sentence within the passage that fits a particular description; others require you to select one or more answer choices to get a question right. In addition, "new" types of logical reasoning questions now appear in the reading comprehension portions of the test. These new logical reasoning questions resemble questions found on the Analytical Ability sections of the old GRE, the Logical Reasoning sections of the LSAT, the verbal sections of the GMAT, and so on. These questions ask you to determine the logical conclusion of an argument, to analyze the function and relationship of individual statements within an argument, to

TIP

Read the question *first*! Know what info you're seeking before you start your search.

'isolate the assumptions underlying an argument, and to distinguish what strengthens an argument from what weakens it.

The reading comprehension questions following each passage are not arranged in order of difficulty. They are arranged to reflect the way the passage's content is organized. A question based on information found at the beginning of the passage generally will come before a question based on information at the passage's end.

Testing Tactics

TACTIC
1
First Read the Question,
Then Read the Passage

In responding to reading comprehension passages on the GRE, you often will have to consider more material than can fit conveniently on a single screen. You will confront a split screen similar to the one on this page. On one-half of the screen you will see the question you must answer; on the other you will see a segment of the passage under consideration. You will have to scroll through the passage in order to read the text in its entirety.

| Quit Test | Exit Section | Review | Mark | Help | Back | Next |

Both societies are territorial: they occupy a particular home range, which they defend against intruders.
Likewise, both are cooperative:
(40) members organize themselves into working groups that observe a clearly-defined division of labor. In addition, members of both groups can convey to each other a range of
(45) basic emotions and personal information: animosity, fright, hunger, rank within a particular caste, and ability to reproduce. Wilson readily concedes that, from a specialist's perspective, such a likeness
(50) may at first appear superficial, even unscientifically glib.
Nonetheless, in this eminent scholar's judgment, "It is out of such deliberate oversimplification that the beginnings of a general theory are made.

Which of the following statements best describes the organization of the author's discussion of the importance of the termite/macaque comparison in the development of a unified science of sociobiology?

○ He provides an example of a comparison and then rejects its implications.

○ He concedes that current data are insufficient and modifies his initial assertion of their importance.

○ He acknowledges hypothetical objections to the comparison, but concludes by reaffirming its significance.

○ He cites critical appraisals of the comparison, but refrains from making an appraisal of his own.

○ He notes an ambiguity in the comparison, but finally concedes its validity.

Click on your choice.

Under these conditions, clearly only one tactic works: first read the question, then read the passage.

It is particularly important to follow this tactic when you are dealing with the logical reasoning questions on the GRE. You must look at the question before you look at the argument.

Rather than jumping in blindly and analyzing each and every aspect of the argument—assumptions, central point, evidence, further application, logical flaws—do no more work than necessary. Look at the question stem. Then examine the argument. Know what aspect of the argument you are to concentrate on, and focus on it. You will save time and effort.

The logical reasoning reading question that follows consists of a short passage followed by the question, "Which of the following best serves as an assumption that would make the argument above logically correct?" If you read the question before you read the passage, you will know that, as presented, the argument is faulty. As a result, you will be looking for the flaw as you read the passage and may already realize what's wrong before reading through the five answer choices. If you read the passage first, you may not catch the subtle flaw, and you may find the conclusion perfectly reasonable. Then when you read the question, and learn that the argument was not logically correct, you will be forced to go back and reread the passage, wasting valuable time.

Caution

Read only the question itself— do not read the answer choices before reading the passage. Doing so will confuse you and waste time.

In order to save $500,000 in this year's budget, the city council voted to freeze the salaries of its school building inspectors. This shortsighted decision is yet another example of the council's being penny wise and pound foolish. The cursory inspections that will result from this action will cause many structural defects to go undetected, resulting in millions more dollars being spent on repairs in the future.

EXAMPLE

In order for his argument to be logically correct, the author of the above argument used which of the following statements as an unstated underlying assumption?

Ⓐ City inspectors are already overpaid and so the wage freeze is warranted.
Ⓑ The city council cares less about the safety of the school children than it does about saving money.
Ⓒ If they do not receive an increase in their wages, school inspectors will become lax in performing their jobs.
Ⓓ The council does not feel that cursory inspections will necessarily result in defects going undetected.
Ⓔ The council will not authorize repairs in the future, so it will never have to incur the extra costs.

The passage attempts to justify the conclusion that the city will eventually have to pay much more than it is now saving. Having first read the question, you were on the lookout for a flaw in the passage's logic (the passage's failure to state an underlying assumption). Therefore, you probably picked up the subtle shift from "freeze the salaries" in the first sentence to perform "cursory inspections" in the third sentence. If you did, you might have said to yourself, "The fact that the wages of the inspectors are not being raised does not necessarily mean that they will retaliate by rendering poorer service." This then is the gap in the passage's logic. To justify the conclusion presented, you need to assume that freezing salaries will result in cursory or slipshod inspections; and this is precisely what Choice C says.

In the preceding example, none of the other choices is an assumption upon which the argument depends. You can read and analyze each of the other choices before eliminating it, but that takes time. It is always better if you can anticipate the correct choice.

READING COMPREHENSION STRATEGIES

1. Read the question carefully, so that you are sure you understand what it is asking. Decide whether it is asking about a specific, readily identifiable detail within the passage, or whether it is asking about the passage as a whole. Note any key words in the question that may help you spot where the answer may be found.

2. Next, turn to the passage. Read as rapidly as you can with understanding, but do not force yourself. Do not worry about the time element. If you worry about not finishing the test, you will begin to take shortcuts and miss the correct answer in your haste.

3. As you read the opening sentences, try to anticipate what the passage will be about. Whom or what is the author talking about? What, in other words, is the *topic* of this passage?

4. As you scroll through the passage, think about what kind of writing this is. What is the author trying to do?

   Is the author trying to *explain* some aspect of the topic?
   Is the author trying to *describe* some aspect of the topic?
   Is the author trying to *argue* or debate some aspect of the topic?

   What does the author feel about this topic? What audience is the author addressing here? Answering these questions will give you a sense of the passage as a whole.

5. Use your scratch paper intelligently. Take brief notes of important words or phrases in different paragraphs so that you can scroll back to them quickly when you want to verify an answer choice. You may also want to note key words in question stems (words like EXCEPT and LEAST, which the test-makers capitalize for emphasis, and that restrict your answer choice).

6. Your first scrolling through the passage should give you a general impression of the scope of the passage and of the location of its major subdivisions. In order to answer the question properly, **you must go back to the passage to verify your answer choice**. Do not rely on your memory. Above all, do not rely on anything you may have learned from your reading or courses about the topic of this passage. Base your answer on what this passage says, not on what you know from other sources.

TACTIC 2

Learn to Spot the Major Reading Question Types

It helps to familiarize yourself with the major types of reading questions on the test. If you can recognize just what a given question is asking for, you will be better able to tell which reading tactic to apply.

Here are seven categories of reading questions you are likely to face:

1. **Main Idea** Questions that test your ability to find the central thought of a passage or to judge its significance often take one of the following forms:

   The main point of the passage is to...
   The passage is primarily concerned with...
   The author's primary purpose in this passage is to...

The chief theme of the passage can best be described as...

Which of the following titles best states the central idea of the passage?

Which of the following statements best expresses the main idea of the passage?

2. **Finding Specific Details** Questions that test your ability to understand what the author states *explicitly* are often worded:

   According to the author,...

   The author states all of the following EXCEPT...

   According to the passage, which of the following is true of the...

   The passage supplies information that would answer which of the following questions?

   Which of the following statements is (are) best supported by the passage?

   Which of the following is NOT cited in the passage as evidence of...?

3. **Drawing Inferences** Questions that test your ability to go beyond the author's explicit statements and see what these statements imply may be worded:

   It can be inferred from the passage that...

   The author implies that...

   The passage suggests that...

   Which of the following statements about...can be inferred from the passage?

4. **Application to Other Situations** (These are logical reasoning questions.) Questions that test your ability to recognize how the author's ideas might apply to other situations often are worded:

   With which of the following statements would the author of the passage be most likely to agree?

   With which of the following aphorisms would the author be in strongest agreement?

   The author's argument would be most weakened by the discovery of which of the following?

   The author's contention would be most clearly strengthened if which of the following were found to be true?

   Which of the following examples could best be substituted for the author's example of...?

   Which of the following statements would be most likely to begin the paragraph immediately following the passage?

   The author is most probably addressing which of the following audiences?

5. **Tone/Attitude** Questions that test your ability to sense an author's emotional state often take the form:

   The author's attitude toward the problem can best be described as...

   The author regards that idea that...with...

   The author's tone in the passage is that of a person attempting to...

   Which of the following best describes the author's tone in the passage?

6. **Technique** Questions that test your ability to recognize a passage's method of organization or technique often are worded:

> Which of the following best describes the development of this passage?
> In presenting the argument, the author does all of the following EXCEPT...
> The relationship between the second paragraph and the first paragraph can best be described as...
> In the passage, the author makes the central point primarily by...
> The organization of the passage can best be described as...

7. **Determining the Meaning of Words from Their Context** Questions that test your ability to work out the meaning of unfamiliar words from their context often are worded:

> As it is used in the passage, the term...can best be described as...
> The phrase...is used in the passage to mean that...
> As used by the author, the term...refers to...
> The author uses the phrase...to describe...

TACTIC

3

When Asked to Find the Main Idea, Be Sure to Check the Opening and Summary Sentences of Each Paragraph

The opening and closing sentences of a paragraph are key sentences for you to read. They can serve as guideposts, pointing out the author's main idea.

When you are asked to determine a passage's main idea, *always* check the opening and summary sentences of each paragraph. Authors typically provide readers with a sentence that expresses a paragraph's main idea succinctly. Although such *topic sentences* may appear anywhere in the paragraph, readers customarily look for them in the opening or closing sentences.

Note that in GRE reading passages topic sentences are sometimes implied rather than stated directly. If you cannot find a topic sentence, ask yourself these questions:

1. Who or what is this passage about?
   (The subject of the passage can be a *person*, *place*, or *thing*. It can be something abstract, such as an *idea*. It can even be a *process*, or something in motion, for which no single-word synonym exists.)

2. What aspect of this subject is the author talking about?

3. What is the author trying to get across about this aspect of the subject?
   (Decide the most important thing that is being said about the subject. Either the subject must be *doing* something, or something is *being done* to it.)

Read the following natural science passage and apply this tactic.

> According to Wilson[1], only when we are able to apply the same parameters and mathematical principles to weighing both troops of rhesus macaques and termite colonies will a unified science of sociobiology
> *Line* finally exist. While recognizing that many of his colleagues question such
> (5) an outcome, Wilson, one of sociobiology's leading proponents, finds himself simultaneously more and more struck by the functional similarities

that characterize both insect and vertebrate societies and less concerned with the structural differences that divide them to such an apparently irreconcilable degree. Thus, he freely compares termites and macaques, (10) pointing out numerous likenesses between them. Both societies are territorial: they occupy a particular home range, which they defend against intruders. Likewise, both are cooperative: members organize themselves into working groups that observe a clearly-defined division of labor. In addition, members of both groups can convey to each other a range of (15) basic emotions and personal information: animosity, fright, hunger, rank within a particular caste, and ability to reproduce. Wilson readily concedes that, from a specialist's perspective, such a likeness may at first appear superficial, even unscientifically glib. Nonetheless, in this eminent scholar's judgment, "it is out of such deliberate oversimplification that the (20) beginnings of a general theory are made."

[1]Edwin O. Wilson, Harvard professor and author of *Sociobiology*.

Now look at a typical main idea question on this passage.

EXAMPLE

Which of the following best summarizes the author's main point?

(A) Facile and simplistic comparisons of animal societies could damage the prospects for the establishment of a unified science of sociobiology.

(B) It is necessary to study both biology and sociology in order to appreciate how animals as different as termites and rhesus macaques can be said to resemble each other.

(C) The majority of animal species arrange themselves in societies whose patterns of group behavior resemble those of human societies.

(D) It is worthwhile noting that animals as dissimilar as termites and rhesus monkeys observe certain analogous and predictable behavior patterns.

(E) An analysis of the ways in which insect and vertebrate societies resemble one another could supply the foundation for a unified science of sociobiology.

Look at the opening and summary sentences of the passage: "only when we are able to apply the same parameters and mathematical principles to weighing both troops of rhesus macaques and termite colonies will a unified science of sociobiology finally exist...it is out of such deliberate oversimplification that the beginnings of a general theory are made." First, is there a person, place, thing, idea, or process that is common to both sentences? Are there any words in the last sentence that repeat something in the first? *A general theory* repeats the idea of *a unified science* of sociobiology. The paragraph's subject seems to be the unified science of sociobiology. Note as well the words pointing to expectations for the future — *will...finally exist, beginnings*. The tone of both sentences appears positive: when certain conditions are met, then, in Wilson's view, a specific result will follow — we will have a unified science or general theory of sociobiology. This result, however, is not guaranteed; it can come about only if the conditions are met.

Now turn to the answer choices. What does Choice A say about a unified science of sociobiology? It states some things could make it less likely, not more likely, to come about. Choice A is incorrect; it contradicts the passage's sense that a unified science of sociobiology is a *likely* outcome. Choices B, C, and D also may be incorrect: not one of them mentions a unified science of sociobiology. On closer inspection, Choice B proves incorrect: it makes an unsupported statement that one needs biological and sociological education to understand the resemblances between insects and vertebrates. Choice C also proves incorrect: it goes far beyond what the passage actually states. Where the passage speaks in terms of termites and rhesus macaques, Choice C speaks in terms of the *majority* of animal species and extends the comparison to include humans as well. Choice D, while factually correct according to the passage, is incorrect because it is too narrow in scope. It ignores the author's main point; it fails to include Wilson's interest in the possibility that a study of such similar patterns of behavior might lead to a general theory of sociobiology. The correct answer is Choice E. It is the only statement that speaks of a unified science of sociobiology as a likely possibility.

TACTIC

4 When Asked to Choose a Title, Watch Out for Choices That Are Too Specific or Too Broad

A paragraph has been defined as a group of sentences revolving around a central theme. An appropriate title for a paragraph, therefore, must express this central theme that each of the sentences in the paragraph develops. It should be neither too broad nor too narrow in scope; it should be specific and yet comprehensive enough to include all the essential ideas presented by the sentences. A good title for a passage of two or more paragraphs should express the thoughts of ALL the paragraphs.

When you are trying to select the best title for a passage, watch out for words that come straight out of the passage. They may not always be your best choice.

This second question on the sociobiology passage is a title question. Note how it resembles questions on the passage's purpose or main idea.

EXAMPLE

Which of the following is the best title for the passage?

Ⓐ Deceptive Comparisons: Oversimplification in Biological Research
Ⓑ An Uncanny Likeness: Termites and Rhesus Macaques
Ⓒ Structural Dissimilarities Between Insects and Vertebrates
Ⓓ Arguments Against a Science of Sociobiology
Ⓔ Sociobiology: Intimations of a General Theory

Choice A is incorrect: it is at once too narrow and too broad. It is too narrow in that the passage refers to *oversimplification* only in passing; it does not have oversimplification as its subject. It is too broad in that the passage emphasizes sociobiology, not the whole realm of biological research. It is also misleading; the passage never asserts that the deliberate oversimplification of the comparison between termites and macaques is intended to deceive.

Choice B is incorrect: it is too narrow. True, the author discusses the resemblance between termite and macaque societies; however, this likeness is not his subject. He discusses it to provide an example of the sort of comparison that may lay the ground-work for a potential science of sociobiology.

Choice C is also incorrect because it is not inclusive enough. It fails to mention the potential science of sociobiology. In addition, while the passage refers to *structural differences* between insect and vertebrate societies, it stresses structural similarities, not structural dissimilarities.

Choices D and E both mention the theory of sociobiology. Which is the better title for the piece? Clearly, Choice E: the author is not arguing against the potential science of sociobiology; he is reporting Wilson's opinions concerning the likelihood of sociobiology's emergence as a unified science. Thus, he finds in the termite-macaque comparison *intimations* or hints of an incipient general theory.

TACTIC 5	When Asked to Determine Questions of Attitude, Mood, or Tone, Look for Words That Convey Emotion, Express Values, or Paint Pictures

In determining the attitude, mood, or tone of an author, examine the specific diction used. Is the author using adjectives to describe the subject? If so, are they words like *fragrant, tranquil, magnanimous* — words with positive connotations? Or are they words like *fetid, ruffled, stingy* — words with negative connotations?

When we speak, our tone of voice conveys our mood — frustrated, cheerful, critical, gloomy, angry. When we write, our images and descriptive phrases get our feelings across.

The next model question on the Wilson passage is an attitude question. Note the range of feelings in the answer choices.

EXAMPLE

According to the author, Wilson's attitude toward the prospect of a unified theory in sociobiology can best be characterized as which of the following?

Ⓐ Unconditional enthusiasm
Ⓑ Cautious optimism
Ⓒ Unbiased objectivity
Ⓓ Resigned acquiescence
Ⓔ Strong displeasure

How does Wilson feel about the possibility of a unified theory of sociobiology? The answer choices range from actively negative (*strong displeasure*) to actively positive (*unconditional enthusiasm*), with passively negative (*resigned acquiescence*), neutral (*unbiased objectivity*), and guardedly positive (*cautious optimism*) in between.

Wilson's attitude toward the possibility of a unified theory of sociobiology is implicit in the author's choice of words. It is clear that Wilson views this possibility positively; the whole thrust of his argument is that the current studies of the similarities between insect and vertebrate societies could mark the beginnings of such a unified theory and that the specialist should not dismiss these studies as glib or simpleminded. Note in the second sentence how the author describes Wilson as a leading proponent or champion of sociobiology, someone whose feelings about the field are by definition positive.

Wilson is certainly not unhappy or *strongly displeased* with this potential unified theory, nor is he merely long-suffering or *resigned* to it. Similarly, he is not *unbiased* and *objective* about it; he actively involves himself in arguing the case for sociobiology. Thus, you can eliminate Choices C, D, and E. But how do you decide between the two positive terms, *enthusiasm* and *optimism*, Choice A and Choice B? To decide between them, you must look carefully at the adjectives modifying them. Is Wilson's enthusiasm unqualified or *unconditional?* You may think so, but look again. The opening sentence states a basic condition that must be met before there can be a unified science of sociobiology: the same parameters and mathematical principles must be used to analyze insect and vertebrate societies. Though a proponent of sociobiology, Wilson is first and foremost a scientist, one who tests hypotheses and comes to logical conclusions about them. *Unconditional enthusiasm* seems to overstate his attitude.

Choice A appears incorrect. What of Choice B? Is Wilson's optimism *cautious* or guarded? Yes. According to the passage, Wilson is aware that specialists may well find fault with the sociobiologist's conclusions; the passage uses terms that convey values, first the negative "superficial, even unscientifically glib" to suggest the specialist's negative attitude toward sociobiology, then the positive "deliberate" to convey Wilson's own more positive response. The correct answer is Choice B.

TACTIC
6
When Asked About Specific Details in the Passage, Spot Key Words in the Question and Scan the Passage to Find Them (or Their Synonyms)

In developing the main idea of a passage, a writer will make statements to support his or her point. To answer questions about such supporting details, you *must* find a word or group of words in the passage supporting your choice of answer. The words "according to the passage" or "according to the author" should focus your attention on what the passage explicitly states. Do not be misled into choosing an answer (even one that makes good sense) if you cannot find it supported by the text.

Detail questions often ask about a particular phrase or line. In such cases, use the following technique:

1. Look for key words (nouns or verbs) in the answer choices.
2. Scroll through the passage, looking for those key words or their synonyms. (This is *scanning*. It is what you do when you look up someone's number in the phone directory.)
3. When you find a key word or its synonym in a sentence, reread that sentence to make sure the test-makers haven't used the original wording to mislead you.

Read the following brief passage and apply this tactic.

What is involved in the process of visual recognition? First, like computer data, visual memories of an object must be stored; then, a mechanism must exist for them to be retrieved. But how does this process work?
Line The eye triggers the nerves into action. This neural activity constructs a
(5) picture in the brain's memory system, an internal image of the object

observed. When the eye once again confronts that object, the object is compared with its internal image; if the two images match, recognition takes place.

(10) Among psychologists, the question as to whether visual recognition is a parallel, single-step operation or a sequential, step-by-step one is the subject of much debate. Gestalt psychologists contend that objects are perceived as wholes in a parallel operation: the internal image is matched with the retinal impression in one single step. Psychologists of other schools, however, suggest the opposite, maintaining that the individual

(15) features of an object are matched serially with the features of its internal image. Some experiments have demonstrated that the more well-known an object is, the more holistic its internal image becomes, and the more parallel the process of recognition tends to be. Nonetheless, the bulk of the evidence appears to uphold the serial hypothesis, at least for simple

(20) objects that are relatively unfamiliar to the viewer.

Now look at the following question on a specific detail in the passage.

EXAMPLE

According to the passage, psychologists of the Gestalt school assume which of the following about the process of visual recognition?

Select *all* that apply.

A The image an object makes on the retina is exactly the same as its internal image.

B The mind recognizes a given object as a whole; it has no need to analyze the object's constituent parts individually.

C The process of matching an object with its internal image takes place in a single step.

You can arrive at the correct answer to this question by elimination.

First, quickly scan the passage looking for the key word *Gestalt*. The sentence mentioning Gestalt psychologists states they maintain that objects are recognized as wholes in a parallel procedure. The sentence immediately preceding defines a parallel procedure as one that takes only one step.

Now examine the statements. Do Gestalt psychologists maintain that an object's retinal image is exactly the same as its internal image? Statement A is unsupported by the passage.

Statement B is supported by the passage: lines 11–12 indicate that Gestalt psychologists believe objects are recognized as wholes.

Statement C is supported by the passage: lines 12–13 indicate that Gestalt psychologists believe matching is a parallel process that occurs in one step.

Choices B and C are both correct.

Note how necessary it is to point to specific lines in the passage when you answer questions on specific details.

TACTIC
7
When Asked to Make Inferences, Base Your Answers on What the Passage Implies, Not What It States Directly

In *Language in Thought and Action*, S. I. Hayakawa defines an inference as "a statement about the unknown made on the basis of the known."

Inference questions require you to use your own judgment. You must not take anything directly stated by the author as an inference. Instead, you must look for clues in the passage that you can use in deriving your own conclusion. You should choose as your answer a statement that is a logical development of the information the author has provided.

Try this relatively easy inference question, based on the previous passage about visual recognition.

EXAMPLE

One can infer from the passage that, in visual recognition, the process of matching

Ⓐ requires neural inactivity
Ⓑ cannot take place if an attribute of a familiar object has been altered in some way
Ⓒ cannot occur when the observer looks at an object for the very first time
Ⓓ has now been proven to necessitate both serial and parallel processes
Ⓔ can only occur when the brain receives a retinal image as a single unit

---

Go through the answer choices, eliminating any choices that obviously contradict what the passage states or implies. Remember that in answering inference questions you must go beyond the obvious, beyond what the authors explicitly state, to look for logical implications of what they say.

Choice A is incorrect. Nothing in the passage suggests that the matching process requires or demands neural inactivity. Rather, the entire process of visual recognition, including the matching of images, requires neural *activity*.

Choice D is incorrect. It is clear from the passage that the matching process is not fully understood; nothing yet has been absolutely *proven*. The weight of the evidence *seems* to support the serial hypothesis, but controversy still surrounds the entire question.

Choice E is incorrect. It can be eliminated because it directly contradicts information in the passage stating that recognition most likely is a serial or step-by-step process rather than a parallel one receiving an image as a single unit.

Choices B and C are left. Which is a possible inference? Choice C seems a possible inference. Although the author never says so, it seems logical that you could not match an object if you had never seen it before. After all, if you had never seen the object before, you would have no prior internal image of it and would have nothing with which to match it. What of Choice B? Nothing in the passage mentions altering any attributes or features of a familiar object. Therefore, *on the basis of the passage* you have no way to deduce whether matching would or would not be possible if such a change took place. There is not enough information in the passage to justify Choice B as an inference. The correct answer is Choice C.

Another, more difficult inference question is based on the previous excerpt reviewing Wilson's *Sociobiology*. Review the passage briefly and see how you do with a question that very few of the examinees would have answered correctly.

According to Wilson, only when we are able to apply the same parameters and mathematical principles to weighing both troops of rhesus macaques and termite colonies will a unified science of sociobiology
Line finally exist. While recognizing that many of his colleagues question such
(5) an outcome, Wilson, one of sociobiology's leading proponents, finds himself simultaneously more and more struck by the functional similarities that characterize both insect and vertebrate societies and less concerned with the structural differences that divide them to such an apparently irreconcilable degree. Thus, he freely compares termites and macaques,
(10) pointing out numerous likenesses between them. Both societies are territorial: they occupy a particular home range, which they defend against intruders. Likewise, both are cooperative: members organize themselves into working groups that observe a clearly-defined division of labor. In addition, members of both groups can convey to each other a range of
(15) basic emotions and personal information: animosity, fright, hunger, rank within a particular caste, and ability to reproduce. Wilson readily concedes that, from a specialist's perspective, such a likeness may at first appear superficial, even unscientifically glib. Nonetheless, in this eminent scholar's judgment, "it is out of such deliberate oversimplification that the
(20) beginnings of a general theory are made."

EXAMPLE

In analyzing insect and vertebrate societies, the passage suggests which of the following?

Ⓐ A clearly-defined division of labor is a distinguishing feature of most insect and vertebrate societies.
Ⓑ The caste structures of insect and vertebrate societies share certain likenesses.
Ⓒ Most insect and vertebrate societies utilize cooperative groups to hold and defend their home range.
Ⓓ The system of communication employed by members of insect societies resembles the system that members of vertebrate societies follow.
Ⓔ Major structural differences exist between insect and vertebrate societies.

Why would most examinees answer this question incorrectly? The reason is simple: it is easy to confuse statements made about specific insect and vertebrate societies with statements made about insect and vertebrate societies in general. In this passage, in the fourth sentence, the author switches from talking about Wilson's views of insect and vertebrate societies in general and refers to his comments on termites and macaques in specific.

Go through the answer choices one by one. Does the passage suggest that a clearly-defined division of labor distinguishes *most* insect and vertebrate societies? No. It merely states that, according to Wilson, a clearcut division of labor is a characteristic of termite and rhesus macaque societies. Choice A is incorrect: you cannot justify leaping from a single type of insect (*termites*) and a single type of vertebrate (*rhesus macaques*) to most insects and most vertebrates.

Does the passage suggest that the caste structure of insect societies shares certain likenesses with that of their counterparts in vertebrate societies? No. It merely states that, according to Wilson, termites and macaques both can communicate rank within a particular caste. Choice B is incorrect. You cannot assume that the caste structure of insect societies is similar to the caste structure of vertebrate societies just because termites and rhesus macaques both have some way to communicate caste status or rank.

Does the passage suggest that *most* insect and vertebrate societies form cooperative groups in order to hold and defend their home range or territory? No. It merely states that termites and macaques organize themselves into cooperative groups, and that both species occupy and defend territories. Choice C is incorrect: again, you cannot justify leaping from termites and rhesus macaques to *most* insects and *most* vertebrates.

Does the passage suggest that the system of communication employed by members of insect societies resembles that employed by members of vertebrate societies? No. It merely states that communication among termites and macaques serves similar ends; it says nothing about the specific systems of communication they use, nor about those systems of communication used by other insects and vertebrates. Choice D is incorrect.

The correct answer is Choice E. In the passage, the author states that Wilson has grown less impressed "with the structural differences that divide them (i.e., insect and vertebrate societies) to such an apparently irreconcilable degree." This suggests that, even though Wilson may be unimpressed with them, these differences exist and are *major*.

TACTIC

8

When Asked to Apply Ideas from the Passage to a New Situation, Put Yourself in the Author's Place

GRE application questions require you to do three things:

1. *Reason* — If X is true, then Y must also be true.
2. *Perceive Feelings* — If the author feels this way about subject A, he probably feels a certain way about subject B.
3. *Sense a Larger Structure* — This passage is part of an argument for a proposal, or part of a description of a process, or part of a critique of a hypothesis.

Like inference questions, application questions require you to go beyond what the author explicitly states. Application questions, however, ask you to go well beyond a simple inference, using clues in the passage to interpret possible reasons for actions and possible outcomes of events. Your concern is to comprehend how the author's ideas might apply to other situations, or be affected by them. To do so, you have to put yourself in the author's place.

Imagine you are the author. What are you arguing for? Given what you have just stated in the passage, what would you want to say next? What might hurt your argument? What might make it stronger? What kind of audience would appreciate what you have to say? Whom are you trying to convince? If you involve yourself personally with the passage, you will be better able to grasp it in its entirety and see its significance.

Answer the following application question based on the previous passage discussing Wilson's *Sociobiology*.

EXAMPLE

Which of the following statements would be most likely to begin the paragraph immediately following the passage?

Ⓐ Wilson has raised a problem in ethical philosophy in order to characterize the essence of the discipline of sociobiology.

Ⓑ It may not be too much to say that sociology and the other social sciences are the last branches of biology waiting to be integrated into neo-Darwinist evolutionary theory.

Ⓒ Although behavioral biology is traditionally spoken of as if it were a unified subject, it is now emerging as two distinct disciplines centered on neurophysiology and sociobiology, respectively.

Ⓓ The formulation of a theory of sociobiology constitutes, in Wilson's opinion, one of the great manageable problems of biology for the next twenty or thirty years.

Ⓔ In the past, the development of sociobiology has been slowed by too close an identification with ethology and behavioral psychology.

As you know from answering the previous main idea and attitude questions, Wilson's point is that students of insect and vertebrate societies may be on the verge of devising a general theory of sociobiology. Like Wilson, the author of the passage appears optimistic about the likelihood of developing this unified science. At the same time, again like Wilson, he is cautious; he too does not wish to overstate the case.

Put yourself in the author's place. What would you be likely to say next? The author has just been describing Wilson's hopeful view of the prospects for putting together a general theory of sociobiology. What would be more natural than for him next to discuss Wilson's opinion of a time frame for formulating this general theory? Choice D, with its confident yet judicious view of the formulation of a theory of sociobiology as "one of the great *manageable* problems of biology for the next twenty or thirty years," seems a logical extension of what the passage has just been saying. While Choices A, B, C, and E all touch on sociobiology in some way, none of them follows as naturally from the passage's immediate argument.

TACTIC

9 **When Asked to Give the Meaning of an Unfamiliar Word, Look for Nearby Context Clues**

When a question in the reading comprehension part of an examination asks for the meaning of a word, that meaning can usually be deduced from the word's context. The purpose of this kind of question is to determine how well you can extract meaning from the text, not how extensive your general vocabulary is.

Sometimes the unknown word is a common word used in one of its special or technical meanings. For example:

> He *threw* the pot in an hour. The wheel turned busily and the shape grew quickly as his fingers worked the wet, spinning clay. (*Throw* here means to shape on a potter's wheel.)

At other times, the unknown word may bear a deceptive resemblance to a known word.

> He fell *senseless* to the ground. (He was unconscious. He did not fall foolishly or nonsensically to the ground.)

Just because you know *one* meaning of a word, do not assume that you know its meaning as it is used in a particular passage. You must look within the passage for clues. Often authors will use an unfamiliar word and then immediately define it within the same sentence. The two words or groups of words are juxtaposed — set beside one another — to make their relationship clear. Commas, hyphens, and parentheses may signal this relationship.

1. The *rebec*, a medieval stringed instrument played with a bow, has only three strings.
2. *Paleontologists* — students of fossil remains — explore the earth's history.
3. Most mammals are *quadrupeds* (four-footed animals).

Often an unfamiliar word in one clause of a sentence will be defined or clarified in the sentence's other clause.

1. The early morning dew had frozen, and everything was covered with a thin coat of *rime.*
2. Cowards, we use *euphemisms* when we cannot bear the truth, calling our dead "the dear departed," as if they have just left the room.

Refer once more to the passage on visual recognition to answer the following question.

> What is involved in the process of visual recognition? First, like computer data, visual memories of an object must be stored; then, a mechanism must exist for them to be retrieved. But how does this process work?
> *Line* The eye triggers the nerves into action. This neural activity constructs a
> *(5)* picture in the brain's memory system, an internal image of the object observed. When the eye once again confronts that object, the object is compared with its internal image; if the two images match, recognition takes place.

Among psychologists, the question as to whether visual recognition is
(10) a parallel, single-step operation or a sequential, step-by-step one is the
subject of much debate. Gestalt psychologists contend that objects are
perceived as wholes in a parallel operation: the internal image is matched
with the retinal impression in one single step. Psychologists of other
schools, however, suggest the opposite, maintaining that the individual
(15) features of an object are matched serially with the features of its internal
image. Some experiments have demonstrated that the more well-known
an object is, the more holistic its internal image becomes, and the more
parallel the process of recognition tends to be. Nonetheless, the bulk of
the evidence appears to uphold the serial hypothesis, at least for simple
(20) objects that are relatively unfamiliar to the viewer.

EXAMPLE

Which of the following phrases could best replace "the more holistic its internal image becomes" (line 17) without significantly changing the sentence's meaning?

Ⓐ the more its internal image increases in detail
Ⓑ the more integrated its internal image grows
Ⓒ the more its internal image decreases in size
Ⓓ the more it reflects its internal image
Ⓔ the more indistinct its internal image appears

What words or phrases in the vicinity of "the more holistic its internal image becomes" give you a clue to the phrase's meaning? The phrase immediately following, "becomes more parallel." If the recognition process becomes more parallel as an object becomes more familiar, then matching takes place in one step in which all the object's features are simultaneously transformed into a single internal representation. Thus, to say that an object's internal image becomes more holistic is to say that it becomes more *integrated* or whole. The correct answer is Choice B.

TACTIC
10   Familiarize Yourself with the Technical Terms Used to Describe a Passage's Organization

Another aspect of understanding the author's point is understanding how the author organizes what he has to say. You have to understand how the author makes his point, figure out whether he begins with his thesis or main idea or works up to it gradually. Often this means observing how the opening sentence or paragraph relates to the passage as a whole.

Here is a technique question based on the last two sentences of the passage about sociobiology. Those lines are repeated here so that you can easily refer to them.

Wilson readily concedes that, from a specialist's perspective, such a likeness may at first appear superficial, even unscientifically glib. Nonetheless, in this eminent scholar's judgment, "it is out of such deliberate oversimplification that the beginnings of a general theory are made."

EXAMPLE

Which of the following statements best describes the organization of the author's discussion of the importance of the termite/macaque comparison in the development of a unified science of sociobiology (lines 16–20)?

(A) He provides an example of a comparison and then rejects its implications.

(B) He concedes that current data are insufficient and modifies his initial assertion of their importance.

(C) He acknowledges hypothetical objections to the comparison, but concludes by reaffirming its significance.

(D) He cites critical appraisals of the comparison, but refrains from making an appraisal of his own.

(E) He notes an ambiguity in the comparison, but finally concedes its validity.

Consider the first clause of each answer choice.

In his comment on how things may seem from the specialist's point of view, does the author *provide an example* of a comparison? No. He refers to a comparison made earlier. Therefore, you can eliminate Choice A.

Does he *concede the insufficiency* of current data? Not quite. He states that some people may quarrel with the comparison because it seems glib to them; he does not grant that they are right or that the data are inadequate. Therefore, you can eliminate Choice B.

Does he *acknowledge hypothetical objections* to the comparison? Definitely. Make a note to come back later to Choice C.

Does he *cite critical appraisals* of the comparison? Possibly. Again, make a note of Choice D.

Does he *note an ambiguity* in the comparison? No. He notes an objection to the comparison; he mentions no ambiguities within it. Therefore, you can eliminate Choice E.

Now consider the second clause of Choices C and D. Does the author *refrain from making an appraisal* of the comparison? No. He calls it a deliberate oversimplification that may bear fruit. Choice D is incorrect. Does the author conclude by *reaffirming the significance* of the termite/macaque comparison? Clearly he does; he quotes Wilson's conclusion that such oversimplified comparisons can provide the basis for an important general theory. The correct answer is Choice C.

TACTIC

In Answering Logical Reasoning Questions, Read Each Argument Very Carefully

Some students, who find that they can answer many reading comprehension questions correctly by skimming the passage without reading every word, attack logical reasoning questions in the same way. This is a very poor strategy.

First of all, the temptation to skim logical argument passages should be less, since these passages are much shorter than the usual run of reading comprehension passages, and skimming them will save less time. More important, in logical reasoning passages, it is not enough to have a general idea about the argument; you must be able to analyze the argument very closely.

A cursory reading is not sufficient to pick up a subtle flaw in logic or to ascertain what unstated premise the author is assuming to be true.

TACTIC

12 **In Tackling Logical Reasoning Questions, Always Identify the Conclusion of the Argument**

It is imperative that you are absolutely clear about what conclusion the author of the argument claims to have reached. The three most common situations are as follows:

- The conclusion is the last sentence of the passage, often introduced by a word such as *therefore, so, thus, hence,* or *consequently.* Here is a simple example of this type of argument:

  Joan Smith has those qualities that we seek in our congressional leaders. She is honest, hardworking, intelligent, and dedicated. Having served for ten years in the House of Representatives, she has the requisite experience to be an effective United States Senator. Therefore, you should enthusiastically vote for Ms. Smith in this year's election.

- The conclusion is the first sentence of the passage, followed by the supporting evidence. In such a case, there is no word such as therefore signaling the conclusion, but it is still very easy to spot. For example, the preceding argument could have been presented as follows:

  Joan Smith deserves your vote for United States Senator. She has those qualities that we seek in our congressional leaders. She is honest, hardworking, intelligent, and dedicated. In addition, having served for ten years in the House of Representatives, she has the requisite congressional experience to be an effective United States Senator.

- The conclusion is not in the passage. In such cases, the question usually asks you to identify the conclusion that is implicit in the argument. For example, if in the two preceding arguments the last or first sentence, respectively, had been omitted, you would have had no difficulty determining that the author of the passage wanted you to vote for Joan Smith. The question might have asked, "Which of the following five statements can most reasonably be inferred from the statements in the given passage?"

TACTIC

13 **In Tackling Logical Reasoning Questions, Pay Particular Attention to Signal Words in the Question (and in the Argument As Well)**

In answering logical reasoning questions, you must read closely both the argument and the question or questions based on it. When you do so, be on the lookout for certain signal words that can clarify the situation. In particular, be alert for:

Cause and Effect Signal Words

The following words often signal the conclusion of an argument:

accordingly	so
consequently	therefore
for this reason	thus
hence	

Contrast Signal Words

The following words often suggest a reversal of thought within an argument or question stem:

although	instead
but	nevertheless
despite	not
even though	on the contrary
except	on the other hand
however	rather than
in contrast	unlike

Notice that in the following logical reasoning problem several of these words are present: the argument contains the words *despite*, *not*, and *consequently*, and the question stem has the word *except*. Each of these words plays a role in your reasoning.

> Despite the fact that River City increased the average class size by more than 15% in all grades two years ago, this year's average SAT scores for the junior class were the highest ever. This shows that class size is not a good determinant of student performance. Consequently, other school districts should follow River City's lead and save money by increasing the size of their classes.

EXAMPLE

Each of the following statements, if true, is a valid objection to this argument EXCEPT:

Ⓐ The advantages of smaller classes are more pronounced in elementary school than in high school.

Ⓑ The number of classroom discipline problems reported by teachers is directly proportional to the number of students in the classroom.

Ⓒ Japanese schools have a lower teacher-to-student ratio than American schools do and have generally better results on international standardized tests.

Ⓓ Three years ago, the eighth graders in River City Middle School had very high scores on their standardized tests.

Ⓔ The effects on students of learning in larger classes take at least three or four years to manifest themselves completely.

It is implicit in the question stem that the argument is not very persuasive, and that there are several possible objections to it that could be raised. In fact, the question stem tells you that four of the five statements listed raise valid objections to the argument presented. Your job is to determine the only one that does not.

The conclusion that larger class sizes are not detrimental to student learning is based on a single piece of data concerning high school juniors.

Choice A raises the objection that looking at the results of high school students on the SAT does not tell the whole story and that elementary school students will suffer from the larger classes.

Choice E raises an even stronger objection. It suggests that all students may suffer the consequences of increased class sizes; it will just take more time until the results are clearly discernible.

Choice B raises a completely different objection. Even if student academic performance is not adversely affected by larger class sizes, there are behavioral disadvantages to having large classes.

Choice D raises still another objection to the argument, the support for which is based on the performance of this year's junior class. Because three years ago, as eighth graders, the members of this class had very high test scores, it is possible that this group of students is brighter than the average. If so, it is likely that they would excel regardless of class size, whereas other students might suffer more.

Choice C is slightly harder to analyze. If the word *lower* makes you think *smaller*, Choice C seems to say that smaller classes, at least in Japan, result in higher test scores, and are thus beneficial. This then would be yet another valid objection to the given argument. If, however, you are confident in your analysis to this point and are sure that Choices A, B, D, and E are incorrect, by the process of elimination, Choice C *must* be the correct answer. So look at Choice C again. In fact, Choice C refers to a lower teacher-to-student ratio. A lower teacher-to-student ratio means more students per teacher, not fewer students. If there are more students per teacher, that means there will be larger class sizes, not smaller. Choice C then is not an objection to the argument; it supports the argument by showing that good results can occur in larger classes.

As this example shows, logical reasoning reading questions must be read very carefully. Do not attempt to analyze them too quickly.

TACTIC 14
Always Use the Process of Elimination to Reject Incorrect Choices

From Tactic 1, you know that in logical reasoning reading questions, as in all computer-based reading questions, you should always read the question first. This, of course, does not guarantee that you will know the correct answer before you read the answer choices; in fact, more often than not, you won't. What do you do then? Use the process of elimination. In the best-case scenario, using the process of elimination will allow you to zoom in on the correct answer; at worst, it will eliminate some obvious wrong choices and allow you to make an educated guess and move on.

See how the process of elimination works on the next logical reasoning reading question.

In the United States between 1993 and 1998, the number of people on death row continued to increase, but at a rate lower than that of the general prison population.

EXAMPLE

Which of the following statements directly contradicts this claim?

(A) The number of death row inmates increased slightly from 1993 to 1998.

(B) Among people convicted of murder, the proportion of those who were sentenced to death decreased from 1993 to 1998.

(C) Each year from 1993 to 1998, more death row inmates were executed than in the previous year.

(D) Each year from 1993 to 1998, fewer people were sentenced to death than in the previous year.

(E) The proportion of death row inmates among the general prison population rose from 0.6% in 1993 to 0.8% in 1998.

Caution

Do not spend even one second deciding whether you think the claim in the passage or any of the choices is true. This is completely irrelevant. Examine only the logic of the argument. Look for a statement that, if true, would mean that the claim is false.

Even though the passage is only one sentence long, you should have read the question "Which of the following statements directly contradicts this claim?" first. Unfortunately, there are many ways to contradict the claim made in that sentence. So there is no point in trying to think of one, and then looking to see if it is one of the five choices. You simply must read each choice, and then, by process of elimination, find the correct one.

- The passage states that the death row population increased. Choice A confirms this (and says nothing about the general prison population). Choice A is incorrect.

- Choice B compares the proportion of new death row inmates to the number of people convicted of murder, not to the general prison population. Choice B is incorrect.

- Choice C states that the number of people executed each year went up. If the number of people executed each year went up, the death row population might have decreased (thereby contradicting the first part of the claim), but not necessarily (not if they were replaced by many more people being sentenced to death). Choice C is incorrect.

- Choice D doesn't guarantee that the claim is true, but it comes closer to confirming it than to contradicting it. Even if fewer people were sentenced to death each year, some still were, so the number of people on death row might have increased. Again, this answer choice makes no reference to the general prison population. Choice D is incorrect.

Choice E is a little harder to analyze. Because it refers to an increase, many students would not choose it, thinking it confirms rather than refutes the claim. However, you must analyze it. Having definitively rejected choices A, B, C, and D, you know, by the process of elimination, that Choice E must be the correct answer. Let's examine why, in fact, it is.

- The passage claims the death row population increased at a slower rate than the prison population did. This means that the proportion of death row inmates in the prison population actually decreased. Choice E, which states that the proportion increased, is a direct contradiction of that claim.

> ### NOTE
> 1. Although any of the choices A, B, C, and D could be true without the claim's being true, none of them is inconsistent with the truth of the claim.
> 2. Choices B, C, and D each introduce an extraneous issue. None of the following—the number of murder convictions, the number of executions, the number of people sentenced to death—is directly relevant to the claim.

TACTIC
15   In Questions About Weakening or Strengthening an Argument, Examine the Argument for Any Unstated Assumptions It Makes

An argument is based upon certain assumptions made by its author. If an argument's basic premises are sound, the argument is strengthened. If the argument's basic premises are flawed, the argument is weakened.

Pinpoint what the argument assumes. Then compare that assumption with the answer choices. If the question asks you to choose an answer that most strengthens the argument, look for the answer choice that is most in keeping with the argument's basic assumption. If the question asks you to choose an answer that most weakens the argument, look for the answer choice that casts the most doubt on that assumption.

Apply this tactic to the following question.

> In a recent speech, the president of a major college said, "It is extremely valuable for college-educated adults entering the workplace to be able to speak at least one foreign language fluently. I am, therefore, proposing that all of our students be encouraged to spend their junior year abroad."

EXAMPLE

Which of the following, if true, most weakens the president's argument?
- Ⓐ Most students who study abroad for a full year return home with a good working knowledge of the language spoken in the country.
- Ⓑ Only students who already know a language well will choose to study in a country where that language is spoken.
- Ⓒ Some colleges do a much better job than others in teaching foreign languages.
- Ⓓ Some students learn to speak foreign languages fluently by taking intensive immersion courses in the United States.
- Ⓔ Many students who spend their junior year abroad learn to speak the language fluently, but cannot read and write with ease.

The argument claims that, in order for students to learn to speak foreign languages well, they should study abroad. It clearly assumes a high correlation between studying in a foreign country and learning to speak the language well. It assumes, at the least, that students who have studied abroad can speak a foreign language well, and, possibly, that students who have not studied abroad cannot.

Choice A is in keeping with the assumption inherent in the president's argument. If true, it would strengthen the argument, not weaken it. Choice E, by stating that many students who study abroad do not learn to read and write the language well, seems to cast doubt on the value of the junior year abroad program. However, since the president talked only about the value of being able to speak a foreign language well, Choice E also strengthens his argument.

Choices B and C are also incorrect. They neither strengthen nor weaken the president's argument. At worst, Choice B suggests that it may be difficult to convince some students to study abroad; however, it does not state that they should not be encouraged to do so. In order to weaken the president's argument, Choice C would have to go much further than it does; it would have to state explicitly that some colleges do such a good job that their students actually learn to speak foreign languages fluently.

The correct answer is Choice D. It states that it is possible for American students to learn to speak foreign languages fluently without studying abroad. Choice D weakens the president's argument. It does so by suggesting an alternative method by which college students could achieve the president's goal of speaking a foreign language fluently.

Practice Exercises

Note: Although the reading passages on the computer-based GRE range from 50 to 400 words in length, the paper-based GRE taken by students in foreign countries includes reading passages of up to 800 words in length. Therefore, the following practice exercises present a selection of long and short passages to help students to prepare for either the computer-based or the paper-based test.

Directions: Each of the following reading comprehension questions is based on the content of the following passage. Read the passage and then determine the best answer choice for each question. Base your choice on what this passage states directly or implies, not on any information you may have gained elsewhere.

One phase of the business cycle is the expansion phase. This phase is a twofold one, including recovery and prosperity. During
Line the recovery period there is ever-growing
(5) expansion of existing facilities, and new facilities for production are created. More businesses are created and older ones expanded. Improvements of various kinds are made. **There is an ever-increasing optimism about**
(10) **the future of economic growth**. Much capital is invested in machinery or "heavy" industry. More labor is employed. More materials are required. As one part of the economy develops, other parts are affected. For exam-
(15) ple, a great expansion in automobiles results in an expansion of the steel, glass, and rubber industries. Roads are required; thus the cement and machinery industries are stimulated. Demand for labor and materials results
(20) in greater prosperity for workers and suppliers of raw materials, including farmers. This increases purchasing power and the volume of goods bought and sold. Thus, prosperity is diffused among the various segments of the
(25) population. This prosperity period may continue to rise and rise without an apparent end. However, a time comes when this phase reaches a peak and stops spiraling upwards. This is the end of the expansion phase.

1. Which of the following statements best exemplifies the optimism mentioned in the bold-faced sentence of the passage as being part of the expansion phase?
   (A) Public funds are designated for the construction of new highways designed to stimulate tourism.
   (B) Industrial firms allocate monies for the purchase of machine tools.
   (C) The prices of agricultural commodities are increased at the producer level.
   (D) Full employment is achieved at all levels of the economy.
   (E) As technology advances, innovative businesses replace antiquated firms.

2. It can be inferred from the passage that the author believes that
   (A) when consumers lose their confidence in the market, a recession follows
   (B) cyclical ends to business expansion are normal
   (C) luxury goods such as jewelry are unaffected by industrial expansion
   (D) with sound economic policies, prosperity can become a fixed pattern
   (E) the creation of new products is essential for prosperity

3. Which of the following statements would be most likely to begin the paragraph immediately following the passage?

   Ⓐ Union demands may also have an effect on business cycles.

   Ⓑ Some industries are, by their very nature, cyclical, having regular phases of expansion and recession.

   Ⓒ Information is a factor that must be taken into consideration in any discussion of the expansion phase.

   Ⓓ The farmer's role during the expansion phase is of vital importance.

   Ⓔ The other phase of the business cycle is called the recession phase.

Both plants and animals of many sorts show remarkable changes in form, structure, growth habits, and even mode of reproduction in
Line becoming adapted to a different climatic envi-
(5) ronment, type of food supply, or mode of living. This divergence in response to evolution is commonly expressed by altering the form and function of some part or parts of the organism, the original identity of which is clearly dis-
(10) cernible. For example, the creeping foot of the snail is seen in related marine pteropods to be modified into a flapping organ useful for swimming, and is changed into prehensile arms that bear suctorial disks in the squids
(15) and other cephalopods. The limbs of various mammals are modified according to several different modes of life—for swift running (cursorial) as in the horse and antelope; for swinging in trees (arboreal) as in the monkeys;
(20) for digging (fossorial) as in the moles and gophers; for flying (volant) as in the bats; for swimming (aquatic) as in the seals, whales, and dolphins; and for other adaptations. The structures or organs that show main change in
(25) connection with this adaptive divergence are commonly identified readily as **homologous**, in spite of great alterations. Thus, the finger and wrist bones of a bat and whale, for instance, have virtually nothing in common
(30) except that they are definitely equivalent elements of the mammalian limb.

Directions: For the following question, consider each question separately and select *all* that apply.

4. The author provides information that would answer which of the following questions?

   A. What factors cause change in organisms?

   B. What is the theory of evolution?

   C. How are horses' legs related to seals' flippers?

5. Which of the following words could best be substituted for the boldfaced word **homologous** without substantially changing the author's meaning?

   Ⓐ altered

   Ⓑ mammalian

   Ⓒ corresponding

   Ⓓ divergent

   Ⓔ tactile

Although there are no physical differences between the visual organs of the two groups, the inhabitants of the Bilge Islands, when shown a card displaying a spectrum of colors, perceived fewer colors than do most persons in the United States.

6. Which of the following conclusions can most reliably be drawn from the information above?

   Ⓐ Human color perception is at least partly determined by factors other than the physical structure of the visual organs.

   Ⓑ The Bilge Islanders are probably taught in childhood to recognize fewer colors than are persons in the United States.

   Ⓒ Differences in social structure probably affect color perception.

   Ⓓ Color perception in humans is influenced by differences in physical environment.

   Ⓔ Bilge Islanders may have fewer terms denoting colors in their language than do English-speaking persons.

The layer of air next to the earth, which extends upward for about 10 miles, is known as the troposphere. On the whole, the tropo-
Line sphere makes up about 75% of all the weight
(5) of the atmosphere. It is the warmest part of the atmosphere because most of the solar radiation is absorbed by the earth's surface, which warms the air immediately surrounding it. A steady decrease of temperature with increasing
(10) elevation is a most striking characteristic of this region, whose upper layers are colder because of their greater distance from the earth's surface and because of the rapid radiation of heat into space. (Temperatures within
(15) the troposphere decrease about 3.5° per 1,000-foot increase in altitude.) Within the troposphere, winds and air currents distribute heat and moisture. Strong winds, called jet streams, are located at the upper levels of the
(20) troposphere. These jet streams are both complex and widespread in occurrence. They normally show a wave-shaped pattern and move from west to east at velocities of 150 mph, but velocities as high as 400 mph have been
(25) noted. The influences of changing locations and strengths of jet streams upon weather conditions and patterns are no doubt considerable. Current intensive research may eventually reveal their true significance.

7. It can be inferred from the passage that a jet plane will usually have its best average rate of speed on its run from

   Ⓐ New York to San Francisco
   Ⓑ Los Angeles to New York
   Ⓒ Boston to Miami
   Ⓓ Bermuda to New York
   Ⓔ London to Washington, DC

8. It can be inferred from the passage that at the top of Jungfrau, which is 12,000 feet above the town of Interlaken in Switzerland, the temperature is usually

   Ⓐ below freezing
   Ⓑ about 42° colder than on the ground
   Ⓒ warmer than in Interlaken
   Ⓓ affected by the ionosphere
   Ⓔ about 75° colder than in Interlaken

9. The passage states that the troposphere is the warmest part of the atmosphere because it

   Ⓐ is closest to the sun
   Ⓑ contains electrically charged particles
   Ⓒ radiates heat into space
   Ⓓ has winds and air currents that distribute the heat
   Ⓔ is warmed by the earth's heat

"The emancipation of women," James Joyce told one of his friends, "has caused the greatest revolution in our time in the most important
Line relationship there is—that between men and
(5) women." Other modernists agreed: Virginia Woolf, claiming that in about 1910, "human character changed," and, illustrating the new balance between the sexes, urged "Read the 'Agamemnon,' and see whether your
(10) sympathies are not almost entirely with Clytemnestra." D. H. Lawrence wrote, "perhaps the deepest fight for 2000 years and more, has been the fight for women's independence."
But if modernist writers considered women's
(15) revolt against men's domination one of their "greatest" and "deepest" themes, only recently—in perhaps the past 15 years—has literary criticism begun to catch up with it. Not that the images of sexual antagonism that
(20) abound in modern literature have gone unremarked; far from it. But what we are able to see in literary works depends on the perspectives we bring to them, and now that women—enough to make a difference—are reforming
(25) canons and interpreting literature, the landscapes of literary history and the features of individual books have begun to change.

10. According to the passage, women are changing literary criticism by
    - Ⓐ noting instances of hostility between men and women ·
    - Ⓑ seeing the literature from fresh points of view
    - Ⓒ studying the works of early 20th-century writers
    - Ⓓ reviewing books written by feminists
    - Ⓔ resisting masculine influence

11. The author quotes James Joyce, Virginia Woolf, and D. H. Lawrence primarily in order to show that
    - Ⓐ these were feminist writers
    - Ⓑ although well-intentioned, they were ineffectual
    - Ⓒ before the 20th century there was little interest in women's literature
    - Ⓓ modern literature is dependent on the women's movement
    - Ⓔ the interest in feminist issues is not new

When you first saw a piece of African art, it impressed you as a unit; you did not see it as a collection of shapes or forms. This, of
Line course, means that the shapes and volumes
(5) within the sculpture itself were coordinated so successfully that the viewer was affected emotionally.

It is entirely valid to ask how, from a purely artistic point of view, this unity was achieved.
(10) And we must also inquire whether there is a recurrent pattern or rules or a plastic language and vocabulary that is responsible for the powerful communication of emotion which the best African sculpture achieves. If there is
(15) such a pattern of rules, are these rules applied consciously or instinctively to obtain so many works of such high artistic quality?

It is obvious from the study of art history that an intense and unified emotional experi-
(20) ence, such as the Christian credo of the Byzantine or 12th or 13th century Europe, when espoused in art forms, gave great unity, coherence, and power to art. But such an integrated feeling was only the inspirational ele-
(25) ment for the artist, only the starting point of the creative act. The expression of this emotion and its realization in the work could be done only with discipline and thorough knowledge of the craft. And the African sculp-
(30) tor was a highly trained workman. He started his apprenticeship with a master when a child, and he learned the tribal styles and the use of tools and the nature of woods so thoroughly that his carving became what Boas calls
(35) "motor action." He carved automatically and instinctively.

12. The information in the passage suggests that a mature African carver might best be compared to a
    - Ⓐ chef following a recipe
    - Ⓑ fluent speaker of English just now beginning to study French
    - Ⓒ batter who hits a home run the first time at bat
    - Ⓓ veteran fiddler expertly varying a traditional tune
    - Ⓔ senior editor correcting the prose of an unidiomatic author

The likelihood of America's exhausting her natural resources is growing less. All kinds of waste are being recycled, and new uses are constantly being found for almost everything. We are getting more use out of what we produce, and are manufacturing many new byproducts out of what we formerly threw away. It is, therefore, unnecessary for us to continue to ban logging in national parks, nature reserves, or areas inhabited by endangered species of animals.

13. Which one of the following most seriously undermines the conclusion of this argument?

   Ⓐ The increasing amount of recycled material made available each year is equal to one-tenth of the increasing amount of natural material consumed annually.

   Ⓑ Recent studies have shown that the number of endangered animals throughout the world fluctuates sharply and is chiefly determined by changes in meteorological conditions.

   Ⓒ The logging industry contributes huge sums of money to political campaigns in states where it has a financial interest.

   Ⓓ The techniques that make recycling possible are constantly improved so that more is reclaimed for lower costs each year.

   Ⓔ Political contributions by the recycling industry are now greater than those of either the logging or animal protection interests.

ANSWER KEY

1. **B**	6. **A**	11. **E**
2. **B**	7. **B**	12. **D**
3. **E**	8. **B**	13. **A**
4. **A, C**	9. **E**	
5. **C**	10. **B**	

PART 3

ANALYTICAL WRITING: TACTICS, STRATEGIES, AND PRACTICE

Introduction to Part 3

What sort of test is this new analytical writing test? First and foremost, it is not a multiple-choice test. It is a performance test—you have to write two analytical essays in one hour.

The new analytical writing section of the GRE is the most substantive of the three sections on the tests. This section is organized in two parts. In Part 1, "Present Your Perspective on an Issue," you have 30 minutes to write an essay expressing your point of view on a particular issue. You will be given a quotation that states an opinion about an issue; you will probably write a better essay if the quotation "grabs" you, but you can write a strong paper even if the topic seems unappealing at first.

Your job is to take a stand and to support it, drawing on your own experiences and on your readings to come up with examples that reinforce your argument. It does not matter what stand you take; there is no "correct" position, no one true answer. Many different approaches can work. You can agree completely with the quotation's point of view or you can dispute it absolutely. You can disagree with some aspects of the quote, but agree with others. What matters is how you present your case.

Part 2 of the analytical writing section asks you to perform a different but complementary task. In Part 2, "Analyze an Argument," you have 30 minutes to write an essay critiquing the logical soundness of an argument. You will be given one short passage in which an author makes a claim and backs it up, giving reasons that may well be flawed. You get no choice of passages to analyze; you must work with whatever passage comes up on your screen.

This time your job is not to advocate a particular point of view. This is not the moment for you to agree or disagree with the author; it is the moment for you to weigh the validity of the author's reasoning. Your approach is analytical and expository, not argumentative or persuasive. It is your task to examine carefully what the author offers as evidence. You will find it helpful to note what the author claims explicitly, and also to note what she or he assumes (not necessarily justifiably!).

If you study the tactics and work through the practice exercises in the following chapter, and take full advantage of the study materials on the GRE's website, *www.gre.org*, you will be well prepared for the analytical writing section of the GRE and should feel confident in your ability to write high-scoring essays.

Analytical Writing

SCORING GUIDELINES

Two readers will judge your GRE analytical essays, awarding each essay a grade ranging from 0 to 6, with 6 the highest possible score. The powers-that-be then calculate your analytical writing score by taking the average of your four grades, rounding up the result to the nearest half-point. If one reader awarded your issues essay a 5 and your argument essay a 4, while the other reader gave both your essays 4's, you'd come out with a score of 4.25, rounded up to 4.5.

You probably have a sense of what score you need to be accepted by the graduate school of your choice. If you're seeking admission to Harvard's Ph.D. program in history, you're clearly aiming for a 5.5 or 6. If you're aiming for a graduate program in a field that favors number-crunching over essay-writing—mathematics or electrical engineering, for instance—you clearly don't need to aim so high. But however high a score you're seeking, you want to come out of the essay-writing section looking good. And to do that, you have to know what the GRE readers are looking for.

What are the GRE readers looking for? In essence, fluency, organization, and a command of technical English. These are the skills they assess.

Fluency

Fluency is smoothness and ease in communicating. In this case, it is your ability to set down a given number of words on paper within a limited period of time. If you freeze on essay examinations, writing only a sentence or two when whole paragraphs are called for, then you need to practice letting your words and ideas *flow*.

Literary fluency, however, involves more than just the number of words you type. The readers tend to award their highest grades to test-takers who use language well, those who employ a variety of sentence types and demonstrate a command of vocabulary. If you invariably use short, simple sentences, you need to practice constructing more complex ones. If you have a limited vocabulary, you need to expand it, working with *Barron's GRE Flash Cards* and other tools to learn the precise meaning of each new word you employ.

Organization

Organization is coherent arrangement. In this case, it is your ability to arrange your thoughts in order, following a clear game plan. In *The Elements of Style,* William Strunk describes certain elementary principles of composition. The paragraph is the basic unit of composition; the beginning of each new paragraph serves to alert readers that they are coming to a new step in the development of the subject. One paragraph leads to the next, drawing readers on to the essay's conclusion.

Organization involves your ability to reason and to marshal evidence to support your viewpoint. If you jump from subject to subject within a single paragraph, if you leave out critical elements, if you misorder your points or never manage to state exactly what you mean, then you need to practice outlining your position briefly before you express it in essay form.

Technical English

Technical English is the part of English that most students hate—grammar, spelling, punctuation, word usage. In this case, it is your ability to produce grammatically correct sentences in standard written English. If your English compositions used to come back to you with the abbreviations "frag" or "agr" or "sp" scribbled all over the margins, then you need to practice reading through your papers to catch any technical mistakes.

There are literally hundreds of handbooks available that will help you handle the mechanics of writing essays. Strunk and White's manual, *The Elements of Style*, provides clear, concise advice, as does William Zinsser's *On Writing Well*. Other good reference tools are *The Harbrace College Handbook*, Edward Johnson's *Handbook of Good English*, and, for the complete grammarphobe, Patricia O'Conner's aptly named *Woe Is I*.

NOTE: Unless you are someone who can't type two words in a row without making a spelling error, do not worry about spelling and punctuation mistakes. The GRE readers generally ignore them. However, if you make so many errors that it becomes difficult for the readers to make sense of what you have written, they will lower your score accordingly.

ESSAY-WRITING: THE 5-STEP APPROACH
How to Handle the Issue-Writing Task

You have 30 minutes to complete the issue-writing task. To earn a top score, you need to produce a smooth, 400–700-word essay with solid content, coherent organization, and few, if any, mechanical errors.

Each issue topic is presented as a 1–2 sentence statement commenting on a subject of general concern. This statement makes a claim. Your essay may support, refute, or qualify the views expressed in the statement. Whatever you write, however, must be relevant to the issue under discussion, and you must support your viewpoint with data—reasons and examples derived from your studies, experience, and reading.

GRE readers will evaluate your essay, grading it on the basis of your effectiveness in the following areas:

- Analysis of the statement's implications
- Organization and articulation of your ideas
- Use of relevant examples and arguments to support your case
- Handling of the mechanics of standard written English

Here is a 5-step plan you can use in writing your issue essay. Suggested times are approximate.

Step One: Begin with Brainstorming (2 minutes)

You do not lack ideas. What you may lack is a direct means of getting in touch with the ideas you already have. One useful technique to "prime the pump" and encourage fluency is *clustering*. Clustering is a method of brainstorming in which you start with a key word or short phrase and let that word or phrase act as a stimulus, triggering all sorts of associations that you jot down. In just a minute or two, you can come up with dozens of associations, some of which you may later be able to incorporate into your essay. (For a thought-provoking discussion of clustering and other brainstorming techniques, see *Writing the Natural Way* by Gabriele Rico.)

Let the issue statement or prompt trigger your brainstorming. As soon as you've clicked on your chosen topic, grab your pencil and sum up the claim the author is making. If, for example, the issue prompt is "Historians and other social scientists are as useful to society as are biochemists and engineers because society's ills cannot be cured by technological progress alone," your quick summation might be "Historians are as useful as scientists." Once you're clear about the author's point, start scribbling. Write down as many reasons that support or weaken the author's claim as you possibly can. Be sure to write both reasons *for* and reasons *against*. Don't worry right now if any of these reasons strike you as flimsy or implausible or clichéd; you can always cut them later or find ways to strengthen them, if you need to. Just note them down on your scratch paper, together with examples supporting both sides of the issue. Stay loose; this is your time for free associations, not self-censorship.

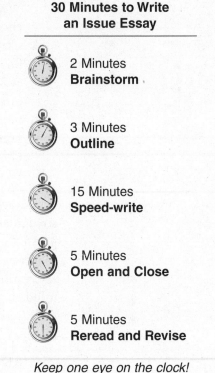

30 Minutes to Write an Issue Essay

2 Minutes
Brainstorm

3 Minutes
Outline

15 Minutes
Speed-write

5 Minutes
Open and Close

5 Minutes
Reread and Revise

Keep one eye on the clock!

Step Two: Organize Your Outline (3 minutes)

According to British rhetorical theorist and philosopher Stephen Toulmin, a sound argument requires three elements: CLAIM, GROUNDS (or data), and WARRANT. Your claim is your thesis; it is an overall statement of the argument you hope to prove. The grounds for your argument are your evidence. Grounds for an argument can include statistics, examples, and even anecdotes. The warrant is the connection between the claim and the grounds. It is an explanation of how the grounds justify the claim.

CLAIM (thesis): Historians and other social scientists are as useful to society as are biochemists and engineers because society's ills cannot be cured by technological progress alone.

Once you have settled on your claim, look to your brainstorming for the arguments that support it. Each of these arguments requires its own claim, grounds, and warrant.

1. CLAIM: War is not prevented by technological progress.
    GROUNDS: Invention of gunpowder, nuclear weapons.
    WARRANT: Technological progress is driven by war; in fact, technology tends to make war more destructive.
2. CLAIM: Historians and social scientists can prevent, or at least discourage, war through their understanding of why wars have occurred in the past.
    GROUNDS: Treaty of Versailles, Marshall Plan.

WARRANT: An understanding of history can allow us to design policies that encourage peace.

3. CLAIM: Technological progress does not prevent poverty.
   GROUNDS: Industrial Revolution, sweatshops.
   WARRANT: Technology changes the distribution of wealth, increasing extreme poverty as it increases wealth for some.

4. CLAIM: Historians and social scientists can prevent poverty through economic policy.
   GROUNDS: New Deal, Social Security.
   WARRANT: Social programs prevent poverty.

Though not a necessary component of the argument, RESERVATIONS can strengthen a claim. A reservation is a rebuttal to the claim that is introduced and granted by the writer. Reservations strengthen arguments in several ways: First, they moderate the writer's claim, thereby decreasing the level of proof required. Second, reservations make the writer appear more reliable by demonstrating that she is open-minded, and that her position is not extreme. Third, reservations allow the writer to defuse criticism before it is made. When you include a reservation in your argument, be sure to take the opportunity to weigh it against your other claims.

5. RESERVATION: Biochemists and engineers do contribute to society.
   WEIGHING: Though technological progress can increase the food supply and cure disease, we will always need historians and social scientists to show us how to use technology without causing more harm than good.

Step Three: Write the Body of Your Essay (15 minutes)

You already know your general line of reasoning, the direction you want your argument to take. You need to spend the bulk of your time writing the body of your essay. As rapidly as you can, type up your points, writing two to three sentences to flesh out each reason or example in your outline. Do not worry if time pressure doesn't allow you to deal with every point you dreamed up. Start with a reason or example that you can easily put into words, preferably your best, most compelling reason or example. Given the 30-minute time limit you're working under, you want to be sure to cover your best points right away, before you run out of time. During the revision period, you can always rearrange your paragraphs, putting the strongest paragraph immediately before the conclusion, so that your essay builds to a solid climax.

Step Four: Now Write Your Opening and Summary Paragraphs (5 minutes)

It may seem strange to write your introductory paragraph after you have written the body of your essay, but it is a useful technique. Many writers launch into writing the introduction, only to find, once they have finished the essay, that their conclusion is unrelated to, or even contradicts, what they had written in the introduction. By writing the introduction *after* you have composed the bulk of the essay, you will avoid having to rewrite the introduction to support the conclusion that you *actually* reached, rather than the conclusion that you *expected* to reach.

This is one area in which the technology of the new GRE will greatly assist you. If the GRE were a hard copy (paper) exam, you would need to save space on your page to insert your introduction, guessing exactly how much room you would need. Instead, because the GRE is computerized, you can simply go back to the top of the page and begin writing the introduction.

What then should your introduction include? Your introductory paragraph should both introduce the topic on which you are writing and clearly indicate your thesis or point. While in some situations it is strategic (or simply more graceful) to reveal your thesis fully only in the conclusion, the GRE is *not* one of those situations. Clarity is key; you do not want to risk leaving your readers uncertain of your line of reasoning, or under the impression that you have strayed from the point.

For a top score, your introductory paragraph should also provide some context for the argument. The GRE readers appear to favor introductions that place the topic in an historical or social context, rather than simply discussing it in a contextual vacuum. The two introductory paragraphs below demonstrate the difference between these two types of introduction.

Introduction with Context

Western society tends to glorify the individual over the group. Our social and political philosophy, based on John Stuart Mill's faith that progress is fostered by competition within the marketplace of ideas, encourages people, as the Apple computer commercial says, to "think different." This cult of the individual overemphasizes the importance of being different and fails to recognize that a healthy person will be both a conformist and an individualist. Ironically, self-conscious dedication to nonconformity will ultimately result in extreme slavishness to custom.

Introduction without Context

A healthy individual is neither a conformist, nor an individualist; he is *both* a conformist and an individualist. Balancing conformity and individualism allows people to follow their interests and passions without wasting time on issues that do not interest them, while a self-conscious dedication to nonconformity ultimately results in an extreme slavishness to custom.

One last note on introductions: While you may have been taught in school that a paragraph must comprise at least three sentences, the GRE readers are not concerned about the length of your introductory paragraph. In fact, they appear willing to grant the highest score to essays whose introduction is only one sentence long. This does not mean that they favor essays with single-sentence introductions, only that they do not discriminate against them. If your introduction makes your thesis clear, it has done its job.

Your conclusion should, however, be longer than one sentence. It should restate your thesis and summarize the arguments that you make in its support. You should mention your supporting arguments in the same order in which they appear in the body of the essay. This technique underscores the organization of your essay, giving it a predictable and orderly appearance.

Step Five: Reread and Revise (5 minutes)

Expert writers often test their work by reading it aloud. In the exam room, you cannot read out loud. However, when you read your essay silently, take your time and listen with your inner ear to how it sounds. Read to get a sense of your essay's logic and rhythm. Does one sentence flow smoothly into the next? Would they flow more smoothly if you were to add a transition word or phrase (*therefore, however, nevertheless, in contrast, similarly*)? Do the sentences follow a logical order? Is any key idea or example missing? Does any sentence seem out of place? How would things sound if you cut out that awkward sentence or inserted that transition word?

Take a minute to act on your response to hearing your essay. If it sounded to you as if a transition word was needed, insert it. If it sounded as if a sentence should be cut, delete it. If it sounded as if a sentence was out of place, move it. Trust your inner ear, but do not attempt to do too much. Have faith in your basic outline for the essay. You have neither the need nor the time to revise everything.

Now think of yourself as an editor, not an auditor. Just as you need to have an ear for problems of logic and language, you also need to have an eye for errors that damage your text. Take a minute to look over your essay for problems in spelling and grammar. From your English classes you should know which words and grammatical constructions have given you trouble in the past. See whether you can spot any of these words or constructions in your essay. Correct any really glaring errors that you find. Do not worry if you fail to catch every mechanical error or awkward phrase. The readers understand that 30 minutes doesn't give you enough time to produce polished, gemlike prose. They won't penalize you for an occasional mechanical glitch.

HOW TO HANDLE THE ARGUMENT-ANALYSIS TASK

You have 30 minutes to complete the argument-analysis task. To earn a top score, you need to produce a smooth, 300–400 word critique with solid content, coherent organization, and few, if any, mechanical errors.

As you critique the argument, think about the writer's underlying assumptions. Ask yourself whether any of them are questionable. Also evaluate any data or evidence the writer brings up. Ask yourself whether this evidence actually supports the writer's conclusion.

In your analysis, you may suggest additional kinds of evidence to reinforce the writer's argument. You may also suggest methods to refute the argument, or additional data that might be useful to you as you assess the soundness of the argument. *You may **not**, however, present your personal views on the topic.* Your job is to analyze the elements of an argument, not to support or contradict that argument.

GRE readers will evaluate your essay, grading it on the basis of your effectiveness in the following areas:

- Identification and assessment of the argument's main elements
- Organization and articulation of your thoughts
- Use of relevant examples and arguments to support your analysis
- Handling of the mechanics of standard written English

Again, follow a 5-step approach in dealing with the argument-analysis task.

Step One: Identify the Claims (2 minutes)

Before you can identify the flaws in an argument essay prompt, you must have a clear understanding of the claims it makes. After reading the prompt once for general understanding, examine it more carefully, one sentence at a time. As you do this, use your scratch paper to write a list of the claims made in the prompt. List the claims in the order in which they are made. GRE argument prompts typically contain at least three flaws in the author's reasoning or use of evidence.

Here is an example of the notes you might take if you were writing on the topic below.

> **Discuss how effective you find the reasoning in this argument.**

The following appeared in an article in the Real Estate section of the Springfield Bugle.

> Springfield is a great place to live. Every year, hundreds of former city dwellers move to Springfield, spurning the sophisticated cultural offerings of the urban setting for Springfield's more relaxed atmosphere. Despite the attractions of big city life, Springfield's new citizens choose their home for its rural setting and small town atmosphere. If Springfield wants to continue to attract these newcomers, it must adopt aggressive planning regulations to keep out chain stores, fast food establishments, bars, and other businesses more appropriate to an urban setting.

Overall Point: Springfield must control the growth of certain types of businesses in order for it to remain attractive to newcomers.
Claim One: People come to Springfield to get away from sophisticated city culture, and to have a relaxed atmosphere.
Claim Two: People come to Springfield for its rural, small-town atmosphere.
Claim Three: Keeping chain stores, bars, and fast food restaurants out of Springfield will maintain its attractiveness to newcomers.

Step Two: Question the Claims (3 minutes)

Once you have identified the claims made in the prompt, you need to assess the strength of those claims. In most cases, their shortcomings will be apparent to you. If, however, you are having trouble figuring out the flaws in a given claim, try applying a few handy questions to it.

1. GROUNDS. Is there any **evidence** to support the claim?
   The first two claims in the prompt above are assertions. Though the author might have survey data to support her claim that newcomers move to Springfield to escape urban culture and enjoy a more relaxed, rural, small-town atmosphere, she presents no such data in her argument.
2. WARRANT. Does the evidence provided support the claim?
   Could **other factors** cause the effect about which the author is writing? In the situation described in the prompt above, there are many possible reasons to

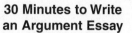

30 Minutes to Write an Argument Essay

 2 Minutes
Spot the Claims

 3 Minutes
Question the Claims

 15 Minutes
Speed-write

 5 Minutes
Open and Close

 5 Minutes
Reread and Revise

Keep one eye on the clock!

choose to move to Springfield. The author gives no reason for readers to believe that she has correctly identified the cause of Springfield's popularity.

Does the author assert a general rule based on an overly **small sample**? For example, if the author of the Springfield argument based her claims about why newcomers generally move to Springfield on the comments of a single new neighbor, her claims would lack adequate support. They would be unwarranted.

Does the author compare **comparable groups**? If, for example, the author of the Springfield argument attempted to support her claims about why new-comers move to Springfield with surveys of residents who moved to Springfield twenty years ago, she would have no basis to make claims about people who have moved to Springfield more recently.

Step Three: Write the Body of Your Critique, Following the Order of the Claims Made in the Prompt (15 minutes)

Organization is an important part of writing a clear and coherent essay. The simplest and best approach is to discuss the claims made in the prompt in the order in which they are presented. There is no reason to try anything tricky or fancy. The test-makers have given you an order. Use it. Using the structure of the prompt will save you time. It will also discourage you from writing a discursive essay that wanders unpredictably from one idea to another. High scores go to test-takers who write clear and well-reasoned essays. Creativity in this context is more likely to confuse your readers than to earn you extra points.

As we recommended in the previous section on the issue essay, spend the bulk of your time writing the body of your critique. Get those ideas onto the screen, allotting two to three sentences to each claim to flesh it out.

Step Four: Then Add Your Introductory and Summary Paragraphs (5 minutes)

While following the structure of the prompt is a handy way to organize the body of your critique, you still need to write an introduction and conclusion to your essay. Your introductory paragraph should provide a general overview of the criticisms you have made in the body of your essay. Do not give too much detail in the introduction; it is where you introduce, rather than explain, your analysis. *Present your points in the introduction in the same order in which they appear in the body of the essay.* By doing so, you will give your reader a clear idea of where you are going and what you intend to demonstrate. *In your conclusion, briefly restate the main points you have made in the body of your critique, and suggest one or two ways the author could have made his or her argument more persuasive.*

Step Five: Reread and Revise (5 minutes)

Once again, our recommendation is: First listen, then look. Begin by reading your essay silently, listening with your inner ear to how it sounds. Ask yourself whether one sentence flows smoothly into the next, and whether any transition words might help the flow. Consider whether any key idea or example might be missing or any sentence seems out of place. Do not make any major changes. Just tweak things slightly to improve your essay's sound and sense.

Now cast an eye over your essay, looking for mechanical errors. You know the sorts of grammatical constructions and spelling words that create problems for you. See whether you can spot any of them in your essay. Correct any errors that jump out at you.

Here is an example of an argument critique that follows the organization of the prompt:

> **Discuss how effective you find the reasoning in this argument.**

The following appeared in an article in the Real Estate section of the Springfield Bugle.
Springfield is a great place to live. Every year, hundreds of former city dwellers move to Springfield, spurning the sophisticated cultural offerings of the urban setting for Springfield's more relaxed atmosphere. Despite the attractions of big city life, Springfield's new citizens choose their home for its rural setting and small town atmosphere. If Springfield wants to continue to attract these newcomers, it must adopt aggressive planning regulations to keep out chain stores, fast food establishments, bars, and other businesses more appropriate to an urban setting.

Response to the Argument

Springfield may well be a great place to live, but the author of this article makes a number of unsubstantiated assumptions about the attributes that make Springfield an attractive home. Based on these assumptions, the author makes a bold proposal regarding zoning and city planning. Though this proposal is intended to maintain the positive attributes that bring new residents to Springfield, it may fail to achieve this goal or even have the perverse effect of worsening the quality of life in the town.

The author's first mistake is to assume that she knows why hundreds of former city dwellers move to Springfield each year. She claims that in moving to Springfield, people are rejecting the culture of the city in favor of Springfield's more relaxed suburban lifestyle. This is a classic case of confusing correlation with causation. While Springfield may in fact be more relaxed than the city, and while the city may have more sophisticated culture than Springfield, it does not follow that those who move from the city to Springfield are choosing relaxation over sophistication. Perhaps they are moving to Springfield for entirely different reasons. High urban property values, with their concomitant high urban property taxes, may be driving potential homeowners to less expensive suburban areas. People may also be moving to Springfield for better schools or a lower crime rate.

The claim that people move to Springfield for its small-town atmosphere and rural setting is similarly unsubstantiated. Yes, Springfield is a small, rural suburb. It does not follow, however, that this is why new residents move to Springfield. They could be moving to Springfield for any of the reasons mentioned above, or for any number of other reasons.

The conclusion that Springfield must keep out businesses that are common in urban areas if it is to remain an attractive community is unsupported. If new residents are really being drawn to Springfield by something other than the ways in which it is different from a big city, there is no reason to believe that keeping Springfield from growing city-like will make it more attractive. In fact, if people move to Springfield in spite of its lack of big-city amenities and because of its lower cost (or some other factor), the addition of big-city businesses may make Springfield more attractive to newcomers.

Ironically, if the author is correct that Springfield's relaxed, small-town feel is what attracts new residents, making Springfield attractive to former city dwellers may, in the long run, destroy Springfield's positive attributes. After all, for how long can Springfield maintain this small-town atmosphere, if hundreds of newcomers are encouraged to move there each year? Ultimately, the author of this article appears to seek the impossible—a quiet small town with sustained, robust population growth.

Despite the flaws in this author's argument, she may be correct in her assessment of why newcomers move to Springfield. She could strengthen her argument by documenting its most important premise with data. If, for example, she provided survey results from newcomers, indicating that they did indeed come to Springfield to escape urban culture and to enjoy a more relaxed, rural, small-town atmosphere, her argument would be far more persuasive. Were this the case, her call for more restrictive zoning might be justified.

Testing Tactics

PREPARING FOR THE WRITING TEST

TACTIC

1   Take Advantage of the GRE's Free Study Aids

TIP

Download
PowerPrep II—
It's *Free!*

When you sign up to take the GRE General Test, you will eventually be sent *PowerPrep II*, a CD-ROM containing test preparation software for the General Test and Writing Assessment. However, you do not have to wait for your copy of *PowerPrep II* to come in the mail. You can download it immediately from the GRE website, *www.gre.org.*

PowerPrep II is helpful because it uses the same GRE word processing software that you will have to use to write your essays when you take your computer-based test. It is a very basic word processor that lets you perform very basic tasks. You can insert text, delete text, and move text around using a cut-and-paste function. You can also undo an action you've just performed.

Familiarize yourself with this word processing software so that, on the test date, you'll be comfortable using it. This software simulates actual testing conditions and presents actual essay topics. Practice writing your essays while you keep one eye on the clock. You need to develop a sense of how much time to allow for thinking over your essay and how much time to set aside for the actual writing.

A WORD OF WARNING

Attention, Mac users: *PowerPrep II* is compatible only with IBMs or PCs. If you own an Apple MacIntosh computer, you'll have to gain access to a PC to run *PowerPrep II*. Do it, even if it means making an extra trip to the campus computer lab or the nearest public library.

TACTIC 2

Practice Taking Shortcuts to Maximize Your Typing Efficiency

Slow and steady is not the way to go, at least not when you're taking the analytical writing test on the GRE. Fast typists have a decided advantage here. Unfortunately, you cannot turn yourself into a typing whiz overnight. However, you can use your time right now to practice some shortcuts to help you on the day of the test.

First, using the GRE's own word processing program (which comes when you download *PowerPrep II*), you can practice using the cut-and-paste function to copy phrases that you want to repeat in your essay. In an argument essay, for example, you might want to reuse such phrases as "the author makes the following assumption" or "another flaw in the author's argument is that...." In an issues essay, if you are running out of time and still haven't written your opening and summary paragraphs (which we advise you to compose *after* you've written the body of your text), you can write just your concluding paragraph, cutting and pasting it to both the beginning and end of the essay. Then, in a few seconds, you can change the wording of that initial paragraph so that it works as an introduction, not as a conclusion. How does that cliché about essay-writing go? "Tell them what you're going to tell them, tell them it, then tell them what you've told them." It's easy to do so, using cut-and-paste.

One thing to note: The GRE word processor currently lacks a copy function. To copy a chunk of text, you must first cut it and then directly paste it back in its original spot; next, you must move the cursor to the place where you want to reproduce the text and paste it there. The process may feel cumbersome at first, but by practicing with the word processor you will quickly build up speed copying using cut-and-paste.

Second, you can also practice abbreviating multiword names or titles. Consider the following argument topic or prompt:

> **Discuss how effective you find the reasoning in this argument.**

The parent of a Collegiate High student included these remarks in a letter to the education page of the Oakville Bugle.

> If you look closely at Oakville's two leading private high schools—Collegiate Preparatory High School and Exover Academy—you must conclude that Collegiate is unmistakably superior to the Academy. Collegiate has a staff of 35 teachers, many of them with doctorates. In contrast, Exover has a staff of 22, several holding only a bachelor's degree. Moreover, Collegiate's average class size is 12, compared to Exover's average class size of 20; Collegiate's students receive much more individual attention than their peers do at the Academy. Students graduating from Collegiate High also are accepted by better universities than Exover graduates are: 40% of last year's Collegiate senior class went on to Ivy League colleges, compared to only 15% of Exover's senior class. Thus, if you want your children to get individual attention from their high school teachers and would like them to get in to good colleges, you should send them to Collegiate Prep.

In critiquing this argument, you can follow the letter writer's example and refer to Exover Academy and Collegiate Preparatory High School simply as Exover and Collegiate. You can also refer to Collegiate by its initials. Be sure, however, to identify the institution fully when you first mention it, inserting its initials in parentheses: Collegiate Preparatory High School (CPHS). Then your readers will know what you mean by future references to CPHS. Similarly, instead of typing out "for example," you can substitute the abbreviation "e.g."

TACTIC
3
Acquaint Yourself with the Actual Essay Topics You Will Face

The GRE has posted its entire selection of potential essay topics on its website. The pool of issue topics can be found at *www.gre.org/issuetop.html*. The pool of argument topics can be found at *www.gre.org/argutop.html*. There is no point in trying to memorize these topics or in trying to write an essay for each one. There are well over 200 items in the pool of issue topics alone. There is, however, a real point to exploring these potential topics and to noting their common themes.

We suggest that you print out both topic pools so that you can go through their contents at leisure. When you do so, you will see that the issue topics fall naturally into groups with common themes. Some of these themes involve contrasts:

- Tradition versus innovation and modernization.
- Competition versus cooperation.
- Present social needs versus future social needs.
- Conformity versus individualism.
- Imagination versus knowledge.
- Pragmatism versus idealism.

Many of the issue topics pose a simple question:

- What makes an effective leader?
- What are education's proper goals?
- How does technology affect our society?
- Why should we study history (or art, literature)?
- What is government's proper role (in education, art, wilderness preservation, and so on)?
- How do we define progress?

Others ask you to question conventional wisdom:

- Is loyalty *always* a virtue?
- Is "moderation in all things" *truly* good advice?
- Does conformity *always* have a negative impact?

Go over these recurrent questions and themes. They relate to all the areas of the college curriculum: political science, sociology, anthropology, economics, history, law, philosophy, psychology, the physical sciences, the fine arts, literature, even media studies. Whether or not you have any special knowledge of a suggested topic's subject area, you most likely have opinions about it. You probably have class notes on it as well.

If you have old notebooks from your general education courses, skim through them to refresh your memory of classroom discussions of typical GRE issues. In the course of flipping through these old notes, you're very likely to come across examples that you might want to note for possible use in writing the issue essay.

WRITING THE ISSUE ESSAY

TACTIC

4 Break Down the Topic Statement into Separate Areas to Consider

Here is an example of an issue topic, modeled on actual topics found in the GRE pool.

> "The end does justify the means,
> if the end is truly meritorious."

Break down the statements into its component elements. Look for key words and phrases. First, consider ***ends*** or goals. These can be divided into personal goals—taking a trip to a foreign country, for example, or providing for one's family—and societal goals—preserving endangered species, for example, or protecting the health of the elderly.

Next, consider what ***means*** you might use to reach these goals. If you have to spend your savings and take a leave of absence from college to travel abroad, thereby postponing or potentially jeopardizing your eventual graduation, then perhaps your goal is insufficiently meritorious to justify the means. If, however, your goal is not simply to take a pleasure trip but to use the time abroad working in a refugee camp, the worthiness of the cause you are serving might well outweigh the expense and the risk of your not graduating. Similarly, while most people would agree that preserving an endangered species is a worthwhile societal goal, the cost to society of doing so can occasionally outweigh the benefits: think about the societal cost in ruined crops and lost income to Klamath Basin farmers when the government cut off water to their farms in an effort to preserve endangered coho salmon and sucker fish, an action later criticized as unnecessary by the National Academy of Sciences.

Finally, consider the phrase ***truly meritorious***. The author is begging the question, qualifying his assertion to make it appear incontrovertible. But what makes an action meritorious? Even more, what makes an action *truly* meritorious? How do you measure merit? Whose standards do you use?

Breaking down the topic statement into its components helps start you thinking analytically about the subject. It's a good way to begin composing your issue essay.

TACTIC

5 Adopt a Balanced Approach

Consider your readers. Who are they? Academics, junior members of college faculties. What are they looking for? They are looking for articulate and persuasive arguments expressed in scholarly, well-reasoned prose. In other words, they are looking for the sort of essay they might write themselves.

How do you go about writing for an academic audience? First, avoid extremes. You want to come across as a mature, evenhanded writer, someone who can take a strong stand on an issue, but who can see others' positions as well. Restrain yourself: don't get so carried away by the "rightness" of your argument that you wind up sounding fanatical or shrill. Second, be sure to acknowledge that other viewpoints exist. Cite them; you'll win points for scholarly objectivity.

Draw examples to support your position from "the great world" and from the academic realm. In writing about teaching methods, for example, you'll win more points citing current newspaper articles about magnet schools or relevant passages from John Dewey and Maria Montessori than telling anecdotes about your favorite gym teacher in junior high school. While it is certainly acceptable for you to offer an occasional example from personal experience, for the most part your object is to show the readers the *breadth* of your knowledge (without showing off by quoting the most obscure sources you can find!).

One additional point: Do not try to second-guess your readers. Yes, they want you to come up with a scholarly, convincing essay. But there is no "one true answer" that they are looking for. You can argue for the position. You can argue against the position. You can strike a middle ground, arguing both for and against the position, hedging your bet. The readers don't care what position you adopt. Don't waste your time trying to psych them out.

TACTIC 6 Make Use of Transitions or Signal Words to Point the Way

TIP

Use Signal Words *Subtly*! Be Precise When You Point the Way.

Assume that typical GRE readers must read hundreds of issue essays in a day. You want to make the readers' job as easy as possible, so that when they come to your essay they breathe a sigh of relief, saying, "Ah! Someone who knows how to write!"

One way to make the readers' job easy is to lead them by the hand from one idea to the next, using signal words to point the way. The GRE readers like it when test-takers use signal words (transitions); in their analyses of sample essays scoring a 5 or 6, they particularly mention the writers' use of transitions as a good thing.

Here are a few helpful transitions. Practice using them precisely: you earn no points for sticking them in at random!

Support Signal Words

Use the following words or abbreviations to signal the reader that you are going to support your claim with an illustration or example:

> *e.g.,* (short for Latin *exempli gratia*, for the sake of an example)
> *for example*
> *for instance*
> *let me illustrate*
> *such as*

Use these words to signal the reader that you are about to add an additional reason or example to support your claim:

additionally	*furthermore*	*likewise*
also	*in addition*	*moreover*

Contrast Signal Words

Use the following words to signal a switch of direction in your argument.

although	*in contrast*	*on the other hand*
but	*in spite of*	*rather than*
despite	*instead of*	*still*
even though	*nevertheless*	*unlike*
except	*not*	*yet*
however	*on the contrary*	

Cause and Effect Signal Words

Use the following words to signal the next step in your line of reasoning or the conclusion of your argument.

accordingly	*in conclusion*	*therefore*
consequently	*in short*	*thus*
for this reason	*in summary*	*when . . . then*
hence	*so . . . that*	

See Tactic 10 for a discussion of how signal words can be helpful to you in the second of your two writing tasks, the argument critique.

WRITING THE ARGUMENT CRITIQUE

TACTIC 7   Learn to Spot Common Logical Fallacies

You may remember studying a list of logical fallacies during your undergraduate education. It probably included Latin terms such as "post hoc ergo propter hoc" and "argumentum ad hominem." Fortunately, you do not need to memorize these terms to perform well on the GRE argument essay. The GRE's essay readers are not concerned with whether you know the name of a given logical fallacy; they are more concerned with whether you can recognize and explain fallacies as they occur in simulated real-world situations. Labeling a claim a "post hoc" fallacy will not win you a 6 (the top score) unless you can *explain* the flaw in the argument. And a straightforward logical explanation of the argument's flaw can get you a 6, whether or not you use the fancy Latin terminology.

This does not mean, however, that brushing up on the common logical fallacies is a waste of your time. A decent understanding of the ways in which arguments can be wrong will help you write a better essay by enabling you to identify more flaws in the assigned argument (GRE argument statements generally include more than one logical error), and by giving you a clearer understanding of the nature of those flaws. Our advice is, therefore, to review the common logical fallacies without spending too much time trying to memorize their names.

Here are two examples of arguments, or prompts, similar to those in the GRE pool. Read them. The discussion following will point out what common logical fallacies they embody.

> **Discuss how effective you find the reasoning in this argument.**

ARGUMENT 1

The school board of the Shadow Valley Unified School District included these remarks in a letter sent to the families of all students attending school in the district.

> Over the past few years, an increase in disciplinary problems and a high drop out rate have plagued District schools. The Ash Lake School District to our north adopted a mandatory uniform policy three years ago. Since that time, suspensions and expulsions in Ash Lake have fallen by 40 percent, while the mean grade point average of Ash Lake students has risen from 2.3 (C+) to 2.7 (B−). In order to improve the discipline and academic performance of Shadow Valley students, we have adopted a mandatory uniform policy effective on the first day of the new school year.

> **Discuss how effective you find the reasoning in this argument.**

ARGUMENT 2

The following is excerpted from a letter to the editor in the Chillington Gazette.

> The recent residential property tax increase to improve park maintenance in Chillington is a waste of money. There is no need to improve Chillington's parks because the people of Chillington do not enjoy outdoor recreation. I live across the street from Green Park in South Chillington, and I've noticed that there is never anyone in the park. Park use did not increase in Warm Springs last year when they implemented a similar tax. There is no reason to improve parks that will not be used.

COMMON LOGICAL FALLACIES

CAUSAL FALLACIES

The classic fallacy of causation is often known by a Latin phrase, "post hoc ergo propter hoc," or its nickname, "the post hoc fallacy." The Latin phrase translates to, "after this, therefore because of this." The post hoc fallacy confuses correlation with causation, assuming that when one event follows another, the second event must have been caused by the first. It is as if you were to say that because your birthday precedes your husband's by one month, your birth must have caused him to be born. The Shadow Valley School District argument presents an excellent example of a post hoc fallacy. The author of this argument assumes that because "suspensions and expulsions in Ash Lake have fallen by 40 percent, while the mean grade point average of Ash Lake students has risen from 2.3 (C+) to 2.7 (B−)" since Ash Lake's adoption of a mandatory uniform policy, the uniform policy has caused the improved student performance. Despite this correlation, it is possible that other factors are responsible for Ash Lake's progress. Perhaps the school uniform policy coincided with a significant decrease in average class size, or the arrival of a new superintendent of schools. Or perhaps the recent improvements were brought about by an increase in federal aid for at-risk students. School uniforms may have been a partial cause of Ash Lake's improvements, or they may have played no role at all. Without further information, no reliable conclusion can be reached.

INDUCTIVE FALLACIES

Fallacies of induction involve the drawing of general rules from specific examples. They are among the most common fallacies found in the GRE argument essay topics. To induce a general rule correctly from specific examples, it is crucial that the specific examples be representative of the larger group. All too often, this is not the case.

The **hasty generalization** (too small sample) is the most common inductive fallacy. A hasty generalization is a general conclusion that is based on too small a sample set. If, for example, you wanted to learn the most popular flavor of ice cream in Italy, you would need to interview a substantial number of Italians. Drawing a conclusion based on the taste of the three Italian tourists you met last week would not be justified. The *Chillington Gazette* argument provides another good example of the hasty generalization. The author of this argument concludes that "the people of Chillington do not enjoy outdoor recreation," but he draws this general conclusion from the lack of visitors to the park across the street from his home. Readers are never told just how many parks there are in Chillington. There could be dozens of parks, all possibly overflowing with happy visitors, despite the unpopularity of the one park viewed by the author.

Small sample size is a problem because it increases the risk of drawing a general conclusion from an **unrepresentative sample**. If, for example, you wanted to learn who was most likely to be elected president of the United States, you could not draw a reliable conclusion based on the preferences of the citizens of a single city, or even a single state. The views of the citizens of Salt Lake City are not necessarily the views of the citizens of the nation as a whole, nor are the views of Californians representative of those of the entire nation. This is why pollsters go to such great lengths to ensure that they interview a representative sample of the entire population.

Unrepresentative samples do not, however, always result from too small a sample. The *Chillington Gazette* argument concludes that the citizens of Chillington will not use improved parks because "Park use did not increase in Warm Springs last year when they implemented a similar tax." The author gives no reason to believe, however, that the two towns' situations are similar. Perhaps park use did not increase in Warm Springs because its parks were already extremely popular, unlike those of

Chillington. Or perhaps Warm Springs is an industrial city with little housing, while Chillington is a bedroom community with a large number of school-aged children. Should we conclude that the experiences of one city will be mirrored by the other?

(To learn more about common logical fallacies, consult standard works on rhetoric and critical reasoning. Two currently popular texts are James Herrick's *Argumentation* and T. Edward Damer's *Attacking Faulty Reasoning*.)

TACTIC 8 — Remember That Your Purpose Is to Analyze, *Not* to Persuade

You are not asked to agree or disagree with the argument in the prompt. Do not be distracted by your feelings on the subject of the prompt, and do not give in to the temptation to write your own argument. Be especially vigilant against this temptation if the topic is on a subject that you know very well. If, for example, the prompt argues that class size reduction is a poor idea because it did not improve test scores in one city, do not answer this argument with data you happen to know about another city in which test scores improved after class sizes were reduced. Instead, point out that one city is not a large enough sample on which to base a general conclusion. Go on to identify other factors that could have caused test scores to remain the same, despite lower class size. (Perhaps test scores in the sample city were already nearly as high as they could go, or the student population in that city was changing at the time class sizes were reduced.) Remember, the readers are not interested in how much you *know* about the subject of the prompt; they want to know how well you *think*.

TACTIC 9 — Examine the Argument for Unstated Assumptions and Missing Information

An argument is based upon certain assumptions made by its author. If an argument's basic premises are sound, the argument is strengthened. If the argument's basic premises are flawed, the argument is weakened.

Pinpoint what the argument assumes but never states. Then consider the validity of these unstated assumptions. For example, the Shadow Valley argument assumes that the populations of Shadow Valley and Ash Lake are analogous. Is this unstated assumption warranted? Not necessarily. The two towns might well have distinctly dissimilar populations—one might be a working-class suburb with high unemployment, while the other might be a suburb populated by wealthy professionals. If that were so, there would be no reason to believe that the same factors would cause poor student performance in both towns.

Ask yourself what additional evidence would strengthen or weaken the claim. Generally, GRE argument prompts are flawed but could be true under some circumstances. Only rarely will you find an argument that is absolutely untrue. Instead, you will find plausible arguments for which support (grounds and warrant) is lacking. Put yourself in the place of the argument's author. If you were trying to prove this argument, what evidence would you need? What missing data should you assemble to support your claim? Use your concluding paragraph to list this evidence and explain how its presence would solve the shortcomings that you identified earlier in your essay.

TACTIC

10 Pay Particular Attention to Signal Words in the Argument

In analyzing arguments, be on the lookout for transitions or signal words that can clarify the structure of the argument. These words are like road signs, pointing out the direction the author wants you to take, showing you the connection between one logical step and the next. When you spot such a word linking elements in the author's argument, ask yourself whether this connection is logically watertight. Does A unquestionably lead to B? These signal words can indicate vulnerable areas in the argument, points you can attack.

In particular, be alert for:

Cause and Effect Signal Words

The following words often signal the conclusion of an argument.

accordingly	*in conclusion*	*therefore*
consequently	*in short*	*thus*
for this reason	*in summary*	
hence	*so*	

Contrast Signal Words

The following words often signal a reversal of thought within an argument.

although	*in contrast*	*rather than*
but	*instead*	*still*
despite	*nevertheless*	*unlike*
even though	*not*	*yet*
except	*on the contrary*	
however	*on the other hand*	

Notice that in the following argument several of these words are present: *despite*, *not*, and *consequently*. Each of these words plays an important role in the argument.

> **Discuss how effective you find the reasoning in this argument.**

ARGUMENT 3

The following is from a letter to the state Department of Education.

> Despite the fact that the River City School District increased the average size by more than 15% in all grades two years ago, this year's average SAT scores for the junior class were the highest ever. This shows that class size is not a good determinant of student performance. Consequently, other school districts should follow River City's lead and save money by increasing the size of their classes.

Think about each link in the chain of reasoning signaled by the three transition words. These words should act like a red flag, alerting you that danger (flawed logic) may lie ahead. Did the average SAT score for the junior class increase *despite* the increase in class size? Maybe. Then again, maybe not; the average score for that year's junior class may have increased because that year's juniors were unusually bright. Do this year's extra-high SAT scores show that class size is *not* a good determinant of student performance? Not necessarily. Many factors could have contributed to the junior class's high scores. Finally, consider the implications of *consequently*. Even if class size were not a good determinant of student performance, does it necessarily follow *as a consequence* that school districts should increase the size of their classes? In the words of the old song, "It ain't necessarily so."

Practice Exercises

Practice for the Issue Task

1. Brainstorm for 5 minutes, jotting down any words and phrases that are triggered by one of the following questions:

   • What should the goals of higher education be?
   • Why should we study history?
   • How does technology affect our society?
   • What is the proper role of art?
   • Which poses the greater threat to society, individualism or conformity?
   • Which is more socially valuable, preserving tradition or promoting innovation?
   • Is it better to be a specialist or a generalist?
   • Can a politician be both honest and effective?

2. In a brief paragraph, define one of the following words:

   • Freedom
   • Originality
   • Honesty
   • Progress

3. To improve your ear for language, read aloud short selections of good prose: editorials from *The New York Times* or *The Christian Science Monitor*, as well as columns or brief essays by prose stylists like Annie Dillard, M. F. K. Fisher, or E. B. White. Listen for the ways in which these authors vary their sentence structure. Note the precision with which they choose their words. The more good prose you hear, the better able you'll be to improve your writing style.

4. Selecting three or four issue topics from the GRE's online pool of topics for the revised test (currently at *http://www.ets.org/gre/revised_general/prepare/analytical_writing/issue/pool*), break down the topic statements in terms of Toulmin's three elements: claim, grounds, and warrant. Ask yourself the following questions. What claims are made in each topic statement? What grounds or data are given to support each of these claims? Is the claim warranted or unwarranted? Why? In what way do the grounds logically justify the claim?

5. Choosing another issue topic from the GRE's published pool of topics, write an essay giving your viewpoint concerning the particular issue raised. Set no time limit; take as long as you want to complete this task, then choose a second issue topic from the pool. *In only 30 minutes*, write an essay presenting your perspective on this second issue.

   Compare your two essays. Ask yourself how working under time pressure affected your second essay. Did its major problems stem from a lack of fluency? A lack of organization? A lack of familiarity with the subject matter under discussion? A lack of knowledge of the mechanics of formal written English? Depending on what problems you spot, review the appropriate sections of this chapter, as well as any style manuals or other texts we suggest.

Practice for the Argument Task

1. Choosing a sample of argument topics from GRE's online pool of topics for the revised test (currently at *http://www.ets.org/gre/revised_general/prepare/analytical_writing/argument/pool*), practice applying the list of logical fallacies to the published prompts. See how many fallacies you can find for each argument. If you have time, write practice essays for some of these arguments. If you are short of time, or would simply like to move more quickly, get together with a friend and explain the fallacies you have found in the argument essay prompts. This will be especially rewarding if you can work with a friend who is also preparing to take the GRE.

2. Write an "original" argument topic, modeling it on one of the argument prompts in the GRE's published pool. Your job is to change the details of the situation (names, figures, and so on) without changing the types of logical fallacies involved. By doing this, you will learn to spot the same old fallacies whenever they crop up in a new guise.

3. Choosing an argument prompt from GRE's online pool of topics for the revised test (currently at *http://www.ets.org/gre/revised_general/prepare/analytical_writing/argument/pool*), write an essay critiquing the particular argument expressed. Set no time limit; take as long as you want to complete this task, then choose a second argument prompt from the pool. *In only 30 minutes*, write an essay critiquing this second argument.

   Compare your two critiques. Ask yourself how working under time pressure affected your second critique. Would more familiarity with the common logical fallacies have helped you? Depending on what problems you spot, review the appropriate sections of this chapter, as well as any other materials we suggest.

PART 4

QUANTITATIVE ABILITY: TACTICS, STRATEGIES, PRACTICE, AND REVIEW

Introduction to Part 4

Part 4 consists of five chapters. Chapter 7 presents several important strategies that can be used on any mathematics questions that appear on the GRE. In Chapters 8, 9, and 10 you will find tactics that are specific to one of the three different types of questions: discrete quantitative questions, quantitative comparison questions, and data interpretation questions, respectively. Chapter 11 contains a complete review of all the mathematics you need to know in order to do well on the GRE, as well as hundreds of sample problems patterned on actual test questions.

FIVE TYPES OF TACTICS

Five different types of tactics are discussed in this book.

1. In Chapters 1 and 2, you learned many basic tactics used by all good test-takers, such as read each question carefully, pace yourself, don't get bogged down on any one question, and never waste time reading the directions. You also learned the specific tactics required to excel on a computerized test. These tactics apply to both the verbal and quantitative sections of the GRE.
2. In Chapters 4 and 5 you learned the important tactics needed for handling each type of verbal question.
3. In Chapter 6 you learned the strategies for planning and writing the two essays that constitute the analytical writing section of the GRE.

4. In Chapters 7–10 you will find all of the tactics that apply to the quantitative sections of the GRE. Chapter 7 contains those techniques that can be applied to all types of mathematics questions; Chapters 8, 9, and 10 present specific strategies to deal with each of the three kinds of quantitative questions found on the GRE: discrete quantitative questions, quantitative comparison questions, and data interpretation questions.

5. In Chapter 11 you will learn or review all of the mathematics that is needed for the GRE, and you will master the specific tactics and key facts that apply to each of the different mathematical topics.

Using these tactics will enable you to answer more quickly many questions that you already know how to do. But the greatest value of these tactics is that they will allow you to correctly answer or make educated guesses on problems that *you do not know how to do.*

WHEN TO STUDY CHAPTER 11

How much time you initially devote to Chapter 11 should depend on how good your math reasoning skills are, how long it has been since you studied math, and how much of the math you learned in middle school and the first two years of high school you remember. If you think that your math skills are quite good, you can initially skip the instructional parts of Chapter 11. If, however, after doing the Model Tests in Part 5 of this book, you find that you made more than one or two mistakes on questions involving the same topic (averages, percents, geometry, etc.) or you spent too much time on them, you should then study the appropriate sections of Chapter 11. Even if your math skills are excellent, you should do the exercises in Chapter 11; they are a good source of additional GRE questions. If your math skills were never very good or if you feel they are rusty, it is advisable to review the material in Chapter 11, including working out the problems, *before* tackling the Model Tests.

AN IMPORTANT SYMBOL

Throughout the rest of this book, the symbol "$\Rightarrow$" is used to indicate that one step in the solution of a problem follows *immediately* from the preceding one, and no explanation is necessary. You should read

$$3x = 12 \Rightarrow x = 4$$

as $\quad\quad\quad 3x = 12$ *implies that* $x = 4$

or $\quad\quad\quad 3x = 12$, *which implies that* $x = 4$

or $\quad\quad$ *since* $3x = 12$, *then* $x = 4$.

Here is a sample solution to the following problem using $\Rightarrow$:

What is the value of $2x^2 - 5$ when $x = -4$?

$$x = -4 \Rightarrow x^2 = (-4)^2 = 16 \Rightarrow 2x^2 = 2(16) = 32 \Rightarrow 2x^2 - 5 = 32 - 5 = \mathbf{27}$$

When the reason for a step is not obvious, $\Rightarrow$ is not used: rather, an explanation is given, often including a reference to a KEY FACT from Chapter 11. In many solutions, some steps are explained, while others are linked by the $\Rightarrow$ symbol, as in the following example.

In the diagram below, if $w = 10$, what is the value of z?

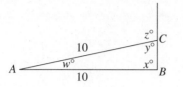

- By KEY FACT J1, $w + x + y = 180$.
- Since $\triangle ABC$ is isosceles, $x = y$ (KEY FACT J5).
- Therefore, $w + 2y = 180 \Rightarrow 10 + 2y = 180 \Rightarrow 2y = 170 \Rightarrow y = 85$.
- Finally, since $y + z = 180$ (KEY FACT I3), $85 + z = 180 \Rightarrow z = \mathbf{95}$.

CALCULATORS ON THE GRE

You may *not* bring your own calculator to use when you take the GRE. However, starting in 2011, for the first time ever, you will have access to an onscreen calculator. While you are working on the math sections, one of the icons at the top of the screen will be a calculator icon. During the verbal and writing sections of the test, either that icon will be greyed out (meaning that you can't click on it) or it will simply not be there at all. During the math sections, however, you will be able to click on that icon at anytime; when you do, a calculator will instantly appear on the screen. Clicking the X in the upper-right-hand corner of the calculator will hide it.

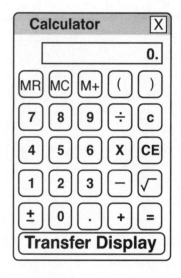

Note that when the calculator appears on the screen, it may cover part of the question or the answer choices. If this occurs, just click on the top of the calculator and drag it to a convenient location. If you use the calculator to answer a question and then click NEXT to go to the next question, the calculator remains on the screen, exactly where it was, with the same numerical readout. This is actually a distraction. So, if you do use the calculator to answer a question, as soon as you have answered that question, click on the X to remove the calculator from the screen. Later, it takes only one click to get it back.

The onscreen calculator is a simple four-function calculator, with a square root key. It is not a graphing calculator; it is not a scientific calculator. The only operations you can perform with the onscreen calculator are adding, subtracting, multiplying, dividing, and taking square roots. Fortunately, these are the only operations you will ever need to answer any GRE question.

At the bottom of the onscreen calculator is a bar labeled TRANSFER DISPLAY. If you are using the calculator on a numeric entry question, and the result of your final calculation is the answer that you want to enter in the box, click on TRANSFER DISPLAY —the number currently displayed in the calculator's readout will instantly appear in the box under the question. This saves the few seconds that it would otherwise take to enter your answer; more important, it guarantees that you won't make an error typing in your answer.

Just because you have a calculator at your disposal does not mean that you should use it very much. In fact, you shouldn't. The vast majority of questions that appear on the GRE do not require any calculations.

Remember

Use your calculator only when you need to.

General Math Strategies

In Chapters 8 and 9, you will learn tactics that are specifically applicable to discrete quantitative questions and quantitative comparison questions, respectively. In this chapter you will learn several important general math strategies that can be used on both of these types of questions.

The directions that appear on the screen at the beginning of the quantitative sections include the following cautionary information:

> Figures that accompany questions are intended to provide information useful in answering the questions.

> However, unless a note states that a figure is drawn to scale, you should solve these problems NOT by estimating sizes by sight or measurement, but by using your knowledge of mathematics.

Despite the fact that they are telling you that you cannot totally rely on *their* diagrams, if you learn how to draw diagrams accurately, *you can trust the ones you draw.* Knowing the best ways of handling diagrams on the GRE is critically important. Consequently, the first five tactics all deal with diagrams.

TACTIC 1.	**Draw a diagram.**
TACTIC 2.	**Trust a diagram that has been drawn to scale.**
TACTIC 3.	**Exaggerate or change a diagram.**
TACTIC 4.	**Add a line to a diagram.**
TACTIC 5.	**Subtract to find shaded regions.**

To implement these tactics, you need to be able to draw line segments and angles accurately, and you need to be able to look at segments and angles and accurately estimate their measures. Let's look at three variations of the same problem.

1. If the diagonal of a rectangle is twice as long as the shorter side, what is the degree measure of the angle it makes with the longer side?
2. In the rectangle below, what is the value of x?

3. In the rectangle below, what is the value of *x*?

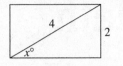

For the moment, let's ignore the correct mathematical way of solving this problem. In the diagram in (3), the side labeled 2 appears to be half as long as the diagonal, which is labeled 4; consequently, you should assume that the diagram has been drawn to scale, and you should see that *x* is about 30, *certainly* between 25 and 35. In (1) you aren't given a diagram, and in (2) the diagram is useless because you can see that it has not been drawn to scale (the side labeled 2 is nearly as long as the diagonal, which is labeled 4). However, if while taking the GRE, you see a question such as (1) or (2), you should be able to quickly draw on your scrap paper a diagram that looks just like the one in (3), and then look at *your* diagram and see that the measure of *x* is just about 30. If the answer choices for these questions were

   Ⓐ 15 Ⓑ 30 Ⓒ 45 Ⓓ 60 Ⓔ 75

you would, of course, choose **30, B**. If the choices were

   Ⓐ 20 Ⓑ 25 Ⓒ 30 Ⓓ 35 Ⓔ 40

you might not be quite as confident, but you should still choose **30**, here **C**.

When you take the GRE, even though you are not allowed to have rulers or protractors, you should be able to draw your diagrams very accurately. For example, in (1) above, you should draw a horizontal line, and then, either freehand or by tracing the corner of a piece of scrap paper, draw a right angle on the line. The vertical line segment will be the width of the rectangle; label it 2.

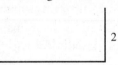

Mark off that distance twice on a piece of scrap paper and use that to draw the diagonal.

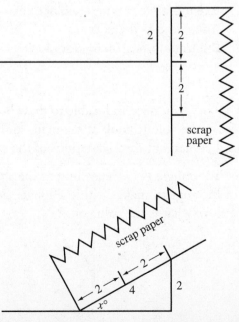

You should now have a diagram that is similar to that in (3), and you should be able to see that *x* is about 30.

By the way, *x* is *exactly* 30. A right triangle in which one leg is half the hypotenuse must be a 30-60-90 triangle, and that leg is opposite the 30° angle [see KEY FACT J11].

Having drawn an accurate diagram, are you still unsure as to how you should know that the value of *x* is 30 just by looking at the diagram? You will now learn not only how to look at *any* angle and know its measure within 5 or 10 degrees, but how to draw any angle that accurately.

You should easily recognize a 90° angle and can probably draw one freehand; but you can always just trace the corner of a piece of scrap paper. To draw a 45° angle, just bisect a 90° angle. Again, you can probably do this freehand. If not, or to be even more accurate, draw a right angle, mark off the same distance on each side, draw a square, and then draw in the diagonal.

To draw other acute angles, just divide the two 45° angles in the above diagram with as many lines as necessary.

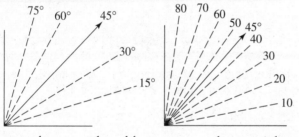

Finally, to draw an obtuse angle, add an acute angle to a right angle.

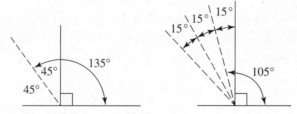

Now, to estimate the measure of a given angle, just draw in some lines.

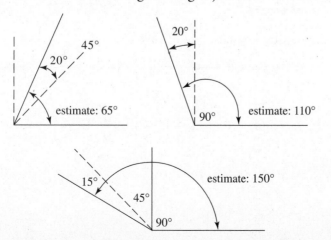

To test yourself, find the measure of each angle shown. The answers are found below.

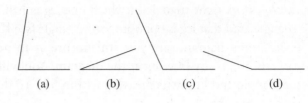

(a)   (b)   (c)   (d)

Answers (a) 80° (b) 20° (c) 115° (d) 160°. Did you come within 10° on each one?

Testing Tactics

TACTIC 1

Draw a Diagram

On *any* geometry question for which a figure is not provided, draw one (as accurately as possible) on your scrap paper — *never attempt a geometry problem without first drawing a diagram.*

EXAMPLE 1

What is the area of a rectangle whose length is twice its width and whose perimeter is equal to that of a square whose area is 1?

(A) 1   (B) 6   (C) $\frac{2}{3}$ (D) $\frac{4}{3}$ (E) $\frac{8}{9}$

SOLUTION. Don't even think of answering this question until you have drawn a square and a rectangle and labeled each of them: each side of the square is 1, and if the width of the rectangle is w, its length (ℓ) is $2w$.

Now, write the required equation and solve it:

$$6w = 4 \Rightarrow w = \frac{4}{6} = \frac{2}{3} \Rightarrow 2w = \frac{4}{3}$$

The area of the rectangle $= \ell w = \left(\frac{4}{3}\right)\left(\frac{2}{3}\right) = \frac{8}{9}$, **E.**

EXAMPLE 2

Betty drove 8 miles west, 6 miles north, 3 miles east, and 6 more miles north. How many miles was Betty from her starting place?

[   ] miles

SOLUTION. Draw a diagram showing Betty's route from *A* to *B* to *C* to *D* to *E*.

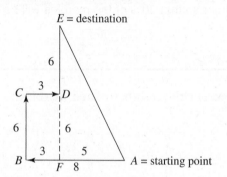

Now, extend line segment *ED* until it intersects *AB* at *F*. Then, *AFE* is a right triangle, whose legs are 5 and 12. The length of hypotenuse *AE* represents the distance from her starting point to her destination. Either recognize that △*AFE* is a 5-12-13 right triangle or use the Pythagorean theorem:

$$5^2 + 12^2 = (AE)^2 \Rightarrow (AE)^2 = 25 + 144 = 169 \Rightarrow AE = \textbf{13}.$$

EXAMPLE 3

What is the difference in the degree measures of the angles formed by the hour hand and the minute hand of a clock at 12:35 and 12:36?

Ⓐ 1°   Ⓑ 5°   Ⓒ 5.5°   Ⓓ 6°   Ⓔ 30°

SOLUTION. Draw a simple picture of a clock. The hour hand makes a complete revolution, 360°, once every 12 hours. So, in 1 hour it goes through 360° ÷ 12 = 30°, and in one minute it advances through 30° ÷ 60 = 0.5°. The minute hand moves through 30° every 5 minutes or 6° per minute. So, in the minute from 12:35 to 12:36 (or any other minute), the *difference* between the hands increased by 6° − 0.5° = **5.5°, C.**

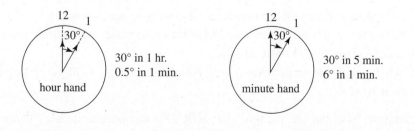

NOTE: It was not necessary, and would have been more time-consuming, to determine the angle between the hands at either 12:35 or 12:36. (See TACTIC 6: Don't do more than you have to.)

Drawings should not be limited to geometry questions; there are many other questions on which drawings will help.

EXAMPLE 4

A jar contains 10 red marbles and 30 green ones. How many red marbles must be added to the jar so that 60% of the marbles will be red?

SOLUTION. Let x represent the number of red marbles to be added, and draw a diagram and label it.

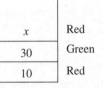

From the diagram it is clear that there are now $40 + x$ marbles in the jar, of which $10 + x$ are red. Since we want the fraction of red marbles to be 60%, we have $\dfrac{10 + x}{40 + x} = 60\% = \dfrac{60}{100} = \dfrac{3}{5}$. Cross-multiplying, we get:

$$5(10 + x) = 3(40 + x) \Rightarrow 50 + 5x = 120 + 3x \Rightarrow 2x = 70 \Rightarrow x = \textbf{35}.$$

Of course, you could have set up the equation and solved it without the diagram, but the diagram makes the solution easier and you are less likely to make a careless mistake.

TACTIC

Trust a Diagram That Has Been Drawn to Scale

Whenever diagrams have been drawn to scale, they can be trusted. This means that you can look at the diagram and use your eyes to accurately estimate the sizes of angles and line segments. For example, in the first problem discussed at the beginning of this chapter, you could "see" that the measure of the angle was about 30°.

To take advantage of this situation:

- If a diagram is given that appears to be drawn to scale, trust it.
- If a diagram is given that has not been drawn to scale, try to draw it to scale on your scrap paper, and then trust it.
- When no diagram is provided, and you draw one on your scrap paper, try to draw it to scale.

In Example 5 below, we are told that *ABCD* is a square and that diagonal *BD* is 3. In the diagram provided, quadrilateral *ABCD* does indeed look like a square, and

BD = 3 does not contradict any other information. We can, therefore, assume that the diagram has been drawn to scale.

EXAMPLE 5

In the figure at the right, diagonal *BD* of square *ABCD* is 3. What is the perimeter of the square?

Ⓐ 4.5　Ⓑ 12　Ⓒ 3√2　Ⓓ 6√2　Ⓔ 12√2

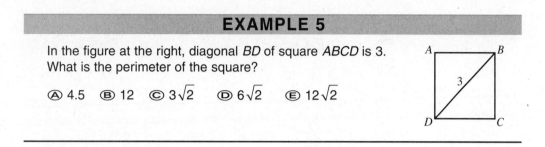

SOLUTION. Since this diagram has been drawn to scale, you can trust it. The sides of the square appear to be about two thirds as long as the diagonal, so assume that each side is about 2. Then the perimeter is about 8. Which of the choices is approximately 8? Certainly not A or B. Since $\sqrt{2} \approx 1.4$, Choices C, D, and E are approximately 4.2, 8.4, and 12.6, respectively. Clearly, the answer must be **D**.

　Direct mathematical solution. Let *s* be a side of the square. Then since $\triangle BCD$ is a 45-45-90 right triangle, $s = \dfrac{3}{\sqrt{2}} = \dfrac{3\sqrt{2}}{2}$, and the perimeter of the square is

$$4s = 4\left(\frac{3\sqrt{2}}{2}\right) = 6\sqrt{2}.$$

　Remember the goal of this book is to help you get credit for *all* the problems you know how to do, and, by using the TACTICS, to get credit for *many* that you don't know how to do. Example 5 is typical. Many students would miss this question. *You*, however, can now answer it correctly, even though you may not remember how to solve it directly.

EXAMPLE 6

In $\triangle ABC$, what is the value of *x*?

Ⓐ 75　Ⓑ 60　Ⓒ 45　Ⓓ 30　Ⓔ 15

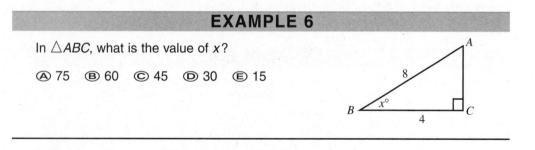

SOLUTION. If you don't see the correct mathematical solution, you should use TACTIC 2 and trust the diagram; but to do that you must be careful that when you copy it onto your scrap paper you *fix it*. What's wrong with the way it is drawn now? *AB* = 8 and *BC* = 4, but in the figure, *AB* and *BC* are almost the same length. Redraw it so that *AB* is *twice* as long as *BC*. Now, just look: *x* is about **60**, **B**.

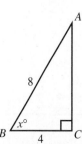

　In fact, *x* is exactly 60. If the hypotenuse of a right triangle is twice the length of one of the legs, then it's a 30-60-90 triangle, and the angle formed by the hypotenuse and that leg is 60° (see Section 11-J).

TACTIC 2 is equally effective on quantitative comparison questions that have diagrams. See pages 9–11 for directions on how to solve quantitative comparison questions.

EXAMPLE 7

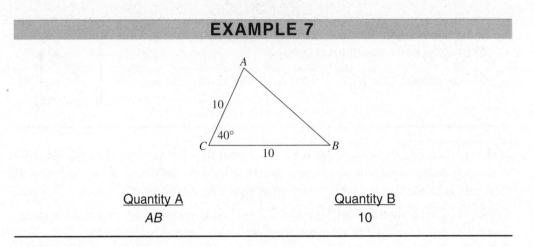

Quantity A	Quantity B
AB	10

SOLUTION. There are two things wrong with the given diagram: $\angle C$ is labeled 40°, but looks much more like 60° or 70°, and *AC* and *BC* are each labeled 10, but *BC* is drawn much longer. When you copy the diagram onto your scrap paper, be sure to correct these two mistakes: draw a triangle that has a 40° angle and two sides of the same length.

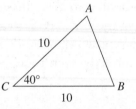

Now, it's clear: *AB* < 10. The answer is **B**.

EXAMPLE 8

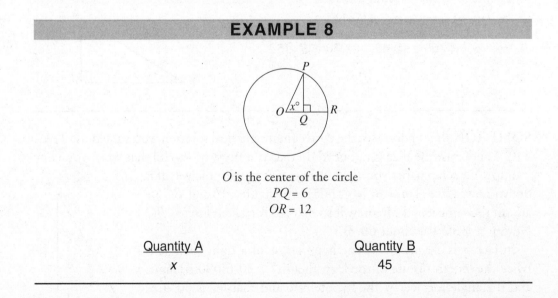

O is the center of the circle
PQ = 6
OR = 12

Quantity A	Quantity B
x	45

SOLUTION. In the diagram on page 154, the value of *x* is at least 60, so if the diagram has been drawn to scale, the answer would be **A**. If, on the other hand, the diagram has not been drawn to scale, we can't trust it. Which is it? The diagram is *not* drawn to scale — *PQ* is drawn almost as long as *OR*, even though *OR* is twice as long. Correct the diagram:

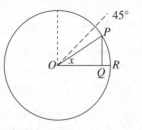

Now you can see that *x* is less than 45. The answer is **B**.

TACTIC

3   **Exaggerate or Otherwise Change a Diagram**

Sometimes it is appropriate to take a diagram that appears to be drawn to scale and intentionally exaggerate it. Why would we do this? Consider the following example.

EXAMPLE 9

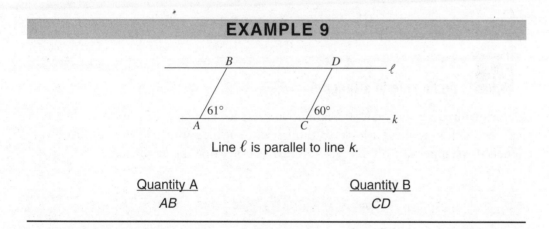

Line ℓ is parallel to line *k*.

<u>Quantity A</u>   <u>Quantity B</u>
AB   *CD*

SOLUTION. In the diagram, which appears to be drawn correctly, *AB* and *CD* look as though they are the same length. However, there *might* be an imperceptible difference due to the fact that angle *C* is slightly smaller than angle *A*. So exaggerate the diagram: redraw it, making angle *C much* smaller than angle *A*. Now, it's clear: *CD* is longer. The answer is **B**.

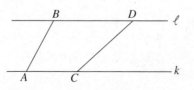

    When you copy a diagram onto your scrap paper, you can change anything you like as long as your diagram is consistent with all the given data.

EXAMPLE 10

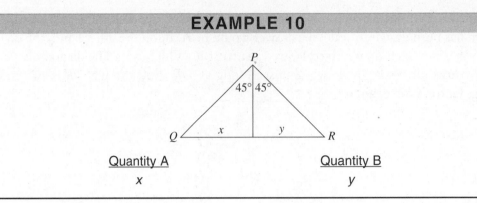

Quantity A	Quantity B
x	*y*

SOLUTION. You may redraw this diagram any way you like, as long as the two angles that are marked 45° remain 45°. If *PQ* and *PR* are equal, as they appear to be in the given diagram, then *x* would equal *y*. Since the given information doesn't state that *PQ* = *PR*, draw a diagram in which *PQ* and *PR* are clearly unequal. In the diagram below, *PR* is much longer than *PQ*, and *x* and *y* are clearly unequal. The answer is **D**.

TACTIC

4   Add a Line to a Diagram

Occasionally, after staring at a diagram, you still have no idea how to solve the problem to which it applies. It looks as though not enough information has been given. When this happens, it often helps to draw another line in the diagram.

EXAMPLE 11

In the figure below, *Q* is a point on the circle whose center is *O* and whose radius is *r*, and *OPQR* is a rectangle. What is the length of diagonal *PR*?

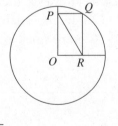

Ⓐ *r*   Ⓑ r^2 Ⓒ $\dfrac{r^2}{\pi}$ Ⓓ $\dfrac{r\sqrt{2}}{\pi}$

Ⓔ It cannot be determined from the information given.

SOLUTION. If after staring at the diagram and thinking about rectangles, circles, and the Pythagorean theorem, you're still lost, don't give up. Ask yourself, "Can I add another line to this diagram?" As soon as you think to draw in *OQ*, the other diagonal, the problem becomes easy: the two diagonals of a rectangle have the same length and, since *OQ* is a radius, it is equal to **r**, **A**.

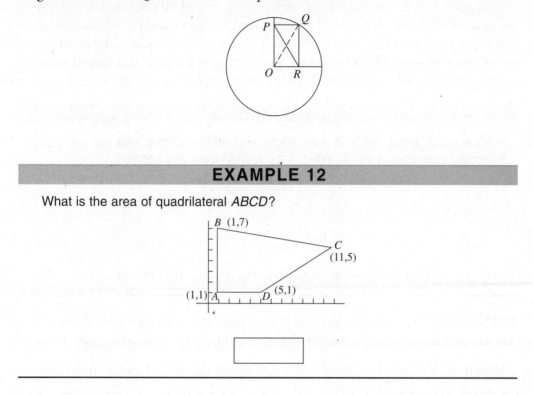

EXAMPLE 12

What is the area of quadrilateral *ABCD*?

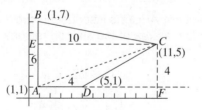

SOLUTION. Since the quadrilateral is irregular, there isn't a formula to find the area. However, if you draw in *AC*, you will divide *ABCD* into two triangles, each of whose areas can be determined.

If you then draw in the height of each triangle, you see that the area of △*ACD* is $\frac{1}{2}(4)(4) = 8$, and the area of △*BAC* is $\frac{1}{2}(6)(10) = 30$, so the area of *ABCD* is $30 + 8 = \textbf{38}$.

Note that this problem could also have been solved by drawing in lines to create rectangle *ABEF*, and subtracting the areas of △*BEC* and △*CFD* from the area of the rectangle.

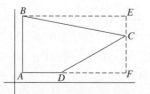

TACTIC

Subtract to Find Shaded Regions

Whenever part of a figure is shaded, the straightforward way to find the area of the shaded portion is to find the area of the entire figure and subtract from it the area of the unshaded region. Of course, if you are asked for the area of the unshaded region, you can, instead, subtract the shaded area from the total area. Occasionally, you may see an easy way to calculate the shaded area directly, but usually you should subtract.

EXAMPLE 13

In the figure below, *ABCD* is a rectangle, and *BE* and *CF* are arcs of circles centered at *A* and *D*. What is the area of the striped region?

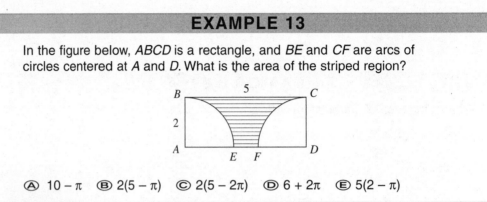

Ⓐ 10 − π   Ⓑ 2(5 − π)   Ⓒ 2(5 − 2π)   Ⓓ 6 + 2π   Ⓔ 5(2 − π)

SOLUTION. The entire region is a 2 × 5 rectangle whose area is 10. Since the white region consists of two quarter-circles of radius 2, the total white area is that of a semicircle of radius 2: $\frac{1}{2}\pi(2)^2 = 2\pi$. Therefore, the area of the striped region is $10 - 2\pi = \mathbf{2(5 - \pi)}$, **B**.

EXAMPLE 14

In the figure below, square *ABCD* is inscribed in circle *O*. If the perimeter of *ABCD* is 24, what is the area of the shaded region?

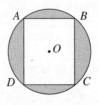

Ⓐ 18π − 36   Ⓑ 18π − 24   Ⓒ 12π − 36   Ⓓ 9π − 36   Ⓔ 9π − 24

SOLUTION. Since the perimeter of square *ABCD* is 24, each of its sides is 6, and its area is $6^2 = 36$. Since diagonal *AC* is the hypotenuse of isosceles right triangle *ABC*, $AC = 6\sqrt{2}$. But *AC* is also a diameter of circle *O*, so the radius of the circle is $3\sqrt{2}$, and its area is $\pi(3\sqrt{2})^2 = 18\pi$. Finally, the area of the shaded region is **18π − 36, A.**

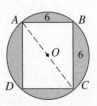

TACTIC
6   Don't Do More Than You Have To

Very often a problem can be solved in more than one way. You should always try to do it in the easiest way possible. Consider the following examples.

EXAMPLE 15

If $5(3x - 7) = 20$, what is $3x - 8$?

Ⓐ $\dfrac{11}{3}$ Ⓑ 0 Ⓒ 3 Ⓓ 14 Ⓔ 19

It is not difficult to solve for x:

$$5(3x - 7) = 20 \Rightarrow 15x - 35 = 20 \Rightarrow 15x = 55 \Rightarrow x = \frac{55}{15} = \frac{11}{3}.$$

But it's too much work. Besides, once you find that $x = \dfrac{11}{3}$, you still have to multiply to get $3x$: $3\left(\dfrac{11}{3}\right) = 11$, and then subtract to get $3x - 8$: $11 - 8 = \textbf{3}$.

SOLUTION. The key is to recognize that you don't need to find x. Finding $3x - 7$ is easy (just divide the original equation by 5), and $3x - 8$ is just 1 less:

$$5(3x - 7) = 20 \Rightarrow 3x - 7 = 4 \Rightarrow 3x - 8 = \textbf{3}, \textbf{C}.$$

EXAMPLE 16

If $7x + 3y = 17$ and $3x + 7y = 19$, what is the average (arithmetic mean) of x and y?

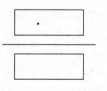

The obvious way to do this is to first find x and y by solving the two equations simultaneously and then to take their average. If you know how to do this, try it now, before reading further. If you worked carefully, you should have found that $x = \dfrac{31}{20}$ and $y = \dfrac{41}{20}$, and their average is $\dfrac{\frac{31}{20} + \frac{41}{20}}{2} = \dfrac{9}{5}$. Enter 9 as the numerator and 5 as the denominator.

This is not too difficult, but it is quite time-consuming, and questions on the GRE never require you to do that much work. Look for a shortcut. Is there a way to find the average without first finding x and y? Absolutely! Here's the best way to do this.

SOLUTION. Add the two equations:

$$7x + 3y = 17$$
$$+\ 3x + 7y = 19$$
$$\overline{10x + 10y = 36}$$

Divide each side by 10: $$x + y = 3.6$$

Calculate the average: $$\frac{x+y}{2} = \frac{3.6}{2} = \mathbf{1.8}$$

Since this numeric entry question requires a fraction for the answer, note that $1.8 = 1\frac{8}{10} = \frac{18}{10}$. So enter 18 for the numerator and 10 for the denominator. Remember that you don't have to reduce fractions to lowest terms.

EXAMPLE 17

Benjamin worked from 9:47 A.M. until 12:11 P.M.
Jeremy worked from 9:11 A.M. until 12:47 P.M.

Quantity A	Quantity B
The number of minutes Benjamin worked	The number of minutes Jeremy worked

---

Do not spend any time calculating how many minutes either of them worked. You only need to know which column is greater, and since Jeremy started earlier and finished later, he clearly worked longer. The answer is **B**.

TACTIC 7   Pay Attention to Units

Often the answer to a question must be in units different from the data given in the question. As you read the question, write on your scratch paper exactly what you are being asked and circle it or put an asterisk next to it. Do they want hours or minutes or seconds, dollars or cents, feet or inches, meters or centimeters? On multiple-choice questions, an answer using the wrong units is almost always one of the choices.

EXAMPLE 18

Driving at 48 miles per hour, how many minutes will it take to drive 32 miles?

Ⓐ $\frac{2}{3}$ Ⓑ $\frac{3}{2}$ Ⓒ 40   Ⓓ 45   Ⓔ 2400

SOLUTION. This is a relatively easy question. Just be attentive. Divide the distance, 32, by the rate, 48: $\frac{32}{48} = \frac{2}{3}$, so it will take $\frac{2}{3}$ of an *hour* to drive 32 miles. Choice A is $\frac{2}{3}$, but that is not the correct answer, because you are asked how many *minutes* it will take. To convert hours to minutes, multiply by 60: it will take $\frac{2}{3}(60) =$ **40** minutes, **C**.

Note that you could have been asked how many *seconds* it would take, in which case the answer would be 40(60) = 2400, Choice E.

EXAMPLE 19

At Nat's Nuts a $2\frac{1}{4}$-pound bag of pistachio nuts costs \$6.00. At this rate, what is the cost in cents of a bag weighing 9 ounces?

Ⓐ 1.5　Ⓑ 24　Ⓒ 150　Ⓓ 1350　Ⓔ 2400

SOLUTION. This is a relatively simple ratio, but make sure you get the units right. To do this you need to know that there are 100 cents in a dollar and 16 ounces in a pound.

$$\frac{\text{price}}{\text{weight}} : \frac{6 \text{ dollars}}{2.25 \text{ pounds}} = \frac{600 \text{ cents}}{36 \text{ ounces}} = \frac{x \text{ cents}}{9 \text{ ounces}}.$$

Now cross-multiply and solve: $36x = 5400 \Rightarrow x =$ **150**, **C**.

TACTIC
8　Systematically Make Lists

When a question asks "how many," often the best strategy is to make a list of all the possibilities. If you do this it is important that you make the list in a *systematic* fashion so that you don't inadvertently leave something out. Usually, this means listing the possibilities in numerical or alphabetical order. Often, shortly after starting the list, you can see a pattern developing and you can figure out how many more entries there will be without writing them all down. Even if the question does not specifically ask "how many," you may need to count something to answer it; in this case, as well, the best plan may be to write out a list.

EXAMPLE 20

A palindrome is a number, such as 93539, that reads the same forward and backward. How many palindromes are there between 100 and 1,000?

SOLUTION. First, write down the numbers that begin and end in 1:

101, 111, 121, 131, 141, 151, 161, 171, 181, 191

Next write the numbers that begin and end in a 2:

202, 212, 222, 232, 242, 252, 262, 272, 282, 292

By now you should see the pattern: there are 10 numbers beginning with 1, 10 beginning with 2, and there will be 10 beginning with 3, 4, ..., 9 for a total of $9 \times 10 =$ **90** palindromes.

EXAMPLE 21

The product of three positive integers is 300. If one of them is 5, what is the least possible value of the sum of the other two?

Ⓐ 16   Ⓑ 17   Ⓒ 19   Ⓓ 23   Ⓔ 32

SOLUTION. Since one of the integers is 5, the product of the other two is 60. Systematically, list all possible pairs, (a, b), of positive integers whose product is 60 and check their sums. First let $a = 1$, then 2, and so on.

a	b	$a + b$
1	60	61
2	30	32
3	20	23
4	15	19
5	12	17
6	10	16

The least possible sum is **16, A**.

Practice Exercises

General Math Strategies

1. At Leo's Lumberyard, an 8-foot long wooden pole costs $3.00. At this rate, what is the cost, in cents, of a pole that is 16 inches long?

   Ⓐ 0.5
   Ⓑ 48
   Ⓒ 50
   Ⓓ 64
   Ⓔ 96

2. In the figure below, vertex Q of square $OPQR$ is on a circle with center O. If the area of the square is 8, what is the area of the circle?

   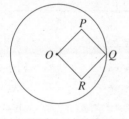

   Ⓐ 8π
   Ⓑ $8\pi\sqrt{2}$
   Ⓒ 16π
   Ⓓ 32π
   Ⓔ 64π

3. In 1999, Diana read 10 English books and 7 French books. In 2000, she read twice as many French books as English books. If 60% of the books that she read during the two years were French, how many books did she read in 2000?

   Ⓐ 16
   Ⓑ 26
   Ⓒ 32
   Ⓓ 39
   Ⓔ 48

4. In writing all of the integers from 1 to 300, how many times is the digit 1 used?

5. In the figure below, if the radius of circle O is 10, what is the length of diagonal AC of rectangle $OABC$?

   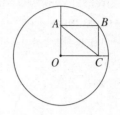

   Ⓐ $\sqrt{2}$
   Ⓑ $\sqrt{10}$
   Ⓒ $5\sqrt{2}$
   Ⓓ 10
   Ⓔ $10\sqrt{2}$

6. In the figure below, $ABCD$ is a square and AED is an equilateral triangle. If $AB = 2$, what is the area of the shaded region?

   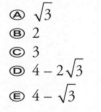

   Ⓐ $\sqrt{3}$
   Ⓑ 2
   Ⓒ 3
   Ⓓ $4 - 2\sqrt{3}$
   Ⓔ $4 - \sqrt{3}$

7. If $5x + 13 = 31$, what is the value of $\sqrt{5x + 31}$?

   Ⓐ $\sqrt{13}$

   Ⓑ $\sqrt{\dfrac{173}{5}}$

   Ⓒ 7
   Ⓓ 13
   Ⓔ 169

8. If $a + 2b = 14$ and $5a + 4b = 16$, what is the average (arithmetic mean) of a and b?

9. In the figure below, equilateral triangle *ABC* is inscribed in circle *O*, whose radius is 4. Altitude *BD* is extended until it intersects the circle at *E*. What is the length of *DE*?

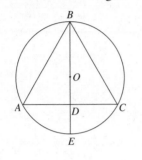

- Ⓐ 1
- Ⓑ $\sqrt{3}$
- Ⓒ 2
- Ⓓ $2\sqrt{3}$
- Ⓔ $4\sqrt{3}$

10. In the figure below, three circles of radius 1 are tangent to one another. What is the area of the shaded region between them?

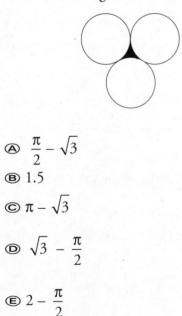

- Ⓐ $\dfrac{\pi}{2} - \sqrt{3}$
- Ⓑ 1.5
- Ⓒ $\pi - \sqrt{3}$
- Ⓓ $\sqrt{3} - \dfrac{\pi}{2}$
- Ⓔ $2 - \dfrac{\pi}{2}$

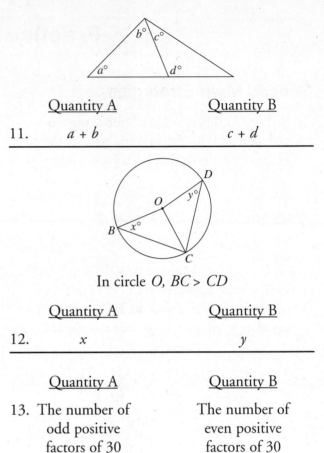

Quantity A	Quantity B

11. $a + b$ $c + d$

In circle *O*, $BC > CD$

Quantity A	Quantity B
12. x	y

Quantity A	Quantity B
13. The number of odd positive factors of 30	The number of even positive factors of 30

Questions 14–15 refer to the following definition.

$\{a, b\}$ represents the remainder when *a* is divided by *b*.

Quantity A	Quantity B
14. $\{10^3, 3\}$	$\{10^5, 5\}$

c and *d* are positive integers with $c < d$.

Quantity A	Quantity B
15. $\{c, d\}$	$\{d, c\}$

ANSWER KEY

1. **C**	6. **E**	11. **B**
2. **C**	7. **C**	12. **B**
3. **E**	8. **2.5**	13. **C**
4. **160**	9. **C**	14. **A**
5. **D**	10. **D**	15. **A**

ANSWER EXPLANATIONS

Two asterisks (**) indicate an alternative method of solving.

1. **(C)** This is a relatively simple ratio problem, but use TACTIC 7 and make sure you get the units right. To do this you need to know that there are 100 cents in a dollar and 12 inches in a foot.

$$\frac{price}{weight} : \frac{3 \text{ dollars}}{8 \text{ feet}} = \frac{300 \text{ cents}}{96 \text{ inches}} = \frac{x \text{ cents}}{16 \text{ inches}}.$$

Now cross-multiply and solve:
$$96x = 4800 \Rightarrow x = 50.$$

2. **(C)** Use TACTICS 2 and 4. On your scrap paper, extend line segments *OP* and *OR*.

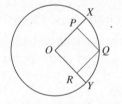

Square *OPQR*, whose area is 8, takes up most of quarter-circle *OXY*. So the area of the quarter-circle is certainly between 11 and 13. The area of the whole circle is 4 times as great: between 44 and 52. Check the five choices: they are approximately 25, 36, 50, 100, 200. The answer is clearly C.

**Another way to use TACTIC 4 is to draw in line segment *OQ*.

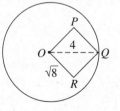

Since the area of the square is 8, each side is $\sqrt{8}$, and diagonal *OQ* is $\sqrt{8} \times \sqrt{2} = \sqrt{16} = 4$. But *OQ* is also a radius, so the area of the circle is $\pi(4)^2 = 16\pi$.

3. **(E)** Use TACTIC 1: draw a picture representing a pile of books or a bookshelf.

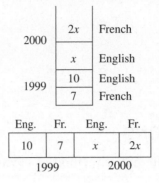

In the two years the number of French books Diana read was $7 + 2x$ and the total number of books was $17 + 3x$. Then 60% or $\dfrac{3}{5} = \dfrac{7 + 2x}{17 + 3x}$. To solve, cross-multiply:

$$5(7 + 2x) = 3(17 + 3x) \Rightarrow 35 + 10x = 51 + 9x \Rightarrow x = 16.$$

In 2000, Diana read 16 English books and 32 French books, a total of 48 books.

4. **160** Use TACTIC 8. Systematically list the numbers that contain the digit 1, writing as many as you need to see the pattern. Between 1 and 99 the digit 1 is used 10 times as the units digit (1, 11, 21, ... , 91) and 10 times as the tens digit (10, 11, 12, ... , 19) for a total of 20 times. From 200 to 299, there are 20 more (the same 20 preceded by a 2). From 100 to 199 there are 20 more plus 100 numbers where the digit 1 is used in the hundreds place. So the total is $20 + 20 + 20 + 100 = 160$.

5. **(D)** Use TACTIC 2. Trust the diagram: AC, which is clearly longer than OC, is approximately as long as radius OE.

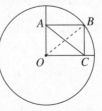

Therefore, AC must be about 10. Check the choices. They are approximately 1.4, 3.1, 7, 10, and 14. The answer must be 10.
**The answer *is* 10. Use TACTIC 4: copy the diagram on your scrap paper and draw in diagonal OB.

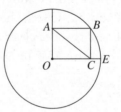

Since the two diagonals of a rectangle are equal, and diagonal OB is a radius, $AC = OB = 10$.

6. **(E)** Use TACTIC 5: subtract to find the shaded area. The area of the square is 4.

The area of the equilateral triangle (see Section 11-J) is $\dfrac{2^2\sqrt{3}}{4}$ = $\dfrac{4\sqrt{3}}{4}$ = $\sqrt{3}$.

So the area of the shaded region is $4 - \sqrt{3}$.

7. **(C)** Use TACTIC 6: don't do more than you have to. In particular, don't solve for *x*.
$$5x + 13 = 31 \Rightarrow 5x = 18 \Rightarrow 5x + 31 =$$
$$18 + 31 = 49 \Rightarrow \sqrt{5x+31} = \sqrt{49} = 7.$$

8. **2.5** Use TACTIC 6: don't do more than is necessary. We don't need to know the values of *a* and *b*, only their average. Adding the two equations, we get

$$6a + 6b = 30 \Rightarrow a + b = 5 \Rightarrow \frac{a+b}{2} = \frac{5}{2} = 2.5.$$

9. **(C)** Use TACTIC 5: to get *DE*, subtract *OD* from radius *OE*, which is 4. Draw *AO* (TACTIC 4).

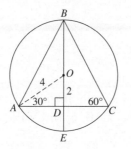

Since $\triangle AOD$ is a 30-60-90 right triangle, *OD* is 2 (one half of *OA*). So, *DE* = 4 − 2 = 2.

10. **(D)** Use TACTIC 4 and add some lines: connect the centers of the three circles to form an equilateral triangle whose sides are 2.

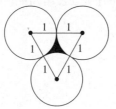

Now use TACTIC 5 and find the shaded area by subtracting the area of the three sectors from the area of the triangle. The area of the triangle is $\dfrac{2^2\sqrt{3}}{4}$ = $\sqrt{3}$ (see Section 11-J).

Each sector is one sixth of a circle of radius 1. Together they form one half of such a circle, so their total area is $\dfrac{1}{2}\pi(1)^2 = \dfrac{\pi}{2}$. Finally, subtract: the shaded

area is $\sqrt{3} - \dfrac{\pi}{2}$.

11. **(B)** If you don't see how to answer this, use TACTIC 2: trust the diagram. Estimate the measure of each angle: for example, $a = 45$, $b = 70$, $c = 30$, and $d = 120$. So $c + d$ (150) is considerably greater than $a + b$ (115). Choose B.

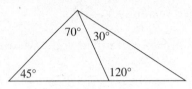

**In fact, d by itself is equal to $a + b$ (an exterior angle of a triangle is equal to the sum of the opposite two interior angles). So $c + d > a + b$.

12. **(B)** From the figure, it appears that x and y are equal, or nearly so. However, the given information states that $BC > CD$, but this is not clear from the diagram. Use TACTIC 3: when you draw the figure on your scrap paper, exaggerate it. Draw it with BC much greater than CD. Now it is clear that y is greater.

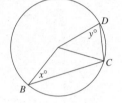

13. **(C)** Use TACTIC 8. Systematically list all the factors of 30, either individually or in pairs: 1, 30; 2, 15; 3, 10; 5, 6. Of the 8 factors, 4 are even and 4 are odd.

14. **(A)** Quantity A: When 10^3 (1000) is divided by 3, the quotient is 333 and the remainder is 1. Quantity B: 10^5 is divisible by 5, so the remainder is 0. Quantity A is greater.

15. **(A)** Quantity A: since $c < d$, the quotient when c is divided by d is 0, and the remainder is c. Quantity B: when d is divided by c the remainder must be less than c.
     So Quantity A is greater.

Discrete Quantitative Questions

About 20 of the 40 questions in the two math sections are what the ETS calls discrete quantitative questions. These questions are of three types:

- Multiple-choice questions
- Multiple-answer questions
- Numeric entry questions

Multiple-choice questions are just the standard multiple-choice questions that you are familiar with. Each one has five answer choices, exactly one of which is the correct answer. To get credit for a multiple-choice question you simply click on the oval in front of the one correct answer choice.

Multiple-answer questions are multiple-choice questions with a twist. These questions could have anywhere from 3 to 12 answer choices, any number of which could be correct, from just one to all of them. To alert you to the fact that there may be, and usually is, more than one correct answer, instead of an oval, a square appears in front of each answer choice. To get credit for a multiple-answer question, you must click on the square in front of each correct answer and leave blank the squares in front of each of the incorrect answers.

Numeric entry questions are the only questions on the test for which no answer choices are given. The answer to such a question may be a positive or negative integer, decimal, or fraction. To get credit for a numeric entry question you must use the keyboard to enter your answer into the box on the screen directly below the question. If in answering a question, you use the onscreen calculator and the digital readout is exactly the answer that you want to enter in the box, you can click on the calculator's TRANSFER DISPLAY bar and the readout will automatically appear in the box. Always enter the exact answer unless the question tells you to round your answer, in which case you must round it to the degree of accuracy asked for.

If the answer is to be entered as a fraction, there will be two boxes, and you are to enter the numerator in the upper box and the denominator in the lower box. Any answer equivalent to a correct answer earns full credit. If the correct answer to a question is 2.5, then 2.50 is equally acceptable, unless you were told to give the answer to the nearest tenth. Also, fractions do not have to be reduced: if the correct answer is $\frac{1}{2}$, then you would receive full credit for $\frac{3}{6}$ or $\frac{13}{26}$, or any other fraction equivalent to $\frac{1}{2}$.

TIP

When you take the GRE, dismiss the instructions for these questions instantly—do not spend even one second reading them—and certainly never accept their offer of clicking on "HELP" to return to them during the test.

TIP

On pages 11–12 you can see a worked out example of each of these three types of questions.

The majority of discrete quantitative questions are of the multiple-choice variety, and all of the tactics discussed in this chapter apply to them. Some of the tactics also apply to multiple-answer questions and numeric entry questions.

The important strategies you will learn in this chapter help you answer many questions on the GRE. However, as invaluable as these tactics are, use them only when you need them. *If you know how to do a problem and are confident that you can do it accurately and reasonably quickly, JUST DO IT!*

As we have done throughout this book, on multiple-choice questions we will continue to label the five answer choices A, B, C, D, and E and to refer to them as such. On multiple-answer questions, the choices will be consecutively labeled A, B, C, etc., using as many letters as there are answer choices. Of course, when you take the GRE, these letters will not appear—there will simply be a blank oval in front of each of the answer choices. When we refer to Choice C—as we do, for example, in TACTIC 1 (below)—we are simply referring to the third answer choice among the five presented.

Testing Tactics

TACTIC
1 Test the Choices, Starting with C

TACTIC 1, often called ***backsolving***, is useful when you are asked to solve for an unknown and you understand what needs to be done to answer the question, but you want to avoid doing the algebra. The idea is simple: test the various choices to see which one is correct.

NOTE: On the GRE the answers to virtually all numerical multiple-choice questions are listed in either increasing or decreasing order. Consequently, C is the middle value, and *in applying TACTIC 1, you should always start with C.* For example, assume that choices A, B, C, D, and E are given in increasing order. Try C. If it works, you've found the answer. If C doesn't work, you should know whether you need to test a larger number or a smaller one, and that permits you to eliminate two more choices. If C is too small, you need a larger number, and so A and B are out; if C is too large, eliminate D and E, which are even larger.

Examples 1 and 2 illustrate the proper use of TACTIC 1.

EXAMPLE 1

If the average (arithmetic mean) of 5, 6, 7, and *w* is 10, what is the value of *w*?

 Ⓐ 8   Ⓑ 13   Ⓒ 18   Ⓓ 22   Ⓔ 28

SOLUTION.
Use TACTIC 1. Test Choice C: $w = 18$.

• Is the average of 5, 6, 7, and 18 equal to 10?

• No: $\dfrac{5+6+7+18}{4} = \dfrac{36}{4} = 9$, which is *too small*.

• Eliminate C, and, since for the average to be 10, w must be *greater* than 18, eliminate A and B, as well.

• Try D: $w = 22$. Is the average of 5, 6, 7, and 22 equal to 10?

• Yes: $\dfrac{5+6+7+22}{4} = \dfrac{40}{4} = 10$. The answer is **D**.

Every problem that can be solved using TACTIC 1 can be solved directly, often in less time. So we stress: *if you are confident that you can solve a problem quickly and accurately, just do so.*

Here are two direct methods for solving Example 1, each of which is faster than backsolving. (See Section 11-E on averages.) If you know either method you should use it, and save TACTIC 1 for those problems that you can't easily solve directly.

DIRECT SOLUTION 1. If the average of four numbers is 10, their sum is 40. So, $5 + 6 + 7 + w = 40 \Rightarrow 18 + w = 40 \Rightarrow w = $ **22.**

DIRECT SOLUTION 2. Since 5 is *5 less than* 10, 6 is *4 less than* 10, and 7 is *3 less than* 10, to compensate, w must be $5 + 4 + 3 = 12$ *more than* 10.
So, $w = 10 + 12 = $ **22.**

EXAMPLE 2

Judy is now twice as old as Adam, but 6 years ago, she was 5 times as old as he was. How old is Judy now?

Ⓐ 10   Ⓑ 16   Ⓒ 20   Ⓓ 24   Ⓔ 32

SOLUTION.
Use TACTIC 1: backsolve starting with C. If Judy is now 20, Adam is 10, and 6 years ago, they would have been 14 and 4. Since Judy would have been less than 5 times as old as Adam, eliminate C, D, and E, and try a smaller value. If Judy is now 16, Adam is 8; 6 years ago, they would have been 10 and 2. That's it; 10 *is* 5 times 2. The answer is **B**.

(See Section 11-H on word problems for the correct algebraic solution.)

Some tactics allow you to eliminate a few choices so you can make an educated guess. On those problems where it can be used, TACTIC 1 *always* gets you the right answer. The only reason not to use it on a particular problem is that you can *easily* solve the problem directly.

TIP

Don't start with C if some of the other choices are much easier to work with. If you start with B and it is too small, you may only get to eliminate two choices (A and B), instead of three, but it will save time if plugging in Choice C would be messy.

EXAMPLE 3

If $3x = 2(5 - 2x)$, then $x =$

Ⓐ $-\dfrac{10}{7}$ Ⓑ 0 Ⓒ $\dfrac{3}{7}$ Ⓓ 1 Ⓔ $\dfrac{10}{7}$

SOLUTION.

Since plugging in 0 is so much easier than plugging in $\dfrac{3}{7}$, start with B: then the left-hand side of the equation is 0 and the right-hand side is 10. The left-hand side is much too small. Eliminate A and B and try something bigger — D, of course; it will be much easier to deal with 1 than with $\dfrac{3}{7}$ or $\dfrac{10}{7}$. Now the left-hand side is 3 and the right-hand side is 6. We're closer, but not there. The answer must be **E**. Notice that we got the right answer without ever plugging in one of those unpleasant fractions. Are you uncomfortable choosing E without checking it? Don't be. If you *know* that the answer is greater than 1, and only one choice is greater than 1, that choice has to be right.

Again, we emphasize that, no matter what the choices are, you backsolve *only* if you can't easily do the algebra. Most students would probably do this problem directly:

$$3x = 2(5 - 2x) \Rightarrow 3x = 10 - 4x \Rightarrow 7x = 10 \Rightarrow x = \frac{10}{7}$$

and save backsolving for a harder problem. You have to determine which method is best for you.

TACTIC

Replace Variables with Numbers

Mastery of TACTIC 2 is critical for anyone developing good test-taking skills. This tactic can be used whenever the five choices involve the variables in the question. There are three steps:

1. Replace each letter with an easy-to-use number.
2. Solve the problem using those numbers.
3. Evaluate each of the five choices with the numbers you picked to see which choice is equal to the answer you obtained.

Examples 4 and 5 illustrate the proper use of TACTIC 2.

EXAMPLE 4

If *a* is equal to the sum of *b* and *c*, which of the following is equal to the difference of *b* and *c*?

Ⓐ $a - b - c$ Ⓑ $a - b + c$ Ⓒ $a - c$ Ⓓ $a - 2c$ Ⓔ $a - b - 2c$

SOLUTION.

- Pick three easy-to-use numbers which satisfy $a = b + c$: for example, $a = 5$, $b = 3$, $c = 2$.
- Then, solve the problem with these numbers: the difference of b and c is $3 - 2 = 1$.
- Finally, check each of the five choices to see which one is equal to 1:

  Ⓐ Does $a - b - c = 1$? NO. $5 - 3 - 2 = 0$
  Ⓑ Does $a - b + c = 1$? NO. $5 - 3 + 2 = 4$
  Ⓒ Does $a - c = 1$? NO. $5 - 2 = 3$
  Ⓓ Does $a - 2c = 1$? YES! $5 - 2(2) = 5 - 4 = 1$
  Ⓔ Does $a - b - 2c = 1$? NO. $5 - 3 - 2(2) = 2 - 4 = -2$

- The answer is **D**.

EXAMPLE 5

If the sum of five consecutive even integers is t, then, in terms of t, what is the greatest of these integers?

Ⓐ $\dfrac{t - 20}{5}$ Ⓑ $\dfrac{t - 10}{5}$ Ⓒ $\dfrac{t}{5}$ Ⓓ $\dfrac{t + 10}{5}$ Ⓔ $\dfrac{t + 20}{5}$

SOLUTION.

- Pick five easy-to-use consecutive even integers: say, 2, 4, 6, 8, 10. Then t, their sum, is 30.
- Solve the problem with these numbers: the greatest of these integers is 10.
- When $t = 30$, the five choices are $\dfrac{10}{5}$, $\dfrac{20}{5}$, $\dfrac{30}{5}$, $\dfrac{40}{5}$, $\dfrac{50}{5}$.

- Only $\dfrac{50}{5}$, Choice **E**, is equal to 10.

Of course, Examples 4 and 5 can be solved without using TACTIC 3 *if your algebra skills are good.* Here are the solutions.

SOLUTION 4. $a = b + c \Rightarrow b = a - c \Rightarrow b - c = (a - c) - c = a - 2c$.

SOLUTION 5. Let n, $n + 2$, $n + 4$, $n + 6$, and $n + 8$ be five consecutive even integers, and let t be their sum. Then,

$$t = n + (n + 2) + (n + 4) + (n + 6) + (n + 8) = 5n + 20$$

So, $n = \dfrac{t - 20}{5} \Rightarrow n + 8 = \dfrac{t - 20}{5} + 8 = \dfrac{t - 20}{5} + \dfrac{40}{5} = \dfrac{t + 20}{5}$.

The important point is that if you can't do the algebra, you can still use TACTIC 2 and *always* get the right answer. Of course, you should use TACTIC 2 even if you can do the algebra, if you think that by using this tactic you will solve the problem faster or will be less likely to make a mistake. This is a good example of what we mean when we say that with the proper use of these tactics, you can correctly answer many questions for which you may not know the correct mathematical solution.

Examples 6 and 7 are somewhat different. You are asked to reason through word problems involving only variables. Most students find problems like these mind-boggling. Here, the use of TACTIC 2 is essential. Without it, Example 6 is difficult and Example 7 is nearly impossible. This is not an easy tactic to master, but with practice you will catch on.

TIP

Replace the letters with numbers that are easy to use, not necessarily ones that make sense. *It is perfectly OK to ignore reality.* A school can have 5 students, apples can cost 10 dollars each, trains can go 5 miles per hour or 1000 miles per hour — it doesn't matter.

EXAMPLE 6

If a school cafeteria needs c cans of soup each week for each student, and if there are s students in the school, for how many weeks will x cans of soup last?

Ⓐ csx Ⓑ $\dfrac{xs}{c}$ Ⓒ $\dfrac{s}{cx}$ Ⓓ $\dfrac{x}{cs}$ Ⓔ $\dfrac{cx}{s}$

SOLUTION.

- Replace c, s, and x with three easy-to-use numbers. If a school cafeteria needs 2 cans of soup each week for each student, and if there are 5 students in the school, how many weeks will 20 cans of soup last?
- Since the cafeteria needs $2 \times 5 = 10$ cans of soup per week, 20 cans will last 2 weeks.
- Which of the choices equals 2 when $c = 2$, $s = 5$, and $x = 20$?

- $csx = 200$; $\dfrac{xs}{c} = 50$; $\dfrac{s}{cx} = \dfrac{1}{8}$; $\dfrac{x}{cs} = 2$; and $\dfrac{cx}{s} = 8$.

The answer is $\dfrac{x}{cs}$, **D**.

NOTE: You do not need to get the exact value of each choice. As soon as you see that a choice does not equal the value you are looking for, stop—eliminate that choice and move on. For example, in the preceding problem, it is clear that csx is much greater than 2, so eliminate it immediately; you do not need to multiply it out to determine that the value is 200.

CAUTION

In this type of problem it is *not* a good idea to replace any of the variables by 1. Since multiplying and dividing by 1 give the same result, you would not be able to distinguish between $\dfrac{cx}{s}$ and $\dfrac{x}{cs}$, both of which are equal to 4 when $c = 1$, $s = 5$, and $x = 20$. It is also not a good idea to use the same number for different variables: $\dfrac{cx}{s}$ and $\dfrac{xs}{c}$ are each equal to x when c and s are equal.

EXAMPLE 7

A vendor sells h hot dogs and s sodas. If a hot dog costs twice as much as a soda, and if the vendor takes in a total of d dollars, how many <u>cents</u> does a soda cost?

(A) $\dfrac{100d}{s+2h}$　(B) $\dfrac{s+2h}{100d}$　(C) $\dfrac{d(s+2h)}{100}$　(D) $100d(s+2h)$　(E) $\dfrac{d}{100(s+2h)}$

SOLUTION.

- Replace h, s, and d with three easy-to-use numbers. Suppose a soda costs 50¢ and a hot dog \$1.00. Then, if he sold 2 sodas and 3 hot dogs, he took in 4 dollars.
- Which of the choices equals 50 when $s = 2$, $h = 3$, and $d = 4$?
- Only $\dfrac{100d}{s+2h}$ (**A**): $\dfrac{100(4)}{2+2(3)} = \dfrac{400}{8} = 50$.

Now, practice TACTIC 3 on the following problems.

EXAMPLE 8

Yann will be x years old y years from now. How old was he z years ago?

(A) $x+y+z$　(B) $x+y-z$　(C) $x-y-z$　(D) $y-x-z$　(E) $z-y-x$

SOLUTION.

Assume that Yann will be 10 in 2 years. How old was he 3 years ago? If he will be 10 in 2 years, he is 8 now and 3 years ago he was 5. Which of the choices equals 5 when $x = 10$, $y = 2$, and $z = 3$? Only $x - y - z$, **C**.

EXAMPLE 9

Stan drove for h hours at a constant rate of r miles per hour. How many miles did he go during the final 20 minutes of his drive?

(A) $20r$　(B) $\dfrac{hr}{3}$　(C) $3rh$　(D) $\dfrac{hr}{20}$　(E) $\dfrac{r}{3}$

SOLUTION.

If Stan drove at 60 miles per hour for 2 hours, how far did he go in the last 20 minutes? Since 20 minutes is $\dfrac{1}{3}$ of an hour, he went 20 ($\dfrac{1}{3}$ of 60) miles. Only Choice **E**, $\dfrac{r}{3}$, is 20 when $r = 60$ and $h = 2$. Notice that h is irrelevant. Whether he had been driving for 2 hours or 20 hours, the distance he covered in the last 20 minutes would be the same.

TACTIC

3   **Choose an Appropriate Number**

TACTIC 3 is similar to TACTIC 2, in that we pick convenient numbers. However, here no variable is given in the problem. TACTIC 3 is especially useful in problems involving fractions, ratios, and percents.

EXAMPLE 10

At Madison High School each student studies exactly one foreign language. Three-fifths of the students take Spanish, and one-fourth of the remaining students take German. If all of the others take French, what <u>percent</u> of the students take French?

Ⓐ 10   Ⓑ 15   Ⓒ 20   Ⓓ 25   Ⓔ 30

SOLUTION.

The least common denominator of $\frac{3}{5}$ and $\frac{1}{4}$ is 20, so assume that there are 20 students at Madison High. (Remember the numbers don't have to be realistic.) The number of students taking Spanish is 12 ($\frac{3}{5}$ of 20). Of the remaining 8 students, 2 of them ($\frac{1}{4}$ of 8) take German. The other 6 take French. Finally, 6 is **30%** of 20. The answer is **E**.

EXAMPLE 11

From 1994 to 1995 the sales of a book decreased by 80%. If the sales in 1996 were the same as in 1994, by what percent did they increase from 1995 to 1996?

Ⓐ 80%   Ⓑ 100%   Ⓒ 120%   Ⓓ 400%   Ⓔ 500%

SOLUTION.

Since this problem involves percents, assume that 100 copies of the book were sold in 1994 (and 1996). Sales dropped by 80 (80% of 100) to 20 in 1995 and then increased by 80, from 20 back to 100, in 1996. The percent increase was

$$\frac{\text{the actual increase}}{\text{the original amount}} \times 100\% = \frac{80}{20} \times 100\% = \mathbf{400\%, D.}$$

TACTIC

4   Eliminate Absurd Choices and Guess

When you have no idea how to solve a multiple-choice question, you can always make an educated guess—simply eliminate all the absurd choices and then guess from among the remaining ones.

During the course of a GRE, you will probably find at least a few multiple-choice questions that you don't know how to solve. Since you are not penalized for wrong answers, you are surely going to enter answers for them. But before taking a wild guess, take a moment to look at the answer choices. Often two or three of them are absurd. Eliminate those and then guess one of the others. Occasionally, four of the choices are absurd. When this occurs, your answer is no longer a guess.

What makes a choice absurd? Lots of things. Here are a few. Even if you don't know how to solve a problem you may realize that

- the answer must be positive, but some of the choices are negative;
- the answer must be even, but some of the choices are odd;
- the answer must be less than 100, but some choices exceed 100;
- a ratio must be less than 1, but some choices are greater than 1.

Let's look at several examples. In a few of them the information given is intentionally insufficient to solve the problem; but you will still be able to determine that some of the answers are absurd. In each case the "solution" will indicate which choices you should have eliminated. At that point you would simply guess. Remember, on the GRE when you guess, don't agonize. Just guess and move on.

EXAMPLE 12

A region inside a semicircle of radius r is shaded and you are asked for its area.

Ⓐ $\frac{1}{4}\pi r^2$ Ⓑ $\frac{1}{3}\pi r^2$ Ⓒ $\frac{1}{2}\pi r^2$ Ⓓ $\frac{2}{3}\pi r^2$ Ⓔ πr^2

SOLUTION.
You may have no idea how to find the area of the shaded region, but you should know that since the area of a circle is πr^2, the area of a semicircle is $\frac{1}{2}\pi r^2$. Therefore, the area of the shaded region must be *less* than $\frac{1}{2}\pi r^2$, so eliminate C, D, and E. On an actual GRE problem, you may be able to make an educated guess between A and B. If so, terrific; if not, just choose one or the other.

EXAMPLE 13

The average (arithmetic mean) of 5, 10, 15, and z is 20. What is z?

Ⓐ 0   Ⓑ 20   Ⓒ 25   Ⓓ 45   Ⓔ 50

SOLUTION.
If the average of four numbers is 20, and three of them are less than 20, the other one must be greater than 20. Eliminate A and B and guess. If you further realize that since 5 and 10 are a *lot less* than 20, z will probably be a *lot more* than 20; eliminate C, as well.

EXAMPLE 14

If 25% of 260 equals 6.5% of *a*, what is *a*?

Ⓐ 10   Ⓑ 65   Ⓒ 100   Ⓓ 130   Ⓔ 1000

SOLUTION.
Since 6.5% of *a* equals 25% of 260, which is surely greater than 6.5% of 260, *a* must be greater than 260. Eliminate A, B, C, and D. The answer *must* be **E**!

Example 14 illustrates an important point. *Even if you know how to solve a problem*, if you immediately see that four of the five choices are absurd, just pick the fifth choice and move on.

EXAMPLE 15

A jackpot of $39,000 is to be divided in some ratio among three people. What is the value of the largest share?

Ⓐ $23,400   Ⓑ $19,500   Ⓒ $11,700   Ⓓ $7800   Ⓔ $3900

SOLUTION.
If the prize were divided equally, each of the three shares would be worth $13,000. If it is divided unequally, the largest share is surely worth *more than* $13,000. Eliminate C, D, and E. In an actual question, you would be told what the ratio is, and that might enable you to eliminate A or B. If not, you just guess.

EXAMPLE 16

In a certain club, the ratio of the number of boys to girls is 5:3. What percent of the members of the club are girls?

Ⓐ 37.5%   Ⓑ 50%   Ⓒ 60%   Ⓓ 62.5%   Ⓔ 80%

SOLUTION.
Since there are 5 boys for every 3 girls, there are fewer girls than boys. Therefore, *fewer than half* (50%) of the members are girls. Eliminate B, C, D, and E. The answer is **A**.

EXAMPLE 17

In the figure below, four semicircles are drawn, each one centered at the midpoint of one of the sides of square *ABCD*. Each of the four shaded "petals" is the intersection of two of the semicircles. If *AB* = 4, what is the total area of the shaded region?

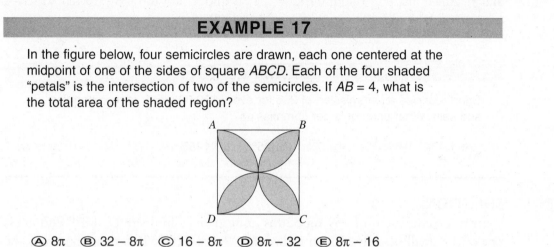

Ⓐ 8π   Ⓑ 32 − 8π   Ⓒ 16 − 8π   Ⓓ 8π − 32   Ⓔ 8π − 16

SOLUTION.
- Since *AB* = 4, the area of the square is 16, and so, obviously, the area of the shaded region must be much less.
- Check each choice. Since π is slightly more than 3 (π ≈ 3.14), 8π is somewhat greater than 24, approximately 25.
- (A) 8π ≈ 25. More than the area of the whole square: way too big.
- (B) 32 − 8π ≈ 32 − 25 = 7.
- (C) 16 − 8π is negative.
- (D) 8π − 32 is also negative.
- (E) 8π − 16 ≈ 25 − 16 = 9.

NOTE: Three of the choices are absurd: A is more than the area of the entire square and C and D are negative; they can be eliminated immediately. The answer must be B or E. If you think the shaded area takes up less than half of the square, guess B; if you think it takes up more than half of the square, guess E. (The answer is **E**).

Now use TACTIC 4 on each of the following problems. Even if you know how to solve them, don't. Practice this technique and see how many choices you can eliminate *without* actually solving.

EXAMPLE 18

In the figure at the right, diagonal *EG* of square *EFGH* is $\frac{1}{2}$ of diagonal *AC* of the square *ABCD*. What is the ratio of the area of the shaded region to the area of *ABCD*?

Ⓐ $\sqrt{2}$:1   Ⓑ 3:4   Ⓒ $\sqrt{2}$:2   Ⓓ 1:2   Ⓔ 1:2$\sqrt{2}$

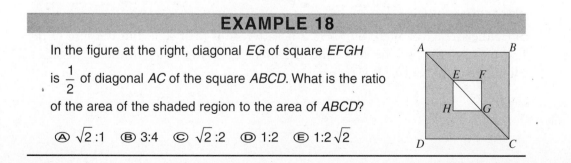

SOLUTION.
Obviously, the shaded region is smaller than square *ABCD*, so the ratio must be less than 1. Eliminate A. Also, from the diagram, it is clear that the shaded region is more than half of square *ABCD*, so the ratio is greater than 0.5. Eliminate D and E. Since 3:4 = .75 and $\sqrt{2}$:2 ≈ .71, B and C are too close to tell which is correct just by looking; so guess. The answer is **B**.

EXAMPLE 19

Shari receives a commission of 25¢ for every $20.00 worth of merchandise she sells. What percent is her commission?

   Ⓐ $1\frac{1}{4}$%   Ⓑ $2\frac{1}{2}$%   Ⓒ 5%   Ⓓ 25%   Ⓔ 125%

SOLUTION.
Clearly, a commission of 25¢ on $20 is quite small. Eliminate D and E and guess one of the small percents. If you realize that 1% of $20 is 20¢, then you know the answer is a little more than 1%, and you should guess A (maybe B, but definitely not C). The answer is **A**.

EXAMPLE 20

From 1980 to 1990, Lior's weight increased by 25%. If his weight was *k* kilograms in 1990, what was it in 1980?

   Ⓐ 1.75*k*   Ⓑ 1.25*k*   Ⓒ 1.20*k*   Ⓓ .80*k*   Ⓔ .75*k*

SOLUTION.
Since Lior's weight increased, his weight in 1980 was *less than k*. Eliminate A, B, and C and guess. The answer is **D**.

EXAMPLE 21

The average of 10 numbers is −10. If the sum of 6 of them is 100, what is the average of the other 4?

   Ⓐ −100   Ⓑ −50   Ⓒ 0   Ⓓ 50   Ⓔ 100

SOLUTION.
Since the average of all 10 numbers is negative, so is their sum. But the sum of the first 6 is positive, so the sum (and the average) of the others must be negative. Eliminate C, D, and E. **B** is correct.

Practice Exercises

Discrete Quantitative Questions

1. Evan has 4 times as many books as David and 5 times as many as Jason. If Jason has more than 40 books, what is the least number of books that Evan could have?

   Ⓐ 200
   Ⓑ 205
   Ⓒ 210
   Ⓓ 220
   Ⓔ 240

2. Judy plans to visit the National Gallery once each month in 2012 except in July and August when she plans to go three times each. A single admission costs $3.50, a pass valid for unlimited visits in any 3-month period can be purchased for $18, and an annual pass costs $60.00. What is the least amount, in dollars, that Judy can spend for her intended number of visits?

    dollars

3. Alison is now three times as old as Jeremy, but 5 years ago, she was 5 times as old as he was. How old is Alison now?

   Ⓐ 10
   Ⓑ 12
   Ⓒ 24
   Ⓓ 30
   Ⓔ 36

4. What is the largest prime factor of 255?

   Ⓐ 5
   Ⓑ 15
   Ⓒ 17
   Ⓓ 51
   Ⓔ 255

5. If c is the product of a and b, which of the following is the quotient of a and b?

   Ⓐ $\dfrac{b^2}{c}$

   Ⓑ $\dfrac{c}{b^2}$

   Ⓒ $\dfrac{b}{c^2}$

   Ⓓ bc^2

   Ⓔ b^2c

6. If w widgets cost c cents, how many widgets can you get for d dollars?

   Ⓐ $\dfrac{100dw}{c}$

   Ⓑ $\dfrac{dw}{100c}$

   Ⓒ $100cdw$

   Ⓓ $\dfrac{dw}{c}$

   Ⓔ cdw

7. If 120% of a is equal to 80% of b, which of the following is equal to $a + b$?

   Ⓐ $1.5a$
   Ⓑ $2a$
   Ⓒ $2.5a$
   Ⓓ $3a$
   Ⓔ $5a$

8. In the figure below, *WXYZ* is a square whose sides are 12. *AB*, *CD*, *EF*, and *GH* are each 8, and are the diameters of the four semicircles. What is the area of the shaded region?

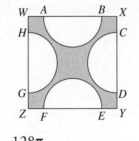

Ⓐ $144 - 128\pi$

Ⓑ $144 - 64\pi$

Ⓒ $144 - 32\pi$

Ⓓ $144 - 16\pi$

Ⓔ 16π

9. If *x* and *y* are integers such that $x^3 = y^2$, which of the following could <u>not</u> be the value of *y*? Indicate *all* such values.

Ⓐ −1

Ⓑ 1

Ⓒ 8

Ⓓ 12

Ⓔ 16

Ⓕ 27

10. What is *a* divided by *a*% of *a*?

Ⓐ $\dfrac{a}{100}$

Ⓑ $\dfrac{100}{a}$

Ⓒ $\dfrac{a^2}{100}$

Ⓓ $\dfrac{100}{a^2}$

Ⓔ $100a$

11. If an object is moving at a speed of 36 kilometers per hour, how many meters does it travel in one second?

| | meters

12. On a certain French-American committee, $\dfrac{2}{3}$ of the members are men, and $\dfrac{3}{8}$ of the men are Americans. If $\dfrac{3}{5}$ of the committee members are French, what fraction of the members are American women?

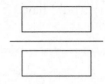

13. For what value of *x* is $8^{2x-4} = 16^x$?

Ⓐ 2

Ⓑ 3

Ⓒ 4

Ⓓ 6

Ⓔ 8

14. If $12a + 3b = 1$ and $7b - 2a = 9$, what is the average (arithmetic mean) of *a* and *b*?

Ⓐ 0.1

Ⓑ 0.5

Ⓒ 1

Ⓓ 2.5

Ⓔ 5

15. If *x*% of *y* is 10, what is *y*?

Ⓐ $\dfrac{10}{.x}$

Ⓑ $\dfrac{100}{x}$

Ⓒ $\dfrac{1000}{x}$

Ⓓ $\dfrac{x}{100}$

Ⓔ $\dfrac{x}{10}$

ANSWER KEY

1. **D**	6. **A**	11. **10**	14. **B**
2. **49.50**	7. **C**	12. $\dfrac{3}{20}$	15. **C**
3. **D**	8. **C**		
4. **C**	9. **D, E**	13. **D**	
5. **B**	10. **B**		

ANSWER EXPLANATIONS

Two asterisks (**) indicate an alternative method of solving.

1. **(D)** Test the answer choices starting with the smallest value. If Evan had 200 books, Jason would have 40. But Jason has more than 40, so 200 is too small. Trying 205 and 210, we see that neither is a multiple of 4, so David wouldn't have a whole number of books. Finally, 220 works. (So does 240, but we shouldn't even test it since we want the least value.)

    **Since Jason has at least 41 books, Evan has at least $41 \times 5 = 205$. But Evan's total must be a multiple of 4 and 5, hence of 20. The smallest multiple of 20 greater than 205 is 220.

2. **49.50** Judy intends to go to the Gallery 16 times during the year. Buying a single admission each time would cost $16 \times \$3.50 = \$56$, which is less than the annual pass. If she bought a 3-month pass for June, July, and August, she would pay \$18 plus \$31.50 for 9 single admissions ($9 \times \$3.50$), for a total expense of \$49.50, which is the least expensive option.

3. **(D)** Use TACTIC 1: backsolve starting with C. If Alison is now 24, Jeremy is 8, and 5 years ago, they would have been 19 and 3, which is more than 5 times as much. Eliminate A, B, and C, and try a bigger value. If Alison is now 30, Jeremy is 10, and 5 years ago, they would have been 25 and 5. That's it; 25 is 5 times 5.

    **If Jeremy is now x, Alison is $3x$, and 5 years ago they were $x - 5$ and $3x - 5$, respectively. Now, solve:

    $3x - 5 = 5(x - 5) \Rightarrow 3x - 5 = 5x - 25 \Rightarrow$
    $2x = 20 \Rightarrow x = 10 \Rightarrow 3x = 30.$

4. **(C)** Test the choices starting with C: 255 *is* divisible by 17 ($255 = 17 \times 15$), so this is a possible answer. Does 255 have a larger prime factor? Neither Choice D nor E is prime, so the answer must be Choice C.

5. **(B)** Use TACTIC 2. Pick simple values for a, b, and c. Let $a = 3$, $b = 2$, and $c = 6$. Then $a \div b = 3/2$. Without these values of a, b, and c, only B is equal to 3/2.

    ** $c = ab \Rightarrow a = \dfrac{c}{b} \Rightarrow a \div b = \dfrac{c}{b} \div b = \dfrac{c}{b} \cdot \dfrac{1}{b} = \dfrac{c}{b^2}.$

6. **(A)** Use TACTIC 2. If 2 widgets cost 10 cents, then widgets cost 5 cents each, and for 3 dollars, you can get 60. Which of the choices equals 60 when $w = 2$, $c = 10$, and $d = 3$? Only A.

    ** $\dfrac{\text{widgets}}{\text{cents}} = \dfrac{w}{c} = \dfrac{x}{100d} \Rightarrow x = \dfrac{100dw}{c}.$

7. **(C)** Since 120% of 80 = 80% of 120, let a = 80 and b = 120. Then $a + b$ = 200, and 200 ÷ 80 = 2.5.

8. **(C)** If you don't know how to solve this, you must use TACTIC 4 and guess after eliminating the absurd choices. Which choices are absurd? Certainly, A and B, both of which are negative. Also, since Choice D is about 94, which is much more than half the area of the square, it is much too big. Guess between Choice C (about 43) and Choice E (about 50). If you remember that the way to find shaded areas is to subtract, guess C.

   **The area of the square is 12^2 = 144. The area of each semicircle is 8π, one-half the area of a circle of radius 4. So together the areas of the semicircles is 32π.

9. **(D)(E)** Test each choice until you find all the correct answers.

   (A) Could $y = -1$? Is there an integer x such that $x^3 = (-1)^2 = 1$? Yes, $x = 1$.
   (B) Similarly, if $y = 1$, $x = 1$.
   (C) Could $y = 8$? Is there an integer x such that $x^3 = (8)^2 = 64$? Yes, $x = 4$.
   (D) Could $y = 12$? Is there an integer such that $x^3 = 12^2 = 144$? No, $5^3 = 125$, which is too small, and $6^3 = 216$, which is too big.
   (E) Could $y = 16$? Is there an integer x such that $x^3 = 16^2 = 256$? No, $6^3 = 216$, which is too small; and $7^3 = 343$, which is too big.
   (F) Could $y = 27$? Is there an integer x such that $x^3 = 27^2 = 729$? Yes, $9^3 = 729$.
   The answer is D and E.

10. **(B)** $a \div (a\% \text{ of } a) = a \div \left(\dfrac{a}{100} \times a \right) = a \div \left(\dfrac{a^2}{100} \right) = a \times \dfrac{100}{a^2} = \dfrac{100}{a}$.

   **Use TACTICS 2 and 3: replace a by a number, and use 100 since the problem involves percents. 100 ÷ (100% of 100) = 100 ÷ 100 = 1. Test each choice; which ones equal 1 when a = 100. Both A and B: $\dfrac{100}{100}$ = 1. Eliminate Choices C, D, and E, and test A and B with another value for a. 50 ÷ (50% of 50) = 50 ÷ (25) = 2. Now, only B works $\left(\dfrac{100}{50} = 2, \text{ whereas } \dfrac{50}{100} = \dfrac{1}{2} \right)$.

11. **10** Set up a ratio:

   $$\frac{\text{distance}}{\text{time}} = \frac{36 \text{ kilometers}}{1 \text{ hour}} = \frac{36,000 \text{ meters}}{60 \text{ minutes}} = \frac{36,000 \text{ meters}}{3600 \text{ seconds}} = 10 \text{ meters/second}.$$

   **Use TACTIC 1: Test choices starting with C:

   100 meters/second = 6000 meters/minute = 360,000 meters/hour = 360 kilometers/hour.

   Not only is that too big, it is too big by a factor of 10. The answer is 10.

12. $\frac{3}{20}$ Use TACTIC 3. The LCM of all the denominators is 120, so assume that the

committee has 120 members. Then there are $\frac{2}{3} \times 120 = 80$ men and 40 women.

Of the 80 men 30 $\left(\frac{3}{8} \times 80 \right)$ are American. Since there are 72 $\left(\frac{3}{5} \times 120 \right)$ French

members, there are $120 - 72 = 48$ Americans, of whom 30 are men, so the other

18 are women. Finally, the fraction of American women is $\frac{18}{120} = \frac{3}{20}$.

This is illustrated in the Venn diagram below.

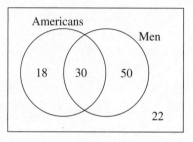

13. **(D)** Use the laws of exponents to simplify the equation, and then solve it:
$8^{2x-4} = 16^x \Rightarrow (2^3)^{2x-4} = (2^4)^x \Rightarrow 3(2x - 4) = 4x \Rightarrow 6x - 12 = 4x \Rightarrow$
$2x = 12 \Rightarrow x = 6$.

14. **(B)** Add the two equations:

$10a + 10b = 10 \Rightarrow a + b = 1 \Rightarrow \dfrac{a+b}{2} = \dfrac{1}{2}$.

Do not waste time solving for a and b.

15. **(C)** Pick easy-to-use numbers. Since 100% of 10 is 10, let $x = 100$ and $y = 10$.
When $x = 100$, Choices C and E are each 10. Eliminate Choices A, B, and D,
and try some other numbers: 50% of 20 is 10. Of Choices C and E, only C = 20
when $x = 50$.

Quantitative Comparison Questions

About 15 of the 40 questions on the two quantitative sections of the GRE are quantitative comparisons. Unless you took the SAT before 2005, it is very likely that you have never seen questions of this type and certainly never learned the correct strategies for answering them. Don't worry. In this chapter you will learn all of the necessary tactics. If you master them, you will quickly realize that quantitative comparisons are the easiest mathematics questions on the GRE and will wish that there were more than 15 of them.

Before the first quantitative comparison question appears on the screen, you will see these instructions.

Directions: In the following question, there are two quantities, labeled Quantity A and Quantity B. You are to compare those quantities, taking into consideration any additional information given and decide which of the following statements is true:

> Quantity A is greater;
> Quantity B is greater;
> The two quantities are equal; or
> It is impossible to determine which quantity is greater.

Note: The given information, if any, is centered above the two quantities. If a symbol appears more than once, it represents the same thing each time.

Before learning the different strategies for solving this type of question, let's clarify these instructions. In quantitative comparison questions there are two quantities, and it is your job to compare them. The correct answer to a quantitative comparison question is one of the four statements listed in the directions above. Of course, on the computer screen those choices will not be listed as A, B, C, and D. Rather, you will see an oval in front of each statement, and you will click on the oval in front of the statement you believe is true.

You should click on the oval in front of	if
Quantity A is greater.	Quantity A is greater *all the time, no matter what.*
Quantity B is greater.	Quantity B is greater *all the time, no matter what.*
The two quantities are equal.	The two quantities are equal *all the time, no matter what.*
It is impossible to determine which quantity is greater.	*The answer is not one of the first three choices.*

This means, for example, that *if you can find a single instance* when Quantity A is greater than Quantity B, then you can immediately eliminate two choices: the answer cannot be "Quantity B is greater," and the answer cannot be "The two quantities are equal." In order for the answer to be "Quantity B is greater," Quantity B would have to be greater *all the time*; but you know of one instance when it isn't. Similarly, since the quantities are not equal *all the time*, the answer can't be "The two quantities are equal." The correct answer, therefore, is either "Quantity A is greater" or "It is impossible to determine which quantity is greater." If it turns out that Quantity A *is* greater all the time, then that is the answer; if, however, you can find a single instance where Quantity A is not greater, the answer is "It is impossible to determine which quantity is greater."

By applying the tactics that you will learn in this chapter, you will probably be able to determine which of the choices is correct; if, however, after eliminating two of the choices, you still cannot determine which answer is correct, quickly guess between the two remaining choices and move on.

Before learning the most important tactics for handling quantitative comparison questions, let's look at two examples to illustrate the preceding instructions.

TIP

Right now, memorize the instructions for answering quantitative comparison questions. *When you take the GRE, dismiss the instructions for these questions immediately—do not spend even one second reading the directions (or looking at a sample problem).*

EXAMPLE 1

$$1 < x < 3$$

Quantity A	Quantity B
x^2	$2x$

○ Quantity A is greater.
○ Quantity B is greater.
○ The two quantities are equal.
○ It is impossible to determine which quantity is greater.

SOLUTION.

Throughout, x represents the same thing — a number between 1 and 3. If x is 2, then x^2 and $2x$ are each 4, and *in this case* the two quantities are equal. We can, therefore, eliminate the first two choices: neither Quantity A nor Quantity B is greater *all the time*. However, in order for the correct answer to be "The two quantities are equal," the quantities would have to be equal *all the time*. Are they? Note that although 2 is the only *integer* between 1 and 3, it is not the only *number* between 2 and 3: *x* could be 1.1 or 2.5 or any of infinitely many other numbers. And in those cases the quantities are not equal (for example, $2.5^2 = 6.25$, whereas $2(2.5) = 5$). The quantities are *not* always equal, and so the correct answer is the fourth choice: It is impossible to determine which quantity is greater.

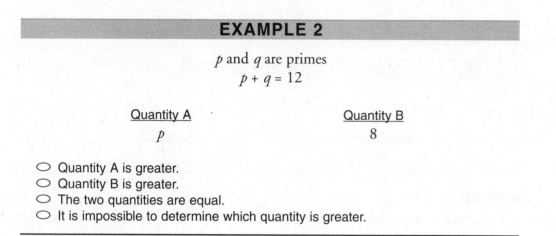

EXAMPLE 2

p and *q* are primes
$p + q = 12$

Quantity A	Quantity B
p	8

○ Quantity A is greater.
○ Quantity B is greater.
○ The two quantities are equal.
○ It is impossible to determine which quantity is greater.

SOLUTION.
Since 5 and 7 are the only primes whose sum is 12, *p* could be 5 or 7. In either case, *p* is less than 8, and so Quantity B is greater, *all the time*. Note that although $1 + 11 = 12$, *p* cannot be 11, because 1 is not a prime [See Section 11-A].

NOTE: To simplify the discussion, throughout the rest of this chapter, in the explanations of the answers to all sample questions and in the Model Tests, the four answer choices will be referred to as A, B, C, and D, respectively. For example, we will write

The correct answer is **B**.

rather than

The correct answer is: Quantity B is greater.

Testing Tactics

TACTIC

 1   **Replace Variables with Numbers**

Many problems that are hard to analyze because they contain variables become easy to solve when the variables are replaced by simple numbers.

TACTIC 1 is the most important tactic in this chapter. Using it properly will earn you more points on the quantitative comparison questions of the GRE than you can gain by applying any of the others. *Be sure to master it!*

Most quantitative comparison questions contain variables. When those variables are replaced by simple numbers such as 0 or 1, the quantities become much easier to compare.

The reason that TACTIC 1 is so important is that it *guarantees* that on any quantitative comparison question that involves variables, you will be able to immediately eliminate two of the four choices, and very often a third choice as well, leaving you with at least a 50% chance of guessing correctly, and often a certainty. Try the following example, and then read the explanation very carefully.

EXAMPLE 3

$$a < b < c < d$$

<u>Quantity A</u>	<u>Quantity B</u>
ab	*cd*

SOLUTION.

* Replace *a*, *b*, *c*, and *d* with easy-to-use numbers which satisfy the condition $a < b < c < d$: for example, $a = 1$, $b = 3$, $c = 6$, $d = 10$. [See the guidelines that follow to learn why 1, 2, 3, 4 is not a good choice.]
* Evaluate the two quantities: $ab = (1)(3) = 3$, and $cd = (6)(10) = 60$.
* So *in this case*, Quantity B is greater.
* Does that mean that B is the correct answer? Not necessarily. Quantity B *is* greater this time, but will it be greater ***every single time, no matter what?***
* What it does mean is that neither A nor C could possibly be the correct answer: Quantity A can't be greater ***every single time, no matter what*** because it isn't greater *this* time; and the quantities aren't equal ***every single time, no matter what*** because they aren't equal *this* time.

So in the few seconds that it took you to plug in 1, 3, 6, and 10 for *a*, *b*, *c*, and *d*, you were able to eliminate two of the four choices. You now know that the correct answer is either B or D, and if you could do nothing else, you would now guess with a 50% chance of being correct.

But, of course, *you will do something else.* You will try some other numbers. But *which* numbers? Since the first numbers you chose were positive, try some negative numbers this time.

* Let $a = -5$, $b = -3$, $c = -2$, and $d = -1$.
* Evaluate: $ab = (-5)(-3) = 15$ and $cd = (-2)(-1) = 2$.
* So *in this case*, Quantity A is greater.
* Quantity B is *not* greater all the time. B is *not* the correct answer.
* The correct answer is **D**: It is impossible to determine which quantity is greater.

NOTES:

1. If for your second substitution you had chosen 3, 7, 8, 10 or 2, 10, 20, 35 or *any* four positive numbers, Quantity B would have been bigger. No matter how many substitutions you made, Quantity B would have been bigger each time, and you would have incorrectly concluded that B was the answer. In fact, if the given condition had been $0 < a < b < c < d$, then B *would have been* the correct answer.

2. Therefore, knowing which numbers to plug in when you use TACTIC 1 is critical. As long as you comply with the conditions given in the question, you have complete freedom in choosing the numbers. Some choices, however, are much better than others.

Here are some guidelines for deciding which numbers to use when applying TACTIC 1.

1. **The very best numbers to use first are: 1, 0, and –1.**

2. **Often, fractions between 0 and 1 are useful.**

3. **Occasionally, "large" numbers such as 10 or 100 can be used.**

4. **If there is more than one letter, it is permissible to replace each with the same number.**

5. **Do not impose any conditions not specifically stated.** In particular, do not assume that variables must be integers. For example, 3 is not the only number that satisfies $2 < x < 4$ (2.1, 3.95, and π all work). The expression $a < b < c < d$ does not mean that a, b, c, d are *integers*, let alone *consecutive* integers (which is why we didn't choose 1, 2, 3, and 4 in Example 3), nor does it mean that any or all of them are *positive*.

When you replace the variables in a quantitative comparison question with numbers, remember:

If the value of Quantity A is ever greater:	eliminate B and C — the answer must be A or D.
If the value of Quantity B is ever greater:	eliminate A and C — the answer must be B or D.
If the two quantities are ever equal:	eliminate A and B — the answer must be C or D.

You have learned that, no matter how hard a quantitative comparison is, as soon as you replace the variables, two choices can *immediately* be eliminated; and if you can't decide between the other two, just guess. This guarantees that in addition to correctly answering all the questions that you know how to solve, you will be able to answer correctly at least half, and probably many more, of the questions that you don't know how to do.

Practice applying TACTIC 1 on these examples.

EXAMPLE 4

$$m > 0 \text{ and } m \neq 1$$

Quantity A	Quantity B
m^2	m^3

SOLUTION.
Use TACTIC 1. Replace m with numbers satisfying $m > 0$ and $m \neq 1$.

	Quantity A	Quantity B	Compare	Eliminate
Let $m = 2$	$2^2 = 4$	$2^3 = 8$	B is greater	A and C
Let $m = \dfrac{1}{2}$	$\left(\dfrac{1}{2}\right)^2 = \dfrac{1}{4}$	$\left(\dfrac{1}{2}\right)^3 = \dfrac{1}{8}$	A is greater	B

The answer is **D**.

EXAMPLE 5

Quantity A	Quantity B
$13y$	$15y$

SOLUTION.
Use TACTIC 1. There are no restrictions on y, so use the best numbers: 1, 0, –1.

	Quantity A	Quantity B	Compare	Eliminate
Let $y = 1$	$13(1) = 13$	$15(1) = 15$	B is greater	A and C
Let $y = 0$	$13(0) = 0$	$15(0) = 0$	They're equal	B

The answer is **D**.

EXAMPLE 6

Quantity A	Quantity B
$w + 11$	$w - 11$

SOLUTION.
Use TACTIC 1. There are no restrictions on w, so use the best numbers: 1, 0, –1.

	Quantity A	Quantity B	Compare	Eliminate
Let $w = 1$	$1 + 11 = 12$	$1 - 11 = -10$	A is greater	B and C
Let $w = 0$	$0 + 11 = 11$	$0 - 11 = -11$	A is greater	
Let $w = -1$	$-1 + 11 = 10$	$-1 - 11 = -12$	A is greater	

Guess **A**. We let w be a positive number, a negative number, and 0. Each time, Quantity A was greater. That's not proof, but it justifies an educated guess. [The answer *is* A. Clearly, $11 > -11$, and if we add w to each side, we get: $w + 11 > w - 11$.]

EXAMPLE 7

Quantity A	Quantity B
The perimeter of a rectangle whose area is 18	The perimeter of a rectangle whose area is 28

SOLUTION.

What's this question doing here? How can we use TACTIC 1? Where are the variables that we're supposed to replace? Well, each quantity is the perimeter of a rectangle, and the variables are the lengths and widths of these rectangles.

Quantity A	Quantity B	Compare	Eliminate
Choose a rectangle whose area is 18:	Choose a rectangle whose area is 28:		
The perimeter here is 9 + 2 + 9 + 2 = **22**	The perimeter here is 7 + 4 + 7 + 4 = **22**	Quantities A and B are equal	A and B

Keep Quantity B, but take a different rectangle of area 18 when evaluating Quantity A:

Perimeter = 3 + 6 + 3 + 6 = **18**	Perimeter = **22**	B is greater	C

The answer is **D**.

EXAMPLE 8

$$a = \frac{2}{3}t \qquad b = \frac{5}{6}t \qquad c = \frac{3}{5}b$$

Quantity A	Quantity B
$3a$	$4c$

SOLUTION.

Use TACTIC 1. First, try the easiest number: let $t = 0$. Then a, b, and c are each 0, and *in this case*, the quantities are equal — they're both 0. Eliminate A and B. Now, try another number for t. The obvious choice is 1, but then a, b, and c will all be fractions. To avoid this, let $t = 6$. Then, $a = \frac{2}{3}(6) = 4$, $b = \frac{5}{6}(6) = 5$, and $c = \frac{3}{5}(5) = 3$. This time, $3a = 3(4) = $ **12** and $4b = 4(3) = $ **12**. *Again, the two quantities are equal.* Choose **C**.

NOTE: You should consider answering this question directly (i.e., without plugging in numbers), *only if you are very comfortable with <u>both</u> fractions and elementary algebra.* Here's the solution:

$$c = \frac{3}{5}b = \frac{3}{5}\left(\frac{5}{6}t\right) = \frac{1}{2}t$$

Therefore, $2c = t$, and $4c = 2t$. Since $a = \frac{2}{3}t$, $3a = 2t$. So, $4c = 3a$. The answer is **C**.

TACTIC
2   Choose an Appropriate Number

This is just like TACTIC 1. We are replacing a variable with a number, but the variable isn't mentioned in the problem.

EXAMPLE 9

Every band member is either 15, 16, or 17 years old.
One third of the band members are 16, and
twice as many band members are 16 as 15.

Quantity A	Quantity B
The number of 17-year-old band members	The total number of 15- and 16-year-old band members

If the first sentence of Example 9 had been "There are n students in the school band, all of whom are 15, 16, or 17 years old," the problem would have been identical to this one. Using TACTIC 1, you could have replaced n with an easy-to-use number, such as 6, and solved: $\frac{1}{3}(6) = 2$ are 16 years old; 1 is 15, and the remaining 3 are 17. The answer is **C**.

The point of TACTIC 2 is that you can plug in numbers even if there are no variables. As discussed in TACTIC 3, Chapter 8, this is especially useful on problems involving percents, in which case 100 is a good number, and problems involving fractions, in which case the LCD of the fractions is a good choice. However, the use of TACTIC 2 is not limited to these situations. Try using TACTIC 2 on the following three problems.

EXAMPLE 10

The perimeter of a square and the
circumference of a circle are equal.

Quantity A	Quantity B
The area of the circle	The area of the square

SOLUTION.
First use TACTIC 1, Chapter 7: draw a diagram.

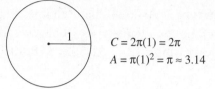

$$C = 2\pi(1) = 2\pi$$
$$A = \pi(1)^2 = \pi \approx 3.14$$

Then use TACTIC 2: choose an easy-to-use number. Let the radius of the circle be 1. Then its area is π. Let s be the side of the square:

$$P = 4s$$
$$A = s^2$$

$$4s = 2\pi \approx 6 \Rightarrow s \approx 1.5 \Rightarrow$$
$$\text{area of the square} \approx (1.5)^2 = 2.25$$

The answer is **A**.

EXAMPLE 11

Jen, Ken, and Len divided a cash prize.

Jen took 50% of the money and spent $\frac{3}{5}$ of what she took.

Ken took 40% of the money and spent $\frac{3}{4}$ of what he took.

Quantity A	Quantity B
The amount that Jen spent	The amount that Ken spent

SOLUTION.
Use TACTIC 2. Assume the prize was $100. Then Jen took $50 and spent $\frac{3}{5}$($50) = $30. Ken took $40 and spent $\frac{3}{4}$($40) = $30. The answer is **C**.

EXAMPLE 12

Eliane types twice as fast as Delphine.
Delphine charges 50% more per page than Eliane.

Quantity A	Quantity B
Amount Eliane earns in 9 hours	Amount Delphine earns in 12 hours

SOLUTION.

Use TACTIC 2. Choose appropriate numbers. Assume Delphine can type 1 page per hour and Eliane can type 2. Assume Eliane charges $1.00 per page and Delphine charges $1.50. Then in 9 hours, Eliane types 18 pages, earning **$18.00**. In 12 hours, Delphine types 12 pages, earning 12 × $1.50 = **$18.00**. The answer is **C**.

TACTIC

3   **Make the Problem Easier: Do the Same Thing to Each Quantity**

A quantitative comparison question can be treated as an equation or an inequality. Either:

> Quantity A < Quantity B, or
> Quantity A = Quantity B, or
> Quantity A > Quantity B

In solving an equation or an inequality, you can always add the same thing to each side or subtract the same thing from each side. Similarly, in solving a quantitative comparison, you can always add the same thing to quantities A and B or subtract the same thing from quantities A and B. You can also multiply or divide each side of an equation or inequality by the same number, *but in the case of <u>inequalities</u> you can do this only if the number is positive*. Since you don't know whether the quantities are equal or unequal, you cannot multiply or divide by a variable *unless you know that it is positive*. If quantities A and B are both positive you may square them or take their square roots.

To illustrate the proper use of TACTIC 3, we will give alternative solutions to examples 4, 5, and 6, which we already solved using TACTIC 1.

EXAMPLE 4

$$m > 0 \text{ and } m \neq 1$$

Quantity A	Quantity B
m^2	m^3

	Quantity A	Quantity B

SOLUTION.

Divide each quantity by m^2 (that's OK — m^2 is positive): $\dfrac{m^2}{m^2} = 1$ $\dfrac{m^3}{m^2} = m$

This is a much easier comparison. Which is greater, m or 1? We don't know. We know $m > 0$ and $m \neq 1$, but it could be greater than 1 or less than 1. The answer is **D**.

EXAMPLE 5

Quantity A	Quantity B
$13y$	$15y$

	Quantity A	Quantity B

SOLUTION.
Subtract $13y$ from each quantity: $13y - 13y = 0$ $15y - 13y = 2y$

   Since there are no restrictions on y, $2y$ could be greater than, less than, or equal to 0. The answer is **D**.

EXAMPLE 6

Quantity A	Quantity B
$w + 11$	$w - 11$

	Quantity A	Quantity B

SOLUTION.
Subtract w from each quantity: $(w + 11) - w = 11$ $(w - 11) - w = -11$

   Clearly, 11 is greater than -11. Quantity **A** is greater.
   Here are five more examples on which to practice TACTIC 3.

EXAMPLE 13

Quantity A	Quantity B
$\dfrac{1}{3} + \dfrac{1}{4} + \dfrac{1}{9}$	$\dfrac{1}{9} + \dfrac{1}{3} + \dfrac{1}{5}$

	Quantity A	Quantity B

SOLUTION.

Subtract $\dfrac{1}{3}$ and $\dfrac{1}{9}$ from each quantity: $\dfrac{\cancel{1}}{\cancel{3}} + \dfrac{1}{4} + \dfrac{\cancel{1}}{\cancel{9}}$ $\dfrac{\cancel{1}}{\cancel{9}} + \dfrac{\cancel{1}}{\cancel{3}} + \dfrac{1}{5}$

Since $\dfrac{1}{4} > \dfrac{1}{5}$, the answer is **A**.

EXAMPLE 14

Quantity A	Quantity B
$(43 + 59)(17 - 6)$	$(43 + 59)(17 + 6)$

	Quantity A	Quantity B

SOLUTION.

Divide each quantity by $(43 + 59)$: $\cancel{(43 + 59)}(17 - 6)$ $\cancel{(43 + 59)}(17 + 6)$

Clearly, $(17 + 6) > (17 - 6)$. The answer is **B**.

EXAMPLE 15

Quantity A	Quantity B
$(43 - 59)(43 - 49)$	$(43 - 59)(43 + 49)$

SOLUTION.

> ### CAUTION
>
> $(43 - 59)$ is negative, and you may not divide the two quantities by a negative number.

The easiest alternative is to note that Quantity A, being the product of 2 negative numbers, is positive, whereas Quantity B, being the product of a negative number and a positive number, is negative, and so Quantity A is greater.

EXAMPLE 16

a is a negative number

Quantity A	Quantity B
a^2	$-a^2$

	Quantity A	Quantity B

SOLUTION.

Add a^2 to each quantity: $a^2 + a^2 = 2a^2$ $-a^2 + a^2 = 0$

Since *a* is negative, $2a^2$ is positive. The answer is **A**.

EXAMPLE 17

Quantity A	Quantity B
$\dfrac{\sqrt{20}}{2}$	$\dfrac{5}{\sqrt{5}}$

	Quantity A	Quantity B

SOLUTION.

Square each quantity: $\left(\dfrac{\sqrt{20}}{2}\right)^2 = \dfrac{20}{4} = 5$ $\left(\dfrac{5}{\sqrt{5}}\right)^2 = \dfrac{25}{5} = 5$

The answer is **C**.

TACTIC

4

Ask "Could They Be Equal?" and "Must They Be Equal?"

TACTIC 4 has many applications, but is most useful when one of the quantities contains a variable and the other contains a number. In this situation ask yourself, "Could they be equal?" If the answer is "yes," eliminate A and B, and then ask, "Must they be equal?" If the second answer is "yes," then C is correct; if the second answer is "no," then choose D. When the answer to "Could they be equal?" is "no," we usually know right away what the correct answer is. In both questions, "Could they be equal" and "Must they be equal," the word *they* refers, of course, to quantities A and B.

Let's look at a few examples.

EXAMPLE 18

The sides of a triangle are 3, 4, and x

Quantity A	Quantity B
x	5

SOLUTION.
Could they be equal? Could $x = 5$? Of course. That's the all-important 3-4-5 right triangle. Eliminate A and B. Must they be equal? Must $x = 5$? If you're not sure, try drawing an acute or an obtuse triangle. The answer is No. Actually, x can be any number satisfying: $1 < x < 7$. (See KEY FACT J12, the triangle inequality, and the figure below.) The answer is **D**.

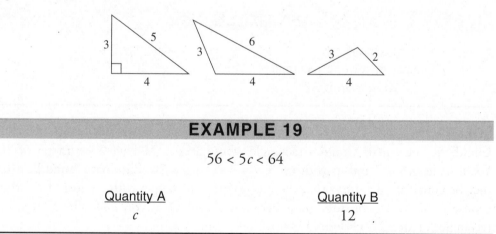

EXAMPLE 19

$$56 < 5c < 64$$

Quantity A	Quantity B
c	12

SOLUTION.
Could they be equal? Could $c = 12$? If $c = 12$, then $5c = 60$, so, yes, they could be equal. Eliminate A and B. Must they be equal? Must $c = 12$? Could c be more or less than 12? BE CAREFUL: $5 \times 11 = 55$, which is too small; and $5 \times 13 = 65$, which is too big. Therefore, the only *integer* that c could be is 12; but *c doesn't have to be an integer*. The *only* restriction is that $56 < 5c < 64$. If $5c$ were 58 or 61.6 or 63, then c would not be 12. The answer is **D**.

EXAMPLE 20

School A has 100 teachers and School B has 200 teachers.
Each school has more female teachers than male teachers.

Quantity A	Quantity B
The number of female teachers at School A	The number of female teachers at School B

SOLUTION.
Could they be equal? Could the number of female teachers be the same in both schools? No. More than half (i.e., more than 100) of School B's 200 teachers are female, but School A has only 100 teachers in all. The answer is **B**.

EXAMPLE 21

$$(m + 1)(m + 2)(m + 3) = 720$$

Quantity A	Quantity B
$m + 2$	10

SOLUTION.
Could they be equal? Could $m + 2 = 10$? No, if $m + 2 = 10$, then $m + 1 = 9$ and $m + 3 = 11$, and $9 \times 10 \times 11 = 990$, which is too big. The answer is *not* C, and since $m + 2$ clearly has to be smaller than 10, the answer is **B**.

EXAMPLE 22

Quantity A	Quantity B
The perimeter of a rectangle whose area is 21	20

SOLUTION.
Could they be equal? Could a rectangle whose area is 21 have a perimeter of 20? Yes, if its length is 7 and its width is 3: $7 + 3 + 7 + 3 = 20$. Eliminate A and B. Must they be equal? If you're *sure* that there is no other rectangle with an area of 21, then choose C; if you're *not* sure, guess between C and D; if you *know* there are other rectangles of area 21, choose D.

There are other possibilities — lots of them; here are a 7×3 rectangle and a few other rectangles whose areas are 21:

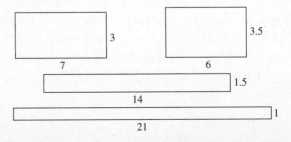

TACTIC
5 Don't Calculate: Compare

Avoid unnecessary calculations. You don't have to determine the exact values of Quantity A and Quantity B; you just have to compare them.

TACTIC 5 is the special application of TACTIC 7, Chapter 10 (Don't do more than you have to) to quantitative comparison questions. Using TACTIC 5 allows you to solve many quantitative comparisons without doing tedious calculations, thereby saving you valuable test time that you can use on other questions. *Before you start calculating,* stop, look at the quantities, and ask yourself, "Can I easily and quickly determine which quantity is greater without doing *any* arithmetic?" Consider Examples 23 and 24, which look very similar, but really aren't.

EXAMPLE 23

Quantity A	Quantity B
37×43	30×53

EXAMPLE 24

Quantity A	Quantity B
37×43	39×47

Example 23 is very easy. Just multiply: $37 \times 43 = 1591$ and $30 \times 53 = 1590$. The answer is **A**.

Example 24 is even easier. *Don't* multiply. In less time than it takes to do the multiplications, even with the calculator, you can see that $37 < 39$ and $43 < 47$, so clearly $37 \times 43 < 39 \times 47$. The answer is **B**. *You don't get any extra credit for taking the time to determine the value of each product!*

Remember: do not start calculating immediately. Always take a second or two to glance at each quantity. In Example 23 it's not at all clear which product is larger, so you have to multiply. In Example 24, however, no calculations are necessary.

These are problems on which poor test-takers do a lot of arithmetic and good test-takers think! Practicing TACTIC 5 will help you become a good test-taker.

Now, test your understanding of TACTIC 5 by solving these problems.

EXAMPLE 25

Quantity A	Quantity B
The number of years from 1776 to 1929	The number of years from 1767 to 1992

EXAMPLE 26

Quantity A	Quantity B
$45^2 + 25^2$	$(45 + 25)^2$

EXAMPLE 27

Quantity A	Quantity B
$45(35 + 65)$	$45 \times 35 + 45 \times 65$

EXAMPLE 28

Marianne earned a 75 on each of her first three math tests and an 80 on her fourth and fifth tests.

Quantity A	Quantity B
Marianne's average after 4 tests	Marianne's average after 5 tests

SOLUTIONS 25–28

Performing the Indicated Calculations	Using TACTIC 5 to Avoid Doing the Calculations
25. Quantity A: 1929 – 1776 = 153 Quantity B: 1992 – 1767 = 225 The answer is **B**.	25. The subtraction is easy enough, but why do it? The dates in Quantity **B** start earlier and end later. Clearly, they span more years. You don't need to know how many years. The answer is **B**.
26. Quantity A: $45^2 + 25^2 =$ 2025 + 625 = 2650 Quantity B: $(45 + 25)^2 =$ $70^2 = 4900$ The answer is **B**.	26. For *any positive numbers a* and *b*: $(a + b)^2 > a^2 + b^2$. You should do the calculations only if you don't know this fact. The answer is **B**.

Performing the Indicated Calculations	Using TACTIC 5 to Avoid Doing the Calculations
27. Quantity A: 45(35 + 65) = 45(100) = 4500 Quantity B: 45 × 35 + 45 × 65 = 1575 + 2925 = 4500 The answer is **C**.	27. This is just the distributive property (KEY FACT A20), which states that, for *any* numbers a, b, c: $a(b + c) = ab + ac$. The answer is **C**.
28. Quantity A: $$\frac{75 + 75 + 75 + 80}{4} = \frac{305}{4} = 76.25$$ Quantity B: $$\frac{75 + 75 + 75 + 80 + 80}{5} = \frac{385}{5} = 77$$ The answer is **B**.	28. Remember, you want to know which average is higher, *not* what the averages are. After 4 tests Marianne's average is clearly less than 80, so an 80 on the fifth test had to *raise* her average (KEY FACT E4). The answer is **B**.

Caution

TACTIC 5 is important, but *don't spend a lot of time looking for ways to avoid a simple calculation.*

TACTIC 6

Know When to Avoid Choice D

If Quantity A and Quantity B are both fixed numbers, the answer cannot be D.

Notice that D was not the correct answer to any of the six examples discussed under TACTIC 5. Those problems had no variables. The quantities were all specific numbers. In each of the next four examples, Quantity A and Quantity B are also fixed numbers. In each case, either the two numbers are equal or one is greater than the other. It can *always* be determined, and so D *cannot be the correct answer to any of these problems*. If, while taking the GRE, you find a problem of this type that you can't solve, just guess: A, B, or C. Now try these four examples.

EXAMPLE 29

Quantity A	Quantity B
The number of seconds in one day	The number of days in one century

---

EXAMPLE 30

Quantity A	Quantity B
The area of a square whose sides are 4	Twice the area of an equilateral triangle whose sides are 4

EXAMPLE 31

Three fair coins are flipped.

Quantity A	Quantity B
The probability of getting one head	The probability of getting two heads

---

EXAMPLE 32

Quantity A	Quantity B
The time it takes to drive 40 miles at 35 mph	The time it takes to drive 35 miles at 40 mph

---

Here's the important point to remember: don't choose D because *you* can't determine which quantity is bigger; choose D only if *nobody* could determine it. *You* may or may not know how to compute the number of seconds in a day, the area of an equilateral triangle, or a certain probability, but *these calculations can be made.*

SOLUTIONS 29–32

Direct Calculation	**Solution Using Various TACTICS**
29. Recall the facts you need and calculate. 60 seconds = 1 minute, 60 minutes = 1 hour, 24 hours = 1 day, 365 days = 1 year, and 100 years = 1 century. Quantity A: $60 \times 60 \times 24 = 86,400$ Quantity B: $365 \times 100 = 36,500$ Even if we throw in some days for leap years, the answer is clearly **A**.	29. The point of TACTIC 6 is that even if you have no idea how to calculate the number of seconds in a day, you can eliminate two choices. The answer *cannot* be D, and it would be an incredible coincidence if these two quantities were actually equal, so don't choose C. *Guess* between A and B.
30. Calculate both areas. (See KEY FACT J15 for the easy way to find the area of an equilateral triangle.) Quantity A: $A = s^2 = 4^2 = 16$ Quantity B: $$A = \frac{s^2\sqrt{3}}{4} = \frac{4^2\sqrt{3}}{4} = 4\sqrt{3};$$ and *twice A* is $8\sqrt{3}$. Since $\sqrt{3} \approx 1.7$, $8\sqrt{3} \approx 13.6$. The answer is **A**.	30. Use TACTIC 5: don't calculate— draw a diagram and then compare. Since the height of the triangle is less than 4, its area is less than $\frac{1}{2}(4)(4) = 8$, and twice its area is less than 16, the area of the square. The answer is **A**. (If you don't see that, and just have to guess in order to move on, be sure not to guess D.)

Direct Calculation	**Solution Using Various TACTICS**
31. When a coin is flipped 3 times, there are 8 possible outcomes: HHH, HHT, HTH, HTT, THH, THT, TTH, and TTT. Of these, 3 have one head and 3 have two heads. Each probability is $\frac{3}{8}$. The answer is **C**.	31. Don't forget TACTIC 5. Even if you know how, you don't *have to* calculate the probabilities. When 3 coins are flipped, getting two heads means getting one tail. Therefore, the probability of two heads equals the probability of one tail, which by symmetry equals the probability of one head. The answer is **C**. (If you don't remember anything about probability, TACTIC 5 at least allows you to eliminate D before you guess.)
32. Since $d = rt$, $t = \dfrac{d}{r}$ [see Sect. 11-H]. Quantity A: $\dfrac{40}{35}$ hours—more than 1 hour. Quantity B: $\dfrac{35}{40}$ hours—less than 1 hour. The answer is **A**.	32. You *do* need to know these formulas, but *not* for this problem. At 35 mph it takes *more than an hour* to drive 40 miles. At 40 mph it takes *less than an hour* to drive 35 miles. Choose **A**.

Practice Exercises

Quantitative Comparison Questions

> Ⓐ Quantity A is greater.
> Ⓑ Quantity B is greater.
> Ⓒ Quantities A and B are equal.
> Ⓓ It is impossible to determine which quantity is greater.

Quantity A	Quantity B
1. 197 + 398 + 586	203 + 405 + 607

$$x > 0$$

Quantity A	Quantity B
2. $10x$	$\dfrac{10}{x}$

Quantity A	Quantity B
The time that it takes to type 7 pages at a rate of 6 pages per hour	The time that it takes to type 6 pages at a rate of 7 pages per hour
3.	

$$cd < 0$$

Quantity A	Quantity B
4. $(c + d)^2$	$c^2 + d^2$

a, *b*, and *c* are the measures of the angles of isosceles triangle *ABC*.
x, *y*, and *z* are the measures of the angles of right triangle *XYZ*.

Quantity A	Quantity B
The average of	The average of
5. *a*, *b*, and *c*	*x*, *y*, and *z*

$$b < 0$$

Quantity A	Quantity B
6. $6b$	b^6

Quantity A	Quantity B
The area of a circle	The area of a circle
7. whose radius is 17	whose diameter is 35

Line *k* goes through (1,1) and (5,2).
Line *m* is perpendicular to *k*.

Quantity A	Quantity B
The slope of	The slope of
8. line *k*	line *m*

x is a positive integer

Quantity A	Quantity B
The number of multiples of 6 between 100 and *x* + 100	The number of multiples of 9 between 100 and *x* + 100
9.	

$$x + y = 5$$
$$y - x = -5$$

Quantity A	Quantity B
10. *y*	0

Quantity A	Quantity B
11. $\dfrac{7}{8}$	$\left(\dfrac{7}{8}\right)^5$

O is the center of the circle of radius 6. *OXYZ* is a square.

Quantity A	Quantity B
The area of the	12
12. shaded region	

The number of square inches in the
surface area of a cube is equal to the
number of cubic inches in its volume.

Quantity A	Quantity B
The length of an edge of the cube	6 inches

13.

$1 < x < 4$

Quantity A	Quantity B
14. πx	x^2

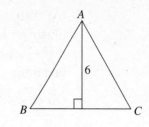

$AB = AC$

Quantity A	Quantity B
The area of $\triangle ABC$	3

15.

ANSWER KEY

1. **B**	4. **B**	7. **B**	10. **C**	13. **C**
2. **D**	5. **C**	8. **A**	11. **A**	14. **D**
3. **A**	6. **B**	9. **D**	12. **B**	15. **D**

ANSWER EXPLANATIONS

The direct mathematical solution to a problem is almost always the preferable one, so it is given first. It is often followed by one or more alternative solutions, indicated by a double asterisk (**), based on the various tactics discussed in this chapter. Occasionally, a solution based on one of the tactics is much easier than the straightforward one. In that case, it is given first.

1. **(B)** Using the onscreen calculator, this can easily be solved in 20 or 30 seconds by adding, but in only 5 seconds by thinking! Use TACTIC 5: don't calculate; compare. Each of the three numbers in Quantity B is greater than the corresponding numbers in Quantity A.

2. **(D)** Use TACTIC 1. When $x = 1$, the quantities are equal; when $x = 2$, they aren't.
   **Use TACTIC 3

	Quantity A	Quantity B
	$10x$	$\dfrac{10}{x}$
Multiply each quantity by x (this is OK since $x > 0$):	$10x^2$	10
Divide each quantity by 10:	x^2	1

   This is a much easier comparison. x^2 *could* equal 1, but doesn't have to. The answer is Choice D.

3. **(A)** You can easily calculate each of the times — divide 7 by 6 to evaluate Quantity A, and 6 by 7 in Quantity B. However, it is easier to just observe that Quantity A is more than one hour, whereas Quantity B is less than one hour.

4. **(B)** Use TACTIC 3

	Quantity A	Quantity B
Expand Quantity A:	$(c + d)^2 =$	
	$c^2 + 2cd + d^2$	$c^2 + d^2$
Subtract $c^2 + d^2$ from each quantity:	$2cd$	0

Since it is given that $cd < 0$, so is $2cd$.

   **If you can't expand $(c + d)^2$, then use TACTIC 1. Replace c and d with numbers satisfying $cd < 0$.

	Quantity A	Quantity B	Compare	Eliminate
Let $c = 1$ and $d = -1$	$(1 + -1)^2 = 0$	$1^2 + (-1)^2 =$ $1 + 1 = 2$	B is greater	A and C
Let $c = 3$ and $d = -5$	$(3 + -5)^2 =$ $(-2)^2 = 4$	$3^2 + (-5)^2 =$ $9 + 25 = 34$	B is greater	

Both times Quantity B was greater: choose B.

5. **(C)** The average of 3 numbers is their sum divided by 3. Since in *any* triangle the sum of the measures of the 3 angles is 180°, the average in each quantity is equal to $180 \div 3 = 60$.

   **Use TACTIC 1. Pick values for the measures of the angles. For example, in isosceles $\triangle ABC$ choose 70, 70, 40; in right $\triangle XYZ$, choose 30, 60, 90. Each average is 60. Choose C.

6. **(B)** Since $b < 0$, $6b$ is negative, whereas b^6 is positive.

   **Use TACTIC 1. Replace b with numbers satisfying $b < 0$.

	Quantity A	Quantity B	Compare	Eliminate
Let $b = -1$	$6(-1) = -6$	$(-1)^6 = 1$	B is greater	A and C
Let $b = -2$	$6(-2) = -12$	$(-2)^6 = 64$	B is greater	

Both times Quantity B was greater: choose B.

7. **(B)** Use TACTIC 5: don't calculate the two areas; compare them. The circle in Quantity A is the area of a circle whose radius is 17 and whose diameter is 34. Quantity B is the area of a circle whose diameter is 35, and so is clearly greater.

8. **(A)** Use TACTIC 5: don't calculate either slope. Quickly, make a rough sketch of line *k*, going through (1,1) and (5,2), and draw line *m* perpendicular to it.

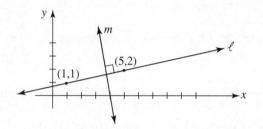

Line *k* has a positive slope (it slopes upward), whereas line *m* has a negative slope (it slopes downward). Quantity A is greater.

[Note: The slope of *k* is $\frac{1}{4}$ and the slope of *m* is –4, but you don't need to calculate either one. See Section 11-N for all the facts you need to know about slopes.]

   **If you don't know this fact about slopes, use TACTIC 6. The answer cannot be Choice D, and if two lines intersect, their slopes cannot be equal, so eliminate Choice C. Guess Choice A or B.

9. **(D)** Every sixth integer is a multiple of 6 and every ninth integer is a multiple of 9, so in a large interval there will be many more multiples of 6. But in a very small interval, there might be none or possibly just one of each.

   **Use TACTIC 1. Let *x* = 1. Between 100 and 101 there are *no* multiples of 6 and *no* multiples of 9. Eliminate Choices A and B. Choose a large number for *x*: 100, for example. Between 100 and 200 there are many more multiples of 6 than there are multiples of 9. Eliminate Choice C.

10. **(C)** Add the equations.

$$x + y = 5$$
$$+ \quad y - x = -5$$
$$\overline{\hphantom{+ \quad} 2y = 0}$$

Since $2y = 0$, $y = 0$.

   **Use TACTIC 4. Could $y = 0$? In each equation, if $y = 0$, then $x = -5$. So, *y* can equal 0. Eliminate Choices A and B, and either guess between Choices C and D or continue. Must $y = 0$? Yes, when you have two linear equations in two variables, there is only one solution, so nothing else is possible.

11. **(A)** With a calculator, you can multiply $\frac{7}{8} \times \frac{7}{8} \times \frac{7}{8} \times \frac{7}{8} \times \frac{7}{8}$, but it is annoying and time-consuming. However, you can avoid the arithmetic, if you know KEY FACT A24:

If $0 < x < 1$ and $n > 1$, then $x^n < x$.

Since $\frac{7}{8} < 1$, then $\left(\frac{7}{8}\right)^5 < \frac{7}{8}$.

12. **(B)** The area of the shaded region is the area of quarter-circle *AOB* minus the area of the square. Since *r* = *OA* = 6, the area of the quarter-circle is $\frac{1}{4}\pi r^2 = \frac{1}{4}36\pi = 9\pi$. *OY*, the diagonal of the square, is 6 (since it is a radius of the circle), so *OZ*, the side of the square, is $\frac{6}{\sqrt{2}}$ [See KEY FACT J8]. So the area of the square is $\left(\frac{6}{\sqrt{2}}\right)^2 = \frac{36}{2} = 18$. Finally, the area of the shaded region is $9\pi - 18$, which is approximately 10.

    **The solution above requires several steps. [See Sections 11-J, K, L to review any of the facts used.] If you can't reason through this, you still should be able to answer this question correctly. Use TACTIC 6. The shaded region has a definite area, which is either 12, more than 12, or less than 12. Eliminate D. Also, the area of a curved region almost always involves π, so assume the area isn't exactly 12. Eliminate Choice C. You can now *guess* between Choices A and B, but if you trust the diagram and know a little bit you can improve your guess. If you know that the area of the circle is 36π, so that the quarter-circle is 9π or about 28, you can estimate the shaded region. It's well less than half of the quarter-circle, so less than 14 and probably less than 12. Guess Choice B.

13. **(C)** Use TACTIC 4. Could the edge be 6? Test it. If each edge is 6, the area of each face is 6 × 6 = 36, and since a cube has 6 faces, the total surface area is 6 × 36 = 216. The volume is 6^3 = 216. So the quantities could be equal. Eliminate Choices A and B. If you have a sense that this is the only cube with this property, choose C. In fact, if you had no idea how to do this, you might use TACTIC 6, assume that there is only one way, eliminate Choice D, and then guess C. The direct solution is simple enough if you know the formulas. If *e* is the length of an edge of the cube, then the area is $6e^2$ and the volume is e^3: $6e^2 = e^3 \Rightarrow 6 = e$.

14. **(D)** There are several ways to answer this question. Use TACTIC 1: plug in a number for *x*. If *x* = 2, Quantity A is 2π, which is slightly more than 6, and Quantity B is 2^2 = 4. Quantity A is greater: eliminate Choices B and C. Must Quantity A be greater? If the only other number you try is *x* = 3, you'll think so, because 3^2 = 9, but $3\pi > 9$. But remember, *x* does not have to be an integer: $3.9^2 > 15$, whereas $3.9\pi < 4\pi$, which is a little over 12.

    **Use TACTIC 4. Could $\pi x = x^2$? Yes, if $x = \pi$. Must $x = \pi$? No.

    **Use TACTIC 3. Divide each quantity by *x*: Now Quantity A is π and Quantity B is *x*. Which is bigger, π or *x*? We cannot tell.

15. **(D)** Use TACTIC 4. Could the area of $\triangle ABC = 3$? Since the height is 6, the area would be 3 only if the base were 1: $\frac{1}{2}(1)(6) = 3$. Could $BC = 1$? Sure (see the figure). Must the base be 1? Of course not.

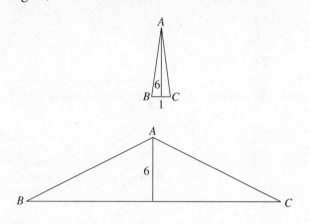

Data Interpretation Questions

Three of the 20 questions in each quantitative section of the GRE are data interpretation questions. As their name suggests, these questions are always based on the information that is presented in some form of a graph or a chart. Occasionally, the data are presented in a chart or table, but much more often, they are presented graphically. The most common types of graphs are

- line graphs
- bar graphs
- circle graphs

In each section, the data interpretation questions are three consecutive questions, say questions 14, 15, and 16, all of which refer to the same set of graphs or charts.

When the first data interpretation question appears, either the graphs will be on the left-hand side of the screen, and the question will be on the right-hand side, or the graphs will be at the top of the screen and the question will be below them. It is possible, but unlikely, that you will have to scroll down in order to see all of the data. After you answer the first question, a second question will replace it on the right-hand side (or the bottom) of the screen; the graphs, of course, will still be on the screen for you to refer to.

The tactics discussed in this chapter can be applied to any type of data, no matter how they are displayed. In the practice exercises at the end of the chapter, there are data interpretation questions based on the types of graphs that normally appear on the GRE. Carefully, read through the answer explanations for each exercise, so that you learn the best way to handle each type of graph.

Infrequently, an easy data interpretation question will require only that you read the graph and find a numerical fact that is displayed. Usually, however, you will have to do some calculation on the data that you are analyzing. In harder questions, you may be given hypothetical situations and asked to make inferences based on the information provided in the given graphs.

Most data interpretation questions are multiple-choice questions, but some could be multiple-answer or numeric entry questions. They are never quantitative comparisons.

Testing Tactics

The four questions that follow will be used to illustrate the tactics that you should use in answering data interpretation questions. Remember, however, that on the GRE there will always be three questions that refer to a particular graph or set of graphs.

Questions 1–4 refer to the following graphs.

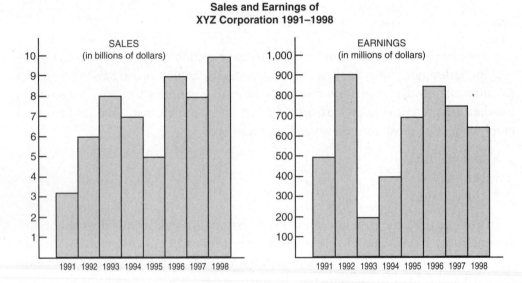

Sales and Earnings of
XYZ Corporation 1991–1998

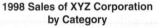

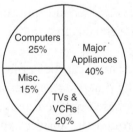

1998 Sales of XYZ Corporation
by Category

1. What is the average (arithmetic mean) in billions of dollars of the sales of XYZ Corporation for the period 1991–1998?
   Ⓐ 5.5   Ⓑ 6.0   Ⓒ 7.0   Ⓓ 8.0   Ⓔ 8.5

2. For which year was the percentage increase in earnings from the previous year the greatest?
   Ⓐ 1992   Ⓑ 1993   Ⓒ 1994   Ⓓ 1995   Ⓔ 1996

3. Which of the following statements can be deduced from the data in the given charts and circle graph?

Indicate *all* such statements.

- [A] Sales of major appliances in 1998 exceeded total sales in 1991.
- [B] Earnings for the year in which earnings were greatest were more than sales for the year in which sales were lowest.
- [C] If in 1998, the sales of major appliances had been 10% less, and the sales of computers had been 10% greater, the sales of major appliances would have been less than the sales of computers.

4. What was the ratio of earnings to sales in 1993?

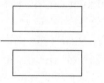

TACTIC

First Read the Titles

When the first data interpretation question appears on the screen, do not even read it! Before you attempt to answer a data interpretation question, take 15 to 30 seconds to study the graphs. Try to get a general idea about the information that is being displayed.

Observe that the bar graphs on which questions 1–4 are based present two different sets of data. The bar graph on the left-hand side provides information about the sales of XYZ Corporation, and the right-hand graph provides information about the corporation's earnings. Also, note that whereas sales are given in billions of dollars, earnings are given in millions of dollars. Finally, the circle graph gives a breakdown by category of the sales of XYZ Corporation for one particular year.

TACTIC

2 Don't Confuse Percents and Numbers

Many students make mistakes on data interpretation questions because they don't distinguish between absolute numbers and percents. Although few students would look at the circle graph shown and think that XYZ Corporation sold 25 computers in 1998, many would mistakenly think that it sold 15% more major appliances than computers.

The problem is particularly serious when the questions involve percent increases or percent decreases. In question 2 you are not asked for the year in which the increase in earnings from the previous year was the greatest. You are asked for the year in which the percent increase in earnings was the greatest. A quick glance at the right-hand graph reveals that the greatest increase occurred from 1991 to 1992 when earnings jumped by $400 million. However, when we solve this problem in the discussion of TACTIC 3, you will see that Choice A is not the correct answer.

NOTE: Since many data interpretation questions involve percents, you should carefully study Section 11-C, and be sure that you know all of the tactics for solving percent problems. In particular, always try to use the number 100 or 1000, since it is so easy to mentally calculate percents of powers of 10.

TACTIC

3   Whenever Possible, Estimate

Although you have access to the onscreen calculator, when you take the GRE, you will not be expected to do complicated or lengthy calculations. Often, thinking and using some common sense can save you considerable time. For example, it may seem that in order to get the correct answer to question 2, you have to calculate five different percents. In fact, you only need to do one calculation, and that one you can do in your head!

Just looking at the Earnings bar graph, it is clear that the only possible answers are 1992, 1994, and 1995, the three years in which there was a significant increase in earnings from the year before. From 1993 to 1994 expenditures doubled, from $200 million to $400 million — an increase of 100%. From 1991 to 1992 expenditures increased by $400 million (from $500 million to $900 million), but that is less than a 100% increase (we don't care how much less). From 1994 to 1995 expenditures increased by $300 million (from $400 million to $700 million); but again, this is less than a 100% increase. The answer is **C**.

TACTIC

4   Do Each Calculation Separately

As in all multiple-answer questions, question 3 requires you to determine which of the statements are true. The key is to work with the statements individually.

To determine whether or not statement A is true, look at both the Sales bar graph and the circle graph. In 1998, total sales were $10 billion, and sales of major appliances accounted for 40% of the total: 40% of $10 billion = $4 billion. This exceeds the $3 billion total sales figure for 1991, so statement A is true.

In 1992, the year in which earnings were greatest, earnings were $900 million. In 1991, the year in which sales were lowest, sales were $3 billion, which is much greater than $900 million. Statement B is false.

In 1998, sales of major appliances were $4 billion. If they had been 10% less, they would have been $3.6 billion. That year, sales of computers were $2.5 billion (25% of $10 billion). If computer sales had increased by 10%, sales would have increased by $0.25 billion to $2.75 billion. Statement C is false.

The answer is **A**.

TACTIC

5   Use Only the Information Given

You must base your answer to each question only on the information in the given charts and graphs. It is unlikely that you have any preconceived notion as to the sales of XYZ Corporation, but you might think that you know the population of the

United States for a particular year or the percent of women currently in the workplace. If your knowledge contradicts any of the data presented in the graphs, ignore what you know. First of all, you may be mistaken; but more important, the data may refer to a different, unspecified location or year. In any event, *always* base your answers on the given data.

TACTIC 6 — Always Use the Proper Units

In answering question 4, observe that earnings are given in millions, while sales are in billions. If you answer too quickly, you might say that in 1993 earnings were 200 and sales were 8, and conclude that the desired ratio is $\frac{200}{8} = \frac{25}{1}$. You will avoid this mistake if you keep track of units: earnings were 200 *million* dollars, whereas sales were 8 *billion* dollars. The correct ratio is

$$\frac{200,000,000}{8,000,000,000} = \frac{2}{80} = \frac{1}{40}.$$

Enter 1 in the box for the numerator and 40 in the box for the denominator.

TACTIC 7 — Be Sure That Your Answer Is Reasonable

Before clicking on your answer, take a second to be sure that it is reasonable. For example, in question 4, from the logic of the situation, you should realize that earnings can't exceed sales. The desired ratio, therefore, must be less than 1. If you use the wrong units (see TACTIC 6, above), your initial thought might be to enter $\frac{25}{1}$. By testing your answer for reasonableness, you will realize that you made a mistake.

Remember that if you don't know how to solve a problem, you should always guess. Before guessing, however, check to see if one or more of the choices are unreasonable. If so, eliminate them. For example, if you forget how to calculate a percent increase, you would have to guess at question 2. But before guessing wildly, you should at least eliminate Choice B, since from 1992 to 1993 earnings decreased.

TACTIC 8 — Try to Visualize the Answer

Because graphs and tables present data in a form that enables you to readily see relationships and to make quick comparisons, you can often avoid doing any calculations. Whenever possible, use your eye instead of your computational skills.

For example, to answer question 1, rather than reading the sales figures in the bar graph on the left for each of the eight years, adding them, and then dividing by 8, visualize the situation. Where could you draw a horizontal line across the graph so that there would be the same amount of gray area above the line as white area below it? Imagine a horizontal line drawn through the 7 on the vertical axis. The portions of the bars above the line for 1993 and 1996–1998 are just about exactly the same size as the white areas below the line for 1991, 1992, and 1994. The answer is **C**.

Practice Exercises

Data Interpretation Questions

On the GRE there will typically be three questions based on any set of graphs. Accordingly, in each section of the model tests in this book, there are three data interpretation questions, each referring to the same set of graphs. However, to illustrate the variety of questions that can be asked, in this exercise set, for some of the graphs there are only two questions.

Questions 1–2 refer to the following graphs.

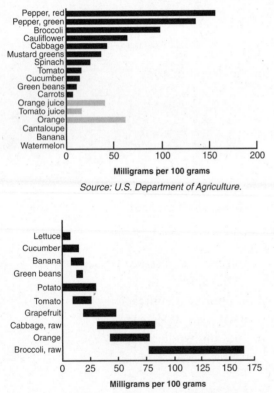

Source: U.S. Department of Agriculture.

Source: U.S. Department of Agriculture.

1. What is the ratio of the amount of Vitamin C in 500 grams of orange to the amount of Vitamin C in 500 grams of orange juice?

   Ⓐ 4:7
   Ⓑ 1:1
   Ⓒ 7:4
   Ⓓ 2:1
   Ⓔ 4:1

2. How many grams of tomato would you have to eat to be certain of getting more vitamin C than you would get by eating 100 grams of raw broccoli?

   Ⓐ 300
   Ⓑ 500
   Ⓒ 750
   Ⓓ 1200
   Ⓔ 1650

Questions 3–4 refer to the following graphs.

Percentage of students who reported spending time on homework and watching television

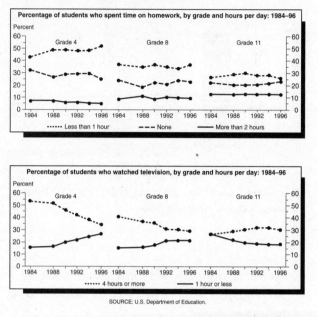

Questions 5–6 refer to the following graph.

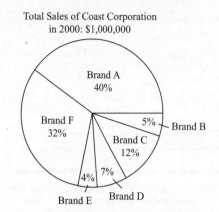

3. In 1996, what percent of fourth-graders did between 1 and 2 hours of homework per day?

   Ⓐ 5%

   Ⓑ 15%

   Ⓒ 25%

   Ⓓ 40%

   Ⓔ 55%

4. If in 1984 there were 2,000,000 eleventh-graders, and if between 1984 and 1996 the number of eleventh-graders increased by 10%, then approximately how many fewer eleventh-graders watched 1 hour or less of television in 1996 than in 1984?

   Ⓐ 25,000

   Ⓑ 50,000

   Ⓒ 75,000

   Ⓓ 100,000

   Ⓔ 150,000

5. If the above circle graph were drawn to scale, then which of the following is closest to the difference in the degree measurements of the central angle of the sector representing Brand C and the central angle of the sector representing Brand D?

   Ⓐ 5°

   Ⓑ 12°

   Ⓒ 18°

   Ⓓ 25°

   Ⓔ 43°

6. The total sales of Coast Corporation in 2005 were 50% higher than in 2000. If the dollar value of the sales of Brand A was 25% higher in 2005 than in 2000, then the sales of Brand A accounted for what percentage of total sales in 2005?

   Ⓐ 20%

   Ⓑ 25%

   Ⓒ $33\frac{1}{3}$%

   Ⓓ 40%

   Ⓔ 50%

Questions 7–8 refer to the following graphs.

Questions 9–10 refer to the following graph.

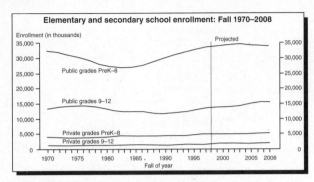

Elementary and secondary school enrollment: Fall 1970–2008

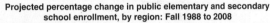

Projected percentage change in public elementary and secondary school enrollment, by region: Fall 1988 to 2008

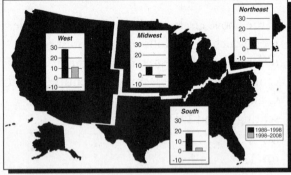

SOURCE: U.S. Department of Education, National Center for Education Statistics.

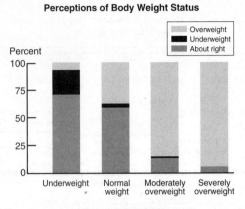

Perceptions of Body Weight Status

Actual weight status

Perceived compared with actual weight status of adult females.

Source: U.S. Department of Agriculture.

7. To the nearest million, how many more students were enrolled in school — both public and private, preK–12 — in 1970 than in 1988?

  Ⓐ 3,000,000
  Ⓑ 6,000,000
  Ⓒ 10,000,000
  Ⓓ 44,000,000
  Ⓔ 51,000,000

8. In 1988 there were 40,000,000 public school students in the United States, of whom 22% lived in the West. Approximately, how many public school students are projected to be living in the West in 2008?

  Ⓐ 9,000,000
  Ⓑ 12,000,000
  Ⓒ 15,000,000
  Ⓓ 24,000,000
  Ⓔ 66,000,000

9. To the nearest 5%, what percent of under-weight adult females perceive themselves to be underweight?

 %

10. The members of which of the four groups had the least accurate perception of their body weight?

  Ⓐ Underweight
  Ⓑ Normal weight
  Ⓒ Moderately overweight
  Ⓓ Severely overweight
  Ⓔ It cannot be determined from the information given in the graph.

Questions 11–12 refer to the following table.

In 1979, residents of New York City paid both New York State and New York City tax. Residents of New York State who lived and worked outside of New York City paid only New York State tax.

Tax Rate Schedules for 1979

New York State						City of New York					
Taxable Income						**Taxable Income**					
over	**but not over**			**Amount of Tax**		**over**	**but not over**			**Amount of Tax**	
$ 0	$1,000			2%	of taxable income	$ 0	$1,000			0.9%	of taxable income
1,000	3,000	$20	plus	3%	of excess over $1,000	1,000	3,000	$ 9	plus	1.4%	of excess over $1,000
3,000	5,000	80	plus	4%	of excess over 3,000	3,000	5,000	37	plus	1.8%	of excess over 3,000
5,000	7,000	160	plus	5%	of excess over 5,000	5,000	7,000	73	plus	2.0%	of excess over 5,000
7,000	9,000	260	plus	6%	of excess over 7,000	7,000	9,000	113	plus	2.3%	of excess over 7,000
9,000	11,000	380	plus	7%	of excess over 9,000	9,000	11,000	159	plus	2.5%	of excess over 9,000
11,000	13,000	520	plus	8%	of excess over 11,000	11,000	13,000	209	plus	2.7%	of excess over 11,000
13,000	15,000	680	plus	9%	of excess over 13,000	13,000	15,000	263	plus	2.9%	of excess over 13,000
15,000	17,000	860	plus	10%	of excess over 15,000	15,000	17,000	321	plus	3.1%	of excess over 15,000
17,000	19,000	1,060	plus	11%	of excess over 17,000	17,000	19,000	383	plus	3.3%	of excess over 17,000
19,000	21,000	1,280	plus	12%	of excess over 19,000	19,000	21,000	449	plus	3.5%	of excess over 19,000
21,000	23,000	1,520	plus	13%	of excess over 21,000	21,000	23,000	519	plus	3.8%	of excess over 21,000
23,000		1,780	plus	14%	of excess over 23,000	23,000	25,000	595	plus	4.0%	of excess over 23,000
						25,000		675	plus	4.3%	of excess over 25,000

11. In 1979 how much tax, in dollars, would a resident of New York State who lived and worked outside New York City have paid on a taxable income of $16,100?

    ☐ dollars

12. In 1979, how much more total tax would a resident of New York City who had a taxable income of $36,500 pay, compared to a resident of New York City who had a taxable income of $36,000?

    Ⓐ $21.50
    Ⓑ $43
    Ⓒ $70
    Ⓓ $91.50
    Ⓔ $183

Questions 13–14 refer to the following tables.

Questions 15–16 refer to the following graph.

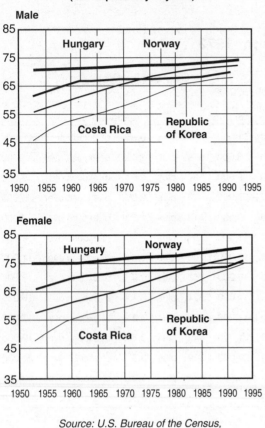

Years of Life Expectancy at Birth
(Life expectancy in years)

Source: U.S. Bureau of the Census,
Center for International Research.

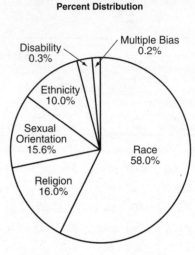

Bias-Motivated Offenses 1998
Percent Distribution

Source: U.S. Department of Justice,
Federal Bureau of Investigation.

13. For how many of the countries listed in the graphs is it true that the life expectancy of a female born in 1955 was higher than the life expectancy of a male born in 1990?

Ⓐ None
Ⓑ 1
Ⓒ 2
Ⓓ 3
Ⓔ 4

14. By sex and nationality, who had the greatest increase in life expectancy between 1955 and 1990?

Ⓐ A Korean female
Ⓑ A Korean male
Ⓒ A Costa Rican female
Ⓓ A Costa Rican male
Ⓔ A Norwegian female

15. If in 1998 there were 10,000 bias-motivated offenses based on ethnicity, how many more offenses were based on religion than on sexual orientation?

Ⓐ 4
Ⓑ 40
Ⓒ 400
Ⓓ 4000
Ⓔ 40,000

16. If after further analysis it was determined that between 25% and 50% of the offenses included under Religion were, in fact, not bias-motivated, and those offenses were removed from the study, which of the following could be the percentage of bias-motivated offenses based on race?

Indicate *all* such percentages.

A 59%
B 60%
C 61%
D 62%
E 63%
F 64%
G 65%

ANSWER KEY

1. **C**	4. **E**	7. **B**	10. **A**	· 13. **B**	16. **C, D, E**
2. **E**	5. **C**	8. **B**	11. **970**	14. **A**	
3. **B**	6. **C**	9. **25**	12. **D**	15. **C**	

ANSWER EXPLANATIONS

1. **(C)** According to the graph on the left, there are approximately 70 milligrams of vitamin C in 100 grams of orange and 40 milligrams in the same amount of orange juice. This is a ratio of 70:40 = 7:4. Since the question refers to the same amount of orange and orange juice (500 grams), the ratio is unchanged.

2. **(E)** From the graph on the right, you can see that by eating 100 grams of raw broccoli, you could receive as much as 165 milligrams of vitamin C. Since 100 grams of tomato could have as little as 10 milligrams of vitamin C, you would have to eat 1650 grams of tomato to be sure of getting 165 milligrams of vitamin C.

3. **(B)** From the top graph, we see that among fourth-graders in 1996:

   25% did no homework;
   55% did less than 1 hour;
    5% did more than 2 hours.

   This accounts for 85% of the fourth-graders; the other 15% did between 1 and 2 hours of homework per day.

4. **(E)** In 1984, approximately 540,000 eleventh-graders watched television 1 hour or less per day (27% of 2,000,000). By 1996, the number of eleventh-graders had increased by 10% to 2,200,000, but the percent of them who watched television 1 hour or less per day decreased to about 18%: 18% of 2,200,000 is 396,000. This is a decrease of 144,000, or approximately 150,000.

5. **(C)** The central angle of the sector representing Brand C is 12% of 360°:

   $(0.12) \times 360° = 43.2°$

   The central angle of the sector representing Brand D is 7% of 360°.

   $(0.7) \times 360° = 25.2°$

   Finally, $43.2° \times 25.2° = 18°$

   ****Note this can be done in one step by noticing that the percentage difference between Brands C and D is 5% and 5% of 360 is $(0.05) \times 380 = 18$.

6. **(C)** Since total sales in 2000 were $1,000,000, in 2005 sales were $1,500,000 (a 50% increase).

   In 2000, sales of Brand A were $400,000 (40% of $1,000,000).

   In 2005 sales of Brand A were $500,000 (25% or $\frac{1}{4}$ more than in 2000).

   Finally, $500,000 is $\frac{1}{3}$ or $33\frac{1}{3}$% of $1,500,000.

7. **(B)** Reading from the top graph, we get the following enrollment figures:

	1970	1988
Public PreK–8	33,000,000	28,000,000
Public 9–12	13,000,000	12,000,000
Private PreK–8	4,000,000	4,000,000
Private 9–12	1,000,000	1,000,000
Total	51,000,000	45,000,000

51,000,000 – 45,000,000 = 6,000,000.

8. **(B)** In 1988, 8,800,000 (22% of 40,000,000) students lived in the West. From 1988–1998 this figure increased by 27% — for simplicity use 25%: an additional 2,200,000 students; so the total was then 11,000,000. The projected increase from 1998–2008 is about 10%, so the number will grow by 1,100,000 to 12,100,000.

9. **25** The bar representing underweight adult females who perceive themselves to be underweight extends from about 70% to about 95%, a range of approximately 25%.

10. **(A)** Almost all overweight females correctly considered themselves to be overweight; and more than half of all females of normal weight correctly considered themselves "about right." But nearly 70% of underweight adult females inaccurately considered themselves "about right."

11. **970** Referring only to the New York State table, we see that the amount of tax on a taxable income between $15,000 and $17,000 was $860 plus 10% of the excess over $15,000. Therefore, the tax on $16,100 is $860 plus 10% of $1,100 = $860 + $110 = $970.

12. **(D)** According to the tables, each additional dollar of taxable income over $25,000 was subject to a New York State tax of 14% and a New York City tax of 4.3%, for a total tax of 18.3%. Therefore, an additional $500 in taxable income would have incurred an additional tax of $0.183 \times 500 = \$91.50$.

13. **(B)** In Norway, the life expectancy of a female born in 1955 was 75 years, which is greater than the life expectancy of a male born in 1990. In Hungary, the life expectancy of a female born in 1955 was 66 years, whereas the life expectancy of a male born in 1990 was greater than 67. In the other two countries, the life expectancy of a female born in 1955 was less than 65 years, and the life expectancy of a male born in 1990 was greater than 65.

14. **(A)** The life expectancy of a Korean female born in 1955 was about 51 and in 1990 it was about 74, an increase of 23 years. This is greater than any other nationality and sex.

15. **(C)** Since there were 10,000 bias-motivated offenses based on ethnicity, and that represents 10% of the total, there were 100,000 bias-motivated offenses in total. Of these, 16,000 (16% of 100,000) were based on religion, and 15,600 (15.6% of 100,000) were based on sexual orientation. The difference is 400.

16. **(C), (D), (E)** Since this is a question about percentages, assume that the total number of bias-motivated offenses in 1998 was 100, of which 16 were based on religion and 58 were based on race.

   - If 8 of the religion-based offenses (50% of 16) were deleted, then there would have been 92 offenses in all, of which 58 were based on race.

   $$\frac{58}{92} = 0.6304 = 63.04\%$$

   - If 4 of the religion-based offenses (25% of 16) were deleted, then there would have been 96 offenses in all, of which 58 were based on race.

   $$\frac{58}{96} = 0.6041 = 60.41\%$$

   Only choices C, D, and E lie between 60.41% and 63.04%.

Mathematics Review

The mathematics questions on the GRE General Test require a working knowledge of mathematical principles, including an understanding of the fundamentals of algebra, plane geometry, and arithmetic, as well as the ability to translate problems into formulas and to interpret graphs. Very few questions require any math beyond what is typically taught in the first two years of high school, and even much of that is not tested. The following review covers those areas that you definitely need to know.

This chapter is divided into 15 sections, labeled 11-A through 11-O. For each question on the Diagnostic Test and the two Model Tests, the Answer Key indicates which section of Chapter 11 you should consult if you need help on a particular topic.

How much time you initially devote to reviewing mathematics should depend on your math skills. If you have always been a good math student and you have taken some math in college and remember most of your high school math, you can skip the instructional parts of this chapter for now. If while doing the Model Tests in Part 5 or on the accompanying CD-ROM, you find that you keep making mistakes on certain types of problems (averages, percents, circles, solid geometry, word problems, for example), or they take you too long, you should then study the appropriate sections here. Even if your math skills are excellent, and you don't need the review, you should complete the sample questions in those sections; they are an excellent source of additional GRE questions. If you know that your math skills are not very good and you have not done much math since high school, then it is advisable to review all of this material, including working out the problems, *before* tackling the model tests.

No matter how good you are in math, *you should carefully read and do the problems* in Chapters 7, 8, 9, and 10. For many of these problems, two solutions are given: the most direct mathematical solution and a second solution using one or more of the special tactics taught in these chapters.

Arithmetic

To do well on the GRE, you need to feel comfortable with most topics of basic arithmetic. In the first five sections of this chapter, we will review the basic arithmetic operations, signed numbers, fractions, decimals, ratios, percents, and averages. Since the GRE uses these concepts to test your reasoning skills, not your ability to perform tedious calculations, we will concentrate on the concepts and not on arithmetic drill. The solutions to more than one-third of the mathematics questions on the GRE depend on your knowing the key facts in these sections. Be sure to review them all.

11-A. BASIC ARITHMETIC CONCEPTS

Let's start by reviewing the most important sets of numbers and their properties. On the GRE the word *number* always means *real number*, a number that can be represented by a point on the number line.

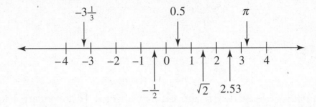

Signed Numbers

The numbers to the right of 0 on the number line are called ***positive*** and those to the left of 0 are called ***negative***. Negative numbers must be written with a *negative sign* (–2); positive numbers can be written with a *plus sign* (+2) but are usually written without a sign (2). All numbers can be called ***signed numbers***.

> **KEY FACT A1**

For any number *a*, exactly one of the following is true:

- *a* is negative
- *a* = 0
- *a* is positive

TIP

The absolute value of a number if *never* negative.

The ***absolute value*** of a number *a*, denoted |*a*|, is the distance between *a* and 0 on the number line. Since 3 is 3 units to the right of 0 on the number line and –3 is 3 units to the left of 0, both have an absolute value of 3:

- $|3| = 3$
- $|-3| = 3$

Two unequal numbers that have the same absolute value are called ***opposites***. So, 3 is the opposite of –3 and –3 is the opposite of 3.

> **KEY FACT A2**

The only number that is equal to its opposite is 0.

EXAMPLE 1

$$a - b = -(a - b)$$

Quantity A	Quantity B
a	b

SOLUTION.
Since –(*a* – *b*) is the opposite of *a* – *b*, *a* – *b* = 0, and so *a* = *b*. The answer is **C**.

In arithmetic we are basically concerned with the addition, subtraction, multiplication, and division of numbers. The third column of the following table gives the terms for the results of these operations.

Operation	Symbol	Result	Example
Addition	+	**Sum**	16 is the sum of 12 and 4 16 = 12 + 4
Subtraction	−	**Difference**	8 is the difference of 12 and 4 8 = 12 − 4
Multiplication*	×	**Product**	48 is the product of 12 and 4 48 = 12 × 4
Division	÷	**Quotient**	3 is the quotient of 12 and 4 3 = 12 ÷ 4

*Multiplication can be indicated also by a dot, parentheses, or the juxtaposition of symbols without any sign: $2^2 \cdot 2^4$, 3(4), 3(x + 2), 3a, 4abc.

Given any two numbers a and b, we can *always* find their sum, difference, product, and quotient, except that we may *never divide by zero.*

- $0 \div 7 = 0$
- $7 \div 0$ is meaningless

EXAMPLE 2

What is the sum of the product and quotient of 8 and 8?

Ⓐ 16   Ⓑ 17   Ⓒ 63   Ⓓ 64   Ⓔ 65

SOLUTION.
Product: $8 \times 8 = 64$. Quotient: $8 \div 8 = 1$. Sum: $64 + 1 = $ **65 (E)**.

KEY FACT A3

- **The product of 0 and any number is 0. For any number a: $a \times 0 = 0$.**
- **Conversely, if the product of two numbers is 0, *at least one* of them must be 0:**

$$ab = 0 \Rightarrow a = 0 \text{ or } b = 0.$$

EXAMPLE 3

Quantity A	Quantity B
The product of the integers from −7 to 2	The product of the integers from −2 to 7

SOLUTION.
Do not multiply. Each quantity is the product of 10 numbers, one of which is 0. So, by KEY FACT A3, each product is 0. The quantities are equal (**C**).

KEY FACT A4

The product and quotient of two positive numbers or two negative numbers are positive; the product and quotient of a positive number and a negative number are negative.

×	+	−
+	+	−
−	−	+

÷	+	−
+	+	−
−	−	+

$6 \times 3 = 18$ $6 \times (-3) = -18$ $(-6) \times 3 = -18$ $(-6) \times (-3) = 18$

$6 \div 3 = 2$ $6 \div (-3) = -2$ $(-6) \div 3 = -2$ $(-6) \div (-3) = 2$

To determine whether a product of more than two numbers is positive or negative, count the number of negative factors.

KEY FACT A5

- **The product of an *even* number of negative factors is positive.**
- **The product of an *odd* number of negative factors is negative.**

EXAMPLE 4

Quantity A	Quantity B
$(-1)(2)(-3)(4)(-5)$	$(1)(-2)(3)(-4)(5)$

SOLUTION.
Don't waste time multiplying. Quantity A is negative since it has 3 negative factors, whereas Quantity B is positive since it has 2 negative factors. The answer is **B**.

KEY FACT A6

- **The *reciprocal* of any nonzero number a is $\frac{1}{a}$.**
- **The product of any number and its reciprocal is 1:**

$$a \times \left(\frac{1}{a}\right) = 1.$$

KEY FACT A7

- The sum of two positive numbers is positive.
- The sum of two negative numbers is negative.
- To find the sum of a positive and a negative number, find the difference of their absolute values and use the sign of the number with the larger absolute value.

$$6 + 2 = 8 \qquad (-6) + (-2) = -8$$

To calculate either $6 + (-2)$ or $(-6) + 2$, take the *difference*, $6 - 2 = 4$, and use the sign of the number whose absolute value is 6. So,

$$6 + (-2) = 4 \qquad (-6) + 2 = -4$$

KEY FACT A8

The sum of any number and its opposite is 0:

$$a + (-a) = 0.$$

Many of the properties of arithmetic depend on the relationship between subtraction and addition and between division and multiplication.

KEY FACT A9

- Subtracting a number is the same as adding its opposite.
- Dividing by a number is the same as multiplying by its reciprocal.

$$a - b = a + (-b) \qquad a \div b = a \times \left(\frac{1}{b}\right)$$

Many problems involving subtraction and division can be simplified by changing them to addition and multiplication problems, respectively.

KEY FACT A10

To subtract signed numbers, change the problem to an addition problem, by changing the sign of what is being subtracted, and use KEY FACT A7.

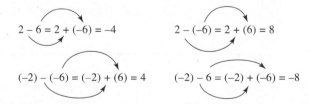

$$2 - 6 = 2 + (-6) = -4 \qquad 2 - (-6) = 2 + (6) = 8$$

$$(-2) - (-6) = (-2) + (6) = 4 \qquad (-2) - 6 = (-2) + (-6) = -8$$

In each case, the minus sign was changed to a plus sign, and either the 6 was changed to –6 or the –6 was changed to 6.

Integers

The ***integers*** are	$\{\dots, -4, -3, -2, -1, 0, 1, 2, 3, 4, \dots\}.$
The ***positive integers*** are	$\{1, 2, 3, 4, 5, \dots\}.$
The ***negative integers*** are	$\{\dots, -5, -4, -3, -2, -1\}.$

There are five integers whose absolute value is less than 3—two negative integers (–2 and –1), two positive integers (1 and 2), and 0.

Consecutive integers are two or more integers written in sequence in which each integer is 1 more than the preceding integer. For example:

$$22, 23 \quad 6, 7, 8, 9 \quad -2, -1, 0, 1 \quad n, n+1, n+2, n+3$$

TIP

0 is neither positive nor negative, but it *is* an integer.

EXAMPLE 5

If the sum of three consecutive integers is less than 75, what is the greatest possible value of the smallest one?

Ⓐ 23 Ⓑ 24 Ⓒ 25 Ⓓ 26 Ⓔ 27

SOLUTION.

Let the numbers be *n*, *n* + 1, and *n* + 2. Then,

$$n + (n + 1) + (n + 2) = 3n + 3 \Rightarrow 3n + 3 < 75 \Rightarrow 3n < 72 \Rightarrow n < 24.$$

So, the most *n* can be is **23 (A)**.

CAUTION

Never assume that *number* means *integer*: 3 is not the only number between 2 and 4; there are infinitely many, including 2.5, 3.99, $\frac{10}{3}$, π, and $\sqrt{10}$.

EXAMPLE 6

If $2 < x < 4$ and $3 < y < 7$, what is the largest integer value of $x + y$?

SOLUTION.

If *x* and *y* are integers, the largest value is 3 + 6 = 9. However, although *x* + *y* is to be an integer, neither *x* nor *y* must be. If *x* = 3.8 and *y* = 6.2, then *x* + *y* = **10**.

The sum, difference, and product of two integers are *always* integers; the quotient of two integers may be an integer, but it is not necessarily one. The quotient 23 ÷ 10 can be expressed as $\frac{23}{10}$ or $2\frac{3}{10}$ or 2.3. If the quotient is to be an integer, we can say that the quotient is 2 and there is a ***remainder*** of 3. It depends upon our point of view. For example, if 23 dollars is to be divided among 10 people, each one will get \$2.30 (2.3 dollars); but if 23 books are to be divided among 10 people, each one will get 2 books and there will be 3 books left over (the remainder).

KEY FACT A11

If *m* and *n* are positive integers and if *r* is the remainder when *n* is divided by *m*, then *n* is *r* more than a multiple of *m*. That is, $n = mq + r$ where *q* is an integer and $0 \le r < m$.

EXAMPLE 7

How many positive integers less than 100 have a remainder of 3 when divided by 7?

SOLUTION.

To leave a remainder of 3 when divided by 7, an integer must be 3 more than a multiple of 7. For example, when 73 is divided by 7, the quotient is 10 and the remainder is 3: $73 = 10 \times 7 + 3$. So, just take the multiples of 7 and add 3. (*Don't forget that 0 is a multiple of 7.*)

$$\underline{0} \times 7 + 3 = 3; \qquad \underline{1} \times 7 + 3 = 10;$$
$$\underline{2} \times 7 + 3 = 17; \qquad \dots ;$$
$$\underline{13} \times 7 + 3 = 94$$

A total of **14** numbers.

Calculator Shortcut

The standard way to find quotients and remainders is to use long division; but on the GRE you *never* do long division: you use the onscreen calculator. To find the remainder when 100 is divided by 7, divide on your calculator: 100 ÷ 7 = 14.285714... . This tells you that the quotient is 14. (Ignore everything to the right of the decimal point.) To find the remainder, multiply 14 × 7 = 98, and then subtract: 100 − 98 = 2.

EXAMPLE 8

If today is Saturday, what day will it be in 500 days?

Ⓐ Friday   Ⓑ Saturday   Ⓒ Sunday   Ⓓ Monday   Ⓔ Tuesday

SOLUTION.

The days of the week form a repeating sequence. Seven days (1 week), 70 days (10 weeks), 700 days (100 weeks) from Saturday it is again Saturday. If 500 were a multiple of 7, then the answer would be Choice B, Saturday. Is it? With your calculator divide 500 by 7: 500 ÷ 7 = 71.428... So, 500 is not a multiple of 7; since $71 \times 7 = 497$, The quotient when 500 is divided by 7 is 71, and the remainder is 3. Therefore, 500 days is 3 days more than 71 complete weeks. 497 days from Saturday it will again be Saturday; three days later it will be **Tuesday, (E)**.

If *a* and *b* are integers, the following four terms are synonymous:

a is a ***divisor*** of *b*	*a* is a ***factor*** of *b*
b is ***divisible*** by *a*	*b* is a ***multiple*** of *a*

They all mean that when *b* is divided by *a* there is no remainder (or, more precisely, the remainder is 0). For example:

3 is a divisor of 12	3 is a factor of 12
12 is divisible by 3	12 is a multiple of 3

KEY FACT A12

Every integer has a finite set of factors (or divisors) and an infinite set of multiples.

The factors of 12:   –12, –6, –4, –3, –2, –1, 1, 2, 3, 4, 6, 12
The multiples of 12:   ... , –48, –36, –24, –12, 0, 12, 24, 36, 48, ...

The only positive divisor of 1 is 1. All other positive integers have at least 2 positive divisors: 1 and itself, and possibly many more. For example, 6 is divisible by 1 and 6, as well as 2 and 3, whereas 7 is divisible only by 1 and 7. Positive integers, such as 7, that have exactly 2 positive divisors are called ***prime numbers*** or ***primes***. The first ten primes are

$$2, 3, 5, 7, 11, 13, 17, 19, 23, 29$$

TIP

1 is *not* a prime.

Memorize this list — it will come in handy.

Positive integers greater than 1 that are not prime are called ***composite numbers***. It follows from the definition that every composite number has at least three distinct positive divisors. The first ten composite numbers are

$$4, 6, 8, 9, 10, 12, 14, 15, 16, 18$$

KEY FACT A13

Every integer greater than 1 that is not a prime (i.e., every composite number) can be written as a product of primes.

To find the prime factorization of any integer, find any two factors; if they're both primes, you are done; if not, factor them. Continue until each factor has been written in terms of primes. A useful method is to make a *factor tree*.

For example, here are the prime factorizations of 108 and 240:

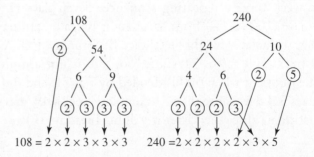

$$108 = 2 \times 2 \times 3 \times 3 \times 3 \qquad 240 = 2 \times 2 \times 2 \times 2 \times 3 \times 5$$

EXAMPLE 9

For any positive integer a, let $\lceil a \rfloor$ denote the smallest prime factor of a. Which of the following is equal to $\lceil 35 \rfloor$?

    (A) $\lceil 10 \rfloor$ (B) $\lceil 15 \rfloor$ (C) $\lceil 45 \rfloor$ (D) $\lceil 55 \rfloor$ (E) $\lceil 75 \rfloor$

SOLUTION.
Check the first few primes; 35 is not divisible by 2 or 3, but is divisible by 5, so 5 is the *smallest* prime factor of 35: $\lceil 35 \rfloor = 5$. Now check the five choices: $\lceil 10 \rfloor = 2$, and $\lceil 15 \rfloor$, $\lceil 45 \rfloor$, and $\lceil 75 \rfloor$ are all equal to 3. Only $\lceil \mathbf{55} \rfloor = 5$. The answer is **D.**

The **least common multiple** (**LCM**) of two or more integers is the smallest positive integer that is a multiple of each of them. For example, the LCM of 6 and 10 is 30. Infinitely many positive integers are multiples of both 6 and 10, including 60, 90, 180, 600, 6000, and 66,000,000, but 30 is the smallest one. The **greatest common factor** (**GCF**) or **greatest common divisor** (**GCD**) of two or more integers is the largest integer that is a factor of each of them. For example, the only positive integers that are factors of both 6 and 10 are 1 and 2, so the GCF of 6 and 10 is 2. For small numbers, you can often find their GCF and LCM by inspection. For larger numbers, KEY FACT A14 is very useful.

KEY FACT A14

The product of the GCF and LCM of two numbers is equal to the product of the two numbers.

An easy way to find the GCF or LCM of two or more integers is to first get their prime factorizations.

- The GCF is the product of all the primes that appear in each factorization, using each prime the smallest number of times it appears in any of the factorizations.
- The LCM is the product of all the primes that appear in any of the factorizations, using each prime the largest number of times it appears in any of the factorizations.

TIP

It is usually easier to find the GCF than the LCM. For example, you might see immediately that the GCF of 36 and 48 is 12. You could then use KEY FACT A14 to find the LCM: since GCF × LCM = 36 × 48, then

$$\text{LCM} = \frac{\overset{3}{\cancel{36}} \times 48}{\underset{1}{\cancel{12}}} = 3 \times 48 = 144.$$

For example, let's find the GCF and LCM of 108 and 240. As we saw:

$$108 = 2 \times 2 \times 3 \times 3 \times 3 \quad \text{and} \quad 240 = 2 \times 2 \times 2 \times 2 \times 3 \times 5.$$

- **GCF.** The primes that appear in both factorizations are 2 and 3: 2 appears twice in the factorization of 108 and 4 times in the factorization of 240, so we take it twice; 3 appears 3 times in the factorization of 108, but only once in the factorization of 240, so we take it just once. The GCF = $2 \times 2 \times 3 = \mathbf{12}$.
- **LCM.** Take one of the factorizations and add to it any primes from the other that are not yet listed. So, start with $2 \times 2 \times 3 \times 3 \times 3$ (108) and look at the primes from 240: there are four 2s; we already wrote two 2s, so we need two more; there is a 3 but we already have that; there is a 5, which we need. So, the LCM = $(2 \times 2 \times 3 \times 3 \times 3) \times (2 \times 2 \times 5) = 108 \times 20 = \mathbf{2,160}$.

EXAMPLE 10

What is the smallest number that is divisible by both 34 and 35?

☐

SOLUTION. We are being asked for the LCM of 34 and 35. By KEY FACT A14,
LCM = $\frac{34 \times 35}{\text{GCF}}$. But the GCF is 1 since no number greater than 1 divides evenly
into both 34 and 35. So, the LCM is $34 \times 35 = $ **1,190**.

The ***even numbers*** are all the multiples of 2:

$$\{..., -4, -2, 0, 2, 4, 6, ...\}$$

The ***odd numbers*** are the integers not divisible by 2:

$$\{..., -5, -3, -1, 1, 3, 5, ...\}$$

NOTE:
- Every integer (positive, negative, or 0) is either odd or even.
- 0 is an even integer; it is a multiple of 2. ($0 = 0 \times 2$)
- 0 is a multiple of *every* integer. ($0 = 0 \times n$)
- 2 is the only even prime number.

TIP

The terms odd
and even apply
only to integers.

KEY FACT A15

The tables below summarize three important facts:

1. If two integers are both even or both odd, their sum and difference are even.
2. If one integer is even and the other odd, their sum and difference are odd.
3. The product of two integers is even unless both of them are odd.

+ and −	even	odd
even	even	odd
odd	odd	even

×	even	odd
even	even	even
odd	even	odd

Exponents and Roots

Repeated addition of the same number is indicated by multiplication:

$$17 + 17 + 17 + 17 + 17 + 17 + 17 = 7 \times 17$$

Repeated multiplication of the same number is indicated by an exponent:

$$17 \times 17 \times 17 \times 17 \times 17 \times 17 \times 17 = 17^7$$

In the expression 17^7, 17 is called the ***base*** and 7 is the ***exponent***.

At some time, you may have seen expressions such as 2^{-4}, $2^{\frac{1}{2}}$, or even $2^{\sqrt{2}}$.
On the GRE, although the base, *b*, can be any number, the exponents you will see
will almost always be positive integers.

KEY FACT A16

For any number b: $b^1 = b$, and $b^n = b \times b \times \cdots \times b$, where b is used as a factor n times.

(i) $2^5 \times 2^3 = (2 \times 2 \times 2 \times 2 \times 2) \times (2 \times 2 \times 2) = 2^8 = 2^{5+3}$

(ii) $\dfrac{2^5}{2^3} = \dfrac{2 \times 2 \times 2 \times 2 \times 2}{2 \times 2 \times 2} = 2 \times 2 = 2^2 = 2^{5-3}$

(iii) $(2^2)^3 = (2 \times 2)^3 = (2 \times 2) \times (2 \times 2) \times (2 \times 2) = 2^6 = 2^{2 \times 3}$

(iv) $2^3 \times 7^3 = (2 \times 2 \times 2) \times (7 \times 7 \times 7) = (2 \times 7)(2 \times 7)(2 \times 7) = (2 \times 7)^3$

These four examples illustrate the following important *laws of exponents* given in KEY FACT A17.

KEY FACT A17

For any numbers b and c and positive integers m and n:

(i) $b^m b^n = b^{m+n}$ (ii) $\dfrac{b^m}{b^n} = b^{m-n}$ (iii) $(b^m)^n = b^{mn}$ (iv) $b^m c^m = (bc)^m$

TIP

Memorize the laws of exponents. They come up often on the GRE.

> **CAUTION**
>
> In (i) and (ii) the bases are the same and in (iv) the exponents are the same. None of these rules applies to expressions such as $7^5 \times 5^7$, in which both the bases and the exponents are different.

EXAMPLE 11

If $2^x = 32$, what is x^2?

Ⓐ 5   Ⓑ 10   Ⓒ 25   Ⓓ 100   Ⓔ 1024

SOLUTION.
To solve $2^x = 32$, just count (and keep track of) how many 2s you need to multiply to get 32: $2 \times 2 \times 2 \times 2 \times 2 = 32$, so $x = 5$ and $x^2 = \mathbf{25}$ **(C)**.

EXAMPLE 12

If $3^a \times 3^b = 3^{100}$, what is the average (arithmetic mean) of a and b?

SOLUTION.

Since $3^a \times 3^b = 3^{a+b}$, we see that $a + b = 100 \Rightarrow \dfrac{a+b}{2} = \mathbf{50}$.

The next KEY FACT is an immediate consequence of KEY FACTS A4 and A5.

KEY FACT A18

For any positive integer *n*:

- $0^n = 0$
- **if *a* is positive, then a^n is positive**
- **if *a* is negative and *n* is even, then a^n is positive**
- **if *a* is negative and *n* is odd, then a^n is negative.**

EXAMPLE 13

Quantity A	Quantity B
$(-13)^{10}$	$(-13)^{25}$

SOLUTION.
Quantity A is positive and Quantity B is negative. So Quantity **A** is greater.

Squares and Square Roots

The exponent that appears most often on the GRE is 2. It is used to form the square of a number, as in πr^2 (the area of a circle), $a^2 + b^2 = c^2$ (the Pythagorean theorem), or $x^2 - y^2$ (the difference of two squares). Therefore, it is helpful to recognize the **perfect squares**, numbers that are the squares of integers. The squares of the integers from 0 to 15 are as follows:

x	0	1	2	3	4	5	6	7
x^2	0	1	4	9	16	25	36	49

x	8	9	10	11	12	13	14	15
x^2	64	81	100	121	144	169	196	225

There are two numbers that satisfy the equation $x^2 = 9$: $x = 3$ and $x = -3$. The positive one, 3, is called the (**principal**) **square root** of 9 and is denoted by the symbol $\sqrt{9}$. Clearly, each perfect square has a square root: $\sqrt{0} = 0$, $\sqrt{36} = 6$, $\sqrt{81} = 9$, and $\sqrt{144} = 12$. But, it is an important fact that *every* positive number has a square root.

KEY FACT A19

For any positive number *a*, there is a positive number *b* that satisfies the equation $b^2 = a$. That number is called the square root of *a* and we write $b = \sqrt{a}$.

So, for any positive number *a*: $(\sqrt{a})^2 = \sqrt{a} \times \sqrt{a} = a$.

The only difference between $\sqrt{9}$ and $\sqrt{10}$ is that the first square root is an integer, while the second one isn't. Since 10 is a little more than 9, we should expect that $\sqrt{10}$ is a little more than $\sqrt{9} = 3$. In fact, $(3.1)^2 = 9.61$, which is close to 10, and $(3.16)^2 = 9.9856$, which is very close to 10. So, $\sqrt{10} \approx 3.16$. On the GRE you will *never* have to evaluate such a square root; if the solution to a problem involves a square root, that square root will be among the answer choices.

EXAMPLE 14

What is the circumference of a circle whose area is 10π?

Ⓐ 5π Ⓑ 10π Ⓒ $\pi\sqrt{10}$ Ⓓ $2\pi\sqrt{10}$ Ⓔ $\pi\sqrt{20}$

SOLUTION.

Since the area of a circle is given by the formula $A = \pi r^2$, we have

$$\pi r^2 = 10\pi \Rightarrow r^2 = 10 \Rightarrow r = \sqrt{10}.$$

The circumference is given by the formula $C = 2\pi r$, so $C = \mathbf{2\pi\sqrt{10}}$ (**D**).

KEY FACT A20

For any positive numbers a and b:

- $\sqrt{ab} = \sqrt{a} \times \sqrt{b}$

- $\sqrt{\dfrac{a}{b}} = \dfrac{\sqrt{a}}{\sqrt{b}}$

CAUTION

$\sqrt{a+b} \neq \sqrt{a} + \sqrt{b}$. For example:

$$5 = \sqrt{25} = \sqrt{9+16} \neq \sqrt{9} + \sqrt{16} = 3 + 4 = 7.$$

CAUTION

Although it is always true that $(\sqrt{a})^2 = a$, $\sqrt{a^2} = a$ is true *only if a is positive*:

$$\sqrt{(-5)^2} = \sqrt{25} = 5, \textit{not} -5.$$

EXAMPLE 15

Quantity A	Quantity B
$\sqrt{x^{20}}$	$(x^5)^2$

SOLUTION.
Quantity A: Since $x^{10}x^{10} = x^{20}$, $\sqrt{x^{20}} = x^{10}$. Quantity B: $(x^5)^2 = x^{10}$. The quantities are equal (**C**).

PEMDAS

When a calculation requires performing more than one operation, it is important to carry them out in the correct order. For decades students have memorized the sentence "<u>P</u>lease <u>E</u>xcuse <u>M</u>y <u>D</u>ear <u>A</u>unt <u>S</u>ally," or just the first letters, PEMDAS, to remember the proper order of operations. The letters stand for:

- <u>P</u>arentheses: first do whatever appears in parentheses, following PEMDAS within the parentheses if necessary.
- <u>E</u>xponents: next evaluate all terms with exponents.
- <u>M</u>ultiplication and <u>D</u>ivision: then do all multiplications and divisions *in order from left to right* — *do not* multiply first and then divide.
- <u>A</u>ddition and <u>S</u>ubtraction: finally, do all additions and subtractions *in order from left to right* — do not add first and then subtract.

Here are some worked-out examples.

1. $12 + 3 \times 2 = 12 + 6 = 18$ [Multiply before you add.]
   $(12 + 3) \times 2 = 15 \times 2 = 30$ [First add in the parentheses.]

2. $12 \div 3 \times 2 = 4 \times 2 = 8$ [Just go from left to right.]
   $12 \div (3 \times 2) = 12 \div 6 = 2$ [First multiply inside the parentheses.]

3. $5 \times 2^3 = 5 \times 8 = 40$ [Do exponents first.]
   $(5 \times 2)^3 = 10^3 = 1000$ [First multiply inside the parentheses.]

4. $4 + 4 \div (2 + 6) = 4 + 4 \div 8 = 4 + .5 = 4.5$
   [First add in the parentheses, then divide, and finally add.]

5. $100 - 2^2(3 + 4 \times 5) = 100 - 2^2(23) = 100 - 4(23) = 100 - 92 = 8$
   [First evaluate what's inside the parentheses (using PEMDAS); then take the exponent; then multiply; and finally subtract.]

There is an important situation when you shouldn't start with what's in the parentheses. Consider the following two examples.

(i) What is the value of $7(100 - 1)$?

   Using PEMDAS, you would write $7(100 - 1) = 7(99)$, and then multiply: $7 \times 99 = 693$. But you can do this even quicker in your head if you think of it this way: $7(100 - 1) = 700 - 7 = 693$.

(ii) What is the value of (77 + 49) ÷ 7?

If you followed the rules of PEMDAS, you would first add, 77 + 49 = 126, and then divide, 126 ÷ 7 = 18. This is definitely more difficult and time-consuming than mentally doing $\frac{77}{7} + \frac{49}{7} = 11 + 7 = 18$.

Both of these examples illustrate the very important distributive law.

Key Fact A21

The distributive law

For any real numbers *a*, *b*, and *c*:

- $a(b + c) = ab + ac$
- $a(b - c) = ab - ac$

and if $a \neq 0$

- $\dfrac{b + c}{a} = \dfrac{b}{a} + \dfrac{c}{a}$

- $\dfrac{b - c}{a} = \dfrac{b}{a} - \dfrac{c}{a}$

TIP

Many students who use the distributive law with multiplication forget about it with division. Don't you do that.

EXAMPLE 16

Quantity A	Quantity B
$5(a - 7)$	$5a - 7$

SOLUTION.

By the distributive law, Quantity A = $5a - 35$. The result of subtracting 35 from a number is *always less* than the result of subtracting 7 from that number. Quantity **B** is greater.

EXAMPLE 17

Quantity A	Quantity B
$\dfrac{50 + x}{5}$	$10 + x$

SOLUTION.

	Quantity A	Quantity B
By the distributive law:	$10 + \dfrac{x}{5}$	$10 + x$
Subtract 10 from each quantity:	$\dfrac{x}{5}$	x

The quantities are equal if $x = 0$, but not if $x = 1$.
The answer is **D**.

Inequalities

The number a is **greater than** the number b, denoted $a > b$, if a is to the right of b on the number line. Similarly, a is **less than** b, denoted $a < b$, if a is to the left of b on the number line. Therefore, if a is positive, $a > 0$, and if a is negative, $a < 0$. Clearly, if $a > b$, then $b < a$.

The following KEY FACT gives an important alternate way to describe greater than and less than.

KEY FACT A22

• For any numbers a and b:

$a > b$ means that $a - b$ is positive.

• For any numbers a and b:

$a < b$ means that $a - b$ is negative.

KEY FACT A23

• For any numbers a and b, exactly one of the following is true:

$a > b$ or $a = b$ or $a < b$.

The symbol $\geq$ means **greater than or equal to** and the symbol $\leq$ means **less than or equal to**. The statement "$x \geq 5$" means that x can be 5 or any number greater than 5; the statement "$x \leq 5$" means that x can be 5 or any number less than 5. The statement "$2 < x < 5$" is an abbreviation for the statement "$2 < x$ and $x < 5$." It means that x is a number between 2 and 5 (greater than 2 and less than 5).

Inequalities are very important on the GRE, especially on the quantitative comparison questions where you have to determine which of two quantities is the greater one. KEY FACTS A24 and A25 give some important facts about inequalities.

If the result of performing an arithmetic operation on an inequality is a new inequality in the same direction, we say that the inequality has been **preserved**. If the result of performing an arithmetic operation on an inequality is a new inequality in the opposite direction, we say that the inequality has been **reversed**.

KEY FACT A24

- Adding a number to an inequality or subtracting a number from an inequality preserves it.

  If $a < b$, then $a + c < b + c$ and $a - c < b - c$.

  $$3 < 7 \Rightarrow 3 + 100 < 7 + 100 \quad (103 < 107)$$
  $$3 < 7 \Rightarrow 3 - 100 < 7 - 100 \quad (-97 < -93)$$

- Adding inequalities in the same direction preserves them.

  If $a < b$ and $c < d$, then $a + c < b + d$.

  $$3 < 7 \text{ and } 5 < 10 \Rightarrow 3 + 5 < 7 + 10 \quad (8 < 17)$$

- Multiplying or dividing an inequality by a positive number preserves it.

  If $a < b$, and c is positive, then $ac < bc$ and $\dfrac{a}{c} < \dfrac{b}{c}$.

  $$3 < 7 \Rightarrow 3 \times 100 < 7 \times 100 \quad (300 < 700)$$
  $$3 < 7 \Rightarrow 3 \div 100 < 7 \div 100 \quad \left(\frac{3}{100} < \frac{7}{100}\right)$$

- Multiplying or dividing an inequality by a negative number reverses it.

  If $a < b$, and c is negative, then $ac > bc$ and $\dfrac{a}{c} > \dfrac{b}{c}$.

  $$3 < 7 \Rightarrow 3 \times (-100) > 7 \times (-100) \quad (-300 > -700)$$
  $$3 < 7 \Rightarrow 3 \div (-100) > 7 \div (-100) \quad \left(-\frac{3}{100} > -\frac{7}{100}\right)$$

- Taking negatives reverses an inequality.

  If $a < b$, then $-a > -b$ and if $a > b$, then $-a < -b$.

  $$3 < 7 \Rightarrow -3 > -7 \text{ and } 7 > 3 \Rightarrow -7 < -3$$

- If two numbers are each positive or negative, then taking reciprocals reverses an inequality.

  If a and b are both positive or both negative and $a < b$, then $\dfrac{1}{a} > \dfrac{1}{b}$.

  $$3 < 7 \Rightarrow \frac{1}{3} > \frac{1}{7} \qquad -7 < -3 \Rightarrow -\frac{1}{7} > -\frac{1}{3}$$

KEY FACT A25

Important inequalities for numbers between 0 and 1.

- If $0 < x < 1$, and a is positive, then $xa < a$. For example: $.85 \times 19 < 19$.
- If $0 < x < 1$, and m and n are positive integers with $m > n$, then

  $x^m < x^n < x$. For example, $\left(\dfrac{1}{2}\right)^5 < \left(\dfrac{1}{2}\right)^2 < \dfrac{1}{2}$.

TIP

Be sure you understand KEY FACT A24; it is very useful. Also, review the important properties listed in KEY FACTS A25 and A26. These properties come up often on the GRE.

- If $0 < x < 1$, then $\sqrt{x} > x$. For example, $\sqrt{\dfrac{3}{4}} > \dfrac{3}{4}$.

- If $0 < x < 1$, then $\dfrac{1}{x} > x$. In fact, $\dfrac{1}{x} > 1$. For example, $\dfrac{1}{0.2} > 1 > 0.2$.

KEY FACT A26

Properties of Zero

- 0 is the only number that is neither positive nor negative.
- 0 is smaller than every positive number and greater than every negative number.
- 0 is an even integer.
- 0 is a multiple of every integer.
- For every number a: $a + 0 = a$ and $a - 0 = a$.
- For every number a: $a \times 0 = 0$.
- For every positive integer n: $0^n = 0$.
- For every number a (including 0): $a \div 0$ and $\dfrac{a}{0}$ are *meaningless symbols*. (They are *undefined*.)
- For every number a other than 0: $0 \div a = \dfrac{0}{a} = 0$.
- 0 is the only number that is equal to its opposite: $0 = -0$.
- If the product of two or more numbers is 0, at least one of them is 0.

Key Fact A27

Properties of 1

- For any number a: $1 \times a = a$ and $\dfrac{a}{1} = a$.
- For any integer n: $1^n = 1$.
- 1 is a divisor of every integer.
- 1 is the smallest positive integer.
- 1 is an odd integer.
- 1 is *not* a prime.

Practice Exercises—Basic Arithmetic

Discrete Quantitative Questions

1. For how many positive integers, a, is it true that $a^2 \leq 2a$?

   Ⓐ None
   Ⓑ 1
   Ⓒ 2
   Ⓓ 4
   Ⓔ More than 4

2. If $0 < a < b < 1$, which of the following statements are true?

   Indicate *all* such statements.

   A⃞ $a - b$ is negative

   B⃞ $\dfrac{1}{ab}$ is positive

   C⃞ $\dfrac{1}{b} - \dfrac{1}{a}$ is positive

3. If the product of 4 consecutive integers is equal to one of them, what is the largest possible value of one of the integers?

4. At 3:00 A.M. the temperature was 13° below zero. By noon it had risen to 32°. What was the average hourly increase in temperature?

   Ⓐ $\left(\dfrac{19}{9}\right)^\circ$

   Ⓑ $\left(\dfrac{19}{6}\right)^\circ$

   Ⓒ 5°
   Ⓓ 7.5°
   Ⓔ 45°

5. If a and b are negative, and c is positive, which of the following statements are true? Indicate *all* such statements.

   A⃞ $a - b < a - c$

   B⃞ If $a < b$, then $\dfrac{a}{c} < \dfrac{b}{c}$

   C⃞ $\dfrac{1}{b} < \dfrac{1}{c}$

6. If $-7 \leq x \leq 7$ and $0 \leq y \leq 12$, what is the greatest possible value of $y - x$?

   Ⓐ −19
   Ⓑ 5
   Ⓒ 7
   Ⓓ 17
   Ⓔ 19

7. If $(7^a)(7^b) = \dfrac{7^c}{7^d}$, what is d in terms of a, b, and c?

   Ⓐ $\dfrac{c}{ab}$

   Ⓑ $c - a - b$
   Ⓒ $a + b - c$
   Ⓓ $c - ab$

   Ⓔ $\dfrac{c}{a + b}$

8. If each of ★ and ❖ can be replaced by +, −, or ×, how many different values are there for the expression 2 ★ 2 ❖ 2?

9. A number is "terrific" if it is a multiple of 2 or 3. How many terrific numbers are there between –11 and 11?

Ⓐ 6
Ⓑ 7
Ⓒ 11
Ⓓ 15
Ⓔ 17

10. If $x \; \bigstar \; y$ represents the number of integers greater than x and less than y, what is the value of $-\pi \; \bigstar \; \sqrt{2}$?

Ⓐ 2
Ⓑ 3
Ⓒ 4
Ⓓ 5
Ⓔ 6

Questions 11 and 12 refer to the following definition.

For any positive integer n, $\tau(n)$ represents the number of positive divisors of n.

11. Which of the following statements are true? Indicate *all* such statements.

A $\tau(5) = \tau(7)$
B $\tau(5) \cdot \tau(7) = \tau(35)$
C $\tau(5) + \tau(7) = \tau(12)$

12. What is the value of $\tau(\tau(\tau(12)))$?

Ⓐ 1
Ⓑ 2
Ⓒ 3
Ⓓ 4
Ⓔ 6

13. If p and q are primes greater than 2, which of the following statements must be true? Indicate *all* such statements.

A $p + q$ is even
B pq is odd
C $p^2 - q^2$ is even

14. If $0 < x < 1$, which of the following lists the numbers in increasing order?

Ⓐ $\sqrt{x}, x, x^2$
Ⓑ $x^2, x, \sqrt{x}$
Ⓒ $x^2, \sqrt{x}, x$
Ⓓ $x, x^2, \sqrt{x}$
Ⓔ $x, \sqrt{x}, x^2$

15. Which of the following is equal to $(7^8 \times 7^9)^{10}$?

Ⓐ 7^{27}
Ⓑ 7^{82}
Ⓒ 7^{170}
Ⓓ 49^{170}
Ⓔ 49^{720}

Quantitative Comparison Questions

> (A) Quantity A is greater.
> (B) Quantity B is greater.
> (C) Quantities A and B are equal.
> (D) It is impossible to determine which quantity is greater.

	Quantity A	Quantity B
16.	The product of the odd integers between −8 and 8	The product of the even integers between −9 and 9

a and *b* are nonzero integers

	Quantity A	Quantity B
17.	$a + b$	ab

	Quantity A	Quantity B
18.	The remainder when a positive integer is divided by 7	7

	Quantity A	Quantity B
19.	$24 \div 6 \times 4$	12

	Quantity A	Quantity B
20.	$\dfrac{2x - 17}{2}$	$x - 17$

n is an integer greater than 1 that leaves a remainder of 1 when it is divided by 2, 3, 4, 5, and 6

	Quantity A	Quantity B
21.	n	60

	Quantity A	Quantity B
22.	The number of primes that are divisible by 2	The number of primes that are divisible by 3

n is a positive integer

	Quantity A	Quantity B
23.	The number of different prime factors of n	The number of different prime factors of n^2

	Quantity A	Quantity B
24.	The number of even positive factors of 30	The number of odd positive factors of 30

n is a positive integer

	Quantity A	Quantity B
25.	$(-10)^n$	$(-10)^{n+1}$

ANSWER KEY

1. **C**	6. **E**	11. **A, B**	16. **A**	21. **A**
2. **A, B**	7. **B**	12. **C**	17. **D**	22. **C**
3. **3**	8. **4**	13. **A, B, C**	18. **B**	23. **C**
4. **C**	9. **D**	14. **B**	19. **A**	24. **C**
5. **B, C**	10. **D**	15. **C**	20. **A**	25. **D**

ANSWER EXPLANATIONS

1. **(C)** Since a is positive, we can divide both sides of the given inequality by a:
   $a^2 \le 2a \Rightarrow a \le 2 \Rightarrow a = 1$ or 2.

2. **(A)(B)** Since $a < b$, $a - b$ is negative (A is true). Since a and b are positive, so is their product, ab; and the reciprocal of a positive number is positive (B is true).
   $\dfrac{1}{b} - \dfrac{1}{a} = \dfrac{a-b}{ab}$, and we have just seen that the numerator is negative and the denominator positive; so the value of the fraction is negative (C is false).

3. **3** If all four integers were negative, their product would be positive, and so could not equal one of them. If all of the integers were positive, their product would be much greater than any of them (even $1 \times 2 \times 3 \times 4 = 24$). So, the integers must include 0, in which case their product *is* 0. The largest set of four consecutive integers that includes 0 is 0, 1, 2, 3.

4. **(C)** In the 9 hours from 3:00 to 12:00, the temperature rose $32 - (-13) = 32 + 13 = 45$ degrees. So, the average hourly increase was $45° \div 9 = 5°$.

5. **(B)(C)** Since b is negative and c is positive, $b < c \Rightarrow -b > -c \Rightarrow a - b > a - c$ (A is false). Since c is positive, dividing by c preserves the inequality. (B is true.) Since b is negative, $\dfrac{1}{b}$ is negative, and so is less than $\dfrac{1}{c}$, which is positive (C is true).

6. **(E)** To make $y - x$ as large as possible, let y be as big as possible (12), and subtract the smallest amount possible ($x = -7$): $12 - (-7) = 19$.

7. **(B)** $(7^a)(7^b) = 7^{a+b}$, and $\dfrac{7^c}{7^d} = 7^{c-d}$. Therefore,
   $a + b = c - d \Rightarrow a + b + d = c \Rightarrow d = c - a - b$

8. **4** Just list the 9 possible outcomes of replacing ★ and ❖ by +, −, and ×, and see that there are 4 different values: −2, 2, 6, 8.
   $2 + 2 + 2 = 6 \quad\quad 2 - 2 - 2 = -2 \quad\quad 2 \times 2 \times 2 = 8$
   $2 + 2 - 2 = 2 \quad\quad 2 - 2 \times 2 = -2 \quad\quad 2 \times 2 + 2 = 6$
   $2 + 2 \times 2 = 6 \quad\quad 2 - 2 + 2 = 2 \quad\quad 2 \times 2 - 2 = 2$

9. **(D)** There are 15 "terrific" numbers: 2, 3, 4, 6, 8, 9, 10, their opposites, and 0.

10. **(D)** There are 5 integers ($1, 0, -1, -2, -3$) that are greater than -3.14 ($-\pi$) and less than 1.41 $\left(\sqrt{2}\right)$.

11. **(A)(B)** Since 5 and 7 have two positive factors each, $\tau(5) = \tau(7)$. (A is true.) Since 35 has 4 divisors (1, 5, 7, and 35) and $\tau(5) \cdot \tau(7) = 2 \times 2 = 4$. (B is true.) Since the positive divisors of 12 are 1, 2, 3, 4, 6, and 12, $\tau(12)$ is 6, which is *not* equal to 2 + 2. (C is false.)

12. **(C)** $\tau(\tau(\tau(12))) = \tau(\tau(6)) = \tau(4) = 3$

13. **(A)(B)(C)** All primes greater than 2 are odd, so p and q are odd, and $p + q$, the sum of two odd numbers, is even (A is true). The product of two odd numbers is odd (B is true). Since p and q are odd, so are their squares, and so the difference of their squares is even (C is true).

14. **(B)** For any number, x, between 0 and 1: $x^2 < x$ and $x < \sqrt{x}$.

15. **(C)** First, multiply inside the parentheses: $7^8 \times 7^9 = 7^{17}$; then, raise to the 10th power: $(7^{17})^{10} = 7^{170}$.

16. **(A)** Since Quantity A has 4 negative factors (–7, –5, –3, –1), it is positive. Quantity B also has 4 negative factors, but be careful—it also has the factor 0, and so Quantity B is 0.

17. **(D)** If a and b are each 1, then $a + b = 2$, and $ab = 1$; so, Quantity A is greater. But, if a and b are each 3, $a + b = 6$, and $ab = 9$, then Quantity B is greater.

18. **(B)** The remainder is *always* less than the divisor.

19. **(A)** According to PEMDAS, you divide and multiply from left to right (do *not* do the multiplication first): $24 \div 6 \times 4 = 4 \times 4 = 16$.

20. **(A)** By the distributive law, $\dfrac{2x - 17}{2} = \dfrac{2x}{2} - \dfrac{17}{2} = x - 8.5$, which is greater than $x - 17$ (the larger the number you subtract, the smaller the difference.)

21. **(A)** The LCM of 2, 3, 4, 5, 6 is 60; and all multiples of 60 are divisible by each of them. So, n could be 61 or 1 more than any multiple of 60.

22. **(C)** The only prime divisible by 2 is 2, and the only prime divisible by 3 is 3. Quantity A and Quantity B are each 1.

23. **(C)** If you make a factor tree for n^2, the first branches would be n and n. Now, when you factor each n, you get exactly the same prime factors. (See the example below.)

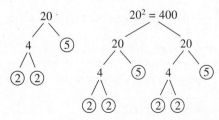

24. **(C)** Just list the factors of 30: 1, 2, 3, 5, 6, 10, 15, 30. Four of them are odd and four are even.

25. **(D)** If n is even, then $n + 1$ is odd, and consequently $(-10)^n$ is positive, whereas $(-10)^{n+1}$ is negative. If n is odd, exactly the opposite is true.

11-B. FRACTIONS AND DECIMALS

Several questions on the GRE involve fractions or decimals. The KEY FACTS in this section cover all of the important facts you need to know for the GRE.

When a whole is *divided* into n equal parts, each part is called *one-nth* of the whole, written $\dfrac{1}{n}$. For example, if a pizza is cut (*divided*) into 8 equal slices, each slice is one-eighth $\left(\dfrac{1}{8}\right)$ of the pizza; a day is *divided* into 24 equal hours, so an hour is one-twenty-fourth $\left(\dfrac{1}{24}\right)$ of a day; and an inch is one-twelfth $\left(\dfrac{1}{12}\right)$ of a foot.

- If Donna slept for 5 hours, she slept for five-twenty-fourths $\left(\dfrac{5}{24}\right)$ of a day.

- If Taryn bought 8 slices of pizza, she bought eight-eighths $\left(\dfrac{8}{8}\right)$ of a pie.

- If Aviva's shelf is 30 inches long, it measures thirty-twelfths $\left(\dfrac{30}{12}\right)$ of a foot.

Numbers such as $\dfrac{5}{24}$, $\dfrac{8}{8}$, and $\dfrac{30}{12}$, in which one integer is written over a second integer, are called **fractions**. The center line is called the fraction bar. The number above the bar is called the **numerator**, and the number below the bar is called the **denominator**.

CAUTION

The denominator of a fraction can *never* be 0.

- A fraction, such as $\dfrac{5}{24}$, in which the numerator is less than the denominator, is called a **proper fraction**. Its value is less than 1.
- A fraction, such as $\dfrac{30}{12}$, in which the numerator is more than the denominator, is called an **improper fraction**. Its value is greater than 1.
- A fraction, such as $\dfrac{8}{8}$, in which the numerator and denominator are the same, is also **improper**, but it is equal to 1.

It is useful to think of the fraction bar as a symbol for division. If three pizzas are divided equally among eight people, each person gets $\dfrac{3}{8}$ of a pizza. If you actually divide 3 by 8, you get that $\dfrac{3}{8} = 0.375$.

KEY FACT B1

Every fraction, proper or improper, can be expressed in decimal form (or as a whole number) by dividing the numerator by the denominator.

$$\frac{3}{10} = 0.3 \qquad \frac{3}{4} = 0.75 \qquad \frac{5}{8} = 0.625 \qquad \frac{3}{16} = 0.1875$$

$$\frac{8}{8} = 1 \qquad \frac{11}{8} = 1.375 \qquad \frac{48}{16} = 3 \qquad \frac{100}{8} = 12.5$$

Note that any number beginning with a decimal point can be written with a 0 to the left of the decimal point. In fact, some calculators will express 3 ÷ 8 as .375, whereas others will print 0.375.

Unlike the examples above, when most fractions are converted to decimals, the division does not terminate after 2 or 3 or 4 decimal places; rather it goes on forever with some set of digits repeating itself.

$$\frac{2}{3} = 0.666666\ldots \qquad \frac{3}{11} = 0.272727\ldots \qquad \frac{5}{12} = 0.416666\ldots \qquad -\frac{17}{15} = -1.133333\ldots$$

A convenient way to represent repeating decimals is to place a bar over the digits that repeat. For example, the decimal equivalent of the four fractions, above, could be written as follows:

$$\frac{2}{3} = 0.\overline{6} \qquad \frac{3}{11} = 0.\overline{27} \qquad \frac{5}{12} = 0.41\overline{6} \qquad -\frac{17}{15} = -1.1\overline{3}$$

A *rational number* is any number that can be expressed as a fraction, $\frac{a}{b}$, where a and b are integers. For example, 2, –2.2, and $2\frac{1}{2}$ are all rational since they can be expressed as $\frac{2}{1}$, $\frac{-22}{10}$, and $\frac{5}{2}$, respectively. When written as decimals, all rational numbers either terminate or repeat. Numbers such as $\sqrt{2}$ and π that cannot be expressed as fractions whose numerators and denominators are integers are called *irrational numbers*. The decimal expansions of irrational numbers neither terminate nor repeat. For example, $\sqrt{2}$ = 1.414213562…. and π = 3.141592654 . . . .

Comparing Fractions and Decimals

KEY FACT B2

To compare two positive decimals, follow these rules.

- **Whichever number has the greater number to the left of the decimal point is greater: since 11 > 9, 11.001 > 9.896; since 1 > 0, 1.234 > 0.8; and since 3 > –3, 3.01 > –3.95. (Recall that if a decimal is written without a number to the left of the decimal point, you may assume that a 0 is there. So, 1.234 > 0.8.)**

• **If the numbers to the left of the decimal point are equal (or if there are no numbers to the left of the decimal point), proceed as follows:**

   1. **If the numbers do not have the same number of digits to the right of the decimal point, add zeros to the end of the shorter one.**
   2. **Now, compare the numbers *ignoring* the decimal point.**

For example, to compare 1.83 and 1.823, add a 0 to the end of 1.83, forming 1.830. Now compare them, *thinking of them as whole numbers*: since, 1830 > 1823, then 1.830 > 1.823.

EXAMPLE 1

Quantity A	Quantity B
.2139	.239

SOLUTION.
Do not think that Quantity A is greater because 2139 > 239. Be sure to add a 0 to the end of 0.239 (forming 0.2390) before comparing. Now, since 2390 > 2139, Quantity **B** is greater.

KEY FACT B3

There are two methods of comparing positive fractions:

   1. **Convert them to decimals (by dividing), and use KEY FACT B2.**
   2. **Cross-multiply.**

For example, to compare $\frac{1}{3}$ and $\frac{3}{8}$, we have two choices.

   1. Write $\frac{1}{3}$ = .3333... and $\frac{3}{8}$ = .375. Since .375 > .333, then $\frac{3}{8} > \frac{1}{3}$.

   2. Cross-multiply: $\frac{1}{3} \diagup \diagdown \frac{3}{8}$. Since $3 \times 3 > 8 \times 1$, then $\frac{3}{8} > \frac{1}{3}$.

KEY FACT B4

When comparing positive fractions, there are three situations in which it is easier just to look at the fractions, and not use either method in KEY FACT B3.

   1. If the fractions have the same denominator, the fraction with the larger numerator is greater. Just as \$9 is more than \$7, and 9 books are more than 7 books, 9 fortieths are more than 7 fortieths: $\frac{9}{40} > \frac{7}{40}$.

   2. If the fractions have the same numerator, the fraction with the smaller denominator is greater.

If you divide a cake into 5 equal pieces, each piece is larger than the pieces you would get if you had divided the cake into

10 equal pieces: $\dfrac{1}{5} > \dfrac{1}{10}$, and similarly $\dfrac{3}{5} > \dfrac{3}{10}$.

3. Sometimes the fractions are so familiar or easy to work with, you just know the answer. For example, $\dfrac{3}{4} > \dfrac{1}{5}$ and $\dfrac{11}{20} > \dfrac{1}{2}$ $\left(\text{since } \dfrac{10}{20} = \dfrac{1}{2} \right)$.

KEY FACTS B2, B3, and B4 apply to *positive* decimals and fractions.

KEY FACT B5

• Clearly, any positive number is greater than any negative number:

$$\frac{1}{2} > -\frac{1}{5} \quad \text{and} \quad 0.123 > -2.56$$

• For negative decimals and fractions, use KEY FACT A24, which states that if $a > b$, then $-a < -b$:

$$\frac{1}{2} > \frac{1}{5} \Rightarrow -\frac{1}{2} < -\frac{1}{5} \quad \text{and} \quad 0.83 > 0.829 \Rightarrow -0.83 < -0.829$$

EXAMPLE 2

Which of the following lists the fractions $\dfrac{2}{3}$, $\dfrac{5}{8}$, and $\dfrac{13}{20}$ in order from least to greatest?

(A) $\dfrac{2}{3}, \dfrac{5}{8}, \dfrac{13}{20}$ (B) $\dfrac{5}{8}, \dfrac{2}{3}, \dfrac{13}{20}$ (C) $\dfrac{5}{8}, \dfrac{13}{20}, \dfrac{2}{3}$ (D) $\dfrac{13}{20}, \dfrac{5}{8}, \dfrac{2}{3}$ (E) $\dfrac{13}{20}, \dfrac{2}{3}, \dfrac{5}{8}$

SOLUTION.
Use your calculator to quickly convert each to a decimal, writing down the first few decimal places: $\dfrac{2}{3} = 0.666$, $\dfrac{5}{8} = 0.625$, and $\dfrac{13}{20} = 0.65$. It is now easy to order the decimals: $0.625 < 0.650 < 0.666$. The answer is **C**.

ALTERNATIVE SOLUTION.
Cross-multiply.

• $\dfrac{2}{3} > \dfrac{5}{8}$ since $8 \times 2 > 3 \times 5$.

• $\dfrac{13}{20} > \dfrac{5}{8}$ since $8 \times 13 > 20 \times 5$.

• $\dfrac{2}{3} > \dfrac{13}{20}$ since $20 \times 2 > 3 \times 13$.

EXAMPLE 3

$$0 < x < y$$

Quantity A	Quantity B
$\dfrac{1}{x} - \dfrac{1}{y}$	0

SOLUTION.

By KEY FACT B4, $x < y \Rightarrow \dfrac{1}{x} > \dfrac{1}{y}$, and so by KEY FACT A22, $\dfrac{1}{x} - \dfrac{1}{y}$ is positive. Quantity **A** is greater.

Equivalent Fractions

If Bill and Al shared a pizza, and Bill ate $\dfrac{1}{2}$ the pizza and Al ate $\dfrac{4}{8}$ of it, they had exactly the same amount.

We express this idea by saying that $\dfrac{1}{2}$ and $\dfrac{4}{8}$ are *equivalent fractions*: they have the exact same value.

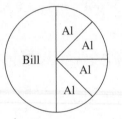

NOTE: If you multiply both the numerator and denominator of $\dfrac{1}{2}$ by 4 you get $\dfrac{4}{8}$; and if you divide both the numerator and denominator of $\dfrac{4}{8}$ by 4 you get $\dfrac{1}{2}$. This illustrates the next KEY FACT.

KEY FACT B6

Two fractions are equivalent if multiplying or dividing both the numerator and denominator of the first one *by the same number* gives the second one.

Consider the following two cases.

1. When the numerator and denominator of $\dfrac{3}{8}$ are each multiplied by 15, the products are $3 \times 15 = 45$ and $8 \times 15 = 120$. Therefore, $\dfrac{3}{8}$ and $\dfrac{45}{120}$ are equivalent fractions.

2. $\dfrac{2}{3}$ and $\dfrac{28}{45}$ are not equivalent fractions because 2 must be multiplied by 14 to get 28, but 3 must be multiplied by 15 to get 45.

KEY FACT B7

To determine if two fractions are equivalent, cross-multiply. The fractions are equivalent if and only if the two products are equal.

For example, since $120 \times 3 = 8 \times 45$, then $\dfrac{3}{8}$ and $\dfrac{45}{120}$ are equivalent.

Since $45 \times 2 \neq 3 \times 28$, then $\dfrac{2}{3}$ and $\dfrac{28}{45}$ are not equivalent fractions.

A fraction is in ***lowest terms*** if no positive integer greater than 1 is a factor of both the numerator and denominator. For example, $\dfrac{9}{20}$ is in lowest terms, since no integer greater than 1 is a factor of both 9 and 20; but $\dfrac{9}{24}$ is not in lowest terms, since 3 is a factor of both 9 and 24.

KEY FACT B8

Every fraction can be *reduced* to lowest terms by dividing the numerator and the denominator by their greatest common factor (GCF). If the GCF is 1, the fraction is already in lowest terms.

For any positive integer n: $n!$, read n *factorial*, is the product of all the integers from 1 to n, inclusive.

EXAMPLE 4

What is the value of $\dfrac{6!}{8!}$?

(A) $\dfrac{1}{56}$ (B) $\dfrac{1}{48}$ (C) $\dfrac{1}{8}$ (D) $\dfrac{1}{4}$ (E) $\dfrac{3}{4}$

SOLUTION.
Even with a calculator, you do not want to calculate 6! ($1 \cdot 2 \cdot 3 \cdot 4 \cdot 5 \cdot 6 = 720$) and 8! ($1 \cdot 2 \cdot 3 \cdot 4 \cdot 5 \cdot 6 \cdot 7 \cdot 8 = 40{,}320$) and then take the time to reduce $\dfrac{720}{40{,}320}$. Here's the easy solution:

$$\frac{6!}{8!} = \frac{\overset{1}{\cancel{6 \times 5 \times 4 \times 3 \times 2 \times 1}}}{8 \times 7 \times \underset{1}{\cancel{6 \times 5 \times 4 \times 3 \times 2 \times 1}}} = \frac{1}{8 \times 7} = \frac{1}{56}$$

Arithmetic Operations with Decimals

Arithmetic operations with decimals should be done on your calculator, unless they are so easy that you can do them in your head.

Multiplying and dividing by powers of 10 is particularly easy and does not require a calculator: they can be accomplished just by moving the decimal point.

KEY FACT B9

To multiply any decimal or whole number by a power of 10, move the decimal point as many places to the *right* as there are 0s in the power of 10, filling in with 0s, if necessary.

$$1.35 \times 10 = 13.5 \qquad 1.35 \times 100 = 135$$
$$1.35 \times 1000 = 1350$$

$$23 \times 10 = 230 \qquad 23 \times 100 = 2300$$
$$23 \times 1{,}000{,}000 = 23{,}000{,}000$$

KEY FACT B10

To divide any decimal or whole number by a power of 10, move the decimal point as many places to the *left* as there are 0s in the power of 10, filling in with 0s, if necessary.

$$67.8 \div 10 = 6.78 \qquad 67.8 \div 100 = 0.678$$
$$67.8 \div 1000 = 0.0678$$

$$14 \div 10 = 1.4 \qquad 14 \div 100 = 0.14$$
$$14 \div 1{,}000{,}000 = 0.000014$$

EXAMPLE 5

Quantity A	Quantity B
3.75×10^4	$37{,}500{,}000 \div 10^3$

SOLUTION.
To evaluate Quantity A, move the decimal point 4 places to the right: **37,500**. To evaluate Quantity B, move the decimal point 3 places to the left: **37,500**. The answer is **C**.

Arithmetic Operations with Fractions

KEY FACT B11

To multiply two fractions, multiply their numerators and multiply their denominators:

$$\frac{3}{5} \times \frac{4}{7} = \frac{3 \times 4}{5 \times 7} = \frac{12}{35} \qquad \frac{3}{5} \times \frac{\pi}{2} = \frac{3 \times \pi}{5 \times 2} = \frac{3\pi}{10}$$

KEY FACT B12

To multiply a fraction by any other number, write that number as a fraction whose denominator is 1:

$$\frac{3}{5} \times 7 = \frac{3}{5} \times \frac{7}{1} = \frac{21}{5} \qquad \frac{3}{5} \times \pi = \frac{3}{5} \times \frac{\pi}{1} = \frac{3\pi}{5}$$

TACTIC

B1

Before multiplying fractions, reduce. You may reduce by dividing any numerator and any denominator by a common factor.

EXAMPLE 6

Express the product, $\frac{3}{4} \times \frac{8}{9} \times \frac{15}{16}$, in lowest terms.

$$\frac{\boxed{}}{\boxed{}}$$

SOLUTION.

You could use your calculator to multiply the numerators and denominators: $\frac{360}{576}$.

It is better, however, to use TACTIC B1 and reduce first:

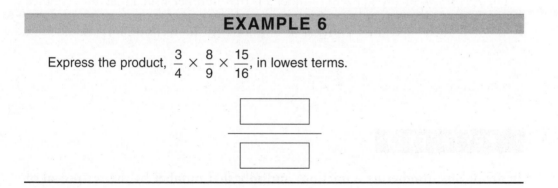

TACTIC

When a problem requires you to find a fraction of a number, multiply.

EXAMPLE 7

If $\frac{4}{7}$ of the 350 sophomores at Monroe High School are girls, and $\frac{7}{8}$ of them play on a team, how many sophomore girls do <u>not</u> play on a team?

$$\boxed{}$$

SOLUTION.

There are $\frac{4}{7} \times 350 = 200$ sophomore girls.

Of these, $\frac{7}{8} \times 200 = 175$ play on a team. So, $200 - 175 = \mathbf{25}$ do not play on a team.

The ***reciprocal*** of any nonzero number x is that number y such that $xy = 1$. Since $x\left(\frac{1}{x}\right) = 1$, then $\frac{1}{x}$ is the reciprocal of x. Similarly, the reciprocal of the fraction

$\frac{a}{b}$ is the fraction $\frac{b}{a}$, since $\frac{a}{b} \cdot \frac{b}{a} = 1$.

KEY FACT B13

To divide any number by a fraction, multiply that number by the reciprocal of the fraction.

$$20 \div \frac{2}{3} = \frac{20}{1} \times \frac{3}{2} = 30 \qquad\qquad \frac{3}{5} \div \frac{2}{3} = \frac{3}{5} \times \frac{3}{2} = \frac{9}{10}$$

$$\sqrt{2} \div \frac{2}{3} = \frac{\sqrt{2}}{1} \times \frac{3}{2} = \frac{3\sqrt{2}}{2} \qquad\qquad \frac{\pi}{5} \div \frac{2}{3} = \frac{\pi}{5} \times \frac{3}{2} = \frac{3\pi}{10}$$

EXAMPLE 8

In the meat department of a supermarket, 100 pounds of chopped meat was divided into packages, each of which weighed $\frac{4}{7}$ of a pound. How many packages were there?

$$\boxed{}$$

SOLUTION.

$$100 \div \frac{4}{7} = \frac{100}{1} \times \frac{7}{4} = \textbf{175}$$

KEY FACT B14

- **To add or subtract fractions with the same denominator, add or subtract the numerators and keep the denominator:**

$$\frac{4}{9} + \frac{1}{9} = \frac{5}{9} \quad \text{and} \quad \frac{4}{9} - \frac{1}{9} = \frac{3}{9} = \frac{1}{3}$$

- **To add or subtract fractions with different denominators, first rewrite the fractions as equivalent fractions with the same denominators:**

$$\frac{1}{6} + \frac{3}{4} = \frac{2}{12} + \frac{9}{12} = \frac{11}{12}$$

NOTE: The *easiest* common denominator to find is the product of the denominators ($6 \times 4 = 24$, in this example), but the best denominator to use is the ***least common denominator,*** which is the least common multiple (LCM) of the denominators (12, in this case). Using the least common denominator minimizes the amount of reducing that is necessary to express the answer in lowest terms.

KEY FACT B15

If $\frac{a}{b}$ is the fraction of a whole that satisfies some property, then $1 - \frac{a}{b}$ is the fraction of that whole that does not satisfy it.

EXAMPLE 9

In a jar, $\frac{1}{2}$ of the marbles are red, $\frac{1}{4}$ are white, and $\frac{1}{5}$ are blue. What fraction of the marbles are neither red, white, nor blue?

SOLUTION.

The red, white, and blue marbles constitute

$$\frac{1}{2} + \frac{1}{4} + \frac{1}{5} = \frac{10}{20} + \frac{5}{20} + \frac{4}{20} = \frac{19}{20}$$

of the total, so $1 - \frac{19}{20} = \frac{20}{20} - \frac{19}{20} = \frac{1}{20}$ of the marbles are neither red, white, nor blue.

Alternatively, you could convert the fractions to decimals and use your calculator.

$$0.5 + 0.25 + 0.2 = 0.95$$

$$1 - 0.95 = 0.05 = \frac{5}{100}$$

Remember, on the GRE you do not have to reduce fractions, so $\frac{5}{100}$ is an acceptable answer.

EXAMPLE 10

Lindsay ate $\frac{1}{3}$ of a cake and Emily ate $\frac{1}{4}$ of it. What fraction of the cake was still uneaten?

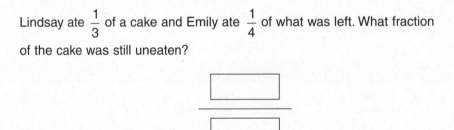

SOLUTION.

$\frac{1}{3} + \frac{1}{4} = \frac{4}{12} + \frac{3}{12} = \frac{7}{12}$ of the cake was eaten, and $1 - \frac{7}{12} = \frac{5}{12}$ was uneaten.

EXAMPLE 11

Lindsay ate $\frac{1}{3}$ of a cake and Emily ate $\frac{1}{4}$ of what was left. What fraction of the cake was still uneaten?

CAUTION: Be sure to read questions carefully. In Example 10, Emily ate $\frac{1}{4}$ of the cake. In Example 11, however, she only ate $\frac{1}{4}$ of the $\frac{2}{3}$ that was left after Lindsay had her piece: she ate $\frac{1}{4} \times \frac{2}{3} = \frac{1}{6}$ of the cake.

SOLUTION.

$\frac{1}{3} + \frac{1}{6} = \frac{2}{6} + \frac{1}{6} = \frac{1}{2}$ of the cake was eaten, and the other $\frac{1}{2}$ was uneaten.

Arithmetic Operations with Mixed Numbers

A ***mixed number*** is a number such as $3\frac{1}{2}$, which consists of an integer followed by a fraction. It is an abbreviation for the *sum* of the number and the fraction; so, $3\frac{1}{2}$ is an abbreviation for $3 + \frac{1}{2}$. Every mixed number can be written as an improper fraction, and every improper fraction can be written as a mixed number:

$$3\frac{1}{2} = 3 + \frac{1}{2} = \frac{3}{1} + \frac{1}{2} = \frac{6}{2} + \frac{1}{2} = \frac{7}{2} \qquad \text{and} \qquad \frac{7}{2} = \frac{6}{2} + \frac{1}{2} = 3 + \frac{1}{2} = 3\frac{1}{2}$$

On the GRE you should perform all arithmetic operations on mixed numbers in one of the following two ways:

- Change the mixed numbers to improper fractions and use the rules you already know for performing arithmetic operations on fractions.
- Change the mixed numbers to decimals and perform the arithmetic on your calculator.

CAUTION

A common mistake for many students is to think that

$$3 \times 5\frac{1}{2} \text{ is } 15\frac{1}{2} \text{— it isn't!}$$

If you need to multiply $3 \times 5\frac{1}{2}$, use one of the two methods mentioned above.

- $3 \times 5\frac{1}{2} = 3\left(5 + \frac{1}{2}\right) = 15 + \frac{3}{2} = 15 + 1\frac{1}{2} = 16\frac{1}{2}$

- $3 \times 5\frac{1}{2} = 3 \times 5.5 = 16.5 = 16\frac{1}{2}$

Complex Fractions

A *complex fraction* is a fraction, such as $\dfrac{1+\dfrac{1}{6}}{2-\dfrac{3}{4}}$, which has one or more fractions in

its numerator or denominator or both.

KEY FACT B16

There are two ways to simplify a complex fraction:

- **Multiply *every* term in the numerator and denominator by the least common multiple of all the denominators that appear in the fraction.**
- **Simplify the numerator and the denominator, and then divide.**

To simplify $\dfrac{1+\dfrac{1}{6}}{2-\dfrac{3}{4}}$

- either multiply each term by 12, the LCM of 6 and 4:

$$\frac{12(1)+12\left(\dfrac{1}{6}\right)}{12(2)-12\left(\dfrac{3}{4}\right)} = \frac{12+2}{24-9} = \frac{14}{15}, \text{ or}$$

- simplify the numerator and denominator:

$$\frac{1+\dfrac{1}{6}}{2-\dfrac{3}{4}} = \frac{\dfrac{7}{6}}{\dfrac{5}{4}} = \frac{7}{6} \times \frac{4}{5} = \frac{14}{15}.$$

Practice Exercises—Fractions and Decimals

Discrete Quantitative Questions

1. A biology class has 12 boys and 18 girls. What fraction of the class are boys?

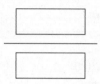

2. For how many integers, *a*, between 30 and 40 is it true that $\frac{5}{a}$, $\frac{8}{a}$, and $\frac{13}{a}$ are all in lowest terms?

   Ⓐ 1
   Ⓑ 2
   Ⓒ 3
   Ⓓ 4
   Ⓔ 5

3. What fractional part of a week is 98 hours?

4. What is the value of the product $\frac{5}{5} \times \frac{5}{10} \times \frac{5}{15} \times \frac{5}{20} \times \frac{5}{25}$?

   Ⓐ $\frac{1}{120}$

   Ⓑ $\frac{1}{60}$

   Ⓒ $\frac{1}{30}$

   Ⓓ $\frac{5}{30}$

   Ⓔ $\frac{1}{2}$

5. If $\frac{3}{11}$ of a number is 22, what is $\frac{6}{11}$ of that number?

   Ⓐ 6
   Ⓑ 11
   Ⓒ 12
   Ⓓ 33
   Ⓔ 44

6. Jason won some goldfish at the state fair. During the first week, $\frac{1}{5}$ of them died, and during the second week, $\frac{3}{8}$ of those still alive at the end of the first week died. What fraction of the original goldfish were still alive after two weeks?

   Ⓐ $\frac{3}{10}$

   Ⓑ $\frac{17}{40}$

   Ⓒ $\frac{1}{2}$

   Ⓓ $\frac{23}{40}$

   Ⓔ $\frac{7}{10}$

7. $\frac{5}{8}$ of 24 is equal to $\frac{15}{7}$ of what number?

   Ⓐ 7
   Ⓑ 8
   Ⓒ 15
   Ⓓ $\frac{7}{225}$
   Ⓔ $\frac{225}{7}$

8. If $7a = 3$ and $3b = 7$, what is the value of $\frac{a}{b}$?

   Ⓐ $\frac{9}{49}$

   Ⓑ $\frac{3}{7}$

   Ⓒ 1

   Ⓓ $\frac{7}{3}$

   Ⓔ $\frac{49}{9}$

9. What is the value of $\dfrac{\frac{7}{9} \times \frac{7}{9}}{\frac{7}{9} + \frac{7}{9} + \frac{7}{9}}$?

   Ⓐ $\frac{7}{27}$

   Ⓑ $\frac{2}{3}$

   Ⓒ $\frac{7}{9}$

   Ⓓ $\frac{9}{7}$

   Ⓔ $\frac{3}{2}$

10. Which of the following expressions are greater than x when $x = \frac{9}{11}$?

   Indicate *all* such expressions.

   Ⓐ $\frac{1}{x}$

   Ⓑ $\frac{x+1}{x}$

   Ⓒ $\frac{x+1}{x-1}$

11. One day at Lincoln High School, $\frac{1}{12}$ of the students were absent, and $\frac{1}{5}$ of those present went on a field trip. If the number of students staying in school that day was 704, how many students are enrolled at Lincoln High?

12. If $a = 0.87$, which of the following expressions are less than a?

   Indicate *all* such expressions.

   Ⓐ $\sqrt{a}$

   Ⓑ a^2

   Ⓒ $\frac{1}{a}$

13. For what value of x is
$$\frac{(34.56)(7.89)}{x} = (.3456)(78.9)?$$

   Ⓐ .001

   Ⓑ .01

   Ⓒ .1

   Ⓓ 10

   Ⓔ 100

14. If $A = \{1, 2, 3\}$, $B = \{2, 3, 4\}$, and C is the set consisting of all the fractions whose numerators are in A and whose denominators are in B, what is the product of all of the numbers in C?

   Ⓐ $\frac{1}{64}$

   Ⓑ $\frac{1}{48}$

   Ⓒ $\frac{1}{24}$

   Ⓓ $\frac{1}{12}$

   Ⓔ $\frac{1}{2}$

15. For the final step in a calculation, Ezra accidentally divided by 1000 instead of multiplying by 1000. What should he do to his incorrect answer to correct it?

Ⓐ Multiply it by 1000.
Ⓑ Multiply it by 100,000.
Ⓒ Multiply it by 1,000,000.
Ⓓ Square it.
Ⓔ Double it.

Quantitative Comparison Questions

Ⓐ Quantity A is greater.
Ⓑ Quantity B is greater.
Ⓒ Quantities A and B are equal.
Ⓓ It is impossible to determine which quantity is greater.

Quantity A	Quantity B
16. $\dfrac{5}{13}$ of 47	$\dfrac{47}{13}$ of 5

$$x = -\frac{2}{3} \text{ and } y = \frac{3}{5}$$

Quantity A	Quantity B
17. xy	$\dfrac{x}{y}$

Quantity A	Quantity B
18. $\dfrac{15}{\frac{1}{15}}$	1

Judy needed 8 pounds of chicken. At the supermarket, the only packages available weighed $\dfrac{3}{4}$ of a pound each.

Quantity A	Quantity B
19. The number of packages Judy needed to buy	11

	Quantity A	Quantity B
20.	$\dfrac{11}{12}$ or $\dfrac{13}{14}$	$\dfrac{14}{15}$

$$a \nabla b = \frac{a}{b} + \frac{b}{a}$$

	Quantity A	Quantity B
21.	$3 \nabla 4$	$\dfrac{1}{2} \nabla \dfrac{2}{3}$

	Quantity A	Quantity B
22.	$\dfrac{100}{2^{100}}$	$\dfrac{100}{3^{100}}$

	Quantity A	Quantity B
23.	$\left(-\dfrac{1}{2}\right)\left(-\dfrac{3}{4}\right)\left(-\dfrac{5}{6}\right)\left(-\dfrac{7}{8}\right)$	$\left(-\dfrac{3}{7}\right)\left(-\dfrac{5}{9}\right)\left(-\dfrac{7}{11}\right)$

$$a = \frac{1}{2} \text{ and } b = \frac{1}{3}$$

	Quantity A	Quantity B
24.	$\dfrac{a}{b}$	$\dfrac{b}{a}$

	Quantity A	Quantity B
25.	$\left(\dfrac{3}{11}\right)^2$	$\sqrt{\dfrac{3}{11}}$

ANSWER KEY

1. $\frac{2}{5}$	4. **A**	9. **A**	14. **A**	19. **C**	24. **A**
	5. **E**	10. **A, B**	15. **C**	20. **B**	25. **B**
2. **C**	6. **C**	11. **960**	16. **C**	21. **C**	
	7. **A**	12. **B**	17. **A**	22. **A**	
3. $\frac{7}{12}$	8. **A**	13. **D**	18. **A**	23. **A**	

Answer Explanations

1. $\frac{2}{5}$ The class has 30 students, of whom 12 are boys. So, the boys make up

$$\frac{12}{30} = \frac{2}{5} \text{ of the class.}$$

2. **(C)** If a is even, then $\frac{8}{a}$ is *not* in lowest terms, since both a and 8 are

divisible by 2. Therefore, the only possibilities are 31, 33, 35, 37, and 39;

but $\frac{5}{35} = \frac{1}{7}$ and $\frac{13}{39} = \frac{1}{3}$, so only 3 integers—31, 33, and 37—satisfy the

given condition.

3. $\frac{7}{12}$ There are 24 hours in a day and 7 days in a week, so there are

$$24 \times 7 = 168 \text{ hours in a week: } \frac{98}{168} = \frac{7}{12}.$$

4. **(A)** Reduce each fraction and multiply:
$$1 \times \frac{1}{2} \times \frac{1}{3} \times \frac{1}{4} \times \frac{1}{5} = \frac{1}{120}.$$

5. **(E)** Don't bother writing an equation for this one; just think. We know that

$\frac{3}{11}$ of the number is 22, and $\frac{6}{11}$ of a number is twice as much as $\frac{3}{11}$ of it:

$2 \times 22 = 44.$

6. **(C)** The *algebra* way is to let x = the number of goldfish Jason won. During

the first week $\frac{1}{5}x$ died, so $\frac{4}{5}x$ were still alive. During week two, $\frac{3}{8}$ of them

died and $\frac{5}{8}$ of them survived:

$$\left(\frac{\overset{1}{\cancel{5}}}{\underset{2}{\cancel{8}}}\right)\left(\frac{\overset{1}{\cancel{4}}}{\underset{1}{\cancel{5}}}x\right) = \frac{1}{2}x.$$

On the GRE, the best way is to assume that the original number of goldfish was 40, the LCM of the denominators (see TACTIC 3, Chapter 9). Then, 8 died the first week $\left(\frac{1}{5}\text{ of }40\right)$, and 12 of the 32 survivors $\left(\frac{3}{8}\text{ of }32\right)$ died the second week. In all, 8 + 12 = 20 died; the other 20 $\left(\frac{1}{2}\text{ the original number}\right)$ were still alive.

7. **(A)** If x is the number, then $\frac{15}{7}x = \frac{5}{\underset{1}{\cancel{8}}} \times \overset{3}{\cancel{24}} = 15$. So, $\frac{15}{7}x = 15$, which

means (dividing by 15) that $\frac{1}{7}x = 1$, and so $x = 7$.

8. **(A)** $7a = 3$ and $3b = 7 \Rightarrow a = \frac{3}{7}$ and $b = \frac{7}{3} \Rightarrow \frac{a}{b} = \frac{3}{7} \div \frac{7}{3} = \frac{3}{7} \times \frac{3}{7} = \frac{9}{49}$.

9. **(A)** Don't start by doing the arithmetic. This is just $\frac{(a)(a)}{a+a+a} = \frac{(a)(\cancel{a})}{3\cancel{a}} = \frac{a}{3}$.

    Now, replacing a with $\frac{7}{9}$ gives $\frac{7}{9} \div 3 = \frac{7}{9} \times \frac{1}{3} = \frac{7}{27}$.

10. **(A)(B)** The reciprocal of a positive number less than 1 is greater than 1 (A is true). $\frac{x+1}{x} = 1 + \frac{1}{x}$, which is greater than 1 (B is true). Since $\frac{9}{11} + 1$ is

    positive and $\frac{9}{11} - 1$ is negative, when $x = \frac{9}{11}$, $\frac{x+1}{x-1} < 0$ and, therefore, less

    than x (C is false).

11. **960** If s is the number of students enrolled, $\frac{1}{12}s$ is the number who were

    absent, and $\frac{11}{12}s$ is the number who were present. Since $\frac{1}{5}$ of them went on a

    field trip, $\frac{4}{5}$ of them stayed in school. Therefore,

    $$704 = \frac{\overset{1}{\cancel{4}}}{5} \times \frac{11}{\underset{3}{\cancel{12}}}s = \frac{11}{15}s \Rightarrow$$

    $$s = 704 \div \frac{11}{15} = 704 \times \frac{15}{11} = 960.$$

12. **(B)** Since $a < 1$, $\sqrt{a} > a$ (A is false). Since $a < 1$, $a^2 < a$ (B is true). The reciprocal of a positive number less than 1 is greater than 1 (C is false).

13. **(D)** There are two easy ways to do this. The first is to see that $(34.56)(7.89)$ has 4 decimal places, whereas $(.3456)(78.9)$ has 5, so the numerator has to be divided by 10. The second is to round off and calculate mentally: since $30 \times 8 = 240$, and $.3 \times 80 = 24$, we must divide by 10.

14. **(A)** Nine fractions are formed:
$$\frac{1}{2}, \frac{1}{3}, \frac{1}{4}, \frac{2}{2}, \frac{2}{3}, \frac{2}{4}, \frac{3}{2}, \frac{3}{3}, \frac{3}{4}$$
Note that although some of these fractions are equivalent, we do have nine distinct fractions.
When you multiply, the three 2s and the three 3s in the numerators cancel with the three 2s and three 3s in the denominators. So, the numerator is 1 and the denominator is $4 \times 4 \times 4 = 64$.

15. **(C)** Multiplying Ezra's incorrect answer by 1000 would undo the final division he made. At that point he should have multiplied by 1000. So, to correct his error, he should multiply again by 1000. In all, Ezra should multiply his incorrect answer by $1000 \times 1000 = 1{,}000{,}000$.

16. **(C)** Each quantity equals $\dfrac{5 \times 47}{3}$.

17. **(A)** Quantity A: $-\dfrac{2}{3} \times \dfrac{3}{5} = -\dfrac{2}{5}$.

Quantity B: $-\dfrac{2}{3} \div \dfrac{3}{5} = -\dfrac{2}{3} \times \dfrac{5}{3} = -\dfrac{10}{9}$.

Finally, $\dfrac{10}{9} > \dfrac{2}{5} \Rightarrow -\dfrac{10}{9} < -\dfrac{2}{5}$.

18. **(A)** Quantity A: $\dfrac{15}{\frac{1}{15}} = 15 \times 15 = 225$.

19. **(C)** $8 \div \dfrac{3}{4} = 8 \times \dfrac{4}{3} = \dfrac{32}{3} = 10\dfrac{2}{3}$. Since 10 packages wouldn't be enough, she had to buy 11. (10 packages would weigh only $7\dfrac{1}{2}$ pounds.)

20. **(B)** You don't need to multiply on this one: since $\dfrac{11}{12} < 1$, $\dfrac{11}{12}$ of $\dfrac{13}{14}$ is less than $\dfrac{13}{14}$, which is already less than $\dfrac{14}{15}$.

21. **(C)** Quantity B is the sum of 2 complex fractions:

$$\frac{\frac{1}{2}}{\frac{2}{3}} + \frac{\frac{2}{3}}{\frac{1}{2}}$$

Simplifying each complex fraction, by multiplying numerator and denominator by 6, or treating these as the quotient of 2 fractions, we get $\frac{3}{4} + \frac{4}{3}$, which is exactly the value of Quantity A.

22. **(A)** When two fractions have the same numerator, the one with the smaller denominator is bigger, and $2^{100} < 3^{100}$.

23. **(A)** Since Quantity A is the product of 4 negative numbers, it is positive, and so is greater than Quantity B, which, being the product of 3 negative numbers, is negative.

24. **(A)** Quantity A: $\frac{1}{2} \div \frac{1}{3} = \frac{1}{2} \times \frac{3}{1} = \frac{3}{2}$.

   Since Quantity B is the reciprocal of Quantity A, Quantity B = $\frac{2}{3}$.

25. **(B)** If $0 < x < 1$, then $x^2 < x < \sqrt{x}$. In this question, $x = \frac{3}{11}$.

11-C. PERCENTS

The word *percent* means hundredth. We use the symbol "%" to express the word "percent." For example, "17 percent" means "17 hundredths," and can be written with a % symbol, as a fraction, or as a decimal:

$$17\% = \frac{17}{100} = 0.17.$$

KEY FACT C1

- To convert a percent to a decimal, drop the % symbol and move the decimal point two places to the left, adding 0s if necessary. (Remember that we assume that there is a decimal point to the right of any whole number.)
- To convert a percent to a fraction, drop the % symbol, write the number over 100, and reduce.

$$25\% = 0.25 = \frac{25}{100} = \frac{1}{4} \qquad 100\% = 1.00 = \frac{100}{100} \qquad 12.5\% = 0.125 = \frac{12.5}{100} = \frac{125}{1000} = \frac{1}{8}$$

$$1\% = 0.01 = \frac{1}{100} \qquad \frac{1}{2}\% = 0.5\% = 0.005 = \frac{.5}{100} = \frac{1}{200} \qquad 250\% = 2.50 = \frac{250}{100} = \frac{5}{2}$$

KEY FACT C2

- To convert a decimal to a percent, move the decimal point two places to the right, adding 0s if necessary, and add the % symbol.
- To convert a fraction to a percent, first convert the fraction to a decimal, then convert the decimal to a percent, as indicated above.

$$0.375 = 37.5\% \qquad 0.3 = 30\% \qquad 1.25 = 125\% \qquad 10 = 1000\%$$

$$\frac{3}{4} = 0.75 = 75\% \qquad \frac{1}{3} = 0.33333... = 33.333...\% = 33\frac{1}{3}\% \qquad \frac{1}{5} = 0.2 = 20\%$$

You should be familiar with the following basic conversions:

$\frac{1}{2} = 50\%$	$\frac{1}{10} = 10\%$	$\frac{6}{10} = \frac{3}{5} = 60\%$
$\frac{1}{3} = 33\frac{1}{3}\%$	$\frac{2}{10} = \frac{1}{5} = 20\%$	$\frac{7}{10} = 70\%$
$\frac{2}{3} = 66\frac{2}{3}\%$	$\frac{3}{10} = 30\%$	$\frac{8}{10} = \frac{4}{5} = 80\%$
$\frac{1}{4} = 25\%$	$\frac{4}{10} = \frac{2}{5} = 40\%$	$\frac{9}{10} = 90\%$
$\frac{3}{4} = 75\%$	$\frac{5}{10} = \frac{1}{2} = 50\%$	$\frac{10}{10} = 1 = 100\%$

Knowing these conversions can help solve many problems more quickly. For example, the fastest way to find 25% of 32 is not to multiply 32 by 0.25; rather, it is to know that 25% = $\frac{1}{4}$, and that $\frac{1}{4}$ of 32 is 8.

Many questions involving percents can actually be answered more quickly in your head than by using paper and pencil. Since 10% = $\frac{1}{10}$, to take 10% of a number, just divide by 10 by moving the decimal point one place to the left: 10% of 60 is 6. Also, since 5% is half of 10%, then 5% of 60 is 3 (half of 6); and since 30% is 3 times 10%, then 30% of 60 is 18 (3 × 6).

Practice doing this, because improving your ability to do mental math will add valuable points to your score on the GRE.

CAUTION

Do not confuse 0.5 and 0.5%.
Just as 5 is 100 times 5%, 0.5 is 100 times 0.5% = 0.005.

CAUTION

Although 35% can be written as $\frac{35}{100}$ or 0.35, x% can *only* be written as $\frac{x}{100}$.

Solving Percent Problems

Consider the following three questions:

   (i) <u>What</u> is 45% of 200?
   (ii) 90 is 45% <u>of what number</u>?
   (iii) 90 is <u>what percent</u> of 200?

The arithmetic needed to answer each of these questions is very easy, but unless you set a question up properly, you won't know whether you should multiply or divide. In each case, there is one unknown, which we will call x. Now just translate each sentence, replacing "is" by "=" and the unknown by x.

   (i) $x = 45\%$ of $200 \Rightarrow x = .45 \times 200 = 90$
   (ii) $90 = 45\%$ of $x \Rightarrow 90 = .45x \Rightarrow x = 90 \div .45 = 200$
   (iii) $90 = x\%$ of $200 \Rightarrow 90 = \frac{x}{\cancel{100}_1}(\cancel{200}^{\,2}) \Rightarrow 90 = 2x \Rightarrow x = 45$

EXAMPLE 1

Charlie gave 20% of his baseball cards to Kenne and 15% to Paulie. If he still had 520 cards, how many did he have originally?

SOLUTION.
Originally, Charlie had 100% of the cards (all of them). Since he gave away 35% of them, he has 100% – 35% = 65% of them left. So, 520 is 65% of what number?

$$520 = .65x \Rightarrow x = 520 \div .65 = \textbf{800}.$$

EXAMPLE 2

After Ruth gave 110 baseball cards to Alison and 75 to Susanna, she still had 315 left. What percent of her cards did Ruth give away?

Ⓐ 25%   Ⓑ $33\frac{1}{3}$%   Ⓒ 37%   Ⓓ 40%   Ⓔ 50%

SOLUTION. Ruth gave away a total of 185 cards and had 315 left. Therefore, she started with 185 + 315 = 500 cards. So, 185 is what percent of 500?

$$185 = \frac{x}{\cancel{100}_{1}}(\cancel{500}^{5}) \Rightarrow 5x = 185 \Rightarrow x = 185 \div 5 = \textbf{37}$$

Ruth gave away 37% of her cards, (**C**).

Since percent means hundredth, the easiest number to use in any percent problem is 100:

$$a\% \text{ of } 100 = \frac{a}{\cancel{100}_{1}} \times \cancel{100}^{1} = a.$$

KEY FACT C3

For any positive number *a*: *a*% of 100 is *a*.

For example: 91.2% of 100 is 91.2; 300% of 100 is 300; and $\frac{1}{2}$% of 100 is $\frac{1}{2}$.

TACTIC

In any problem involving percents, use the number 100. (It doesn't matter whether or not 100 is a realistic number—a country can have a population of 100; an apple can cost $100; a man can run 100 miles per hour.)

EXAMPLE 3

In 1985 the populations of town A and town B were the same. From 1985 to 1995 the population of town A increased by 60% while the population of town B decreased by 60%. In 1995, the population of town B was what percent of the population of town A?

Ⓐ 25%   Ⓑ 36%   Ⓒ 40%   Ⓓ 60%   Ⓔ 120%

SOLUTION.

On the GRE, do not waste time with a nice algebraic solution. Simply, assume that in 1985 the population of each town was 100. Then, since 60% of 100 is 60, in 1995, the populations were 100 + 60 = 160 and 100 − 60 = 40. So, in 1995, town B's population was $\frac{40}{160} = \frac{1}{4} = $ **25**% of town A's (**A**).

Since a% of b is $\frac{a}{100} \times b = \frac{ab}{100}$, and b% of a is $\frac{b}{100} \times a = \frac{ba}{100}$, we have the result shown in KEY FACT C4.

KEY FACT C4

For any positive numbers a and b: a% of b = b% of a.

KEY FACT C4 often comes up on the GRE in quantitative comparison questions: Which is greater, 13% of 87 or 87% of 13? Don't multiply — they're equal.

Percent Increase and Decrease

KEY FACT C5

- **The *percent increase* of a quantity is**

$$\frac{\text{actual increase}}{\text{original amount}} \times 100\%.$$

- **The *percent decrease* of a quantity is**

$$\frac{\text{actual decrease}}{\text{original amount}} \times 100\%.$$

For example:

- If the price of a lamp goes from $80 to $100, the actual increase is $20, and the percent increase is $\frac{20}{80} \times 100\% = \frac{1}{4} \times 100\% = 25\%$.

- If a $100 lamp is on sale for $80, the actual decrease in price is $20, and the percent decrease is $\frac{20}{100} \times 100\% = 20\%$.

Notice that the percent increase in going from 80 to 100 is not the same as the percent decrease in going from 100 to 80.

KEY FACT C6

If $a < b$, the percent increase in going from a to b is *always* greater than the percent decrease in going from b to a.

KEY FACT C7

- **To increase a number by k%, multiply it by $(1 + k\%)$.**
- **To decrease a number by k%, multiply it by $(1 - k\%)$.**

For example:

- The value of a $1600 investment after a 25% increase is
  $1600(1 + 25\%) = \$1600(1.25) = \$2000$.
- If the investment then loses 25% of its value, it is worth
  $2000(1 - 25\%) = \$2000(.75) = \$1500$.

Note that, after a 25% increase followed by a 25% decrease, the value is $1500, $100 *less* than the original amount.

KEY FACT C8

An increase of k% followed by a decrease of k% is equal to a decrease of k% followed by an increase of k%, and is *always* less than the original value. The original value is never regained.

EXAMPLE 4

Store B always sells CDs at 60% off the list price.
Store A sells its CDs at 40% off the list price, but often runs
a special sale during which it reduces its prices by 20%.

Quantity A	Quantity B
The price of a CD when it is on sale at store A	The price of the same CD at store B

SOLUTION.

Assume the list price of the CD is $100. Store B always sells the CD for $40 ($60 off the list price). Store A normally sells the CD for $60 ($40 off the list price), but on sale reduces its price by 20%. Since 20% of 60 is 12, the sale price is $48 ($60 − $12). The price is greater at Store A.

Notice that a decrease of 40% followed by a decrease of 20% is not the same as a single decrease of 60%; it is less. In fact, a decrease of 40% followed by a decrease of 30% wouldn't even be as much as a single decrease of 60%.

KEY FACT C9

- A decrease of $a\%$ followed by a decrease of $b\%$ *always* results in a smaller decrease than a single decrease of $(a + b)\%$.
- An increase of $a\%$ followed by an increase of $b\%$ *always* results in a larger increase than a single increase of $(a + b)\%$.
- An increase (or decrease) of $a\%$ followed by another increase (or decrease) of $a\%$ is *never* the same as a single increase (or decrease) of $2a\%$.

EXAMPLE 5

Sally and Heidi were both hired in January at the same salary. Sally got two 40% raises, one in July and another in November. Heidi got one 90% raise in October.

Quantity A	Quantity B
Sally's salary at the end of the year	Heidi's salary at the end of the year

SOLUTION.
Since this is a percent problem, assume their salaries were $100. Quantity A: Sally's salary rose to $100(1.40) = 140$, and then to $140(1.40) = \$196$. Quantity B: Heidi's salary rose to $100(1.90) = \$190$. Quantity **A** is greater.

EXAMPLE 6

In January, the value of a stock increased by 25%, and in February, it decreased by 20%. How did the value of the stock at the end of February compare with its value at the beginning of January?

(A) It was less.
(B) It was the same.
(C) It was 5% greater.
(D) It was more than 5% greater.
(E) It cannot be determined from the information given.

SOLUTION. Assume that at the beginning of January the stock was worth $100. Then at the end of January it was worth $125. Since 20% of 125 is 25, during February its value decreased from $125 to $100. The answer is **B**.

KEY FACT C10

- If a number is the result of increasing another number by $k\%$, to find the original number, divide by $(1 + k\%)$.
- If a number is the result of decreasing another number by $k\%$, to find the original number, divide it by $(1 - k\%)$.

For example, if the population of a town in 1990 was 3000, and this represents an increase of 20% since 1980, to find the population in 1980, divide 3000 by (1 + 20%): 3000 ÷ 1.20 = 2500.

EXAMPLE 7

From 1989 to 1990, the number of applicants to a college increased 15% to 5060. How many applicants were there in 1989?

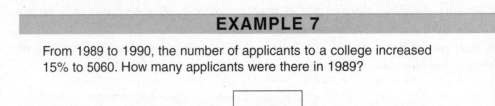

SOLUTION.

The number of applicants in 1989 was 5060 ÷ 1.15 = **4400**.

CAUTION

Percents over 100%, which come up most often on questions involving percent increases, are often confusing for students. First of all, be sure you understand that 100% of a number is that number, 200% of a number is 2 times the number, and 1000% of a number is 10 times the number. If the value of an investment goes from $1000 to $5000, it is now worth 5 times, or 500%, as much as it was originally; but there has only been a *400%* increase in value:

$$\frac{\text{actual increase}}{\text{original amount}} \times 100\% = \frac{4000}{1000} \times 100\% = 4 \times 100\% = 400\%.$$

EXAMPLE 8

The population of a country doubled every 10 years from 1960 to 1990. What was the percent increase in population during this time?

(A) 200% (B) 300% (C) 700% (D) 800% (E) 1000%

SOLUTION.

The population doubled three times (once from 1960 to 1970, again from 1970 to 1980, and a third time from 1980 to 1990). Assume that the population was originally 100. Then it increased from 100 to 200 to 400 to 800. So the population in 1990 was 8 times the population in 1960, but this was an increase of 700 people, or **700% (C)**.

Practice Exercises — Percents

Discrete Quantitative Questions

1. If 25 students took an exam and 4 of them failed, what percent of them passed?

    Ⓐ 4%
    Ⓑ 21%
    Ⓒ 42%
    Ⓓ 84%
    Ⓔ 96%

2. Amanda bought a $60 sweater on sale at 5% off. How much did she pay, including 5% sales tax?

    Ⓐ $54.15
    Ⓑ $57.00
    Ⓒ $57.75
    Ⓓ $59.85
    Ⓔ $60.00

3. What is 10% of 20% of 30%?

    Ⓐ 0.006%
    Ⓑ 0.6%
    Ⓒ 6%
    Ⓓ 60%
    Ⓔ 6000%

4. If c is a positive number, 500% of c is what percent of $500c$?

    Ⓐ 0.01
    Ⓑ 0.1
    Ⓒ 1
    Ⓓ 10
    Ⓔ 100

5. What percent of 50 is b?

    Ⓐ $\dfrac{b}{50}$

    Ⓑ $\dfrac{b}{2}$

    Ⓒ $\dfrac{50}{b}$

    Ⓓ $\dfrac{2}{b}$

    Ⓔ $2b$

6. 8 is $\dfrac{1}{3}$% of what number?

7. During his second week on the job, Mario earned $110. This represented a 25% increase over his earnings of the previous week. How much did he earn during his first week of work?

    Ⓐ $82.50
    Ⓑ $85.00
    Ⓒ $88.00
    Ⓓ $137.50
    Ⓔ $146.67

8. At Bernie's Bargain Basement everything is sold for 20% less than the price marked. If Bernie buys radios for $80, what price should he mark them if he wants to make a 20% profit on his cost?

    Ⓐ $96
    Ⓑ $100
    Ⓒ $112
    Ⓓ $120
    Ⓔ $125

9. Mrs. Fisher usually deposits the same amount of money each month into a vacation fund. This year she decided not to make any contributions during November and December. To make the same annual contribution that she had originally planned, by what percent should she increase her monthly deposits from January through October?

   Ⓐ $16\frac{2}{3}\%$

   Ⓑ 20%

   Ⓒ 25%

   Ⓓ $33\frac{1}{3}\%$

   Ⓔ It cannot be determined from the information given.

10. The price of a loaf of bread was increased by 20%. How many loaves can be purchased for the amount of money that used to buy 300 loaves?

    Ⓐ 240

    Ⓑ 250

    Ⓒ 280

    Ⓓ 320

    Ⓔ 360

11. If 1 micron = 10,000 angstroms, then 100 angstroms is what percent of 10 microns?

    Ⓐ 0.0001%

    Ⓑ 0.001%

    Ⓒ 0.01%

    Ⓓ 0.1%

    Ⓔ 1%

12. There are twice as many girls as boys in an English class. If 30% of the girls and 45% of the boys have already handed in their book reports, what percent of the students have not yet handed in their reports?

     %

13. An art dealer bought a Ming vase for $1000 and later sold it for $10,000. By what percent did the value of the vase increase?

    Ⓐ 10%

    Ⓑ 90%

    Ⓒ 100%

    Ⓓ 900%

    Ⓔ 1000%

14. During a sale a clerk was putting a new price tag on each item. On one jacket, he accidentally raised the price by 15% instead of lowering the price by 15%. As a result the price on the tag was $45 too high. What was the original price of the jacket?

    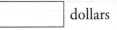 dollars

15. On a test consisting of 80 questions, Eve answered 75% of the first 60 questions correctly. What percent of the other 20 questions does she need to answer correctly for her grade on the entire exam to be 80%?

    Ⓐ 85%

    Ⓑ 87.5%

    Ⓒ 90%

    Ⓓ 95%

    Ⓔ 100%

Quantitative Comparison Questions

> Ⓐ Quantity A is greater.
> Ⓑ Quantity B is greater.
> Ⓒ Quantities A and B are equal.
> Ⓓ It is impossible to determine which quantity is greater.

	Quantity A	Quantity B
16.	400% of 3	300% of 4

n% of 25 is 50

	Quantity A	Quantity B
17.	50% of *n*	75

	Quantity A	Quantity B
18.	The price of a television when it is on sale at 25% off	The price of that television when it's on sale at $25 off

The price of cellular phone 1 is 20% more than the price of cellular phone 2.

	Quantity A	Quantity B
19.	The price of cellular phone 1 when it is on sale at 20% off	The price of cellular phone 2

	Quantity A	Quantity B
20.	$\frac{2}{3}$% of $\frac{3}{4}$	$\frac{3}{4}$% of $\frac{2}{3}$

	Quantity A	Quantity B
21.	*a*% of $\frac{1}{b}$	*b*% of $\frac{1}{a}$

Bank A pays 5% interest on its savings accounts. Bank B pays 4% interest on its savings accounts.

	Quantity A	Quantity B
22.	Percent by which bank B would have to raise its interest rate to match bank A	20%

A mixture of sugar and cinnamon is 20% sugar by weight. To make it sweeter, the amount of sugar is doubled.

	Quantity A	Quantity B
23.	The percent of sugar in the new mixture	40%

b is an integer greater than 1, and *b* equals *n*% of b^2

	Quantity A	Quantity B
24.	*n*	50

After Ali gave Lior 50% of her money, she had 20% as much as he did.

	Quantity A	Quantity B
25.	75% of the amount Lior had originally	150% of the amount Ali had originally

ANSWER KEY

1. **D**	6. **2400**	11. **D**	16. **C**	21. **D**
2. **D**	7. **C**	12. **65**	17. **A**	22. **A**
3. **B**	8. **D**	13. **D**	18. **D**	23. **B**
4. **C**	9. **B**	14. **150**	19. **B**	24. **D**
5. **E**	10. **B**	15. **D**	20. **C**	25. **C**

Answer Explanations

1. **(D)** If 4 students failed, then the other $25 - 4 = 21$ students passed, and $\frac{21}{25} = 0.84 = 84\%$.

2. **(D)** Since 5% of 60 is 3, Amanda saved $3, and thus paid $57 for the sweater. She then had to pay 5% sales tax on the $57: $.05 \times 57 = 2.85$, so the total cost was $57 + $2.85 = $59.85.

3. **(B)** 10% of 20% of 30% $= .10 \times .20 \times .30 = .006 = .6\%$.

4. **(C)** 500% of $c = 5c$, which is 1% of $500c$.

5. **(E)** $b = \frac{x}{\overset{\;}{\underset{2}{100}}}(\overset{1}{\cancel{50}}) \Rightarrow b = \frac{x}{2} \Rightarrow x = 2b$.

6. **2400** $8 = \dfrac{\frac{1}{3}}{100}x = \dfrac{1}{300}x \Rightarrow x = 8 \times 300 = 2400$.

7. **(C)** To find Mario's earnings during his first week, divide his earnings from the second week by 1.25: $110 \div 1.25 = 88$.

8. **(D)** Since 20% of 80 is 16, Bernie wants to get $96 for each radio he sells. What price should the radios be marked so that after a 20% discount, the customer will pay $96? If x represents the marked price, then $.80x = 96 \Rightarrow x = 96 \div .80 = 120$.

9. **(B)** Assume that Mrs. Fisher usually contributed $100 each month, for an annual total of $1200. Having decided not to contribute for 2 months, the $1200 will have to be paid in 10 monthly deposits of $120 each. This is an increase of $20, and a percent increase of

$$\frac{\text{actual increase}}{\text{original amount}} \times 100\% = \frac{20}{100} \times 100\% = 20\%.$$

10. **(B)** Assume that a loaf of bread used to cost $1 and that now it costs $1.20 (20% more). Then 300 loaves of bread used to cost $300. How many loaves costing $1.20 each can be bought for $300? $300 \div 1.20 = 250$.

11. **(D)** 1 micron = 10,000 angstroms $\Rightarrow$ 10 microns = 100,000 angstroms;

dividing both sides by 1000, we get 100 angstroms = $\dfrac{1}{1000}$ (10 microns);

and $\dfrac{1}{1000}$ = .001 = 0.1%.

12. **65** Assume that there are 100 boys and 200 girls in the class. Then, 45 boys and 60 girls have handed in their reports. So 105 students have handed them in, and 300 − 105 = 195 have not handed them in. What percent of 300 is 195?

$$\dfrac{195}{300} = .65 = 65\%.$$

13. **(D)** The increase in the value of the vase was $9,000. So the percent increase is $\dfrac{\text{actual increase}}{\text{original cost}} \times 100\% = \dfrac{9000}{1000} = 9 = 900\%.$

14. **150** If p represents the original price, the jacket was priced at $1.15p$ instead of $.85p$. Since this was a $45 difference, $45 = 1.15p - .85p = .30p \Rightarrow p = 45 \div .30 = \$150.$

15. **(D)** To earn a grade of 80% on the entire exam, Eve needs to correctly answer 64 questions (80% of 80). So far, she has answered 45 questions correctly (75% of 60). Therefore, on the last 20 questions she needs 64 − 45 = 19 correct answers; and $\dfrac{19}{20} = 95\%.$

16. **(C)** Quantity A: 400% of 3 = 4 × 3 = 12.
Quantity B: 300% of 4 = 3 × 4 = 12.

17. **(A)** Since $n\%$ of 25 is 50, then 25% of n is also 50, and 50% of n is twice as much: 100. If you don't see that, just solve for n:

$$\dfrac{n}{\cancel{100}\,4} \times \cancel{25}^{1} = 50 \Rightarrow \dfrac{n}{4} = 50 \Rightarrow n = 200 \text{ and } 50\% \text{ of } n = 100.$$

18. **(D)** A 25% discount on a $10 television is much less than $25, whereas a 25% discount on a $1000 television is much more than $25. (They would be equal only if the regular price of the television were $100.)

19. **(B)** Assume that the list price of cellular phone 2 is $100; then the list price of cellular phone 1 is $120, and on sale at 20% off it costs $24 less: $96.

20. **(C)** For *any* numbers a and b: $a\%$ of b is equal to $b\%$ of a.

21. **(D)**

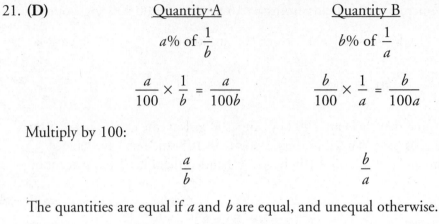

Quantity A	Quantity B
$a\%$ of $\dfrac{1}{b}$	$b\%$ of $\dfrac{1}{a}$
$\dfrac{a}{100} \times \dfrac{1}{b} = \dfrac{a}{100b}$	$\dfrac{b}{100} \times \dfrac{1}{a} = \dfrac{b}{100a}$

Multiply by 100:

$$\dfrac{a}{b} \qquad\qquad \dfrac{b}{a}$$

The quantities are equal if a and b are equal, and unequal otherwise.

22. **(A)** Bank B would have to increase its rate from 4% to 5%, an actual increase of 1%. This represents a percent increase of $\dfrac{1\%}{4\%} \times 100\% = 25\%$.

23. **(B)** Assume that the original mixture consists of 20 grams of sugar and 80 grams of cinnamon. If the amount of sugar is doubled, there would be 40 grams of sugar and 80 grams of cinnamon.

The sugar will then comprise $\dfrac{40}{120} = \dfrac{1}{3} = 33\dfrac{1}{3}\%$ of the mixture.

24. **(D)** If $b = 2$, then $b^2 = 4$, and 2 = 50% of 4; in this case, the quantities are equal. If $b = 4$, $b^2 = 16$, and 4 is not 50% of 16; in this case, the quantities are not equal.

25. **(C)** Avoid the algebra and just assume Ali started with $100. After giving Lior $50, she had $50 left, which was 20% or one-fifth of what he had. So, Lior had 5 × $50 = $250, which means that originally he had $200.
Quantity A: 75% of $200 = $150.
Quantity B: 150% of $100 = $150.
The quantities are equal.

11-D. RATIOS AND PROPORTIONS

A *ratio* is a fraction that compares two quantities that are measured in the same units. The first quantity is the numerator and the second quantity is the denominator.

For example, if there are 4 boys and 16 girls on the debate team, we say that the ratio of the number of boys to the number of girls on the team is 4 to 16, or $\frac{4}{16}$.

This is often written 4:16. Since a ratio is just a fraction, it can be reduced or converted to a decimal or a percent. The following are all different ways to express the same ratio:

$$4 \text{ to } 16 \quad 4{:}16 \quad \frac{4}{16} \qquad 2 \text{ to } 8 \quad 2{:}8 \quad \frac{2}{8} \qquad 1 \text{ to } 4 \quad 1{:}4 \quad \frac{1}{4} \qquad 0.25 \quad 25\%$$

CAUTION

Saying that the ratio of boys to girls on the team is 1:4 does *not* mean that $\frac{1}{4}$ of the team members are boys. It means that for each boy on the team there are 4 girls; so for every 5 members of the team, there are 4 girls and 1 boy. Boys, therefore, make up $\frac{1}{5}$ of the team, and girls $\frac{4}{5}$.

KEY FACT D1

If a set of objects is divided into two groups in the ratio of *a:b*, then the first group contains $\frac{a}{a+b}$ of the objects and the second group contains $\frac{b}{a+b}$ of the objects.

EXAMPLE 1

Last year, the ratio of the number of tennis matches that Central College's women's team won to the number of matches they lost was 7:3. What percent of their matches did the team win?

[___] %

SOLUTION.

The team won $\frac{7}{7+3} = \frac{7}{10} = \mathbf{70}\%$ of their matches.

EXAMPLE 2

If 45% of the students at a college are male, what is the ratio of male students to female students?

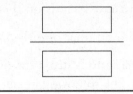

TIP

In problems involving percents the best number to use is 100.

SOLUTION.

Assume that there are 100 students. Then 45 of them are male, and $100 - 45 = 55$ of them are female. So, the ratio of males to females is $\dfrac{45}{55} = \dfrac{9}{11}$.

If we know how many boys and girls there are in a club, then, clearly, we know not only the ratio of boys to girls, but several other ratios too. For example, if the club has 7 boys and 3 girls: the ratio of boys to girls is $\dfrac{7}{3}$, the ratio of girls to boys is $\dfrac{3}{7}$, the ratio of boys to members is $\dfrac{7}{10}$, the ratio of members to girls is $\dfrac{10}{3}$, and so on.

However, if we know a ratio, we *cannot* determine how many objects there are. For example, if a jar contains only red and blue marbles, and if the ratio of red marbles to blue marbles is 3:5, there *may* be 3 red marbles and 5 blue marbles, but *not necessarily*. There may be 300 red marbles and 500 blue ones, since the ratio 300:500 reduces to 3:5. In the same way, all of the following are possibilities for the distribution of marbles.

Red	6	12	33	51	150	3000	**3x**
Blue	10	20	55	85	250	5000	**5x**

The important thing to observe is that the number of red marbles can be *any* multiple of 3, as long as the number of blue marbles is the *same* multiple of 5.

KEY FACT D2

If two numbers are in the ratio of *a:b*, then for some number *x*, the first number is *ax* and the second number is *bx*. If the ratio is in lowest terms, and if the quantities must be integers, then *x* is also an integer.

TACTIC

D1

In any ratio problem, write the letter *x* after each number and use some given information to solve for *x*.

EXAMPLE 3

If the ratio of men to women in a particular dormitory is 5:3, which of the following could not be the number of residents in the dormitory?

Ⓐ 24 Ⓑ 40 Ⓒ 96 Ⓓ 150 Ⓔ 224

SOLUTION.

If $5x$ and $3x$ are the number of men and women in the dormitory, respectively, then the number of residents in the dormitory is $5x + 3x = 8x$. So, the number of students must be a multiple of 8. Of the five choices, only **150 (D)** is not divisible by 8.

NOTE: Assume that the ratio of the number of pounds of cole slaw to the number of pounds of potato salad consumed in the dormitory's cafeteria was 5:3. Then, it is possible that a total of exactly 150 pounds was eaten: 93.75 pounds of cole slaw and 56.25 pounds of potato salad. In Example 3, 150 wasn't possible because there had to be a *whole* number of men and women.

EXAMPLE 4

The measures of the two acute angles in a right triangle are in the ratio of 5:13. What is the measure of the larger angle?

Ⓐ 25° Ⓑ 45° Ⓒ 60° Ⓓ 65° Ⓔ 75°

SOLUTION.

Let the measure of the smaller angle be $5x$ and the measure of the larger angle be $13x$. Since the sum of the measures of the two acute angles of a right triangle is 90° (KEY FACT J1), $5x + 13x = 90 \Rightarrow 18x = 90 \Rightarrow x = 5$.

Therefore, the measure of the larger angle is $13 \times 5 = $ **65° (D)**.

Ratios can be extended to three or four or more terms. For example, we can say that the ratio of freshmen to sophomores to juniors to seniors in a college marching band is 6:8:5:8, which means that for every 6 freshmen in the band there are 8 sophomores, 5 juniors, and 8 seniors.

TIP

TACTIC D1 applies to extended ratios, as well.

EXAMPLE 5

The concession stand at Cinema City sells popcorn in three sizes: large, super, and jumbo. One day, Cinema City sold 240 bags of popcorn, and the ratio of large to super to jumbo was 8:17:15. How many super bags of popcorn were sold that day?

SOLUTION.
Let $8x$, $17x$, and $15x$ be the number of large, super, and jumbo bags of popcorn sold, respectively. Then $8x + 17x + 15x = 240 \Rightarrow 40x = 240 \Rightarrow x = 6$.
The number of super bags sold was $17 \times 6 = \mathbf{102}$.

KEY FACT D3

KEY FACT D1 applies to extended ratios, as well. If a set of objects is divided into 3 groups in the ratio $a:b:c$, then the first group contains $\dfrac{a}{a+b+c}$ of the objects, the second $\dfrac{b}{a+b+c}$, and the third $\dfrac{c}{a+b+c}$.

EXAMPLE 6

If the ratio of large to super to jumbo bags of popcorn sold at Cinema City was 8:17:15, what percent of the bags sold were super?

Ⓐ 20%   Ⓑ 25%   Ⓒ $33\frac{1}{3}$%   Ⓓ 37.5%   Ⓔ 42.5%

SOLUTION.
Super bags made up $\dfrac{17}{8+17+15} = \dfrac{17}{40} = \mathbf{42.5\%}$ of the total (**E**).

A jar contains a number of red (R), white (W), and blue (B) marbles. Suppose that R:W = 2:3 and W:B = 3:5. Then, for every 2 red marbles, there are 3 white ones, and for those 3 white ones, there are 5 blue ones. So, R:B = 2:5, and we can form the extended ratio R:W:B = 2:3:5.

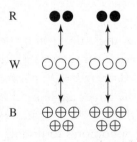

If the ratios were R:W = 2:3 and W:B = 4:5, however, we wouldn't be able to combine them as easily. From the diagram below, you see that for every 8 reds there are 15 blues, so R:B = 8:15.

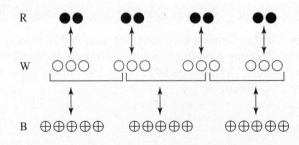

To see this without drawing a picture, we write the ratios as fractions: $\dfrac{R}{W} = \dfrac{2}{3}$ and $\dfrac{W}{B} = \dfrac{4}{5}$. Then, we multiply the fractions:

$$\frac{R}{\cancel{W}} \times \frac{\cancel{W}}{B} = \frac{2}{3} \times \frac{4}{5} = \frac{8}{15}, \quad \text{so} \quad \frac{R}{B} = \frac{8}{15}.$$

Not only does this give us R:B = 8:15, but also, if we multiply both W numbers, $3 \times 4 = 12$, we can write the extended ratio: R:W:B = 8:12:15.

EXAMPLE 7

Jar A and jar B each have 70 marbles,
all of which are red, white, or blue.
In jar A, R:W = 2:3 and W:B = 3:5.
In jar B, R:W = 2:3 and W:B = 4:5.

Quantity A	Quantity B
The number of white marbles in jar A	The number of white marbles in jar B

SOLUTION.
From the discussion immediately preceding this example, in jar A the extended ratio R:W:B is 2:3:5, which implies that the white marbles constitute $\dfrac{3}{2+3+5} = \dfrac{3}{10}$ of the total: $\dfrac{3}{10} \times 70 = \mathbf{21}$.

In jar B the extended ratio R:W:B is 8:12:15, so the white marbles are $\dfrac{12}{8+12+15} = \dfrac{12}{35}$ of the total: $\dfrac{12}{35} \times 70 = \mathbf{24}$. The answer is **B**.

A **_proportion_** is an equation that states that two ratios are equivalent. Since ratios are just fractions, any equation such as $\dfrac{4}{6} = \dfrac{10}{15}$ in which each side is a single fraction is a proportion. Usually the proportions you encounter on the GRE involve one or more variables.

TACTIC

Solve proportions by cross-multiplying: if $\dfrac{a}{b} = \dfrac{c}{d}$, then $ad = bc$.

Setting up a proportion is a common way of solving a problem on the GRE.

EXAMPLE 8

If $\dfrac{3}{7} = \dfrac{x}{84}$, what is the value of x?

$\boxed{}$

SOLUTION.
Cross-multiply: $3(84) = 7x \Rightarrow 252 = 7x \Rightarrow x = \mathbf{36}$.

EXAMPLE 9

If $\dfrac{x+2}{17} = \dfrac{x}{16}$, what is the value of $\dfrac{x+6}{19}$?

Ⓐ $\dfrac{1}{2}$ Ⓑ 1 Ⓒ $\dfrac{3}{2}$ Ⓓ 2 Ⓔ 3

SOLUTION.
Cross-multiply: $16(x+2) = 17x \Rightarrow 16x + 32 = 17x \Rightarrow x = 32$.

So, $\dfrac{x+6}{19} = \dfrac{32+6}{19} = \dfrac{38}{19} = \mathbf{2}\ (\mathbf{D})$.

EXAMPLE 10

A state law requires that on any field trip the ratio of the number of chaperones to the number of students must be at least 1:12. If 100 students are going on a field trip, what is the minimum number of chaperones required?

Ⓐ 6 Ⓑ 8 Ⓒ $8\dfrac{1}{3}$ Ⓓ 9 Ⓔ 12

SOLUTION.
Let x represent the number of chaperones required, and set up a proportion: $\dfrac{\text{number of chaperones}}{\text{number of students}} = \dfrac{1}{12} = \dfrac{x}{100}$. Cross-multiply: $100 = 12x \Rightarrow x = 8\dfrac{1}{3}$. This, of course, is *not* the answer since, clearly, the number of chaperones must be a whole number. Since x is greater than 8, 8 chaperones would not be enough. The answer is **9 (D)**.

A *rate* is a fraction that compares two quantities measured in different units. The word "per" often appears in rate problems: miles per hour, dollars per week, cents per ounce, students per classroom, and so on.

TIP

A rate can always be written as a fraction.

TACTIC
D3

Set up rate problems just like ratio problems. Solve the proportions by cross-multiplying.

EXAMPLE 11

Brigitte solved 24 math problems in 15 minutes. At this rate, how many problems can she solve in 40 minutes?

Ⓐ 25   Ⓑ 40   Ⓒ 48   Ⓓ 60   Ⓔ 64

SOLUTION.

Handle this rate problem exactly like a ratio problem. Set up a proportion and cross-multiply:

$$\frac{\text{problems}}{\text{minutes}} = \frac{24}{15} = \frac{x}{40} \Rightarrow 15x = 40 \times 24 = 960 \Rightarrow x = \mathbf{64}\ (\mathbf{E}).$$

When the denominator in the given rate is 1 unit (1 minute, 1 mile, 1 dollar), the problem can be solved by a single division or multiplication. Consider Examples 12 and 13.

EXAMPLE 12

If Stefano types at the rate of 35 words per minute, how long will it take him to type 987 words?

SOLUTION.

Set up a proportion and cross-multiply:

$$\frac{\text{words typed}}{\text{minutes}} = \frac{35}{1} = \frac{987}{x} \Rightarrow 35x = 987 \Rightarrow x = \frac{987}{35} = \mathbf{28.2}\ \text{minutes}.$$

EXAMPLE 13

If Mario types at the rate of 35 words per minute, how many words can he type in 85 minutes?

SOLUTION.
Set up a proportion and cross-multiply:

$$\frac{\text{words typed}}{\text{minutes}} = \frac{35}{1} = \frac{x}{85} \Rightarrow x = 35 \times 85 = \mathbf{2975} \text{ words.}$$

Notice that in Example 12, all we did was divide 987 by 35, and in Example 13, we multiplied 35 by 85. If you realize that, you don't have to introduce *x* and set up a proportion. You must know, however, whether to multiply or divide. If you're not absolutely positive which is correct, write the proportion; then you can't go wrong.

CAUTION

In rate problems it is essential that the units in both fractions be the same.

EXAMPLE 14

If 3 apples cost 50¢, how many apples can you buy for $20?

Ⓐ 20   Ⓑ 60   Ⓒ 120   Ⓓ 600   Ⓔ 2000

SOLUTION.
We have to set up a proportion, but it is *not* $\frac{3}{50} = \frac{x}{20}$. In the first fraction, the denominator represents *cents*, whereas in the second fraction, the denominator represents *dollars*. The units must be the same. We can change 50 cents to 0.5 dollar or we can change 20 dollars to 2000 cents:

$$\frac{3}{50} = \frac{x}{2000} \Rightarrow 50x = 6000 \Rightarrow x = \mathbf{120} \text{ apples } (\mathbf{C}).$$

On the GRE, some rate problems involve only variables. They are handled in exactly the same way.

EXAMPLE 15

If *a* apples cost *c* cents, how many apples can be bought for *d* dollars?

Ⓐ 100*acd*   Ⓑ $\frac{100d}{ac}$ Ⓒ $\frac{ad}{100c}$ Ⓓ $\frac{c}{100ad}$ Ⓔ $\frac{100ad}{c}$

SOLUTION.
First change *d* dollars to 100*d* cents, and set up a proportion: $\frac{\text{apples}}{\text{cents}} = \frac{a}{c} = \frac{x}{100d}$.

Now cross-multiply: $100ad = cx \Rightarrow x = \frac{100ad}{c}$ (**E**).

Most students find problems such as Example 15 very difficult. If you get stuck on such a problem, use TACTIC 2, Chapter 8, which gives another strategy for handling these problems.

Notice that in rate problems, as one quantity increases or decreases, so does the other. If you are driving at 45 miles per hour, the more hours you drive, the further you go; if you drive fewer miles, it takes less time. If chopped meat cost $3.00 per pound, the less you spend, the fewer pounds you get; the more meat you buy, the more it costs.

In some problems, however, as one quantity increases, the other decreases. These *cannot* be solved by setting up a proportion. Consider the following two examples, which look similar but must be handled differently.

EXAMPLE 16

A hospital needs 150 pills to treat 6 patients for a week. How many pills does it need to treat 10 patients for a week?

$$\boxed{}$$

SOLUTION.
Example 16 is a standard rate problem. The more patients there are, the more pills are needed.

The *ratio* or *quotient* remains constant: $\dfrac{150}{6} = \dfrac{x}{10} \Rightarrow 6x = 1500 \Rightarrow x = \mathbf{250}$.

EXAMPLE 17

A hospital has enough pills on hand to treat 10 patients for 14 days. How long will the pills last if there are 35 patients?

$$\boxed{}$$

SOLUTION.
In Example 17, the situation is different. With more patients, the supply of pills will last for a shorter period of time; if there were fewer patients, the supply would last longer. It is not the ratio that remains constant, it is the *product*.

There are enough pills to last for $10 \times 14 = 140$ patient-days:

$$\frac{140 \text{ patient-days}}{10 \text{ patients}} = 14 \text{ days} \qquad \frac{140 \text{ patient-days}}{35 \text{ patients}} = 4 \text{ days}$$

$$\frac{140 \text{ patient-days}}{70 \text{ patients}} = 2 \text{ days} \qquad \frac{140 \text{ patient-days}}{1 \text{ patient}} = 140 \text{ days}$$

There are many mathematical situations in which one quantity increases as another decreases, but their product is not constant. Those types of problems, however, do not appear on the GRE.

TACTIC

D4

If one quantity increases as a second quantity decreases, multiply them; their product will be a constant.

EXAMPLE 18

If 15 workers can pave a certain number of driveways in 24 days, how many days will 40 workers take, working at the same rate, to do the same job?

Ⓐ 6   Ⓑ 9   Ⓒ 15   Ⓓ 24   Ⓔ 40

SOLUTION.

Clearly, the more workers there are, the less time it will take, so use TACTIC D4: multiply. The job takes $15 \times 24 = 360$ worker-days:

$$\frac{360 \text{ worker-days}}{40 \text{ workers}} = \mathbf{9} \text{ days } (\mathbf{B}).$$

Note that it doesn't matter how many driveways have to be paved, as long as the 15 workers and the 40 workers are doing the same job. Even if the question had said, "15 workers can pave 18 driveways in 24 days," the number 18 would not have entered into the solution. This number would be important only if the second group of workers was going to pave a different number of driveways.

EXAMPLE 19

If 15 workers can pave 18 driveways in 24 days, how many days would it take 40 workers to pave 22 driveways?

Ⓐ 6   Ⓑ 9   Ⓒ 11   Ⓓ 15   Ⓔ 18

SOLUTION.

This question is similar to Example 18, except that now the jobs that the two groups of workers are doing are different. The solution, however, starts out exactly the same way. Just as in Example 18, 40 workers can do in 9 days the *same* job that 15 workers can do in 24 days. Since that job is to pave 18 driveways, 40 workers can pave $18 \div 9 = 2$ driveways every day. So, it will take **11** days for them to pave 22 driveways (**C**).

Practice Exercises—Ratios and Proportions

Discrete Quantitative Questions

1. If $\frac{3}{4}$ of the employees in a supermarket are not college graduates, what is the ratio of the number of college graduates to those who are not college graduates?

   Ⓐ 1:3
   Ⓑ 3:7
   Ⓒ 3:4
   Ⓓ 4:3
   Ⓔ 3:1

2. If $\frac{a}{9} = \frac{10}{2a}$, what is the value of a^2?

   Ⓐ $3\sqrt{6}$
   Ⓑ $3\sqrt{5}$
   Ⓒ $9\sqrt{6}$
   Ⓓ 45
   Ⓔ 90

3. If 80% of the applicants to a program were rejected, what is the ratio of the number accepted to the number rejected?

4. Scott can read 50 pages per hour. At this rate, how many pages can he read in 50 minutes?

   Ⓐ 25
   Ⓑ $41\frac{2}{3}$
   Ⓒ $45\frac{1}{2}$
   Ⓓ 48
   Ⓔ 60

5. If all the members of a team are juniors or seniors, and if the ratio of juniors to seniors on the team is 3:5, what percent of the team members are seniors?

   Ⓐ 37.5%
   Ⓑ 40%
   Ⓒ 60%
   Ⓓ 62.5%
   Ⓔ It cannot be determined from the information given.

6. The measures of the three angles in a triangle are in the ratio of 1:1:2. Which of the following statements must be true?

   Indicate *all* such statements.

   Ⓐ The triangle is isosceles.
   Ⓑ The triangle is a right triangle.
   Ⓒ The triangle is equilateral.

7. What is the ratio of the circumference of a circle to its radius?

   Ⓐ 1
   Ⓑ $\frac{\pi}{2}$
   Ⓒ $\sqrt{\pi}$
   Ⓓ π
   Ⓔ 2π

8. The ratio of the number of freshmen to sophomores to juniors to seniors on a college basketball team is 4:7:6:8. What percent of the team are sophomores?

   Ⓐ 16%
   Ⓑ 24%
   Ⓒ 25%
   Ⓓ 28%
   Ⓔ 32%

9. At Central State College the ratio of the number of students taking Spanish to the number taking French is 7:2. If 140 students are taking French, how many are taking Spanish?

 students

10. If $a:b = 3:5$ and $a:c = 5:7$, what is the value of $b:c$?

Ⓐ 3:7
Ⓑ 21:35
Ⓒ 21:25
Ⓓ 25:21
Ⓔ 7:3

11. If x is a positive number and $\dfrac{x}{3} = \dfrac{12}{x}$, then $x =$

Ⓐ 3
Ⓑ 4
Ⓒ 6
Ⓓ 12
Ⓔ 36

12. In the diagram below, $b:a = 7:2$. What is $b - a$?

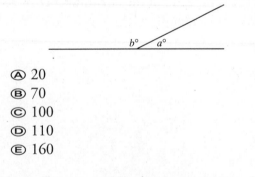

Ⓐ 20
Ⓑ 70
Ⓒ 100
Ⓓ 110
Ⓔ 160

13. A snail can move i inches in m minutes. At this rate, how many feet can it move in h hours?

Ⓐ $\dfrac{5hi}{m}$

Ⓑ $\dfrac{60hi}{m}$

Ⓒ $\dfrac{hi}{12m}$

Ⓓ $\dfrac{5m}{hi}$

Ⓔ $5him$

14. Gilda can grade t tests in $\dfrac{1}{x}$ hours. At this rate, how many tests can she grade in x hours?

Ⓐ tx
Ⓑ tx^2
Ⓒ $\dfrac{1}{t}$

Ⓓ $\dfrac{x}{t}$

Ⓔ $\dfrac{1}{tx}$

15. A club had 3 boys and 5 girls. During a membership drive the same number of boys and girls joined the club. How many members does the club have now if the ratio of boys to girls is 3:4?

Ⓐ 12
Ⓑ 14
Ⓒ 16
Ⓓ 21
Ⓔ 28

16. If $\dfrac{3x-1}{25} = \dfrac{x+5}{11}$, what is the value of x?

Ⓐ $\dfrac{3}{4}$

Ⓑ 3
Ⓒ 7
Ⓓ 17
Ⓔ 136

17. If 4 boys can shovel a driveway in 2 hours, how many minutes will it take 5 boys to do the job?

Ⓐ 60
Ⓑ 72
Ⓒ 96
Ⓓ 120
Ⓔ 150

18. If 500 pounds of mush will feed 20 pigs for a week, for how many days will 200 pounds of mush feed 14 pigs?

```
┌──────────┐
│          │
└──────────┘
```

Quantitative Comparison Questions

Ⓐ Quantity A is greater.
Ⓑ Quantity B is greater.
Ⓒ Quantities A and B are equal.
Ⓓ It is impossible to determine which quantity is greater.

The ratio of red to blue marbles in a jar was 3:5. The same number of red and blue marbles were added to the jar.

Quantity A	Quantity B
19. The ratio of red to blue marbles now	3:5

Three associates agreed to split the $3000 profit of an investment in the ratio of 2:5:8.

Quantity A	Quantity B
20. The difference between the largest and the smallest share	$1200

The ratio of the number of boys to girls in the chess club is 5:2. The ratio of the number of boys to girls in the glee club is 11:4.

Quantity A	Quantity B
21. The number of boys in the chess club	The number of boys in the glee club

Sally invited the same number of boys and girls to her party. Everyone who was invited came, but 5 additional boys showed up. This caused the ratio of girls to boys at the party to be 4:5.

Quantity A	Quantity B
22. The number of people she invited to her party	40

A large jar is full of marbles. When a single marble is drawn at random from the jar, the probability that it is red is $\frac{3}{7}$.

Quantity A	Quantity B
23. The ratio of the number of red marbles to non-red marbles in the jar	$\frac{1}{2}$

$3a = 2b$ and $3b = 5c$

Quantity A	Quantity B
24. The ratio of a to c	1

The radius of circle II is 3 times the radius of circle I

Quantity A	Quantity B
25. $\dfrac{\text{area of circle II}}{\text{area of circle I}}$	3π

ANSWER KEY

1. **A**	6. **A, B**	12. **C**	18. **4**	24. **A**
2. **D**	7. **E**	13. **A**	19. **A**	25. **B**
3. $\frac{1}{4}$	8. **D**	14. **B**	20. **C**	
	9. **490**	15. **B**	21. **D**	
4. **B**	10. **D**	16. **D**	22. **C**	
5. **D**	11. **C**	17. **C**	23. **A**	

Answer Explanations

1. **(A)** Of every 4 employees, 3 are not college graduates, and 1 is a college graduate. So the ratio of graduates to nongraduates is 1:3.

2. **(D)** Cross-multiplying, we get: $2a^2 = 90 \Rightarrow a^2 = 45$.

3. $\frac{1}{4}$ If 80% were rejected, 20% were accepted, and the ratio of accepted to rejected is 20:80 = 1:4.

4. **(B)** Set up a proportion: $\dfrac{50 \text{ pages}}{1 \text{ hour}} = \dfrac{50 \text{ pages}}{60 \text{ minutes}} = \dfrac{x \text{ pages}}{50 \text{ minutes}}$,

   and cross-multiply: $50 \times 50 = 60x \Rightarrow 2500 = 60x \Rightarrow x = 41\dfrac{2}{3}$.

5. **(D)** Out of every 8 team members, 3 are juniors and 5 are seniors. Seniors, therefore, make up $\dfrac{5}{8}$ = 62.5% of the team.

6. **(A)(B)** It is worth remembering that if the ratio of the measures of the angles of a triangle is 1:1:2, the angles are 45-45-90 (see Section 11-J). Otherwise, the first step is to write $x + x + 2x = 180 \Rightarrow 4x = 180 \Rightarrow x = 45$.

   Since two of the angles have the same measure, the triangle is isosceles, and since one of the angles measures 90°, it is a right triangle. I and II are true, and, of course, III is false.

7. **(E)** By definition, π is the ratio of the circumference to the diameter of a circle (see Section 11-L). Therefore, $\pi = \dfrac{C}{d} = \dfrac{C}{2r} \Rightarrow 2\pi = \dfrac{C}{r}$.

8. **(D)** The *fraction* of the team that is sophomores is $\dfrac{7}{4+7+6+8} = \dfrac{7}{25}$, and $\dfrac{7}{25} \times 100\% = 28\%$.

9. **490** Let the number of students taking Spanish be $7x$, and the number taking French be $2x$. Then, $2x = 140 \Rightarrow x = 70 \Rightarrow 7x = 490$.

10. **(D)** Since $\frac{a}{b} = \frac{3}{5}$, $\frac{b}{a} = \frac{5}{3}$. So, $b:c = \frac{b}{c} = \frac{b}{c} \times \frac{a^1}{a_1} = \frac{5}{3} \times \frac{5}{7} = \frac{25}{21} = 25:21$.

Alternatively, we could write equivalent ratios with the same value for a:

$$a:b = 3:5 = 15:25 \text{ and } a:c = 5:7 = 15:21.$$

So, when $a = 15$, $b = 25$, and $c = 21$.

11. **(C)** To solve a proportion, cross-multiply: $\frac{x}{3} = \frac{12}{x} \Rightarrow x^2 = 36 \Rightarrow x = 6$.

12. **(C)** Let $b = 7x$ and $a = 2x$. Then, $7x + 2x = 180 \Rightarrow 9x = 180 \Rightarrow x = 20 \Rightarrow$ $b = 140$ and $a = 40 \Rightarrow b - a = 140 - 40 = 100$.

13. **(A)** Set up the proportion, keeping track of

units: $\frac{x \text{ feet}}{h \text{ hours}} = \frac{\overset{1}{\cancel{12}}x \text{ inches}}{\underset{5}{\cancel{60}}h \text{ minutes}} = \frac{i \text{ inches}}{m \text{ minutes}} \Rightarrow \frac{x}{5h} = \frac{i}{m} \Rightarrow x = \frac{5hi}{m}$.

14. **(B)** Gilda grades at the rate of $\dfrac{t \text{ tests}}{\frac{1}{x}\text{ hours}} = \dfrac{tx \text{ tests}}{1 \text{ hour}}$.

Since she can grade tx tests each hour, in x hours she can grade $x(tx) = tx^2$ tests.

15. **(B)** Suppose that x boys and x girls joined the club. Then, the new ratio of boys to girls would be $(3 + x):(5 + x)$, which we are told is 3:4.

So, $\dfrac{3+x}{5+x} = \dfrac{3}{4} \Rightarrow 4(3 + x) = 3(5 + x) \Rightarrow 12 + 4x = 15 + 3x \Rightarrow x = 3$.

Therefore, 3 boys and 3 girls joined the other 3 boys and 5 girls: a total of 14.

16. **(D)** Cross-multiplying, we get:
$11(3x - 1) = 25(x + 5) \Rightarrow 33x - 11 = 25x + 125 \Rightarrow 8x = 136 \Rightarrow x = 17$.

17. **(C)** Since 4 boys can shovel the driveway in 2 hours, or $2 \times 60 = 120$ minutes, the job takes $4 \times 120 = 480$ boy-minutes; and so 5 boys would need $\dfrac{480 \text{ boy-minutes}}{5 \text{ boys}} = 96$ minutes.

18. **4** Since 500 pounds will last for 20 pig-weeks = 140 pig-days, 200 pounds will last for $\dfrac{2}{5} \times 140$ pig-days = 56 pig-days, and $\dfrac{56 \text{ pig-days}}{14 \text{ pigs}} = 4$ days.

19. **(A)** Assume that to start there were $3x$ red marbles and $5x$ blue ones and that y of each color were added.

	Quantity A	Quantity B
	$\dfrac{3x + y}{5x + y}$	$\dfrac{3}{5}$
Cross-multiply:	$5(3x + y)$	$3(5x + y)$
Distribute:	$15x + 5y$	$15x + 3y$
Subtract $15x$:	$5y$	$3y$

Since y is positive, Quantity A is greater.

20. **(C)** The shares are $2x$, $5x$, and $8x$, and their sum is 3000:
    $2x + 5x + 8x = 3000 \Rightarrow 15x = 3000 \Rightarrow x = 200$, and so $8x - 2x = 6x = 1200$.

21. **(D)** Ratios alone can't answer the question, "How many?" There could be 5 boys in the chess club or 500. We can't tell.

22. **(C)** Assume that Sally invited x boys and x girls. When she wound up with x girls and $x + 5$ boys, the girl:boy ratio was 4:5. So,
    $$\frac{x}{x+5} = \frac{4}{5} \Rightarrow 5x = 4x + 20 \Rightarrow x = 20$$
    Sally invited 40 people (20 boys and 20 girls).

23. **(A)** If the probability of drawing a red marble is $\frac{3}{7}$, 3 out of every 7 marbles are red, and 4 out of every 7 are non-red. So the ratio of red:non-red = 3:4, which is greater than $\frac{1}{2}$.

24. **(A)** Multiplying the first equation by 3 and the second by 2 to get the same coefficient of b, we have: $9a = 6b$ and $6b = 10c$. So, $9a = 10c$ and $\frac{a}{c} = \frac{10}{9}$.

25. **(B)** Assume the radius of circle I is 1 and the radius of circle II is 3. Then the areas are π and 9π, respectively. So, the area of circle II is 9 times the area of circle I, and $3\pi > 9$.

11-E. AVERAGES

The *average* of a set of *n* numbers is the sum of those numbers divided by *n*.

$$\text{average} = \frac{\text{sum of the } n \text{ numbers}}{n} \quad \text{or simply} \quad A = \frac{\text{sum}}{n}.$$

If the weights of three children are 80, 90, and 76 pounds, respectively, to calculate the average weight of the children, you would add the three weights and divide by 3:

$$\frac{80 + 90 + 76}{3} = \frac{246}{3} = 82$$

The technical name for this type of average is "arithmetic mean," and on the GRE those words always appear in parentheses—for example, "What is the average (arithmetic mean) of 80, 90, and 76?"

Usually, on the GRE, you are not asked to find an average; rather, you are given the average of a set of numbers and asked for some other information. The key to solving all of these problems is to first find the sum of the numbers. Since $A = \frac{\text{sum}}{n}$, multiplying both sides by *n* yields the equation: sum = *nA*.

TACTIC

E1

If you know the average, *A*, of a set of *n* numbers, multiply *A* by *n* to get their sum.

EXAMPLE 1

One day a supermarket received a delivery of 25 frozen turkeys. If the average (arithmetic mean) weight of a turkey was 14.2 pounds, what was the total weight, in pounds, of all the turkeys?

SOLUTION.
Use TACTIC E1: $25 \times 14.2 = $ **355**.

NOTE: We do not know how much any individual turkey weighed nor how many turkeys weighed more or less than 14.2 pounds. All we know is their total weight.

EXAMPLE 2

Sheila took five chemistry tests during the semester and the average (arithmetic mean) of her test scores was 85. If her average after the first three tests was 83, what was the average of her fourth and fifth tests?

Ⓐ 83 Ⓑ 85 Ⓒ 87 Ⓓ 88 Ⓔ 90

SOLUTION.
• Use TACTIC E1: On her five tests, Sheila earned $5 \times 85 = 425$ points.
• Use TACTIC E1 again: On her first three tests she earned $3 \times 83 = 249$ points.

- Subtract: On her last two tests Sheila earned 425 − 249 = 176 points.
- Calculate her average on her last two tests: $\frac{176}{2}$ = **88 (D)**.

NOTE: We cannot determine Sheila's grade on even one of the tests.

KEY FACT E1

- **If all the numbers in a set are the same, then that number is the average.**
- **If the numbers in a set are not all the same, then the average must be greater than the smallest number and less than the largest number. Equivalently, at least one of the numbers is less than the average and at least one is greater.**

If Jessica's test grades are 85, 85, 85, and 85, her average is 85. If Gary's test grades are 76, 83, 88, and 88, his average must be greater than 76 and less than 88. What can we conclude if, after taking five tests, Kristen's average is 90? We know that she earned exactly 5 × 90 = 450 points, and that either she got a 90 on every test or at least one grade was less than 90 and at least one was over 90. Here are a few of the thousands of possibilities for Kristen's grades:

(a) 90, 90, 90, 90, 90   (b) 80, 90, 90, 90, 100   (c) 83, 84, 87, 97, 99
(d) 77, 88, 93, 95, 97   (e) 50, 100, 100, 100, 100

In (b), 80, the one grade below 90, is *10 points below*, and 100, the one grade above 90, is *10 points above*. In (c), 83 is 7 points below 90, 84 is 6 points below 90, and 87 is 3 points below 90, for a total of 7 + 6 + 3 = *16 points below 90*; 97 is 7 points above 90, and 99 is 9 points above 90, for a total of 7 + 9 = *16 points above 90*.

These differences from the average are called ***deviations***, and the situation in these examples is not a coincidence.

KEY FACT E2

The total deviation below the average is equal to the total deviation above the average.

EXAMPLE 3

If the average (arithmetic mean) of 25, 31, and *x* is 37, what is the value of *x*?

```
┌─────────┐
│         │
└─────────┘
```

SOLUTION 1.
Use KEY FACT E2. Since 25 is 12 less than 37 and 31 is 6 less than 37, the total deviation below the average is 12 + 6 = 18. Therefore, the total deviation above must also be 18. So, *x* = 37 + 18 = **55**.

SOLUTION 2.
Use TACTIC E1. Since the average of the three numbers is 37, the sum of the 3 numbers is 3 × 37 = 111. Then,

$$25 + 31 + x = 111 \Rightarrow 56 + x = 111 \Rightarrow x = \textbf{55}.$$

KEY FACT E3

Assume that the average of a set of numbers is *A*. If a number *x* is added to the set and a new average is calculated, then the new average will be less than, equal to, or greater than *A*, depending on whether *x* is less than, equal to, or greater than *A*, respectively.

EXAMPLE 4

Quantity A	Quantity B
The average (arithmetic mean) of the integers from 0 to 12	The average (arithmetic mean) of the integers from 1 to 12

TIP

Remember TACTIC 5 from Chapter 9. We don't have to *calculate* the averages, we just have to *compare* them.

SOLUTION 1.

Quantity B is the average of the integers from 1 to 12, which is surely greater than 1. Quantity A is the average of those same 12 numbers and 0. Since the extra number, 0, is less than Quantity B, Quantity A must be *less* [KEY FACT E3]. The answer is **B**.

SOLUTION 2.

Clearly the sum of the 13 integers from 0 to 12 is the same as the sum of the 12 integers from 1 to 12. Since that sum is positive, dividing by 13 yields a smaller quotient than dividing by 12 [KEY FACT B4].

Although in solving Example 4 we didn't calculate the averages, we could have:

$$0 + 1 + 2 + 3 + 4 + 5 + \mathbf{6} + 7 + 8 + 9 + 10 + 11 + 12 = 78 \text{ and } \frac{78}{13} = 6.$$

$$1 + 2 + 3 + 4 + 5 + \mathbf{6} + \mathbf{7} + 8 + 9 + 10 + 11 + 12 = 78 \text{ and } \frac{78}{12} = 6.5.$$

Notice that the average of the 13 *consecutive* integers 0, 1,...,12 is the *middle integer*, **6**, and the average of the 12 *consecutive* integers 1, 2,...,12 is the *average of the two middle integers*, **6** and **7**. This is a special case of KEY FACT E4.

KEY FACT E4

Whenever *n* numbers form an arithmetic sequence (one in which the difference between any two consecutive terms is the same): (i) if *n* is odd, the average of the numbers is the middle term in the sequence and (ii) if *n* is even, the average of the numbers is the average of the two middle terms, which is the same as the average of the first and last terms.

For example, in the arithmetic sequence 6, 9, 12, 15, 18, the average is the middle number, **12**; in the sequence 10, 20, 30, 40, 50, 60, the average is **35**, the average of the two middle numbers — 30 and 40. Note that 35 is also the average of the first and last terms—10 and 60.

EXAMPLE 5

On Thursday, 20 of the 25 students in a chemistry class took a test and their average was 80. On Friday, the other 5 students took the test, and their average was 90. What was the average (arithmetic mean) for the entire class?

SOLUTION.

The class average is calculated by dividing the sum of all 25 test grades by 25.

- The first 20 students earned a total of: $20 \times 80 = 1600$ points
- The other 5 students earned a total of: $5 \times 90 = 450$ points
- Add: altogether the class earned: $1600 + 450 = 2050$ points

- Calculate the class average: $\dfrac{2050}{25} = \mathbf{82}$.

Notice that the answer to Example 5 is *not* 85, which is the average of 80 and 90. This is because the averages of 80 and 90 were earned by different numbers of students, and so the two averages had to be given different weights in the calculation. For this reason, this is called a ***weighted average***.

KEY FACT E5

To calculate the weighted average of a set of numbers, multiply each number in the set by the number of times it appears, add all the products, and divide by the total number of numbers in the set.

So, the solution to Example 5 should look like this:

$$\frac{20(80) + 5(90)}{25} = \frac{1600 + 450}{25} = \frac{2050}{25} = 82$$

Problems involving *average speed* will be discussed in Section 11-H, but we mention them briefly here because they are closely related to problems on weighted averages.

TIP

Without doing any calculations, you should immediately realize that since the grade of 80 is being given more weight than the grade of 90, the average will be closer to 80 than to 90 — certainly *less than 85.*

EXAMPLE 6

For the first 3 hours of his trip, Justin drove at 50 miles per hour. Then, due to construction delays, he drove at only 40 miles per hour for the next 2 hours. What was his average speed, in miles per hour, for the entire trip?

Ⓐ 40   Ⓑ 43   Ⓒ 46   Ⓓ 48   Ⓔ 50

SOLUTION.

This is just a weighted average:

$$\frac{3(50) + 2(40)}{5} = \frac{150 + 80}{5} = \frac{230}{5} = \mathbf{46}.$$

Note that in the fractions above, the numerator is the total distance traveled and the denominator the total time the trip took. This is *always* the way to find an average speed. Consider the following slight variation on Example 6.

EXAMPLE 6A

For the first 100 miles of his trip, Justin drove at 50 miles per hour, and then due to construction delays, he drove at only 40 miles per hour for the next 120 miles. What was his average speed, in miles per hour, for the entire trip?

| | miles per hour

SOLUTION.
This is not a *weighted* average. Here we immediately know the total distance traveled, 220 miles. To get the total time the trip took, we find the time for each portion and add: the first 100 miles took 100 ÷ 50 = 2 hours, and the next 120 miles took 120 ÷ 40 = 3 hours. So the average speed was $\frac{220}{5}$ = **44** miles per hour.

Notice that in Example 6, since Justin spent more time traveling at 50 miles per hour than at 40 miles per hour, his average speed was closer to 50; in Example 6a, he spent more time driving at 40 miles per hour than at 50 miles per hour, so his average speed was closer to 40.

Two other terms that are associated with averages are *median* and *mode*. In a set of *n* numbers that are arranged in increasing order, the *median* is the middle number (if *n* is odd), or the average of the two middle numbers (if *n* is even). The *mode* is the number in the set that occurs most often.

EXAMPLE 7

During a 10-day period, Jorge received the following number of phone calls each day: 2, 3, 9, 3, 5, 7, 7, 10, 7, 6. What is the average (arithmetic mean) of the median and mode of this set of data?
Ⓐ 6　Ⓑ 6.25　Ⓒ 6.5　Ⓓ 6.75　Ⓔ 7

SOLUTION.
The first step is to write the data in increasing order:

$$2, 3, 3, 5, 6, 7, 7, 7, 9, 10.$$

- The median is 6.5, the average of the middle two numbers.
- The mode is 7, the number that appears more times than any other.

- The average of the median and the mode is $\frac{6.5+7}{2}$ = **6.75 (D)**.

The median is actually a special case of a measure called a ***percentile***. In the same way that the median divides a set of data into two roughly equal groups, percentiles divide a set of data into 100 roughly equal groups. P_{63}, the 63rd percentile, for example, is a number with the property that 63% of the data in the group is less than or equal to that number and the rest of the data is greater than that number. Clearly, percentiles are mainly used for large groups of data—it doesn't make much sense to talk about the 63rd percentile of a set of data with 5 or 10 or 20 numbers in it. When you receive your GRE scores in the mail, you will receive a percentile ranking for each of your scores. If you are told that your Verbal score is at the 63rd percentile, that means that your score was higher than the scores of approximately 63% of all GRE test takers (and, therefore, that your score was lower than those of approximately 37% of GRE test takers).

From the definition of percentile, it follows that the median is exactly the same as the 50th percentile. Another term that is often used in analyzing data is ***quartile***. There are three quartiles, Q_1, Q_2, and Q_3, which divide a set of data into four roughly equal groups. Q_1, Q_2, and Q_3 are called the first, second, and third quartiles and are equal to P_{25}, P_{50}, and P_{75}, respectively. So, if M represents the median, then $M = Q_2 = P_{50}$. A measure that is sometimes used to show how spread out the numbers in a set of data are is the ***interquartile range***, which is defined as the difference between the first and third quartiles: $Q_3 - Q_1$.

The interquartile range shows where the middle half of all the data lies. The interquartile range can be graphically illustrated in a diagram called a ***boxplot***. A boxplot extends from the smallest number in the set of data (S) to the largest number in the set of data (L) and has a box representing the interquartile range. The box, which begins and ends at the first and third quartiles, also shows the location of the median (Q_2). The box may be symmetric about the median, but does not need to be, as is illustrated in the two boxplots, below. The upper boxplot shows the distribution of math SAT scores for all students who took the SAT in 2010, while the lower boxplot shows the distribution of math scores for the students at a very selective college.

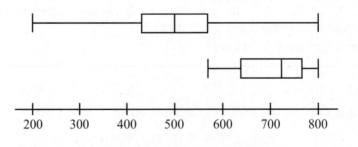

EXAMPLE 8

Twelve hundred 18-year-old boys were weighed, and their weights, in pounds, are summarized in the following boxplot.

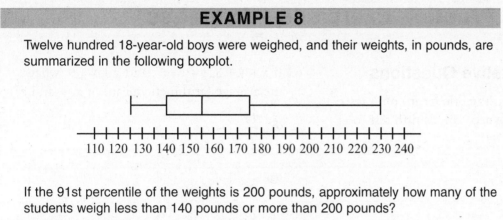

110 120 130 140 150 160 170 180 190 200 210 220 230 240

If the 91st percentile of the weights is 200 pounds, approximately how many of the students weigh less than 140 pounds or more than 200 pounds?

Ⓐ 220   Ⓑ 280   Ⓒ 350   Ⓓ 410   Ⓔ 470

SOLUTION.

From the boxplot, we see that the first quartile is 140. So, approximately 25% of the boys weigh less than 140. And since the 91st percentile is 200, approximately 9% of the boys weigh more than 200. So 25% + 9% = 34% of the 1,200 boys fall within the range we are considering.

Finally, 34% of 1,200 = 0.34 × 1200 = 408, or approximately **410** (**D**).

Practice Exercises—Averages

Discrete Quantitative Questions

1. Michael's average (arithmetic mean) on 4 tests is 80. What does he need on his fifth test to raise his average to 84?

   Ⓐ 82
   Ⓑ 84
   Ⓒ 92
   Ⓓ 96
   Ⓔ 100

2. Maryline's average (arithmetic mean) on 4 tests is 80. Assuming she can earn no more than 100 on any test, what is the least she can earn on her fifth test and still have a chance for an 85 average after seven tests?

   Ⓐ 60
   Ⓑ 70
   Ⓒ 75
   Ⓓ 80
   Ⓔ 85

3. Sandrine's average (arithmetic mean) on 4 tests is 80. Which of the following <u>cannot</u> be the number of tests on which she earned exactly 80 points?

   Ⓐ 0
   Ⓑ 1
   Ⓒ 2
   Ⓓ 3
   Ⓔ 4

4. What is the average (arithmetic mean) of the positive integers from 1 to 100, inclusive?

   Ⓐ 49
   Ⓑ 49.5
   Ⓒ 50
   Ⓓ 50.5
   Ⓔ 51

5. If $10a + 10b = 35$, what is the average (arithmetic mean) of a and b?

6. If $x + y = 6$, $y + z = 7$, and $z + x = 9$, what is the average (arithmetic mean) of x, y, and z?

   Ⓐ $\dfrac{11}{3}$

   Ⓑ $\dfrac{11}{2}$

   Ⓒ $\dfrac{22}{3}$

   Ⓓ 11

   Ⓔ 22

7. If the average (arithmetic mean) of 5, 6, 7, and w is 8, what is the value of w?

   Ⓐ 8
   Ⓑ 12
   Ⓒ 14
   Ⓓ 16
   Ⓔ 24

8. What is the average (arithmetic mean) in degrees of the measures of the five angles in a pentagon?

   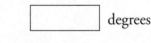 degrees

9. If $a + b = 3(c + d)$, which of the following is the average (arithmetic mean) of a, b, c, and d?

   Ⓐ $\dfrac{c + d}{4}$

   Ⓑ $\dfrac{3(c + d)}{8}$

   Ⓒ $\dfrac{c + d}{2}$

   Ⓓ $\dfrac{3(c + d)}{4}$

   Ⓔ $c + d$

10. In the diagram below, lines ℓ and m are *not* parallel.

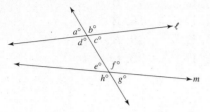

If A represents the average (arithmetic mean) of the degree measures of all eight angles, which of the following is true?

Ⓐ $A = 45$

Ⓑ $45 < A < 90$

Ⓒ $A = 90$

Ⓓ $90 < A < 180$

Ⓔ $A = 180$

11. What is the average (arithmetic mean) of 2^{10} and 2^{20}?

Ⓐ 2^{15}

Ⓑ $2^5 + 2^{10}$

Ⓒ $2^9 + 2^{19}$

Ⓓ 2^{29}

Ⓔ 30

12. Let M be the median and m the mode of the following set of numbers: 10, 70, 20, 40, 70, 90. What is the average (arithmetic mean) of M and m?

Ⓐ 50

Ⓑ 55

Ⓒ 60

Ⓓ 62.5

Ⓔ 65

Quantitative Comparison Questions

Ⓐ Quantity A is greater.
Ⓑ Quantity B is greater.
Ⓒ Quantities A and B are equal.
Ⓓ It is impossible to determine which quantity is greater.

Quantity A	Quantity B
13. The average (arithmetic mean) of the measures of the three angles of an equilateral triangle	The average (arithmetic mean) of the measures of the three angles of a right triangle

10 students took a test and the average grade was 80. No one scored exactly 80.

Quantity A	Quantity B
14. The number of grades over 80	5

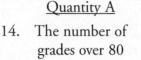

Quantity A	Quantity B
15. The average (arithmetic mean) of $2x$ and $2y$	180

There are the same number of boys and girls in a club. The average weight of the boys is 150 pounds. The average weight of the girls is 110 pounds.

Quantity A	Quantity B
16. The number of boys weighing over 150	The number of girls weighing over 110

The average (arithmetic mean) of 22, 38, x, and y is 15. $x > 0$

Quantity A	Quantity B
17. y	0

Quantity A	Quantity B
18. The average (arithmetic mean) of the even numbers between 1 and 11	The average (arithmetic mean) of the odd numbers between 2 and 12

Quantity A	Quantity B
19. The average (arithmetic mean) of 17, 217, 417	The average (arithmetic mean) of 0, 17, 217, 417

$y > 0$

Quantity A	Quantity B
20. The average (arithmetic mean) of x and y	The average (arithmetic mean) of x, y, and $2y$

ANSWER KEY

1. **E**	5. **1.75**	9. **E**	13. **C**	17. **B**
2. **C**	6. **A**	10. **C**	14. **D**	18. **B**
3. **D**	7. **C**	11. **C**	15. **C**	19. **A**
4. **D**	8. **108**	12. **D**	16. **D**	20. **D**

Answer Explanations

1. **(E)** Use TACTIC E1. For Michael's average on five tests to be an 84, he needs a total of $5 \times 84 = 420$ points. So far, he has earned $4 \times 80 = 320$ points. Therefore, he needs 100 points more.

2. **(C)** Use TACTIC E1. So far, Maryline has earned 320 points. She can survive a low grade on test five if she gets the maximum possible on both the sixth and seventh tests. So, assume she gets two 100s. Then her total for tests 1, 2, 3, 4, 6, and 7 would be 520. For her seven-test average to be 85, she needs a total of $7 \times 85 = 595$ points. Therefore, she needs at least $595 - 520 = 75$ points.

3. **(D)** Since Sandrine's 4-test average is 80, she earned a total of $4 \times 80 = 320$ points. Could Sandrine have earned a total of 320 points with:
   0 grades of 80?   Easily; for example, 20, 100, 100, 100 or 60, 70, 90, 100.
   1 grade of 80?   Lots of ways; 80, 40, 100, 100, for instance.
   2 grades of 80?   Yes; 80, 80, 60, 100.
   4 grades of 80?   Sure: 80, 80, 80, 80.
   3 grades of 80?   NO! $80 + 80 + 80 + x = 320 \Rightarrow x = 80$, as well.

4. **(D)** Clearly, the sequence of integers from 1 to 100 has 100 terms, and so by KEY FACT E4, we know that the average of all the numbers is the average of the two middle ones: 50 and 51. The average, therefore, is 50.5.

5. **1.75** Since $10a + 10b = 35$, dividing both sides of the equation by 10, we get that $a + b = 3.5$. Therefore, the average of a and b is $3.5 \div 2 = 1.75$.

6. **(A)** Whenever a question involves three equations, add them:
$$\begin{array}{r} x + y = 6 \\ y + z = 7 \\ + \quad z + x = 9 \\ \hline 2x + 2y + 2z = 22 \end{array}$$
   Divide by 2: $x + y + z = 11$
   The average of x, y, and z is $\dfrac{x + y + z}{3} = \dfrac{11}{3}$.

7. **(C)** Use TACTIC E1: the sum of the 4 numbers is 4 times their average:
   $5 + 6 + 7 + w = 4 \times 8 = 32 \Rightarrow 18 + w = 32 \Rightarrow w = 14$.

8. **108** The average of the measures of the five angles is the sum of their measures divided by 5. The sum is $(5 - 2) \times 180 = 3 \times 180 = 540$ (see Section 11-K). So, the average is $540 \div 5 = 108$.

9. **(E)** Calculate the average:

$$\frac{a+b+c+d}{4} = \frac{3(c+d)+c+d}{4} = \frac{3c+3d+c+d}{4} = \frac{4c+4d}{4} = c+d$$

10. **(C)** Since $a + b + c + d = 360$, and $e + f + g + h = 360$ (see Section 11-I), the sum of the measures of all 8 angles is $360 + 360 = 720$, and their average is $720 \div 8 = 90$.

11. **(C)** The average of 2^{10} and 2^{20} is $\dfrac{2^{10} + 2^{20}}{2} = \dfrac{2^{10}}{2} + \dfrac{2^{20}}{2} = 2^9 + 2^{19}$.

12. **(D)** Arrange the numbers in increasing order: 10, 20, 40, 70, 70, 90. M, the median, is the average of the middle two numbers: $\dfrac{40+70}{2} = 55$; the mode, m, is 70, the number that appears most frequently. The average of M and m, therefore, is the average of 55 and 70, which is 62.5.

13. **(C)** In *any* triangle, the sum of the measures of the three angles is $180°$, and the average of their measures is $180 \div 3 = 60$.

14. **(D)** From KEY FACT E1, we know only that *at least one grade was above 80*. In fact, there may have been only one (9 grades of 79 and 1 grade of 89, for example). But there could have been five or even nine (for example, 9 grades of 85 and 1 grade of 35).
Alternative solution. The ten students scored exactly 800 points. Ask, "Could they be equal?" Could there be exactly five grades above 80? Sure, five grades of 100 for 500 points and five grades of 60 for 300 points. Must they be equal? No, eight grades of 100 and two grades of 0 also total 800.

15. **(C)** The average of $2x$ and $2y$ is $\dfrac{2x+2y}{2} = x + y$, which equals 180.

16. **(D)** It is possible that no boy weighs over 150 (if every single boy weighs exactly 150); on the other hand, it is possible that almost every boy weighs over 150. The same is true for the girls.

17. **(B)** Use TACTIC E1: $22 + 38 + x + y = 4(15) = 60 \Rightarrow 60 + x + y = 60 \Rightarrow x + y = 0$.
Since it is given that x is positive, y must be negative.

18. **(B)** Don't calculate the averages. Quantity A is the average of 2, 4, 6, 8, and 10. Quantity B is the average of 3, 5, 7, 9, and 11. Since each of the five numbers from Quantity A is less than the corresponding number from Quantity B, Quantity A must be less than Quantity B.

19. **(A)** You don't have to calculate the averages. Quantity A is clearly positive, and by KEY FACT E3, adding 0 to the set of numbers being averaged must lower the average.

20. **(D)** Use KEY FACT E3: If $x < y$, then the average of x and y is less than y, and surely less than $2y$. So, $2y$ has to raise the average. On the other hand, if x is much larger than y, then $2y$ would lower the average.

Algebra

For the GRE you need to know only a small portion of the algebra normally taught in a high school elementary algebra course and none of the material taught in an intermediate or advanced algebra course. Sections 11-F, 11-G, and 11-H review only those topics that you absolutely need for the GRE.

11-F. POLYNOMIALS

Even though the terms *monomial*, *binomial*, *trinomial*, and *polynomial* are not used on the GRE, you must be able to work with simple polynomials, and the use of these terms will make it easier for us to discuss the important concepts.

A ***monomial*** is any number or variable or product of numbers and variables. Each of the following is a monomial:

$$3 \quad -4 \quad x \quad y \quad 3x \quad -4xyz \quad 5x^3 \quad 1.5xy^2 \quad a^3b^4$$

The number that appears in front of the variables in a monomial is called the *coefficient*. The coefficient of $5x^3$ is 5. If there is no number, the coefficient is 1 or –1, because x means $1x$ and $-ab^2$ means $-1ab^2$.

On the GRE, you could be asked to evaluate a monomial for specific values of the variables.

EXAMPLE 1

What is the value of $-3a^2b$ when $a = -4$ and $b = 0.5$?

Ⓐ –72   Ⓑ –24   Ⓒ 24   Ⓓ 48   Ⓔ 72

SOLUTION.

Rewrite the expression, replacing the letters a and b with the numbers –4 and 0.5, respectively. Make sure to write each number in parentheses. Then evaluate:
$-3(-4)^2(0.5) = -3(16)(0.5) = $ **–24 (B)**.

CAUTION

Be sure you follow PEMDAS (see Section 11-A): handle exponents before the other operations. In Example 1, you *cannot* multiply –4 by –3, get 12, and then square the 12; you must first square –4.

A ***polynomial*** is a monomial or the sum of two or more monomials. Each monomial that makes up the polynomial is called a ***term*** of the polynomial. Each of the following is a polynomial:

$$2x^2 \quad 2x^2 + 3 \quad 3x^2 - 7 \quad x^2 + 5x - 1 \quad a^2b + b^2a \quad x^2 - y^2 \quad w^2 - 2w + 1$$

The first polynomial in the above list is a monomial; the second, third, fifth, and sixth polynomials are called *binomials*, because each has two terms; the fourth and seventh polynomials are called *trinomials*, because each has three terms. Two terms are called *like terms* if they have exactly the same variables and exponents; they can differ only in their coefficients: $5a^2b$ and $-3a^2b$ are like terms, whereas a^2b and b^2a are not.

The polynomial $3x^2 + 4x + 5x + 2x^2 + x - 7$ has 6 terms, but some of them are like terms and can be combined:

$$3x^2 + 2x^2 = 5x^2 \quad \text{and} \quad 4x + 5x + x = 10x.$$

So, the original polynomial is equivalent to the trinomial $5x^2 + 10x - 7$.

KEY FACT F1

The only terms of a polynomial that can be combined are like terms.

KEY FACT F2

To add two polynomials, put a plus sign between them, erase the parentheses, and combine like terms.

EXAMPLE 2

What is the sum of $5x^2 + 10x - 7$ and $3x^2 - 4x + 2$?

SOLUTION.
$(5x^2 + 10x - 7) + (3x^2 - 4x + 2)$
$= 5x^2 + 10x - 7 + 3x^2 - 4x + 2$
$= (5x^2 + 3x^2) + (10x - 4x) + (-7 + 2)$
$= \mathbf{8x^2 + 6x - 5}.$

KEY FACT F3

To subtract two polynomials, change the minus sign between them to a plus sign and change the sign of every term in the second parentheses. Then just use KEY FACT F2 to add them: erase the parentheses and then combine like terms.

CAUTION
Make sure you get the order right in a subtraction problem.

TIP

To add, subtract, multiply, and divide polynomials, use the usual laws of arithmetic. To avoid careless errors, before performing any arithmetic operations, write each polynomial in parentheses.

EXAMPLE 3

Subtract $3x^2 - 4x + 2$ from $5x^2 + 10x - 7$.

SOLUTION.

Be careful. Start with the second polynomial and subtract the first:

$$(5x^2 + 10x - 7) - (3x^2 - 4x + 2) = (5x^2 + 10x - 7) + (-3x^2 + 4x - 2) = \boldsymbol{2x^2 + 14x - 9}.$$

EXAMPLE 4

What is the average (arithmetic mean) of $5x^2 + 10x - 7$, $3x^2 - 4x + 2$, and $4x^2 + 2$?

SOLUTION.

As in any average problem, add and divide:

$$(5x^2 + 10x - 7) + (3x^2 - 4x + 2) + (4x^2 + 2) = 12x^2 + 6x - 3,$$

and by the distributive law (KEY FACT A21), $\dfrac{12x^2 + 6x - 3}{3} = \boldsymbol{4x^2 + 2x - 1}$.

KEY FACT F4

To multiply monomials, first multiply their coefficients, and then multiply their variables (letter by letter), by adding the exponents (see Section 11-A).

EXAMPLE 5

What is the product of $3xy^2z^3$ and $-2x^2y^2$?

SOLUTION.

$(3xy^2z^3)(-2x^2y^2) = 3(-2)(x)(x^2)(y^2)(y^2)(z^3) = \boldsymbol{-6x^3y^4z^3}$.

All other polynomials are multiplied by using the distributive law.

KEY FACT F5

To multiply a monomial by a polynomial, just multiply each term of the polynomial by the monomial.

EXAMPLE 6

What is the product of $2a$ and $3a^2 - 6ab + b^2$?

SOLUTION.

$2a(3a^2 - 6ab + b^2) = \mathbf{6a^3 - 12a^2b + 2ab^2}$.

On the GRE, the only other polynomials that you could be asked to multiply are two binomials.

KEY FACT F6

To multiply two binomials, use the so-called FOIL method, which is really nothing more than the distributive law: Multiply each term in the first parentheses by each term in the second parentheses and simplify by combining terms, if possible.

$$(2x - 7)(3x + 2) = (2x)(3x) + (2x)(2) + (-7)(3x) + (-7)(2) =$$
$$\quad\quad\quad\quad\quad \text{First terms}\quad \text{Outer terms}\quad \text{Inner terms}\quad \text{Last terms}$$

$$6x^2 + 4x - 21x - 14 = 6x^2 - 17x - 14$$

EXAMPLE 7

What is the value of $(x - 2)(x + 3) - (x - 4)(x + 5)$?

SOLUTION.
First, multiply both pairs of binomials:

$$(x - 2)(x + 3) = x^2 + 3x - 2x - 6 = x^2 + x - 6$$
$$(x - 4)(x + 5) = x^2 + 5x - 4x - 20 = x^2 + x - 20$$

Now, subtract:

$$(x^2 + x - 6) - (x^2 + x - 20) = x^2 + x - 6 - x^2 - x + 20 = \mathbf{14}.$$

KEY FACT F7

The three most important binomial products on the GRE are these:

- $(x - y)(x + y) = x^2 + xy - yx - y^2 = x^2 - y^2$
- $(x - y)^2 = (x - y)(x - y) = x^2 - xy - yx + y^2 = x^2 - 2xy + y^2$
- $(x + y)^2 = (x + y)(x + y) = x^2 + xy + yx + y^2 = x^2 + 2xy + y^2$

TIP

If you memorize these, you won't have to multiply them out each time you need them.

EXAMPLE 8

If $a - b = 7$ and $a + b = 13$, what is the value of $a^2 - b^2$?

$$\boxed{}$$

SOLUTION.

In Section 11-G, we will review how to solve such a pair of equations; but even if you know how, *you should not do it here.* You do not need to know the values of a and b to answer this question. The moment you see $a^2 - b^2$, you should think $(a - b)(a + b)$. Then:

$$a^2 - b^2 = (a - b)(a + b) = (7)(13) = \mathbf{91}.$$

EXAMPLE 9

If $x^2 + y^2 = 36$ and $(x + y)^2 = 64$, what is the value of xy?

$$\boxed{}$$

SOLUTION.

$$64 = (x + y)^2 = x^2 + 2xy + y^2 = x^2 + y^2 + 2xy = 36 + 2xy.$$

Therefore, $2xy = 64 - 36 = 28 \Rightarrow xy = \mathbf{14}$.

On the GRE, the only division of polynomials you might have to do is to divide a polynomial by a monomial. You will *not* have to do long division of polynomials.

KEY FACT F8

To divide a polynomial by a monomial, use the distributive law. Then simplify each term by reducing the fraction formed by the coefficients to lowest terms and applying the laws of exponents.

EXAMPLE 10

What is the quotient when $32a^2b + 12ab^3c$ is divided by $8ab$?

SOLUTION.

By the distributive law, $\dfrac{32a^2b + 12ab^3c}{8ab} = \dfrac{32a^2b}{8ab} + \dfrac{12ab^3c}{8ab}$.

Now reduce each fraction: $4a + \dfrac{3}{2}b^2c$.

On the GRE, the most important way to use the three formulas in KEY FACT F7 is to recognize them in reverse. In other words, whenever you see $x^2 - y^2$, you should realize that it can be rewritten as $(x - y)(x + y)$. This process, which is the reverse of multiplication, is called *factoring*.

EXAMPLE 11

Quantity A	Quantity B
The value of $x^2 + 4x + 4$ when $x = 95.9$	The value of $x^2 - 4x + 4$ when $x = 99.5$

SOLUTION.
Obviously, you don't want to plug in 95.9 and 99.5 (remember that the GRE *never* requires you to do tedious arithmetic). Recognize that $x^2 + 4x + 4$ is equal to $(x + 2)^2$ and that $x^2 - 4x + 4$ is equal to $(x - 2)^2$. So, Quantity A is just $(95.9 + 2)^2 = 97.9^2$, whereas Quantity B is $(99.5 - 2)^2 = 97.5^2$. Quantity **A** is greater.

EXAMPLE 12

What is the value of $(1,000,001)^2 - (999,999)^2$?

$$\boxed{}$$

SOLUTION.
Do not even consider squaring 999,999. You know that there has to be an easier way to do this. In fact, if you stop to think, you can get the right answer in a few seconds. This is just $a^2 - b^2$ where $a = 1,000,001$ and $b = 999,999$, so change it to $(a - b)(a + b)$:

$$(1,000,001)^2 - (999,999)^2 = (1,000,001 - 999,999)(1,000,001 + 999,999) =$$
$$(2)(2,000,000) = \mathbf{4,000,000}.$$

Although the coefficients of any of the terms in a polynomial can be fractions, as in $\frac{2}{3}x^2 - \frac{1}{2}x$, the variable itself cannot be in the denominator. An expression such as $\frac{3 + x}{x^2}$, which does have a variable in the denominator, is called an ***algebraic fraction***. Fortunately, you should have no trouble with algebraic fractions, since they are handled just like regular fractions. The rules that you reviewed in Section 11-B for adding, subtracting, multiplying, and dividing fractions apply to algebraic fractions, as well.

EXAMPLE 13

What is the sum of the reciprocals of x^2 and y^2?

SOLUTION.

To add $\dfrac{1}{x^2} + \dfrac{1}{y^2}$, you need a common denominator, which is x^2y^2.

Multiply the numerator and denominator of $\dfrac{1}{x^2}$ by y^2 and the numerator and denominator of $\dfrac{1}{y^2}$ by x^2, and then add:

$$\frac{1}{x^2} + \frac{1}{y^2} = \frac{y^2}{x^2 y^2} + \frac{x^2}{x^2 y^2} = \frac{x^2 + y^2}{x^2 y^2}.$$

Often, the way to simplify algebraic fractions is to factor the numerator or the denominator or both. Consider the following example, which is harder than anything you will see on the GRE, but still quite manageable.

EXAMPLE 14

What is the value of $\dfrac{4x^3 - x}{(2x+1)(6x-3)}$ when $x = 9999$?

$$\boxed{}$$

SOLUTION.

Don't use FOIL to multiply the denominator. That's going the wrong way. We want to simplify this fraction by factoring everything we can. First factor an x out of the numerator and notice that what's left is the difference of two squares, which can be factored. Then factor out the 3 in the second factor in the denominator:

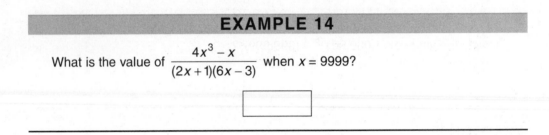

$$\frac{4x^3 - x}{(2x+1)(6x-3)} = \frac{x(4x^2-1)}{(2x+1)3(2x-1)} = \frac{x\cancel{(2x-1)}\cancel{(2x+1)}}{3\cancel{(2x+1)}\cancel{(2x-1)}} = \frac{x}{3}.$$

So, instead of plugging 9999 into the original expression, plug it into $\dfrac{x}{3}$: $9999 \div 3 = \textbf{3333}$.

Practice Exercises—Polynomials

Discrete Quantitative Questions

1. What is the value of $\dfrac{a^2 - b^2}{a - b}$ when $a = 117$ and $b = 118$?

2. If $a^2 - b^2 = 21$ and $a^2 + b^2 = 29$, which of the following could be the value of ab? Indicate *all* possible values.

   [A] -10

   [B] $5\sqrt{2}$

   [C] 10

3. What is the average (arithmetic mean) of $x^2 + 2x - 3$, $3x^2 - 2x - 3$, and $30 - 4x^2$?

   Ⓐ $\dfrac{8x^2 + 4x + 24}{3}$

   Ⓑ $\dfrac{8x^2 + 24}{3}$

   Ⓒ $\dfrac{24 - 4x}{3}$

   Ⓓ -12

   Ⓔ 8

4. What is the value of $x^2 + 12x + 36$ when $x = 994$?

   Ⓐ 11,928
   Ⓑ 98,836
   Ⓒ 100,000
   Ⓓ 988,036
   Ⓔ 1,000,000

5. If $c^2 + d^2 = 4$ and $(c - d)^2 = 2$, what is the value of cd?

   Ⓐ 1
   Ⓑ $\sqrt{2}$
   Ⓒ 2
   Ⓓ 3
   Ⓔ 4

6. What is the value of $(2x + 3)(x + 6) - (2x - 5)(x + 10)$?

   Ⓐ 32
   Ⓑ 16
   Ⓒ 68
   Ⓓ $4x^2 + 30x + 68$
   Ⓔ $4x^2 + 30x - 32$

7. If $\dfrac{1}{a} + \dfrac{1}{b} = \dfrac{1}{c}$ and $ab = c$, what is the average of a and b?

   Ⓐ 0

   Ⓑ $\dfrac{1}{2}$

   Ⓒ 1

   Ⓓ $\dfrac{c}{2}$

   Ⓔ $\dfrac{a + b}{2c}$

8. If $x^2 - y^2 = 28$ and $x - y = 8$, what is the average of x and y?

   Ⓐ 1.75
   Ⓑ 3.5
   Ⓒ 7
   Ⓓ 8
   Ⓔ 10

9. Which of the following is equal to

$$\left(\frac{1}{a} + a\right)^2 - \left(\frac{1}{a} - a\right)^2 ?$$

Ⓐ 0

Ⓑ 4

Ⓒ $\dfrac{1}{a^2} - a^2$

Ⓓ $\dfrac{2}{a^2} - 2a^2$

Ⓔ $\dfrac{1}{a^2} - 4 - a^2$

10. If $\left(\dfrac{1}{a} + a\right)^2 = 100$, what is the value of $\dfrac{1}{a^2} + a^2$?

Ⓐ 10

Ⓑ 64

Ⓒ 98

Ⓓ 100

Ⓔ 102

Quantitative Comparison Questions

Ⓐ Quantity A is greater.
Ⓑ Quantity B is greater.
Ⓒ Quantities A and B are equal.
Ⓓ It is impossible to determine which quantity is greater.

$$n < 0$$

	Quantity A	Quantity B
11.	$-2n^2$	$(-2n)^2$

$$d < c$$

	Quantity A	Quantity B
12.	$(c - d)(c + d)$	$(c - d)(c - d)$

$$x = -3 \text{ and } y = 2$$

	Quantity A	Quantity B
13.	$-x^2 y^3$	0

	Quantity A	Quantity B
14.	$(r + s)(r - s)$	$r(s + r) - s(r + s)$

	Quantity A	Quantity B
15.	$\dfrac{5x^2 - 20}{x - 2}$	$4x + 8$

ANSWER KEY

1. **235**	4. **E**	7. **B**	10. **C**	13. **B**
2. **A, C**	5. **A**	8. **A**	11. **B**	14. **C**
3. **E**	6. **C**	9. **B**	12. **D**	15. **D**

Answer Explanations

1. **235** $\dfrac{a^2 - b^2}{a-b} = \dfrac{\cancel{(a-b)}(a+b)}{\cancel{a-b}} = a + b = 117 + 118 = 235.$

2. **(A)(C)** Adding the two equations, we get that $2a^2 = 50 \Rightarrow a^2 = 25 \Rightarrow b^2 = 4$. So, $a = 5$ or -5 and $b = 2$ or -2. The only possibilities for their product are 10 and -10. (Only A and C are true.)

3. **(E)** To find the average, take the sum of the three polynomials and then divide by 3. Their sum is
$(x^2 + 2x - 3) + (3x^2 - 2x - 3) + (30 - 4x^2) = 24$, and $24 \div 3 = 8$.

4. **(E)** You can avoid messy, time-consuming arithmetic if you recognize that $x^2 + 12x + 36 = (x + 6)^2$. The value is $(994 + 6)^2 = 1000^2 = 1{,}000{,}000$.

5. **(A)** Start by squaring $c - d$: $2 = (c - d)^2 = c^2 - 2cd + d^2 = c^2 + d^2 - 2cd = 4 - 2cd$.
So, $2 = 4 - 2cd \Rightarrow 2cd = 2 \Rightarrow cd = 1$.

6. **(C)** First multiply out both pairs of binomials: $(2x + 3)(x + 6) = 2x^2 + 15x + 18$ and $(2x - 5)(x + 10) = 2x^2 + 15x - 50$.
Now subtract: $(2x^2 + 15x + 18) - (2x^2 + 15x - 50) = 18 - (-50) = 68$.

7. **(B)** $\dfrac{1}{c} = \dfrac{1}{a} + \dfrac{1}{b} = \dfrac{a+b}{ab} = \dfrac{a+b}{c} \Rightarrow 1 = a + b \Rightarrow \dfrac{a+b}{2} = \dfrac{1}{2}.$

8. **(A)** $x^2 - y^2 = (x - y)(x + y) \Rightarrow 28 = 8(x + y) \Rightarrow x + y = 28 \div 8 = 3.5$.

   Finally, the average of x and y is $\dfrac{x+y}{2} = \dfrac{3.5}{2} = 1.75$.

9. **(B)** Expand each square: $\left(\dfrac{1}{a} + a\right)^2 = \dfrac{1}{a^2} + 2\left(\dfrac{1}{a}\right)(a) + a^2 = \dfrac{1}{a^2} + 2 + a^2.$

   Similarly, $\left(\dfrac{1}{a} - a\right)^2 = \dfrac{1}{a^2} - 2 + a^2.$

   Subtract: $\left(\dfrac{1}{a^2} + 2 + a^2\right) - \left(\dfrac{1}{a^2} - 2 + a^2\right) = 4.$

10. **(C)** $100 = \left(\dfrac{1}{a} + a\right)^2 = \dfrac{1}{a^2} + 2 + a^2 \Rightarrow \dfrac{1}{a^2} + a^2 = 98.$

11. **(B)** Since n is negative, n^2 is positive, and so $-2n^2$ is negative. Therefore, Quantity A is negative, whereas Quantity B is positive.

	Quantity A	Quantity B

12. **(D)** $c > d \Rightarrow c - d$ is positive,
so divide each side by $c - d$: $c + d$ $c - d$
Subtract c from each quantity: d $-d$
If $d = 0$ the quantities are equal; if $d = 1$, they aren't.

13. **(B)** Quantity A: $-(-3)^2 2^3 = -(9)(8) = -72$.

14. **(C)** Quantity B: $r(s + r) - s(r + s) = rs + r^2 - sr - s^2 = r^2 - s^2$
Quantity A: $(r + s)(r - s) = r^2 - s^2$.

15. **(D)** Quantity A: $\dfrac{5x^2 - 20}{x - 2} = \dfrac{5(x^2 - 4)}{x - 2} = \dfrac{5(x - 2)(x + 2)}{x - 2} = 5(x + 2)$.

Quantity B: $4x + 8 = 4(x + 2)$. If $x = -2$, both quantities are 0; for any other value of x the quantities are unequal.

11-G. SOLVING EQUATIONS AND INEQUALITIES

The basic principle that you must adhere to in solving any *equation* is that you can manipulate it in any way, as long as *you do the same thing to both sides.* For example, you may always add the same number to each side; subtract the same number from each side; multiply or divide each side by the same number (except 0); square each side; take the square root of each side (if the quantities are positive); or take the reciprocal of each side. These comments apply to inequalities, as well, except you must be very careful, because some procedures, such as multiplying or dividing by a negative number and taking reciprocals, reverse inequalities (see Section 11-A).

Most of the equations and inequalities that you will have to solve on the GRE have only one variable and no exponents. The following simple six-step method can be used on all of them.

EXAMPLE 1

If $\frac{1}{2}x + 3(x - 2) = 2(x + 1) + 1$, what is the value of x?

[ ]

SOLUTION.
Follow the steps outlined in the following table.

Step	What to Do	Example 1
1	Get rid of fractions and decimals by multiplying both sides by the Lowest Common Denominator (LCD).	Multiply each term by 2: $x + 6(x - 2) = 4(x + 1) + 2$.
2	Get rid of all parentheses by using the distributive law.	$x + 6x - 12 = 4x + 4 + 2$.
3	Combine like terms on each side.	$7x - 12 = 4x + 6$.
4	By adding or subtracting, get all the variables on one side.	Subtract $4x$ from each side: $3x - 12 = 6$.
5	By adding or subtracting, get all the plain numbers on the other side.	Add 12 to each side: $3x = 18$.
6	Divide both sides by the coefficient of the variable.*	Divide both sides by 3: $x = \mathbf{6}$.

*Note: If you start with an inequality and in Step 6 you divide by a negative number, remember to reverse the inequality (see KEY FACT A24).

Example 1 is actually harder than any equation on the GRE, because it required all six steps. On the GRE that never happens. Think of the six steps as a list of questions that must be answered. Ask if each step is necessary. If it isn't, move on to the next one; if it is, do it.

Let's look at Example 2, which does not require all six steps.

EXAMPLE 2

For what real number *n* is it true that $3(n - 20) = n$?

☐

SOLUTION. Do whichever of the six steps are necessary.

Step	Question	Yes/No	What to Do
1	Are there any fractions or decimals?	No	
2	Are there any parentheses?	Yes	Get rid of them: $3n - 60 = n$.
3	Are there any like terms to combine?	No	
4	Are there variables on both sides?	Yes	Subtract *n* from each side: $2n - 60 = 0$.
5	Is there a plain number on the same side as the variable?	Yes	Add 60 to each side: $2n = 60$.
6	Does the variable have a coefficient?	Yes	Divide both sides by 2: $n = \mathbf{30}$.

TACTIC

Memorize the six steps *in order* and use this method whenever you have to solve this type of equation or inequality.

EXAMPLE 3

Three brothers divided a prize as follows. The oldest received $\frac{2}{5}$ of it, the middle brother received $\frac{1}{3}$ of it, and the youngest received the remaining $120. What was the value of the prize?

☐

SOLUTION.

If *x* represents the value of the prize, then $\frac{2}{5}x + \frac{1}{3}x + 120 = x$.

Solve this equation using the six-step method.

Step	Question	Yes/No	What to Do
1	Are there any fractions or decimals?	Yes	To get rid of them, multiply by 15. $15\left(\dfrac{2}{5}x\right) + 15\left(\dfrac{1}{3}x\right) +$ $15(120) = 15(x)$ $6x + 5x + 1800 = 15x$
2	Are there any parentheses?	No	
3	Are there any like terms to combine?	Yes	Combine them: $11x + 1800 = 15x$.
4·	Are there variables on both sides?	Yes	Subtract $11x$ from each side: $1800 = 4x$.
5	Is there a plain number on the same side as the variable?	No	
6	Does the variable have a coefficient?	Yes	Divide both sides by 4: $x = \mathbf{450}$.

Sometimes on the GRE, you are given an equation with several variables and asked to solve for one of them in terms of the others.

TACTIC

When you have to solve for one variable in terms of the others, treat all of the others as if they were numbers, and apply the six-step method.

EXAMPLE 4

If $a = 3b - c$, what is the value of b in terms of a and c?

SOLUTION.

To solve for b, treat a and c as numbers and use the six-step method with b as the variable.

Step	Question	Yes/No	What to Do
1	Are there any fractions or decimals?	No	
2	Are there any parentheses?	No	
3	Are there any like terms to combine?	No	
4	Are there variables on both sides?	No	Remember: the only variable is b.
5	Is there a plain number on the same side as the variable?	Yes	Remember: we're considering c as a number, and it is on the same side as b, the variable. Add c to both sides: $a + c = 3b$.
6	Does the variable have a coefficient?	Yes	Divide both sides by 3: $b = \dfrac{a + c}{3}$.

TIP

In applying the six-step method, you shouldn't actually write out the table, as we did in Examples 1–4, since it would be too time consuming. Instead, use the method as a guideline and mentally go through each step, doing whichever ones are required.

Sometimes when solving equations, you may see a shortcut. For example, to solve $7(w - 3) = 42$, it saves time to start by dividing both sides by 7, getting $w - 3 = 6$, rather than by using the distributive law to eliminate the parentheses. Similarly, if you have to solve a proportion such as $\frac{x}{7} = \frac{3}{5}$, it is easier to cross-multiply, getting $5x = 21$, than to multiply both sides by 35 to get rid of the fractions (although that's exactly what cross-multiplying accomplishes). Other shortcuts will be illustrated in the problems at the end of the section. If you spot such a shortcut, use it; but if you don't, be assured that the six-step method *always* works.

EXAMPLE 5

If $x - 4 = 11$, what is the value of $x - 8$?
Ⓐ −15   Ⓑ −7   Ⓒ −1   Ⓓ 7   Ⓔ 15

SOLUTION.

Going immediately to Step 5, add 4 to each side: $x = 15$. But this is *not* the answer. You need the value not of x, but of $x - 8$: $15 - 8 = \mathbf{7}$ (**D**).

As in Example 5, on the GRE you are often asked to solve for something other than the simple variable. In Example 5, you could have been asked for the value of x^2 or $x + 4$ or $(x - 4)^2$, and so on.

TACTIC

G3

TIP

Very often, solving the equation is not the quickest way to answer the question. Consider Example 6.

As you read each question on the GRE, on your scrap paper write down whatever you are looking for, and circle it. This way you will always be sure that you are answering the question that is asked.

EXAMPLE 6

If $2x - 5 = 98$, what is the value of $2x + 5$?

SOLUTION.

The first thing you should do is write $2x + 5$ on your paper and circle it. The fact that you are asked for the value of something other than x should alert you to look at the question carefully to see if there is a shortcut.

- The best approach here is to observe that $2x + 5$ is 10 more than $2x - 5$, so the answer is **108** (10 more than 98).
- Next best would be to do only one step of the six-step method, add 5 to both sides: $2x = 103$. Now, add 5 to both sides: $2x + 5 = 103 + 5 = 108$.
- The *worst* method would be to divide $2x = 103$ by 2, get $x = 51.5$, and then use that to calculate $2x + 5$.

EXAMPLE 7

If *w* is an integer, and the average (arithmetic mean) of 3, 4, and *w* is less than 10, what is the greatest possible value of *w*?

Ⓐ 9 Ⓑ 10 Ⓒ 17 Ⓓ 22 Ⓔ 23

SOLUTION.

Set up the inequality: $\dfrac{3+4+w}{3} < 10$. Do Step 1 (get rid of fractions by multiplying by 3): $3 + 4 + w < 30$. Do Step 3 (combine like terms): $7 + w < 30$. Finally, do Step 5 (subtract 7 from each side): $w < 23$. Since *w* is an integer, the most it can be is **22 (D)**.

The six-step method also works when there are variables in denominators.

EXAMPLE 8

For what value of *x* is $\dfrac{4}{x} + \dfrac{3}{5} = \dfrac{10}{x}$?

Ⓐ 5 Ⓑ 10 Ⓒ 20 Ⓓ 30 Ⓔ 50

SOLUTION. Multiply each side by the LCD, $5x$:

$$5x\left(\frac{4}{x}\right) + 5x\left(\frac{3}{5}\right) = 5x\left(\frac{10}{x}\right) \Rightarrow 20 + 3x = 50.$$

Now solve normally: $20 + 3x = 50 \Rightarrow 3x = 30$ and so $x = $ **10 (B)**.

EXAMPLE 9

If *x* is positive, and $y = 5x^2 + 3$, which of the following is an expression for *x* in terms of *y*?

Ⓐ $\sqrt{\dfrac{y}{5} - 3}$ Ⓑ $\sqrt{\dfrac{y-3}{5}}$ Ⓒ $\dfrac{\sqrt{y-3}}{5}$ Ⓓ $\dfrac{\sqrt{y}-3}{5}$ Ⓔ $\dfrac{\sqrt{y}-\sqrt{3}}{5}$

SOLUTION.

The six-step method works when there are no exponents. However, we can treat x^2 as a single variable, and use the method as far as possible:

$$y = 5x^2 + 3 \Rightarrow y - 3 = 5x^2 \Rightarrow \frac{y-3}{5} = x^2.$$

Now take the square root of each side; since *x* is positive, the only solution is

$x = \sqrt{\dfrac{y-3}{5}}$ **(B)**.

CAUTION

Doing the same thing to each *side* of an equation does *not* mean doing the same thing to each *term* of the equation. Study Examples 10 and 11 carefully.

EXAMPLE 10

If $\dfrac{1}{a} = \dfrac{1}{b} + \dfrac{1}{c}$, what is a in terms of b and c?

SOLUTION 1.

First add the fractions on the right hand side:

$$\frac{1}{a} = \frac{1}{b} + \frac{1}{c} = \frac{b+c}{bc}.$$

Now, take the reciprocal of each *side*: $a = \dfrac{bc}{b+c}$.

SOLUTION 2.

Use the six-step method. Multiply each term by abc, the LCD:

$$abc\left(\frac{1}{a}\right) = abc\left(\frac{1}{b}\right) + abc\left(\frac{1}{c}\right) \Rightarrow bc = ac + ab = a(c + b) \Rightarrow a = \frac{bc}{c+b}.$$

EXAMPLE 11

If $a > 0$ and $a^2 + b^2 = c^2$, what is a in terms of b and c?

SOLUTION. $a^2 + b^2 = c^2 \Rightarrow a^2 = c^2 - b^2$. Be careful: you *cannot* now take the square root of each *term* and write, $a = c - b$. Rather, you must take the square root of each *side*: $a = \sqrt{a^2} = \sqrt{c^2 - b^2}$.

There are a few other types of equations that you could have to solve on the GRE. Fortunately, they are quite easy. You probably will not have to solve a quadratic equation. However, if you do, you will *not* need the quadratic formula, and you will not have to factor a trinomial. Here are two examples.

EXAMPLE 12

If x is a positive number and $x^2 + 64 = 100$, what is the value of x?

(A) 6　(B) 12　(C) 13　(D) 14　(E) 36

SOLUTION. When there is an x^2-term, but no x-term, we just have to take a square root:

$$x^2 + 64 = 100 \Rightarrow x^2 = 36 \Rightarrow x = \sqrt{36} = 6 \text{ (A)}.$$

EXAMPLE 13

What is the largest value of x that satisfies the equation $2x^2 - 3x = 0$?

Ⓐ 0   Ⓑ 1.5   Ⓒ 2   Ⓓ 2.5   Ⓔ 3

SOLUTION.

When an equation has an x^2-term and an x-term but no constant term, the way to solve it is to factor out the x and to use the fact that if the product of two numbers is 0, one of them must be 0 (KEY FACT A3):

$$2x^2 - 3x = 0 \Rightarrow x(2x - 3) = 0$$
$$x = 0 \ \text{ or } \ 2x - 3 = 0$$
$$x = 0 \ \text{ or } \ 2x = 3$$
$$x = 0 \ \text{ or } \ x = 1.5.$$

The largest value is **1.5 (B)**.

In another type of equation that occasionally appears on the GRE, the variable is in the exponent. These equations are particularly easy and are basically solved by inspection.

EXAMPLE 14

If $2^{x+3} = 32$, what is the value of 3^{x+2}?

Ⓐ 5   Ⓑ 9   Ⓒ 27   Ⓓ 81   Ⓔ 125

SOLUTION.

How many 2s do you have to multiply together to get 32? If you don't know that it's 5, just multiply and keep track. Count the 2s on your fingers as you say to yourself, "2 times 2 is 4, times 2 is 8, times 2 is 16, times 2 is 32." Then

$$2^{x+3} = 32 = 2^5 \Rightarrow x + 3 = 5 \Rightarrow x = 2.$$

Therefore, $x + 2 = 4$, and $3^{x+2} = 3^4 = 3 \times 3 \times 3 \times 3 = \mathbf{81 \ (D)}$.

Occasionally, both sides of an equation have variables in the exponents. In that case, it is necessary to write both exponentials with the same base.

EXAMPLE 15

If $4^{w+3} = 8^{w-1}$, what is the value of w?

Ⓐ 0   Ⓑ 1   Ⓒ 2   Ⓓ 3   Ⓔ 9

SOLUTION.

Since it is necessary to have the same base on each side of the equation, write $4 = 2^2$ and $8 = 2^3$. Then

$$4^{w+3} = (2^2)^{w+3} = 2^{2(w+3)} = 2^{2w+6} \quad \text{and} \quad 8^{w-1} = (2^3)^{w-1} = 2^{3(w-1)} = 2^{3w-3}.$$

So, $2^{2w+6} = 2^{3w-3} \Rightarrow 2w + 6 = 3w - 3 \Rightarrow w = \mathbf{9 \ (E)}$.

Systems of Linear Equations

The equations $x + y = 10$ and $x - y = 2$ each have lots of solutions (infinitely many, in fact). Some of them are given in the tables below.

$x + y = 10$

x	5	6	4	1	1.2	10	20
y	5	4	6	9	8.8	0	−10
$x + y$	10	10	10	10	10	10	10

$x - y = 2$

x	5	6	2	0	2.5	19	40
y	3	4	0	−2	.5	17	38
$x - y$	2	2	2	2	2	2	2

However, only one pair of numbers, $x = 6$ and $y = 4$, satisfy both equations simultaneously: $6 + 4 = 10$ and $6 - 4 = 2$. This then is the only solution of the

system of equations: $\begin{cases} x + y = 10 \\ x - y = 2 \end{cases}$.

A system of equations is a set of two or more equations involving two or more variables. To solve such a system, you must find values for each of the variables that will make each equation true. In an algebra course you learn several ways to solve systems of equations. On the GRE, the most useful way to solve them is to add or subtract (usually add) the equations. After demonstrating this method, we will show in Example 19 one other way to handle some systems of equations.

TACTIC

To solve a system of equations, add or subtract them. If there are more than two equations, add them.

EXAMPLE 16

$$x + y = 10$$
$$x - y = 2$$

Quantity A	Quantity B
x	y

SOLUTION.

Add the two equations:

$$x + y = 10$$
$$+ \ x - y = \ 2$$
$$\overline{2x \qquad = 12}$$
$$x = \ 6$$

Replacing x with 6 in $x + y = 10$ yields $y = 4$. So, Quantity **A** is greater.

TIP

On the GRE, most problems involving systems of equations do not require you to solve the system. They usually ask for something other than the values of each variable. Read the questions very carefully, circle what you need, and do no more than is required.

EXAMPLE 17

If $3a + 5b = 10$ and $5a + 3b = 30$, what is the average (arithmetic mean) of a and b?

SOLUTION.

Add the two equations:

$$3a + 5b = 10$$
$$+ \ 5a + 3b = 30$$
$$\overline{8a + 8b = 40}$$

Divide both sides by 8: $a + b = 5$

The average of a and b is: $\dfrac{a+b}{2} = \dfrac{5}{2} = \mathbf{2.5}$

NOTE: It is not only unnecessary to first solve for a and b ($a = 7.5$ and $b = -2.5$.), but, because that procedure is so much more time-consuming, it would be foolish to do so.

EXAMPLE 18

$$7a - 3b = 200$$
$$7a + 3b = 100$$

Quantity A	Quantity B
a	b

TIP

Remember TACTIC 5, Chapter 9. On quantitative comparison questions, you don't need to know the value of the quantity in each column; you only need to know which one is greater.

SOLUTION.

Don't actually solve the system. Add the equations:

$$14a = 300 \Rightarrow 7a = 150.$$

So, replacing $7a$ with 150 in the second equation, we get $150 + 3b = 100$; so $3b$, and hence b, must be negative, whereas a is positive. Therefore, $a > b$, and Quantity **A** is greater.

Occasionally on the GRE, it is as easy, or easier, to solve the system by substitution.

TACTIC

G5

If one of the equations in a system of equations consists of a single variable equal to some expression, substitute that expression for the variable in the other equation.

EXAMPLE 19

$$x + y = 10$$
$$y = x - 2$$

Quantity A	Quantity B
x	y

SOLUTION.

Since the second equation states that a single variable (y), is equal to some expression ($x - 2$), substitute that expression for y in the first equation: $x + y = 10$ becomes $x + (x - 2) = 10$. Then, $2x - 2 = 10$, $2x = 12$, and $x = 6$. As always, to find the value of the other variable (y), plug the value of x into one of the two original equations: $y = 6 - 2 = 4$. Quantity **A** is greater.

Practice Exercises — Equations/Inequalities

Discrete Quantitative Questions

1. If $4x + 12 = 36$, what is the value of $x + 3$?

   (A) 3
   (B) 6
   (C) 9
   (D) 12
   (E) 18

2. If $7x + 10 = 44$, what is the value of $7x - 10$?

   (A) $-6\dfrac{6}{7}$

   (B) $4\dfrac{6}{7}$

   (C) $14\dfrac{6}{7}$

   (D) 24

   (E) 34

3. If $4x + 13 = 7 - 2x$, what is the value of x?

   (A) $-\dfrac{10}{3}$

   (B) -3
   (C) -1
   (D) 1

   (E) $\dfrac{10}{3}$

4. If $x - 4 = 9$, what is the value of $x^2 - 4$?

   [   ]

5. If $ax - b = c - dx$, what is the value of x in terms of a, b, c, and d?

   (A) $\dfrac{b+c}{a+d}$

   (B) $\dfrac{c-b}{a-d}$

   (C) $\dfrac{b+c-d}{a}$

   (D) $\dfrac{c-b}{a+d}$

   (E) $\dfrac{c}{b} - \dfrac{d}{a}$

6. If $\dfrac{1}{3}x + \dfrac{1}{6}x + \dfrac{1}{9}x = 33$, what is the value of x?

   (A) 3
   (B) 18
   (C) 27
   (D) 54
   (E) 72

7. If $3x - 4 = 11$, what is the value of $(3x - 4)^2$?

   (A) 22
   (B) 36
   (C) 116
   (D) 121
   (E) 256

8. If $64^{12} = 2^{a-3}$, what is the value of a?

   (A) 9
   (B) 15
   (C) 69
   (D) 72
   (E) 75

9. If the average (arithmetic mean) of $3a$ and $4b$ is less than 50, and a is twice b, what is the largest possible integer value of a?

   Ⓐ 9
   Ⓑ 10
   Ⓒ 11
   Ⓓ 19
   Ⓔ 20

10. If $\dfrac{1}{a-b} = 5$, then $a =$

   Ⓐ $b + 5$
   Ⓑ $b - 5$
   Ⓒ $b + \dfrac{1}{5}$

   Ⓓ $b - \dfrac{1}{5}$

   Ⓔ $\dfrac{1-5b}{5}$

11. If $x = 3a + 7$ and $y = 9a^2$, what is y in terms of x?

   Ⓐ $(x - 7)^2$
   Ⓑ $3(x - 7)^2$
   Ⓒ $\dfrac{(x - 7)^2}{3}$

   Ⓓ $\dfrac{(x + 7)^2}{3}$
   Ⓔ $(x + 7)^2$

12. If $4y - 3x = 5$, what is the smallest integer value of x for which $y > 100$?

Quantitative Comparison Questions

> Ⓐ Quantity A is greater.
> Ⓑ Quantity B is greater.
> Ⓒ Quantities A and B are equal.
> Ⓓ It is impossible to determine which quantity is greater.

$$a + b = 13$$
$$a - b = 13$$

	Quantity A	Quantity B
13.	b	13

$$\frac{2^{a-1}}{2^{b+1}} = 8$$

	Quantity A	Quantity B
14.	a	b

$$4x^2 = 3x$$

	Quantity A	Quantity B
15.	x	1

$$a + b = 1$$
$$b + c = 2$$
$$c + a = 3$$

	Quantity A	Quantity B
16.	The average (arithmetic mean) of a, b, and c	1

$$3x - 4y = 5$$
$$y = 2x$$

	Quantity A	Quantity B
17.	x	y

$$\frac{x}{2} - 2 > \frac{x}{3}$$

	Quantity A	Quantity B
18.	x	12

$$3r - 5s = 17$$
$$2r - 6s = 7$$

$$\frac{1}{c} = 1 + \frac{1}{d}$$

c and d are positive

	Quantity A	Quantity B		Quantity A	Quantity B
19.	The average (arithmetic mean) of r and s	10	20.	c	d

ANSWER KEY

1. **C**	5. **A**	9. **D**	13. **B**	17. **A**
2. **D**	6. **D**	10. **C**	14. **A**	18. **A**
3. **C**	7. **D**	11. **A**	15. **B**	19. **B**
4. **165**	8. **E**	12. **132**	16. **C**	20. **B**

Answer Explanations

1. **(C)** The easiest method is to recognize that $x + 3$ is $\frac{1}{4}$ of $4x + 12$ and,

   therefore, equals $\frac{1}{4}$ of 36, which is 9. If you don't see that, solve normally:

   $$4x + 12 = 36 \Rightarrow 4x = 24 \Rightarrow x = 6 \text{ and so } x + 3 = 9.$$

2. **(D)** Subtracting 20 from each side of $7x + 10 = 44$ gives $7x - 10 = 24$. If you don't see that, subtract 10 from each side, getting $7x = 34$. Then subtract 10 to get $7x - 10 = 24$. The worst alternative is to divide both sides of

   $7x = 34$ by 7 to get $x = \frac{34}{7}$; then you have to multiply by 7 to get back

   to 34, and then subtract 10.

3. **(C)** Add $2x$ to each side: $6x + 13 = 7$. Subtract 13 from each side: $6x = -6$. Divide by 6: $x = -1$.

4. **165** $x - 4 = 9 \Rightarrow x = 13 \Rightarrow x^2 = 169$ and so $x^2 - 4 = 165$.

5. **(A)** Treat a, b, c, and d as constants, and use the six-step method to solve for x:

   $$ax - b = c - dx \Rightarrow ax - b + dx = c \Rightarrow ax + dx = c + b \Rightarrow x(a + d) = b + c \Rightarrow$$

   $$x = \frac{b + c}{a + d}.$$

6. **(D)** Multiply both sides by 18, the LCD:

$$18\left(\frac{1}{3}x + \frac{1}{6}x + \frac{1}{9}x\right) = 18(33) \Rightarrow 6x + 3x + 2x = 594 \Rightarrow 11x = 594 \Rightarrow x = 54.$$

It's actually easier not to multiply out 18×33; leave it in that form, and then divide by 11: $\dfrac{18 \times \cancel{33}^{3}}{\cancel{11}_{1}} = 3 \times 18 = 54$.

7. **(D)** Be alert. Since you are given the value of $3x - 4$, and want the value of $(3x - 4)^2$, just square both sides: $11^2 = 121$. If you don't see that, you'll waste time solving $3x - 4 = 11$ ($x = 5$), only to use that value to calculate that $3x - 4$ is equal to 11, which you aready knew.

8. **(E)** $2^{a-3} = 64^{12} = (2^6)^{12} = 2^{72} \Rightarrow a - 3 = 72$, and so $a = 75$.

9. **(D)** Since $a = 2b$, $2a = 4b$. Therefore, the average of $3a$ and $4b$ is the average of $3a$ and $2a$, which is $2.5a$. Therefore, $2.5a < 50 \Rightarrow a < 20$. So the largest *integer* value of a is 19.

10. **(C)** Taking the reciprocal of each side, we get $a - b = \dfrac{1}{5}$. So $a = b + \dfrac{1}{5}$.

11. **(A)** $x = 3a + 7 \Rightarrow x - 7 = 3a \Rightarrow a = \dfrac{x-7}{3}$.

Therefore, $y = 9a^2 = 9\left(\dfrac{x-7}{3}\right)^2 = 9\dfrac{(x-7)^2}{3^2} = (x-7)^2$.

12. **132** Solving for y yields $y = \dfrac{5 + 3x}{4}$.

Then, since $y > 100$: $\dfrac{5 + 3x}{4} > 100 \Rightarrow 5 + 3x > 400 \Rightarrow 3x > 395 \Rightarrow$

$x > 131.666$.

The smallest integer value of x is 132.

13. **(B)** Adding the two equations, we get that $2a = 26$. Therefore, $a = 13$ and $b = 0$.

14. **(A)** Express each side of $\dfrac{2^{a-1}}{2^{b+1}} = 8$ as a power of 2:

$8 = 2^3$ and $\dfrac{2^{a-1}}{2^{b+1}} = 2^{(a-1)-(b+1)} = 2^{a-b-2}$.

Therefore, $a - b - 2 = 3 \Rightarrow a = b + 5$, and so a is greater.

15. **(B)** $4x^2 = 3x \Rightarrow 4x^2 - 3x = 0 \Rightarrow x(4x - 3) = 0.$
So,

$$x = 0 \quad \text{or} \quad 4x - 3 = 0 \Rightarrow$$
$$x = 0 \quad \text{or} \quad 4x = 3 \Rightarrow$$
$$x = 0 \quad \text{or} \quad x = \frac{3}{4}.$$

There are two possible values of x, both of which are less than 1.

16. **(C)** When we add all three equations, we get

$$2a + 2b + 2c = 6 \Rightarrow a + b + c = 3, \text{ and so } \frac{a + b + c}{3} = 1.$$

17. **(A)** Use substitution. Replace y in the first equation with $2x$:

$$3x - 4(2x) = 5 \Rightarrow 3x - 8x = 5 \Rightarrow -5x = 5 \Rightarrow x = -1 \Rightarrow y = -2.$$

18. **(A)** Multiply both sides by 6, the LCD:

$$6\left(\frac{x}{2} - 2\right) > 6\left(\frac{x}{3}\right) \Rightarrow 3x - 12 > 2x \Rightarrow -12 > -x \Rightarrow x > 12.$$

19. **(B)** The first thing to try is to add the equations. That yields $5r - 11s = 24$, which does not appear to be useful. So now try to subtract the equations. That yields $r + s = 10$.

So the average of r and s is $\dfrac{r + s}{2} = \dfrac{10}{2} = 5$.

20. **(B)** Multiply both sides of the given equation by cd, the LCD of the fractions:

$$cd\left(\frac{1}{c}\right) = cd\left(1 + \frac{1}{d}\right) \Rightarrow d = cd + c = c(d + 1) \Rightarrow c = \frac{d}{d+1}.$$

Since d is positive, $d + 1 > 1$, and so $\dfrac{d}{d+1} < d$.

So $c < d$.

11-H. WORD PROBLEMS

On a typical GRE you will see several word problems, covering almost every math topic for which you are responsible. In this chapter you have already seen word problems on consecutive integers in Section A; fractions and percents in Sections B and C; ratios and rates in Section D; and averages in Section E. Later in this chapter you will see word problems involving probability, circles, triangles, and other geometric figures. A few of these problems can be solved with just arithmetic, but most of them require basic algebra.

   To solve word problems algebraically, you must treat algebra as a foreign language and learn to translate "word for word" from English into algebra, just as you would from English into French or Spanish or any other language. When translating into algebra, we use some letter (often *x*) to represent the unknown quantity we are trying to determine. It is this translation process that causes difficulty for some students. Once translated, solving is easy using the techniques we have already reviewed. Consider the following pairs of typical GRE questions. The first ones in each pair (1A and 2A) would be considered easy, whereas the second ones (1B and 2B) would be considered harder.

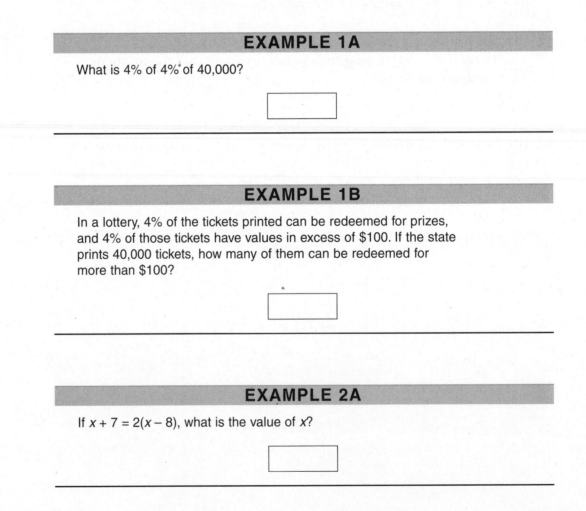

EXAMPLE 1A

What is 4% of 4% of 40,000?

EXAMPLE 1B

In a lottery, 4% of the tickets printed can be redeemed for prizes, and 4% of those tickets have values in excess of $100. If the state prints 40,000 tickets, how many of them can be redeemed for more than $100?

EXAMPLE 2A

If $x + 7 = 2(x - 8)$, what is the value of *x*?

EXAMPLE 2B

In 7 years Erin will be twice as old as she was 8 years ago. How old is Erin now?

Once you translate the words into arithmetic expressions or algebraic equations, Examples 1A and 1B and 2A and 2B are identical. The problem that many students have is doing the translation. It really isn't very difficult, and we'll show you how. First, though, look over the following English to algebra "dictionary."

English Words	Mathematical Meaning	Symbol
Is, was, will be, had, has, will have, is equal to, is the same as	Equals	=
Plus, more than, sum, increased by, added to, exceeds, received, got, older than, farther than, greater than	Addition	+
Minus, fewer, less than, difference, decreased by, subtracted from, younger than, gave, lost	Subtraction	−
Times, of, product, multiplied by	Multiplication	×
Divided by, quotient, per, for	Division	$\div, \frac{a}{b}$
More than, greater than	Inequality	>
At least	Inequality	≥
Fewer than, less than	Inequality	<
At most	Inequality	≤
What, how many, etc.	Unknown quantity	x (or some other variable)

Let's use our dictionary to translate some phrases and sentences.

1. The <u>sum</u> of 5 and some number <u>is</u> 13. $5 + x = 13$

2. John <u>was</u> 2 years <u>younger than</u> Sam. $J = S - 2$

3. Bill has <u>at most</u> \$100. $B \le 100$

4. The <u>product</u> of 2 and a number <u>exceeds</u> that number by 5 (is 5 more than). $2N = N + 5$

In translating statements, you first must decide what quantity the variable will represent. Often it's obvious. Other times there is more than one possibility.

Let's translate and solve the two questions from the beginning of this section, and then we'll look at a few new ones.

TIP

In all word problems on the GRE, remember to write down and circle what you are looking for. Don't answer the wrong question!

EXAMPLE 1B

In a lottery, 4% of the tickets printed can be redeemed for prizes, and 4% of those tickets have values in excess of $100. If the state prints 40,000 tickets, how many of them can be redeemed for more than $100?

SOLUTION.

Let x = the number of tickets worth more than $100. Then

$$x = 4\% \text{ of } 4\% \text{ of } 40{,}000 = .04 \times .04 \times 40{,}000 = \mathbf{64},$$

which is also the solution to Example 1a.

EXAMPLE 2B

In 7 years Erin will be twice as old as she was 8 years ago. How old is Erin now?

TIP

In problems involving ages, remember that "years ago" means you need to subtract, and "years from now" means you need to add.

SOLUTION.

Let x = Erin's age now. Then 8 years ago she was $x - 8$, and 7 years from now she will be $x + 7$. So,

$$x + 7 = 2(x - 8) \Rightarrow x + 7 = 2x - 16 \Rightarrow 7 = x - 16 \Rightarrow x = \mathbf{23},$$

which is also the solution to Example 2a.

Most algebraic word problems on the GRE are not too difficult, and if you can do the algebra, that's usually the best way. But if, after studying this section, you still get stuck on a question during the test, don't despair. Use the tactics that you learned in Chapter 8, especially TACTIC 1—backsolving.

Age Problems

TIP

It is often very useful to organize the data from a word problem in a table.

EXAMPLE 3

In 1980, Judy was 3 times as old as Adam, but in 1984 she was only twice as old as he was. How old was Adam in 1990?

Ⓐ 4   Ⓑ 8   Ⓒ 12   Ⓓ 14   Ⓔ 16

SOLUTION.

Let x be Adam's age in 1980 and fill in the table below.

Year	Judy	Adam
1980	$3x$	x
1984	$3x + 4$	$x + 4$

Now translate: Judy's age in 1984 was twice Adam's age in 1984:

$$3x + 4 = 2(x + 4) = 2x + 8$$

$$3x + 4 = 2x + 8 \Rightarrow x + 4 = 8, \text{ and so } x = 4.$$

So, Adam was 4 in 1980. However, 4 is *not* the answer to this question. Did you remember to circle what you're looking for? The question *could have* asked for Adam's age in 1980 (Choice A) or 1984 (Choice B) or Judy's age in any year whatsoever (Choice C is 1980 and Choice E is 1984); but it didn't. It asked for *Adam's age in 1990.* Since he was 4 in 1980, then 10 years later, in 1990, he was **14** (**D**).

Distance Problems

Distance problems all depend on three variations of the same formula:

$$\textbf{distance} = \textbf{rate} \times \textbf{time} \qquad \textbf{rate} = \frac{\text{distance}}{\text{time}} \qquad \textbf{time} = \frac{\text{distance}}{\text{rate}}$$

These are usually abbreviated, $\boldsymbol{d = rt}$, $\boldsymbol{r = \dfrac{d}{t}}$, and $\boldsymbol{t = \dfrac{d}{r}}$.

EXAMPLE 4

How much longer, in *seconds*, is required to drive 1 mile at 40 miles per hour than at 60 miles per hour?

	seconds

SOLUTION.

The time to drive 1 mile at 40 miles per hour is given by

$$t = \frac{1}{40} \text{ hour} = \frac{1}{\underset{2}{\cancel{40}}} \times \overset{3}{\cancel{60}} \text{ minutes} = 1\frac{1}{2} \text{ minutes.}$$

The time to drive 1 mile at 60 miles per hour is given by $t = \dfrac{1}{60}$ hour = 1 minute.

The difference is $\dfrac{1}{2}$ minute = **30** seconds.

Note that this solution used the time formula given, but required only arithmetic, not algebra. Example 5 requires an algebraic solution.

EXAMPLE 5

Avi drove from his home to college at 60 miles per hour. Returning over the same route, there was a lot of traffic, and he was only able to drive at 40 miles per hour. If the return trip took 1 hour longer, how many miles did he drive each way?

(A) 2   (B) 3   (C) 5   (D) 120   (E) 240

SOLUTION.

Let x = the number of hours Avi took going to college and make a table.

	rate	time	. distance
Going	60	x	$60x$
Returning	40	$x + 1$	$40(x + 1)$

Since he drove the same distance going and returning,

$$60x = 40(x + 1) \Rightarrow 60x = 40x + 40 \Rightarrow 20x = 40, \text{ and so } x = 2.$$

Now be sure to answer the correct question. When $x = 2$, Choices A, B, and C are the time in hours that it took going, returning, and round-trip; Choices D and E are the distances each way and round-trip. You could have been asked for any of the five. If you circled what you're looking for, you won't make a careless mistake. Avi drove **120** miles each way, and so the correct answer is **D**.

The d in $d = rt$ stands for "distance," but it could really be any type of work that is performed at a certain rate, r, for a certain amount of time, t. Example 5 need not be about distance. Instead of driving 120 miles at 60 miles per hour for 2 hours, Avi could have read 120 pages at a rate of 60 pages per hour for 2 hours; or planted 120 flowers at the rate of 60 flowers per hour for 2 hours; or typed 120 words at a rate of 60 words per minute for 2 minutes.

Examples 6 and 7 illustrate two additional word problems of the type that you might find on the GRE.

EXAMPLE 6

Lindsay is trying to collect all the cards in a special commemorative set of baseball cards. She currently has exactly $\frac{1}{4}$ of the cards in that set.

When she gets 10 more cards, she will then have $\frac{1}{3}$ of the cards. How many cards are in the set?

Ⓐ 30   Ⓑ 60   Ⓒ 120   Ⓓ 180   Ⓔ 240

SOLUTION.

Let x be the number cards in the set. First, translate this problem from English into algebra: $\frac{1}{4}x + 10 = \frac{1}{3}x$. Now, use the six-step method of Section 11-G to solve the equation. Multiply by 12 to get, $3x + 120 = 4x$, and then subtract $3x$ from each side: $x = $ **120 (C)**.

EXAMPLE 7

Jen, Ken, and Len have a total of $390. Jen has 5 times as much as Len, and Ken has $\frac{3}{4}$ as much as Jen. How much money does Ken have?

Ⓐ $40   Ⓑ $78   Ⓒ $150   Ⓓ $195   Ⓔ $200

Suppose, for example, that in this problem you let x represent the amount of money that Ken has. Then since Ken has $\frac{3}{4}$ as much as Jen, Jen has $\frac{4}{3}$ as much as Ken: $\frac{4}{3}x$; and Jen would have $\frac{1}{5}$ of that: $\left(\frac{1}{5}\right)\left(\frac{4}{3}x\right)$. It is much easier here to let x represent the amount of money Len has.

SOLUTION.

Let x represent the amount of money Len has. Then $5x$ is the amount that Jen has, and $\frac{3}{4}(5x)$ is the amount that Ken has. Since the total amount of money is $390, $x + 5x + \frac{15}{4}x = 390$.

Multiply by 4 to get rid of the fraction: $4x + 20x + 15x = 1560$.
Combine like terms and then divide: $39x = 1560 \Rightarrow x = 40$.

So Len has $40, Jen has $5 \times 40 = \$200$, and Ken has $\frac{3}{4}(200) = \mathbf{\$150}$ **(C)**.

TIP
You often have a choice as to what to let the variable represent. Don't necessarily let it represent what you're looking for; rather, choose what will make the problem easiest to solve.

Practice Exercises — Word Problems

Discrete Quantitative Questions

1. Howard has three times as much money as Ronald. If Howard gives Ronald $50, Ronald will then have three times as much money as Howard. How much money, in dollars, do the two of them have together?

   [_____] dollars

2. In the afternoon, Beth read 100 pages at the rate of 60 pages per hour; in the evening, when she was tired, she read another 100 pages at the rate of 40 pages per hour. What was her average rate of reading for the day?

   (A) 45
   (B) 48
   (C) 50
   (D) 52
   (E) 55

3. If the sum of five consecutive integers is *S*, what is the largest of those integers in terms of *S*?

   (A) $\dfrac{S-10}{5}$

   (B) $\dfrac{S+4}{4}$

   (C) $\dfrac{S+5}{4}$

   (D) $\dfrac{S-5}{2}$

   (E) $\dfrac{S+10}{5}$

4. As a fund-raiser, the school band was selling two types of candy: lollipops for 40 cents each and chocolate bars for 75 cents each. On Monday, they sold 150 candies and raised 74 dollars. How many lollipops did they sell?

   (A) 75
   (B) 90
   (C) 96
   (D) 110
   (E) 120

5. A jar contains only red, white, and blue marbles. The number of red marbles is $\dfrac{4}{5}$ the number of white ones, and the number of white ones is $\dfrac{3}{4}$ the number of blue ones. If there are 470 marbles in all, how many of them are blue?

   (A) 120
   (B) 135
   (C) 150
   (D) 184
   (E) 200

6. The number of shells in Judy's collection is 80% of the number in Justin's collection. If Justin has 80 more shells than Judy, how many shells do they have altogether?

   [_____] shells

7. What is the greater of two numbers whose product is 900, if the sum of the two numbers exceeds their difference by 30?

   (A) 15
   (B) 60
   (C) 75
   (D) 90
   (E) 100

8. On a certain project the only grades awarded were 80 and 100. If 10 students completed the project and the average of their grades was 94, how many earned 100?

   Ⓐ 2
   Ⓑ 3
   Ⓒ 5
   Ⓓ 7
   Ⓔ 8

9. If $\frac{1}{2}x$ years ago Adam was 12, and $\frac{1}{2}x$ years from now he will be $2x$ years old, how old will he be $3x$ years from now?

   Ⓐ 18
   Ⓑ 24
   Ⓒ 30
   Ⓓ 54
   Ⓔ It cannot be determined from the information given.

10. Since 1950, when Barry was discharged from the army, he has gained 2 pounds every year. In 1980 he was 40% heavier than in 1950. What percent of his 1995 weight was his 1980 weight?

    Ⓐ 80
    Ⓑ 85
    Ⓒ 87.5
    Ⓓ 90
    Ⓔ 95

Quantitative Comparison Questions

Ⓐ Quantity A is greater.
Ⓑ Quantity B is greater.
Ⓒ Quantities A and B are equal.
Ⓓ It is impossible to determine which quantity is greater.

Lindsay is twice as old as she was 10 years ago. Kimberly is half as old as she will be in 10 years.

	Quantity A	Quantity B
11.	Lindsay's age now	Kimberly's age now

Boris spent $\frac{1}{4}$ of his take-home pay on Saturday and $\frac{1}{3}$ of what was left on Sunday. The rest he put in his savings account.

	Quantity A	Quantity B
12.	The amount of his take-home pay that he spent	The amount of his take-home pay that he saved

In 8 years, Tiffany will be 3 times as old as she is now.

	Quantity A	Quantity B
13.	The number of years until Tiffany will be 6 times as old as she is now	16

Rachel put exactly 50 cents worth of postage on an envelope using only 4-cent stamps and 7-cent stamps.

	Quantity A	Quantity B
14.	The number of 4-cent stamps she used	The number of 7-cent stamps she used

Car A and Car B leave from the same spot at the same time. Car A travels due north at 40 mph. Car B travels due east at 30 mph.

	Quantity A	Quantity B
15.	Distance from Car A to Car B 9 hours after they left	450 miles

ANSWER KEY

1. **100**	4. **D**	7. **B**	10. **C**	13. **A**
2. **B**	5. **E**	8. **D**	11. **A**	14. **D**
3. **E**	6. **720**	9. **D**	12. **C**	15. **C**

Answer Explanations

1. **100**

	Ronald	Howard
At the beginning	x	$3x$
After the gift	$x + 50$	$3x - 50$

After the gift, Ronald will have 3 times as much money as Howard:
$x + 50 = 3(3x - 50) \Rightarrow x + 50 = 9x - 150 \Rightarrow 8x = 200$, and so $x = 25$.
So Ronald has $25 and Howard has $75, for a total of $100.

2. **(B)** Beth's average rate of reading is determined by dividing the total number of pages she read (200) by the total amount of time she spent reading. In the afternoon she read for $\dfrac{100}{60} = \dfrac{5}{3}$ hours, and in the evening for $\dfrac{100}{40} = \dfrac{5}{2}$ hours,

for a total time of $\dfrac{5}{3} + \dfrac{5}{2} = \dfrac{10}{6} + \dfrac{15}{6} = \dfrac{25}{6}$ hours. So, her average rate was

$200 \div \dfrac{25}{6} = 200 \times \dfrac{6}{25} = 48$ pages per hour.

3. **(E)** Let the 5 consecutive integers be n, $n + 1$, $n + 2$, $n + 3$, $n + 4$. Then,
$S = n + n + 1 + n + 2 + n + 3 + n + 4 = 5n + 10 \Rightarrow 5n = S - 10 \Rightarrow n = \dfrac{S - 10}{5}$.
Choice A, therefore, is the *smallest* of the integers; the *largest* is
$n + 4 = \dfrac{S - 10}{5} + 4 = \dfrac{S - 10}{5} + \dfrac{20}{5} = \dfrac{S + 10}{5}$.

4. **(D)** Let x represent the number of chocolate bars sold; then $150 - x$ is the number of lollipops sold. We must use the same units, so we could write 75 cents as .75 dollars or 74 dollars as 7400 cents. Let's avoid the decimals: x chocolates sold for $75x$ cents and $(150 - x)$ lollipops sold for $40(150 - x)$ cents. So,
$7400 = 75x + 40(150 - x) = 75x + 6000 - 40x = 6000 + 35x \Rightarrow$
$1400 = 35x \Rightarrow x = 40$ and $150 - 40 = 110$.

5. **(E)** If b is the number of blue marbles, then there are $\dfrac{3}{4}b$ white ones, and

$\dfrac{4}{5}\left(\dfrac{3}{4}b\right) = \dfrac{3}{5}b$ red ones.

Therefore, $470 = b + \dfrac{3}{4}b + \dfrac{3}{5}b = b\left(1 + \dfrac{3}{4} + \dfrac{3}{5}\right) = \dfrac{47}{20}b$.

So, $b = 470 \div \dfrac{47}{20} = \overset{10}{\cancel{470}} \times \dfrac{20}{\underset{1}{\cancel{47}}} = 200$.

6. **720** If x is the number of shells in Justin's collection, then Judy has $.80x$. Since Justin has 80 more shells than Judy,

$x = .80x + 80 \Rightarrow .20x = 80 \Rightarrow x = 80 \div .20 = 400$.

So Justin has 400 and Judy has 320: a total of 720.

7. **(B)** If x represents the greater and y the smaller of the two numbers, then $(x + y) = 30 + (x - y) \Rightarrow y = 30 - y \Rightarrow 2y = 30$, and so $y = 15$. Since $xy = 900$, $x = 900 \div 15 = 60$.

8. **(D)** If x represents the number of students earning 100, then $10 - x$ is the number of students earning 80. So

$$94 = \frac{100x + 80(10 - x)}{10} \Rightarrow 94 = \frac{100x + 800 - 80x}{10} = \frac{20x + 800}{10} \Rightarrow$$

$94 \times 10 = 940 = 20x + 800 \Rightarrow 140 = 20x$, and $x = 7$.

9. **(D)** Since $\frac{1}{2}x$ years ago, Adam was 12, he is now $12 + \frac{1}{2}x$. So $\frac{1}{2}x$ years from

now, he will be $12 + \frac{1}{2}x + \frac{1}{2}x = 12 + x$. But, we are told that at that time

he will be $2x$ years old. So, $12 + x = 2x \Rightarrow x = 12$.

Thus, he is now $12 + 6 = 18$, and $3x$ or 36 years from now he will be $18 + 36 = 54$.

10. **(C)** Let x be Barry's weight in 1950. By 1980, he had gained 60 pounds (2 pounds per year for 30 years) and was 40% heavier: $60 = .40x \Rightarrow$ $x = 60 \div .4 = 150$. So in 1980, he weighed 210. Fifteen years later, in 1995,

he weighed 240: $\frac{210}{240} = \frac{7}{8} = 87.5\%$.

11. **(A)** You can do the simple algebra, but you might realize that if in the past 10 years Lindsay's age doubled, she was 10 and is now 20. Similarly, Kimberly is now 10 and in 10 years will be 20.

Here is the algebra: if x represents Lindsay's age now, $x = 2(x - 10) \Rightarrow x = 2x - 20 \Rightarrow x = 20$. Similarly, Kimberly is now 10 and will be 20 in 10 years.

12. **(C)** Let x represent the amount of Boris's take-home pay. On Saturday, he

spent $\frac{1}{4}x$ and still had $\frac{3}{4}x$; but on Sunday, he spent $\frac{1}{3}$ of that:

$\frac{1}{3}\left(\frac{3}{4}x\right) = \frac{1}{4}x$. Therefore, he spent $\frac{1}{4}$ of his take-home pay each day.

So, he spent $\frac{1}{2}$ of his pay and saved $\frac{1}{2}$ of his pay.

13. **(A)** If x represents Tiffany's age now, then in 8 years she will be $x + 8$, and so $x + 8 = 3x \Rightarrow 8 = 2x \Rightarrow x = 4$.

    Tiffany will be 6 times as old 20 years from now, when she will be 24.

14. **(D)** If x and y represent the number of 4-cent stamps and 7-cent stamps that Rachel used, respectively, then $4x + 7y = 50$. This equation has infinitely many solutions but only 2 in which x and y are both positive integers: $y = 2$ and $x = 9$ or $y = 6$ and $x = 2$.

15. **(C)** Draw a diagram. In 9 hours Car A drove 360 miles north and Car B drove 270 miles east. These are the legs of a right triangle, whose hypotenuse is the distance between them. Use the Pythagorean theorem if you don't recognize that this is just a $3x$–$4x$–$5x$ right triangle: the legs are 90×3 and 90×4, and the hypotenuse is $90 \times 5 = 450$.

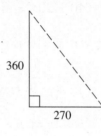

360

270

Geometry

Although about 30% of the math questions on the GRE have to do with geometry, there are only a relatively small number of facts you need to know — far less than you would learn in a geometry course — and, of course, there are no proofs. In the next six sections we will review all of the geometry that you need to know to do well on the GRE. We will present the material exactly as it appears on the GRE, using the same vocabulary and notation, which might be slightly different from the terminology you learned in your high school math classes. The numerous examples in the next six sections will show you exactly how these topics are treated on the GRE.

11-I. LINES AND ANGLES

An ***angle*** is formed by the intersection of two line segments, rays, or lines. The point of intersection is called the ***vertex***. On the GRE, angles are always measured in degrees.

KEY FACT I1

Angles are classified according to their degree measures.

- **An acute angle measures less than 90°.**
- **A right angle measures 90°.**
- **An obtuse angle measures more than 90° but less than 180°.**
- **A straight angle measures 180°.**

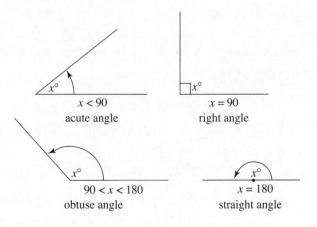

$x < 90$
acute angle

$x = 90$
right angle

$90 < x < 180$
obtuse angle

$x = 180$
straight angle

NOTE: The small square in the second angle in the figure above is *always* used to mean that the angle is a right angle. On the GRE, if an angle has a square in it, it must measure exactly 90°, *whether or not you think that the figure has been drawn to scale.*

KEY FACT I2

If two or more angles form a straight angle, the sum of their measures is 180°.

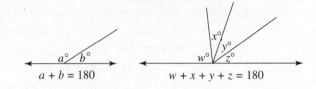

$a + b = 180$ $w + x + y + z = 180$

EXAMPLE 1

In the figure below, *R*, *S*, and *T* are all on line ℓ. What is the average of *a*, *b*, *c*, *d*, and *e*?

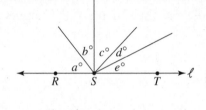

SOLUTION.

Since $\angle RST$ is a straight angle, by KEY FACT I2, the sum of *a*, *b*, *c*, *d*, and *e* is 180, and so their average is $\dfrac{180}{5} = \mathbf{36}$.

In the figure below, since $a + b + c + d = 180$ and $e + f + g = 180$, $a + b + c + d + e + f + g = 180 + 180 = 360$.

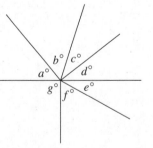

It is also true that $u + v + w + x + y + z = 360$, even though none of the angles forms a straight angle.

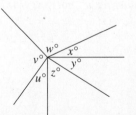

KEY FACT 13

The sum of all the measures of all the angles around a point is 360°.

NOTE: This fact is particularly important when the point is the center of a circle, as we shall see in Section 11-L.

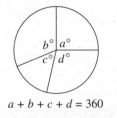

$$a + b + c + d = 360$$

When two lines intersect, four angles are formed. The two angles in each pair of opposite angles are called ***vertical angles***.

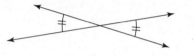

KEY FACT 14

Vertical angles have equal measures.

EXAMPLE 2

In the figure at the right, what is the value of x?

Ⓐ 6   Ⓑ 8   Ⓒ 10   Ⓓ 20   Ⓔ 40

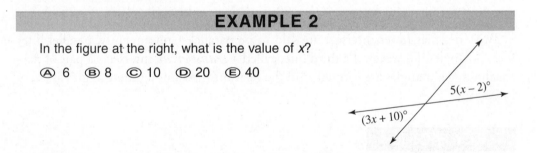

SOLUTION.
Since the measures of vertical angles are equal, $3x + 10 = 5(x - 2) \Rightarrow 3x + 10 = 5x - 10 \Rightarrow 3x + 20 = 5x \Rightarrow 20 = 2x \Rightarrow x = $ **10 (C)**.

KEY FACT 15

If one of the angles formed by the intersection of two lines (or line segments) is a right angle, then all four angles are right angles.

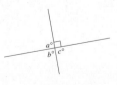

$$a = b = c = 90$$

Two lines that intersect to form right angles are called ***perpendicular***.

In the figures below, line ℓ divides ∠*ABC* into two equal parts, and line *k* divides line segment *DE* into two equal parts. Line ℓ is said to **bisect** the angle, and line *k* **bisects** the line segment. Point *M* is called the **midpoint** of segment *DE*.

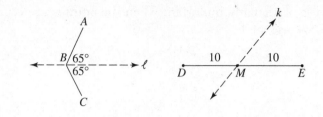

EXAMPLE 3

In the figure at the right, lines *k*, ℓ, and *m* intersect at *O*. If line *m* bisects ∠*AOB*, what is the value of *x*?

Ⓐ 25   Ⓑ 35   Ⓒ 45   Ⓓ 50   Ⓔ 60

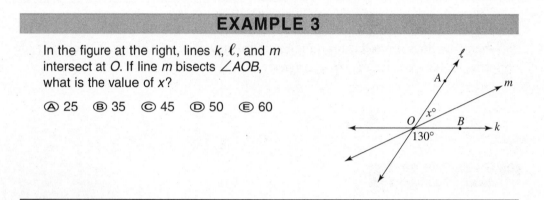

SOLUTION.
m∠*AOB* + 130 = 180 ⇒ m∠*AOB* = 50; and since *m* bisects ∠*AOB*, *x* = **25 (A)**.

Two lines that never intersect are said to be parallel. Consequently, parallel lines form no angles. However, if a third line, called a **transversal**, intersects a pair of parallel lines, eight angles are formed, and the relationships among these angles are very important.

KEY FACT I6

If a pair of parallel lines is cut by a transversal that is perpendicular to the parallel lines, all eight angles are right angles.

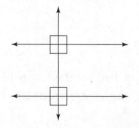

KEY FACT I7

If a pair of parallel lines is cut by a transversal that is not perpendicular to the parallel lines,

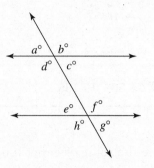

- Four of the angles are acute and four are obtuse;
- The four acute angles are equal: $a = c = e = g$;
- The four obtuse angles are equal: $b = d = f = h$;
- The sum of any acute angle and any obtuse angle is 180°: for example, $d + e = 180$, $c + f = 180$, $b + g = 180$, ...

KEY FACT I8

If a pair of lines that are not parallel is cut by a transversal, *none* of the properties listed in KEY FACT I7 is true.

You must know KEY FACT I7 — virtually every GRE has at least one question based on it. However, you do *not* need to know the special terms you learned in high school for these pairs of angles; those terms are not used on the GRE.

EXAMPLE 4

In the figure below, *AB* is parallel to *CD*. What is the value of *x*?

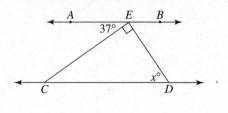

SOLUTION.

Let *y* be the measure of $\angle BED$. Then by KEY FACT I2:

$$37 + 90 + y = 180 \Rightarrow 127 + y = 180 \Rightarrow y = 53.$$

Since *AB* is parallel to *CD*, by KEY FACT I7, $x = y \Rightarrow x =$ **53**.

EXAMPLE 5

In the figure below, lines ℓ and k are parallel. What is the value of $a + b$?

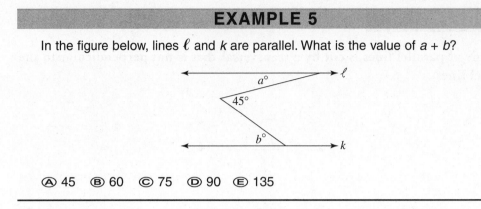

Ⓐ 45   Ⓑ 60   Ⓒ 75   Ⓓ 90   Ⓔ 135

SOLUTION.

It is impossible to determine the value of either a or b. We can, however, find the value of $a + b$. We draw a line through the vertex of the angle parallel to ℓ and k. Then, looking at the top two lines, we see that $a = x$, and looking at the bottom two lines, we see that $b = y$. So, $a + b = x + y = $ **45 (A)**.

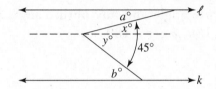

Alternative solution. Draw a different line and use a Key Fact from Section 11-J on triangles. Extend one of the line segments to form a triangle. Since ℓ and k are parallel, the measure of the third angle in the triangle equals a. Now, use the fact that the sum of the measures of the three angles in a triangle is 180° or, even easier, that the given 45° angle is an external angle of the triangle, and so is equal to the sum of a and b.

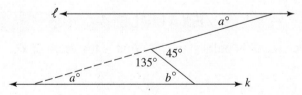

Practice Exercises — Lines and Angles

Discrete Quantitative Questions

1. In the figure below, what is the average (arithmetic mean) of the measures of the five angles?

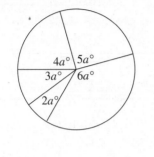

- Ⓐ 36
- Ⓑ 45
- Ⓒ 60
- Ⓓ 72
- Ⓔ 90

2. In the figure below, what is the value of $\dfrac{b+a}{b-a}$?

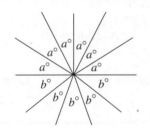

- Ⓐ 1
- Ⓑ 10
- Ⓒ 11
- Ⓓ 30
- Ⓔ 36

3. In the figure below, what is the value of b?

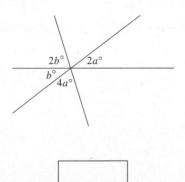

4. In the figure below, what is the value of x if $y:x = 3:2$?

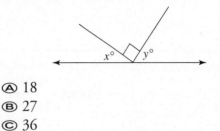

- Ⓐ 18
- Ⓑ 27
- Ⓒ 36
- Ⓓ 45
- Ⓔ 54

5. What is the measure, in degrees, of the angle formed by the minute and hour hands of a clock at 1:50?

 degrees

6. Concerning the figure below, if $a = b$, which of the following statements must be true?

Indicate *all* such statements.

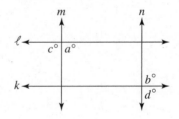

- A $c = d$
- B ℓ and k are parallel
- C m and ℓ are perpendicular

7. In the figure below, $a:b = 3:5$ and $c:b = 2:1$. What is the measure of the largest angle?

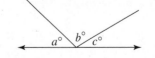

- Ⓐ 30
- Ⓑ 45
- Ⓒ 50
- Ⓓ 90
- Ⓔ 100

8. *A*, *B*, and *C* are points on a line with *B* between *A* and *C*. Let *M* and *N* be the midpoints of *AB* and *BC*, respectively. If *AB*:*BC* = 3:1, what is *MN*:*BC*?

- Ⓐ 1:2
- Ⓑ 2:3
- Ⓒ 1:1
- Ⓓ 3:2
- Ⓔ 2:1

9. In the figure below, lines *k* and *ℓ* are parallel. What is the value of *y* − *x*?

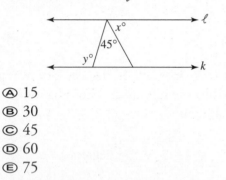

- Ⓐ 15
- Ⓑ 30
- Ⓒ 45
- Ⓓ 60
- Ⓔ 75

10. In the figure below, line *m* bisects ∠*AOC* and line *ℓ* bisects ∠*AOB*. What is the measure of ∠*DOE*?

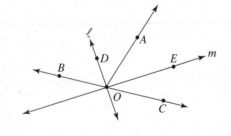

- Ⓐ 75
- Ⓑ 90
- Ⓒ 100
- Ⓓ 105
- Ⓔ 120

Quantitative Comparison Questions

> Ⓐ Quantity A is greater.
> Ⓑ Quantity B is greater.
> Ⓒ Quantities A and B are equal.
> Ⓓ It is impossible to determine which quantity is greater.

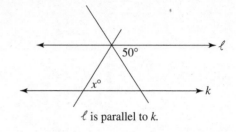

ℓ is parallel to *k*.

	Quantity A	Quantity B
11.	*x*	50

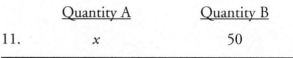

AB is parallel to *CD*.

	Quantity A	Quantity B
12.	*a*	*b*

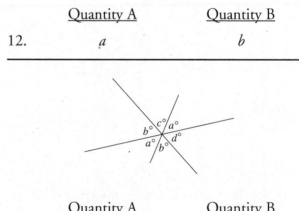

	Quantity A	Quantity B
13.	*a* + *b* + *c* + *d*	2*a* + 2*b*

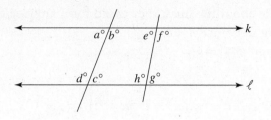

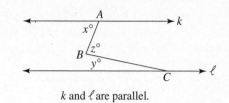

k and *ℓ* are parallel.

	Quantity A	Quantity B			Quantity A	Quantity B
14.	$a + b + c + d$	$e + f + g + h$		15.	z	$x + y$

ANSWER KEY

1. **D**	4. **C**	7. **E**	10. **B**	13. **D**
2. **C**	5. **115**	8. **E**	11. **D**	14. **C**
3. **36**	6. **A**	9. **C**	12. **B**	15. **C**

Answer Explanations

1. **(D)** The markings in the five angles are irrelevant. The sum of the measures of the five angles is 360°, and 360 ÷ 5 = 72. If you calculated the measure of each angle you should have gotten 36, 54, 72, 90, and 108; but you would have wasted time.

2. **(C)** From the diagram, we see that $6a = 180$, which implies that $a = 30$, and that $5b = 180$, which implies that $b = 36$. So, $\dfrac{b + a}{b - a} = \dfrac{36 + 30}{36 - 30} = \dfrac{66}{6} = 11$.

3. **36** Since vertical angles are equal, the two unmarked angles are $2b$ and $4a$. Since the sum of all six angles is 360°,
   $360 = 4a + 2b + 2a + 4a + 2b + b = 10a + 5b$.

   However, since vertical angles are equal, $b = 2a \Rightarrow 5b = 10a$. Hence, $360 = 10a + 5b = 10a + 10a = 20a$, so $a = 18$ and $b = 36$.

4. **(C)** Since $x + y + 90 = 180$, $x + y = 90$. Also, since $y{:}x = 3{:}2$, $y = 3t$ and $x = 2t$. Therefore, $3t + 2t = 90 \Rightarrow 5t = 90$. So $t = 18$, and $x = 2(18) = 36$.

5. **115** For problems such as this, always draw a diagram. The measure of each of the 12 central angles from one number to the next on the clock is 30°. At 1:50 the minute hand is pointing at 10, and the hour hand has gone $\dfrac{50}{60} = \dfrac{5}{6}$ of the way from 1 to 2. So from 10 to 1 on the clock is 90°, and from 1 to

   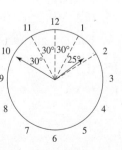

   the hour hand is $\dfrac{5}{6}(30°) = 25°$, for a total of $90° + 25° = 115°$.

6. **(A)** No conclusions can be made about the lines; they could form any angles whatsoever. (B and C are both false.) Since $a = b$,

$$c = 180 - a = 180 - b = d.$$

(A is true.)

7. **(E)** Since $a:b = 3:5$, then $a = 3x$ and $b = 5x$. $c:b = c:5x = 2:1 \Rightarrow c = 10x$. Then, $3x + 5x + 10x = 180 \Rightarrow 18x = 180$. So, $x = 10$ and $c = 10x = 100$.

8. **(E)** If a diagram is not provided on a geometry question, draw one on your scrap paper. From the figure below, you can see that $MN:BC = 2:1$.

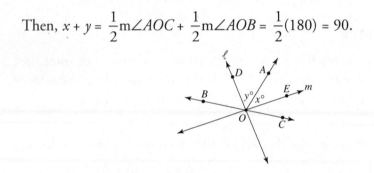

9. **(C)** Since the lines are parallel, the angle marked y and the sum of the angles marked x and 45 are equal: $y = x + 45 \Rightarrow y - x = 45$.

10. **(B)** Let $x = \frac{1}{2}\text{m}\angle AOC$, and $y = \frac{1}{2}\text{m}\angle AOB$.

Then, $x + y = \frac{1}{2}\text{m}\angle AOC + \frac{1}{2}\text{m}\angle AOB = \frac{1}{2}(180) = 90$.

11. **(D)** No conclusion can be made: x could equal 50 or be more or less.

12. **(B)** Since $\text{m}\angle A + 32 + 75 = 180$, $\text{m}\angle A = 73$; and since AB is parallel to CD, $a = 73$, whereas, because vertical angles are equal, $b = 75$.

13. **(D)**

	Quantity A	Quantity B
	$a + b + c + d$	$2a + 2b$
Subtract a and b from each quantity:	$c + d$	$a + b$
Since $b = d$, subtract them:	c	a

There is no way to determine whether a is less than, greater than, or equal to c.

14. **(C)** Whether the lines are parallel or not, $a + b = c + d = e + f = g + h = 180$. Each quantity is equal to 360.

15. **(C)** Extend line segment AB to form a transversal. Since $w + z = 180$ and $w + (x + y) = 180$, it follows that $z = x + y$.

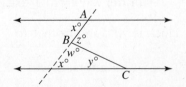

11-J. TRIANGLES

More geometry questions on the GRE pertain to triangles than to any other topic. To answer them, there are several important facts that you need to know about the angles and sides of triangles. The KEY FACTS in this section are extremely useful. Read them carefully, a few times if necessary, and *make sure you learn them all.*

KEY FACT J1

In any triangle, the sum of the measures of the three angles is 180°:

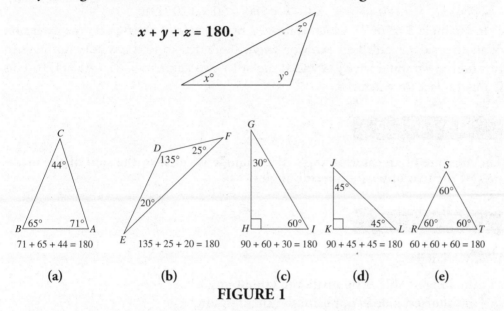

$$x + y + z = 180.$$

71 + 65 + 44 = 180   135 + 25 + 20 = 180   90 + 60 + 30 = 180   90 + 45 + 45 = 180   60 + 60 + 60 = 180

(a)   (b)   (c)   (d)   (e)

FIGURE 1

Figure 1 (a–e) illustrates KEY FACT J1 for five different triangles, which will be discussed below.

EXAMPLE 1

In the figure below, what is the value of *x*?

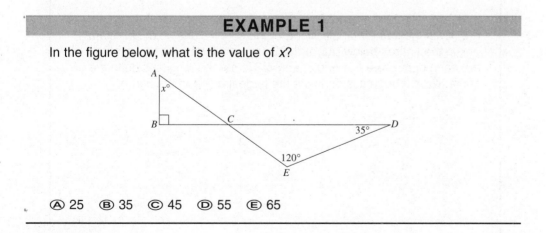

Ⓐ 25   Ⓑ 35   Ⓒ 45   Ⓓ 55   Ⓔ 65

SOLUTION.
Use KEY FACT J1 twice: first, for $\triangle CDE$ and then for $\triangle ABC$.

- $m\angle DCE + 120 + 35 = 180 \Rightarrow m\angle DCE + 155 = 180 \Rightarrow m\angle DCE = 25.$
- Since vertical angles are equal, $m\angle ACB = 25$ (see KEY FACT I6).
- $x + 90 + 25 = 180 \Rightarrow x + 115 = 180$, and so $x = $ **65** (**E**).

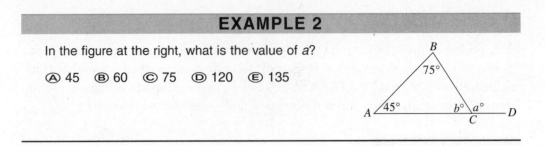

EXAMPLE 2

In the figure at the right, what is the value of *a*?

(A) 45   (B) 60   (C) 75   (D) 120   (E) 135

SOLUTION.

First find the value of *b*: $180 = 45 + 75 + b = 120 + b \Rightarrow b = 60$.

Then, $a + b = 180 \Rightarrow a = 180 - b = 180 - 60 = \mathbf{120} \ (\mathbf{D})$.

In Example 2, $\angle BCD$, which is formed by one side of $\triangle ABC$ and the extension of another side, is called an ***exterior angle***. Note that to find *a* we did not have to first find *b*; we could have just added the other two angles: $a = 75 + 45 = 120$. This is a useful fact to remember.

KEY FACT J2

The measure of an exterior angle of a triangle is equal to the sum of the measures of the two opposite interior angles.

KEY FACT J3

In any triangle:

- **the longest side is opposite the largest angle;**
- **the shortest side is opposite the smallest angle;**
- **sides with the same length are opposite angles with the same measure.**

CAUTION

In KEY FACT J3 the condition "in any triangle" is crucial. If the angles are not in the same triangle, none of the conclusions hold. For example, in the figures below, *AB* and *DE* are *not* equal even though they are each opposite a 90° angle, and *QS* is not the longest side in the figure, even though it is opposite the largest angle in the figure.

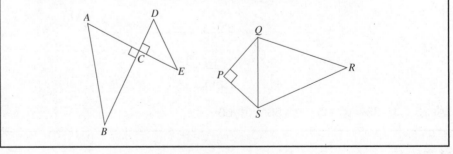

Consider triangles *ABC*, *JKL*, and *RST* in Figure 1 on the previous page.

- In $\triangle ABC$: *BC* is the longest side since it is opposite angle *A*, the largest angle (71°). Similarly, *AB* is the shortest side since it is opposite angle *C*, the smallest angle (44°). So $AB < AC < BC$.

- In $\triangle JKL$: angles J and L have the same measure (45°), so $JK = KL$.
- In $\triangle RST$: since all three angles have the same measure (60°), all three sides have the same length: $RS = ST = TR$.

EXAMPLE 3

Which of the following statements concerning the length of side *YZ* is true?

Indicate *all* such statements.

[A] $YZ < 9$

[B] $YZ = 9$

[C] $9 < YZ < 10$

[D] $YZ = 10$

[E] $YZ > 10$

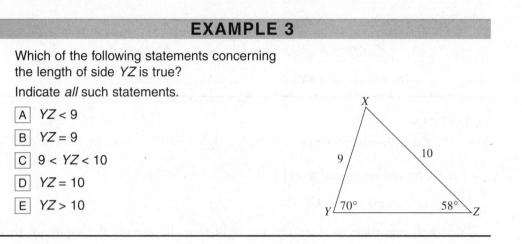

SOLUTION.

Since the five answer choices are mutually exclusive, only one of them can be true.

- By KEY FACT J1, $m\angle X + 70 + 58 = 180 \Rightarrow m\angle X = 52$.
- So, X is the smallest angle.
- Therefore, by KEY FACT J3, YZ is the shortest side. So **YZ < 9** (**A**).

Classification of Triangles

Name	Lengths of the Sides	Measures of the Angles	Examples from Figure 1
scalene	all 3 different	all 3 different	*ABC, DEF, GHI*
isosceles	2 the same	2 the same	*JKL*
equilateral	all 3 the same	all 3 the same	*RST*

Acute triangles are triangles such as *ABC* and *RST*, in which all three angles are acute. An acute triangle could be scalene, isosceles, or equilateral.

Obtuse triangles are triangles such as *DEF*, in which one angle is obtuse and two are acute. An obtuse triangle could be scalene or isosceles.

Right triangles are triangles such as *GHI* and *JKL*, which have one right angle and two acute ones. A right triangle could be scalene or isosceles. The side opposite the 90° angle is called the *hypotenuse*, and by KEY FACT J3, it is the longest side. The other two sides are called the *legs*.

If x and y are the measures of the acute angles of a right triangle, then by KEY FACT J1, $90 + x + y = 180 \Rightarrow x + y = 90$.

KEY FACT J4

In any right triangle, the sum of the measures of the two acute angles is 90°.

EXAMPLE 4

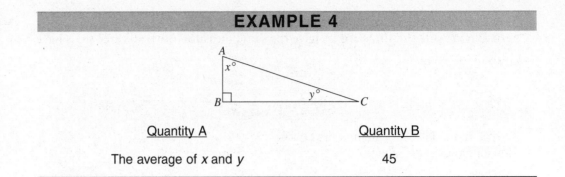

Quantity A	Quantity B
The average of x and y	45

SOLUTION.
Since the diagram indicates that $\triangle ABC$ is a right triangle, then, by KEY FACT J1, $x + y = 90$. So the average of x and $y = \dfrac{x+y}{2} = \dfrac{90}{2} = 45$.

The quantities are equal (**C**).

The most important facts concerning right triangles are the **Pythagorean theorem** and its converse, which are given in KEY FACT J5 and repeated as the first line of KEY FACT J6.

KEY FACT J5

Let a, b, and c be the sides of $\triangle ABC$, with $a \le b \le c$. If $\triangle ABC$ is a right triangle, $a^2 + b^2 = c^2$; and if $a^2 + b^2 = c^2$, then $\triangle ABC$ is a right triangle.

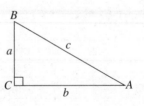

KEY FACT J6

Let a, b, and c be the sides of $\triangle ABC$, with $a \le b \le c$.

- $a^2 + b^2 = c^2$ if and only if angle C is a right angle. ($\triangle ABC$ is a right triangle.)
- $a^2 + b^2 < c^2$ if and only if angle C is obtuse. ($\triangle ABC$ is an obtuse triangle.)
- $a^2 + b^2 > c^2$ if and only if angle C is acute. ($\triangle ABC$ is an acute triangle.)

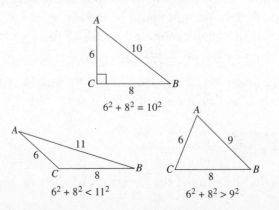

EXAMPLE 5

Which of the following triples are *not* the sides of a right triangle?
Indicate *all* such triples.

[A] 3, 4, 5

[B] 1, 1, $\sqrt{3}$

[C] 1, $\sqrt{3}$, 2

[D] $\sqrt{3}$, $\sqrt{4}$, $\sqrt{5}$

[E] 30, 40, 50

SOLUTION.
Just check each choice.

(A) $3^2 + 4^2 = 9 + 16 = 25 = 5^2$ These *are* the sides of a right triangle.

(B) $1^2 + 1^2 = 1 + 1 = 2 \neq (\sqrt{3})^2$ These *are not* the sides of a right triangle.

(C) $1^2 + (\sqrt{3})^2 = 1 + 3 = 4 = 2^2$ These *are* the sides of a right triangle.

(D) $(\sqrt{3})^2 + (\sqrt{4})^2 = 3 + 4 = 7 \neq (\sqrt{5})^2$ These *are not* the sides of a right triangle.

(E) $30^2 + 40^2 = 900 + 1600 = 2500 = 50^2$ These *are* the sides of a right triangle.

The answer is **B** and **D**.

Below are the right triangles that appear most often on the GRE. You should recognize them immediately whenever they come up in questions. Carefully study each one, and memorize KEY FACTS J7–J11.

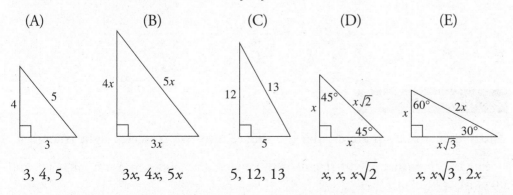

(A)   (B)   (C)   (D)   (E)

3, 4, 5   3x, 4x, 5x   5, 12, 13   x, x, x$\sqrt{2}$ x, x$\sqrt{3}$, 2x

On the GRE, the most common right triangles whose sides are integers are the 3-4-5 triangle (A) and its multiples (B).

KEY FACT J7

For any positive number x, there is a right triangle whose sides are $3x$, $4x$, $5x$.

For example:

$x = 1$	3, 4, 5	$x = 5$	15, 20, 25
$x = 2$	6, 8, 10	$x = 10$	30, 40, 50
$x = 3$	9, 12, 15	$x = 50$	150, 200, 250
$x = 4$	12, 16, 20	$x = 100$	300, 400, 500

TIP

KEY FACT J7 applies even if x is not an integer. For example:
$x = .5$ 1.5, 2, 2.5
$x = \pi$ 3π, 4π, 5π

NOTE: The only other right triangle with integer sides that you should recognize immediately is the one whose sides are 5, 12, 13 (C).

Let x = length of each leg, and h = length of the hypotenuse, of an isosceles right triangle (D). By the Pythagorean theorem (KEY FACT J5), $x^2 + x^2 = h^2$.

So, $2x^2 = h^2$, and $h = \sqrt{2x^2} = x\sqrt{2}$.

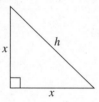

KEY FACT J8

In a 45-45-90 right triangle, the sides are x, x, and $x\sqrt{2}$. So,

- **by multiplying the length of a leg by $\sqrt{2}$, you get the hypotenuse.**

- **by dividing the hypotenuse by $\sqrt{2}$, you get the length of each leg.**

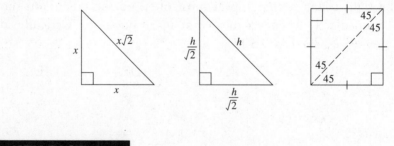

KEY FACT J9

The diagonal of a square divides the square into two isosceles right triangles.

The last important right triangle is the one whose angles measure 30°, 60°, and 90°. (E)

KEY FACT J10

An altitude divides an equilateral triangle into two 30-60-90 right triangles.

Let $2x$ be the length of each side of equilateral $\triangle ABC$ in which altitude AD is drawn. Then $\triangle ABD$ is a 30-60-90 right triangle, and its sides are x, $2x$, and h.

By the Pythagorean theorem,

$$x^2 + h^2 = (2x)^2 = 4x^2.$$

So $h^2 = 3x^2$, and $h = \sqrt{3x^2} = x\sqrt{3}$.

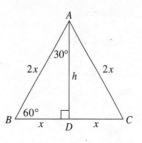

KEY FACT J11

In a 30-60-90 right triangle the sides are

x, $x\sqrt{3}$, and $2x$.

If you know the length of the shorter leg (x),

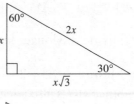

- multiply it by $\sqrt{3}$ to get the longer leg, and
- multiply it by 2 to get the hypotenuse.

If you know the length of the longer leg (a),

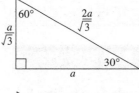

- divide it by $\sqrt{3}$ to get the shorter leg, and
- multiply the shorter leg by 2 to get the hypotenuse.

If you know the length of the hypotenuse (h),

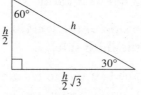

- divide it by 2 to get the shorter leg, and
- multiply the shorter leg by $\sqrt{3}$ to get the longer leg.

EXAMPLE 6

What is the area of a square whose diagonal is 10?

SOLUTION.

Draw a diagonal in a square of side s, creating a 45-45-90 right triangle. By KEY FACT J8:

$$s = \frac{10}{\sqrt{2}} \quad \text{and} \quad A = s^2 = \left(\frac{10}{\sqrt{2}}\right)^2 = \frac{100}{2} = \mathbf{50}.$$

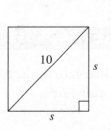

EXAMPLE 7

In the diagram at the right, if $BC = \sqrt{6}$, what is the value of CD?

Ⓐ $2\sqrt{2}$

Ⓑ $4\sqrt{2}$

Ⓒ $2\sqrt{3}$

Ⓓ $2\sqrt{6}$

Ⓔ 4

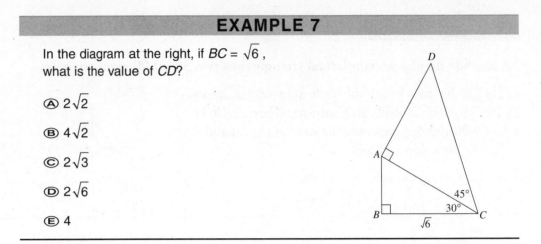

SOLUTION.

Since $\triangle ABC$ and $\triangle DAC$ are 30-60-90 and 45-45-90 right triangles, respectively, use KEY FACTS J11 and J8.

- Divide the longer leg, BC, by $\sqrt{3}$ to get the shorter leg, AB: $\dfrac{\sqrt{6}}{\sqrt{3}} = \sqrt{2}$.

- Multiply AB by 2 to get the hypotenuse: $AC = 2\sqrt{2}$.
- Since AC is also a leg of isosceles right $\triangle DAC$, to get hypotenuse CD, multiply AC by $\sqrt{2}$: $CD = 2\sqrt{2} \times \sqrt{2} = 2 \times 2 = 4$ (**E**).

Key Fact J12

Triangle Inequality

The sum of the lengths of any two sides of a triangle is greater than the length of the third side.

The best way to remember this is to see that $x + y$, the length of the path from A to C through B, is greater than z, the length of the direct path from A to C.

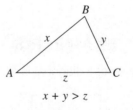

$$x + y > z$$

NOTE: If you subtract x from each side of $x + y > z$, you see that $z - x < y$.

KEY FACT J13

The difference of the lengths of any two sides of a triangle is less than the length of the third side.

EXAMPLE 8

If the lengths of two of the sides of a triangle are 6 and 7, which of the following could be the length of the third side?

Indicate *all* possible lengths.

A 1	C π	E 12	G 15
B 2	D 7	F 13	

SOLUTION.
Use KEY FACTS J12 and J13.

- The third side must be *less* than 6 + 7 = 13. (Eliminate F and G.)
- The third side must be *greater* than 7 − 6 = 1. (Eliminate A.)
- *Any* number between 1 and 13 could be the length of the third side.

The answer is **B, C, D, E**.

The following diagram illustrates several triangles, two of whose sides have lengths of 6 and 7.

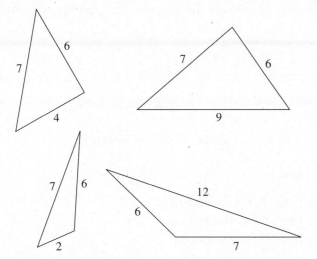

On the GRE, two other terms that appear regularly in triangle problems are *perimeter* and *area* (see Section 11-K).

EXAMPLE 9

In the figure at the right, what is the perimeter of △*ABC*?

Ⓐ 20 + 10√2

Ⓑ 20 + 10√3

Ⓒ 25

Ⓓ 30

Ⓔ 40

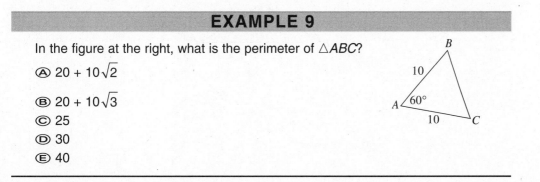

SOLUTION.
First, use KEY FACTS J3 and J1 to find the measures of the angles.

- Since $AB = AC$, m$\angle B$ = m$\angle C$. Represent each of them by x.
- Then, $x + x + 60 = 180 \Rightarrow 2x = 120 \Rightarrow x = 60$.
- Since the measure of each angle of $\triangle ABC$ is 60, the triangle is equilateral.
- So $BC = 10$, and the perimeter is $10 + 10 + 10 = \mathbf{30}$ (**D**).

KEY FACT J14

The area of a triangle is given by $A = \dfrac{1}{2}\,bh$, where b is the base and h is the height.

NOTE:

1. *Any* side of the triangle can be taken as the **base**.
2. The **height** or **altitude** is a line segment drawn to the base or, if necessary, to an extension of the base from the opposite vertex.
3. In a right triangle, either leg can be the base and the other the height.
4. The height may be outside the triangle. [See the figure below.]

TIP

If one endpoint of the base of a triangle is the vertex of an obtuse angle, then the height drawn to that base will be outside the triangle.

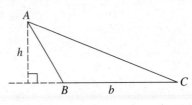

Note: $\triangle ABC$ is obtuse.

In the figure below:

- If AC is the base, BD is the height.
- If AB is the base, CE is the height.
- If BC is the base, AF is the height.

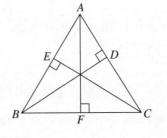

EXAMPLE 10

What is the area of an equilateral triangle whose sides are 10?

Ⓐ 30   Ⓑ $25\sqrt{3}$ Ⓒ 50   Ⓓ $50\sqrt{3}$ Ⓔ 100

SOLUTION.
Draw an equilateral triangle and one of its altitudes.

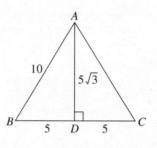

- By KEY FACT J10, $\triangle ABD$ is a 30-60-90 right triangle.

- By KEY FACT J11, $BD = 5$ and $AD = 5\sqrt{3}$.

- The area of $\triangle ABC = \dfrac{1}{2}(10)(5\sqrt{3}) = \mathbf{25\sqrt{3}}$ (**B**).

Replacing 10 by *s* in Example 10 yields a very useful result.

KEY FACT J15

If *A* represents the area of an equilateral triangle with side *s*, then $A = \dfrac{s^2\sqrt{3}}{4}$.

TIP

Learn this formula for the area of an equilateral triangle. It can save you time.

Practice Exercises — Triangles

Discrete Quantitative Questions

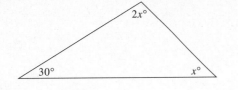

1. In the triangle above, what is the value of *x*?
   - Ⓐ 20
   - Ⓑ 30
   - Ⓒ 40
   - Ⓓ 50
   - Ⓔ 60

2. If the difference between the measures of the two smaller angles of a right triangle is 8°, what is the measure, in degrees, of the smallest angle?
   - Ⓐ 37
   - Ⓑ 41
   - Ⓒ 42
   - Ⓓ 49
   - Ⓔ 53

3. What is the area of an equilateral triangle whose altitude is 6?
   - Ⓐ 18
   - Ⓑ $12\sqrt{3}$
   - Ⓒ $18\sqrt{3}$
   - Ⓓ 36
   - Ⓔ $24\sqrt{3}$

4. Two sides of a right triangle are 12 and 13. Which of the following *could be* the length of the third side?

   Indicate *all* possible lengths.
   - Ⓐ 2
   - Ⓑ 5
   - Ⓒ $\sqrt{31}$
   - Ⓓ 11
   - Ⓔ $\sqrt{313}$

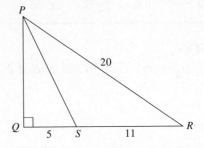

5. What is the value of *PS* in the triangle above?
   - Ⓐ $5\sqrt{2}$
   - Ⓑ 10
   - Ⓒ 11
   - Ⓓ 13
   - Ⓔ $12\sqrt{2}$

6. If the measures of the angles of a triangle are in the ratio of 1:2:3, and if the length of the smallest side of the triangle is 10, what is the length of the longest side?
   - Ⓐ $10\sqrt{2}$
   - Ⓑ $10\sqrt{3}$
   - Ⓒ 15
   - Ⓓ 20
   - Ⓔ 30

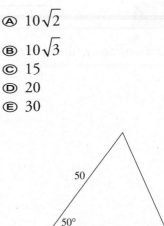

7. What is the value of *x* in the figure above?

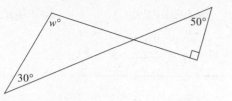

8. In the figure above, what is the value of *w*?

Questions 9–10 refer to the following figure.

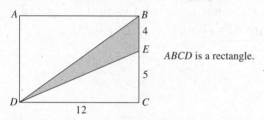

ABCD is a rectangle.

9. What is the area of △*BED*?

Ⓐ 12
Ⓑ 24
Ⓒ 36
Ⓓ 48
Ⓔ 60

10. What is the perimeter of △*BED*?

Ⓐ $19 + 5\sqrt{2}$
Ⓑ 28
Ⓒ $17 + \sqrt{185}$
Ⓓ 32
Ⓔ 36

Questions 11–12 refer to the following figure.

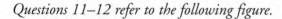

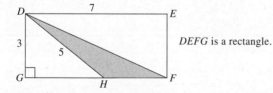

DEFG is a rectangle.

11. What is the area of △*DFH*?

Ⓐ 3
Ⓑ 4.5
Ⓒ 6
Ⓓ 7.5
Ⓔ 10

12. What is the perimeter of △*DFH*?

Ⓐ $8 + \sqrt{41}$
Ⓑ $8 + \sqrt{58}$
Ⓒ 16
Ⓓ 17
Ⓔ 18

13. Which of the following expresses a true relationship between *x* and *y* in the figure above?

Ⓐ $y = 60 - x$
Ⓑ $y = x$
Ⓒ $x + y = 90$
Ⓓ $y = 180 - 3x$
Ⓔ $x = 90 - 3y$

Questions 14–15 refer to the following figure.

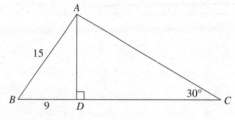

14. What is the perimeter of △*ABC*?

Ⓐ 48
Ⓑ $48 + 12\sqrt{2}$
Ⓒ $48 + 12\sqrt{3}$
Ⓓ 60
Ⓔ $60 + 6\sqrt{3}$

15. What is the area of △*ABC*?

Ⓐ 108
Ⓑ $54 + 72\sqrt{2}$
Ⓒ $54 + 72\sqrt{3}$
Ⓓ 198
Ⓔ 216

Quantitative Comparison Questions

Ⓐ Quantity A is greater.
Ⓑ Quantity B is greater.
Ⓒ Quantities A and B are equal.
Ⓓ It is impossible to determine which quantity is greater.

The lengths of two sides of a triangle are 7 and 11.

	Quantity A	Quantity B
16.	The length of the third side	4

	Quantity A	Quantity B
17.	The ratio of the length of a diagonal to the length of a side of a square	$\sqrt{2}$

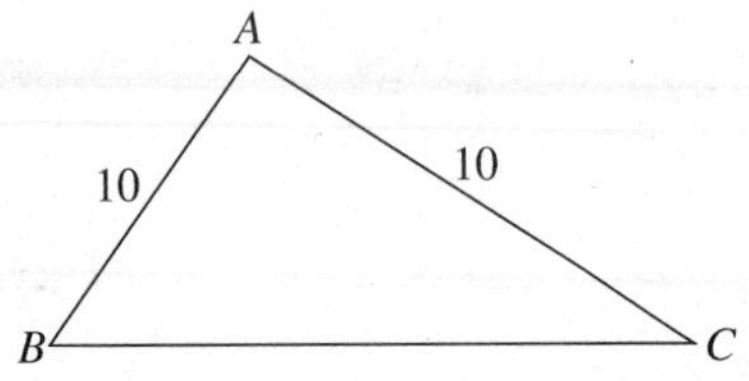

	Quantity A	Quantity B
18.	The perimeter of △ABC	30

Questions 19–20 refer to the following figure.

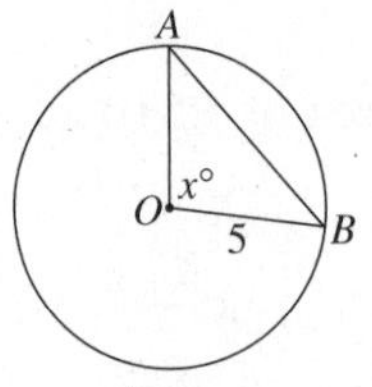

$90 < x$

	Quantity A	Quantity B
19.	The length of AB	7

	Quantity A	Quantity B
20.	The perimeter of △AOB	20

	Quantity A	Quantity B
21.	The area of an equilateral triangle whose sides are 10	The area of an equilateral triangle whose altitude is 10

Questions 22–23 refer to the following figure in which the horizontal and vertical lines divide square *ABCD* into 16 smaller squares.

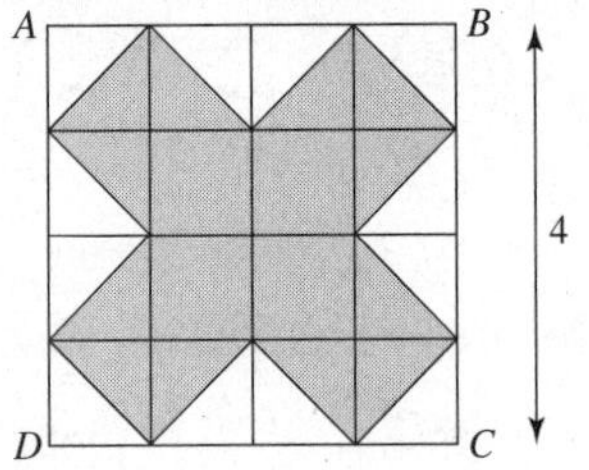

	Quantity A	Quantity B
22.	The perimeter of the shaded region	The perimeter of the square

	Quantity A	Quantity B
23.	The area of the shaded region	The area of the white region

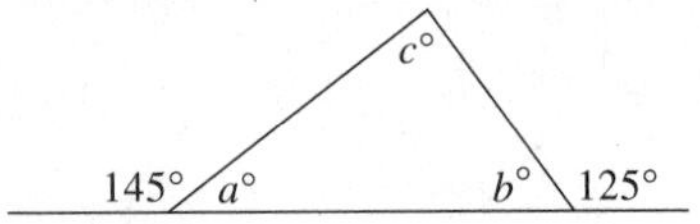

	Quantity A	Quantity B
24.	$a + b$	c

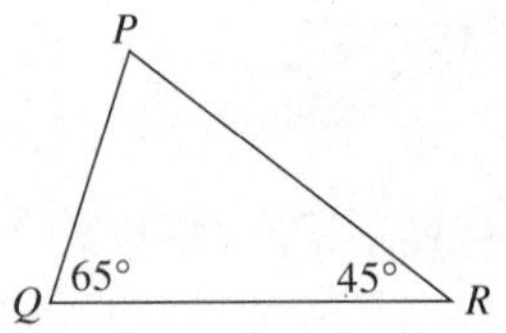

	Quantity A	Quantity B
25.	PR	QR

ANSWER KEY

1. **D**	6. **D**	11. **B**	16. **A**	21. **B**
2. **B**	7. **115**	12. **B**	17. **C**	22. **A**
3. **B**	8. **110**	13. **A**	18. **D**	23. **A**
4. **B, E**	9. **B**	14. **C**	19. **A**	24. **C**
5. **D**	10. **D**	15. **C**	20. **B**	25. **B**

Answer Explanations

1. **(D)** $x + 2x + 30 = 180 \Rightarrow 3x + 30 = 180 \Rightarrow 3x = 150 \Rightarrow x = 50$.

2. **(B)** Draw a diagram and label it.

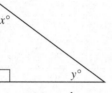

   Then write the equations: $x + y = 90$ and $x - y = 8$.
   Add the equations:
$$\begin{array}{r} x + y = 90 \\ + \underline{x - y = 8} \\ 2x = 98 \end{array}$$

   So $x = 49$ and $y = 90 - 49 = 41$.

3. **(B)** Draw altitude AD in equilateral $\triangle ABC$.

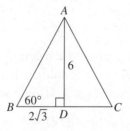

   By KEY FACT J11, $BD = \dfrac{6}{\sqrt{3}} = \dfrac{6\sqrt{3}}{3} = 2\sqrt{3}$, and BD is one half the base.

   So, the area is $2\sqrt{3} \times 6 = 12\sqrt{3}$.

4. **(B)(E)** If the triangle were not required to be a right triangle, by KEY FACTS J11 and J12 *any* number greater than 1 and less than 25 could be the length of the third side, and the answer would be A, B, C, D, E. But for a right triangle, there are only *two* possibilities:
   - If 13 is the hypotenuse, then the legs are 12 and 5. (B is true.) (If you didn't recognize the 5-12-13 triangle, use the Pythagorean theorem: $12^2 + x^2 = 13^2$, and solve.)
   - If 12 and 13 are the two legs, then use the Pythagorean theorem to find the hypotenuse: $12^2 + 13^2 = c^2 \Rightarrow c^2 = 144 + 169 = 313 \Rightarrow c = \sqrt{313}$. (E is true.)

5. **(D)** Use the Pythagorean theorem twice, unless you recognize the common right triangles in this figure (*which you should*). Since $PR = 20$ and $QR = 16$, $\triangle PQR$ is a 3x-4x-5x right triangle with $x = 4$. So $PQ = 12$, and $\triangle PQS$ is a right triangle whose legs are 5 and 12. The hypotenuse, *PS*, therefore, is 13.

6. **(D)** If the measures of the angles are in the ratio of 1:2:3,

   $x + 2x + 3x = 180 \Rightarrow 6x = 180 \Rightarrow x = 30.$

   So the triangle is a 30-60-90 right triangle, and the sides are a, $2a$, and $a\sqrt{3}$. Since $a = 10$, then $2a$, the length of the longest side, is 20.

7. **115** Label the other angles in the triangle.

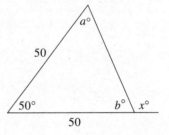

   $50 + a + b = 180 \Rightarrow a + b = 130$, and since the triangle is isosceles, $a = b$. Therefore, a and b are each 65, and $x = 180 - 65 = 115$.

8. **110** Here, $50 + 90 + a = 180 \Rightarrow a = 40$, and since vertical angles are equal, $b = 40$. Then, $40 + 30 + w = 180 \Rightarrow w = 110$.

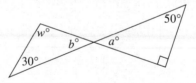

9. **(B)** You *could* calculate the area of the rectangle and subtract the area of the two white right triangles, but you shouldn't. It is easier to solve this problem if you realize that the shaded area is a triangle whose base is 4 and whose height is 12. The area is $\frac{1}{2}(4)(12) = 24$.

10. **(D)** Since both *BD* and *ED* are the hypotenuses of right triangles, their lengths can be calculated by the Pythagorean theorem, but these are triangles you should recognize: the sides of $\triangle DCE$ are 5-12-13, and those of $\triangle BAD$ are 9-12-15 (3x-4x-5x, with $x = 3$). So the perimeter of $\triangle BED$ is $4 + 13 + 15 = 32$.

11. **(B)** Since $\triangle DGH$ is a right triangle whose hypotenuse is 5 and one of whose legs is 3, the other leg, *GH*, is 4. Since $GF = DE$ is 7, *HF* is 3. Now, $\triangle DFH$ has a base of 3 (*HF*) and a height of 3 (*DG*), and its area is $\frac{1}{2}(3)(3) = 4.5$.

12. **(B)** In $\triangle DFH$, we already have that $DH = 5$ and $HF = 3$; we need only find DF, which is the hypotenuse of $\triangle DEF$. By the Pythagorean theorem,

$$(DF)^2 = 3^2 + 7^2 = 9 + 49 = 58 \Rightarrow DF = \sqrt{58}.$$

So the perimeter is $3 + 5 + \sqrt{58} = 8 + \sqrt{58}$.

13. **(A)** $x + 2x + 3y = 180 \Rightarrow 3x + 3y = 180$. So $x + y = 60$, and $y = 60 - x$.

14. **(C)** $\triangle ABD$ is a right triangle whose hypotenuse is 15 and one of whose legs is 9, so this is a $3x$-$4x$-$5x$ triangle with $x = 3$; so $AD = 12$. Now $\triangle ADC$ is a 30-60-90 triangle, whose shorter leg is 12. Hypotenuse AC is 24, and leg CD is $12\sqrt{3}$. So the perimeter is $24 + 15 + 9 + 12\sqrt{3} = 48 + 12\sqrt{3}$.

15. **(C)** From the solution to 14, we have the base $(9 + 12\sqrt{3})$ and the height (12) of $\triangle ABC$. Then, the area is $\frac{1}{2}(12)(9 + 12\sqrt{3}) = 54 + 72\sqrt{3}$.

16. **(A)** Any side of a triangle must be greater than the difference of the other two sides (KEY FACT J13), so the third side is greater than $11 - 7 = 4$.

17. **(C)** Draw a diagram. A diagonal of a square is the hypotenuse of each of the two 45-45-90 right triangles formed. The ratio of the length of the hypotenuse to the length of the leg in such a triangle is $\sqrt{2}$:1, so the quantities are equal.

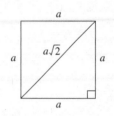

18. **(D)** BC can be any positive number less than 20 (by KEY FACTS J12 and J13, $BC > 10 - 10 = 0$ and $BC < 10 + 10 = 20$). So the perimeter can be *any* number greater than 20 and less than 40.

19. **(A)** Since OA and OB are radii, they are each equal to 5. With no restrictions on x, AB could be any positive number less than 10, and the bigger x is, the bigger AB is. If x were 90, AB would be $5\sqrt{2}$, but we are told that $x > 90$, so $AB > 5\sqrt{2} > 7$.

20. **(B)** Since AB must be less than 10, the perimeter is *less* than 20.

21. **(B)** Don't calculate either area. The length of a side of an equilateral triangle is *greater* than the length of an altitude. So Quantity B is larger since it is the area of a triangle whose sides are greater.

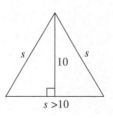

22. **(A)** Quantity A: The perimeter of the shaded region consists of 12 line segments, each of which is the hypotenuse of a 45-45-90 right triangle whose legs are 1. So each line segment is $\sqrt{2}$, and the perimeter is $12\sqrt{2}$. Quantity B: The perimeter of the square is 16.

    To compare $12\sqrt{2}$ and 16, square them: $(12\sqrt{2})^2 = 144 \times 2 = 288$; $16^2 = 256$.

23. **(A)** The white region consists of 12 right triangles, each of which has an area of $\frac{1}{2}$, for a total area of 6. Since the area of the large square is 16, the area of the shaded region is $16 - 6 = 10$.

24. **(C)** Since $a = 180 - 145 = 35$ and $b = 180 - 125 = 55$, $a + b = 35 + 55 = 90$. Therefore, $180 = a + b + c = 90 + c \Rightarrow c = 90$.

25. **(B)** Since $65 + 45 = 110$, $m\angle P = 70$. Since $\angle P$ is the largest angle, QR, the side opposite it, is the largest side.

11-K. QUADRILATERALS AND OTHER POLYGONS

A *polygon* is a closed geometric figure made up of line segments. The line segments are called *sides* and the endpoints of the line segments are called *vertices* (each one is called a *vertex*). Line segments inside the polygon drawn from one vertex to another are called *diagonals*. The simplest polygons, which have three sides, are the triangles, which you just studied in Section J. A polygon with four sides is called a *quadrilateral*. The only other terms you should be familiar with are *pentagon*, *hexagon*, *octagon*, and *decagon*, which are the names for polygons with five, six, eight, and ten sides, respectively.

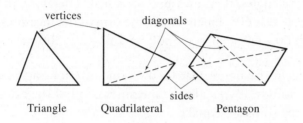

In this section we will present a few facts about polygons and quadrilaterals in general, but the emphasis will be on reviewing the key facts you need to know about four special quadrilaterals.

Every quadrilateral has two diagonals. If you draw in either one, you will divide the quadrilateral into two triangles. Since the sum of the measures of the three angles in each of the triangles is 180°, the sum of the measures of the angles in the quadrilateral is 360°.

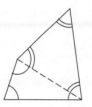

KEY FACT K1

In any quadrilateral, the sum of the measures of the four angles is 360°.

In exactly the same way, any polygon can be divided into triangles by drawing in all of the diagonals emanating from one vertex.

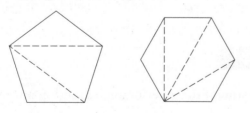

Notice that the pentagon is divided into three triangles, and the hexagon is divided into four triangles. In general, an *n*-sided polygon is divided into $(n-2)$ triangles, which leads to KEY FACT K2.

KEY FACT K2

The sum of the measures of the *n* angles in a polygon with *n* sides is $(n-2) \times 180°$.

EXAMPLE 1

In the figure at the right, what is the value of *x*?

Ⓐ 60   Ⓑ 90   Ⓒ 100   Ⓓ 120   Ⓔ 150

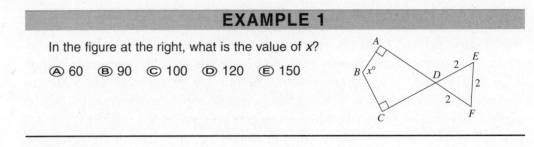

SOLUTION.

Since △*DEF* is equilateral, all of its angles measure 60°; also, since the two angles at vertex *D* are vertical angles, their measures are equal. Therefore, the measure of ∠*D* in quadrilateral *ABCD* is 60°. Finally, since the sum of the measures of all four angles of *ABCD* is 360°, $60 + 90 + 90 + x = 360 \Rightarrow 240 + x = 360 \Rightarrow x = \mathbf{120}$ (**D**).

In the polygons in the figure that follows, one exterior angle has been drawn at each vertex. Surprisingly, if you add the measures of all of the exterior angles in any of the polygons, the sums are equal.

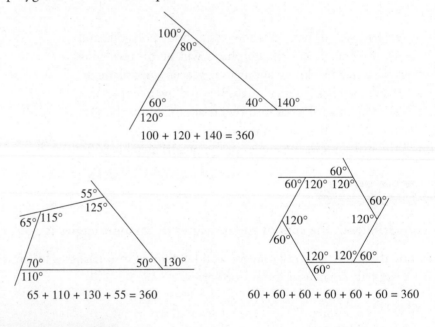

$100 + 120 + 140 = 360$

$65 + 110 + 130 + 55 = 360$

$60 + 60 + 60 + 60 + 60 + 60 = 360$

KEY FACT K3

In any polygon, the sum of the exterior angles, taking one at each vertex, is 360°.

A *regular polygon* is a polygon in which all of the sides are the same length and each angle has the same measure. KEY FACT K4 follows immediately from this definition and from KEY FACTS K2 and K3.

KEY FACT K4

In any regular polygon the measure of each interior angle is $\dfrac{(n-2) \times 180°}{n}$ and the measure of each exterior angle is $\dfrac{360°}{n}$.

EXAMPLE 2

What is the measure, in degrees, of each interior angle in a regular decagon?

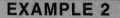 degrees

---

SOLUTION 1.

The measure of each of the 10 interior angles is

$$\frac{(10-2)\times180°}{10} = \frac{8\times180°}{10} = \frac{1440°}{10} = \mathbf{144°}.$$

SOLUTION 2.

The measure of each of the 10 exterior angles is 36° (360° ÷ 10). Therefore, the measure of each interior angle is 180° − 36° = **144°**.

A *parallelogram* is a quadrilateral in which both pairs of opposite sides are parallel.

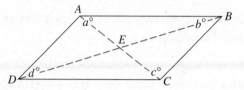

KEY FACT K5

Parallelograms have the following properties:

- **Opposite sides are equal:** $AB = CD$ and $AD = BC$.
- **Opposite angles are equal:** $a = c$ and $b = d$.
- **Consecutive angles add up to 180°:** $a + b = 180$, $b + c = 180$, $c + d = 180$, and $a + d = 180$.
- **The two diagonals bisect each other:** $AE = EC$ and $BE = ED$.
- **A diagonal divides the parallelogram into two triangles that have the exact same size and shape. (The triangles are congruent.)**

EXAMPLE 3

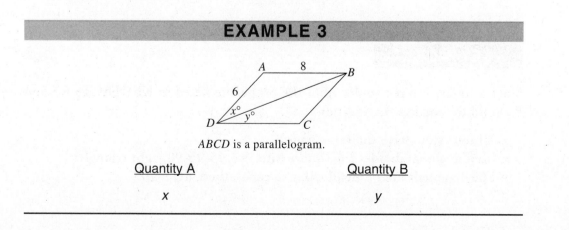

ABCD is a parallelogram.

Quantity A	Quantity B
x	*y*

SOLUTION.
In △*ABD* the larger angle is opposite the larger side (KEY FACT J2); so
x > m∠*ABD*. However, since *AB* and *CD* are parallel sides cut by transversal *BD*,
y = m∠*ABD*. Therefore, *x* > *y*. Quantity **A** is greater.

A ***rectangle*** is a parallelogram in which all four angles are right angles. Two adja-
cent sides of a rectangle are usually called the ***length*** (ℓ) and the ***width*** (*w*). Note
in the right-hand figure that the length is not necessarily greater than the width.

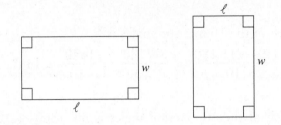

KEY FACT K6

TIP

A rectangle is a
parallelogram.

**Since a rectangle is a parallelogram, all of the properties listed in KEY FACT
K5 hold for rectangles. In addition:**

- **The measure of each angle in a rectangle is 90°.**
- **The diagonals of a rectangle have the same length: *AC* = *BD*.**

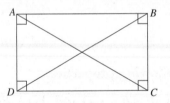

A ***square*** is a rectangle in which all four sides have the same length.

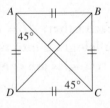

KEY FACT K7

TIP

A square is a
rectangle and,
hence, a
parallelogram.

**Since a square is a rectangle, all of the properties listed in KEY FACTS K5 and
K6 hold for squares. In addition:**

- **All four sides have the same length.**
- **Each diagonal divides the square into two 45-45-90 right triangles.**
- **The diagonals are perpendicular to each other: *AC* ⊥ *BD*.**

EXAMPLE 4

What is the length of each side of a square if its diagonals are 10?

Ⓐ 5   Ⓑ 7   Ⓒ $5\sqrt{2}$ Ⓓ $10\sqrt{2}$ Ⓔ $10\sqrt{3}$

SOLUTION.
Draw a diagram.

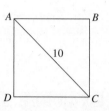

In square *ABCD*, diagonal *AC* is the hypotenuse of △*ABC* a 45-45-90 right triangle, and side *AB* is a leg of that triangle. By KEY FACT J7,

$$AB = \frac{AC}{\sqrt{2}} = \frac{10}{\sqrt{2}} \times \frac{\sqrt{2}}{\sqrt{2}} = \frac{10\sqrt{2}}{2} = 5\sqrt{2} \ \textbf{(C)}.$$

A *trapezoid* is a quadrilateral in which one pair of sides is parallel and the other pair of sides is not parallel. The parallel sides are called the *bases* of the trapezoid. The two bases are never equal. In general, the two nonparallel sides are not equal; if they are the trapezoid is called an *isosceles trapezoid*.

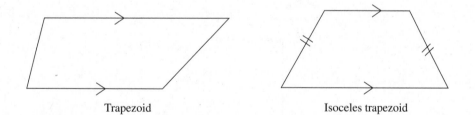

Trapezoid   Isoceles trapezoid

The *perimeter* (*P*) of any polygon is the sum of the lengths of all of its sides.

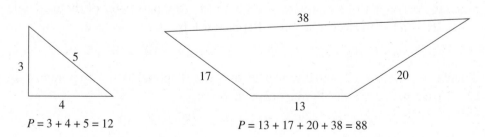

$P = 3 + 4 + 5 = 12$ $P = 13 + 17 + 20 + 38 = 88$

KEY FACT K8

In a rectangle, $P = 2(\ell + w)$; in a square, $P = 4s$.

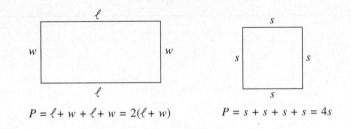

$$P = \ell + w + \ell + w = 2(\ell + w) \qquad P = s + s + s + s = 4s$$

EXAMPLE 5

The length of a rectangle is 7 more than its width. If the perimeter of the rectangle is the same as the perimeter of a square of side 8.5, what is the length of a diagonal of the rectangle?

SOLUTION.
Don't do anything until you have drawn a diagram.

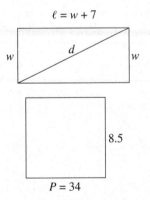

Since the perimeter of the square = $4 \times 8.5 = 34$, the perimeter of the rectangle is also 34: $2(\ell + w) = 34 \Rightarrow \ell + w = 17$. Replacing ℓ by $w + 7$, we get:

$$w + 7 + w = 17 \Rightarrow 2w + 7 = 17 \Rightarrow 2w = 10 \Rightarrow w = 5$$

Then $\ell = 5 + 7 = 12$. Finally, realize that the diagonal is the hypotenuse of a 5-12-13 triangle, or use the Pythagorean theorem:

$$d^2 = 5^2 + 12^2 = 25 + 144 = 169 \Rightarrow d = \mathbf{13}.$$

In Section 11-J we reviewed the formula for the area of a triangle. The only other figures for which you need to know area formulas are the parallelogram, rectangle, square, and trapezoid.

KEY FACT K9

Here are the area formulas you need to know:

- For a parallelogram: $A = bh$.
- For a rectangle: $A = \ell w$.
- For a square: $A = s^2$ or $A = \dfrac{1}{2}d^2$.
- For a trapezoid: $A = \dfrac{1}{2}(b_1 + b_2)h$.

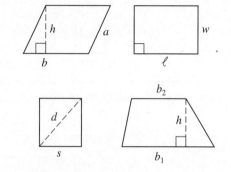

TIP

Be sure to learn the alternative formula for the area of a square: $A = 1/2\,d^2$, where d is the length of a diagonal.

EXAMPLE 6

In the figure below, the area of parallelogram *ABCD* is 40. What is the area of rectangle *AFCE*?

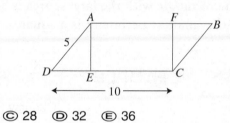

Ⓐ 20 Ⓑ 24 Ⓒ 28 Ⓓ 32 Ⓔ 36

SOLUTION.
Since the base, *CD*, is 10 and the area is 40, the height, *AE*, must be 4. Then △*AED* must be a 3-4-5 right triangle with *DE* = 3, which implies that *EC* = 7. So the area of the rectangle is $7 \times 4 = $ **28** (**C**).

Two rectangles with the same perimeter can have different areas, and two rectangles with the same area can have different perimeters. These facts are a common source of questions on the GRE.

RECTANGLES WHOSE PERIMETERS ARE 100

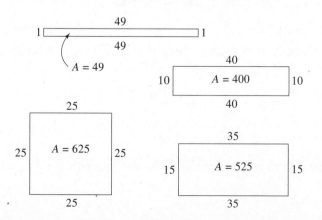

RECTANGLES WHOSE AREAS ARE 100

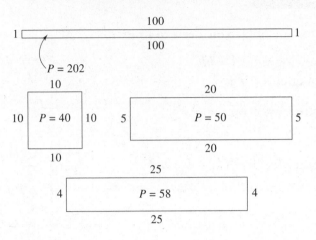

KEY FACT K10

For a given perimeter, the rectangle with the largest area is a square. For a given area, the rectangle with the smallest perimeter is a square.

EXAMPLE 7

Quantity A	Quantity B
The area of a rectangle whose perimeter is 12	The area of a rectangle whose perimeter is 14

SOLUTION.

Draw any rectangles whose perimeters are 12 and 14 and compute their areas. As drawn below, Quantity A = 8 and Quantity B = 12.

This time Quantity B is greater. Is it always? Draw a different rectangle whose perimeter is 14.

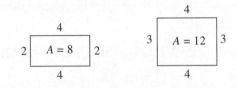

The one drawn here has an area of 6. Now Quantity B isn't greater. The answer is **D**.

EXAMPLE 8

Quantity A	Quantity B
The area of a rectangle whose perimeter is 12	10

SOLUTION.
There are many rectangles of different areas whose perimeters are 12. But the largest area is 9, when the rectangle is a 3 × 3 square. Quantity **B** is greater.

Practice Exercises — Quadrilaterals

Discrete Quantitative Questions

1. If the length of a rectangle is 4 times its width, and if its area is 144, what is its perimeter?

Questions 2–3 refer to the diagram below in which the diagonals of square *ABCD* intersect at *E*.

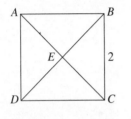

2. What is the area of △*DEC*?

    Ⓐ $\dfrac{1}{2}$

    Ⓑ 1

    Ⓒ $\sqrt{2}$

    Ⓓ 2

    Ⓔ $2\sqrt{2}$

3. What is the perimeter of △*DEC*?

    Ⓐ $1 + \sqrt{2}$

    Ⓑ $2 + \sqrt{2}$

    Ⓒ 4

    Ⓓ $2 + 2\sqrt{2}$

    Ⓔ 6

4. If the angles of a five-sided polygon are in the ratio of 2:3:3:5:5, what is the measure of the smallest angle?

    Ⓐ 20

    Ⓑ 40

    Ⓒ 60

    Ⓓ 80

    Ⓔ 90

5. If in the figures below, the area of rectangle *ABCD* is 100, what is the area of rectangle *EFGH*?

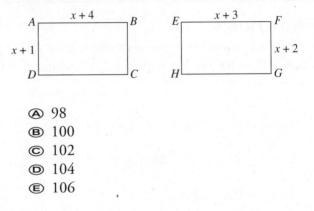

    Ⓐ 98

    Ⓑ 100

    Ⓒ 102

    Ⓓ 104

    Ⓔ 106

Questions 6–7 refer to a rectangle in which the length of each diagonal is 12, and one of the angles formed by the diagonal and a side measures 30°.

6. What is the area of the rectangle?

    Ⓐ 18

    Ⓑ 72

    Ⓒ $18\sqrt{3}$

    Ⓓ $36\sqrt{3}$

    Ⓔ $36\sqrt{2}$

7. What is the perimeter of the rectangle?

    Ⓐ 18

    Ⓑ 24

    Ⓒ $12 + 12\sqrt{3}$

    Ⓓ $18 + 6\sqrt{3}$

    Ⓔ $24\sqrt{2}$

8. How many sides does a polygon have if the measure of each interior angle is 8 times the measure of each exterior angle?

   Ⓐ 8
   Ⓑ 9
   Ⓒ 10
   Ⓓ 12
   Ⓔ 18

9. The length of a rectangle is 5 more than the side of a square, and the width of the rectangle is 5 less than the side of the square. If the area of the square is 45, what is the area of the rectangle?

   Ⓐ 20
   Ⓑ 25
   Ⓒ 45
   Ⓓ 50
   Ⓔ 70

Questions 10–11 refer to the following figure, in which *M*, *N*, *O*, and *P* are the midpoints of the sides of rectangle *ABCD*.

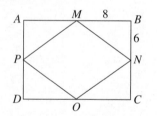

10. What is the perimeter of quadrilateral *MNOP*?

    Ⓐ 24
    Ⓑ 32
    Ⓒ 40
    Ⓓ 48
    Ⓔ 60

11. What is the area of quadrilateral *MNOP*?

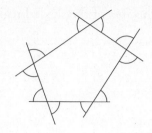

12. In the figure above, what is the sum of the measures of all of the marked angles?

    Ⓐ 360
    Ⓑ 540
    Ⓒ 720
    Ⓓ 900
    Ⓔ 1080

13. In quadrilateral *WXYZ*, the measure of angle *Z* is 10 more than twice the average of the measures of the other three angles. What is the measure of angle *Z*?

    Ⓐ 100
    Ⓑ 105
    Ⓒ 120
    Ⓓ 135
    Ⓔ 150

Questions 14–15 refer to the following figure, in which *M* and *N* are the midpoints of two of the sides of square *ABCD*.

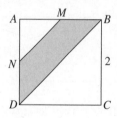

14. What is the perimeter of the shaded region?

    Ⓐ 3
    Ⓑ $2 + 3\sqrt{2}$
    Ⓒ $3 + 2\sqrt{2}$
    Ⓓ 5
    Ⓔ 8

15. What is the area of the shaded region?

ⓐ 1.5

ⓑ 1.75

ⓒ 3

ⓓ $2\sqrt{2}$

ⓔ $3\sqrt{2}$

Quantitative Comparison Questions

ⓐ Quantity A is greater.

ⓑ Quantity B is greater.

ⓒ Quantities A and B are equal.

ⓓ It is impossible to determine which quantity is greater.

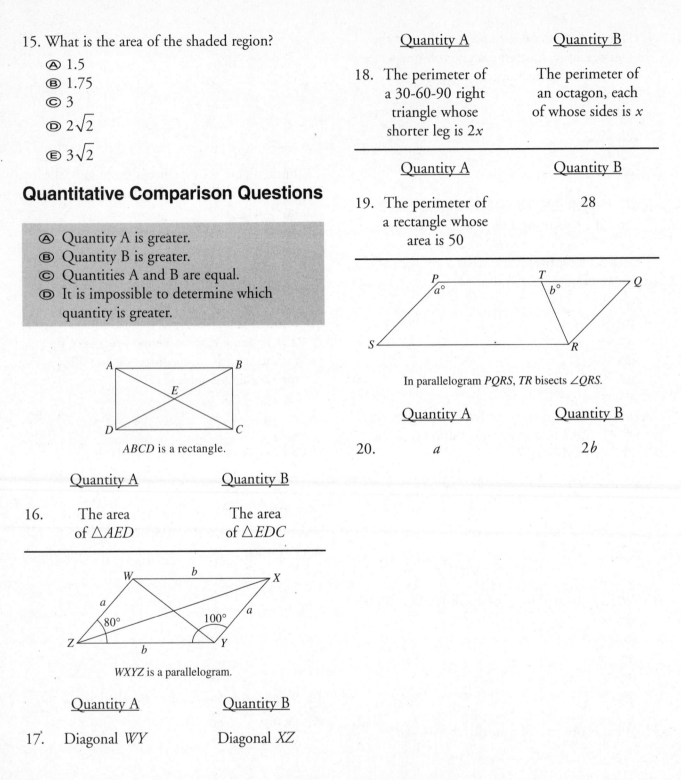

ABCD is a rectangle.

Quantity A	Quantity B
16. The area of △*AED*	The area of △*EDC*

WXYZ is a parallelogram.

Quantity A	Quantity B
17. Diagonal *WY*	Diagonal *XZ*

Quantity A	Quantity B
18. The perimeter of a 30-60-90 right triangle whose shorter leg is 2x	The perimeter of an octagon, each of whose sides is x

Quantity A	Quantity B
19. The perimeter of a rectangle whose area is 50	28

In parallelogram *PQRS*, *TR* bisects ∠*QRS*.

Quantity A	Quantity B
20. *a*	2*b*

ANSWER KEY

1. **60**	5. **C**	9. **A**	13. **150**	17. **B**
2. **B**	6. **D**	10. **C**	14. **B**	18. **A**
3. **D**	7. **C**	11. **96**	15. **A**	19. **A**
4. **C**	8. **E**	12. **C**	16. **C**	20. **C**

Answer Explanations

1. **60** Draw a diagram and label it.

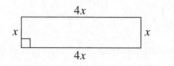

   Since the area is 144, then $144 = (4x)(x) = 4x^2 \Rightarrow x^2 = 36 \Rightarrow x = 6$.
   So the width is 6, the length is 24, and the perimeter is 60.

2. **(B)** The area of the square is $2^2 = 4$, and each triangle is one-fourth of the square. So the area of $\triangle DEC$ is 1.

3. **(D)** $\triangle DEC$ is a 45-45-90 right triangle whose hypotenuse, DC, is 2.

   Therefore, each of the legs is $\dfrac{2}{\sqrt{2}} = \sqrt{2}$. So the perimeter is $2 + 2\sqrt{2}$.

4. **(C)** The sum of the angles of a five-sided polygon is $(5 - 2) \times 180 = 3 \times 180 = 540$. Therefore, $540 = 2x + 3x + 3x + 5x + 5x = 18x$.
   So, $x = 540 \div 18 = 30$.
   The measure of the smallest angle is $2x = 2 \times 30 = 60$.

5. **(C)** The area of rectangle $ABCD$ is $(x + 1)(x + 4) = x^2 + 5x + 4$.

   The area of rectangle $EFGH$ is $(x + 2)(x + 3) = x^2 + 5x + 6$, which is exactly 2 more than the area of rectangle $ABCD$: $100 + 2 = 102$.

6. **(D)** Draw a picture and label it.

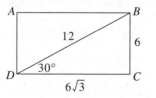

   Since $\triangle BCD$ is a 30-60-90 right triangle, BC is 6 (half the hypotenuse) and CD is $6\sqrt{3}$.

   So the area is $\ell w = 6(6\sqrt{3}) = 36\sqrt{3}$.

7. **(C)** The perimeter of the rectangle is $2(\ell + w) = 2(6 + 6\sqrt{3}) = 12 + 12\sqrt{3}$.

8. **(E)** The sum of the degree measures of an interior and exterior angle is 180, so $180 = 8x + x = 9x \Rightarrow x = 20$.

   Since the sum of the measures of all the exterior angles is 360, there are $360 \div 20 = 18$ angles and 18 sides.

   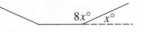

9. **(A)** Let x represent the side of the square. Then the dimensions of the rectangle are $(x + 5)$ and $(x - 5)$, and its area is $(x + 5)(x - 5) = x^2 - 25$. Since the area of the square is 45, $x^2 = 45 \Rightarrow x^2 - 25 = 45 - 25 = 20$.

10. **(C)** Each triangle surrounding quadrilateral *MNOP* is a 6-8-10 right triangle. So each side of *MNOP* is 10, and its perimeter is 40.

11. **96** The area of each of the triangles is $\frac{1}{2}(6)(8) = 24$, so together the four triangles have an area of 96. The area of the rectangle is $16 \times 12 = 192$. Therefore, the area of quadrilateral *MNOP* is $192 - 96 = 96$.
    Note: Joining the midpoints of the four sides of *any* quadrilateral creates a parallelogram whose area is one-half the area of the original quadrilateral.

12. **(C)** Each of the 10 marked angles is an exterior angle of the pentagon. If we take one angle at each vertex, the sum of those five angles is 360; the sum of the other five is also 360: $360 + 360 = 720$.

13. **150** Let W, X, Y, and Z represent the measures of the four angles. Since $W + X + Y + Z = 360$, $W + X + Y = 360 - Z$. Also,

$$Z = 10 + 2\left(\frac{W + X + Y}{3}\right) = 10 + 2\left(\frac{360 - Z}{3}\right).$$

So $Z = 10 + \frac{2}{3}(360) - \frac{2}{3}Z = 10 + 240 - \frac{2}{3}Z \Rightarrow \frac{5}{3}Z = 250 \Rightarrow Z = 150$.

14. **(B)** Since M and N are midpoints of sides of length 2, *AM*, *MB*, *AN*, and *ND* are all 1. $MN = \sqrt{2}$, since it's the hypotenuse of an isosceles right triangle whose legs are 1; and $BD = 2\sqrt{2}$, since it's the hypotenuse of an isosceles right triangle whose legs are 2. So the perimeter of the shaded region is $1 + \sqrt{2} + 1 + 2\sqrt{2} = 2 + 3\sqrt{2}$.

15. **(A)** The area of $\triangle ABD = \frac{1}{2}(2)(2) = 2$, and the area of $\triangle AMN$ is $\frac{1}{2}(1)(1) = 0.5$.

So the area of the shaded region is $2 - 0.5 = 1.5$.

16. **(C)** The area of $\triangle AED$ is $\frac{1}{2}w\left(\frac{\ell}{2}\right) = \frac{\ell w}{4}$.

The area of $\triangle EDC$ is $\frac{1}{2}\ell\left(\frac{w}{2}\right) = \frac{\ell w}{4}$.

Note: Each of the four small triangles has the same area.

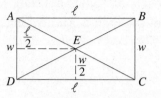

17. **(B)** By KEY FACT J5, since $\angle Z$ is acute and $\angle Y$ is obtuse, $(WY)^2 < a^2 + b^2$, whereas $(XZ)^2 > a^2 + b^2$.

18. **(A)** Since an octagon has eight sides, Quantity B is $8x$.
Quantity A: By KEY FACT J10, the hypotenuse of the triangle is $4x$, and the longer leg is $2x\sqrt{3}$. So the perimeter is $2x + 4x + 2x\sqrt{3}$. Since $\sqrt{3} > 1$, then $2x + 4x + 2x\sqrt{3} > 2x + 4x + 2x = 8x$.

19. **(A)** The perimeter of a rectangle of area 50 can be as large as we like, but the least it can be is when the rectangle is a square. In that case, each side is $\sqrt{50}$, which is greater than 7, and so the perimeter is greater than 28.

20. **(C)** TR is a transversal cutting the parallel sides PQ and RS. So $b = x$ and $2b = 2x$. But since the opposite angles of a parallelogram are equal, $a = 2x$. So $a = 2b$.

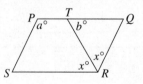

11-L. CIRCLES

A *circle* consists of all the points that are the same distance from one fixed point called the *center*. That distance is called the *radius* of the circle. The figure below is a circle of radius 1 unit whose center is at the point *O. A, B, C, D,* and *E,* which are each 1 unit from *O,* are all points on circle *O.* The word *radius* is also used to represent any of the line segments joining the center and a point on the circle. The plural of *radius* is *radii.* In circle *O,* below, *OA, OB, OC, OD,* and *OE* are all radii. If a circle has radius *r,* each of the radii is *r* units long.

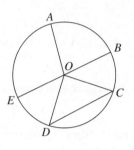

KEY FACT L1

Any triangle, such as △*COD* **in the figure above, formed by connecting the endpoints of two radii, is isosceles.**

EXAMPLE 1

If *P* and *Q* are points on circle *O,* what is the value of *x*?

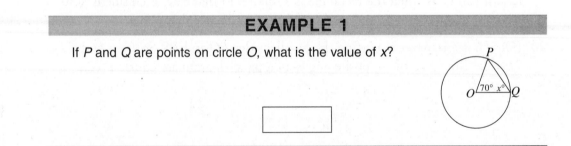

SOLUTION.
Since △*POQ* is isosceles, angles *P* and *Q* have the same measure. Then, $70 + x + x = 180 \Rightarrow 2x = 110 \Rightarrow x = \mathbf{55}$.

A line segment, such as *CD* in circle *O* at the beginning of this section, both of whose endpoints are on a circle is called a *chord.* A chord such as *BE,* which passes through the center of the circle, is called a *diameter.* Since *BE* is the sum of two radii, *OB* and *OE,* it is twice as long as a radius.

KEY FACT L2

If *d* is the diameter and *r* the radius of a circle, *d* = 2*r*.

KEY FACT L3

A diameter is the longest chord that can be drawn in a circle.

EXAMPLE 2

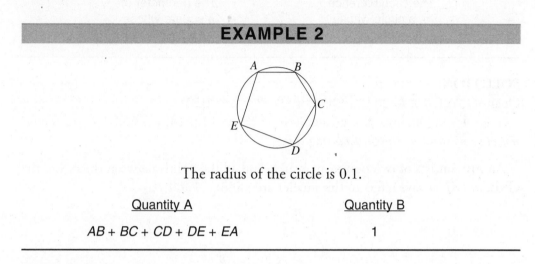

The radius of the circle is 0.1.

Quantity A	Quantity B
AB + BC + CD + DE + EA	1

SOLUTION.
Since the radius of the circle is 0.1, the diameter is 0.2. Therefore, the length of each of the five sides of pentagon *ABCDE* is less than 0.2, and the sum of their lengths is less than 5 × 0.2 = 1. The answer is **B**.

The total length around a circle, from *A* to *B* to *C* to *D* to *E* and back to *A*, is called the ***circumference*** of the circle. In every circle the ratio of the circumference to the diameter is exactly the same and is denoted by the symbol π (the Greek letter "pi").

KEY FACT L4

- $\pi = \dfrac{\text{circumference}}{\text{diameter}} = \dfrac{C}{d}$
- $C = \pi d$
- $C = 2\pi r$

KEY FACT L5

The value of π is approximately 3.14.

On GRE questions that involve circles, you are almost always expected to leave your answer in terms of π. So *don't* multiply by 3.14 until the final step, and then only if you have to. If you are ever stuck on a problem whose answers involve π, use your calculator to evaluate the answer or to test the answers. For example, assume that you think that an answer is about 50, and the answer choices are 4π, 6π, 12π, 16π, and 24π. Since π is slightly greater than 3, these choices are a little greater than 12, 18, 36, 48, and 72. The answer must be 16π. (To the nearest hundredth, 16π is actually 50.27, but approximating it by 48 was close enough.)

EXAMPLE 3

Quantity A	Quantity B
The circumference of a circle whose diameter is 12	The perimeter of a square whose side is 12

SOLUTION.
Quantity A: $C = \pi d = \pi(12)$. Quantity B: $P = 4s = 4(12)$.

Since $4 > \pi$, Quantity **B** is greater. (Note: $12\pi = 12(3.14) = 37.68$, but *you should not have wasted any time calculating this.*)

An *arc* consists of two points on a circle and all the points between them. On the GRE, *arc AB* always refers to the smaller arc joining *A* and *B*.

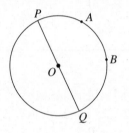

If we wanted to refer to the large arc going from *A* to *B* through *P* and *Q*, we would refer to it as arc *APB* or arc *AQB*. If two points, such as *P* and *Q* in circle *O*, are the endpoints of a diameter, they divide the circle into two arcs called *semicircles*.

An angle whose vertex is at the center of a circle is called a *central angle*.

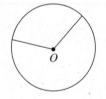

KEY FACT L6

The degree measure of a complete circle is 360°.

KEY FACT L7

The degree measure of an arc equals the degree measure of the central angle that intercepts it.

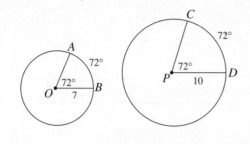

CAUTION

Degree measure is *not* a measure of length. In the circles above, arc *AB* and arc *CD* each measure 72°, even though arc *CD* is much longer.

How long *is* arc *CD?* Since the radius of Circle *P* is 10, its diameter is 20, and its circumference is 20π. Since there are 360° in a circle, arc *CD* is $\dfrac{72}{360}$, or $\dfrac{1}{5}$, of the circumference: $\dfrac{1}{5}(20\pi) = 4\pi$.

KEY FACT L8

The formula for the area of a circle of radius *r* is $A = \pi r^2$.

The area of Circle *P*, below KEY FACT L7, is $\pi(10)^2 = 100\pi$ square units. The area of sector *CPD* is $\dfrac{1}{5}$ of the area of the circle: $\dfrac{1}{5}(100\pi) = 20\pi$.

KEY FACT L9

If an arc measures $x°$, the length of the arc is $\dfrac{x}{360}(2\pi r)$, and the area of the

sector formed by the arc and 2 radii is $\dfrac{x}{360}(\pi r^2)$.

Examples 4 and 5 refer to the circle below.

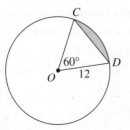

EXAMPLE 4

What is the area of the shaded region?

Ⓐ $144\pi - 144\sqrt{3}$

Ⓑ $144\pi - 36\sqrt{3}$

Ⓒ $144 - 72\sqrt{3}$

Ⓓ $24\pi - 36\sqrt{3}$

Ⓔ $24\pi - 72\sqrt{3}$

SOLUTION.

The area of the shaded region is equal to the area of sector *COD* minus the area of $\triangle COD$. The area of the circle is $\pi(12)^2 = 144\pi$.

- Since $\dfrac{60}{360} = \dfrac{1}{6}$, the area of sector *COD* is $\dfrac{1}{6}(144\pi) = 24\pi$.

- Since m$\angle O = 60°$, m$\angle C + \angle D = 120°$ and since $\triangle COD$ is isosceles, m$\angle C =$ m$\angle D$. So, they each measure $60°$, and the triangle is equilateral.

- By KEY FACT J15, area of $\triangle COD = \dfrac{12^2\sqrt{3}}{4} = \dfrac{144\sqrt{3}}{4} = 36\sqrt{3}$. So the area

  of the shaded region is $\mathbf{24\pi - 36\sqrt{3}}$ (**D**).

EXAMPLE 5

What is the perimeter of the shaded region?

Ⓐ $12 + 4\pi$

Ⓑ $12 + 12\pi$

Ⓒ $12 + 24\pi$

Ⓓ $12\sqrt{2} + 4\pi$

Ⓔ $12\sqrt{2} + 24\pi$

SOLUTION.

Since $\triangle COD$ is equilateral, $CD = 12$. Since the circumference of the circle is $2\pi(12) = 24\pi$, arc $CD = \dfrac{1}{6}(24\pi) = 4\pi$. So the perimeter is $\mathbf{12 + 4\pi}$ (**A**).

Suppose that in Example 5 you see that $CD = 12$, but you don't remember how to find the length of arc *CD*. From the diagram, it is clear that it is slightly longer than *CD*, say 13. So you know that the perimeter is *about* 25. Now, mentally, using 3 for π, or with your calculator, using 3.14 for π, approximate the value of each of the choices and see which one is closest to 25. Only Choice A is even close.

A line and a circle or two circles are ***tangent*** if they have only one point of inter-section. A circle is ***inscribed*** in a triangle or square if it is tangent to each side. A polygon is ***inscribed*** in a circle if each vertex is on the circle.

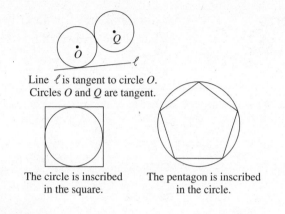

Line ℓ is tangent to circle *O*.
Circles *O* and *Q* are tangent.

The circle is inscribed
in the square.

The pentagon is inscribed
in the circle.

KEY FACT L10

If a line is tangent to a circle, a radius (or diameter) drawn to the point where the tangent touches the circle is perpendicular to the tangent line.

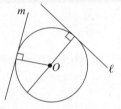

Lines ℓ and *m* are tangent to circle *O*.

EXAMPLE 6

A is the center of a circle whose radius is 8, and *B* is the center of a circle whose diameter is 8. If these two circles are tangent to one another, what is the area of the circle whose diameter is *AB*?

Ⓐ 12π Ⓑ 36π Ⓒ 64π Ⓓ 144π Ⓔ 256π

SOLUTION.
Draw a diagram.

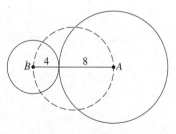

Since the diameter, *AB*, of the dotted circle is 12, its radius is 6, and its area is $\pi(6)^2 = \mathbf{36\pi}$ **(B)**.

Practice Exercises — Circles

Discrete Quantitative Questions

1. What is the circumference of a circle whose area is 100π?

   Ⓐ 10
   Ⓑ 20
   Ⓒ 10π
   Ⓓ 20π
   Ⓔ 25π

2. What is the area of a circle whose circumference is π?

   Ⓐ $\dfrac{\pi}{4}$

   Ⓑ $\dfrac{\pi}{2}$

   Ⓒ π
   Ⓓ 2π
   Ⓔ 4π

3. What is the area of a circle that is inscribed in a square of area 2?

   Ⓐ $\dfrac{\pi}{4}$

   Ⓑ $\dfrac{\pi}{2}$

   Ⓒ π

   Ⓓ $\pi\sqrt{2}$

   Ⓔ 2π

4. A square of area 2 is inscribed in a circle. What is the area of the circle?

   Ⓐ $\dfrac{\pi}{4}$

   Ⓑ $\dfrac{\pi}{2}$

   Ⓒ π

   Ⓓ $\pi\sqrt{2}$

   Ⓔ 2π

5. A 5×12 rectangle is inscribed in a circle. What is the radius of the circle?

6. If, in the figure below, the area of the shaded sector is 85% of the area of the entire circle, what is the value of w?

   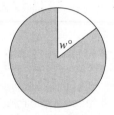

   Ⓐ 15
   Ⓑ 30
   Ⓒ 45
   Ⓓ 54
   Ⓔ 60

7. The circumference of a circle is $a\pi$ units, and the area of the circle is $b\pi$ square units. If $a = b$, what is the radius of the circle?

   Ⓐ 1
   Ⓑ 2
   Ⓒ 3
   Ⓓ π
   Ⓔ 2π

Questions 8–9 refer to the following figure.

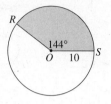

8. What is the length of arc *RS*?
   Ⓐ 8
   Ⓑ 20
   Ⓒ 8π
   Ⓓ 20π
   Ⓔ 40π

9. What is the area of the shaded sector?
   Ⓐ 8
   Ⓑ 20
   Ⓒ 8π
   Ⓓ 20π
   Ⓔ 40π

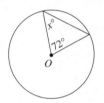

10. In the figure above, what is the value of *x*?

    [ ]

11. If *A* is the area and *C* the circumference of a circle, which of the following is an expression for *A* in terms of *C*?
    Ⓐ $\dfrac{C^2}{4\pi}$

    Ⓑ $\dfrac{C^2}{4\pi^2}$

    Ⓒ $2C$

    Ⓓ $2C^2\sqrt{\pi}$

    Ⓔ $\dfrac{C^2\sqrt{\pi}}{4}$

12. What is the area of a circle whose radius is the diagonal of a square whose area is 4?
    Ⓐ 2π
    Ⓑ $2\pi\sqrt{2}$
    Ⓒ 4π
    Ⓓ 8π
    Ⓔ 16π

Quantitative Comparison Questions

> Ⓐ Quantity A is greater.
> Ⓑ Quantity B is greater.
> Ⓒ Quantities A and B are equal.
> Ⓓ It is impossible to determine which quantity is greater.

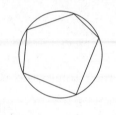

	Quantity A	Quantity B
13.	The perimeter of the pentagon	The circumference of the circle

The circumference of a circle is *C* inches. The area of the same circle is *A* square inches.

	Quantity A	Quantity B
14.	$\dfrac{C}{A}$	$\dfrac{A}{C}$

	Quantity A	Quantity B
15.	The area of a circle of radius 2	The area of a semicircle of radius 3

C is the circumference of a circle of radius *r*

	Quantity A	Quantity B
16.	$\dfrac{C}{r}$	6

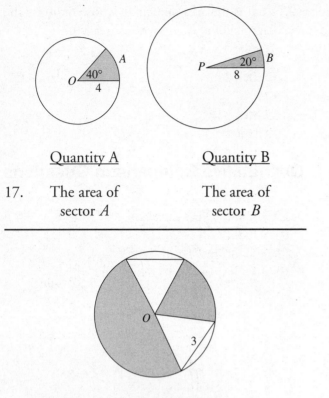

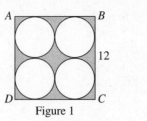

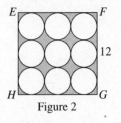

Figure 1   Figure 2

ABCD and *EFGH* are squares,
and all the circles are tangent to one
another and to the sides of the squares.

	Quantity A	Quantity B
19.	The area of the shaded region in Figure 1	The area of the shaded region in Figure 2

A square and a circle have equal areas.

	Quantity A	Quantity B
20.	The perimeter of the square	The circumference of the circle

	Quantity A	Quantity B
17.	The area of sector *A*	The area of sector *B*

Each of the triangles is equilateral.

	Quantity A	Quantity B
18.	The area of the shaded region	6π

ANSWER KEY

1. **D**	5. **6.5**	9. **E**	13. **B**	17. **B**
2. **A**	6. **D**	10. **54**	14. **D**	18. **C**
3. **B**	7. **B**	11. **A**	15. **B**	19. **C**
4. **C**	8. **C**	12. **D**	16. **A**	20. **A**

Answer Explanations

1. **(D)** $A = \pi r^2 = 100\pi \Rightarrow r^2 = 100 \Rightarrow r = 10 \Rightarrow C = 2\pi r = 2\pi(10) = 20\pi$.

2. **(A)** $C = 2\pi r = \pi \Rightarrow 2r = 1 \Rightarrow r = \dfrac{1}{2} \Rightarrow A = \pi r^2 = \pi\left(\dfrac{1}{2}\right)^2 = \dfrac{1}{4}\pi = \dfrac{\pi}{4}$.

3. **(B)** Draw a diagram.

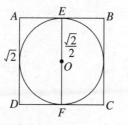

Since the area of square $ABCD$ is 2, $AD = \sqrt{2}$.

Then diameter $EF = \sqrt{2}$ and radius $OE = \dfrac{\sqrt{2}}{2}$. Then the area of the

circle is $\pi\left(\dfrac{\sqrt{2}}{2}\right)^2 = \dfrac{2}{4}\pi = \dfrac{\pi}{2}$

4. **(C)** Draw a diagram.

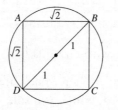

Since the area of square $ABCD$ is 2, $AD = \sqrt{2}$. Then, since $\triangle ABD$ is an isosceles right triangle, diagonal $BD = \sqrt{2} \times \sqrt{2} = 2$.

But BD is also a diameter of the circle. So the diameter is 2 and the radius is 1. Therefore, the area is $\pi(1)^2 = \pi$.

5. **6.5** Draw a diagram.

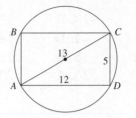

By the Pythagorean theorem (or by recognizing a 5-12-13 triangle), we see that diagonal *AC* is 13. But *AC* is also a diameter of the circle, so the diameter is 13 and the radius is 6.5.

6. **(D)** Since the shaded area is 85% of the circle, the white area is 15% of the circle. So, *w* is 15% of 360°: $0.15 \times 360 = 54$.

7. **(B)** Since $C = a\pi = b\pi = A$, we have $2\pi r = \pi r^2 \Rightarrow 2r = r^2 \Rightarrow r = 2$.

8. **(C)** The length of arc *RS* is $\dfrac{144}{360}$ of the circumference:

$$\left(\frac{144}{360}\right)2\pi(10) = \left(\frac{2}{5}\right)20\pi = 8\pi.$$

9. **(E)** The area of the shaded sector is $\left(\dfrac{144}{360}\right)$ of the area of the circle:

$$\left(\frac{144}{360}\right)\pi(10)^2 = \left(\frac{2}{5}\right)100\pi = 40\pi.$$

10. **54** Since two of the sides are radii of the circles, the triangle is isosceles. So the unmarked angle is also *x*:

$$180 = 72 + 2x \Rightarrow 2x = 108 \Rightarrow x = 54.$$

11. **(A)** $C = 2\pi r \Rightarrow r = \dfrac{C}{2\pi} \Rightarrow A = \pi\left(\dfrac{C}{2\pi}\right)^2 = \pi\left(\dfrac{C^2}{4\pi^2}\right) = \dfrac{C^2}{4\pi}$

12. **(D)** If the area of the square is 4, each side is 2, and the length of a diagonal is $2\sqrt{2}$. The area of a circle whose radius is $2\sqrt{2}$ is $\pi(2\sqrt{2})^2 = 8\pi$.

13. **(B)** There's nothing to calculate here. Each arc of the circle is clearly longer than the corresponding chord, which is a side of the pentagon. So the circumference, which is the sum of all the arcs, is greater than the perimeter, which is the sum of all the chords.

14. **(D)** Quantity A: $\dfrac{C}{A} = \dfrac{2\pi r}{\pi r^2} = \dfrac{2}{r}$.

Quantity B: $\dfrac{A}{C} = \dfrac{r}{2}$.

If $r = 2$, the quantities are equal; otherwise, they're not.

15. **(B)** Quantity A: $A = \pi(2)^2 = 4\pi$.

   Quantity B: The area of a semicircle of radius 3 is $\frac{1}{2}\pi(3)^2 = \frac{1}{2}(9\pi) = 4.5\pi$.

16. **(A)** By KEY FACT L4, $\pi = \frac{C}{d} = \frac{C}{2r} \Rightarrow \frac{C}{r} = 2\pi$, which is greater than 6.

17. **(B)** The area of sector A is $\frac{40}{360}(16\pi) = \frac{16\pi}{9}$.

   The area of sector B is $\frac{20}{360}(64\pi) = \frac{64\pi}{18} = \frac{32\pi}{9}$.

   So sector B is twice as big as sector A.

18. **(C)** Since the triangles are equilateral, the two white central angles each measure 60°, and their sum is 120°. So the white area is $\frac{120}{360} = \frac{1}{3}$ of the circle, and the shaded area is $\frac{2}{3}$ of the circle. The area of the circle is $\pi(3)^2 = 9\pi$, so the shaded area is $\frac{2}{3}(9\pi) = 6\pi$.

19. **(C)** In Figure 1, since the radius of each circle is 3, the area of each circle is 9π, and the total area of the 4 circles is 36π. In Figure 2, the radius of each circle is 2, and so the area of each circle is 4π, and the total area of the 9 circles is 36π. In the two figures, the white areas are equal, as are the shaded areas.

20. **(A)** Let A represent the area of the square and the circle.

   Quantity A: $A = s^2 \Rightarrow s = \sqrt{A} \Rightarrow P = 4\sqrt{A}$.

   Quantity B: $A = \pi r^2 \Rightarrow r = \sqrt{\frac{A}{\pi}} = \frac{\sqrt{A}}{\sqrt{\pi}}$.

   So $C = 2\pi\left(\frac{\sqrt{A}}{\sqrt{\pi}}\right) = 2\sqrt{\pi}\sqrt{A}$.

   Since $\pi \approx 3.14$, $\sqrt{\pi} \approx 1.77 \Rightarrow 2\sqrt{\pi} \approx 3.54$. Quantity A is $4\sqrt{A}$; Quantity B is $3.54\sqrt{A}$. Quantity A is greater.

11-M. SOLID GEOMETRY

There are very few solid geometry questions on the GRE, and they cover only a few elementary topics. Basically, all you need to know are the formulas for the volume and surface areas of rectangular solids (including cubes) and cylinders.

A *rectangular solid* or *box* is a solid formed by six rectangles, called *faces*. The sides of the rectangles are called *edges*. As shown in the diagram below (left), the edges are called the *length*, *width*, and *height*. A *cube* is a rectangular solid in which the length, width, and height are equal; so all the edges are the same length.

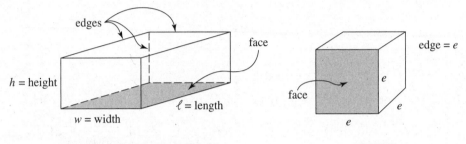

RECTANGULAR SOLID   **CUBE**

The *volume* of a solid is the amount of space it takes up and is measured in *cubic units*. One cubic unit is the amount of space occupied by a cube all of whose edges are one unit long. In the figure above (right), if each edge of the cube is 1 inch long, then the area of each face is 1 square inch, and the volume of the cube is 1 cubic inch.

KEY FACT M1

- The formula for the volume of a rectangular solid is $V = \ell wh$.
- The formula for the volume of a cube is $V = e \cdot e \cdot e = e^3$.

EXAMPLE 1

The base of a rectangular tank is 12 feet long and 8 feet wide; the height of the tank is 30 inches. If water is pouring into the tank at the rate of 2 cubic feet per second, how many <u>minutes</u> will be required to fill the tank?

Ⓐ 1   Ⓑ 2   Ⓒ 10   Ⓓ 120   Ⓔ 240

SOLUTION.

Draw a diagram. In order to express all of the dimensions of the tank in the same units, convert 30 inches to 2.5 feet. Then the volume of the tank is $12 \times 8 \times 2.5 = 240$ cubic feet. At 2 cubic feet per second, it will take $240 \div 2 = 120$ seconds = **2** minutes to fill the tank (**B**).

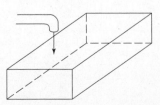

The ***surface area*** of a rectangular solid is the sum of the areas of the six faces. Since the top and bottom faces are equal, the front and back faces are equal, and the left and right faces are equal, we can calculate the area of one from each pair and then double the sum. In a cube, each of the six faces has the same area.

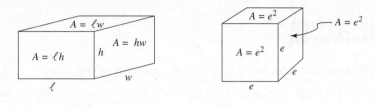

KEY FACT M2

- The formula for the surface area of a rectangular solid is $A = 2(\ell w + \ell h + wh)$.
- The formula for the surface area of a cube is $A = 6e^2$.

EXAMPLE 2

The volume of a cube is v cubic *yards*, and its surface area is a square *feet*. If $v = a$, what is the length in *inches* of each edge?

	inches

SOLUTION.
Draw a diagram.

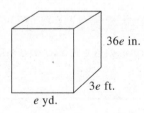

36e in.
3e ft.
e yd.

If e is the length of the edge in yards, $3e$ is the length in feet, and $36e$ the length in inches. Therefore, $v = e^3$ and $a = 6(3e)^2 = 6(9e^2) = 54e^2$. Since $v = a$, $e^3 = 54e^2$, and $e = 54$. So the length of each edge is $36(54) = $ **1,944** inches.

A ***diagonal*** of a box is a line segment joining a vertex on the top of the box to the opposite vertex on the bottom. A box has 4 diagonals, all the same length. In the box below they are line segments AG, BH, CE, and DF.

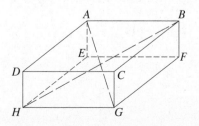

KEY FACT M3

A diagonal of a box is the longest line segment that can be drawn between two points on the box.

KEY FACT M4

If the dimensions of a box are ℓ, w, and h, and if d is the length of a diagonal, then $d^2 = \ell^2 + w^2 + h^2$ and $d = \sqrt{\ell^2 + w^2 + h^2}$.

For example, in the box below: $d^2 = 3^2 + 4^2 + 12^2 = 9 + 16 + 144 = 169 \Rightarrow d = 13$.

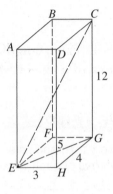

This formula is really just an extended Pythagorean theorem. *EG* is the diagonal of rectangular base *EFGH*. Since the sides of the base are 3 and 4, *EG* is 5. Now, $\triangle CGE$ is a right triangle whose legs are 12 and 5, so diagonal *CE* is 13.

EXAMPLE 3

What is the length of a diagonal of a cube whose edges are 1?

Ⓐ 1   Ⓑ 2   Ⓒ 3   Ⓓ $\sqrt{2}$ Ⓔ $\sqrt{3}$

SOLUTION.
Use the formula:

$$d^2 = 1^2 + 1^2 + 1^2 = 3 \Rightarrow d = \sqrt{3} \ \textbf{(E)}.$$

Without the formula you would draw a diagram and label it. Since the base is a 1×1 square, its diagonal is $\sqrt{2}$. Then the diagonal of the cube is the hypotenuse of a right triangle whose legs are 1 and $\sqrt{2}$, so

$$d^2 = 1^2 + (\sqrt{2})^2 = 1 + 2 = 3, \text{ and } d = \sqrt{3}.$$

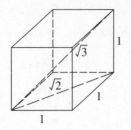

A *cylinder* is similar to a rectangular solid except that the base is a circle instead of a rectangle. The volume of a cylinder is the area of its circular base (πr^2) times its height (h). The surface area of a cylinder depends on whether you are envisioning a tube, such as a straw, without a top or bottom, or a can, which has both a top and a bottom.

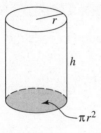

KEY FACT M5

- **The formula for the volume, V, of a cylinder whose circular base has radius r and whose height is h is $V = \pi r^2 h$.**
- **The surface area, A, of the side of the cylinder is the circumference of the circular base times the height: $A = 2\pi rh$.**
- **The area of the top and bottom are each πr^2, so the total area of a can is $2\pi rh + 2\pi r^2$.**

EXAMPLE 4

The radius of cylinder II equals the height of cylinder I.
The height of cylinder II equals the radius of cylinder I.

Quantity A	Quantity B
The volume of cylinder I	The volume of cylinder II

SOLUTION.
Let r and h be the radius and height, respectively, of cylinder I. Then

	Quantity A	Quantity B
	$\pi r^2 h$	$\pi h^2 r$
Divide each quantity by πrh:	r	h

Either r or h could be greater, or the two could be equal. The answer is **D**.

These are the only formulas you need to know. Any other solid geometry questions that might appear on the GRE would require you to visualize a situation and reason it out, rather than to apply a formula.

EXAMPLE 5

How many small cubes are needed to construct the tower in the figure below?

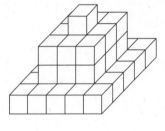

SOLUTION.
You need to "see" the answer. The top level consists of 1 cube, the second and third levels consist of 9 cubes each, and the bottom layer consists of 25 cubes. The total is $1 + 9 + 9 + 25 = \textbf{44}$.

Practice Exercises — Solid Geometry

Discrete Quantitative Questions

1. The sum of the lengths of all the edges of a cube is 6 centimeters. What is the volume, in cubic centimeters, of the cube?

    Ⓐ $\dfrac{1}{8}$

    Ⓑ $\dfrac{1}{4}$

    Ⓒ $\dfrac{1}{2}$

    Ⓓ 1

    Ⓔ 8

2. What is the volume of a cube whose surface area is 150?

    ☐

3. What is the surface area of a cube whose volume is 64?

    Ⓐ 16
    Ⓑ 64
    Ⓒ 96
    Ⓓ 128
    Ⓔ 384

4. What is the number of cubic inches in one cubic foot?

    Ⓐ 12
    Ⓑ 24
    Ⓒ 144
    Ⓓ 684
    Ⓔ 1728

5. A solid metal cube of edge 3 feet is placed in a rectangular tank whose length, width, and height are 3, 4, and 5 feet, respectively. What is the volume, in cubic feet, of water that the tank can now hold?

    Ⓐ 20
    Ⓑ 27
    Ⓒ 33
    Ⓓ 48
    Ⓔ 60

6. A 5-foot-long cylindrical pipe has an inner diameter of 6 feet and an outer diameter of 8 feet. If the total surface area (inside and out, including the ends) is $k\pi$, what is the value of k?

    Ⓐ 7
    Ⓑ 40
    Ⓒ 48
    Ⓓ 70
    Ⓔ 84

7. The height, h, of a cylinder is equal to the edge of a cube. If the cylinder and cube have the same volume, what is the radius of the cylinder?

    Ⓐ $\dfrac{h}{\sqrt{\pi}}$

    Ⓑ $h\sqrt{\pi}$

    Ⓒ $\dfrac{\sqrt{\pi}}{h}$

    Ⓓ $\dfrac{h^2}{\pi}$

    Ⓔ πh^2

8. A rectangular tank has a base that is 10 centimeters by 5 centimeters and a height of 20 centimeters. If the tank is half full of water, by how many centimeters will the water level rise if 325 cubic centimeters of water are poured into the tank?

Ⓐ 3.25

Ⓑ 6.5

Ⓒ 16.25

Ⓓ 32.5

Ⓔ 65

9. If the height of a cylinder is 4 times its circumference, what is the volume of the cylinder in terms of its circumference, C?

Ⓐ $\dfrac{C^3}{\pi}$

Ⓑ $\dfrac{2C^3}{\pi}$

Ⓒ $\dfrac{2C^2}{\pi^2}$

Ⓓ $\dfrac{\pi C^2}{4}$

Ⓔ $4\pi C^3$

10. Three identical balls fit snugly into a cylindrical can: the radius of the spheres equals the radius of the can, and the balls just touch the bottom and the top of the can. If the formula for the volume of a sphere is $V = \dfrac{4}{3}\pi r^3$, what fraction of the volume of the can is taken up by the balls?

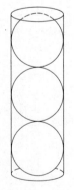

$$\dfrac{\boxed{}}{\boxed{}}$$

Quantitative Comparison Questions

Ⓐ Quantity A is greater.
Ⓑ Quantity B is greater.
Ⓒ Quantities A and B are equal.
Ⓓ It is impossible to determine which quantity is greater.

Jack and Jill each roll a sheet of 9×12 paper to form a cylinder. Jack tapes the two 9-inch edges together. Jill tapes the two 12-inch edges together.

Quantity A	Quantity B
11. The volume of Jack's cylinder	The volume of Jill's cylinder

Quantity A	Quantity B
12. The volume of a cube whose edges are 6	The volume of a box whose dimensions are 5, 6, and 7

A is the surface area of a rectangular box in square units.
V is the volume of the same box in cubic units.

Quantity A	Quantity B
13. A	V

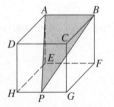

P is a point on edge GH of cube $ABCDEFGH$. Each edge of the cube is 1.

Quantity A	Quantity B
14. The area of $\triangle ABP$	1

Quantity A	Quantity B

15. The volume of
a sphere whose
radius is 1

The volume of
a cube whose
edge is 1

ANSWER KEY

1. **A**	4. **E**	7. **A**	10. $\dfrac{2}{3}$	12. **A**	15. **A**
2. **125**	5. **C**	8. **B**		13. **D**	
3. **C**	6. **E**	9. **A**	11. **A**	14. **B**	

Answer Explanations

1. **(A)** Since a cube has 12 edges, we have $12e = 6 \Rightarrow e = \dfrac{1}{2}$.

   Therefore, $V = e^3 = \left(\dfrac{1}{2}\right)^3 = \dfrac{1}{8}$.

2. **125** Since the surface area is 150, each of the 6 faces is a square whose area is $150 \div 6 = 25$. So the edges are all 5, and the volume is $5^3 = 125$.

3. **(C)** Since the volume of the cube is 64, we have $e^3 = 64 \Rightarrow e = 4$. The surface area is $6e^2 = 6 \times 16 = 96$.

4. **(E)** The volume of a cube whose edges are 1 foot can be expressed in either of two ways:

   $$(1 \text{ foot})^3 = 1 \text{ cubic foot or}$$
   $$(12 \text{ inches})^3 = 1728 \text{ cubic inches.}$$

5. **(C)** The volume of the tank is $3 \times 4 \times 5 = 60$ cubic units, but the solid cube is taking up $3^3 = 27$ cubic units. Therefore, the tank can hold $60 - 27 = 33$ cubic units of water.

6. **(E)** Draw a diagram and label it.

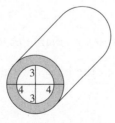

   Since the surface of a cylinder is given by $A = 2\pi rh$, the area of the exterior is $2\pi(4)(5) = 40\pi$, and the area of the interior is $2\pi(3)(5) = 30\pi$. The area of *each* shaded end is the area of the outer circle minus the area of the inner circle: $16\pi - 9\pi = 7\pi$, so the total surface area is

   $$40\pi + 30\pi + 7\pi + 7\pi = 84\pi \Rightarrow k = 84.$$

7. **(A)** Since the volumes are equal, $\pi r^2 h = e^3 = b^3$.

Therefore, $\pi r^2 = b^2 \Rightarrow r^2 = \dfrac{b^2}{\pi} \Rightarrow r = \dfrac{b}{\sqrt{\pi}}$.

8. **(B)** Draw a diagram.

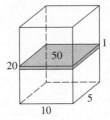

Since the area of the base is $5 \times 10 = 50$ square centimeters, each 1 centimeter of depth has a volume of 50 cubic centimeters. Therefore, 325 cubic centimeters will raise the water level $325 \div 50 = 6.5$ centimeters.

(Note that we didn't use the fact that the tank was half full, except to be sure that the tank didn't overflow. Since the tank was half full, the water was 10 centimeters deep, and the water level could rise by 6.5 centimeters. Had the tank been three-fourths full, the water would have been 15 centimeters deep and the extra water would have caused the level to rise 5 centimeters, filling the tank; the rest of the water would have spilled out.)

9. **(A)** Since $V = \pi r^2 h$, we need to express r and h in terms of C. It is given that $h = 4C$ and since $C = 2\pi r$, then $r = \dfrac{C}{2\pi}$. Therefore,

$$V = \pi \left(\frac{C}{2\pi}\right)^2 (4C) = \pi \left(\frac{C^2}{4\pi^2}\right)(4C) = \frac{C^3}{\pi}.$$

10. $\dfrac{2}{3}$ To avoid using r, assume that the radii of the spheres and the can are 1.

Then the volume of each ball is $\dfrac{4}{3}\pi(1)^3 = \dfrac{4}{3}\pi$, and the total volume of the

3 balls is $3\left(\dfrac{4}{3}\pi\right) = 4\pi$.

Since the height of the can is 6 (the diameter of each sphere is 2), the volume of the can is $\pi(1)^2(6) = 6\pi$. So the balls take up $\dfrac{4\pi}{6\pi} = \dfrac{2}{3}$ of the can.

11. **(A)** Drawing a diagram makes it easier to visualize the problem. The volume of a cylinder is $\pi r^2 h$. In each case, we know the height but have to determine the radius in order to calculate the volume.

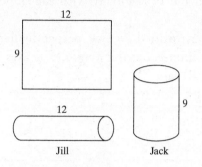

Jill   Jack

Jack's cylinder has a circumference of 12:

$$2\pi r = 12 \Rightarrow r = \frac{12}{2\pi} = \frac{6}{\pi} \Rightarrow V = \pi\left(\frac{6}{\pi}\right)^2 (9) = \pi\left(\frac{36}{\pi^2}\right)(9) = \frac{324}{\pi}.$$

Jill's cylinder has a circumference of 9:

$$2\pi r = 9 \Rightarrow r = \frac{9}{2\pi} \Rightarrow V = \pi\left(\frac{9}{2\pi}\right)^2 (12) = \pi\left(\frac{81}{4\pi^2}\right)(12) = \frac{243}{\pi}.$$

12. **(A)** Quantity A: $V = 6^3 = 216$. Quantity B: $V = 5 \times 6 \times 7 = 210$.

13. **(D)** There is no relationship between the two quantities. If the box is a cube of edge 1, $A = 6$ and $V = 1$. If the box is a cube of edge 10, $A = 600$ and $V = 1000$.

14. **(B)** The base, AB, of $\triangle ABP$ is 1. Since the diagonal is the longest line segment in the cube, the height, h, of the triangle is definitely less than the diagonal, which is $\sqrt{1^2 + 1^2 + 1^2} = \sqrt{3}$.

So the area of the triangle is less than $\frac{1}{2}(1)\sqrt{3} \approx .87$, which is less than 1.

(You could also have just calculated the area: $h = BG = \sqrt{2}$, so the area is $\frac{1}{2}\sqrt{2} \approx .71$.)

15. **(A)** You probably don't know how to find the volume of a sphere; fortunately, you don't need to. You should be able to visualize that the sphere is *much* bigger than the cube. (In fact, it is more than 4 times the size.)

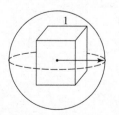

11-N. COORDINATE GEOMETRY

The GRE has very few questions on coordinate geometry. Most often they deal with the coordinates of points and occasionally with the slope of a line. You will *never* have to draw a graph.

The coordinate plane is formed by two perpendicular number lines called the **x-axis** and **y-axis**, which intersect at the **origin**. The axes divide the plane into four **quadrants**, labeled I, II, III, and IV.

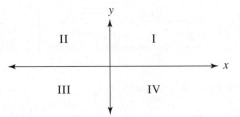

Each point in the plane is assigned two numbers, an **x-coordinate** and a **y-coordinate**, which are written as an ordered pair, *(x, y)*.

- Points to the right of the *y*-axis have positive *x*-coordinates, and those to the left have negative *x*-coordinates.
- Points above the *x*-axis have positive *y*-coordinates, and those below it have negative *y*-coordinates.
- If a point is on the *x*-axis, its *y*-coordinate is 0.
- If a point is on the *y*-axis, its *x*-coordinate is 0.

For example, point *A* in the following figure is labeled (2, 3), since it is 2 units to the right of the *y*-axis and 3 units above the *x*-axis. Similarly, *B*(–3, –5) is in Quadrant III, 3 units to the left of the *y*-axis and 5 units below the *x*-axis.

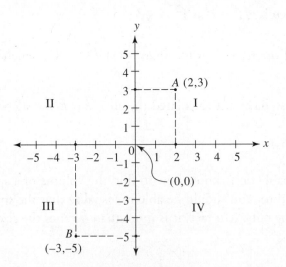

EXAMPLE 1

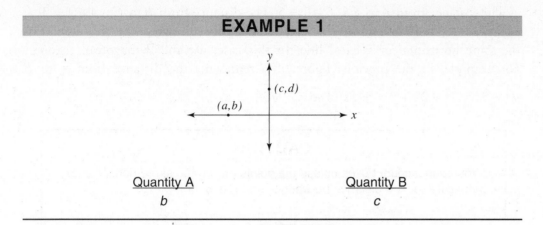

Quantity A	Quantity B
b	c

SOLUTION.
Since (a, b) lies on the *x*-axis, $b = 0$. Since (c, d) lies on the *y*-axis, $c = 0$. The answer is **C**.

EXAMPLE 2

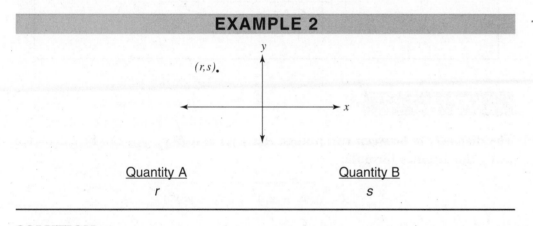

Quantity A	Quantity B
r	s

SOLUTION.
Since (r, s) is in Quadrant II, r is negative and s is positive. The answer is **B**.

Often a question requires you to calculate the distance between two points. This is easiest when the points lie on the same horizontal or vertical line.

KEY FACT N1

- **All the points on a horizontal line have the same *y*-coordinate. To find the distance between them, subtract their *x*-coordinates.**
- **All the points on a vertical line have the same *x*-coordinate. To find the distance between them, subtract their *y*-coordinates.**

 TIP

If the points have been plotted on a graph, you can find the distance between them by counting boxes.

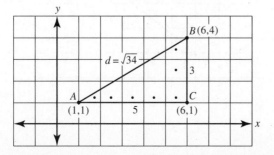

The distance from *A* to *C* is 6 – 1 = 5. The distance from *B* to *C* is 4 – 1 = 3.

It is a little more difficult to find the distance between two points that are not on the same horizontal or vertical line. In this case, use the Pythagorean theorem. For example, in the previous figure, if *d* represents the distance from *A* to *B*, $d^2 = 5^2 + 3^2 = 25 + 9 = 34$, and so $d = \sqrt{34}$.

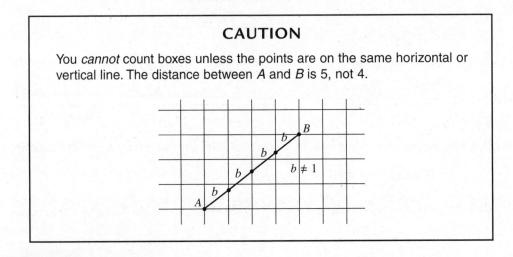

CAUTION

You *cannot* count boxes unless the points are on the same horizontal or vertical line. The distance between *A* and *B* is 5, not 4.

KEY FACT N2

The distance, *d*, between two points, $A(x_1, y_1)$ and $B(x_2, y_2)$, can be calculated using the distance formula:

$$d = \sqrt{(x_2 - x_1)^2 + (y_2 - y_1)^2}.$$

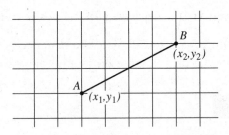

TIP

The "distance formula" is nothing more than the Pythagorean theorem. If you ever forget the formula, and you need the distance between two points that do not lie on the same horizontal or vertical line, do as follows: create a right triangle by drawing a horizontal line through one of the points and a vertical line through the other, and then use the Pythagorean theorem.

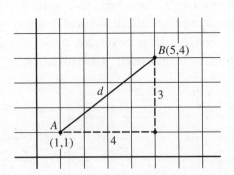

Examples 3–4 refer to the triangle in the following figure.

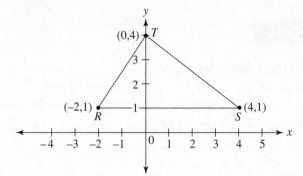

EXAMPLE 3

What is the area of △*RST*?

$$\boxed{}$$

SOLUTION.
$R(-2, 1)$ and $S(4, 1)$ lie on the same horizontal line, so $RS = 4 - (-2) = 6$. Let that be the base of the triangle. Then the height is the distance along the vertical line from T to RS: $4 - 1 = 3$. The area is $\frac{1}{2}(6)(3) = $ **9**.

EXAMPLE 4

What is the perimeter of △*RST*?

Ⓐ 13   Ⓑ 14   Ⓒ 16   Ⓓ $11 + \sqrt{13}$ Ⓔ $11 + \sqrt{61}$

SOLUTION.
The perimeter is $RS + ST + RT$. From the solution to Example 3, you know that $RS = 6$. Also, $ST = 5$, since it is the hypotenuse of a 3-4-5 right triangle. To calculate RT, either use the distance formula:

$$RT = \sqrt{(-2-0)^2 + (1-4)^2} = \sqrt{(-2)^2 + (-3)^2} = \sqrt{4+9} = \sqrt{13}$$

or the Pythagorean theorem: $RT^2 = 2^2 + 3^2 = 4 + 9 = 13 \Rightarrow RT = \sqrt{13}$.

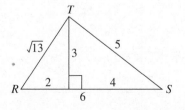

So the perimeter is: $6 + 5 + \sqrt{13} = $ **$11 + \sqrt{13}$** (**D**).

The *slope* of a line is a number that indicates how steep the line is.

KEY FACT N3

- **Vertical lines *do not have slopes*.**
- **To find the slope of any other line proceed as follows:**
  1. **Choose any two points $A(x_1, y_1)$ and $B(x_2, y_2)$ on the line.**
  2. **Take the differences of the *y*-coordinates, $y_2 - y_1$, and the *x*-coordinates, $x_2 - x_1$.**
  3. **Divide: slope = $\dfrac{y_2 - y_1}{x_2 - x_1}$.**

We will illustrate the next KEY FACT by using this formula to calculate the slopes of *RS*, *RT*, and *ST* from Example 3: $R(-2, 1)$, $S(4, 1)$, $T(0, 4)$.

Key Fact N4

- **The slope of any horizontal line is 0: slope of $RS = \dfrac{1-1}{4-(-2)} = \dfrac{0}{6} = 0$**

- **The slope of any line that goes up as you move from left to right is positive:**

  slope of $RT = \dfrac{4-1}{0-(-2)} = \dfrac{3}{2}$

- **The slope of any line that goes down as you move from left to right is negative: slope of $ST = \dfrac{1-4}{4-0} = \dfrac{-3}{4} = -\dfrac{3}{4}$**

EXAMPLE 5

Line ℓ passes through (1, 2) and (3, 5)
Line m is perpendicular to ℓ

Quantity A	Quantity B
The slope of ℓ	The slope of m

SOLUTION.

First, make a quick sketch.

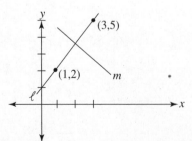

Do not use the formula to calculate the slope of ℓ. Simply notice that ℓ slopes upward, so its slope is positive, whereas m slopes downward, so its slope is negative. Quantity **A** is greater.

Practice Exercises — Coordinate Geometry

Discrete Quantitative Questions

1. What is the slope of the line that passes through points (0, –2) and (3, 0)?

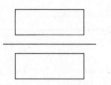

2. If the coordinates of △*RST* are *R*(0, 0), *S*(7, 0), and *T*(2, 5), what is the sum of the slopes of the three sides of the triangle?

    Ⓐ –1.5
    Ⓑ 0
    Ⓒ 1.5
    Ⓓ 2.5
    Ⓔ 3.5

3. If *A*(–1, 1) and *B*(3, –1) are the endpoints of one side of square *ABCD*, what is the area of the square?

    Ⓐ 12
    Ⓑ 16
    Ⓒ 20
    Ⓓ 25
    Ⓔ 36

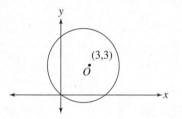

4. If the area of circle *O* above is *k*π, what is the value of *k*?

    Ⓐ 3
    Ⓑ 6
    Ⓒ 9
    Ⓓ 18
    Ⓔ 27

5. If *P*(2, 1) and *Q*(8, 1) are two of the vertices of a rectangle, which of the following could *not* be another of the vertices?

    Ⓐ (2, 8)
    Ⓑ (8, 2)
    Ⓒ (2, –8)
    Ⓓ (–2, 8)
    Ⓔ (8, 8)

6. A circle whose center is at (6, 8) passes through the origin. Which of the following points is *not* on the circle?

    Ⓐ (12, 0)
    Ⓑ (6, –2)
    Ⓒ (16, 8)
    Ⓓ (–2, 12)
    Ⓔ (–4, 8)

Questions 7–8 concern parallelogram *JKLM*, whose coordinates are *J*(–5, 2), *K*(–2, 6), *L*(5, 6), *M*(2, 2).

7. What is the area of parallelogram *JKLM*?

    Ⓐ 35
    Ⓑ 28
    Ⓒ 24
    Ⓓ 20
    Ⓔ 12

8. What is the perimeter of parallelogram *JKLM*?

9. If (a, b) and $\left(\dfrac{1}{a}, b\right)$ are two distinct points, what is the slope of the line that passes through them?

Ⓐ 0

Ⓑ $\dfrac{1}{b}$

Ⓒ $\dfrac{1-a^2}{a}$

Ⓓ $\dfrac{a^2-1}{a}$

Ⓔ undefined

10. If $c \neq 0$ and the slope of the line passing through $(-c, c)$ and $(3c, a)$ is 1, which of the following is an expression for a in terms of c?

Ⓐ $-3c$

Ⓑ $-\dfrac{c}{3}$

Ⓒ $2c$

Ⓓ $3c$

Ⓔ $5c$

Quantitative Comparison Questions

Ⓐ Quantity A is greater.
Ⓑ Quantity B is greater.
Ⓒ Quantities A and B are equal.
Ⓓ It is impossible to determine which quantity is greater.

m is the slope of one of the diagonals of a square.

Quantity A	Quantity B
11. m^2	1

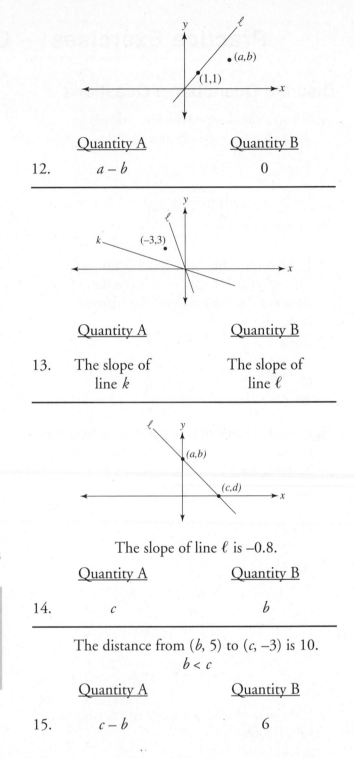

	Quantity A	Quantity B
12.	$a - b$	0

	Quantity A	Quantity B
13.	The slope of line k	The slope of line ℓ

The slope of line ℓ is -0.8.

	Quantity A	Quantity B
14.	c	b

The distance from $(b, 5)$ to $(c, -3)$ is 10.
$$b < c$$

	Quantity A	Quantity B
15.	$c - b$	6

ANSWER KEY

1. $\dfrac{2}{3}$ 3. **C** 6. **D** 9. **A** 12. **A** 15. **C**

2. **C** 4. **D** 7. **B** 10. **E** 13. **A**

  5. **D** 8. **24** 11. **D** 14. **A**

Answer Explanations

1. $\dfrac{2}{3}$ If you sketch the line, you see immediately that the slope of the line is positive. Without even knowing the slope formula, therefore, you can eliminate Choices A, B, and C. To determine the actual slope, use the formula: $\dfrac{y_2 - y_1}{x_2 - x_1} = \dfrac{0 - (-2)}{3 - 0} = \dfrac{2}{3}$.

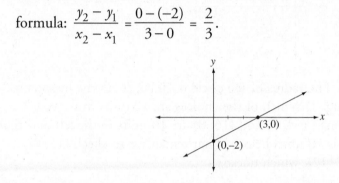

2. **(C)** Sketch the triangle, and then calculate the slopes.

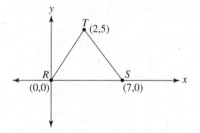

Since RS is horizontal, its slope is 0.

The slope of $RT = \dfrac{5 - 0}{2 - 0} = 2.5$. The slope of $ST = \dfrac{5 - 0}{2 - 7} = \dfrac{5}{-5} = -1$.

Now add: $0 + 2.5 + (-1) = 1.5$

3. **(C)** Draw a diagram and label it. The area of square $ABCD$ is s^2, where $s = AB$, the length of a side. By the Pythagorean theorem:

$$s^2 = 2^2 + 4^2 = 4 + 16 = 20.$$

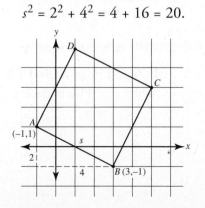

4. **(D)** Since the line segment joining (3, 3) and (0, 0) is a radius of the circle, $r^2 = 3^2 + 3^2 = 18$. Therefore, area $= \pi r^2 = 18\pi \Rightarrow k = 18$. Note that you do not actually have to find that the value of r is $3\sqrt{2}$.

5. **(D)** Draw a diagram. Any point whose x-coordinate is 2 or 8 could be another vertex. Of the choices, only (−2, 8) is *not* possible.

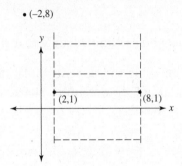

6. **(D)** Draw a diagram. The radius of the circle is 10 (since it's the hypotenuse of a 6-8-10 right triangle). Which of the choices are 10 units from (6, 8)? First, check the easy ones: (−4, 8) and (16, 8) are 10 units to the left and right of (6, 8), and (6, −2) is 10 units below. What remains is to check (12, 0), which works, and (−2, 12), which doesn't.

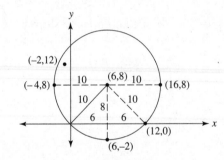

Here is the diagram for solutions 7 and 8.

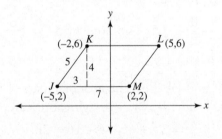

7. **(B)** The base is 7 and the height is 4. So, the area is $7 \times 4 = 28$.

8. **24** Sides *JM* and *KL* are each 7, and sides *JK* and *LM* are each the hypotenuse of a 3-4-5 right triangle, so they are 5. The perimeter is $2(7 + 5) = 24$.

9. **(A)** The formula for the slope is $\dfrac{y_2 - y_1}{x_2 - x_1}$, but before using it, look.

Since the y-coordinates are equal and the x-coordinates are not equal, the numerator is 0 and the denominator is not 0. So the value of the fraction is 0.

10. **(E)** The slope is equal to $\dfrac{y_2 - y_1}{x_2 - x_1} = \dfrac{a - c}{3c - (-c)} = \dfrac{a - c}{4c} = 1$.

So $a - c = 4c$ and $a = 5c$.

11. **(D)** If the sides of the square are horizontal and vertical, then m is 1 or −1, and m^2 is 1. But the square could be positioned any place, and the slope of a diagonal could be any number.

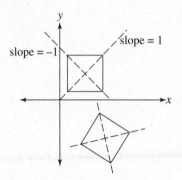

12. **(A)** Line ℓ, which goes through (0, 0) and (1, 1), also goes through (a, a), and since (a, b) is below (a, a), $b < a$. Therefore, $a - b$ is positive. Quantity A is greater.

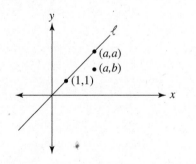

13. **(A)** The line going through (−3, 3) and (0, 0) has slope −1. Since ℓ is steeper, its slope is a number such as −2 or −3; since k is less steep, its slope is a number such as −0.5 or −0.3. Therefore, the slope of k is greater.

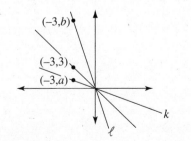

14. **(A)** Since (a, b) is on the y-axis, $a = 0$; and since (c, d) is on the x-axis, $d = 0$.
Then by the slope formula, $-0.8 = \dfrac{0-b}{c-0} = -\dfrac{b}{c} \Rightarrow b = 0.8c$.

Since b and c are both positive, $b < c$.

15. **(C)** Draw a diagram.

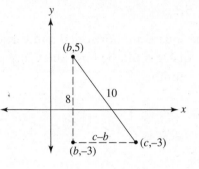

Since the distance between the two points is 10, by the distance formula:

$10 = \sqrt{(c-b)^2 + (-3-5)^2} = \sqrt{(c-b)^2 + (-8)^2} = \sqrt{(c-b)^2 + 64}$.

Squaring both sides gives $100 = (c-b)^2 + 64 \Rightarrow (c-b)^2 = 36$. So $c - b = 6$.

Notice that the equation $100 = (c-b)^2 + 64$ is exactly what you could have gotten immediately by using the Pythagorean theorem: $10^2 = (c-b)^2 + 8^2$.

11-O. COUNTING AND PROBABILITY

Some questions on the GRE begin, "How many ... ." In these problems you are being asked to count something: how many apples can she buy, how many dollars did he spend, how many pages did she read, how many numbers satisfy a certain property, or how many ways are there to complete a particular task. Sometimes these problems can be handled by simple arithmetic. Other times it helps to use TACTIC 8 from Chapter 7 and systematically make a list. Occasionally it helps to know the counting principle and other strategies that we will review in this section.

COUNTING

USING ARITHMETIC TO COUNT

The following three examples require only arithmetic. But be careful; they are not the same.

EXAMPLE 1

Brian bought some apples. If he entered the store with $113 and left with $109, how much, in dollars, did the apples cost?

EXAMPLE 2

Scott was selling tickets for the school play. One day he sold tickets numbered 109 through 113. How many tickets did he sell that day?

EXAMPLE 3

Brian is the 109th person in a line and Scott is the 113th person. How many people are there between Brian and Scott?

SOLUTIONS 1–3.

- It may seem that each of these examples requires a simple subtraction: $113 - 109 = 4$. In Example 1, Brian did spend **$4** on apples; in Example 2, however, Scott sold **5** tickets; and in Example 3, only **3** people are on line between Brian and Scott!

- Assume that Brian went into the store with 113 one-dollar bills, numbered 1 through 113; he spent the 4 dollars numbered 113, 112, 111, and 110, and still had the dollars numbered 1 through 109; Scott sold the 5 tickets numbered 109, 110, 111, 112, and 113; and between Brian and Scott the 110th, 111th, and 112th persons — 3 people — were on line.

In Example 1, you just needed to subtract: 113 – 109 = 4. In Example 2, you need to subtract *and then add 1*: 113 – 109 + 1 = 4 + 1 = 5. And in Example 3, you need to subtract and then *subtract 1 more*: 113 – 109 – 1 = 3. Although Example 1 is too easy for the GRE, questions such as Examples 2 and 3 do appear, because they're not as obvious and they require that little extra thought. *When do you have to add or subtract 1?*

The issue is whether or not the first and last numbers are included. In Example 1, Brian spent dollar number 113, but he still had dollar number 109 when he left the store. In Example 2, Scott sold both ticket number 109 and ticket 113. In Example 3, neither Scott (the 113th person) nor Brian (the 109th person) was to be counted.

KEY FACT O1

To count how many integers there are between two integers, follow these rules:

- **If exactly one of the endpoints is included, subtract.**
- **If both endpoints are included, subtract and add 1.**
- **If neither endpoint is included, subtract and subtract 1 more.**

EXAMPLE 4

From 1:09 to 1:13, Adam read pages 109 through 113 in his English book. What was his rate of reading, in pages per minute?

SOLUTION.
Since Adam read both pages 109 and 113, he read 113 – 109 + 1 = 5 pages. He started reading during the minute that started at 1:09 (and ended at 1:10). Since he stopped reading at 1:13, he did not read during the minute that began at 1:13 (and ended at 1:14). So he read for 1:13 – 1:09 = 4 minutes. He read at the rate of $\frac{5}{4}$ pages per minute.

SYSTEMATICALLY MAKING A LIST

TACTIC

When a question asks "How many...?" and the numbers in the problem are small, just systematically list all of the possibilities.

Proper use of TACTIC O1 eliminates the risk of making an error in arithmetic. In Example 4, rather than even thinking about whether or not to add 1 or subtract 1 after subtracting the number of pages, you could have just quickly jotted down the numbers of the pages Adam read (109, 110, 111, 112, 113), and then counted them.

EXAMPLE 5

Ariel has 4 paintings in the basement. She is going to bring up 2 of them and hang 1 in her den and 1 in her bedroom. In how many ways can she choose which paintings go in each room?

SOLUTION.
Label the paintings 1, 2, 3, and 4, write B for bedroom and D for den, and make a list.

B-D	B-D	B-D	B-D
1-2	2-1	3-1	4-1
1-3	2-3	3-2	4-2
1-4	2-4	3-4	4-3

There are **12** ways to choose which paintings go in each room.

In Example 5, making a list was feasible, but if Ariel had 10 paintings and needed to hang 4 of them, it would be impossible to list all the different ways of hanging them. In such cases, we need the *counting principle*.

THE COUNTING PRINCIPLE

KEY FACT O2

If two jobs need to be completed and there are *m* ways to do the first job and *n* ways to do the second job, then there are *m* × *n* ways to do one job followed by the other. This principle can be extended to any number of jobs.

In Example 5, the first job was to pick 1 of the 4 paintings and hang it in the bedroom. That could be done in 4 ways. The second job was to pick a second painting to hang in the den. That job could be accomplished by choosing any of the remaining 3 paintings. So there are 4 × 3 = **12** ways to hang 2 of the paintings.

Now, assume that there are 10 paintings to be hung in 4 rooms. The first job is to choose one of the 10 paintings for the bedroom. The second job is to choose one of the 9 remaining paintings to hang in the den. The third job is to choose one of the 8 remaining paintings for the living room. Finally, the fourth job is to pick one of the 7 remaining paintings for the dining room. These 4 jobs can be completed in $10 \times 9 \times 8 \times 7 = $ **5040** ways.

EXAMPLE 6

How many integers are there between 100 and 1000 all of whose digits are odd?

SOLUTION.
We're looking for three-digit numbers, such as 135, 711, 353, and 999, in which all three digits are odd. Note that we are *not* required to use three different digits. Although you certainly wouldn't want to list all of them, you could count them by listing some of them and seeing if a pattern develops.

- In the 100s there are 5 numbers that begin with 11: 111, 113, 115, 117, 119.
- Similarly, there are 5 numbers that begin with 13: 131, 133, 135, 137, 139.
- There are 5 that begin with 15; 5 that begin with 17; and 5 that begin with 19.
- A total of $5 \times 5 = 25$ in the 100s.
- In the same way there are 25 in the 300s, 25 in the 500s, 25 in the 700s, and 25 in the 900s, for a grand total of $5 \times 25 = $ **125**.

You can actually do this in less time than it takes to read this paragraph.

The best way to solve Example 6, however, is to use the counting principle. Think of writing a three-digit number as three jobs that need to be done. The first job is to select one of the five odd digits and use it as the digit in the hundreds place. The second job is to select one of the five odd digits to be the digit that goes in the tens place. Finally, the third job is to select one of the five odd digits to be the digit in the units place. Each of these jobs can be done in 5 ways. So the total number of ways is $5 \times 5 \times 5 = $ **125**.

EXAMPLE 7

How many different arrangements are there of the letters *A*, *B*, *C*, and *D*?
Ⓐ 4   Ⓑ 6   Ⓒ 8   Ⓓ 12   Ⓔ 24

Since from the choices given, we know that the answer is a relatively small number, we could just use TACTIC O1 and systematically list them: *ABCD*, *ABDC*, *ACBD*, ... However, this method would not be suitable if you had to arrange as few as 5 or 6 letters and would be essentially impossible if you had to arrange 10 or 20 letters.

SOLUTION.

Think of the act of arranging the four letters as four jobs that need to be done, and use the counting principle. The first job is to choose one of the four letters to write in the first position; there are 4 ways to complete that job. The second job is to choose one of the remaining three letters to write in the second position; there are 3 ways to complete that job. The third job is to choose one of the two remaining letters to write in the third position; there are 2 ways to complete that job. Finally, the fourth job is to choose the only remaining letter and to write it: $4 \times 3 \times 2 \times 1 = \mathbf{24}$.

VENN DIAGRAMS

A ***Venn diagram*** is a figure with two or three overlapping circles, usually enclosed in a rectangle, which is used to solve certain counting problems. To illustrate this, assume that a school has 100 seniors. The following Venn diagram, which divides the rectangle into four regions, shows the distribution of those students in the band and the orchestra.

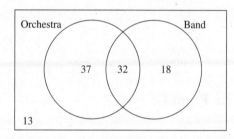

The 32 written in the part of the diagram where the two circles overlap represents the 32 seniors who are in both band and orchestra. The 18 written in the circle on the right represents the 18 seniors who are in band but not in orchestra, while the 37 written in the left circle represents the 37 seniors who are in orchestra but not in band. Finally, the 13 written in the rectangle outside of the circles represents the 13 seniors who are in neither band nor orchestra. The numbers in all four regions must add up to the total number of seniors: 32 + 18 + 37 + 13 = 100. Note that there are 50 seniors in the band — 32 who are also in the orchestra and 18 who are not in the orchestra. Similarly, there are 32 + 37 = 69 seniors in the orchestra. Be careful: the 50 names on the band roster and the 69 names on the orchestra roster add up to 119 names — more than the number of seniors. That's because 32 names are on both lists and so have been counted twice. The number of seniors who are in band or orchestra is only 119 − 32 = 87. Those 87 together with the 13 seniors who are in neither make up the total of 100.

On the GRE, Venn diagrams are used in two ways. It is possible to be given a Venn diagram and asked a question about it, as in Example 8. More often, you will come across a problem, such as Example 9, that you will be able to solve more easily if you think to draw a Venn diagram.

EXAMPLE 8

If the integers from 1 through 15 are each placed in the diagram at the right, which regions are empty?

Indicate *all* such regions.

- [A] A
- [B] B
- [C] C
- [D] D
- [E] E
- [F] F
- [G] G
- [H] H

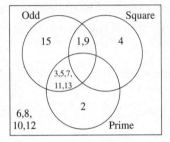

SOLUTION. The easiest way is just to put each of the numbers from 1 through 15 in the appropriate region.

The empty regions are **F and G**.

EXAMPLE 9

Of the 410 students at H. S. Truman High School, 240 study Spanish and 180 study French. If 25 students study neither language, how many study both?

SOLUTION.
Draw a Venn diagram.

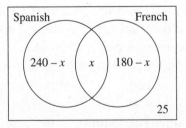

Let x represent the number of students who study both languages, and write x in the part of the diagram where the two circles overlap. Then the number who study only Spanish is $240 - x$, and the number who study only French is $180 - x$. The number who study at least one of the languages is $410 - 25 = 385$, so we have

$$385 = (240 - x) + x + (180 - x) = 420 - x \Rightarrow x = 420 - 385 = \mathbf{35}$$

students who study both.

NOTE: No problem *requires* the use of a Venn diagram. On some problems you might even find it easier not to use one. In Example 9, you could have reasoned that if there were 410 students in the school and 25 didn't study either language, then there were 410 − 25 = 385 students who studied at least one language. There are 240 names on the Spanish class lists and 180 on the French class lists, a total of 240 + 180 = 420 names. But those 420 names belong to only 385 students. It must be that 420 − 385 = 35 names were repeated. In other words, 35 students are in both French and Spanish classes.

PROBABILITY

The ***probability*** that an ***event*** will occur is a number between 0 and 1, usually written as a fraction, which indicates how likely it is that the event will happen. For example, if you spin the spinner in the diagram, there are 4 possible outcomes. It is equally likely that the spinner will stop in any of the 4 regions. There is 1 chance in 4 that it will stop in the region marked 2. So we say that the probability of spinning a 2 is one-fourth and

write $P(2) = \dfrac{1}{4}$. Since 2 is the only even number on

the spinner we could also say $P(\text{even}) = \dfrac{1}{4}$. There are

3 chances in 4 that the spinner will land in a region

with an odd number in it, so $P(\text{odd}) = \dfrac{3}{4}$.

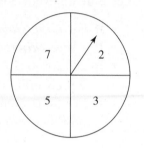

> ### KEY FACT O3

If *E* is any event, the probability that *E* will occur is given by

$$P(E) = \frac{\textbf{number of favorable outcomes}}{\textbf{total number of possible outcomes}},$$

assuming that the possible outcomes are all equally likely.

In the preceding example, each of the 4 regions is the same size, so it is equally likely that the spinner will land on the 2, 3, 5, or 7. Therefore,

$$P(\text{odd}) = \frac{\text{number of ways of getting an odd number}}{\text{total number of possible outcomes}} = \frac{3}{4}$$

Note that the probability of *not* getting an odd number is 1 minus the probability

of getting an odd number: $1 - \dfrac{3}{4} = \dfrac{1}{4}$. Let's look at some other probabilities associated with spinning this spinner once.

$$P(\text{number} > 10) = \frac{\text{number of ways of getting a number} > 10}{\text{total number of possible outcomes}} = \frac{0}{4} = 0.$$

$$P(\text{prime number}) = \frac{\text{number of ways of getting a prime number}}{\text{total number of possible outcomes}} = \frac{4}{4} = 1.$$

$$P(\text{number} < 4) = \frac{\text{number of ways of getting a number} < 4}{\text{total number of possible outcomes}} = \frac{2}{4} = \frac{1}{2}.$$

KEY FACT O4

Let E be an event, and $P(E)$ the probability it will occur.

- If E is *impossible* (such as getting a number greater than 10), $P(E) = 0$.
- If it is *certain* that E will occur (such as getting a prime number), $P(E) = 1$.
- In all cases $0 \le P(E) \le 1$.
- The probability that event E will not occur is $1 - P(E)$.
- If 2 or more events are mutually exclusive and constitute all the outcomes, the sum of their probabilities is 1.

  [For example, $P(\text{even}) + P(\text{odd}) = \frac{1}{4} + \frac{3}{4} = 1$.]

- The more likely it is that an event will occur, the higher its probability (the closer to 1 it is); the less likely it is that an event will occur, the lower its probability (the closer to 0 it is).

Even though probability is defined as a fraction, we can write probabilities as decimals or percents, as well.

Instead of writing $P(E) = \frac{1}{2}$, we can write $P(E) = .50$ or $P(E) = 50\%$.

EXAMPLE 10

An integer between 100 and 999, inclusive, is chosen at random. What is the probability that all the digits of the number are odd?

SOLUTION.
By KEY FACT O1, since both endpoints are included, there are $999 - 100 + 1 = 900$ integers between 100 and 999. In Example 6, we saw that there are 125 three-digit numbers all of whose digits are odd. So the probability is

$$\frac{\text{number of favorable outcomes}}{\text{total number of possible outcomes}} = \frac{125}{900} = \frac{5}{36}.$$

NOTE: On a numeric entry question it is *not* necessary to reduce fractions, so $\frac{125}{900}$ is perfectly acceptable.

KEY FACT O5

If an experiment is done two (or more) times, the probability that first one event will occur and then a second event will occur is the product of the probabilities.

EXAMPLE 11

A fair coin is flipped three times. What is the probability that the coin lands heads each time?

SOLUTION.
When a fair coin is flipped:

$$P(\text{head}) = \frac{1}{2} \text{ and } P(\text{tail}) = \frac{1}{2}.$$

By KEY FACT O5, $P(3 \text{ heads}) =$

$$P(\text{head 1st time}) \times P(\text{head 2nd time}) \times P(\text{head 3rd time}) = \frac{1}{2} \times \frac{1}{2} \times \frac{1}{2} = \frac{1}{8}.$$

Another way to handle problems such as Example 11 is to make a list of all the possible outcomes. For example, if a coin is tossed three times, the possible outcomes are

head, head, head	head, head, tail
head, tail, head	head, tail, tail
tail, head, head	tail, head, tail
tail, tail, head	tail, tail, tail

On the GRE, of course, if you choose to list the outcomes on your scrap paper, you should abbreviate and just write HHH, HHT, and so on. In any event, there are eight possible outcomes, and only one of them (HHH) is favorable. So the probability is $\frac{1}{8}$.

EXAMPLE 12

Three fair coins are flipped.

Quantity A	Quantity B
The probability of getting more heads than tails	The probability of getting more tails than heads

SOLUTION.

From the list of the 8 possible outcomes mentioned, you can see that in 4 of them (HHH, HHT, HTH, THH) there are more heads than tails, and that in 4 of them (TTT, TTH, THT, HTT) there are more tails than heads. Each probability is $\frac{4}{8}$. The answer is **C**.

In Example 12, it wasn't even necessary to calculate the two probabilities. Since heads and tails are equally likely, when several coins are flipped, it is just as likely to have more heads as it is to have more tails. This is typical of quantitative comparison questions on probability; you usually can tell which of the two probabilities is greater without having to calculate either one. This is another instance where you can use TACTIC 5 from Chapter 10: don't calculate, compare.

EXAMPLE 13

The numbers from 1 to 1000 are each written on a slip of paper and placed in a box. Then 1 slip is removed.

Quantity A	Quantity B
The probability that the number drawn is a multiple of 5	The probability that the number drawn is a multiple of 7

SOLUTION.

Since there are many more multiples of 5 than there are of 7, it is more likely that a multiple of 5 will be drawn. Quantity **A** is greater.

Practice Exercises — Counting and Probability

Discrete Quantitative Questions

1. Alyssa completed exercises 6–20 on her math review sheet in 30 minutes. At this rate, how long, in minutes, will it take her to complete exercises 29–57?

    Ⓐ 56
    Ⓑ 57
    Ⓒ 58
    Ⓓ 60
    Ⓔ 65

2. A diner serves a lunch special, consisting of soup or salad, a sandwich, coffee or tea, and a dessert. If the menu lists 3 soups, 2 salads, 7 sandwiches, and 8 desserts, how many different lunches can you choose? (*Note*: Two lunches are different if they differ in any aspect.)

    Ⓐ 22
    Ⓑ 280
    Ⓒ 336
    Ⓓ 560
    Ⓔ 672

3. Dwight Eisenhower was born on October 14, 1890 and died on March 28, 1969. What was his age, in years, at the time of his death?

    Ⓐ 77
    Ⓑ 78
    Ⓒ 79
    Ⓓ 80
    Ⓔ 81

4. How many four-digit numbers have only even digits?

5. There are 27 students on the college debate team. What is the probability that at least 3 of them have their birthdays in the same month?

    Ⓐ 0
    Ⓑ $\dfrac{3}{27}$
    Ⓒ $\dfrac{3}{12}$
    Ⓓ $\dfrac{1}{2}$
    Ⓔ 1

6. Let A be the set of primes less than 6, and B be the set of positive odd numbers less than 6. How many different sums of the form $a + b$ are possible, if a is in A and b is in B?

    Ⓐ 6
    Ⓑ 7
    Ⓒ 8
    Ⓓ 9
    Ⓔ 10

7. There are 100 people on a line. Aviva is the 37th person and Naomi is the 67th person. If a person on line is chosen at random, what is the probability that the person is standing between Aviva and Naomi?

8. A jar has 5 marbles, 1 of each of the colors red, white, blue, green, and yellow. If 4 marbles are removed from the jar, what is the probability that the yellow one was removed?

Ⓐ $\dfrac{1}{20}$

Ⓑ $\dfrac{1}{5}$

Ⓒ $\dfrac{1}{4}$

Ⓓ $\dfrac{4}{5}$

Ⓔ $\dfrac{5}{4}$

9. Josh works on the second floor of a building. There are 10 doors to the building and 8 staircases from the first to the second floor. Josh decided that each day he would enter by one door and leave by a different one, and go up one staircase and down another. How many days could Josh do this before he had to repeat a path he had previously taken?

Ⓐ 80
Ⓑ 640
Ⓒ 800
Ⓓ 5040
Ⓔ 6400

10. A jar contains 20 marbles: 4 red, 6 white, and 10 blue. If you remove marbles one at a time, randomly, what is the minimum number that must be removed to be certain that you have at least 2 marbles of each color?

Ⓐ 6
Ⓑ 10
Ⓒ 12
Ⓓ 16
Ⓔ 18

11. At the audition for the school play, *n* people tried out. If *k* people went before Judy, who went before Liz, and *m* people went after Liz, how many people tried out between Judy and Liz?

Ⓐ $n - m - k - 2$
Ⓑ $n - m - k - 1$
Ⓒ $n - m - k$
Ⓓ $n - m - k + 1$
Ⓔ $n - m - k + 2$

12. In a group of 100 students, more students are on the fencing team than are members of the French club. If 70 are in the club and 20 are neither on the team nor in the club, what is the minimum number of students who could be both on the team and in the club?

Ⓐ 10
Ⓑ 49
Ⓒ 50
Ⓓ 60
Ⓔ 61

13. In a singles tennis tournament that has 125 entrants, a player is eliminated whenever he loses a match. How many matches are played in the entire tournament?

[   ]

Questions 14–15 refer to the following diagram.

A is the set of positive integers less than 20;
B is the set of positive integers that contain the
digit 7; and C is the set of primes.

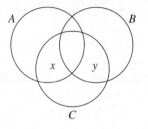

14. How many numbers are in the region
    labeled *x*?

    Ⓐ 4
    Ⓑ 5
    Ⓒ 6
    Ⓓ 7
    Ⓔ 8

15. What is the sum of all the numbers less than
    50 that are in the region labeled *y*?

    ⬚

Quantitative Comparison Questions

> Ⓐ Quantity A is greater.
> Ⓑ Quantity B is greater.
> Ⓒ Quantities A and B are equal.
> Ⓓ It is impossible to determine which
>   quantity is greater.

Quantity A	Quantity B
16. The probability of getting no heads when a fair coin is flipped 7 times	The probability of getting 7 heads when a fair coin is flipped 7 times

A jar contains 4 marbles: 2 red and 2 white.
2 marbles are chosen at random.

Quantity A	Quantity B
17. The probability that the marbles chosen are the same color	The probability that the marbles chosen are different colors

Quantity A	Quantity B
18. The number of ways to assign a number from 1 to 5 to each of 4 people	The number of ways to assign a number from 1 to 5 to each of 5 people

Quantity A	Quantity B
19. The probability that 2 people chosen at random were born on the same day of the week	The probability that 2 people chosen at random were born in the same month

Quantity A	Quantity B
20. The probability a number chosen at random from the primes between 100 and 199 is odd.	.99

ANSWER KEY

1. **C**	5. **E**	8. **D**	12. **E**	16. **C**	20. **A**
2. **D**	6. **B**	9. **D**	13. **124**	17. **B**	
3. **B**	7. $\dfrac{29}{100}$	10. **E**	14. **C**	18. **C**	
4. **500**		11. **A**	15. **84**	19. **A**	

Answer Explanations

1. **(C)** Alyssa completed 20 – 6 + 1 = 15 exercises in 30 minutes, which is a rate of 1 exercise every 2 minutes. Therefore, to complete 57 – 29 + 1 = 29 exercises would take her 58 minutes.

2. **(D)** You can choose your soup or salad in any of 5 ways, your beverage in any of 2 ways, your sandwich in 7 ways, and your dessert in 8 ways. The counting principle says to multiply: $5 \times 2 \times 7 \times 8 = 560$. (Note that if you got soup *and* a salad, then instead of 5 choices for the first course there would have been $2 \times 3 = 6$ choices for the first two courses.)

3. **(B)** His last birthday was in October 1968, when he turned 78: 1968 – 1890 = 78.

4. **500** The easiest way to solve this problem is to use the counting principle. The first digit can be chosen in any of 4 ways (2, 4, 6, 8), whereas the second, third, and fourth digits can be chosen in any of 5 ways (0, 2, 4, 6, 8). Therefore, the total number of four-digit numbers all of whose digits are even is $4 \times 5 \times 5 \times 5 = 500$.

5. **(E)** If there were no month in which at least 3 students had a birthday, then each month would have the birthdays of at most 2 students. But that's not possible. Even if there were 2 birthdays in January, 2 in February, ..., and 2 in December, that would account for only 24 students. It is guaranteed that with more than 24 students, at least one month will have 3 or more birthdays. The probability is 1.

6. **(B)** $A = \{2, 3, 5\}$ and $B = \{1, 3, 5\}$. Any of the 3 numbers in A could be added to any of the 3 numbers in B, so there are 9 sums that could be formed. However, there could be some duplication. List the sums systematically; first add 1 to each number in A, then 3, and then 5: 3, 4, 6; 5, 6, 10; 7, 8, 10. There are 7 different sums.

7. $\dfrac{29}{100}$ There are 67 – 37 – 1 = 29 people between Aviva and Naomi, so, the probability that one of them is chosen is $\dfrac{29}{100}$.

8. **(D)** It is equally likely that any one of the 5 marbles will be the one that is not removed. So, the probability that the yellow one is left is $\dfrac{1}{5}$ and the probability that it is removed is $\dfrac{4}{5}$.

9. **(D)** This is the counting principle at work. Each day Josh has four jobs to do: choose 1 of the 10 doors to enter and 1 of the 9 other doors to exit; choose 1 of the 8 staircases to go up and 1 of the other 7 to come down. This can be done in $10 \times 9 \times 8 \times 7 = 5040$ ways. So on each of 5040 days Josh could choose a different path.

10. **(E)** In a problem like this the easiest thing to do is to see what could go wrong in your attempt to get 2 marbles of each color. If you were really unlucky, you might remove 10 blue ones in a row, followed by all 6 white ones. At that point you would have 16 marbles, and you still wouldn't have even 1 red one. The next 2 marbles, however, must both be red. The answer is 18.

11. **(A)** It may help to draw a line and label it:

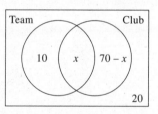

    Since k people went before Judy, she was number $k + 1$ to try out; and since m people went after Liz, she was number $n - m$ to try out. So the number of people to try out between them was $(n - m) - (k + 1) - 1 = n - m - k - 2$.

12. **(E)** Draw a Venn diagram, letting x be the number of students who are on the team and in the club.

    Of the 100 students, 70 are in the club, so 30 are not in the club. Of these 30, 20 are also not on the team, so 10 are on the team but not in the club. Since more students are on the team than in the club, $10 + x > 70 \Rightarrow x > 60$. Since x must be an integer, the least it can be is 61.

13. **124** You could try to break it down by saying that first 124 of the 125 players would be paired off and play 62 matches. The 62 losers would be eliminated and there would still be 63 people left, the 62 winners and the 1 person who didn't play yet. Then continue until only 1 person was left. This is too time-consuming. An easier way is to observe that the winner never loses and the other 124 players each lose once. Since each match has exactly one loser, there must be 124 matches.

14. **(C)** The region labeled x contains all of the primes less than 20 that do *not* contain the digit 7. They are 2, 3, 5, 11, 13, 19.

15. **84** Region y consists of primes that contain the digit 7 and are greater than 20. There are two of them that are less than 50: 37 and 47. Their sum is 84.

16. **(C)** Don't calculate the probabilities. The probability of no heads is equal to the probability of no tails; but no tails means all heads.

17. **(B)** The simplest solution is to notice that whatever color the first marble is, there is only 1 more marble of that color, but there are 2 of the other color, so it is twice as likely that the marbles will be of different colors.

18. **(C)** By the counting principle, Quantity A is 5·4·3·2 and Quantity B is 5·4·3·2·1. Clearly, the quantities are equal.

19. **(A)** Quantity A: the probability is $\frac{1}{7}$. Quantity B: the probability is $\frac{1}{12}$.

20. **(A)** Every prime between 100 and 199 is odd (the only even prime is 2). So Quantity A is 1, which is greater than .99.

PART 5

MODEL TESTS

Model Tests

This chapter is designed to give you further experience in what to expect on the verbal, quantitative, and analytical writing sections of the Graduate Record Examination General Test. These tests should serve as a basis for analysis, which for some may signal the need for further drill before taking the actual test, and for others, may indicate that preparation for this part of the test is adequate. For the best results, take these tests only after reviewing your weak areas, found as a result of completing our Diagnostic Test.

Remember that the actual GRE Test you take will be done on a computer. Therefore, we strongly recommend that, if you purchased this book with a CD-ROM, in addition to completing these model tests, you take a computer-based model test using the CD-ROM. Note that the model tests in this book follow the exact same format as the test you will be taking. In each of the model tests in this book, the order of the five sections is analytical writing, verbal, quantitative, verbal, quantitative. On the actual computerized GRE that you take, the sections can appear in any order, except that Section 1 will definitely be the writing section.

To best simulate actual test conditions, find a quiet place to work. Have a stopwatch or a clock handy so that you can keep perfect track of the time. Go through each section by answering the questions in the order in which they appear. If you don't know the answer to a question, guess, making an educated guess, if possible, and move on. Practice pacing yourself so that you use all your time and just finish each section in the time allowed. Do not spend too much time on any one question. If you get stuck, just guess and go on to the next question.

After you have devoted the specified time allowed for each section of a model examination, refer to the correct answers furnished, determine your raw score, judge your progress, and plan further study. You should then carefully study the explanations for the correct answers of those questions that gave you difficulty. If you find that a particular topic needs further review, refer to the earlier part of the book where this topic is treated before attempting to take the next model test. If you follow this procedure, by the time you complete the second test in this chapter you will feel confident about your success.

Answer Sheet

MODEL TEST 1

Remove answer sheet by cutting on dotted line

Section 2

1. Ⓐ Ⓑ Ⓒ Ⓓ Ⓔ Ⓕ
2. Ⓐ Ⓑ Ⓒ Ⓓ Ⓔ Ⓕ
3. Ⓐ Ⓑ Ⓒ Ⓓ Ⓔ Ⓕ
4. Ⓐ Ⓑ Ⓒ Ⓓ Ⓔ Ⓕ
5. Ⓐ Ⓑ Ⓒ Ⓓ Ⓔ Ⓕ

6. Ⓐ Ⓑ Ⓒ Ⓓ Ⓔ
7. Ⓐ Ⓑ Ⓒ Ⓓ Ⓔ
8. Ⓐ Ⓑ Ⓒ Ⓓ Ⓔ
9. Ⓐ Ⓑ Ⓒ Ⓓ Ⓔ
10. Ⓐ Ⓑ Ⓒ Ⓓ Ⓔ

11. Ⓐ Ⓑ Ⓒ Ⓓ Ⓔ Ⓕ
12. Ⓐ Ⓑ Ⓒ Ⓓ Ⓔ Ⓕ
13. Ⓐ Ⓑ Ⓒ Ⓓ Ⓔ Ⓕ Ⓖ Ⓗ Ⓘ
14. Ⓐ Ⓑ Ⓒ Ⓓ Ⓔ Ⓕ
15. Ⓐ Ⓑ Ⓒ Ⓓ Ⓔ Ⓕ Ⓖ Ⓗ Ⓘ

16. Ⓐ Ⓑ Ⓒ Ⓓ Ⓔ
17. Ⓐ Ⓑ Ⓒ Ⓓ Ⓔ
18. Ⓐ Ⓑ Ⓒ Ⓓ Ⓔ
19. Ⓐ Ⓑ Ⓒ Ⓓ Ⓔ
20. Ⓐ Ⓑ Ⓒ Ⓓ

Section 3

1. Ⓐ Ⓑ Ⓒ Ⓓ
2. Ⓐ Ⓑ Ⓒ Ⓓ
3. Ⓐ Ⓑ Ⓒ Ⓓ
4. Ⓐ Ⓑ Ⓒ Ⓓ
5. Ⓐ Ⓑ Ⓒ Ⓓ

6. Ⓐ Ⓑ Ⓒ Ⓓ
7. Ⓐ Ⓑ Ⓒ Ⓓ
8. Ⓐ Ⓑ Ⓒ Ⓓ
9. Ⓐ Ⓑ Ⓒ Ⓓ Ⓔ
10. [ ]

11. [ ]
12. Ⓐ Ⓑ Ⓒ Ⓓ Ⓔ
13. Ⓐ Ⓑ Ⓒ Ⓓ Ⓔ Ⓕ
14. Ⓐ Ⓑ Ⓒ Ⓓ Ⓔ
15. Ⓐ Ⓑ Ⓒ Ⓓ Ⓔ

16. Ⓐ Ⓑ Ⓒ
17. Ⓐ Ⓑ Ⓒ Ⓓ Ⓔ
18. Ⓐ Ⓑ Ⓒ
19. Ⓐ Ⓑ Ⓒ Ⓓ Ⓔ
20. Ⓐ Ⓑ Ⓒ Ⓓ Ⓔ

Answer Sheet

MODEL TEST 1

Section 4

1 Ⓐ Ⓑ Ⓒ Ⓓ Ⓔ Ⓕ   6 Ⓐ Ⓑ Ⓒ Ⓓ Ⓔ   11 Ⓐ Ⓑ Ⓒ Ⓓ Ⓔ   16 Ⓐ Ⓑ Ⓒ Ⓓ Ⓔ Ⓕ

2 Ⓐ Ⓑ Ⓒ Ⓓ Ⓔ Ⓕ   7 Ⓐ Ⓑ Ⓒ Ⓓ Ⓔ   12 Ⓐ Ⓑ Ⓒ Ⓓ Ⓔ Ⓕ   17 Ⓐ Ⓑ Ⓒ Ⓓ Ⓔ

3 Ⓐ Ⓑ Ⓒ Ⓓ Ⓔ Ⓕ   8 Ⓐ Ⓑ Ⓒ Ⓓ Ⓔ   13 Ⓐ Ⓑ Ⓒ Ⓓ Ⓔ Ⓕ   18 Ⓐ Ⓑ Ⓒ Ⓓ Ⓔ

4 Ⓐ Ⓑ Ⓒ Ⓓ Ⓔ Ⓕ   9 Ⓐ Ⓑ Ⓒ Ⓓ Ⓔ   14 Ⓐ Ⓑ Ⓒ Ⓓ Ⓔ Ⓕ   19 Ⓐ Ⓑ Ⓒ Ⓓ Ⓔ

5 Ⓐ Ⓑ Ⓒ Ⓓ Ⓔ Ⓕ   10 Ⓐ Ⓑ Ⓒ Ⓓ Ⓔ   15 Ⓐ Ⓑ Ⓒ Ⓓ Ⓔ Ⓕ   20 Ⓐ Ⓑ Ⓒ Ⓓ Ⓔ

Section 5

1 Ⓐ Ⓑ Ⓒ Ⓓ   6 Ⓐ Ⓑ Ⓒ Ⓓ   11 Ⓐ Ⓑ Ⓒ Ⓓ Ⓔ   14 Ⓐ Ⓑ Ⓒ Ⓓ Ⓔ

2 Ⓐ Ⓑ Ⓒ Ⓓ   7 Ⓐ Ⓑ Ⓒ Ⓓ   12 Ⓐ Ⓑ Ⓒ Ⓓ Ⓔ   15 Ⓐ Ⓑ Ⓒ Ⓓ Ⓔ

3 Ⓐ Ⓑ Ⓒ Ⓓ   8 Ⓐ Ⓑ Ⓒ Ⓓ Ⓔ   13 [_____]   16 Ⓐ Ⓑ Ⓒ Ⓓ Ⓔ

4 Ⓐ Ⓑ Ⓒ Ⓓ   9 Ⓐ Ⓑ Ⓒ Ⓓ Ⓔ   [_____]   17 [_____]

5 Ⓐ Ⓑ Ⓒ Ⓓ   10 Ⓐ Ⓑ Ⓒ Ⓓ Ⓔ Ⓕ   18 Ⓐ Ⓑ Ⓒ Ⓓ Ⓔ

   19 [_____]

   20 Ⓐ Ⓑ Ⓒ Ⓓ Ⓔ

Model Test 1

Section 1 Analytical Writing

TIME: 60 MINUTES—2 WRITING TASKS

Task 1: Issue Exploration
30 MINUTES

Directions: In 30 minutes, compose an essay on the topic below. You may not write on any other topic. Write your essay on the lined page that follows.

The topic is presented in a one- to two-sentence quotation commenting on an issue of general concern. Your essay may support, refute, or qualify the views expressed in the quotation. Whatever you write, however, must be relevant to the issue under discussion, and you must support your viewpoint with reasons and examples derived from your studies and/or experience.

Faculty members from various institutions will evaluate your essay, judging it on the basis of your skill in the following areas.

- Analysis of the quotation's implications
- Organization and articulation of your ideas
- Use of relevant examples and arguments to support your case
- Handling of the mechanics of standard written English

Topic

"Question authority. Only by questioning accepted wisdom can we advance our understanding of the world."

Task 2: Argument Analysis
30 MINUTES

Directions: In 30 minutes, prepare a critical analysis of an argument expressed in a short paragraph. You may not offer an analysis of any other argument. Write your essay on the lined page that follows.

As you critique the argument, think about the author's underlying assumptions. Ask yourself whether any of them are questionable. Also evaluate any evidence the author brings up. Ask yourself whether it actually supports the author's conclusion.

In your analysis, you may suggest additional kinds of evidence to reinforce the author's argument. You may also suggest methods to refute the argument, or additional data that might be useful to you as you assess the soundness of the argument. *You may **not**, however, present your personal views on the topic.* Your job is to analyze the elements of an argument, not to support or contradict that argument.

Faculty members from various institutions will judge your essay, assessing it on the basis of your skill in the following areas:

- Identification and assessment of the argument's main elements
- Organization and articulation of your thoughts
- Use of relevant examples and arguments to support your case
- Handling of the mechanics of standard written English

Topic

The following appeared in a petition presented by Classen University students to the school's administration.

> The purpose of higher education is to prepare students for the future, but Classen students are at a serious disadvantage in the competition for post-college employment due to the University's burdensome breadth requirements. Classen's job placement rate is substantially lower than placement rates of many top-ranked schools. Classen students would be more attractive to employers if they had more time to take advanced courses in their specialty, rather than being required to spend fifteen percent of their time at Classen taking courses outside of their subject area. We demand, therefore, that the University abandon or drastically cut back on its breadth requirements.

Section 2 Verbal Reasoning

TIME: 30 MINUTES—20 QUESTIONS

Directions: For each of the following sentences, select the **two** answers of the six choices given that, when substituted in the sentence, both logically complete the sentence as a whole **and** create sentences that are equivalent to one another in meaning.

Questions 1–5

1. It seems ironic that the preacher's sermon, intended to reconcile the feuding brothers, served only to _____ them further.

   A intimidate
   B estrange
   C avenge
   D arbitrate
   E commiserate
   F disaffect

2. In recent years, the British seem to have become _____ Americanisms: even members of Parliament fall into baseball metaphors, although very few Britons understand the rules of the game.

   A critical of
   B indifferent to
   C enamored of
   D aggrieved by
   E tired of
   F hooked on

3. The general was such a contrarian that, at times when it appeared that the only sane action would be to _____, he became all the more determined to fight to the bitter end.

   A capitulate
   B remonstrate
   C exonerate
   D submit
   E repeat
   F resist

4. Some critics of the administration maintained that it was _____ of the White House to describe its proposal to reduce welfare payments to single parents as "tough love": the plan, in their opinion, while decidedly tough, was not loving at all.

   A witty
   B accurate
   C disingenuous
   D diplomatic
   E mendacious
   F salient

5. A perfectionist is someone who feels _____ when he makes even the most minuscule of errors.

   A vexation
   B hostility
   C indifference
   D chagrin
   E condemnation
   F bafflement

Directions: The next questions are based on the content of the following passage. Read the passage and then determine the best answer choice for each question. Base your choice on what this passage *states directly* or *implies*, not on any information you may have gained elsewhere.

For each of Questions 6–10, select *one* answer choice unless otherwise instructed.

Questions 6–10 are based on the following passage.

There can be no doubt that the emergence of the Negro writer in the post-war period stemmed, in part, from the fact that
Line he was inclined to exploit the opportunity to
(5) write about himself. It was more than that, however. The movement that has variously been called the "Harlem Renaissance," the "Blank Renaissance," and the "New Negro Movement" was essentially a part of the
(10) growing interest of American literary circles in the immediate and pressing social and economic problems. This growing interest coincided with two developments in Negro life that fostered the growth of the New
(15) Negro Movement. These two factors, the keener realization of injustice and the improvement of the capacity for expression, produced a crop of Negro writers who constituted the "Harlem Renaissance."
(20)   The literature of the Harlem Renaissance was, for the most part, the work of a race-conscious group. Through poetry, prose, and song, the writers cried out against social and economic wrongs. They protested against
(25) segregation and lynching. They demanded higher wages, shorter hours, and better conditions of work. They stood for full social equality and first-class citizenship. The new vision of social and economic freedom that
(30) they had did not force them to embrace the several foreign ideologies that sought to sink their roots in some American groups during the period.
    The writers of the Harlem Renaissance,
(35) bitter and cynical as some of them were, gave little attention to the propaganda of the socialists and communists. The editors of the *Messenger* ventured the opinion that the New

Negro was the "product of the same world-
(40) wide forces that have brought into being the great liberal and radical movements that are now seizing the reins of power in all the civilized countries of the world." Such forces may have produced the New Negro, but the
(45) more articulate of the group did not resort to advocating the type of political action that would have subverted American constitutional government. Indeed, the writers of the Harlem Renaissance were not so much
(50) revolting against the system as they were protesting its inefficient operation. In this approach they proved as characteristically American as any writers of the period.

6. Which of the following is implied by the statement that the writers of the Harlem Renaissance "were not so much revolting against the system as they were protesting its inefficient operation" (lines 48–51)?
   Ⓐ Black writers played only a minor part in protesting the injustices of the period.
   Ⓑ Left to itself, the system was certain to function efficiently.
   Ⓒ Black writers in general were not opposed to the system as such.
   Ⓓ In order for the system to operate efficiently, blacks must seize the reins of power in America.
   Ⓔ Black writers were too caught up in aesthetic questions to identify the true nature of the conflict.

7. With which of the following statements regarding the writers of the Harlem Renaissance would the author most likely agree?
   Ⓐ They needed to increase their commitment to international solidarity.
   Ⓑ Their awareness of oppression caused them to reject American society.
   Ⓒ They transformed their increasing social and political consciousness into art.
   Ⓓ Their art suffered from their overinvolvement in political crusades.
   Ⓔ Their detachment from their subject matter lessened the impact of their work.

8. The information in the passage suggests that the author is most likely
   Ⓐ a historian concerned with presenting socially conscious black writers of the period as loyal Americans
   Ⓑ a literary critic who questions the conclusions of historians about the Harlem Renaissance
   Ⓒ an educator involved in fostering creating writing programs for minority youths
   Ⓓ a black writer of fiction bent on discovering new facts about his literary roots
   Ⓔ a researcher with questions about the validity of his sources

9. Which of the following statements best describes the organization of lines 34–48) of the passage ("The writers. . . constitutional government")?
   Ⓐ The author cites an authority supporting a previous statement and then qualifies the original statement to clarify its implications.
   Ⓑ The author makes a point, quotes an observation apparently contradicting that point, and then resolves the inconsistency by limiting the application of his original statement.
   Ⓒ The author makes a negative comment and then modifies it by rephrasing his original comment to eliminate its negative connotations.
   Ⓓ The author summarizes an argument, quotes an observation in support of that argument, and then advances an alternative hypothesis to explain potential contradictions in that argument.
   Ⓔ The author states a thesis, quotes a statement relevant to that thesis, and then presents two cases, both of which corroborate the point of the original statement.

10. The passage supplies information for answering which of the following questions?
   Ⓐ What factors led to the stylistic improvement in the literary work of black writers in the post-war period?
   Ⓑ Who were the leading exponents of protest literature during the Harlem Renaissance?
   Ⓒ Why were the writers of the Harlem Renaissance in rebellion against foreign ideological systems?
   Ⓓ How did black writers in the post-war period define the literary tradition to which they belonged?
   Ⓔ With what specific socioeconomic causes did the black writers of the post-war period associate themselves?

Model Test 1

Directions: Each of the following sentences or groups of sentences contains one, two, or three blanks. These blanks signify that a word or set of words has been left out. Below each sentence are columns of words or sets of words. For each blank, pick the *one* word or set of words from the corresponding column that *best* completes the text.

11. Like the theory of evolution, the big-bang model of the universe's formation has undergone modification and (i) _____, but it has (ii) _____ all serious challenges.

Blank (i)
Ⓐ refinement
Ⓑ evaluation
Ⓒ refutation

Blank (ii)
Ⓓ resisted
Ⓔ acknowledged
Ⓕ misdirected

12. A rigid and conventional thinker, he lacked both the (i) _____ to adapt to changing conditions and the (ii) _____ to be innovative.

Blank (i)
Ⓐ volatility
Ⓑ refinement
Ⓒ flexibility

Blank (ii)
Ⓓ creativity
Ⓔ discipline
Ⓕ impertinence

13. Perugino's initial fame brought him considerable wealth and prestige, if not (i) _____ glory: some years after having been lauded as the most famous artist in Italy, his reputation having suffered a decline, Perugino was (ii) _____ by the acerbic Michelangelo as an artistic (iii) _____.

Blank (i)
Ⓐ mundane
Ⓑ enduring
Ⓒ ephemeral

Blank (ii)
Ⓓ derided
Ⓔ claimed
Ⓕ emulated

Blank (iii)
Ⓖ virtuoso
Ⓗ bumpkin
Ⓘ precursor

14. Rather than portraying Joseph II as a radical reformer whose reign was strikingly (i) _____, the play *Amadeus* depicts him as (ii) _____ thinker, too wedded to orthodox theories of musical composition to appreciate an artist of Mozart's genius.

Blank (i)

Ⓐ	dissipated
Ⓑ	enlightened
Ⓒ	placid

Blank (ii)

Ⓓ	a revolutionary
Ⓔ	an iconoclastic
Ⓕ	a doctrinaire

15. Some critics maintain that fixed poetic forms, which require a specific number of lines and syllables, invite and may even (i) _____ wordiness; when no such (ii) _____ exists, the poet can easily spot and (iii) _____ superfluities.

Blank (i)

Ⓐ	curtail
Ⓑ	encourage
Ⓒ	juxtapose

Blank (ii)

Ⓓ	constraint
Ⓔ	lyricism
Ⓕ	subterfuge

Blank (iii)

Ⓖ	foster
Ⓗ	brandish
Ⓘ	eliminate

16. A university training enables a graduate to see things as they are, to go right to the point, to disentangle a twisted _____ of thought.

Ⓐ	line
Ⓑ	lack
Ⓒ	mass
Ⓓ	plethora
Ⓔ	skein

Directions: The next questions are based on the content of the following passage. Read the passage and then determine the best answer choice for each question. Base your choice on what this passage *states directly* or *implies*, not on any information you may have gained elsewhere.

For each of Questions 17–20, select one answer choice unless otherwise instructed.

Questions 17–19 are based on the following passage.

As the works of dozens of women writers have been rescued from what E. P. Thompson calls "the enormous condescen-
Line sion of posterity," and considered in relation
(5) to each other, the lost continent of the female tradition has risen like Atlantis from the sea of English literature. It is now becoming clear that, contrary to Mill's theory, women have had a literature of their
(10) own all along. The woman novelist, according to Vineta Colby, was "really neither single nor anomalous," but she was also more than a "register and spokesman for her age." She was part of a tradition that had its ori-
(15) gins before her age, and has carried on through our own.

Many literary historians have begun to reinterpret and revise the study of women writers. Ellen Moers sees women's literature
(20) as an international movement, "apart from, but hardly subordinate to the mainstream: an undercurrent, rapid and powerful. This 'movement' began in the late eighteenth century, was multinational, and produced some
(25) of the greatest literary works of two centuries, as well as most of the lucrative pot-boilers." Patricia Meyer Spacks, in *The Female Imagination*, finds that "for readily discernible historical reasons women have characteristi-
(30) cally concerned themselves with matters more or less peripheral to male concerns, or at least slightly skewed from them. The differences between traditional female preoccupations and roles and male ones make a difference in
(35) female writing." Many other critics are beginning to agree that when we look at women writers collectively we can see an imaginative continuum, the recurrence of certain patterns, themes, problems, and images from generation to generation.

17. In the second paragraph of the passage the author's attitude toward the literary historians cited can best be described as one of
Ⓐ irony
Ⓑ ambivalence
Ⓒ disparagement
Ⓓ receptiveness
Ⓔ awe

Directions: For the following question, consider each of the choices separately and select *all* that apply.

18. The passage supplies information for answering which of the following questions?
A̲ Does the author believe the female literary tradition to be richer in depth than its masculine counterpart?
B̲ Which literary historian maintains that the female literary tradition transcends national boundaries?
C̲ Does Moers share Mill's concern over the ephemeral nature of female literary renown?
D̲ What patterns, themes, images, and problems recur sufficiently in the work of women writers to belong to the female imaginative continuum?
E̲ Did Mill acknowledge the existence of a separate female literary tradition?

19. In the first paragraph, the author makes use of all the following techniques EXCEPT
Ⓐ extended metaphor
Ⓑ enumeration and classification
Ⓒ classical allusion
Ⓓ direct quotation
Ⓔ comparison and contrast

Question 20 is based on the following passage.

In 1798 Thomas Malthus wrote "An Essay on the Principle of Population," in which he postulates that food supply never can keep
Line pace with the rate of increase in human pop-
(5) ulation. Increase the supply of food, Malthus argues, and population will rise to meet this increase. This, he asserts, means that the race between population and resources can never be truly won by any sociocultural system.
(10) Therefore, some measure of social inequality is inevitable in all human societies.

20. Which of the following statements, if true, would tend to undermine Malthus's argument?

A The rate of population increase has begun to decline in Northern Europe, but the food supply has not diminished.

B In many nations, the increase in human population has far outstripped the food-producing capacity.

C Human population growth may be limited by the use of contraception.

D For many ethnic and religious groups, artificial control of conception is morally unacceptable.

Section 3 Quantitative Ability

TIME: 35 MINUTES—20 QUESTIONS

Directions: In each of Questions 1–8, there are two quantities—Quantity A and Quantity B. You are to compare those quantities, taking into consideration any additional information given. The correct answer to such a question is

Ⓐ if Quantity A is greater;
Ⓑ if Quantity B is greater;
Ⓒ if the two quantities are equal;
Ⓓ if it is impossible to determine which quantity is greater.

Note: The given information, if any, is always centered above the two quantities. In any question, if a symbol or letter appears more than once, it represents the same thing each time.

	Quantity A	Quantity B
1.	The sum of the positive divisors of 19	The product of the positive divisors of 19

	Quantity A	Quantity B
2.	$a + b$	$c + d$

	Quantity A	Quantity B
3.	$5(r + t)$	$5r + t$

	Quantity A	Quantity B
4.	The average (arithmetic mean) of all the positive multiples of 5 less than 26	The average (arithmetic mean) of all the positive multiples of 7 less than 26

c and *d* are positive

$$\frac{1}{c} = 1 + \frac{1}{d}$$

	Quantity A	Quantity B
5.	c	d

A number is a *palindrome* if it reads exactly the same from right to left as it does from left to right. For example, 959 and 24742 are palindromes.

	Quantity A	Quantity B
6.	The probability that a three-digit number chosen at random is a palindrome	$\frac{1}{10}$

Jack and Jill each bought the same TV set using a 10% off coupon. Jack's cashier took 10% off the price and then added 8.5% sales tax. Jill's cashier first added the tax and then took 10% off the total price.

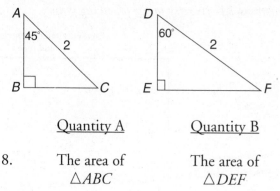

	Quantity A	Quantity B
7.	The amount Jack paid	The amount Jill paid

	Quantity A	Quantity B
8.	The area of △ABC	The area of △DEF

Directions: Questions 9–20 have three different formats. Unless a question has its own directions that specifically state otherwise, each question has five answer choices, exactly one of which is correct.

9. If it is now June, what month will it be 400 months from now?

Ⓐ January
Ⓑ April
Ⓒ June
Ⓓ October
Ⓔ December

Directions: The answer to the following question is a fraction. Enter the numerator in the upper box and the denominator in the lower box.

10. If $\frac{5}{9}$ of the members of the school chorus are boys, what is the ratio of girls to boys in the chorus?

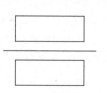

Directions: For the following question, enter your answer in the box.

11. What is the volume of a cube whose total surface area is 54?

12. If A is 25 kilometers east of B, which is 12 kilometers south of C, which is 9 kilometers west of D, how far is it, in kilometers, from A to D?

Ⓐ 20
Ⓑ $5\sqrt{34}$
Ⓒ $5\sqrt{41}$
Ⓓ $10\sqrt{13}$
Ⓔ 71

Directions: For the following question, consider each of the choices separately and select *all* that apply.

13. In triangle ABC, $AB = AC = 2$. Which of the following could be the area of triangle ABC? Indicate *all* possible areas.

A 0.5
B 1.0
C 1.5
D 2.0
E 2.5
F 3.0

Questions 14–16 refer to the following graphs.

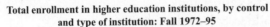

Total enrollment in higher education institutions, by control and type of institution: Fall 1972–95

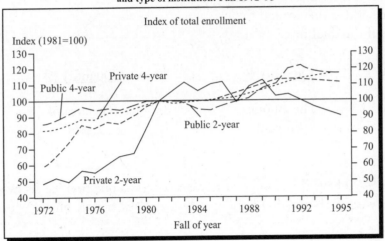

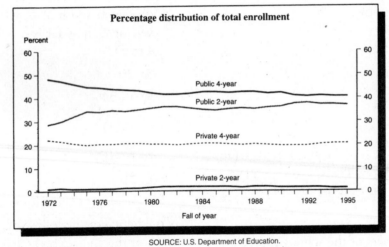

SOURCE: U.S. Department of Education.

14. In 1995 the number of students enrolled in public institutions of higher education was approximately how many times the number of students enrolled in private institutions of higher education?

Ⓐ 2

Ⓑ 2.5

Ⓒ 3

Ⓓ 3.5

Ⓔ 4

15. If the total enrollment in institutions of higher education in 1972 was 5,000,000, approximately how many students were enrolled in private 4-year institutions in 1995?

Ⓐ 1,000,000

Ⓑ 1,100,000

Ⓒ 1,250,000

Ⓓ 1,500,000

Ⓔ 1,650,000

Directions: For the following question, consider each of the choices separately and select *all* that apply.

16. Based on the information in the two graphs, which of the following statements are true?

    Indicate *all* such statements.

    A The number of students enrolled in private 2-year institutions was approximately the same in 1981 and 1987.

    B The percentage of students enrolled in private 2-year institutions was approximately the same in 1981 and 1987.

    C From 1972 to 1995, the percentage of college students who were enrolled in 2-year institutions rose by more than 25%.

17. Which of the following expresses the area of a circle in terms of C, its circumference?

    Ⓐ $\dfrac{C^2}{4\pi}$

    Ⓑ $\dfrac{C^2}{2\pi}$

    Ⓒ $\dfrac{\sqrt{C}}{2\pi}$

    Ⓓ $\dfrac{C\pi}{4}$

    Ⓔ $\dfrac{C}{4\pi}$

Directions: For the following question, consider each of the choices separately and select *all* that apply.

18. If the lengths of two of the sides of a triangle are 9 and 10, which of the following could be the length of the third side?

    Indicate *all* such lengths.

    A 1

    B 11

    C 21

19. If p pencils cost c cents at the same rate, how many pencils can be bought for d dollars?

    Ⓐ cdp

    Ⓑ $100\, cdp$

    Ⓒ $\dfrac{dp}{100c}$

    Ⓓ $\dfrac{100cd}{p}$

    Ⓔ $\dfrac{100dp}{c}$

20. Because her test turned out to be more difficult than she intended it to be, a teacher decided to adjust the grades by deducting only half the number of points a student missed. For example, if a student missed 10 points, she received a 95 instead of a 90. Before the grades were adjusted the class average was A. What was the average after the adjustment?

    Ⓐ $50 + \dfrac{A}{2}$

    Ⓑ $\dfrac{1}{2}(100 - A)$

    Ⓒ $100 - \dfrac{A}{2}$

    Ⓓ $\dfrac{50 + A}{2}$

    Ⓔ $A + 25$

Section 4 Verbal Reasoning

TIME: 30 MINUTES—20 QUESTIONS

Directions: For each of the following sentences, select the **two** answers of the six choices given that, when substituted in the sentence, both logically complete the sentence as a whole **and** create sentences that are equivalent to one another in meaning.

Questions 1–5

1. From papayas in Hawaii to canola in Canada, the spread of pollen or seeds from genetically engineered plants is evolving from _____ scientific worry into a significant practical problem.

   [A] a toxic

   [B] a theoretical

   [C] a radical

   [D] an abstract

   [E] an overblown

   [F] an analogous

2. When facts are _____ and data hard to come by, even scientists occasionally throw aside the professional pretense of objectivity and tear into each other with shameless appeals to authority and arguments that are unabashedly ad hominem.

   [A] elusive

   [B] established

   [C] demonstrable

   [D] ineluctable

   [E] uncertain

   [F] relevant

3. You may wonder how the expert on fossil remains is able to trace descent through teeth, which seem _____ pegs upon which to hang whole ancestries.

   [A] novel

   [B] reliable

   [C] flimsy

   [D] specious

   [E] inadequate

   [F] academic

4. During the military takeover, the constitution was not abolished, but some of its clauses temporarily were _____ as the armed forces took over the administration.

   [A] suspended

   [B] notarized

   [C] under construction

   [D] put in abeyance

   [E] left undefined

   [F] widely promulgated

5. Woolf _____ conventional notions of truth: in her words, one cannot receive from any lecture "a nugget of pure truth" to wrap up between the pages of one's notebook and keep on the mantelpiece forever.

   [A] anticipates

   [B] articulates

   [C] makes light of

   [D] mocks

   [E] pays heed to

   [F] puts up with

Directions: The next questions are based on the content of the following passages. Read each passage and then determine the best answer choice for each question. Base your choice on what the passages *state directly* or *imply*, not on any information you may have gained elsewhere.

For each of Questions 6–10, select one answer choice unless otherwise instructed.

Question 6 is based on the following passage.

Contemporary literary scholars have come to discard the once-conventional image of English theater in the time of Elizabeth I as an anomalous literary wonder, a sudden flowering of creativity rooted not in the dramatic traditions of England but the theater of ancient Greece and Rome. While acknowledging the debt of the Elizabethan playwrights to the dramas of Terence, Plautus, and Seneca, and to the *Poetics* of Aristotle, the majority of theater scholars today regard Elizabethan drama as being organically related to traditional English drama, above all to the medieval cycles of mystery and morality plays.

Directions: For the following question, consider each of the choices separately and select *all* that apply.

6. Which of the following is NOT consistent with the passage above?

[A] Theater historians have significantly altered their views of the origins of Elizabethan drama.

[B] England had a native dramatic tradition antedating the Elizabethan era.

[C] Although Elizabethan drama deals with English subject matter, it derives its form and method solely from classical Greek and Roman theater.

[D] Once envisioned as a historical and literary anomaly, Elizabethan drama now is interpreted as part of a historical continuum.

[E] Modern theater scholars view Elizabethan drama as a direct offshoot of Greek and Roman dramatic traditions.

Question 7 is based on the following passage.

The current trend toward specialization in nearly all occupational groups is exactly the opposite of what the educational system needs. World problems today are so diverse, complex, and interrelated that only the generalist stands a chance of understanding the broad picture. Unless our schools stress a truly broad, liberal education, the world will crumble around us as we each expertly perform our own narrow function.

7. Each of the following, if true, would weaken the conclusion drawn above, EXCEPT:

Ⓐ Many of the world's problems can be solved only by highly specialized experts working on specific problems.

Ⓑ Relatively few generalists are needed to coordinate the work of the many specialists.

Ⓒ Specialization does not necessarily entail losing the ability to see the broad picture.

Ⓓ Increasingly complex problems require a growing level of technical expertise that can be acquired only through specialization.

Ⓔ Even the traditional liberal education is becoming more highly specialized today.

Questions 8–10 are based on the following passage.

Given the persistent and intransigent nature of the American race system, which proved quite impervious to black attacks, Du Bois in his speeches and writings moved from one proposed solution to another, and the salience of various parts of his philosophy changed as his perceptions of the needs and strategies of black America shifted over time. Aloof and autonomous in his personality, Du Bois did not hesitate to depart markedly from whatever was the current mainstream of black thinking when he perceived that the conventional wisdom being enunciated by black spokesmen was proving inadequate to the task of advancing the race. His willingness to seek different solutions often placed him well in advance of his contemporaries, and this, combined with a strong-willed, even arrogant personality made his career as a black leader essentially a series of stormy conflicts.

Thus Du Bois first achieved his role as a major black leader in the controversy that arose over the program of Booker T. Washington, the most prominent and influential black leader at the opening of the twentieth century. Amidst the wave of lynchings, disfranchisement, and segregation laws, Washington, seeking the good will of powerful whites, taught blacks not to protest against discrimination, but to elevate themselves through industrial education, hard work, and property accumulation; then, they would ultimately obtain recognition of their citizenship rights. At first Du Bois agreed with this gradualist strategy, but in 1903 with the publication of his most influential book, *Souls of Black Folk*, he became the chief leader of the onslaught against Washington that polarized the black community into two wings—the "conservative" supporters of Washington and his "radical" critics.

(Line markers in passage: Line, (5), (10), (15), (20), (25), (30), (35), (40))

8. Which of the following statements about W. E. B. Du Bois does the passage best support?
   Ⓐ He sacrificed the proven strategies of earlier black leaders to his craving for political novelty.
   Ⓑ Preferring conflict to harmony, he followed a disruptive course that alienated him from the bulk of his followers.
   Ⓒ He proved unable to change with the times in mounting fresh attacks against white racism.
   Ⓓ He relied on the fundamental benevolence of the white population for the eventual success of his movement.
   Ⓔ Once an adherent of Washington's policies, he ultimately lost patience with them for their inefficacy.

9. It can be inferred that Booker T. Washington in comparison with W. E. B. Du Bois could be described as all of the following EXCEPT
   Ⓐ submissive to the majority
   Ⓑ concerned with financial success
   Ⓒ versatile in adopting strategies
   Ⓓ traditional in preaching industry
   Ⓔ respectful of authority

10. The author's attitude towards Du Bois's departure from conventional black policies can best be described as
   Ⓐ skeptical
   Ⓑ derisive
   Ⓒ shocked
   Ⓓ approving
   Ⓔ resigned

Directions: Each of the following pieces of text contains one, two, or three blanks. These blanks signify that a word or set of words has been left out. Below each piece of text are columns of choices. For each blank, select the word or set of words from the corresponding column of choices that *best* reflects the overall meaning of the text.

11. As any visitor to Claude Monet's final home at Giverny can _____, Japanese prints were the artist's passion: his home overflows with works by Hiroshige, Utamaro, and other Japanese masters.

Ⓐ portray
Ⓑ attest
Ⓒ contest
Ⓓ rectify
Ⓔ invalidate

12. Breaking with established musical traditions, Stravinsky was (i) _____ composer whose (ii) _____ works infuriated the traditionalists of his day.

Blank (i)

Ⓐ a derivative
Ⓑ an uncontroversial
Ⓒ an iconoclastic

Blank (ii)

Ⓓ hackneyed
Ⓔ heterodox
Ⓕ euphonious

13. While the disease is in (i) _____ state it is almost impossible to determine its existence by (ii) _____ .

Blank (i)

Ⓐ a critical
Ⓑ a latent
Ⓒ an overt

Blank (ii)

Ⓓ postulate
Ⓔ methodology
Ⓕ observation

14. The paleontologist's (i) _____ orthodoxy meant that the evidence he had so painstakingly gathered would inevitably be (ii) _____ by his more conventional colleagues.

Blank (i)

Ⓐ break with
Ⓑ dependence on
Ⓒ reputation for

Blank (ii)

Ⓓ considered
Ⓔ contested
Ⓕ classified

15. An essential purpose of the criminal justice system is to enable purgation to take place; that is, to provide a (i) _____ by which a community expresses its collective (ii) _____ the transgression of the criminal.

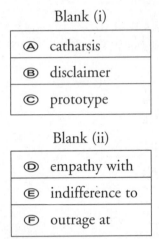

Blank (i)	
Ⓐ	catharsis
Ⓑ	disclaimer
Ⓒ	prototype

Blank (ii)	
Ⓓ	empathy with
Ⓔ	indifference to
Ⓕ	outrage at

16. In a classic example of scholarly (i) _____, the poet and scholar A. E. Housman once assailed a German rival for relying on manuscripts "as a drunkard relies on lampposts, for support rather than (ii) _____."

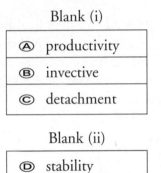

Blank (i)	
Ⓐ	productivity
Ⓑ	invective
Ⓒ	detachment

Blank (ii)	
Ⓓ	stability
Ⓔ	illumination
Ⓕ	credibility

Directions: The next questions are based on the content of the following passages. Read each passage and then determine the best answer choice for each question. Base your choice on what the passages *state directly* or *imply*, not on any information you may have gained elsewhere.

For each of Questions 17–20, select *one* answer choice unless otherwise instructed.

Question 17 is based on the following passage.

Exquisitely adapted for life in one of Earth's harshest environments, polar bears can survive for 20 years or more on the Arctic Circle's glacial ice. At home in a waste where temperatures reach minus 50 degrees Fahrenheit, these largest members of the bear family are a striking example of natural selection at work. With two layers of fur over a subcutaneous layer of blubber, polar bears are well adapted to resist heat loss. Their broad, snowshoe-like paws and sharp, curved claws enable them to traverse the ice with ease. Formidable hunters, these monarchs of the icy waste even possess the capacity to scent prey from a distance of 20 miles.

17. In the context of the passage's final sentence, "capacity" most nearly means
   Ⓐ faculty
   Ⓑ stature
   Ⓒ dimensions
   Ⓓ spaciousness
   Ⓔ intelligence

Questions 18–20 are based on the following passage.

At night, schools of prey and predators are almost always spectacularly illuminated by the bioluminescence produced by the micro-
Line scopic and larger plankton. The reason for
(5) the ubiquitous production of light by the microorganisms of the sea remains obscure, and suggested explanations are controversial. It has been suggested that light is a kind of inadvertent by-product of life in transparent
(10) organisms. It has also been hypothesized that the emission of light on disturbance is advantageous to the plankton in making the predators of the plankton conspicuous to *their* predators! Unquestionably, it does act
(15) this way. Indeed, some fisheries base the detection of their prey on the biolumines-cence that the fish excite. It is difficult, how-ever, to defend the thesis that this effect was the direct factor in the original development
(20) of bioluminescence, since the effect was of no advantage to the individual microorgan-ism that first developed it. Perhaps the lumi-nescence of a microorganism also discourages attack by light-avoiding predators and is of
(25) initial survival benefit to the individual. As it then becomes general in the population, the effect of revealing plankton predators to their predators would also become important.

18. The primary topic of the passage is which of the following?
Ⓐ The origin of bioluminescence in plank-ton predators
Ⓑ The disadvantages of bioluminescence in microorganisms
Ⓒ The varieties of marine bioluminescent life forms
Ⓓ Symbiotic relationships between predators and their prey
Ⓔ Hypotheses on the causes of biolumines-cence in plankton

19. The author mentions the activities of fisheries in order to provide an example of
Ⓐ how ubiquitous the phenomenon of bio-luminescence is coastally
Ⓑ how predators do make use of biolumines-cence in locating their prey
Ⓒ how human intervention imperils biolu-minescent microorganisms
Ⓓ how nocturnal fishing expeditions are becoming more and more widespread
Ⓔ how limited bioluminescence is as a source of light for human use

20. The passage provides an answer to which of the following questions?
Ⓐ What is the explanation for the phenome-non of bioluminescence in marine life?
Ⓑ Does the phenomenon of plankton bioluminescence have any practical applications?
Ⓒ Why do only certain specimens of marine life exhibit the phenomenon of bioluminescence?
Ⓓ How does underwater bioluminescence differ from atmospheric bioluminescence?
Ⓔ What are the steps that take place as an individual microorganism becomes bioluminescent?

Section 5 Quantitative Ability

TIME: 35 MINUTES—20 QUESTIONS

Directions: In each of Questions 1–7, there are two quantities—Quantity A and Quantity B. You are to compare those quantities, taking into consideration any additional information given. The correct answer to such a question is

- Ⓐ if Quantity A is greater;
- Ⓑ if Quantity B is greater;
- Ⓒ if the two quantities are equal;
- Ⓓ if it is impossible to determine which quantity is greater.

Note: The given information, if any, is always centered above the two quantities. In any question, if a symbol or letter appears more than once, it represents the same thing each time.

Model Test 1

	Quantity A	Quantity B
1.	$\dfrac{1}{\pi}$	$\dfrac{1}{\sqrt{10}}$

n is an odd positive integer
$700 < n < 800$

	Quantity A	Quantity B
2.	The number of the prime factors of *n*	The number of prime factors of 2*n*

$x < y$

	Quantity A	Quantity B
3.	The average (arithmetic mean) of *x* and *y*	The average (arithmetic mean) of *x*, *y*, and *y*

	Quantity A	Quantity B
4.	*c*	*d*

$0 < a < b$

	Quantity A	Quantity B
5.	*a*% of $\dfrac{1}{b}$	*b*% of $\dfrac{1}{a}$

	Quantity A	Quantity B
6.	*x*	*y*

Line *l* passes

through $\left(-\sqrt{2},\sqrt{3}\right)$ and $\left(\sqrt{2},-\sqrt{3}\right)$.

Line *m* is perpendicular to line *l*.

	Quantity A	Quantity B
7.	The slope of *l*	The slope of *m*

Directions: Questions 8–20 have three different formats. Unless a question has its own directions that specifically state otherwise, each question has five answer choices, exactly one of which is correct.

8. In the figure below, what is the average (arithmetic mean) of the measures of the five angles?

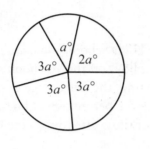

Ⓐ 36

Ⓑ 45

Ⓒ 60

Ⓓ 72

Ⓔ 90

9. Camille's average on her 6 math tests this marking period is 75. Fortunately for Camille, her teacher drops each student's lowest grade, and this raises her average to 85. What was her lowest grade?

Ⓐ 20

Ⓑ 25

Ⓒ 30

Ⓓ 40

Ⓔ 50

Directions: For questions 10 and 11, consider each of the choices separately and select *all* that apply.

10. If the area of a rectangle is 40, which of the following could be the perimeter of the rectangle?

Indicate *all* such areas.

A 20

B 40

C 200

D 400

E 2,000

F 4,000

11. Which of the following is an equation of a line that is perpendicular to the line whose equation is $2x + 3y = 4$?

Indicate *all* such equations.

A $3x + 2y = 4$

B $3x - 2y = 4$

C $2x - 3y = 4$

D $4 - 3x = -2y$

E $4 + 2x = 3y$

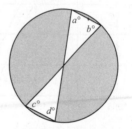

12. In the figure above, the diameter of the circle is 20 and the area of the shaded region is 80π. What is the value of $a + b + c + d$?

Ⓐ 144

Ⓑ 216

Ⓒ 240

Ⓓ 270

Ⓔ 288

Directions: The answer to the following question is a fraction. Enter the numerator in the upper box and the denominator in the lower box.

13. Each integer from 1 to 50 whose units digit is a 3 is written on a slip of paper and placed in a box. If two slips of paper are drawn at random, what is the probability that both the numbers picked are prime?

Questions 14–16 refer to the following graph.

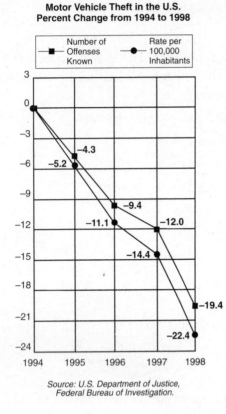

**Motor Vehicle Theft in the U.S.
Percent Change from 1994 to 1998**

Source: U.S. Department of Justice,
Federal Bureau of Investigation.

14. If 1,000,000 vehicles were stolen in 1994,
how many were stolen in 1996?
- Ⓐ 889,000
- Ⓑ 906,000
- Ⓒ 940,000
- Ⓓ 1,094,000
- Ⓔ 1,100,000

15. By what percent did the number of vehicles
stolen decrease from 1997 to 1998?
- Ⓐ 7.4%
- Ⓑ 8.0%
- Ⓒ 8.4%
- Ⓓ 12.0%
- Ⓔ 19.4%

16. To the nearest percent, by what percent did
the population of the United States increase
from 1994 to 1998?
- Ⓐ 1%
- Ⓑ 2%
- Ⓒ 3%
- Ⓓ 4%
- Ⓔ 5%

Directions: For the following question enter
your answer in the box.

17. If the average (arithmetic mean) of v, w, x, y,
and z is 12.3, and the average of v and w is
45.6, what is the average of x, y, and z?

18. At Tyler High School, there are twice as many
girls than boys on the yearbook staff. At one
staff meeting, the percentage of girls attending
was twice the percentage of boys. What
percent of those attending were boys?
- Ⓐ 20
- Ⓑ 25
- Ⓒ 30
- Ⓓ 33
- Ⓔ 50

Directions: For the following question enter
your answer in the box.

19. If four boys can shovel a driveway in two
hours, how many minutes would it take five
boys to shovel that driveway? (Assume that
each boy works at the same rate.)

 minutes

20. In 1950 Roberto was four times as old as
Juan. In 1955, Roberto was three times as
old as Juan. How old was Roberto when
Juan was born?
- Ⓐ 5
- Ⓑ 10
- Ⓒ 20
- Ⓓ 30
- Ⓔ 40

Model Test 1
ANSWER KEY

Section 1–Analytical Writing

There are no "correct answers" to this section.

Section 2–Verbal Reasoning

1. **B, F**	6. **C**	11. **A, D**	16. **E**
2. **C, F**	7. **C**	12. **C, D**	17. **D**
3. **A, D**	8. **A**	13. **B, D, H**	18. **B, E**
4. **C, E**	9. **B**	14. **B, F**	19. **B**
5. **A, D**	10. **E**	15. **B, D, I**	20. **A, C**

Note: The letters in brackets following the Quantitative Ability answers in Sections 3 and 5 refer to the sections of Chapter 11 in which you can find the information you need to answer the questions. For example, 12. A [J] means that the answer to question 12 is A, and that the solution requires information found in Section 11-J: Triangles. Also, 14. D [10] means that the answer to question 14 is D and is based on information in Chapter 10: Data Interpretation.

Section 3–Quantitative Ability

1. **A** [A]	6. **C** [O]	11. **27** [M]	16. **A, B, C** [10]
2. **A** [N]	7. **C** [C]	12. **A** [J]	17. **A** [L]
3. **D** [A]	8. **A** [J]	13. **A, B, C, D** [J]	18. **B** [J]
4. **A** [A, E]	9. **D** [A]	14. **D** [10]	19. **E** [D]
5. **B** [B]	10. **4/5** [B, D]	15. **E** [10]	20. **A** [E, H]

Section 4–Verbal Reasoning

1. **B, D**	6. **C, E**	11. **B**	16. **B, E**
2. **A, E**	7. **E**	12. **C, E**	17. **A**
3. **C, E**	8. **E**	13. **B, F**	18. **E**
4. **A, D**	9. **C**	14. **A, E**	19. **B**
5. **C, D**	10. **D**	15. **A, F**	20. **B**

Section 5–Quantitative Ability

1. **A** [A]	6. **D** [J]	11. **B, D** [N]	16. **D** [10]
2. **B** [A]	7. **B** [N]	12. **E** [L]	17. **–9.9** [E]
3. **B** [E]	8. **D** [E, L]	13. **3/5** [O]	18. **A** [C]
4. **A** [J]	9. **B** [E]	14. **B** [10]	19. **96** [D]
5. **B** [C]	10. **B, C, D, E, F** [L]	15. **C** [10]	20. **D** [H]

ANSWER EXPLANATIONS

Section 1—Analytical Writing

There are no "correct answers" to this section.

Section 2—Verbal Reasoning

1. **(B)(F)** The verbs *estrange* and *disaffect* are synonyms; both mean to make unfriendly or to distance. The two words can be used interchangeably here. Think of "estranged couples" getting a divorce and "disaffected voters" leaving a political party.

2. **(C)(F)** Baseball metaphors are examples of Americanisms, American idioms enthusiastically embraced by Britons despite the British lack of understanding of the original context of these terms. The Britons are *hooked on* or *enamored of* them.

3. **(A)(D)** A contrarian is someone who takes a contrary view or action, one who makes decisions that contradict prevailing wisdom. Because he is a contrarian, the general is resolved to fight to the bitter end; clearly, the wise or sane course would be to *capitulate* or *submit*. Note that *submit* here is a synonym for yielding or giving in, not for asserting or proposing something.

4. **(C)(E)** If the plan, though tough, is not loving, then it certainly would not be *accurate* for the White House to describe it as tough love. It would not be particularly *witty* or *salient* (strikingly conspicuous) for the White House to do so. It might indeed have been *diplomatic* (tactful) for the White House to describe the plan as tough love. However, critics of the administration would be unlikely to put such a positive spin on the administration's description. Also, none of the other choices are synonyms for *diplomatic*. Only two choices remain: *disingenuous* and *mendacious*. To be disingenuous is to be insincere or untruthful. Likewise, to be mendacious is to be untruthful.

5. **(A)(D)** Perfectionists expect perfection of themselves. Therefore, when they make even tiny errors, they feel *vexation* (annoyance with themselves) and *chagrin* (annoyance mixed with humiliation).

6. **(C)** The fact that the writers were more involved with fighting problems in the system than with attacking the system itself suggests that fundamentally they *were not opposed to the* democratic system of government.

   Choice A is incorrect. The fact that the writers did not revolt against the system does not necessarily imply that they played a minor role in fighting abuses of the system.

   Choice B is incorrect. There is nothing in the statement that would imply that, *left to itself, the system was certain to function efficiently*.

   Choice D is incorrect. There is nothing in the statement that would imply that *in order for the system to operate efficiently, blacks must seize the reins of power in America*.

   Choice E is incorrect. There is nothing in the statement that would imply that *Black writers were too caught up in aesthetic questions to identify the true nature of the conflict*.

7. **(C)** In lines 6–12, the author mentions the growing interest in social and economic problems among the writers of the Harlem Renaissance. They used poetry, prose, and song to cry out against social and economic wrongs. Thus, they *transformed their increasing social and political consciousness into art.*

   Choice A is incorrect. The author distrusts the foreign ideologies (lines 28–34) with their commitment to international solidarity.

   Choice B is incorrect. The author states that the writers wished to contribute to American culture; they did not totally reject American society, but wished to improve it.

   Choices D and E are incorrect. Neither is implied by the author.

8. **(A)** The author's evident concern to distinguish Negro writers from those who "embraced" socialist and communist propaganda (lines 28–34) suggest that he is a historian concerned with presenting these writers as loyal Americans.

   Choice B is incorrect. The author touches on literature only in relationship to historical events.

   Choice C, D, and E are incorrect. There is nothing in the passage to suggest any of these interpretations.

9. **(B)** The author makes the point that the writers essentially ignored socialist and communist propaganda. This point is apparently contradicted by the *Messenger* quote asserting that the same forces that produced socialism and communism *produced* the New Negro (and thus the new black writer). The author then *limits the application of his original* assertion by giving only qualified assent to that assertion ("Such forces *may* have produced the New Negro.").

10. **(E)** Choice E is answerable on the basis of this passage.

    The passage cites the battles for better working conditions, desegregation, and social and political equality in which the black writers of the period were engaged. These were *specific socioeconomic causes* with which the writers associated themselves.

    Choice A is unanswerable on the basis of this passage. The passage mentions an "improvement in the capacity for expression" in the period, but cites no factors leading to this stylistic improvement.

    Choice B is unanswerable on the basis of this passage. The passage mentions no specific names.

    Choice C is unanswerable on the basis of this passage. The passage states the writers did not "embrace the several foreign ideologies that sought to sink their roots" in America. However, it nowhere suggests that the writers were *in rebellion* against these foreign ideologies.

    Choice D is unanswerable on the basis of this passage. No such information is supplied by the passage.

11. **(A)(D)** The author concedes that the big-bang theory has been changed somewhat: it has undergone *refinement* or polishing. However, he denies that its validity has been threatened seriously by any rival theories: it has *resisted* or defied all challenges.

The use of the support signal *and* indicates that the first missing word is similar in meaning to "modification." The use of the contrast signal *but* indicates that the second missing word is contrary in meaning to "undergone modification."

12. **(C)(D)** Someone described as "rigid and conventional" would lack both the *flexibility* (adaptability) to adjust to changes and the *creativity* (inventiveness; imagination) to come up with new, innovative ideas.

13. **(B)(D)(H)** The phrases "some years after having been lauded" and "his reputation having suffered a decline" provide the key to unlocking this sentence. The subject here is the change in Perugino's reputation. In the beginning, he received wealth and status, but his fame did not last: he did not win *enduring* glory. Instead, Michaelangelo *derided* (ridiculed; mocked) him as an artistic *bumpkin* (clod; oaf).

14. **(B)(F)** The play *Amadeus* portrays Joseph II as "wedded to orthodox theories of musical composition." Thus, it depicts him as a *doctrinaire* thinker, dogmatic about which theories or doctrines he accepts. This view of Emperor Joseph is in contrast with his image as a reformer whose reign was impressively *enlightened* (liberal; civilized) for the period. The best way to attack this sentence is to complete the second blank first. Note that the second blank immediately precedes a long descriptive phrase that clarifies what kind of thinker Joseph II was.

15. **(B)(D)(I)** The adverb *even* (indeed) is used here as an intensive to stress something. Not only do fixed poetic forms *invite* wordiness, they may even *encourage* it. Because these fixed forms require the poet to write a specific number of lines or syllables, they place a *constraint* (limitation; restriction) on the poet. Without that constraint, the poet might have an easier time spotting and *eliminating* unnecessary syllables and words.

16. **(E)** One would have to disentangle a *skein* or coiled and twisted bundle of yarn. Note how the presence of the verb *disentangle*, which may be used both figuratively and literally, influences the writer's choice of words. In this case, while *line* is a possible choice, the word does not possess the connotations of twistings and tangled contortions that make *skein* a more suitable choice.

17. **(D)** The author opens the paragraph by stating that many literary critics have begun reinterpreting the study of women's literature. She then goes on to cite individual comments that support her assertion. Clearly, she is *receptive* or open to the ideas of these writers, for they and she share a common sense of the need to reinterpret their common field.

Choices A and B are incorrect. The author cites the literary critics straightforwardly, presenting their statements as evidence supporting her thesis.

Choice C is incorrect. The author does not *disparage* or belittle these critics. By quoting them respectfully she implicitly acknowledges their competence.

Choice E is incorrect. The author quotes the critics as acknowledged experts in the field. However, she does not look on these critics with *awe* (an overwhelming feeling of reverence, admiration, or fear).

18. **(B)(E)** Question B is answerable on the basis of the passage. According to lines 19–22, Ellen Moers "sees women's literature as an international move-ment," in other words, as a movement that *transcends national boundaries.*

    Likewise, Question E is answerable on the basis of the passage. According to lines 7–10, Mill disbelieved in the idea that women "have had a literature of their own all along."

19. **(B)** The writer neither lists (*enumerates*) nor sorts (*classifies*) anything in the opening paragraph.

    Choice A is incorrect. The writer likens the female tradition to a lost conti-nent and develops the metaphor by describing the continent "rising...from the sea of English literature."

    Choice C is incorrect. The author refers or *alludes* to the classical legend of Atlantis.

    Choice D is incorrect. The author quotes Colby and Thompson.

    Choice E is incorrect. The author contrasts the revised view of women's lit-erature with Mill's view.

20. **(A)(C)** The statement that "The rate of population increase has begun to decline in Northern Europe, but the food supply has not diminished" weak-ens Malthus's postulate that food supply cannot keep pace with the rate of increase of human population. Likewise, if "[h]uman population growth may be limited by the use of contraception," then it is possible that increasing the supply of food might not necessarily be followed by an increase in human population.

Section 3—Quantitative Ability

Two asterisks (**) indicate an alternative method of solving.

1. **(A)** The only positive divisors of 19 are 1 and 19. Quantity A: $1 + 19 = 20$. Quantity B: $1 \times 19 = 19$. Quantity A is greater.

2. **(A)** Since (a, b) is on the positive portion of the x-axis, a is positive and $b = 0$; so $a + b$ is positive. Also, since (c, d) is on the negative portion of the y-axis, c is negative and $d = 0$; so $c + d$ is negative. Quantity A is greater.

3. **(D)** By the distributive law, Quantity A is $5r + 5t$. Subtract $5r$ from each quantity, and compare $5t$ and t. They are equal if $t = 0$ and unequal other-wise. Neither quantity is always greater, and the two quantities are not always equal (D).

4. **(A)** Quantity A: there are 5 positive multiples of 5 less than 26: 5, 10, 15, 20, 25; their average is 15, the middle one [KEY FACT E5].

    Quantity B: there are 3 positive multiples of 7 less than 26: 7, 14, 21; their average is 14.

    Quantity A is greater.

5. **(B)** Since $\dfrac{1}{c} = 1 + \dfrac{1}{d}$, then $1 = \dfrac{1}{c} - \dfrac{1}{d} = \dfrac{d - c}{cd}$.

    Therefore, $d - c = cd$, which is positive. Then, $d - c$ is positive, and so $d > c$.
    Quantity B is greater.

6. **(C)** The simplest solution is to realize that there is one palindrome between 100 and 109 (101), one between 390 and 399 (393), one between 880 and 889 (888), and in general, one out of every 10 numbers. So the probability is $\frac{1}{10}$. The answer is (C).

   **The more direct solution is to count the number of palindromes. Either systematically make a list and notice that there are 10 of them between 100 and 199, and 10 in each of the hundreds from the 100s to the 900s, for a total of 90; or use the counting principle: the first digit can be chosen in any of 9 ways, the second in any of 10 ways, and the third, since it must match the first, can be chosen in only 1 way ($9 \times 10 \times 1 = 90$). Since there are 900 three-digit numbers, the probability is $\frac{90}{900} = \frac{1}{10}$.

7. **(C)** Let P = the price of the TV set. Then Jack paid $1.085(.90P)$, whereas Jill paid $.90(1.085P)$. The quantities are equal (C).

   **Use TACTIC 2, Chapter 9, and choose a convenient number: assume the TV cost $100. Jack paid $90 plus $7.65 tax (8.5% of $90) for a total of $97.65. Jill's cashier rang up $100 plus $8.50 tax and then deducted $10.85 (10% of $108.50) for a final cost of $97.65.

8. **(A)** Quantity A: Since the hypotenuse is 2, the length of each leg is $\frac{2}{\sqrt{2}} = \sqrt{2}$, and the area is $\frac{1}{2}(\sqrt{2})(\sqrt{2}) = \frac{1}{2}(2) = 1$.

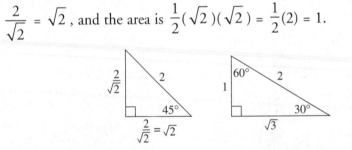

   Quantity B: Since the hypotenuse is 2, the shorter leg is 1, the longer leg is $\sqrt{3}$, and the area is $\frac{1}{2}(1)(\sqrt{3}) = \frac{\sqrt{3}}{2}$, which is less than 1 because $\sqrt{3}$ is less than 2.

   Quantity A is greater.

9. **(D)** Since $400 = 12 \times 33 + 4$, 100 months is 4 months more than 33 years. 33 years from June it will again be June, and 4 months later it will be October. [See Section 11-P]

   **Look for a pattern. Since there are 12 months in a year, after every 12 months it will again be June; i.e., it will be June after 12, 24, 36, 48,..., 120,..., 360 months. So, 396 (33×12) months from now, it will again be June. Count 4 more months to October.

10. $\frac{4}{5}$ Use TACTIC 3 in Chapter 8: pick an easy-to-use number. Since $\frac{5}{9}$ of the members are boys, assume there are 9 members, 5 of whom are boys. Then the other 4 are girls, and the ratio of girls to boys is 4 to 5, or $\frac{4}{5}$.

11. **27** Since the surface area of the cube is 54, the area of each of the six square faces is: $54 \div 6 = 9$. Therefore, each edge is 3, and the volume is $3^3 = 27$.

12. **(A)** Use TACTIC 1 in Chapter 7: draw a diagram. In the figure below, form rectangle *BCDE* by drawing $DE \perp AB$.

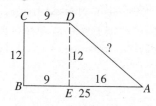

Then, *BE* = 9, *AE* = 16, and *DE* = 12. Finally, *DA* = 20, because right triangle *AED* is a 3-4-5 triangle in which each side is multiplied by 4. If you don't realize that, use the Pythagorean theorem to get *DA*:

$$(DA)^2 = (AE)^2 + (DE)^2 = 256 + 144 = 400 \Rightarrow DA = 20.$$

13. **(A)(B)(C)(D)**

- If m$\angle A$ = 90°, then the area of triangle *ABC* is $\frac{1}{2}(2)(2) = 2$.

  So choice D is possible.

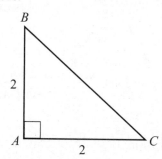

- If angle *A* is either acute or obtuse and we treat *AC* as the base of the triangle, then the height, *h*, is less than 2, and so

$$A = \frac{1}{2}(b)(h) = \frac{1}{2}(2)(h) = h < 2.$$

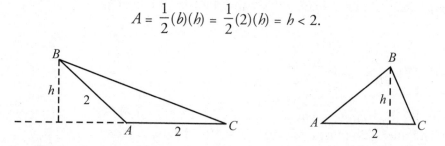

In fact, *h* can be any positive number less than 2. So choices A, B, and C are also possible. Since *h* cannot be greater than 2, choices E and F are *not* possible.

14. **(D)** From the bottom graph, we can estimate the percentage distribution of total enrollment to be:

Public 4-year   41%   Private 4-year   21%
Public 2-year   37%   Private 2-year   1%
Total public   78%   Total private   22%

$78 \div 22 \approx 3.5$, so there were 3.5 times as many students enrolled in public institutions as private ones.

15. **(E)** In 1972, enrollment in private 4-year institutions was approximately 1,100,000 (22% of the total enrollment of 5,000,000). By 1995, the index for private 4-year institutions had increased from 80 to 120, a 50% increase. Therefore, the number of private 4-year students enrolled in 1995 was approximately 1,650,000 (50% more than the 1,100,000 students enrolled in 1972).

16. **(A)(B)(C)**
    - From the top graph, we see that for every 100 students enrolled in private 2-year institutions in 1981, the number increased to about 110 in 1983, stayed between 105 and 110 until 1986, and then dropped back to 100 in 1987. Statement A is true.
    - From the bottom graph, we see that the percentage of students enrolled in 2-year private institutions remained constant at about 2% from 1981 to 1987. Statement B is true.
    -

	1972	1995
Public 2-year	28%	37%
Private 2-year	1%	1%
Total	29%	38%

The percent increase from 29 to 38 is $\dfrac{\text{actual increase}}{\text{original amount}} \times 100\% =$

$\dfrac{9}{29} \times 100\% = 31\%$, well more than 25%. Statement C is true.

17. **(A)** Since $C = 2\pi r$, then $r = \dfrac{C}{2\pi}$, and the area of the circle is

$$\pi r^2 = \pi \left(\frac{C}{2\pi} \right)^2 = \pi \left(\frac{C^2}{4\pi^2} \right) = \frac{C^2}{4\pi}$$

18. **(B)** By the triangle inequality (KEY FACTS J12 and J13),
    - The third side must be *less* than 9 + 10 = 19. (C is false.)
    - The third side must be *greater* than 10 − 9 = 1. (A is false.)
    - *Any* number between 1 and 19 could be the length of the third side. (B is true.)

19. **(E)** Since p pencils cost c cents, each pencil costs $\dfrac{c}{p}$ cents. By dividing the number of cents we have by $\dfrac{c}{p}$, we find out how many pencils we can buy.

Since d dollars equals $100d$ cents, we divide $100d$ by $\dfrac{c}{p}$, which is equivalent to multiplying $100d$ by $\dfrac{p}{c}$: $100d\left(\dfrac{p}{c}\right) = \dfrac{100dp}{c}$.

You will probably prefer the alternate solution below.

**Use TACTIC 2, Chapter 9. Assume 2 pencils cost 10 cents. So, pencils cost 5 cents each or 20 for one dollar. So, for 3 dollars, we can buy 60 pencils. Which of the choices equals 60 when $p = 2$, $c = 10$, and $d = 3$?

Only $\dfrac{100dp}{c}$.

20. **(A)** If a student earned a grade of g, she missed $(100 - g)$ points. In adjusting the grades, the teacher decided to deduct only half that number: $\dfrac{100 - g}{2}$.

So the student's new grade was $100 - \left(\dfrac{100 - g}{2}\right) = 100 - 50 + \dfrac{g}{2} = 50 + \dfrac{g}{2}$.

Since this was done to each student's grade, the effect on the average was exactly the same.

The new average was $50 + \dfrac{A}{2}$.

Section 4—Verbal Reasoning

1. **(B)(D)** The spread of genetically engineered matter has become "a significant practical problem." Thus, it is no longer merely a *theoretical* (hypothetical; lacking practical application) or *abstract* worry.

2. **(A)(E)** Under certain circumstances scientists attack each other with *ad hominem* arguments (personal attacks) and shameless appeals to authority. When is this likely to occur? When facts are *established* or *demonstrable* or *ineluctable* (unavoidable) or *relevant*? Hardly. Under such circumstances they would rely on the facts to establish their case. It is when facts prove *elusive* (hard to pin down) or *uncertain* that they lose control and, in doing so, abandon their pretense of objectivity.

3. **(C)(E)** If "you may wonder" how the expert reaches his conclusions, it appears that it is questionable to rely on teeth for guidance in interpreting fossils. Choices C and E, *flimsy* and *inadequate*, create the element of doubt that the clause tries to develop. Choice D, *specious*, also creates an element of doubt; however, nothing in the context justifies the idea that the reasoning is specious or false.

Note that here you are dealing with an extended metaphor. Picture yourself hanging a heavy winter coat on a slim wooden peg. Wouldn't you worry that the peg might prove inadequate or flimsy?

4. **(A)(D)** If armed forces take over a country's administration, then that country is under military law rather than constitutional law. However, in this military takeover, the constitution has *not* been abolished or stamped out. Instead, some of its provisions merely have been *suspended* (rendered inoperative for a time) or *put in abeyance* (temporarily set aside).

5. **(C)(D)** The second clause presents an example of literary mockery or sarcastic jesting. The abstract idea of preserving a nugget of pure truth is appealing; the concrete example of setting it up on the mantelpiece *makes light of* or *mocks* the whole idea.

6. **(C)(E)** The passage asserts that literary scholars now *reject* the idea that Elizabethan drama has it roots in classical Greek and Roman drama. Therefore, it would be inconsistent with the passage to assert Statement C ("Although Elizabethan drama deals with English subject matter, it derives its form and method solely from classical Greek and Roman theater"). Likewise, it would be inconsistent with the passage to assert Statement E ("Modern theater scholars view Elizabethan drama as a direct offshoot of Greek and Roman dramatic traditions").

7. **(E)** Choice E does not weaken the argument, because the argument specifically calls for "a truly broad, liberal education." Choice E, however, merely refers to "the traditional liberal education," which is not necessarily the truly broad and liberal education the author has in mind.

   Choice A weakens the argument: it exposes the argument's failure to acknowledge that many specific problems may be solved by persons who don't understand the broad picture.

   Choice B weakens the argument: it exposes the assumption that because generalists are needed, *all* persons should be educated as generalists.

   Choice C weakens the argument: it exposes the false dichotomy between specialization and seeing the broad picture.

   Choice D weakens the argument: it attacks the implicit assumption that fewer specialists are needed.

8. **(E)** The last sentence points out that Du Bois originally agreed with Washington's program.

   Choice A is incorrect. Nothing in the passage suggests that Du Bois sacrificed effective strategies out of a desire to try something new.

   Choice B is incorrect. Du Bois gained in influence, effectively winning away large numbers of blacks from Washington's policies.

   Choice C is incorrect. Du Bois's quickness to depart from conventional black wisdom when it proved inadequate to the task of advancing the race shows him to be well able to change with the times.

   Choice D is incorrect. Washington, not Du Bois, is described as seeking the good will of powerful whites.

9. **(C)** The author does *not* portray Washington as versatile. Instead, he portrays Du Bois as versatile.

Choice A is incorrect. The author portrays Washington as submissive to the majority; he shows him teaching blacks not to protest.

Choice B is incorrect. The author portrays Washington as concerned with financial success; he shows him advocating property accumulation.

Choice D is incorrect. The author portrays Washington as traditional in preaching industry; he shows him advocating hard work.

Choice E is incorrect. The author portrays Washington as respectful of authority; he shows him deferring to powerful whites.

10. **(D)** Although the author points out that Du Bois's methods led him into conflicts, he describes Du Bois as "often . . . well in advance of his contemporaries" and stresses that his motives for departing from the mainstream were admirable. Thus, his attitude can best be described as *approving*.

11. **(B)** The fact that Monet's home was filled to overflowing with works by Japanese artists would be sufficient reason for someone to *attest* (declare; bear witness) that Japanese prints were Monet's passion.

12. **(C)(E)** The key phrase here is "Breaking with established musical traditions." Someone who breaks with traditions is by definition *iconoclastic* (unorthodox; radical; irreverent of tradition). The musical creations of an iconoclastic composer would most likely be *heterodox* or unorthodox as well.

13. **(B)(F)** A disease in a *latent* state has yet to manifest itself and emerge into view. Therefore it is almost impossible to determine its existence by *observation*.

    The key phrase here is "almost impossible to determine its existence." By its very nature, it would *not* be almost impossible to determine the existence of a disease in its *critical* (acute) or *overt* (apparent; unconcealed) state.

14. **(A)(E)** The key phrase here is "his more conventional colleagues." The paleontologist described here is less conventional than his colleagues. What then is his relationship to orthodoxy (conventionality)? He has departed from conventional ways, has made a *break with* orthodoxy. Therefore, his more conventional colleagues would *contest* (challenge) the evidence he has gathered.

15. **(A)(F)** Here the task is to determine the communal reaction to crime. The writer maintains that the criminal justice system of punishments allows the community to purge itself of its anger, its sense of *outrage* at the criminal's acts. Thus, it provides a *catharsis* or purgation for the community.

    It is unlikely that an essential purpose of the criminal justice system would be the provision of either a *disclaimer* (denial or disavowal, as in disavowing responsibility for a legal claim) or a *prototype* (model; exemplar).

16. **(B)(E)** The key word here is *assailed*. Housman is attacking his rival. Thus he is in the tradition of scholarly *invective* (vehement verbal attack), criticizing his foe for turning to manuscripts merely for confirmation or support of old theories and not for enlightenment or *illumination*. Again, note the use of figurative language, in this case the simile of the drunkard.

17. **(A)** The capacity of polar bears to scent prey at a great distance is their *faculty* or ability to do so. Note that *faculty* here is being used with a secondary meaning.

18. **(E)** The author first states that the reason for bioluminescence in underwater microorganisms is obscure and then proceeds to enumerate various hypotheses.

19. **(B)** The author does not deny that predators make use of bioluminescence in locating their prey. Instead, he gives an example of human predators (fishers) who are drawn to their prey (the fish that prey on plankton) by the luminescence of the plankton.

20. **(B)** As the previous answer makes clear, the phenomenon of plankton bioluminescence does have practical applications. It is a valuable tool for fisheries interested in increasing their catch of fish that prey on plankton.

Section 5—Quantitative Ability

Two asterisks (**) indicate an alternative method of solving.

1. **(A)** $\pi \approx 3.14$ and $\sqrt{10} \approx 3.16$. So $\pi < \sqrt{10}$.

   For any positive numbers a and b, if $a < b$, then $\frac{1}{a} > \frac{1}{b}$.

   So $\frac{1}{\pi} > \frac{1}{\sqrt{10}}$.

2. **(B)** It is irrelevant that $700 < n < 800$. Every factor of n is a factor of $2n$, but 2 is a prime factor of $2n$, which is not a factor of n (since n is odd). $2n$ has one more prime factor than n. Quantity B is greater.

3. **(B)** Since $x < y$, the average of x and y is less than y, so having another y raises the average. Quantity B is greater.
   ** Plug in the numbers: say $x = 2$ and $y = 4$.
   Quantity A: the average of 2 and 4 is 3.
   Quantity B: the average of 2, 4, and 4 is $10 \div 3 = 3.333$, which is more than 3; the second 4 raised the average.

4. **(A)** In any triangle, if one side is longer than a second side, the angle opposite the longer side is greater than the angle opposite the shorter side, so $c > d$. Quantity A is greater. (It is irrelevant that the third angle is $135°$.)

5. **(B)**

   Quantity A: $a\%$ of $\frac{1}{b} = \frac{a}{100} \times \frac{1}{b} = \frac{a}{100b} = \frac{1}{100} \times \frac{a}{b}$

   Quantity B: $a\%$ of $\frac{1}{a} = \frac{b}{100} \times \frac{1}{a} = \frac{b}{100a} = \frac{1}{100} \times \frac{b}{a}$

   Since a and b are positive and $b > a$, $\frac{b}{a} > 1$, and $\frac{a}{b} < 1$.

   So Quantity B is greater.

6. **(D)** Could x and y be equal? Yes, the two small triangles could be right triangles, and x and y could each be 40. Must they be equal? No, see the figure below, in which clearly $x < y$. Neither quantity is *always* greater, and the quantities are not *always* equal.

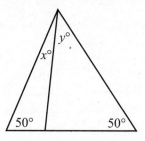

7. **(B)** Don't waste time using the slope formula; just make a quick sketch.

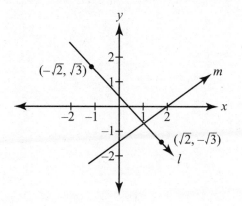

Note that l slopes downward, so its slope is negative, whereas m slopes upward, so its slope is positive. Quantity B is greater.

8. **(D)** The markings in the five angles are irrelevant. The sum of the five angles is 360°, and $360 \div 5 = 72$.

   **If you solve the equation $a + 2a + 3a + 3a + 3a = 360$, you get that $12a = 360 \Rightarrow a = 30$, and so the degree measures of the five angles are 30, 60, 90, 90, and 90. You would then find that the average of those five numbers is 72; but all of that is a waste of time.

9. **(B)** On her six tests combined, Camille earned a total of $6 \times 75 = 450$ points. The total of her five best grades is $5 \times 85 = 425$ points, so her lowest grade was $450 - 425 = 25$.

   **Assume that Camille's five best grades were each 85. Then each one has a deviation of 10 points above the average of 75, and the total deviation above 75 is $5 \times 10 = 50$ points. Therefore, her one bad grade must have been 50 points below 75.

10. **(B)(C)(D)(E)(F)** The perimeter of a rectangle whose area is 40 can be as large as we like (for example, if the length is 4,000 and the width is 0.01, the perimeter is 8,000.02). However, the perimeter is the smallest when the rectangle is a square, in which case each side is $\sqrt{40}$ and the perimeter is

   $4\sqrt{40}$. Since $\sqrt{40} > 6$, the perimeter is greater than $4 \times 6 = 24$.

   So Choice A, 20, is not possible. All of the other choices are possible.

11. **(B)(D)** Rewriting the equation of the given line, $2x + 3y = 4$, in slope-intercept form, we get that $y = -\frac{2}{3}x + \frac{4}{3}$. So the slope of the given line is $-\frac{2}{3}$.

The slope of any line perpendicular to that line must have a slope of $\frac{3}{2}$, the negative reciprocal of $-\frac{2}{3}$.

Rewrite each of the answer choices in slope-intercept form, and see which ones also have a slope of $\frac{3}{2}$.

A: $y = -\frac{3}{2}x + 2$

B: $y = \frac{3}{2}x - 2$

C: $y = \frac{2}{3}x - \frac{4}{3}$

D: $y = \frac{3}{2}x - 2$

E: $y = \frac{2}{3}x + \frac{4}{3}$

Only choices B and D are the equations of lines whose slope is $\frac{3}{2}$.

12. **(E)** Since the diameter of the circle is 20, the radius is 10 and the area is 100π. Since the area of the shaded region is 80π, it is $\frac{80}{100} = \frac{4}{5}$ of the circle, and the white area is $\frac{1}{5}$ of the circle. So the sum of the measures of the two white central angles is $\frac{1}{5}$ of 360°, or 72°. The sum of the measures of all six angles in the two triangles is 360°, so $a + b + c + d + 72 = 360 \Rightarrow a + b + c + d =$ **288**.

13. $\frac{\mathbf{3}}{\mathbf{5}}$ The five numbers are 3, 13, 23, 33, and 43, four of which are prime (all except 33). So the probability that the first number drawn is prime is $\frac{4}{5}$.

If the first number is prime, then three of the remaining four numbers are prime, and the probability is $\frac{3}{4}$ that the second number will be prime.

P(both numbers are prime) =

P(1st number is prime) $\times$ P(2nd number is prime) $= \dfrac{4}{5} \times \dfrac{3}{4} = \dfrac{3}{5}$.

14. **(B)** From 1994 to 1996 there was a 9.4% decrease in the number of vehicles stolen. Since 9.4% of 1,000,000 = 94,000, the number of vehicles stolen in 1996 was 1,000,000 – 94,000 = 906,000. If you can't solve problems such as this, you have to guess. But since the number of stolen vehicles is clearly decreasing, be sure to eliminate Choices D and E first.

15. **(C)** For simplicity, assume that 1000 vehicles were stolen in 1994. By 1997, the number had decreased by 12.0% to 880 (12% of 1000 = 120, and 1000 – 120 = 880); by 1998, the number had decreased 19.4% to 806 (19.4% of 1000 = 194 and 1000 – 194 = 806). So from 1997 to 1998, the number of vehicles stolen decreased by 74 from 880 to 806. This represents a decrease of $\dfrac{74}{880} = .084 = 8.4\%$.

16. **(D)** Simplify the situation by assuming that in 1994 the population was 100,000 and there were 1000 vehicles stolen. As in the solution to question 15, in 1998 the number of stolen vehicles was 806. At the same time, the number of thefts per 100,000 inhabitants decreased 22.4% from 1000 to 776. So if there were 776 vehicles stolen for every 100,000 inhabitants, and 806 cars were stolen, the number of inhabitants must have increased. To know by how much, solve the proportion: $\dfrac{776}{100,000} = \dfrac{806}{x}$. Cross-multiplying, we get

$776x = 80,600,000$.

So, $x = 103,800$. Then for every 100,000 inhabitants in 1994, there were 103,800 in 1998, an increase of 3.8%.

17. **–9.9**
- Since the average of the 5 numbers v, w, x, y, and z is 12.3, their sum is $5 \times 12.3 = 61.5$.
- Since the average of v and w is 45.6, their sum is $2 \times 45.6 = 91.2$.
- Then $x + y + z = 61.5 - 91.2 = -29.7$, and $\dfrac{x+y+z}{3} = \dfrac{-29.7}{3} = -9.9$.

18. **(A)** Even if you can do the algebra, this type of problem is easier if you plug in some easy-to-use numbers, Assume that there are 100 girls and 50 boys on staff and that 20% of the girls and 10% of the boys attended the meeting. Then, 20 girls and 5 boys were there, and 5 is 20% of 25, the total number attending.

Of course, you *can* do this algebraically. If x represents the number of boys on staff, then $2x$ is the number of girls. If $y\%$ of the boys attended the meeting, then $2y\%$ of the girls did. So, the number of boys attending was

$x\left(\dfrac{y}{100}\right) = \dfrac{xy}{100}$, whereas the number of girls attending was $2x\left(\dfrac{2y}{100}\right) = \dfrac{4xy}{100}$.

Therefore, there were 4 times as many girls in attendance as boys:

$\frac{4}{5}$ of those at the meeting were girls and $\frac{1}{5}$ or 20% were boys.

19. **96** Since 4 boys can shovel the driveway in 2 hours or $2 \times 60 = 120$ minutes, the job takes $4 \times 120 = 480$ boy-minutes to complete. Therefore, 5 boys

will need $\dfrac{480 \text{ boy-minutes}}{5 \text{ boys}} = 96$ minutes.

20. **(D)** Make a table to determine Roberto's and Juan's ages. Let x represent Juan's age in 1950, and fill in the table as shown.

	1950	1955
Roberto	$4x$	$4x + 5$
Juan	x	$x + 5$

In 1955, Roberto was 3 times as old as Juan, so $4x + 5 = 3(x + 5) = 3x + 15$, and so $x = 10$. Therefore, in 1950, Juan was 10 and Roberto was 40. Because Roberto is 30 years older than Juan, Roberto was 30 when Rob was born.

Answer Sheet
MODEL TEST 2

Section 2

1 Ⓐ Ⓑ Ⓒ Ⓓ Ⓔ Ⓕ   6 Ⓐ Ⓑ Ⓒ Ⓓ Ⓔ Ⓕ   11 Ⓐ Ⓑ Ⓒ Ⓓ Ⓔ Ⓕ   16 Ⓐ Ⓑ Ⓒ Ⓓ Ⓔ

2 Ⓐ Ⓑ Ⓒ Ⓓ Ⓔ Ⓕ   7 Ⓐ Ⓑ Ⓒ Ⓓ Ⓔ   12 Ⓐ Ⓑ Ⓒ Ⓓ Ⓔ Ⓕ   17 Ⓐ Ⓑ Ⓒ

3 Ⓐ Ⓑ Ⓒ Ⓓ Ⓔ Ⓕ   8 Ⓐ Ⓑ Ⓒ Ⓓ Ⓔ   13 Ⓐ Ⓑ Ⓒ Ⓓ Ⓔ Ⓕ   18 Ⓐ Ⓑ Ⓒ Ⓓ Ⓔ

4 Ⓐ Ⓑ Ⓒ Ⓓ Ⓔ Ⓕ   9 Ⓐ Ⓑ Ⓒ Ⓓ Ⓔ   14 Ⓐ Ⓑ Ⓒ Ⓓ Ⓔ Ⓕ   19 Ⓐ Ⓑ Ⓒ Ⓓ Ⓔ

5 Ⓐ Ⓑ Ⓒ Ⓓ Ⓔ Ⓕ   10 Ⓐ Ⓑ Ⓒ Ⓓ Ⓔ   15 Ⓐ Ⓑ Ⓒ Ⓓ Ⓔ Ⓕ   20 Ⓐ Ⓑ Ⓒ Ⓓ Ⓔ
                                                Ⓖ Ⓗ Ⓘ

Section 3

1 Ⓐ Ⓑ Ⓒ Ⓓ   6 Ⓐ Ⓑ Ⓒ Ⓓ   12 Ⓐ Ⓑ Ⓒ Ⓓ Ⓔ   17 Ⓐ Ⓑ Ⓒ Ⓓ Ⓔ

2 Ⓐ Ⓑ Ⓒ Ⓓ   7 Ⓐ Ⓑ Ⓒ Ⓓ   13 [____]   18 Ⓐ Ⓑ Ⓒ Ⓓ Ⓔ

3 Ⓐ Ⓑ Ⓒ Ⓓ   8 Ⓐ Ⓑ Ⓒ Ⓓ   14 Ⓐ Ⓑ Ⓒ Ⓓ Ⓔ   19 Ⓐ Ⓑ Ⓒ Ⓓ Ⓔ

4 Ⓐ Ⓑ Ⓒ Ⓓ   9 Ⓐ Ⓑ Ⓒ Ⓓ Ⓔ   15 Ⓐ Ⓑ Ⓒ Ⓓ Ⓔ   20 [____]

5 Ⓐ Ⓑ Ⓒ Ⓓ   10 Ⓐ Ⓑ Ⓒ Ⓓ Ⓔ   16 [____]   [____]

                   11 [____]

                      [____]

Answer Sheet

MODEL TEST 2

Section 4

1 Ⓐ Ⓑ Ⓒ Ⓓ Ⓔ Ⓕ   6 Ⓐ Ⓑ Ⓒ Ⓓ Ⓔ Ⓕ   11 Ⓐ Ⓑ Ⓒ Ⓓ Ⓔ Ⓕ   16 Ⓐ Ⓑ Ⓒ Ⓓ Ⓔ

2 Ⓐ Ⓑ Ⓒ Ⓓ Ⓔ Ⓕ   7 Ⓐ Ⓑ Ⓒ Ⓓ Ⓔ   12 Ⓐ Ⓑ Ⓒ Ⓓ Ⓔ Ⓕ   17 Ⓐ Ⓑ Ⓒ Ⓓ Ⓔ

3 Ⓐ Ⓑ Ⓒ Ⓓ Ⓔ Ⓕ   8 Ⓐ Ⓑ Ⓒ Ⓓ Ⓔ   13 Ⓐ Ⓑ Ⓒ Ⓓ Ⓔ Ⓕ   18 Ⓐ Ⓑ Ⓒ Ⓓ Ⓔ

4 Ⓐ Ⓑ Ⓒ Ⓓ Ⓔ Ⓕ   9 Ⓐ Ⓑ Ⓒ Ⓓ Ⓔ   14 Ⓐ Ⓑ Ⓒ Ⓓ Ⓔ Ⓕ   19 Ⓐ Ⓑ Ⓒ Ⓓ Ⓔ

5 Ⓐ Ⓑ Ⓒ Ⓓ Ⓔ Ⓕ   10 Ⓐ Ⓑ Ⓒ Ⓓ Ⓔ   15 Ⓐ Ⓑ Ⓒ Ⓓ Ⓔ   20 Ⓐ Ⓑ Ⓒ Ⓓ Ⓔ

Section 5

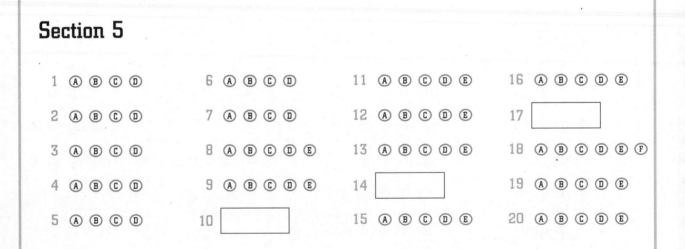

1 Ⓐ Ⓑ Ⓒ Ⓓ   6 Ⓐ Ⓑ Ⓒ Ⓓ   11 Ⓐ Ⓑ Ⓒ Ⓓ Ⓔ   16 Ⓐ Ⓑ Ⓒ Ⓓ Ⓔ

2 Ⓐ Ⓑ Ⓒ Ⓓ   7 Ⓐ Ⓑ Ⓒ Ⓓ   12 Ⓐ Ⓑ Ⓒ Ⓓ Ⓔ   17 [   ]

3 Ⓐ Ⓑ Ⓒ Ⓓ   8 Ⓐ Ⓑ Ⓒ Ⓓ Ⓔ   13 Ⓐ Ⓑ Ⓒ Ⓓ Ⓔ   18 Ⓐ Ⓑ Ⓒ Ⓓ Ⓔ Ⓕ

4 Ⓐ Ⓑ Ⓒ Ⓓ   9 Ⓐ Ⓑ Ⓒ Ⓓ Ⓔ   14 [   ]   19 Ⓐ Ⓑ Ⓒ Ⓓ Ⓔ

5 Ⓐ Ⓑ Ⓒ Ⓓ   10 [   ]   15 Ⓐ Ⓑ Ⓒ Ⓓ Ⓔ   20 Ⓐ Ⓑ Ⓒ Ⓓ Ⓔ

Answer Sheet

Model Test 2

Section 1 Analytical Writing

TIME: 60 MINUTES—2 WRITING TASKS

Task 1: Issue Exploration
30 MINUTES

Directions: In 30 minutes, compose an essay on the following topic . You may not write on any other topic. Write your essay on the lined page that follows.

The topic is presented in a one- to two-sentence quotation commenting on an issue of general concern. Your essay may support, refute, or qualify the views expressed in the quotation. Whatever you write, however, must be relevant to the issue under discussion, and you must support your viewpoint with reasons and examples derived from your studies and/or experience.

Faculty members from various institutions will evaluate your essay, judging it on the basis of your skill in the following areas.

- Analysis of the quotation's implications
- Organization and articulation of your ideas
- Use of relevant examples and arguments to support your case
- Handling of the mechanics of standard written English

Topic

"If rituals did not exist, we would have to invent them. We need ceremonies and rituals to help us define ourselves socially and culturally."

Task 2: Argument Analysis
30 MINUTES

Directions: In 30 minutes, prepare a critical analysis of an argument expressed in a short paragraph. You may not offer an analysis of any other argument. Write your essay on the lined page that follows.

As you critique the argument, think about the author's underlying assumptions. Ask yourself whether any of them are questionable. Also evaluate any evidence the author brings up. Ask yourself whether it actually supports the author's conclusion.

In your analysis, you may suggest additional kinds of evidence to reinforce the author's argument. You may also suggest methods to refute the argument, or additional data that might be useful to you as you assess the soundness of the argument. *You may **not**, however, present your personal views on the topic.* Your job is to analyze the elements of an argument, not to support or contradict that argument.

Faculty members from various institutions will judge your essay, assessing it on the basis of your skill in the following areas:

- Identification and assessment of the argument's main elements
- Organization and articulation of your thoughts
- Use of relevant examples and arguments to support your case
- Handling of the mechanics of standard written English

Topic

The following appeared in a letter to the editor in the journal *Health Matters.*

Statistics gathered over the past three decades show that the death rate is higher among those who do not have jobs than among those with regular employment. Unemployment, just like heart disease and cancer, is a significant health issue. While many health care advocates promote increased government funding for medical research and public health care, it would be folly to increase government spending if doing so were to affect the nation's economy adversely and ultimately cause a rise in unemployment. A healthy economy means healthy citizens.

Section 2 Verbal Reasoning

TIME: 30 MINUTES—20 QUESTIONS

Directions: For each of the following sentences, select the **two** answers of the six choices given that, when substituted in the sentence, both logically complete the sentence as a whole **and** create sentences that are equivalent to one another in meaning.

Questions 1–6

1. Given the human tendency to suspect and disbelieve in processes that take place below the level of consciousness, it is unsurprising that many students of organizational development _____ the impact of the unconscious on business and political behavior and social dynamics.

   [A] intimate

   [B] acclaim

   [C] applaud

   [D] deny

   [E] gainsay

   [F] acknowledge

2. Although the young author had the reputation of being excessively taciturn, he seemed not at all _____ conversation.

   [A] inclined to

   [B] averse from

   [C] capable of

   [D] skilled at

   [E] opposed to

   [F] enamored of

3. To Mrs. Trollope, writing in the 1830s, nothing more clearly illustrated the _____ pervading "the land of the free" than the institution of slavery.

   [A] sanctimoniousness

   [B] conservatism

   [C] hypocrisy

   [D] rationality

   [E] liberality

   [F] orthodoxy

4. To someone as phlegmatic as Paul, it was a shock to find himself attracted to a woman so clearly his opposite in every way: a passionate activist, as _____ in her enthusiasms as in her dislikes.

   [A] dogmatic

   [B] ardent

   [C] haphazard

   [D] wholehearted

   [E] abstracted

   [F] mistaken

5. Soap operas and situation comedies, though given to distortion, are so derivative of contemporary culture that they are inestimable _____ the attitudes and values of our society in any particular decade.

   A contraventions of

   B antidotes to

   C indices of

   D prerequisites for

   E evidence of

   F determinants of

6. Slander is like counterfeit money: many people who would not coin it _____ without qualms.

   A hoard it

   B invest it

   C withdraw it

   D circulate it

   E spread it around

   F complain about it

Directions: The next questions are based on the content of the following passage. Read the passage and then determine the best answer choice for each question. Base your choice on what this passage *states directly* or *implies*, not on any information you may have gained elsewhere.

For each of Questions 7–10, select *one* answer choice unless otherwise instructed.

Questions 7–10 are based on the following passage.

With Meredith's *The Egoist* we enter into a critical problem that we have not yet before faced in these studies. That is the problem
Line offered by a writer of recognizably impressive
(5) stature, whose work is informed by a muscular intelligence, whose language has splendor, whose "view of life" wins our respect, and yet for whom we are at best able to feel only a passive appreciation which amounts, prac-
(10) tically, to indifference. We should be unjust to Meredith and to criticism if we should, giving in to the inertia of indifference, simply avoid dealing with him and thus avoid the problem along with him. He does not
(15) "speak to us," we might say; his meaning is not a "meaning for us"; he "leaves us cold." But do not the challenge and the excitement of the critical problem as such lie in that ambivalence of attitude which allows us to
(20) recognize the intelligence and even the splendor of Meredith's work, while, at the same time, we experience a lack of sympathy, a failure of any enthusiasm of response?

7. According to the passage, the work of Meredith is noteworthy for its elements of

   Ⓐ sensibility and artistic fervor

   Ⓑ ambivalence and moral ambiguity

   Ⓒ tension and sense of vitality

   Ⓓ brilliance and linguistic grandeur

   Ⓔ wit and whimsical frivolity

8. All of the following can be found in the author's discussion of Meredith EXCEPT

   Ⓐ an indication of Meredith's customary effect on readers

   Ⓑ an enumeration of the admirable qualities in his work

   Ⓒ a selection of hypothetical comments at Meredith's expense

   Ⓓ an analysis of the critical ramifications of Meredith's effect on readers

   Ⓔ a refutation of the claim that Meredith evokes no sympathy

9. It can be inferred from the passage that the author finds the prospect of appraising Meredith's work critically to be
   Ⓐ counterproductive
   Ⓑ overly formidable
   Ⓒ somewhat tolerable
   Ⓓ markedly unpalatable
   Ⓔ clearly invigorating

10. It can be inferred from the passage that the author would be most likely to agree with which of the following statements about the role of criticism?
    Ⓐ Its prime office should be to make our enjoyment of the things that feed the mind as conscious as possible.
    Ⓑ It should be a disinterested endeavor to learn and propagate the best that is known and thought in the world.
    Ⓒ It should enable us to go beyond personal prejudice to appreciate the virtues of works antipathetic to our own tastes.
    Ⓓ It should dwell upon excellencies rather than imperfections, ignoring such deficiencies as irrelevant.
    Ⓔ It should strive both to purify literature and to elevate the literary standards of the reading public.

Directions: Each of the following sentences or groups of sentences contains one, two, or three blanks. These blanks signify that a word or set of words has been left out. Below each sentence are columns of words or sets of words. For each blank, pick the *one* word or set of words from the corresponding column that *best* completes the text.

11. Whereas off-Broadway theatre over the past several seasons has clearly (i) _____ a talent for experimentation and improvisation, one deficiency in the commercial stage of late has been its marked incapacity for (ii) _____.

Blank (i)
Ⓐ manifested
Ⓑ lampooned
Ⓒ disavowed

Blank (ii)
Ⓓ orthodoxy
Ⓔ spontaneity
Ⓕ burlesque

12. Although she had received many compliments for her (i) _____ in debate, at her inauguration as president of the student body she was surprisingly (ii) _____.

Blank (i)
Ⓐ candor
Ⓑ analysis
Ⓒ fluency

Blank (ii)
Ⓓ inarticulate
Ⓔ inattentive
Ⓕ inconsiderate

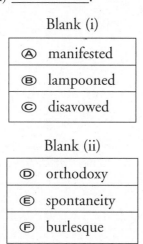

Model Test 2

13. Even though their subjects and approaches are quite different, each of these filmmakers takes great care to (i) _____ a strong sense of place. In this way, they make their films intimate portraits of not only the characters but also the (ii) _____.

Blank (i)

Ⓐ reject
Ⓑ impart
Ⓒ vitiate

Blank (ii)

Ⓓ settings they emulate
Ⓔ families they abandon
Ⓕ spaces they inhabit

14. In England after 1600, small bass viols called division viols began to (i) _____ larger consort basses. They remained the dominant viol size until they (ii) _____ during the eighteenth century.

Blank (i)

Ⓐ impede
Ⓑ displace
Ⓒ circumvent

Blank (ii)

Ⓓ went out of fashion
Ⓔ gained prominence
Ⓕ achieved closure

15. The perpetual spinning of particles is much like that of a top, with one significant (i) _____: unlike the top, the particles have no need to be wound up, for (ii) _____ is one of their (iii) _____ properties.

Blank (i)

Ⓐ difference
Ⓑ correlation
Ⓒ result

Blank (ii)

Ⓓ circuitousness
Ⓔ rotation
Ⓕ collision

Blank (iii)

Ⓖ intrinsic
Ⓗ hypothetical
Ⓘ intangible

Directions: The passage below is followed by questions based on its content. Once you have read the passage, select the answer choice that *best* answers each question. Answer all questions on the basis of what is *stated* or *implied* in the passage.

For each of Questions 16–20, select one answer choice unless otherwise instructed.

Questions 16–17 are based on the following passage.

How is a newborn star formed? For the answer to this question, we must look to the familiar physical concept of gravitational
Line instability. It is a simple concept, long
(5) known to scientists, having been first recognized by Isaac Newton in the late 1600s.

Let us envision a cloud of interstellar atoms and molecules, slightly admixed with dust. This cloud of interstellar gas is static
(10) and uniform. Suddenly, something occurs to disturb the gas, causing one small area within it to condense. As this small area increases in density, becoming slightly denser than the gas around it, its gravitational field likewise
(15) increases somewhat in strength. More matter now is attracted to the area, and its gravity becomes even stronger; as a result, it starts to contract, in process increasing in density even more. This in turn further increases its grav-
(20) ity, so that it accumulates still more matter and contracts further still. And so the process continues, until finally the small area of gas gives birth to a gravitationally bound object, a newborn star.

16. It can be inferred from the passage that the author views the information contained within it as
    Ⓐ controversial but irrefutable
    Ⓑ speculative and unprofitable
    Ⓒ uncomplicated and traditional
    Ⓓ original but obscure
    Ⓔ sadly lacking in elaboration

Directions: For the following question, consider each of the choices separately and select *all* that apply.

17. The author provides information that answers which of the following questions?
    A How does the small area's increasing density affect its gravitational field?
    B What causes the disturbance that changes the cloud from its original static state?
    C What is the end result of the gradually increasing concentration of the small area of gas?

Questions 18–20 are based on the following passage.

The Quechua world is submerged, so to speak, in a cosmic magma that weighs heavily upon it. It possesses the rare quality of
Line being as it were interjected into the midst of
(5) antagonistic forces, which in turn implies a whole body of social and aesthetic structures whose innermost meaning must be the administration of energy. This gives rise to the social organism known as the *ayllu*, the
(10) agrarian community that regulates the procurement of food. The *ayllu* formed the basic structure of the whole Inca empire.

The central idea of this organization was a kind of closed economy, just the opposite of
(15) our economic practices, which can be described as open. The closed economy rested on the fact that the Inca controlled both the production and consumption of food. When one adds to this fact the reli-
(20) gious ideas noted in the Quechua texts cited

by the chronicler Santa Cruz Pachacuti, one comes to the conclusion that in the Andean zone the margin of life was minimal and was made possible only by the system of
(25) magic the Quechua constructed through his religion.

Adversities, moreover, were numerous, for the harvest might fail at any time and bring starvation to millions. Hence the
(30) whole purpose of the Quechua administrative and ideological system was to carry on the arduous task of achieving *abundance* and staving off shortages. This kind of structure presupposes a state of unremitting anxiety,
(35) which could not be resolved by action. The Quechua could not do so because his primordial response to problems was the use of magic, that is, recourse to the unconscious for the solution of external problems. Thus
(40) the struggle against the world was a struggle against the dark depths of the Quechua's own psyche, where the solution was found. By overcoming the unconscious, the outer world was also vanquished.
(45) These considerations permit us to classify Quechua culture as absolutely static or, more accurately, as the expression of a mere state of being. Only in this way can we understand the refuge that it took in the germina-
(50) tive center of the cosmic *mandala* as revealed by Quechua art. The Quechua empire was nothing more than a *mandala,* for it was divided into four zones, with Cuzco in the center. Here the Quechua ensconced himself
(55) to contemplate the decline of the world as though it were caused by an alien and autonomous force.

18. The term "mandala" as used in the last paragraph most likely means
Ⓐ an agrarian community
Ⓑ a kind of superstition
Ⓒ a closed economic pattern
Ⓓ a philosophy or way of regarding the world
Ⓔ a figure composed of four divisions

19. The author implies that the Quechua world was
Ⓐ uncivilized
Ⓑ highly introspective
Ⓒ vitally energetic
Ⓓ free of major worries
Ⓔ well organized

20. With which of the following statements would the author most likely agree?
Ⓐ Only psychological solutions can remedy economic ills.
Ⓑ The Quechua were renowned for equanimity and unconcern.
Ⓒ The Quechua limited themselves to realizable goals.
Ⓓ Much of Quechua existence was harsh and frustrating.
Ⓔ Modern Western society should adopt some Quechua economic ideas.

Section 3 Quantitative Ability

TIME: 35 MINUTES—20 QUESTIONS

Directions: In each of Questions 1–8, there are two quantities—Quantity A and Quantity B. You are to compare those quantities, taking into consideration any additional information given. The correct answer to such a question is

Ⓐ if Quantity A is greater;
Ⓑ if Quantity B is greater;
Ⓒ if the two quantities are equal;
Ⓓ if it is impossible to determine which quantity is greater.

Note: The given information, if any, is always centered above the two quantities. In any question, if a symbol or letter appears more than once, it represents the same thing each time.

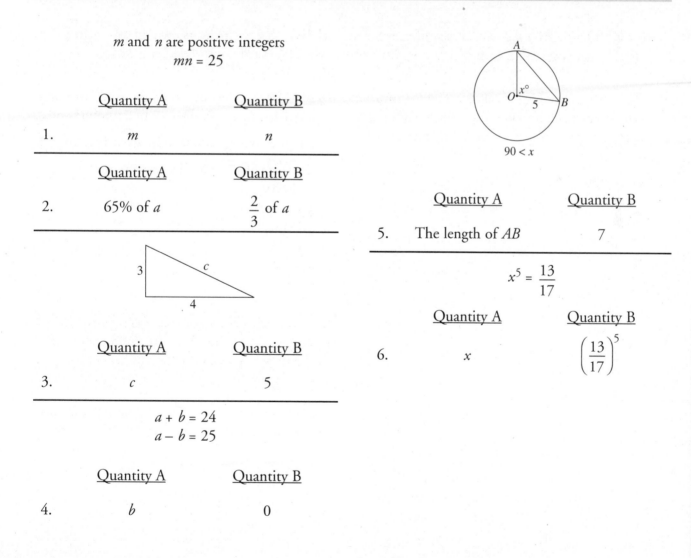

m and *n* are positive integers
$mn = 25$

	Quantity A	Quantity B
1.	m	n

	Quantity A	Quantity B
2.	65% of a	$\dfrac{2}{3}$ of a

	Quantity A	Quantity B
3.	c	5

$a + b = 24$
$a - b = 25$

	Quantity A	Quantity B
4.	b	0

$90 < x$

	Quantity A	Quantity B
5.	The length of AB	7

$x^5 = \dfrac{13}{17}$

	Quantity A	Quantity B
6.	x	$\left(\dfrac{13}{17}\right)^5$

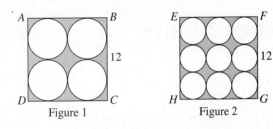

Figure 1   Figure 2

ABCD and *EFGH* are both squares, whose sides are 12. All the circles are tangent to one another and to the sides of the squares.

Quantity A	Quantity B
7. The area of the shaded region in Figure 1	The area of the shaded region in Figure 2

A school group charters three identical buses and occupies $\frac{4}{5}$ of the seats. After $\frac{1}{4}$ of the passengers leave, the remaining passengers use only two of the buses.

Quantity A	Quantity B
8. The fraction of the seats on the two buses that are now occupied	$\frac{9}{10}$

Directions: Questions 9–20 have three different formats. Unless a question has its own directions that specifically state otherwise, each question has five answer choices, exactly one of which is correct.

---

9. The Center City Little League is divided into *d* divisions. Each division has *t* teams, and each team has *p* players. How many players are there in the entire league?

Ⓐ $d + t + p$

Ⓑ dtp

Ⓒ $\dfrac{pt}{d}$

Ⓓ $\dfrac{dt}{p}$

Ⓔ $\dfrac{d}{pt}$

10. In 1980, the cost of *p* pounds of potatoes was *d* dollars. In 1990, the cost of 2*p* pounds of potatoes was $\frac{1}{2} d$ dollars. By what percent did the price of potatoes decrease from 1980 to 1990?

Ⓐ 25%
Ⓑ 50%
Ⓒ 75%
Ⓓ 100%
Ⓔ 400%

Directions: The answer to the following question is a fraction. Enter the numerator in the upper box and the denominator in the lower box.

---

11. A number *x* is chosen at random from the set of positive integers less than 10. What is the probability that $\frac{9}{x} > x$?

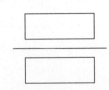

12. A bag contains 3 red, 4 white, and 5 blue marbles. Jason begins removing marbles from the bag at random, one at a time. What is the least number of marbles he must remove to be sure that he has at least one of each color?

Ⓐ 3
Ⓑ 6
Ⓒ 8
Ⓓ 10
Ⓔ 12

Directions: For the following question, enter your answer in the box.

13. Jordan has taken 5 math tests so far this semester. If he gets a 70 on his next test, it will lower the average (arithmetic mean) of his test scores by 4 points. What is his average now?

[ ]

Questions 14–16 refer to the following graphs.

Adult education participation rates in the past 12 months: 1991 and 1995

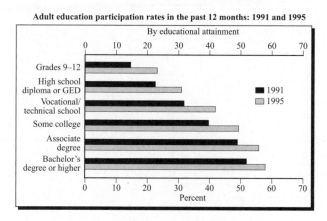

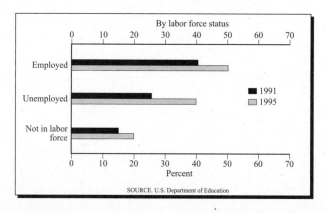

SOURCE. U.S. Department of Education

Directions: For the following question, consider each of the choices separately and select *all* that apply.

14. Which of the following is a valid conclusion from the graphs and the fact that the population of the United States was greater in 1995 than in 1991?

Indicate *all* such conclusions.

Ⓐ In 1991, adults whose highest degree was at least a bachelor's were more than twice as likely to participate in adult education than those whose highest educational attainment was a high school diploma or GED (high school equivalency diploma).

Ⓑ On a percentage basis, from 1991 to 1995, the greatest increase in the adult education participation rate was among those adults whose highest educational attainment was grades 9–12, without earning a high school diploma.

Ⓒ In 1995, more people participated in adult education programs than in 1991.

Ⓓ From 1991 to 1995 the rate of participation in adult education among the groups represented in the graphs increased the least for those who attained at least a bachelor's degree.

Ⓔ In 1995, more adults with at least a bachelor's degree participated in adult education than did adults who attended some college but did not earn a college degree.

15. If, in the United States in 1995, there were 100 million employed adults and 40 million adults not in the labor force, then approximately what was the ratio of the number of employed adults participating in adult education to the number of people not in the labor force participating in adult education?

Ⓐ 5:4
Ⓑ 5:2
Ⓒ 10:3
Ⓓ 5:1
Ⓔ 6:1

Directions: For the following question, enter your answer in the box.

16. Assume that in 1996 the unemployment rate was 8%, meaning that 8 out of every 100 adults in the workforce were unemployed. What percentage of adults in the labor force participated in adult education? Round your answer to the nearest whole percent.

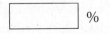 %

17. If a and b are the lengths of the legs of a right triangle whose hypotenuse is 10 and whose area is 20, what is the value of $(a + b)^2$?

   Ⓐ 100
   Ⓑ 120
   Ⓒ 140
   Ⓓ 180
   Ⓔ 200

18. What is the average (arithmetic mean) of 3^{30}, 3^{60}, and 3^{90}?

   Ⓐ 3^{60}
   Ⓑ 3^{177}
   Ⓒ $3^{10} + 3^{20} + 3^{30}$
   Ⓓ $3^{27} + 3^{57} + 3^{87}$
   Ⓔ $3^{29} + 3^{59} + 3^{89}$

19. The figure below consists of four semicircles in a large semicircle. If the small semicircles have radii of 1, 2, 3, and 4, what is the perimeter of the shaded region?

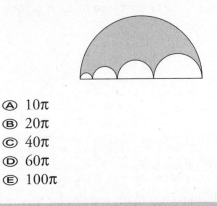

   Ⓐ 10π
   Ⓑ 20π
   Ⓒ 40π
   Ⓓ 60π
   Ⓔ 100π

Directions: The answer to the following question is a fraction. Enter the numerator in the upper box and the denominator in the lower box.

20. If a is increased by 25% and b is decreased by 25%, the resulting numbers will be equal. What is the ratio of a to b?

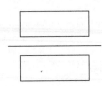

Section 4 Verbal Reasoning

TIME: 30 MINUTES—20 QUESTIONS

Directions: For each of the following sentences, select the **two** answers of the six choices given that, when substituted in the sentence, both logically complete the sentence as a whole **and** create sentences that are equivalent to one another in meaning.

Questions 1–6

1. Ironically, the same mayor who preached _____ to his constituents was noted for his extravagance and his free-spending lifestyle.

   - [A] righteousness
   - [B] radicalism
   - [C] economy
   - [D] austerity
   - [E] repentance
   - [F] honesty

2. The portrait painter was disinclined to accept a commission unless she was assured of adequate _____ for the task.

   - [A] recompense
   - [B] illumination
   - [C] personnel
   - [D] remuneration
   - [E] equipment
   - [F] expertise

2. Beginning with the music and dance of the antebellum plantation, jazz, born from a slave culture, would eventually _____ a musical industry that African musicians would dominate for years to come.

   - [A] preclude
   - [B] spawn
   - [C] withstand
   - [D] advocate
   - [E] disenfranchise
   - [F] generate

4. To a sophisticated audience conversant with the wide range of contemporary literary criticism, this brief essay would have been seen as a _____ version of arguments rehearsed in much more detail elsewhere.

   - [A] synoptic
   - [B] perceptive
   - [C] condensed
   - [D] generic
   - [E] censored
   - [F] forensic

5. Among contemporary writers of fiction, Mrs. Woolf is _____ figure, in some ways as radical as James Joyce, in others no more modern than Jane Austen.

   - [A] a curious
   - [B] an introspective
   - [C] a peripheral
   - [D] a disinterested
   - [E] an anomalous
   - [F] a doctrinaire

6. Book publishing has long been _____ profession, partly because for younger editors the best way to win a raise or a promotion was to move on to another publishing house.

   - [A] an innovative
   - [B] a prestigious
   - [C] an itinerant
   - [D] a mobile
   - [E] a rewarding
   - [F] an insular

Directions: The passage below is followed by questions based on its content. Once you have read the passage, select the answer choice that *best* answers each question. Answer all questions on the basis of what is *stated* or *implied* in the passage.

For each of Questions 7–9, select *one* answer choice unless otherwise instructed.

Questions 7–9 are based on the following passage.

Mary Shelley herself was the first to point to her fortuitous immersion in the literary and scientific revolutions of her day as the
Line source of her novel *Frankenstein.* Her
(5) extreme youth, as well as her sex, have contributed to the generally held opinion that she was not so much an author in her own right as a transparent medium through which passed the ideas of those around her.
(10) "All Mrs. Shelley did," writes Mario Praz, "was to provide a passive reflection of some of the wild fantasies which were living in the air about her."

Passive reflections, however, do not pro-
(15) duce original works of literature, and *Frankenstein*, if not a great novel, was unquestionably an original one. The major Romantic and minor Gothic tradition to which it *should* have belonged was to the lit-
(20) erature of the overreacher: the superman who breaks through normal human limitations to defy the rules of society and infringe upon the realm of God. In the Faust story, hypertrophy of the individual will is symbolized by
(25) a pact with the devil. Byron's and Balzac's heroes; the Wandering Jew; the chained and unchained Prometheus: all are overreachers, all are punished by their own excesses—by a surfeit of sensation, of experience, of knowl-
(30) edge and, most typically, by the doom of eternal life. But Mary Shelley's overreacher is different. Frankenstein's exploration of the forbidden boundaries of human science does not cause the prolongation and extension of
(35) his own life, but the creation of a new one. He defies mortality not by living forever, but by giving birth.

7. The author quotes Mario Praz primarily in order to
   (A) support her own perception of Mary Shelley's uniqueness
   (B) illustrate recent changes in scholarly opinions of Shelley
   (C) demonstrate Praz's unfamiliarity with Shelley's *Frankenstein*
   (D) provide an example of the predominant critical view of Shelley
   (E) contrast Praz's statement about Shelley with Shelley's own self-appraisal

8. The author of the passage concedes which of the following about Mary Shelley as an author?
   (A) She was unaware of the literary and mythological traditions of the overreacher.
   (B) She intentionally parodied the scientific and literary discoveries of her time.
   (C) She was exposed to radical artistic and scientific concepts which influenced her work.
   (D) She lacked the maturity to create a literary work of absolute originality.
   (E) She was not so much an author in her own right as an imitator of the literary works of others.

9. According to the author, Frankenstein parts from the traditional figure of the overreacher in
   (A) his exaggerated will
   (B) his atypical purpose
   (C) the excesses of his method
   (D) the inevitability of his failure
   (E) his defiance of the deity

Directions: Each of the following sentences or groups of sentences contains one, two, or three blanks. These blanks signify that a word or set of words has been left out. Below each sentence are columns of words or sets of words. For each blank, pick the *one* word or set of words from the corresponding column that *best* completes the text.

Questions 10–14

10. With units covering such topics as euthanasia, organ transplantation, and patient rights, the course *Religion, Ethics, and Medicine* explores the ways in which religious ideas and concepts _____ the practice of medicine and delivery of health care.

Ⓐ inform
Ⓑ obviate
Ⓒ reiterate
Ⓓ preclude
Ⓔ deny

11. To the embittered ex-philanthropist, all the former recipients of his charity were (i) _____, as stingy with their thanks as they were wasteful of his (ii) _____.

Blank (i)

Ⓐ misers
Ⓑ ingrates
Ⓒ prigs

Blank (ii)

Ⓓ gratitude
Ⓔ largesse
Ⓕ equanimity

12. For centuries, physicists have had good reason to believe in the principle of equivalence propounded by Galileo: it has (i) _____ many rigorous tests that (ii) _____ its accuracy to extraordinary precision.

Blank (i)

Ⓐ predicted
Ⓑ survived
Ⓒ postulated

Blank (ii)

Ⓓ established
Ⓔ compromised
Ⓕ equated

13. The actress had (i) _____ getting people to do things for her, and, to her delight, her new friends proved quite (ii) _____ in finding new ways to meet her needs.

Blank (i)

Ⓐ a knack for
Ⓑ a disinclination for
Ⓒ an indifference to

Blank (ii)

Ⓓ assiduous
Ⓔ dilatory
Ⓕ stoical

14. Although he did not consider himself
(i) _____, he felt that the
inconsistencies in her story (ii) _____
a certain degree of incredulity on his part.

Blank (i)

Ⓐ an apostate
Ⓑ a skeptic
Ⓒ a hypocrite

Blank (ii)

Ⓓ intimated
Ⓔ dignified
Ⓕ warranted

Directions: The passage below is followed by questions based on its content. Once you have read the passage, select the answer choice that *best* answers each question. Answer all questions on the basis of what is *stated* or *implied* in the passage.

For each of Questions 15–20, select *one* answer choice unless otherwise instructed.

Questions 15–17 are based on the following passage.

(The passage was written in the latter half of the 20th century.)

The coastlines on the two sides of the Atlantic Ocean present a notable parallelism: the easternmost region of Brazil, in
Line Pernambuco, has a convexity that corre-
(5) sponds almost perfectly with the concavity of the African Gulf of Guinea, while the contours of the African coastline between Rio de Oro and Liberia would, by the same approximation, match those of the Caribbean Sea.
(10) Similar correspondences are also observed in many other regions of the Earth. This observation began to awaken scientific interest about sixty years ago, when Alfred Wegener, a professor at the University of
(15) Hamburg, used it as a basis for formulating a revolutionary theory in geological science.

According to Wegener, there was originally only one continent or land mass, which he called Pangaea. Inasmuch as continental

(20) masses are lighter than the base on which they rest, he reasoned, they must float on the substratum of igneous rock, known as sima, as ice floes float on the sea. Then why, he asked, might continents not be subject to
(25) drifting? The rotation of the globe and other forces, he thought, had caused the cracking and, finally, the breaking apart of the original Pangaea, along an extensive line represented today by the longitudinal submerged
(30) mountain range in the center of the Atlantic. While Africa seems to have remained static, the Americas apparently drifted toward the west until they reached their present position after more than 100 million years. Although
(35) the phenomenon seems fantastic, accustomed as we are to the concept of the rigidity and immobility of the continents, on the basis of the distance that separates them it is possible to calculate that the continental
(40) drift would have been no greater than two inches per year.

15. The primary purpose of the passage is to
    - Ⓐ describe the relative speed of continental movement
    - Ⓑ predict the future configuration of the continents
    - Ⓒ refute a radical theory postulating continental movement
    - Ⓓ describe the reasoning behind a geological theory
    - Ⓔ explain how to calculate the continental drift per year

16. It can be inferred from the passage that evidence for continental drift has been provided by the
    - Ⓐ correspondences between coastal contours
    - Ⓑ proof of an original solitary land mass
    - Ⓒ level of sima underlying the continents
    - Ⓓ immobility of the African continent
    - Ⓔ relative heaviness of the continental masses

17. The passage presents information that would answer which of the following questions?
    - Ⓐ In what ways do the coastlines of Africa and South America differ from one another?
    - Ⓑ How much lighter than the substratum of igneous rock below them are the continental masses?
    - Ⓒ Is the rotation of the globe affecting the stability of the present day continental masses?
    - Ⓓ According to Wegener's theory, in what direction have the Americas tended to move?
    - Ⓔ How does Wegener's theory account for the apparent immobility of the African continent?

Questions 18–20 are based on the following passage.

During the 1930s, National Association for the Advancement of Colored People (NAACP) attorneys Charles H. Houston,
Line William Hastie, James M. Nabrit, Leon
(5) Ransom, and Thurgood Marshall charted a legal strategy designed to end segregation in education. They developed a series of legal cases challenging segregation in graduate and professional schools. Houston believed that
(10) the battle against segregation had to begin at the highest academic level in order to mitigate fear of race mixing that could create even greater hostility and reluctance on the part of white judges. After establishing a
(15) series of favorable legal precedents in higher education, NAACP attorneys planned to launch an all-out attack on the separate-but-equal doctrine in primary and secondary schools. The strategy proved successful. In
(20) four major United States Supreme Court decisions precedents were established that would enable the NAACP to construct a solid legal foundation upon which the Brown case could rest: *Missouri ex rel.*
(25) *Gaines* v. *Canada, Registrar of the University of Missouri* (1938); *Sipuel* v. *Board of Regents of the University of Oklahoma* (1948); *McLaurin* v. *Oklahoma State Regents for Higher Education* (1950); and *Sweatt* v.
(30) *Painter* (1950).

In the Oklahoma case, the Supreme Court held that the plaintiff was entitled to enroll in the University. The Oklahoma Regents responded by separating black and white stu-
(35) dents in cafeterias and classrooms. The 1950 McLaurin decision ruled that such internal separation was unconstitutional. In the Sweatt ruling, delivered on the same day, the Supreme Court held that the maintenance of
(40) separate law schools for whites and blacks was unconstitutional. A year after Herman Sweatt entered the University of Texas law school, desegregation cases were filed in the states of Kansas, South Carolina, Virginia,

(45) and Delaware and in the District of
Columbia asking the courts to apply the
qualitative test of the Sweatt case to the
elementary and secondary schools and to
declare the separate-but-equal doctrine
(50) invalid in the area of public education.

The 1954 *Brown* v. *Board of Education*
decision declared that a classification based
solely on race violated the 14th Amendment
to the United States Constitution. The
(55) decision reversed the 1896 *Plessy* v. *Ferguson*
ruling, which had established the separate-
but-equal doctrine. The *Brown* decision
more than any other case launched the
"equalitarian revolution" in American
(60) jurisprudence and signalled the emerging
primacy of equality as a guide to constitutional decisions; nevertheless, the decision
did not end state sanctioned segregation.
Indeed, the second *Brown* decision, known
(65) as *Brown II* and delivered a year later, played
a decisive role in limiting the effectiveness
and impact of the 1954 case by providing
southern states with the opportunity to delay
the implementation of desegregation.

18. According to the passage, Houston aimed his
legislative challenge at the graduate and professional school level on the basis of the
assumption that
Ⓐ the greatest inequities existed at the highest academic and professional levels
Ⓑ the separate-but-equal doctrine applied
solely to the highest academic levels
Ⓒ there were clear precedents for reform in
existence at the graduate school level
Ⓓ the judiciary would feel less apprehension
at desegregation on the graduate level
Ⓔ the consequences of desegregation would
become immediately apparent at the
graduate school level

19. Which of the following statements is most
compatible with the principles embodied in
Plessy v. *Ferguson* as described in the passage?
Ⓐ Internal separation of whites and blacks
within a given school is unconstitutional.
Ⓑ Whites and blacks may be educated in
separate schools so long as they offer
comparable facilities.
Ⓒ The maintenance of separate professional
schools for blacks and whites is
unconstitutional.
Ⓓ The separate-but-equal doctrine is
inapplicable to the realm of private
education.
Ⓔ Blacks may be educated in schools with
whites whenever the blacks and whites
have equal institutions.

20. The aspect of Houston's work most extensively discussed in the passage is its
Ⓐ psychological canniness
Ⓑ judicial complexity
Ⓒ fundamental efficiency
Ⓓ radical intellectualism
Ⓔ exaggerated idealism

Section 5 Quantitative Ability

TIME: 35 MINUTES—20 QUESTIONS

Directions: In each of Questions 1–7, there are two quantities—Quantity A and Quantity B. You are to compare those quantities, taking into consideration any additional information given. The correct answer to such a question is

Ⓐ if Quantity A is greater;
Ⓑ if Quantity B is greater;
Ⓒ if the two quantities are equal;
Ⓓ if it is impossible to determine which quantity is greater.

Note: The given information, if any, is always centered above the two quantities. In any question, if a symbol or letter appears more than once, it represents the same thing each time.

	Quantity A	Quantity B
1.	$(-8)^8$	$(-9)^9$

$$a > 0$$

	Quantity A	Quantity B
2.	$\sqrt{a^{18}}$	$(a^2)(a^3)(a^4)$

The price of a large pizza is 30% more than the price of a small pizza.

	Quantity A	Quantity B
3.	The price of a large pizza when it is on sale for 30% off.	The price of a small pizza.

	Quantity A	Quantity B
4.	The average (arithmetic mean) of a, b, c, d, e, f, and g.	50

In 9 years, Katie will be 4 times as old as she is now.

	Quantity A	Quantity B
5.	The number of years until Katie will be 8 times as old as she is now.	20

	Quantity A	Quantity B
6.	The area of an equilateral triangle whose sides are 6	The area of an isosceles right triangle whose legs are 6

A bag contains four slips of paper, two of which have the number 1 written on them and two of which have the number −1 on them. Two of the slips are chosen at random.

	Quantity A	Quantity B
7.	The probability that the product of the two numbers chosen is −1	The probability that the product of the two numbers chosen in 1

Directions: Questions 8–20 have three different formats. Unless a question has its own directions that specifically state otherwise, each question has five answer choices, exactly one of which is correct.

8. John bought a $100 DVD player on sale at 8% off. How much did he pay including 8% sales tax?
   Ⓐ $84.64
   Ⓑ $92.00
   Ⓒ $96.48
   Ⓓ $99.36
   Ⓔ $100.00

9. The sum of the lengths of all the edges of a cube is 3 feet. What is the volume, in cubic feet, of the cube?

   Ⓐ $\dfrac{1}{64}$

   Ⓑ $\dfrac{1}{8}$

   Ⓒ $\dfrac{1}{4}$

   Ⓓ 8

   Ⓔ 27

Directions: For the following question enter your answer in the box.

10. Mary read from the top of page 10 to the bottom of page 24 in 30 minutes, At this rate, how long, in minutes, will it take her to read from the top of page 25 to the bottom of page 50?

   [ ] minutes

11. For how many positive integers $m \le 100$ is $(m - 5)(m - 45)$ positive?
   Ⓐ 45
   Ⓑ 50
   Ⓒ 58
   Ⓓ 59
   Ⓔ 60

12. The magazine *Modern Crafts* published the instructions for making a circular mosaic whose diameter is 20 centimeters. Geraldine wants to use tiles of the same size as those listed in the magazine article to make a larger mosaic—one that is 30 centimeters in diameter. To have the correct number of tiles for her mosaic, by what factor must she multiply the number of tiles that were listed in the magazine's directions?
   Ⓐ 2.25
   Ⓑ 2.00
   Ⓒ 1.50
   Ⓓ 1.44
   Ⓔ 0.67

Directions: For the following question, consider each of the choices separately and select *all* that apply.

13. Every year between 70% and 85% of the students at Central High School attend the homecoming rally. If one year 1435 students attended the rally, which of the following could have been the number of students at Central High School that year?

   Indicate *all* possible numbers of students.
   Ⓐ 1675
   Ⓑ 1775
   Ⓒ 1875
   Ⓓ 1975
   Ⓔ 2075

Questions 14–16 refer to the following graphs.

College Enrollment, by Age and Gender: 1975 and 1995

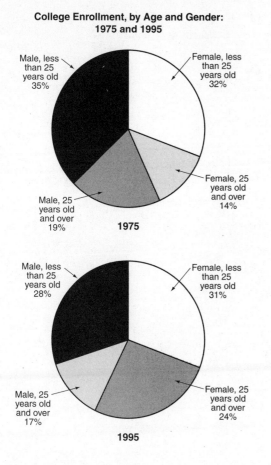

Source: U.S. Bureau of the Census, Current Population Survey.

Directions: For the following question enter your answer in the box.

14. If there were 10,000,000 college students in 1975, how many more male students were there than female students?

15. In 1975 what percent of female college students were at least 25 years old?

  Ⓐ 14%

  Ⓑ 30%

  Ⓒ 45%

  Ⓓ 69%

  Ⓔ 76%

16. If the total number of students enrolled in college was 40% higher in 1995 than in 1975, what is the ratio of the number of male students in 1995 to the number of male students in 1975?

  Ⓐ 5:6

  Ⓑ 6:7

  Ⓒ 7:6

  Ⓓ 6:5

  Ⓔ 7:5

Directions: For the following question enter your answer in the box.

17. Eric can address 40 envelopes per hour. At this rate, how many envelopes can he address in 99 minutes?

Directions: For the following question, consider each of the choices separately and select *all* that apply.

18. At Florence Pizza, the only slices of pizza available are plain and pepperoni, which cost $1.50 and $2.00, respectively. Small, medium, and large cups of soda cost $1.00, $1.50, and $1.75, respectively. Which of the following could be the total cost of two slices of pizza and two sodas?

Indicate *all* such costs.

  A $5.00

  B $5.25

  C $6.00

  D $6.25

  E $7.00

  F $7.25

19. In a normal distribution, 68% of the scores lie within one standard deviation of the mean. If the SAT scores of all the high school juniors in Center City followed a normal distribution with a mean of 500 and a standard deviation of 100, and if 10,200 students scored between 400 and 500, approximately how many students scored above 600?

Ⓐ 2,400
Ⓑ 4,800
Ⓒ 5,100
Ⓓ 7,200
Ⓔ 9,600

20. If $x + y = 10$, and $xy = 20$, what is the value of $\dfrac{1}{x} + \dfrac{1}{y}$?

Ⓐ $\dfrac{1}{20}$

Ⓑ $\dfrac{1}{15}$

Ⓒ $\dfrac{1}{10}$

Ⓓ $\dfrac{1}{2}$

Ⓔ 2

Model Test 2
ANSWER KEY

Section 1–Analytical Writing

There are no "correct answers" to this section.

Section 2–Verbal Reasoning

1. D, E	6. D, E	11. A, E	16. C
2. B, E	7. D	12. C, D	17. A, C
3. A, C	8. E	13. B, F	18. E
4. B, D	9. E	14. B, D	19. B
5. C, E	10. C	15. A, E, G	20. D

Note: The letters in brackets following the Quantitative Ability answers in Sections 3 and 5 refer to the sections of Chapter 11 in which you can find the information you need to answer the questions. For example, 3. D [J] means that the answer to question 3 is D, and that the solution requires information found in Section 11-J: Triangles. Also, 15. B [10] means that the answer to question 15 is B and is based on information in Chapter 10: Data Interpretation.

Section 3–Quantitative Ability

1. D [A]	6. A [B]	11. 2/9 [O]	16. 49 [10]
2. D [B, C]	7. C [K, L]	12. D [O]	17. D [G, J]
3. D [J]	8. C [B]	13. 94 [E]	18. E [A]
4. B [G]	9. B [D]	14. A, B, C, D [10]	19. B [L]
5. A [J, L]	10. C [C, D]	15. E [10]	20. 3/5 [C]

Section 4–Verbal Reasoning

1. C, D	6. C, D	11. B, E	16. A
2. A, D	7. D	12. B, D	17. D
3. B, F	8. C	13. A, D	18. D
4. A, C	9. B	14. B, F	19. B
5. A, E	10. A	15. D	20. A

Section 5–Quantitative Ability

1. A [A]	6. B [J]	11. D [A, G]	16. C [10]
2. C [A]	7. A [O]	12. A [L]	17. 66 [H]
3. B [C]	8. D [C]	13. B, C, D [C, H]	18. A, C, D, E, F [A]
4. A [E, L]	9. A [M]	14. 800,000 [10]	19. B [D]
5. A [H]	10. 52 [O]	15. B [10]	20. D [G]

ANSWER EXPLANATIONS

Section 1—Analytical Writing

There are no "correct answers" to this section.

Section 2—Verbal Reasoning

1. **(D)(E)** Note the two key phrases "Given the human tendency to suspect and disbelieve in" and "it is unsurprising that." People who view the unconscious with suspicion or disbelieve in it are as a consequence likely to *deny* or *gainsay* (contradict) its effect on human interactions.

2. **(B)(E)** In contrast to his reputation, the author is not markedly taciturn (uncommunicative; disinclined to talk). In fact, he seems inclined to talk. In other words, he is not at all *averse from* or *opposed to* conversation.

3. **(A)(C)** To call a country "the land of the free" while allowing the institution of slavery to exist struck Mrs. Trollope as evidence of *hypocrisy* or *sanctimoniousness* (the act of making a false display of righteousness or piety).

4. **(B)(D)** The key word here is "passionate." Paul finds himself attracted to a woman who is *ardent* (fervent; keen) and *wholehearted* (fully enthusiastic) about her likes and dislikes.

5. **(C)(E)** Soap operas and situation comedies are derivative of contemporary culture: they take their elements from that culture. Therefore, they serve as *evidence* or *indices* (signs, indications) of what is going on in that culture; they both point to and point up the social attitudes and values they portray.

    Note that the soap operas and comedies here cannot be *determinants* of our society's attitudes and values: they derive from these attitudes and values; they do not determine them.

6. **(D)(E)** Whatever word or phrase you choose here must apply equally well both to slander and to counterfeit money. People who would not make up a slanderous statement *circulate* or *spread* slander by passing it on. So too people who would not coin or make counterfeit money *circulate* or *spread around* counterfeit money by passing it on.

    Note how the extended metaphor here influences the writer's choice of words.

7. **(D)** The author cites Meredith's intelligence (*brilliance*) and his splendor of language (*linguistic grandeur*).

8. **(E)** Rather than refuting the claim, the author clearly acknowledges Meredith's inability to evoke the reader's sympathy.

    Choice A is incorrect. From the start the author points out how Meredith leaves readers cold.

    Choice B is incorrect. The author reiterates Meredith's virtues, citing muscular intelligence and literary merit.

    Choice C is incorrect. The author quotes several such imagined criticisms.

    Choice D is incorrect. The author indicates that if readers choose to avoid dealing with Meredith they shall be doing a disservice to the cause of criticism.

    Only Choice E remains. It is the correct answer.

9. **(E)** Speaking of the "challenge and excitement of the critical problem as such," the author clearly finds the prospect of appraising Meredith critically to be stirring and *invigorating*.

10. **(C)** The author wishes us to be able to recognize the good qualities of Meredith's work while at the same time we continue to find it personally unsympathetic. Thus, she would agree that criticism should enable us to appreciate the virtues of works we dislike.

    Choices A, B, and E are unsupported by the passage.

    Choice D is incorrect. While the author wishes the reader to be aware of Meredith's excellences, she does not suggest that the reader should ignore those qualities in Meredith that make his work unsympathetic. Rather, she wishes the reader to come to appreciate the very ambivalence of his critical response.

11. **(A)(E)** The off-Broadway and Broadway theatres are contrasted here. The former has *manifested* or shown a talent for improvisation, extemporaneous or spontaneous performance. The latter has manifested no such talent for *spontaneity*.

    Note the use of *whereas* to establish the contrast.

12. **(C)(D)** People had complimented her for her *fluency* or eloquence; it was therefore surprising that she proved *inarticulate* or tongue-tied at her inauguration.

    Note the use of *although* and *surprisingly* to signal the contrast.

13. **(B)(F)** The filmmakers wish neither to *reject* nor to *vitiate* (impair; weaken) a strong sense of place. Instead, they take pains to *impart* (communicate; convey) a strong sense of the places they film as well as of the characters they film. Thus, their films become portraits of the *spaces* their characters *inhabit*.

14. **(B)(D)** The key phrase here is "they remained the dominant viol size." The text is discussing changes over time in the popularity of different sizes of bass viols. Before 1600, larger consort bass viols were in fashion. After 1600, the larger consort bass viols were *displaced* by the smaller division viols. The division viols continued to be popular until some time in the 1700s, when they *went out of fashion*.

15. **(A)(E)(G)** Particles have no need to be wound up because the property of spinning (*rotation*) is built into their makeup: it is *intrinsic*. That is the significant *difference* between the spinning of particles and the spinning of tops.

16. **(C)** To the author the concept is both simple and traditional, dating as it does from Newton's time.

17. **(A)(C)** Question A is answerable on the basis of the passage. As the area's density increases, its gravitational field increases in strength. Likewise, Question C is answerable on the basis of the passage. The end result of the process is the formation of a gravitationally bound object, a newborn star. Remember, you must have selected *both* A and C to receive credit for this question.

    Question B is not answerable on the basis of the passage. The passage nowhere states what disturbs the gas.

18. **(E)** The passage compares the Quechua empire to a *mandala* because "it was divided into four parts." Thus, a *mandala* is most likely a "figure composed of four divisions."

19. **(B)** The author refers to the Quechua as existing in "a state of unremitting anxiety, which could not be resolved by action" and which the Quechua could only deal with by looking into himself and struggling with the depths of his own psyche. This suggests that the Quechua world was *highly introspective*.

20. **(D)** Both the unremitting anxiety of Quechua life and the recurring harvest failures that brought starvation to millions illustrate the *harshness and frustration* of Quechua existence.

Section 3—Quantitative Ability

Two asterisks (**) indicate an alternative method of solving.

1. **(D)** Use TACTIC 4, Chapter 9. Could *m* and *n* be equal? Sure, if each is 5. Eliminate Choices A and B. Must they be equal? No, not if $m = 1$ and $n = 25$. Eliminate Choice C, as well. Neither quantity is always greater, and the two quantities are not always equal (D).

2. **(D)** Since $\frac{2}{3} = 66\frac{2}{3}\%$, which is clearly more than 65%, it *appears* that Quantity B is greater. *Be careful!* That would be true if *a* were positive, but no restrictions are placed on *a*. If $a = 0$, the columns are equal; if *a* is negative, Quantity A is greater. Neither quantity is always greater, and the two quantities are not always equal (D).
   **Use TACTIC 1, Chapter 9. Just let $a = 0$, and then let $a = 1$.

3. **(D)** Use TACTIC 4, Chapter 9. Could the quantities be equal? Could $c = 5$? Sure, if this is a 3-4-5 right triangle. Must $c = 5$? No; if the triangle is not a right triangle, *c* could be less than or more than 5.

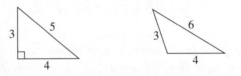

   Neither quantity is *always* greater, and the quantities are not *always* equal (D). (*Note*: Since the figure may not be drawn to scale, do *not* assume that the triangle has a right angle.)

4. **(B)** You don't *have* to solve for *a* and *b*. If $a - b > a + b$, then *b* is negative and Quantity B is greater.
   **You *could* solve. Adding the two equations yields $2a = 49 \Rightarrow a = 24.5 \Rightarrow b = -.5$.

5. **(A)** Since in the given figure *OA* and *OB* are radii, each is equal to 5. With no restrictions on *x*, *AB* could be any positive number less than 10; and the larger *x* is, the larger *AB* is.

If *x* were 90, *AB* would be $5\sqrt{2}$, but we are told that $x > 90$, so

$$AB > 5\sqrt{2} > 7.$$

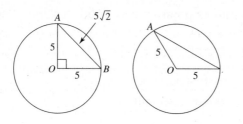

6. **(A)** Quantity B = $\left(\dfrac{13}{17}\right)^5 = (x^5)^5 = x^{25}$. Since $0 < x < 1$, $x^{25} < x$.

7. **(C)** In Figure 1, since the radius of each circle is 3, the area of each circle is 9π, and the total area of the four circles is 36π. In Figure 2, the radius of each circle is 2, and so the area of each circle is 4π, and the total area of the nine circles is 36π. Since the area of both squares is $12^2 = 144$, and the area of both white regions is 36π, the areas of both shaded regions is $144 - 36\pi$. The quantities are equal (C).

8. **(C)** If there are *x* seats on each bus, then the group is using $\dfrac{4}{5}(3x) = \dfrac{12}{5}x$

seats. After $\dfrac{1}{4}$ of them get off, $\dfrac{3}{4}$ of them, or $\dfrac{3}{4}\left(\dfrac{12}{5}x\right) = \dfrac{9}{5}x$ remain.

What fraction of the $2x$ seats on the two buses are now being used?

$$\dfrac{\dfrac{9}{5}x}{2x} = \dfrac{\dfrac{9}{5}}{2} = \dfrac{9}{10}.$$

   **To avoid the algebra, assume there are 20 seats on each bus. At the beginning, the group is using 48 of the 60 seats on the three buses. When 12 people left, the 36 remaining people used $\dfrac{36}{40} = \dfrac{9}{10}$ of the 40 seats on two buses.

9. **(B)** Since *d* divisions each have *t* teams, multiply to get *dt* teams; and since each team has *p* players, multiply the number of teams (*dt*) by *p* to get the total number of players: *dtp*.
   **Use TACTIC 2, Chapter 8. Pick three easy-to-use numbers for *t*, *d*, and *p*. Assume that there are 2 divisions, each consisting of 4 teams, so, there are $2 \times 4 = 8$ teams. Then assume that each team has 10 players, for a total of $8 \times 10 = 80$ players. Now check the choices. Which one is equal to 80 when $d = 2$, $t = 4$, and $p = 10$? Only *dtp*.

10. **(C)** Since, in 1990, $2p$ pounds of potatoes cost $\frac{1}{2}d$ dollars, p pounds cost

half as much: $\frac{1}{2}\left(\frac{1}{2}d\right) = \frac{1}{4}d$. This is $\frac{1}{4}$, or 25%, as much as the cost in 1980, which represents a decrease of 75%.

    **In this type of problem it is *often* easier to use TACTIC 2, Chapter 8. Assume that 1 pound of potatoes cost $100 in 1980. Then in 1990, 2 pounds cost $50, so 1 pound cost $25. This is a decrease of $75 in the cost of 1 pound of potatoes, and

$$\% \text{ decrease} = \frac{\text{actual decrease}}{\text{original amount}} \times 100\% = \frac{75}{100} \times 100\% = 75\%.$$

11. $\frac{2}{9}$ There are nine positive integers less than 10: 1, 2, ... , 9. For which of

them is $\frac{9}{x} > x$?

Only 1 and 2: $\frac{9}{1} > 1$ and $\frac{9}{2} > 2$. When $x = 3$, $\frac{9}{x} = x$, and for all the others

$\frac{9}{x} < x$. The probability is $\frac{2}{9}$.

12. **(D)** If Jason were really unlucky, what could go wrong in his attempt to get one marble of each color? Well, his first nine picks *might* yield five blue marbles and four white ones. But then the tenth marble would be red, and now he would have at least one of each color. The answer is 10.

13. **94** If a represents Jordan's average after 5 tests, then he has earned a total of $5a$ points [TACTIC E1]. A grade of 70 on the sixth test will lower his average 4 points to $a - 4$. Therefore,

$$a - 4 = \frac{5a + 70}{6} \Rightarrow 6(a - 4) = 5a + 70 \Rightarrow$$

$6a - 24 = 5a + 70 \Rightarrow 6a = 5a + 94 \Rightarrow a = 94.$

    **Assume Jordan's average is a because he earned a on each of his first 5 tests. Since after getting a 70 on his sixth test his average will be $a - 4$, the deviation on each of the first 5 tests is 4, for a total deviation above the average of 20 points. So, the total deviation below must also be 20 [KEY FACT E3]. Therefore, 70 is 20 less than the new average of $a - 4$:

$$70 = (a - 4) - 20 \Rightarrow a = 94.$$

    **Use TACTIC 1, Chapter 8: backsolve. Start with Choice C, 86. If his 5-test average was 90, he had 450 points and a 70 on the sixth test would give him a total of 520 points, and an average of $520 \div 6 = 86.666$. So, the 70 lowered his average 3.333 points. That's not enough. Eliminate Choices A, B, and C. Try Choices D or E. Choice E, 94, works.

14. **(A)(B)(C)(D)**

   (A) In 1991, more than 50% of the adults whose highest degree was at least a bachelor's degree participated in adult education, whereas those whose highest educational attainment was a high school diploma or GED (high school equivalency diploma) fewer than 25% participated. (A is true.)

   (B) From 1991 to 1995, among those adults whose highest educational attainment was grades 9–12, without earning a high school diploma, the rate of participation in adult education increased from about 15% to 23%, an increase of about 50%. None of the other groups had nearly that great an increase. (B is true.)

   (C) Since the population of the country grew between 1991 and 1995, and the rate of participation in adult education programs increased in every category, the total number of people participating had to increase. (C is true.)

   (D) From 1991 to 1995 the rate of participation in adult education for those who had attained at least a bachelor's degree increased from about 52% to 58%, the least increase of any group on both an absolute and percent basis. (D is true.)

   (E) Without knowing how many adults have earned a college degree and how many have attended some college without earning a college degree, it is impossible to make this conclusion. For example, 50% of 100,000,000 is much more than 585 of 50,000,000. (E is false.)

15. **(E)** 50% of 100,000,000 = 50,000,000; 20% of 40,000,000 = 8,000,000. 50,000,000:8,000,000 = 50:8 = 6.25:1, which is closest to choice E, 6:1.

16. **(49)** Assume that there were 1,000 adults in the workforce. Then 80 were unemployed and 920 were employed. Since 50% of the employed adults and 40% of the unemployed adults participated in adult education, the number of participants was 50% of 920 + 40% of 80 = 460 + 32 = 492.

   So, the rate of participation was $\dfrac{492}{1000} = \dfrac{49.2}{100} = 49.2\%$.

   Rounded to the nearest whole percent, the answer is 49.

17. **(D)**

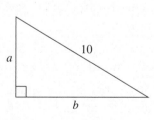

By the Pythagorean theorem,
$$a^2 + b^2 = 10^2 = 100;$$

and since the area is 20, $\dfrac{1}{2}ab = 20 \Rightarrow ab = 40$.

Expand:
$$(a + b)^2 = a^2 + 2ab + b^2 = (a^2 + b^2) + 2ab.$$

Then
$$(a^2 + b^2) + 2ab = 100 + 2(40) = 180.$$

18. **(E)** To find the average of three numbers, divide their sum by 3:

$\dfrac{3^{30} + 3^{60} + 3^{90}}{3}$. Now use the distributive law and divide each term in the

numerator by 3: $\dfrac{3^{30}}{3} + \dfrac{3^{60}}{3} + \dfrac{3^{90}}{3} = 3^{29} + 3^{59} + 3^{89}$.

19. **(B)** In the given figure, the diameters of the four small semicircles are 2, 4, 6, and 8, so the diameter of the large semicircle is 2 + 4 + 6 + 8 = 20, and its radius is 10. The perimeter of the shaded region is the sum of the circumferences of all five semicircles. Since the circumference of a semicircle is π times its radius, the perimeter is $\pi + 2\pi + 3\pi + 4\pi + 10\pi = 20\pi$.

20. $\dfrac{3}{5}$ $a + 25\%(a) = 1.25a$, and $b - 25\%(b) = 0.75b$.

So, $1.25a = .75b$, and $\dfrac{a}{b} = \dfrac{.75}{1.25} = \dfrac{3}{5}$

   **If after increasing a and decreasing b the results are equal, a must be smaller than b. So, *the ratio of* a *to* b *must be less than 1*. Eliminate Choices C, D, and E. Now, either test Choices A and B or just guess. To test Choice B, pick two numbers in the ratio of 3 to 4—30 and 40, for example. Then, 30 increased by 25% is 37.5, and 40 decreased by 25% is 30. The results are not equal, so eliminate Choice B. The answer is $\dfrac{3}{5}$. (50 decreased by 25% *is* 37.5.)

Section 4—Verbal Reasoning

1. **(C)(D)** The key phrase here is "his extravagance and his free-spending lifestyle." *Ironically* is an implicit contrast signal: it indicates that you are looking for an antonym or near-antonym to *extravagance*. The mayor practices extravagance but preaches thrift, that is, *economy* (financial prudence) or *austerity* (strict economy; restraint).

2. **(A)(D)** Working on commission, the portrait painter seeks proper *recompense* or *remuneration* (payment or reward for services) for undertaking the job.

3. **(B)(F)** Stripped of descriptive phrases, the sentence simply states that jazz would *spawn* or *generate* (give rise to) an industry. Note that the verb *spawn* occurs here with a secondary meaning.

4. **(A)(C)** Several clues suggest that this *brief* essay is an abridgment or synopsis of more extensive critiques ("arguments rehearsed in much more detail elsewhere"). Thus, it can be described as a *condensed* (shortened) or *synoptic* (concise; summary) version.

5. **(A)(E)** If Mrs. Woolf combines both radical and non-radical elements in her fictions, then she presents *an anomalous* (unusual; not fitting into a common or familiar pattern) or *curious* (highly unusual) image. Here *curious* occurs

with its secondary meaning (arousing interest or curiosity) rather than with its primary meaning (inquisitive).

6. **(C)(D)** The key phrase here is "move on." If editors have to travel from firm to firm to succeed in their field, then publishing can be classified as an *itinerant* or *mobile* profession, a profession marked by traveling.

7. **(D)** Immediately before quoting Praz, the author states that the general view of Shelley depicts her as "a transparent medium through which passed the ideas of those around her." The quotation from Praz provides an excellent example of this particular point of view.

   To answer this question correctly, you do not need to read the passage in its entirety. Quickly scroll through the passage, scanning for the name Praz; read only the context in which it appears.

8. **(C)** The opening sentence points out that Shelley herself acknowledged the influence of her unplanned immersion in the scientific and literary revolutions of her time. Clearly, the author of the passage concedes this as true of Shelley.

9. **(B)** The concluding paragraph distinguishes Frankenstein from the other overreachers in his desire not to extend his own life but to impart life to another (by creating his monster). Thus, his purpose is *atypical* of the traditional overreacher.

   To say that someone *parts from* the traditional figure of the overreacher is to say that he *differs* from it. Thus, to answer this question quickly, scan the passage looking for *overreacher* and *different* (or their synonyms).

10. **(A)** Clearly religious ideas and concepts do not *obviate* (hinder), *preclude* (rule out), or *deny* the practice of medicine and delivery of health care. Neither do they *reiterate* (repeat) the practice of medicine. However, religious ideas and concepts do *inform* (pervade; permeate, with obvious effect) medical practices.

11. **(B)(E)** The embittered benefactor thinks of them as *ingrates* (ungrateful persons) because they do not thank him sufficiently for his generosity. He does not think of them as *misers* (hoarders of wealth): although they are stingy in expressing thanks, they are extravagant in spending money, that is, being "wasteful of his largesse." He certainly does not think of them as *prigs* (self-righteous fuss-budgets): the specific attribute he resents in them is ingratitude, not self-righteousness, or exaggerated propriety.

12. **(B)(D)** The physicists have had good reason to believe in the principle because it has *survived* rigorous or strict tests. These tests have *established* (proved) that the principle is accurate.

   Note how the second clause supports the first, explaining why the physicists have had reason to be confident in the principle.

13. **(A)(D)** The actress had *a knack* or talent for getting people to do things for her and was delighted that her new friends were *assiduous* (diligent) in finding new ways to meet her needs.

   Note that it is useful to focus first on the second blank as you answer this question. The key phrase here is "to her delight." The actress would have no particular cause for delight if her new friends proved *dilatory* (tardy; slow) or *stoical* (impassive; unemotional) in finding new ways to meet her needs.

14. **(B)(F)** The presence of inconsistencies (discrepancies; contradictions) in someone's story would *warrant* (justify) some incredulity (disbelief) on anyone's part. Even someone who was not a *skeptic* (person who maintains a doubting attitude) would be justified in doubting such a tale.

15. **(D)** The author takes the reader through Wegener's reasoning step by step, describing what led Wegener to reach his conclusions.

16. **(A)** Since the existence of the correspondences between the various coastal contours was used by Wegener as a basis for formulating his theory of continental drift, it can be inferred that the correspondences provide evidence for the theory.

    Choice B is incorrect. The passage does not indicate that Pangaea's existence has been proved.

    Choice C is incorrect. It is the relative heaviness of sima, not the level or depth of sima, that suggested the possibility of the lighter continents drifting.

    Choice D is incorrect. Mobility rather than immobility would provide evidence for continental drift.

    Choice E is incorrect. The continents are lighter than the underlying sima.

17. **(D)** Choice D is answerable on the basis of the passage. The next-to-the-last sentence of the second paragraph states that the Americas "apparently drifted toward the west."

18. **(D)** Houston believed that the battle had to begin at the graduate level "to mitigate fear" (relieve *apprehension*) of race-mixing and miscegenation that might otherwise have caused the judges to rule against the NAACP-sponsored complaints.

19. **(B)** The separate-but-equal doctrine established by *Plessy* v. *Ferguson* allows the existence of racially segregated schools.

20. **(A)** In assessing the possible effects on judges of race-mixing in the lower grades, Houston was *psychologically canny*, shrewd in seeing potential dangers and in figuring strategies to avoid these dangers.

Section 5—Quantitative Ability

Two asterisks (**) indicate an alternative method of solving.

1. **(A)** Quantity A is positive and Quantity B is negative. So, Quantity A is greater.

2. **(C)**
   Quantity A: Since $(a^9)(a^9) = (a^{18})$, and since $a > 0$, $\sqrt{a^{18}} = a^9$.
   Quantity B: $(a^2)(a^3)(a^4) = a^{2+3+4} = a^9$.
   The quantities are equal.

3. **(B)** Assume that the price of a small pizza is $10; then the price of a large pizza is $10 + 0.30($10) = $10 + $3 = $13.
   On sale at 30% off, a large pizza costs 30% less than $13.

   $$\$13 - 0.30(\$13) = \$13 - \$3.90 = \$9.10$$

   So, Quantity B is $10 and Quantity A is $9.10.

4. **(A)** There is not enough information provided to determine the values of *a*, *b*, *c*, *d*, *e*, *f*, and *g*, but they are irrelevant. Since the sum of the measures of the seven angles is 360°, their average is 360° ÷ 7 ≈ 51.4°. Quantity A is greater.

5. **(A)** If *x* represents Katie's age now, then in 9 years she will be *x* + 9, and so *x* + 9 = 4*x*. Therefore, 9 = 3*x*, and *x* = 3. So, Katie is now 3 and will be 8 times as old as she is now when she is 24, which will happen in 21 years.

   Quantity A is greater.

6. **(B)**

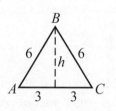

   Quantity A: If *h* is the height of equilateral triangle *ABC*, then by the Pythagorean theorem $3^2 + h^2 = 6^2 \Rightarrow h^2 = 27 \Rightarrow h = 3\sqrt{3}$. So the area of

   triangle *ABC* is $A = \frac{1}{2}bh = \frac{1}{2}(6)(3\sqrt{3}) = 9\sqrt{3} \approx 15.59$.

   Quantity B:

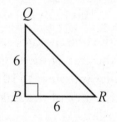

   The area of isosceles triangle *PQR* is $\frac{1}{2}(6)(6) = 18$.

7. **(A)** The simplest solution is to notice that if a 1 is chosen first, of the remaining three slips, two of them have –1 on them and one of them has 1 on it. So there are 2 chances in 3 that the second number will be –1 and the product will be –1. Similarly, if a –1 is chosen first, there are 2 chances in 3 that the second number will be 1 and, again, the product will be –1.

   Quantity A is $\frac{2}{3}$ and Quantity B is $\frac{1}{3}$.

8. **(D)** Since 8% of 100 is 8, John saved $8, and thus paid $92 for the DVD player. He then had to pay 8% sales tax on the $92: 0.08 × 92 = 7.36, so the total cost was $92 + $7.36 = $99.36.

9. **(A)**

A cube has 12 edges. (In the diagram, each shaded square base has 4 edges, and there are 4 edges connecting the two bases.) So, we have that

$$12e = 3 \Rightarrow e = \frac{1}{4}.$$

Therefore, $V = e^3 = \left(\frac{1}{4}\right)^3 = \frac{1}{64}$ cubic feet.

10. **52** How many pages did Mary read in 30 minutes? Since Mary started on page 10, she read the first 24 pages, except pages 1–9: She read 24 – 9 = 15 pages. So she read at the rate of 15 pages every 30 minutes, or 1 page every 2 minutes. Similarly, if Mary reads pages 25 through 50, she will read 50 – 24 = 26 pages. At the rate of 1 page every 2 minutes it will take her 52 minutes to read 26 pages.

11. **(D)** If $(m - 5)(m - 45)$ is positive, either both factors are positive or both factors are negative. If $(m - 5)$ is negative, m must be less than 5, so m could be 1, 2, 3, or 4 (4 values). For $(m - 45)$ to be positive, m must be greater than 45, so m could be 46, 47,… . 100 (55 values). The answer is 59.

12. **(A)** Since the diameters of the two mosaics are 30 and 20, the radii are 15 and 10, respectively. So the area of the larger mosaic is $\pi(15)^2 = 225\pi$, whereas the area of the smaller mosaic is $\pi(10)^2 = 100\pi$. So the area of the larger mosaic is 2.25 times the area of the smaller mosaic, and hence will require 2.25 times as many tiles.

13. **(B)(C)(D)** Let S = the number of students at Central High School that year.
    If 70% of the students attended the rally, then $0.70S = 1,435$, and so $S = 1,435 \div 0.70 = 2,050$.
    If 85% of the students attended the rally, then $0.85S = 1,435$, and so $S = 1,435 \div 0.85 = 1,688$.
    So, S must satisfy the inequality $1,688 < S < 2,050$.

14. **800,000** From the top graph, we see that in 1975, 54% (35% + 19%) of all college students were male, and the other 46% were female. So there were 5,400,000 males and 4,600,000 females — a difference of 800,000.

15. **(B)** In 1975, of every 100 college students, 46 were female — 32 of whom were less than 25 years old, and 14 of whom were 25 years old and over. So, 14 of every 46 female students were at least 25 years old. Finally,
    $$\frac{14}{46} = .30 = 30\%.$$

16. **(C)** From the two graphs, we see that in 1975 54% (35% + 19%) of all college students were male, whereas in 1995 the corresponding figure was 45% (28% + 17%). For simplicity, assume that there were 100 college students in 1975, 54 of whom were male. Then in 1995, there were 140 college students, 63 of whom were male (45% of 140 = 63). So the ratio of the number of male students in 1995 to the number of male students in 1975 is 63:54 = 7:6.

17. **66** Let x represent the number of envelopes Eric can address in 99 minutes and set up a proportion:

$$\frac{40 \text{ envelopes}}{1 \text{ hour}} = \frac{40 \text{ envelopes}}{60 \text{ minutes}} = \frac{2 \text{ envelopes}}{3 \text{ minutes}} = \frac{x \text{ envelopes}}{99 \text{ minutes}} \Rightarrow$$

$$2 \times 99 = 3x \Rightarrow 198 = 3x \Rightarrow x = 66$$

18. **(A)(C)(D)(E)(F)** Start with the least expensive option: 2 regular slices and 2 small sodas.
   - This option costs $5.00. (A is true.)
   - Changing anything would add at least 50 cents to the cost so $5.25 is *not* possible. (B is false.)
   - Increasing two items by 50 cents each—say, buying 2 medium sodas instead of 2 small sodas—brings the cost to $6.00. (C is true.)
   - Now replacing a medium soda with a large soda adds 25 cents, so $6.25 is also possible. (D is true.)
   - 2 pepperoni slices and 2 medium sodas cost $7.00. (E is true.)
   - Replacing one of those medium sodas with a large soda adds 25 cents, so $7.25 is possible, too. (F is true.)

19. **(B)** Since a normal distribution is symmetric about the mean, and since in a normal distribution 68% of the scores are within one standard deviation of the mean, 34% are within one standard deviation below the mean and 34% are within one standard deviation above the mean. The other 32% are more than one standard deviation from the mean, 16% are more than one standard deviation below the mean, and 16% are more than one standard deviation above the mean.

   So 16% score below 400, 34% between 400 and 500, 34% between 500 and 600, and 16% above 600. Set up a proportion.

$$\frac{\text{number of students}}{\text{percent of total}} = \frac{10,200}{34} = \frac{x}{16} \Rightarrow \frac{16 \times 10,200}{34} = x \Rightarrow x = 4,800.$$

20. **(D)** $\dfrac{1}{x} + \dfrac{1}{y} = \dfrac{y}{xy} + \dfrac{x}{xy} = \dfrac{x+y}{xy} = \dfrac{10}{20} = \dfrac{1}{2}.$